THE GLOBAL PAST

VOLUME ONE,
PREHISTORY TO 1500

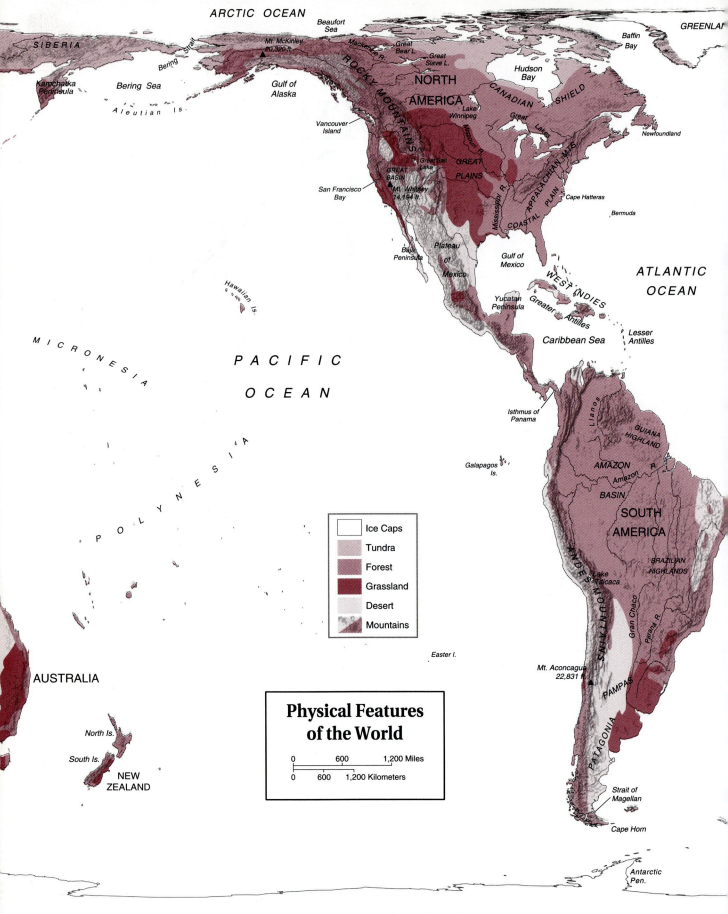

ARCTIC OCEAN

SIBERIA

Beaufort Sea

GREENLAND

Baffin Bay

Kamchatka Peninsula

Bering Sea

Bering Strait

Mt. McKinley 20,320 ft

Mackenzie R.

Great Bear L.

Great Slave L.

Hudson Bay

NORTH AMERICA

CANADIAN SHIELD

Aleutian Is.

Gulf of Alaska

ROCKY MOUNTAINS

Lake Winnipeg

Great Lakes

Newfoundland

Vancouver Island

GREAT BASIN

Great Salt Lake

Missouri R.

GREAT PLAINS

APPALACHIAN MTS.

Cape Hatteras

San Francisco Bay

Mt. Whitney 14,194 ft

Bermuda

Mississippi R.

COASTAL PLAIN

Baja Peninsula

Plateau of Mexico

Gulf of Mexico

WEST INDIES

ATLANTIC OCEAN

Hawaiian Is.

Yucatan Peninsula

Greater Antilles

Lesser Antilles

Caribbean Sea

MICRONESIA

PACIFIC OCEAN

Isthmus of Panama

Galapagos Is.

Llanos

GUIANA HIGHLAND

POLYNESIA

AMAZON

Amazon R.

BASIN

SOUTH AMERICA

Easter I.

BRAZILIAN HIGHLANDS

AUSTRALIA

ANDES MOUNTAINS

Lake Titicaca

Gran Chaco

Parana R.

North Is.

South Is.

NEW ZEALAND

Mt. Aconcagua 22,831 ft

PAMPAS

PATAGONIA

	Ice Caps
	Tundra
	Forest
	Grassland
	Desert
	Mountains

Physical Features of the World

0	600	1,200 Miles
0	600	1,200 Kilometers

Strait of Magellan

Cape Horn

Antarctic Pen.

ANTARCTICA

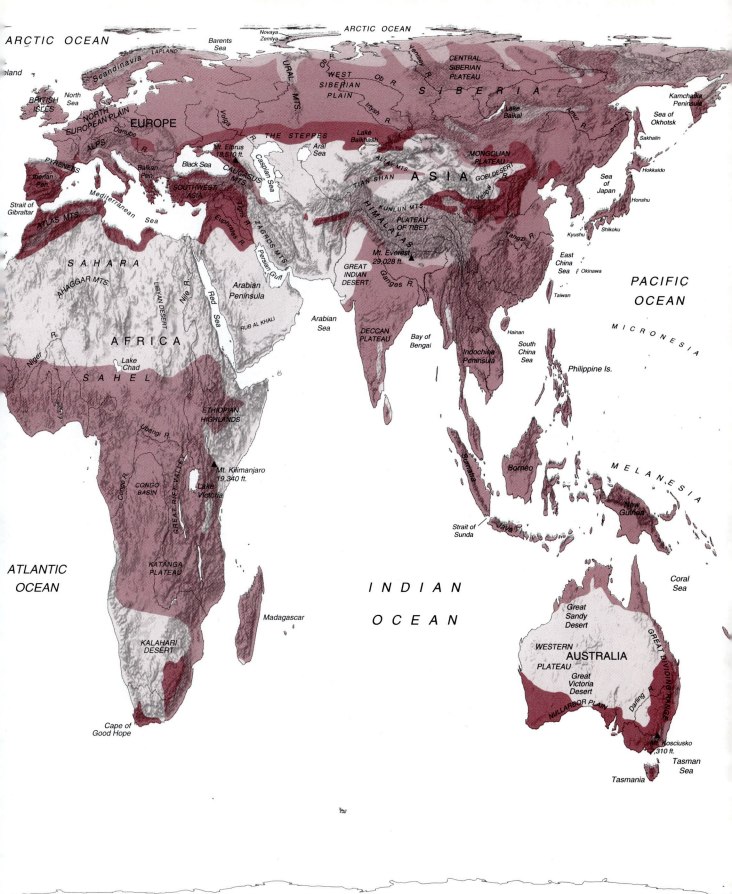

ARCTIC OCEAN

RUSSIA

Alaska
(U.S.)

Greenland
(Den.)

CANADA

PACIFIC
OCEAN

UNITED STATES

ATLANTIC
OCEAN

Gulf of
Mexico

BAHAMAS

MEXICO

CUBA

DOMINICAN REPUBLIC
PUERTO RICO
ANTIGUA & BARBUDA

JAMAICA

BELIZE

HAITI
ST. KITTS & NEVIS

DOMINICA

Hawaii
(U.S.)

GUATEMALA
HONDURAS
EL SALVADOR
NICARAGUA
COSTA RICA

ST. LUCIA
ST. VINCENT &
THE GRENADINES

BARBADOS
GRENADA

GAM

MARSHALL
ISLANDS

TRINIDAD &
TOBAGO

GUINEA-BISS

VENEZUELA

GUYANA

SIERRA LEO

SURINAME

LIBE

PANAMA

COLOMBIA

French Guiana
(Fr.)

FEDERATED
STATES
OF MICRONESIA

KIRIBATI

ECUADOR

NAURU

Tokelau
(N.Z.)

Galapagos Is.
(Ecua.)

BRAZIL

SOLOMON
ISLANDS

TUVALU

PACIFIC
OCEAN

PERU

American
Samoa
(U.S.)

SAMOA

VANUATU

Cook Is.
(N.Z.)

French
Polynesia
(Fr.)

BOLIVIA

FIJI

Niue
(N.Z.)

PARAGUAY

TONGA

New
Caledonia
(Fr.)

CHILE

AUSTRALIA

URUGUAY

**Political Divisions
of the World**

ARGENTINA

0   600   1,200 Miles

0   600   1,200 Kilometers

NEW
ZEALAND

Falkland Is.
(U.K.)

South Ge
(U.K.)

ANTARCTICA

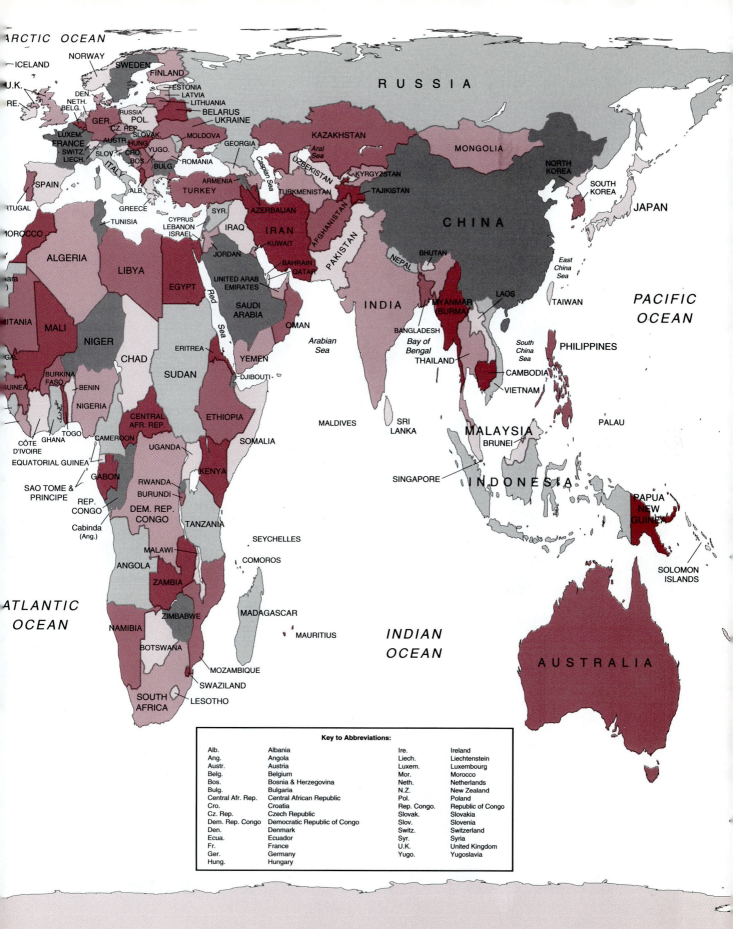

ARCTIC OCEAN

ICELAND
NORWAY
SWEDEN
FINLAND
U.K.
RE.
DEN.
NETH.
BELG.
ESTONIA
LATVIA
LITHUANIA
BELARUS
UKRAINE
RUSSIA
GER.
POL.
CZ. REP.
SLOVAK.
MOLDOVA
LUXEM.
FRANCE
SWITZ.
LIECH.
AUSTR.
SLOV.
HUNG.
CRO.
BOS.
YUGO.
BULG.
ITALY
ALB.
ROMANIA
GEORGIA
ARMENIA
AZERBAIJAN
TURKEY
SPAIN
GREECE
TUNISIA
RTUGAL
CYPRUS
LEBANON
ISRAEL
SYR.
IRAQ
JORDAN
KUWAIT
IRAN
BAHRAIN
QATAR
UNITED ARAB
EMIRATES
OMAN
YEMEN
DJIBOUTI
MOROCCO
ORACCO
ALGERIA
LIBYA
EGYPT
ara
SAUDI
ARABIA
Red
Sea

RUSSIA

KAZAKHSTAN
Aral
Sea
UZBEKISTAN
TURKMENISTAN
KYRGYZSTAN
TAJIKISTAN
AFGHANISTAN
PAKISTAN
NEPAL
BHUTAN

MONGOLIA

CHINA

NORTH
KOREA
SOUTH
KOREA
JAPAN

East
China
Sea

TAIWAN

PACIFIC
OCEAN

Caspian Sea

ITANIA
MALI
NIGER
CHAD
SUDAN
ERITREA
ETHIOPIA
SOMALIA
GAL
BURKINA
FASO
BENIN
GUINEA
NIGERIA
CÔTE
D'IVOIRE
TOGO
GHANA
CAMEROON
EQUATORIAL GUINEA
GABON
SAO TOME &
PRINCIPE
REP.
CONGO
Cabinda
(Ang.)
DEM. REP.
CONGO
UGANDA
RWANDA
BURUNDI
KENYA
TANZANIA
SEYCHELLES
COMOROS
MALAWI
ANGOLA
ZAMBIA
ZIMBABWE
NAMIBIA
BOTSWANA
MADAGASCAR
MAURITIUS

Arabian
Sea

INDIA

MALDIVES

SRI
LANKA

BANGLADESH
Bay of
Bengal
MYANMAR
(BURMA)
THAILAND
LAOS
CAMBODIA
VIETNAM

South
China
Sea

PHILIPPINES

PALAU

MALAYSIA
BRUNEI
SINGAPORE
INDONESIA

PAPUA
NEW
GUINEA

SOLOMON
ISLANDS

ATLANTIC
OCEAN

MOZAMBIQUE
SWAZILAND
SOUTH
AFRICA
LESOTHO

INDIAN
OCEAN

AUSTRALIA

Key to Abbreviations:

Alb.	Albania	Ire.	Ireland
Ang.	Angola	Liech.	Liechtenstein
Austr.	Austria	Luxem.	Luxembourg
Belg.	Belgium	Mor.	Morocco
Bos.	Bosnia & Herzegovina	Neth.	Netherlands
Bulg.	Bulgaria	N.Z.	New Zealand
Central Afr. Rep.	Central African Republic	Pol.	Poland
Cro.	Croatia	Rep. Congo	Republic of Congo
Cz. Rep.	Czech Republic	Slovak.	Slovakia
Dem. Rep. Congo	Democratic Republic of Congo	Slov.	Slovenia
Den.	Denmark	Switz.	Switzerland
Ecua.	Ecuador	Syr.	Syria
Fr.	France	U.K.	United Kingdom
Ger.	Germany	Yugo.	Yugoslavia
Hung.	Hungary		

ANTARCTICA

THE GLOBAL PAST

VOLUME ONE, PREHISTORY TO 1500

Lanny B. Fields
California State University–San Bernardino

Russell J. Barber
California State University–San Bernardino

Cheryl A. Riggs
California State University–San Bernardino

BEDFORD BOOKS **Boston**

For Bedford Books

President and Publisher: Charles H. Christensen
General Manager and Associate Publisher: Joan E. Feinberg
History Editor: Katherine E. Kurzman
Developmental Editor: Jane Betz
Editorial Assistants: Thomas Pierce and Maura Shea
Managing Editor: Elizabeth M. Schaaf
Production Editor: Lori Chong Roncka
Production Assistants: Ellen C. Thibault and Ara Salibian
Copyeditor: Eric Newman
Proofreader: Paula Woolley
Text Design: Wanda Kossak
Photo Researcher: Carole Frohlich, The Visual Connection
Cartography: GeoSystems Global Corporation
Page Layout: DeNee Reiton Skipper
Indexer: Steve Csipke
Cover Design: Hannus Design Associates
Cover Art: Mask, c. 1150–550 B.C. (detail). Olmec, Veracruz, Middle Preclassic. Gift of Landon T. Clay.
    Courtesy of the Museum of Fine Arts, Boston. Yu bronze vase, 1100–1000 B.C. (detail). China, end of the
    Shang-ying period, beginning of the Zhou period. Courtesy of the Tokyo National Museum.
Composition: Ruttle, Shaw & Wetherill, Inc.
Printing and Binding: Quebecor Printing Kingsport

Library of Congress Catalog Card Number: 97–72370

Manufactured in the United States of America.

2   1   0   9   8
f   e   d   c   b   a

For information, write: Bedford Books, 75 Arlington Street, Boston, MA 02116 (617–426–7440)

ISBN: 0–312–10332–8 (hardcover comprehensive vol.)
ISBN: 0–312–10330–1 (paperback Vol. 1)
ISBN: 0–312–10331–X (paperback Vol. 2)

*On the Title Page: This image adorns a wall of the tomb of Ipuy, a member of the Egyptian
elite. Painted in Thebes around 1250 B.C., it shows Ipuy and his wife, seated on the left, receiving offerings of goods and food from their children.*   The Metropolitan Museum of Art (30.4.1114).

Brief Contents

Contents

CHAPTER 15

Regional Kingdoms of Sub-Saharan Africa, around 200–around 1600   371

ISSUE 3

Feudalism   393

PART FOUR
THE REEMERGENCE OF EXPANSIVE SOCIETIES   400

CHAPTER 21
Population Sparks Human Change   527

Special Features

Maps

Preface for Instructors

In 1991, Lanny Fields, who had been teaching world history for more than ten years, wrote an article criticizing the books then available for this course, urging both publishers and professors to be bolder in their goals and methods for teaching a global history. This brief piece was published in *Perspectives,* the newsletter of the American Historical Association, where it came to the attention of an editor who had also been searching for a way to approach a course that was clearly growing. The conversations thus started branched out to include two more professors at California State University–San Bernardino; Cheryl Riggs, also in the Department of History, joined Lanny Fields to add her own experiences in the classroom and to strengthen a commitment to social and religious history. Russell Barber, an anthropologist-archaeologist, was recruited when it became clear that to write something "truly global" meant to move beyond what history alone could encompass; his research and understanding of other social science models has proved invaluable to the project. After the efforts of many years, we are pleased to present a book that is global in scope, practically structured, and designed with our students in mind.

As instructors in world history courses, we have found that the most difficult part of teaching these courses is finding a way to cover such a huge topic: deciding what to leave out, how to integrate diverse strands, and how to give the course shape. We have written *The Global Past* with this essential problem in mind and used a variety of approaches to make the text comprehensive and coherent and to help make the introductory world history course a valuable learning experience for students.

Truly Global Approach

From the beginning, *The Global Past* has been designed to provide truly global coverage of world history. Many world history textbooks were born as Western civilization texts and expanded to incorporate sections on other parts of the world; these sections, however, are often poorly integrated into the textbook and overly brief. In contrast, these topics are given more extensive treatment in *The Global Past*—as their global significance demands—and are integrated into broader discussions throughout the book. In Part Three, for example, an examination of the rise of regional states opens with a full chapter on Islamic expansion. This early chapter provides the context students need for later coverage of the Byzantine Empire.

This broad geographical coverage gives students a better picture of the range of unique world events and encourages them to make comparisons that lead to insights about recurring patterns in world history. Indeed, comparison of events and processes in disparate places and times is an important theme of the book, a theme that is reinforced in the "Issue" chapters and in the special features.

Multidisciplinary Perspectives

Many disciplines have made significant contributions to the study of the human past, and *The Global Past* draws freely on anthropology, geography, and other social sciences to complement the insights of historians. Models and other intellectual tools of the social sciences help to frame discussions, making recurrent patterns more evident and understandable. Models are a widely misunderstood tool of the social sciences. A discussion on p. 17 explains to students that models are ideal constructs created by scholars and that real-world deviations from the expectations derived from models are revealing and frequently lead to new insights.

The presence of an anthropologist-archaeologist among the authors signals a commitment to examining human history before the existence of written records and in places where documents can be complemented with material evidence. The interests of modern archaeologists range from reconstructing past environments to exploring technological capabilities to explaining social change. *The Global Past* incorporates their findings throughout. Archaeological contributions are most obvious in chapters that discuss ancient times, such as those on human origins and the earliest civilizations, but they also enrich our understanding of more recent times and events, such as medieval reactions to the Black Death, plantation slavery in the Americas, the Industrial Revolution, and West African urbanization.

Balanced Coverage

In recognition that history is more than kings and battles, *The Global Past* explores political, economic, cultural, and social developments, attempting to provide balanced and integrated coverage. We have devoted entire chapters, for example, to such topics as "The Development of Civilizations in the Americas" (before European contact) and "Technology and Science before 1500." Shorter treatments are integrated into chapters, linking political-economic events and cultural-social events. This recognition of connections between people, places, and different arenas of activity has been praised by reviewers.

A Variety of Special Features

A number of short sidebar essays are interspersed throughout the text to give students a sense of how people lived in the past, what their concerns were, and how historians interpret the past. These special features, which help to flesh out the coverage and provide a welcome change of pace, are of five types:

- "In Their Own Words," excerpts from primary sources, appear in every chapter. Aztec accounts allow students to glimpse what it was like to be an Aztec king in "It's Good to Be the Aztec Emperor."

- "Paths to the Past," historiographic and methodological discussions, help students understand how historians know what they know. For example, "The Bog People" describes archaeological detective work on bog bodies found in Europe.

- "Encounters," narrative accounts of contacts between peoples, examine the places where cultures met. "The Sicilian Caterer," for example,

discusses food catering in Sicily as a reflection of the interconnectedness of the ancient eastern Mediterranean.

- "Parallels and Divergences," comparisons of particular topics across time and space, examine similarities and differences between cultures. "Economic and Political Uses for Temples," for example, discusses the various functions of temples built in China, India, and Japan in ancient times.

- "Under the Lens" boxes examine individual events, people, or objects in depth. "Nalanda: An Important Indian University," for example, focuses on the famous Buddhist center of learning and traces the paths by which knowledge traveled to distant lands.

Topical-Chronological Organization

As longtime teachers of the world history survey, we are well aware of the dilemma instructors face in such courses. On the one hand, students need to see the chronological pattern of history in order to organize all the information covered in a text of this size; on the other hand, students need to make connections *across* time in order to make the information meaningful. A textbook organized strictly according to chronology can, of course, become encyclopedic and mired in the minutiae of specific cases. One organized strictly according to topics, on the other hand, can obscure the basic and important temporal relationships that are central to understanding causality. *The Global Past* steers a middle course, maintaining a largely chronological structure in this five-part volume while emphasizing important themes within each part in order to give the material coherence and meaning.

One of the great values of a topical treatment is its economy. Writing a truly global text means including sections often omitted in other books; providing balanced treatment of economic, cultural, and social history also adds length. The topical approach allows space for these essential elements while keeping the length of the book manageable; it is a way to emphasize important links without going into endless detail. It also encourages comparison, an important goal of this text. To make space for these new goals, we have scaled back on the traditional European coverage characteristic of the previous generation of world history texts. We hope instructors will agree that this tradeoff is more than compensated for in the truly global coverage that results.

The treatment of the Mongols in a single chapter provides a good example. Focusing on this power that dominated much of Asia for over 250 years allows students to concentrate on Chinggis Khan's forces while also suggesting comparisons with other imperial powers of the era. Further, the discussion of empires in general need not be confined to a single chapter and, instead, benefits from the comparison this focused treatment makes possible.

To give them coherence and thematic unity, each of the main parts of *The Global Past* closes with a brief chapter devoted to an issue—such as trade, empire, religion, or technology—that has shaped the events discussed in that part. These "Issue" chapters encourage students to step back and consider how events occurring in distant cultures connect to one another, and how they connect to events that occurred earlier and later in time.

Features to Assist the Student

The Global Past includes a variety of features to help students make sense of what they read, organize their thoughts, and study.

- An equal-area map at the beginning of each chapter, often with detail inserts, shows what geographical areas will be discussed in that chapter.

- 57 maps within the chapters are accompanied by detailed captions to encourage critical thinking.

- Full-color maps at the back of the book dedicate a two-page spread to each major geographical area and summarize the changes in each area over the period covered in the text.

- An outline at the beginning of each chapter helps students see how the topics covered relate to one another.

- Pronunciation guides, at the bottoms of text pages, give easy-to-read phonetic respellings for non-English words.

- Abundant, good-sized figures and charts are always accompanied by substantial captions to encourage critical thinking.

- Part and chapter timelines place significant events and processes in time, helping students recognize the chronological relationships within and between geographical areas.

- End-of-chapter summaries are ideal for study and review.

- Suggested readings at the end of each chapter offer carefully selected, annotated lists of classic, recent, and specialized studies for students to explore.

In addition to the full-color map appendix, *The Global Past* includes two other reference tools:

- a glossary of significant terms (which appear in boldface in the text), including pronunciation glosses where appropriate; and

- a full index, including cross-references, brief identifications, dates, and pronunciation glosses where appropriate.

Useful Ancillaries

Bedford Books has made available to the student three major ancillaries: a reader, a map workbook, and a study guide. The two-volume reader, *Reading THE GLOBAL PAST* (edited by Russell J. Barber, Lanny B. Fields, and Cheryl A. Riggs) is geared specifically to *The Global Past* and organized into similar parts. Each part offers an integrated set of readings organized around a critical theme of that part, such as the rise of civilization or the role of economics in empires. Most of the readings are primary sources such as travelers' accounts or political documents, but a few important secondary readings are included as examples of current historical thinking. Each part also contains a visual portfolio.

The two-volume map workbook, *Mapping THE GLOBAL PAST: Historical Geography Workbook* (written by Mark Newman at the University of Illinois–Chicago) gives students additional practice working with maps and analyzing the significance of geography in historical events.

The two-volume study guide, *Making the Most of THE GLOBAL PAST: A Study Guide* (written by Jay Boggis) gives students valuable practice in working with art, maps, timelines, outlines, summaries, essays, and test questions of all kinds.

Ancillaries for instructors help manage the formidable task of teaching an introductory world history course. An instructor's resource manual, *Teaching THE GLOBAL PAST* (written by Cheryl A.

Riggs) offers summaries; sample syllabi; lecture suggestions; suggestions for student projects and paper topics; a general bibliography on teaching world history; a variety of references to books, films, and other teaching materials; tips for incorporating the other ancillaries; and more. A testbank (available in print, Macintosh, and Windows formats) offers multiple choice, true/false, fill in the blanks, short answer, reading art, and essay questions of graduated difficulty for all chapters. Color transparencies for maps and selected illustrations in the text allow instructors to focus on particular images in class. A unique *Audio Pronunciation Guide* lets instructors hear how unusual non-English words and phrases are pronounced, so they can speak confidently in class.

History has developed an increased awareness of how critical it is to study the totality of the human past: all arenas of human endeavor at all times and places. *The Global Past* will initiate students into that awareness as soon as they take their first survey course in world history.

Acknowledgments

It is trite but true to state that every book is a group effort; a textbook raises that statement to new heights. We have imposed on our colleagues at California State University–San Bernardino and elsewhere, regularly requesting information and comments. The School of Social and Behavioral Sciences at CSUSB and Deans Aubrey Bonnett and Ellen Gruenbaum assisted us by providing funds to facilitate the project.

At Bedford Books, Publisher Charles Christensen and General Manager Joan Feinberg have been both supportive and demanding, and their dedication to producing a quality book has been exemplary; Jane Betz has guided the text through its evolution; and Lori Chong Roncka has been responsible for its production. Carole Frohlich of The Visual Connection applied her skills and taste in researching the illustrations.

Louise Waller, formerly of St. Martin's Press, holds a special place in our gratitude. Her initial interest in and guidance of this project were very influential in shaping it, and we consider her an honorary author.

Finally, we extend our thanks to the various reviewers who read parts or all of the manuscript and shared their expertise and judgment with us. Not every comment was always welcome at the time, but it would be difficult to find one that did not ultimately help improve the text. We extend our thanks to that legion of reviewers: Roger Adelson, Arizona State University; Ruth Aurelius, Des Moines Area Community College; Norman Bennett, Boston University; Gail Bossenga, University of Kansas; Fritz Blockwell, Washington State University; Thomas W. Burkman, State University of New York–Buffalo; Captain Robert Carriedo, United States Air Force Academy; Ronald Coons, University of Connecticut; Captain Robert Cummings, United States Air Force Academy; R. Hunt Davis, University of Florida; Michael Fisher, Oberlin College; Vernard Foley, Purdue University; Robert D. Friedel, University of Maryland; Robert Garfield, DePaul University; Suzanne Gay, Oberlin College; Frank Garosi, California State University–Sacramento; Laura Gellot, University of Wisconsin–Parkside; Marc Gellot, University of Wisconsin–La Crosse; Marc Gilbert, North Georgia College; Christopher Gutherie, Tarleton State University; John S. Innes, Eastern Washington University; Doug Klepper, Santa Fe Community College; Gregory Kozlowski, DePaul University; James Krippner-Martinez, Haverford College; David Lelyveld, Columbia University; John Mandaville, Portland State University; C. Nicole Martin, Germanna Community College; David McComb, Colorado State University; Rebecca McCoy, University of Idaho; John Mears, Southern Methodist University; Gail Minault, University of Texas–Austin; David T. Morgan, University of Montevallo; Les Muray, Lansing Community College; Vera Reber, Shippensburg University; Donald Roper, State University of New York–New Paltz; Paul Scherer, Indiana State University–South Bend; James Shenton, Columbia University; Amos E. Simpson, University of Southwestern Louisiana; Leonard Smith, Oberlin College; Robert Tignor, Princeton University; Joseph Warren, Lansing Community College; Samuel Wells, Pearl River Community College; Allan Winkler, Miami University of Ohio; John Williams, Indiana State University; Marcia Wright, Columbia University. We would especially like to thank Marian Nelson of the University of Nebraska–Omaha and Robert Berry for their extensive help.

Lanny B. Fields
Russell J. Barber
Cheryl A. Riggs
San Bernardino, California
June 1997

THE GLOBAL PAST

THE HUMAN PAST IS OLD, VERY OLD. By 3 million years ago, recognizable human ancestors lived in Africa, and by 500,000 years ago they had evolved to have significant intelligence and cultural potential. By 100,000 years ago they had become biologically modern human beings like us.

From the achievement of biological modernity to shortly after 10,000 B.C., things stayed much the same for human beings, who lived in small groups of hunters and gatherers with simple organization. But populations slowly were growing, partly as a result of more favorable climatic conditions and partly as a result of expanded and refined technology that permitted human beings to earn their livelihoods more effectively. This growth would lead to more complex societies and eventually to civilizations, with their cities, complicated governments, and sophisticated technology. As children of civilization, we believe civilization to be the normal way of life; but if human existence were an apple, the period of civilization would be no thicker than its skin.

	SOUTHWEST ASIA		EGYPT	EASTERN MEDITERRANEAN	
3000 B.C.	Sumerians		Archaic Egypt		
2500 B.C.			Old Kingdom		
2000 B.C.	Akkadians	Babylonians	Middle Kingdom		Minoans
1500 B.C.	Hittites		Hyksos / New Kingdom	Mycenaeans	
1000 B.C.	Hebrew Kingdom	Assyrians		Phoenicians	Dorians
500 B.C.		Persian Empire			
A.D. 1					
A.D. 500					
A.D. 1000					
A.D. 1500					

PART ONE

EARLY TIMES

Part One of *The Global Past* takes you from our near-human and human ancestors to the earliest civilizations that developed around the world. Chapter 1 introduces concepts about the past and the study of it, concepts that will be used throughout the text. The vast period during which human beings evolved, as well as the cultural achievements of our early ancestors, is discussed in Chapter 2. Chapter 3 presents the idea of civilization, defining it and distinguishing it from other ways that human beings have organized themselves. The earliest civilizations of Mesopotamia, Egypt, and the eastern Mediterranean—including the first civilizations in the world—are discussed in Chapter 4. Chapter 5 treats the earliest civilizations of India and China, and Chapter 6 discusses the development of civilization in the Americas. Finally, Issue 1 probes trade, a powerful force in shaping civilizations.

INDIA	CHINA	MESOAMERICA	PERU	
				3000 B.C.
Indus Valley civilizations				2500 B.C.
				2000 B.C.
				1500 B.C.
Aryans/Gangetic civilizations	Shang Dynasty	Olmecs	Chavín	1000 B.C.
	Early Zhou Dynasty			
				500 B.C.
		Maya / Teotihuacán	Regional states	A.D. 1
				A.D. 500
			Wari Empire	
		Toltecs		A.D. 1000
				A.D. 1500

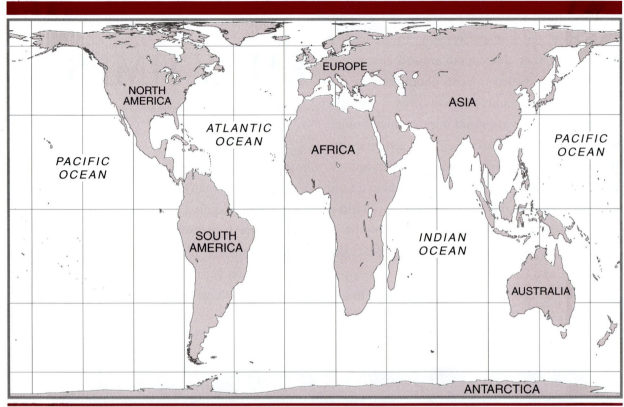

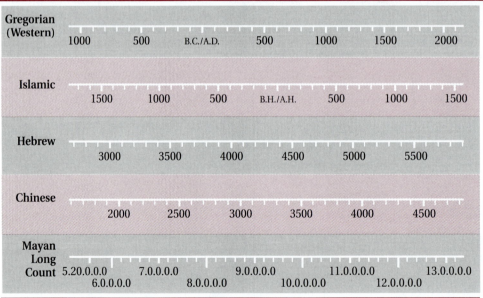

Some Calendric Equivalents. *Around the world, different societies have developed various ways to keep track of time and label dates. This chart shows a few of those methods and how they relate to one another. The Hebrew, Chinese, and Mayan systems start with an ancient date and simply move forward; the Gregorian and Islamic calendars calculate forward and backward from a more recent reference point, hence requiring modifiers (B.C. and A.D. or B.H. and A.H.) to indicate whether a date is before or after the reference point. Dates have been converted to the Gregorian calendar throughout this textbook, but at least forty separate calendric systems have been used by the peoples discussed in* The Global Past.

The Study of the Global Past

"*History*, n. An account mostly false, of events mostly unimportant, which are brought about by rulers mostly knaves, and soldiers mostly fools." So wrote Ambrose Bierce in *The Devil's Dictionary*, his cynical review of the human condition. Our knowledge of the past is necessarily flawed by the human failings of the scholars who study it—Bierce called historians "broad-gauge gossips"—but people nonetheless remain absorbed with the human past.

The Aztecs were fascinated by their Toltec forebears in Mexico and invented fictional links to them to legitimize their empire. Medieval Europeans elevated the ancient Greeks to a lofty status, using their philosophies as the basis for both social and scientific theories of the world; the medieval Roman Catholic Church even established a special dispensation for illustrious Greeks to be admitted to Heaven, despite the fact that they were not Christians. And in Japan and China, ancestor veneration and respect for one's predecessors have been basic and integral parts of everyday life for centuries.

Have these and other people been drawn to the past by a quaint and irrelevant captivation, by a pragmatic interest in exploiting earlier events to their own political advantage, or by an intellectual urge to understand how their age came to be? Probably all of these and many other factors have gone into every people's interest in the past, but every known society devotes itself to the perpetuation of its past in one way or another.

FIGURE 1.1   *George Washington and the Cherry Tree.*   *Fictitious stories about famous people abound, such as the tale of George Washington as a child cutting down a cherry tree and honestly admitting his misdeed to his father. This anecdote has been used to teach children the value of honesty, but it was a fabrication itself, invented by Mason Locke Weems and recorded in his 1806 biography of Washington. Historians since then have tried to root out this false story, but its cultural value to Americans makes it unlikely they will succeed. This 1867 painting by John C. MacRae commemorates the event that never happened.* Corbis/Bettmann.

The academic study of the past draws upon this human interest in one's own history, both in the narrow sense of the ancestors of one's nation or ethnic group and in the broader sense of the ancestors of all people. But academic study distinguishes itself by its keen concern with accuracy and understanding. In the everyday world of the United States, it is a perfectly satisfactory story that young George Washington chopped down a cherry tree and was so honest that he told his parents. It serves as a model for children's behavior and helps foster patriotism by perpetuating a heroic image of one of its founders. The fact that the story is untrue in no way detracts from these purposes; in fact, a historically accurate account of the past might serve these purposes less well. The search for true accounts of the past and ways of understanding why events and processes occurred as they did, however, is the province of academic studies of the past and is the subject of this book.

WHY STUDY THE PAST?

If myths and folklore are more satisfying than the more complicated stories of the past that scholars produce, why bother with the scholarly accounts? There are several reasons.

Most scholars believe that we should be able to learn from the past. Of course events never really repeat themselves; after all, times and circumstances change, so the same event could never recur in just the same way and for just the same reasons. But certainly there are patterns to events.

For example, there have been dozens of cases in which a civilization has run short of resources, often with devastating effects. What are the common threads among the scarcity of wood in Great Britain of the seventeenth century, Ireland's food shortage during the potato famine of 1846, and the dearth of agricultural land and produce among the Central American Maya[1] of the eighth century? Can knowledge of these common threads help modern society cope with impending shortages of raw materials, such as energy sources or food? If studying the past helps us understand the range of ways in which people have met challenges and the relative success of those solutions, it may also help today's policymakers respond to the problems of the modern world in an informed manner.

Studying the past can inform us about the present in another basic way. Many conflicts and issues of any age are rooted in developments of earlier periods. The Cold War of the second half of the twentieth century would make little sense without an understanding of the Russian Revolution, the Stalinist era, World War II, and the Chinese Revolution. The Gulf War of 1991 and other regional conflicts of the latter half of the twentieth century would appear to be irrational squabbles without some understanding of the colonial history of the region and the creation of Israel, Jordan, Kuwait, and other states. The current economic woes of most Latin American countries would seem to be a product of mere mismanagement without knowledge of the colonial exploitation, external military pressures, and puppet regimes that form the background of the current governments. Earlier conflicts and friendships—sometimes in the quite distant past—often have profound effects on the politics of the modern world, and it is foolish to try to understand today's world without studying the world of yesterday.

The academic study of the past also can help us recognize fictitious accounts, concocted as justification for a particular political agenda. For example, Nazi Germany before World War II looked to historians, archaeologists, and anthropologists for reconstructions of the past population movements of different European ethnic groups. If ancestral Aryans (whom the Nazis argued were Germans) could be shown to have occupied

Poland or Russia, it was argued, this would be justification for a German reconquest of these "lost provinces." The reconstructions provided by the Nazi scholars were at best speculations, at worst pure fabrications; they were advanced as sound justifications for political policy, however, and required refutation by more reliable, less biased scholarship. If policymakers are to use knowledge of the past to help them make better decisions today, they must be scrupulously sure that their knowledge of the past is the most accurate possible. Critical scholarship can distinguish between the legitimate use of the past (to advise us about future policies) and the invention of a past to justify preconceived policies.

Perhaps most important, studying the past can inform us better about the human condition. Our personal experience is often so intense and so limited to our own country and period that it can blind us to the recognition that there have been other places and times with people whose lives have been just as full as ours with experiences, events, and crises. By studying the whole range of human experience—past and present—we are in a better position to understand the human world around us and, thereby, ourselves.

WHO STUDIES THE PAST?

Many people assume that the study of the past is the exclusive domain of historians. Historians, of course, are one of the major types of scholars who study the past, but they certainly are not the only ones. In fact, virtually all of the **social sciences**—the disciplines that study human culture and behavior—also have some stake in investigating the past. Political scientists may study ancient Greek ideas of democracy or the thinking of the architects of the French Revolution in order to better understand the historical underpinnings of today's conceptions of democracy. Economists may choose to study the social programs enacted in the United States during the Great Depression to gain insight into what course of action should be followed in subsequent depressions and recessions. But the social sciences most interested in the past—the disciplines that devote most or all of their attention to the past—are history, archaeology, and geography.

[1] **Maya:** MY yuh

History studies the human past primarily through the interpretation of documents. In the broad sense, a document is any written message, and historians may use such diverse sources as diaries, censuses, gravestone epitaphs, and notes written in the margins of books. Historians are interested in the whole range of human events and activities. In the past, however, most of historians' energies were spent in the study of political and sometimes economic issues, such as wars, revolutions, and struggles for power. Indeed, historical documents in many periods are predominantly concerned with these issues, making information on them more easily accessible to historians than information on the day-to-day activities of people. Nonetheless, historians in the past few decades have turned their attentions increasingly to **social history**, the study of everyday life in the past.

On the other hand, **archaeology** operates largely without recourse to documents. Instead, archaeologists study the human past primarily through material remains. These remains include the ruins of buildings and settlements, seeds and bones and other items that indicate the foodstuffs consumed by a people, imported objects that shed light on trade connections, and everyday items cast off after their usefulness has passed. In brief, archaeology studies the refuse left behind by past peoples. Archaeological remains are the clues that, after careful and thoughtful study, can be used to draw conclusions about everyday life. Archaeology is virtually the only window on the first many thousands of years of the human past, because the earliest writing was developed only a few thousand years ago. But even in examining the more recent past, archaeology can prove a valuable adjunct to documentary history.

The line between history and archaeology, drawn so sharply in the foregoing paragraphs, is really somewhat blurred. Historians sometimes draw on physical remains—especially art, architecture, and coinage—to help formulate and support their interpretations. Similarly, archaeologists may use documents when they are available. The difference between the two fields lies largely in the differing emphasis on either documents or physical remains. In this text, we will deal with the integrated study of the past, attempting to transcend the boundaries between history and archaeology.

Fortunately for those who study the past, documents and physical remains often provide com-

FIGURE 1.2 *Archaeological Remains at Pompeii.* *When Mount Vesuvius suddenly erupted in A.D. 79, it buried the ancient Roman city of Pompeii in volcanic ash and lava. People, dogs, and livestock were engulfed by these materials, sometimes caught in midstride, as was the case with these victims crawling up a stairway when overwhelmed by ash. Tragic events such as this one can create a record that reveals details in a manner unparalleled by most archaeological remains.* Sopraintendenza alla Antichita della Campania, Naples.

plementary information. Documents are relatively rich in detail, often providing a wealth of information on individuals, motives, and ideas. Physical remains, on the other hand, provide much more general information, often frustratingly lacking in detail. The conclusions drawn from physical remains often relate to material issues, such as economics and technology; scholars, however, can be very clever about interpreting the material clues and sometimes provide vivid reconstructions of social and ideological aspects of past **lifeways**, typical behaviors for a society. The physical remains that archaeologists examine usually are anonymous and can be related to no specific individual; in contrast, historians often can provide a name and personality to go with an individual involved in an event. Whereas the best written documentation frequently deals with the elite, physical remains frequently are best able to shed light on the everyday life of common people. Finally, while scholars must question the accuracy of the information in a document they study and the motives of its author, archaeologists normally can be assured that no one has manipulated ancient trash with an eye toward finding a favorable place in history.

Geography differs from history and archaeology in that it is defined by its theoretical focus, not its sources of data. To the geographer, the human past is of interest in terms of how people have used the planet's land and resources. The geographical perspective draws attention to the ways that human beings have exploited various resources (such as wood, food species, and minerals), how they have arranged their settlements over the face of the earth (both in relationship to resources and to one another), and how they have transported goods and communicated messages from one place to another. These interests can be addressed with either historical or archaeological data.

Is one of these approaches inherently better than the others? No, each can help solve one part of the puzzle of the past. Modern research tries to use these and other approaches in order to provide the fullest and most balanced possible picture of the past. In fact, most scholars of the past use interpretations of all the different types of evidence and draw on various approaches, calling the composite result "history." The problem of understanding the past is far too difficult to warrant restricting the tools available to solve it.

THE SOURCES OF INFORMATION ON THE PAST

The study of the past, if it is to have any credibility, has to be based on solid evidence. Scholars have three major sources of information on which they can draw to do their work: documents, oral accounts, and physical remains.

Documents

Documents are written records of all sorts. They typically are divided into primary and secondary sources. **Primary sources** are documents that have been written by a participant in the event, activity, or process described or analyzed. For example, an account of the assassination of Abraham Lincoln by a witness in Ford's Theater the evening of the killing would be a primary source, as would be the diary of John Wilkes Booth, the assassin. Clearly, any primary source might include biased reporting and even untruths, but it remains a primary source because it was written by participants or direct observers. Census reports, memoirs of an officer in the U.S. Civil War, and bills of lading for ships are all primary sources. Some primary sources are included as boxes in this textbook, under the heading "In Their Own Words."

In contrast, **secondary sources** are documents for which information is gathered from primary sources, analyzed, and digested, providing an interpretation of the event or process. A newspaper account of the Lincoln assassination, prepared by a reporter on the basis of interviews with witnesses but no firsthand knowledge, is a secondary source. This textbook also is a secondary source, because we, the authors, were neither direct participants in nor recorders of the events and processes discussed in it; rather, we have collected information from primary sources (as well as other secondary sources), selected those portions we have felt most important, and presented an integrated interpretation. Most scholarly books and articles are secondary sources. Most (but by no means all) secondary sources are written long after an event.

There are, of course, documents that do not fall easily into one category or the other. These works are neither primary nor secondary sources but are mixtures of both. For example, an explorer

FIGURE 1.3 *Temple Scroll. Documents such as this one are the most important sources of information for historians. This document, one of the Dead Sea Scrolls, came to the attention of scholars in the 1950s after it had been found in a dry cave by desert nomads in Palestine. It is composed of well-preserved animal skin sewn into a twenty-seven-foot strip and describes the rights and duties of the king of Israel. It dates back to around 100 B.C.* Courtesy of Professor John C. Trever.

of sixteenth-century South America might have included in a book describing that continent both accounts of personal travels and experiences (primary) and stories heard from others (secondary); an attempt to reconcile these differing tales into a consistent interpretation (secondary) might also have been included.

Historians recognize the need to use both primary and secondary sources. Primary sources are preferred for the facts on which an interpretation is based. Those facts may have been restated in secondary sources, and, although it may be easier to use those restatements than to return to the primary sources, there is always a chance of distortion when information from a primary source is restated in a secondary source. Consequently, historians believe strongly that scholars should return to the original, primary sources to collect their

facts. Secondary sources, on the other hand, can provide valuable insights about how other scholars have interpreted particular facts and may serve as the embarkation point for new interpretations.

Primary sources, as noted previously, are not all equal in terms of their accuracy or completeness. In recognition of this, historians have developed a set of procedures often known as **source analysis**. Source analysis is concerned with two issues. First, is the document a legitimate example of what it is purported to be, or is it a fake or something other than what it is claimed to be? Second, to what degree should the document be believed? How accurate is it likely to be?

The first task, largely that of detecting fakes, is often a very technical one. Sometimes fakes are betrayed by physical characteristics of the documents. For example, the Horn Papers, alleged to be an eighteenth-century account of Euro-American settlers west of the Allegheny Mountains, were found to have been written with a metal pen tip, something that was not invented until about one hundred years after the supposed date of the writing of the Horn Papers. Types of paper, types of ink, styles of handwriting, use of vocabulary inappropriate to the time when a document was supposed to have been written, references to events that had not yet occurred—these and other clues have exposed documents as forgeries.

The second task, that of deciding to what degree a document should be believed, is more complex and less likely to yield so simple an answer. The historian must consider factors that affect either the writer's ability to observe and

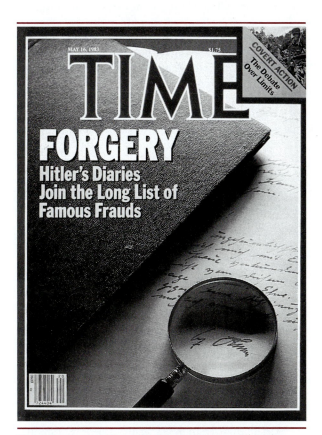

FIGURE 1.4 *Forged Hitler Diaries.* *Historians and other scholars are often wary of unauthenticated documents. In 1983, historians showed that a much-publicized diary of Adolf Hitler was a recent forgery, apparently contrived for economic profit. The methods of source analysis discussed in this chapter are the tools that historians can use to recognize such fakes.*
© 1983 Time Inc. Reprinted by permission.

understand the events transpiring around him or her or the writer's willingness to give a thoroughly honest account. These factors, considered together, constitute what historians call **bias**.

Bias is present in every account, regardless of how hard the writer tries to avoid it. Because all writers are limited by their experiences and preconceptions, they will see and interpret events in terms that make sense to them. Some writers have biases with limited impact on most of their reporting, and others are skilled at recognizing and overcoming much of their bias. The works of other writers, however, are sometimes permeated with biases that have profound effects on the reliability of what they report.

The biases and other circumstances affecting a document must be considered by a historian using that document. Consider, for example, a simple eyewitness account of the assassination of Abraham Lincoln. Was the witness physically in a position to observe the incident? (Factors such as the person's height, seat in the theater, and vision would affect the answer to this question.) Was the witness biased? (A Southern sympathizer would be expected to have a different emotional state from that of a Northern abolitionist at the sight of the assassination of the president, and this could shape a person's perception.) Did the witness have a vested interest in producing a certain sort of account? (If the story was being sold to a newspaper or magazine, there might be incentive to embellish details or create dramatic circumstances.) Had the witness read other accounts before presenting his or her account? Was the witness fluent in English and able to understand others' comments? Was the witness's account recorded shortly after the event, or had memory had time to fade? Are the claims of the accounts corroborated by other information?

These and similar questions have to be asked of every document or other account before the historian can decide which portions probably can be taken at face value and which are more likely to be distorted, fanciful, or simply untrue. Documents may have portions that are of little historical value because of their considerable bias, while other portions may be highly reliable. Source analysis attempts to identify these portions, but the nature of the problem is such that there can be scholarly disagreement about the reliability of a document or part of a document.

IN THEIR
OWN WORDS

*Views of
the Death of
Montezuma*

Historians often are faced with accounts of the same event by different observers, accounts that may not agree particularly well. The historian, then, must use source analysis to evaluate these accounts and try to establish which portions are probably accurate and which are not. Following are excerpts from various accounts of the death of Montezuma,[a] the emperor of the Aztec Empire in Mexico at the time of the Spanish conquest in 1521. These accounts, all describing the same event, underscore how divergent the information given in documents can be.

HERNANDO CORTÉS'S ACCOUNT

Hernando Cortés[b] led the Spanish forces against the Aztecs and wrote letters to Charles V, his king, about his successes. His second letter describes the capture of Montezuma and fierce fighting before the event described in the following passage:

> Montezuma, who with one of his sons and many other chiefs who had been captured at the beginning, was still a prisoner, asked to be carried to the roof of the fort where he could speak to the captains and the [Aztec] people, and cause the war to cease. I had him taken thither, and when he reached the parapet on the top of the fort, intending to speak to the people who were fighting there, one of his own subjects struck him on the head with a stone, with such force that within three days he died. I then had him taken out, dead as he was, by two of the Indian prisoners, who bore him away to his people; but I do not know what they did with him. . . .

SAHAGÚN'S AZTEC ACCOUNT

Bernardino de Sahagún,[c] a Spanish clergyman, collected native accounts of the conquest of Mexico in Nahuatl, the language of the Aztecs, and translated them into Spanish. These accounts were collected from Aztecs shortly after the conquest and presumably were altered minimally by Sahagún. After discussing the battles, the account describes how Montezuma and Itzquauhtzin[d] (a noble in Montezuma's service) mounted the roof and Itzquauhtzin harangued the Aztec crowd to surrender to the superior Spanish military might. The account continues:

> In the increasing outcry which followed, arrows fell upon the roof terrace. The Spaniards protected Montezuma and Itzquauhtzin with their shields so that the Mexicans [Aztecs] might not injure them. But the Mexicans were beside themselves with rage because the Spaniards had completely annihilated our brave warriors—had slain them without warning by treachery. . . . It was after another four days that the Spaniards threw the dead bodies of Montezuma and Itzquauhtzin out of the palace at a place called Teoayoc,[e] the stone turtle carving. As soon as they were recognized, men quickly took up Montezuma's body and carried it to Copulco,[f] placed it on a pile of wood, and fired it. The flames crackled and flared up into many tongues; the body seemed to lie sizzling, sending up a foul stench.

DURÁN'S AZTEC ACCOUNT

Diego Durán read a native account of the conquest, the *Chronicle X* (which since has been lost), and published his secondary account based on it in 1581. His account describes the battles and places Itzquauhtzin on the roof and stoned to death. He wrote:

> The *Chronicle* tells us that once the Spaniards had fled from Mexico [a temporary setback] and those who had remained behind [had] been killed, the Aztecs entered the chambers of King Montezuma in order to treat him more cruelly than they had dealt with the Spaniards. There they found him dead with a chain about his feet and five dagger wounds in his chest. Near him lay many noblemen and great lords who had been held prisoners with him. All of them had been slain shortly before the Spaniards abandoned the building.

---

[a] **Montezuma:** mon tuh ZOO muh
[b] **Hernando Cortés:** ehr NAHN doh kawr TEZ
[c] **Sahagún:** sah hah GOON

[d] **Itzquauhtzin:** eetz kwah OOT zihn
[e] **Teoayoc:** tay oh EYE ohk
[f] **Copulco:** koh PULL koh

Oral Accounts

Although written documents are the most important source for historians, **oral accounts** (stories and descriptions of the past preserved by word of mouth) also can be of considerable importance. For the study of events in the recent past, interviews with individuals who witnessed or participated in them can be invaluable. Oral accounts also can be of great value in the study of the history of nonliterate peoples (peoples who have no written language). In Nigeria, for example, oral histories have traditionally been kept by specialists who have memorized extremely long accounts and passed them on to the next generation. The fact that the same account, word for word, has been reported by different keepers of oral history suggests that the accounts may have been preserved with minimal distortion for several centuries and that they can be used (with appropriate source analysis) as a valuable source of precolonial history there. Similarly, among the Norse (Vikings), a literate people who maintained a strong oral tradition, the epics (histories) were kept by "singers" for whom the penalty of misremembering or altering a tale was death; with this strong incentive for accuracy, it appears that the Norse epics also were kept with great accuracy. The value of these epics as historical documents was demonstrated by their use in locating the archaeological remains of what is almost certainly Vinland, the famous Norse colony in North America.

Even in cases where an oral history has been distorted, elaborated, or exaggerated, it may be of use to the historian. In Hawaii, for example, accounts of native ruling dynasties are intertwined with mythology, and the rulers and gods merge. The myths, of course, are just as real and accurate as the history in the minds of the people who believe them, but to the historian, disentangling historically accurate and inaccurate information is a critical task. These accounts are the only ones available to the historian, and, despite the difficulty of separating accuracy from inaccuracy,

FIGURE 1.5 *Telling an Oral Account. In preliterate societies and sometimes in literate ones, accounts of the past have been preserved primarily in oral form. This has been true especially in Africa, where storytellers like the one shown in this photograph have preserved detailed accounts of events from centuries or even millennia earlier. Such accounts, of course, must be evaluated by source analysis (as must any source of information), but they constitute a valuable store of information about the past.* N. R. Farbman, *Life* Magazine, © 1947 Time Inc.

the careful analysis of these oral accounts has led to probable reconstructions of Hawaii's pre-European past.

Physical Remains

The final category of evidence that can be brought to bear on the study of the past consists of **physical remains**, material items left behind by past people and preserved. The study of physical remains is largely the province of specialists, though some types of physical evidence, such as architecture, can be studied without resorting to technical analysis. On the other hand, drawing conclusions about the trade networks of Iron Age Europeans, for example, requires identifying their artifacts and determining where they were manufactured, a process that demands special skills ranging from stylistic to chemical analysis. These special skills are part of the archaeologist's training, and most scholars in other fields must rely on their expertise for the interpretation of many archaeological remains. The accompanying box on bog people illustrates how archaeologists use their special skills to coax information out of physical remains.

Under the best of circumstances, the scholar studying the past will be able to use several of these types of information. Sometimes one type will be able to bridge gaps left by the others. Sometimes examination of a new class of information will lead to interpretations that conflict with traditional ones, leading to new insights or at least a critical reevaluation of traditional interpretations.

HISTORICAL FACT AND HISTORICAL INTERPRETATION

The preceding discussion of historical sources has referred to "facts" and "interpretations." Now we will explore the differences between them and discuss why both are critical to history.

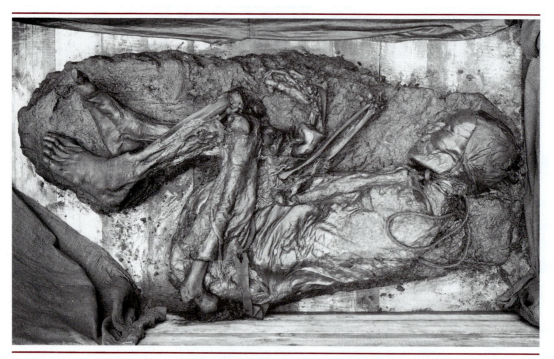

FIGURE 1.6 **Tolland Man.** *From around 500 B.C. to around A.D. 800, the ancient inhabitants of Denmark periodically killed members of their society and placed their bodies in bogs, where the acidic water preserved them. This individual died about 2,000 years ago, having been stabbed, strangled, and beaten in the head. The exceptional preservation of the body permits us to know that the victim ate barley porridge for his last meal and had fingernails that were inconsistent with someone who did manual labor. This may have been a member of the elite sacrificed for religious reasons.* National Museum, Copenhagen.

PATHS TO THE PAST

The Bog People

For centuries, Europeans have been cutting peat, a spongy mat of decayed plant fibers forming in bogs, and have used it for fuel. Occasionally, bog bodies have been found embedded in the peat. Remarkably preserved by the acidic bog water, these human bodies usually have intact skin, hair, organs, and clothing—materials that rarely are preserved in the archaeological record. These rare, archaeologically valuable bog bodies illustrate how archaeologists use physical remains to reconstruct the past.

Most bog bodies date to the Iron Age (about 1000 B.C.–A.D. 100), their age determined primarily through the use of radiocarbon dating, discussed in Chapter 2. In northern Europe, almost seven hundred bog bodies have been reported, although many were found before modern techniques of preservation or analysis were available, so the information about them is often scant. Much of the information that follows comes from the analysis of a recent find, the Lindow Man of England.

The mode of death of a bog person can be determined by searching for signs of disease or violence. The bog bodies are distinctive in the high degree of violence evident. Lindow Man is fairly typical, showing a chest wound (probably from a sword), a fractured skull, facial damage, and strangulation with a thong still around the neck. Other bog bodies also have slit throats. The number of violent acts committed against bog people has been called "murderous overkill," because any of the wounds would have been sufficient to cause death.

The bog people are anonymous, of course, but certain deductions can be made about them. Both men and women became bog people, and they were usually in their twenties or thirties at the times of their deaths. The bodies usually were naked or nearly so with no artifacts that could give an indication of a person's status in life. The fingernails, however, provide telltale clues. Modern laborers' fingernails have distinctive scratches and tiny splits in the ends; modern bank clerks, on the other hand, have smooth nails with few blemishes. Bog body fingernails have their closest parallels among bank clerks, suggesting that the bog people were individuals whose station placed them above the necessity of providing manual labor.

Of the bog bodies that have been fully analyzed, most seem to have died in the late spring. This is indicated by the species of pollen in the intestines. This pollen would have been in the air and consumed with food; its hard silica casings resisted digestion and remained intact in the body.

The last meal of the deceased also can be determined by analyzing remains in the intestine. In the case of Lindow Man, several types of grain were present. Electron spin resonance, a technique pioneered by physicists, revealed that the grains were heated to the temperature required for baking bread. Fragments of the grains indicate that part of the bread was burnt.

Taken together, these facts lead to an interpretation of what happened to these bog people. The number and nature of the violent acts committed against many of the bog people suggest that they were human sacrifices—ritually killed, then disposed of in the approved manner in a bog, perhaps in an attempt to ensure the springtime renewal. Those sacrificed were not commoners but rather members of the elite, perhaps nobility. Even the charring of the bread may be significant. During the Beltain festivals of seventeenth-century England, bread was distributed and the person who received a burnt piece by chance was referred to as being given to the gods as a sacrifice and was called "dead" during the rest of the ceremony. The Beltain festival probably was a bloodless carryover of an ancient Iron Age ritual that extended through much of northern Europe.

A **fact** is a description of an event or action that is generally agreed to be true on the basis of present evidence. It is a fact that Lincoln was shot while attending the theater; it is a fact that wheat and barley were the main foodstuffs in ancient Assyria.

Although facts are generally agreed upon, they can be reassessed with new information or ideas. Domestic cotton, for example, once was believed to have originated in Africa and somehow to have arrived in South America several thousand years before Columbus. New information on the genetic structure of cotton, however, has revealed that there were independent domestications of wild cotton in Africa and South America. One fact has been discarded and replaced with a new one. Facts are our best approximations of truth, not truth itself, so it is understandable that the facts should change as our knowledge improves. It also is understandable that different scholars might have somewhat different conceptions of facts, depending on how they evaluate the sources.

At one time, many historians thought that history could and should concern itself only with facts. Leopold von Ranke[2] (1795–1886), a German historian, argued that historians should simply collect facts, which would speak for themselves. The history he argued for was straightforward and—though a little dry—unambiguous.

Unfortunately, von Ranke's approach suffered from a major flaw, one that has caused its rejection by modern scholars: The facts simply do not speak for themselves. In order for facts to take on any importance, someone must use them to create an **interpretation**, an inference that is consistent with the facts and extends knowledge beyond them by the use of logic, analogy, or some other method of reasoning. An interpretation provides some bit of understanding that otherwise would not have been possible, such as a cause, motivation, or consequence. A string of facts will lead to an interpretation only if the historian accumulating them states how they relate to one another and constructs an argument. Knowing all the facts leading to the beginning of World War I does not automatically provide any insight into why that war occurred; only by using those facts and general notions about how the world works (theory or philosophy) can the historian construct an interpretation of why the war began.

Distinguishing between a fact and an interpretation can be tricky, but the distinction is an important one. Facts are concerned primarily with actions and events, while interpretations are concerned primarily with causes, motives, and processes. It is a fact, for instance, that Abraham Lincoln was shot, but it is an interpretation that he was shot because John Wilkes Booth was a disgruntled Southern sympathizer, just as it is an interpretation that Lincoln's death made reconstruction in the South following the Civil War more harsh than it would have been otherwise. It is a fact that the government of ancient Egypt used military personnel to build the pyramids, but it is an interpretation to argue that the pyramids were a clever

political stratagem to keep a huge standing army in readiness.

By their very nature, interpretations are more subject to differing opinions than are facts. Scholars may emphasize different facts or may approach their interpretation with divergent theoretical ideas about the world. Two scholars, for example, might accept the same facts regarding the Russian Revolution. The one who sees a nation as a set of factions competing with one another for power and resources will probably produce a very different interpretation from that of the scholar who sees a nation as a harmonious entity working for greater cooperation and unity. And, while new information sometimes can lay to rest all disagreements about the truth of a fact, differences of interpretation rarely, if ever, can be resolved so simply.

Interpretations are dependent on assumptions and rarely are subject to objective testing, but this statement should not be misconstrued to mean that all interpretations are created equal. Some interpretations are more likely than others to be correct because they accord better with the facts, they are more logically argued, or they are based on more reasonable assumptions. Bias, of course, can affect interpretation strongly.

Some of the most serious biases in historical reporting relate to race. Many European explorers of the sixteenth, seventeenth, and eighteenth centuries, for example, were committed to the notion that Europeans were superior to all other races; their accounts of other peoples were tainted accordingly. Many European explorers in Africa failed utterly to recognize the complexity of the governments that they encountered, largely because they were sure of the inherent "inferiority" of the Africans. These European accounts suffered from both inaccuracy and omissions, presumably because their writers expected nothing complex and simply never asked the appropriate questions. Chinese accounts of Southeast Asia and ancient Peruvian accounts of the peoples of the Amazonian jungles suffered from similar racial biases.

Gender is another area where serious biases have entered the documentary record. In most societies, men have been the primary leaders in politics, economics, religion, and scholarship. As a result, they have produced the vast majority of documents available to the historian, and these documents often suffer from gender bias. If

[2] **von Ranke:** fahn RAHNG kuh

women were believed (by men) to be delicate beings with no head for business, a male writer was likely to spend little effort describing women who headed businesses, because they would be considered merely aberrations from the norm. Similarly, arenas considered the province of women, particularly domestic life and household management, might be considered less interesting and therefore omitted from description. In some cases where women's lives were discussed by male writers, the resulting caricature speaks more to the writer's ignorance than to the actual state of affairs for women. As with racial bias, changing attitudes and recognition of the pervasiveness of such biases have made writers more aware of them in recent years, and at least some accounts show much less race and gender bias than in earlier times.

Recognizing the distinction between fact and interpretation is absolutely crucial to the successful study of history, and a large proportion of historical misinterpretation is the result of a confusion of the two. Facts are our best attempts to discover what really happened in the past; interpretations are the creations of scholars trying to understand the significance of the facts. Facts can be attacked only on the basis of whether or not they are true; because interpretations can never be proven or disproven, they can be criticized on the basis of whether they fit the facts and whether they follow in a reasonable manner from reasonable assumptions. Although facts are the building blocks of history, they are of limited value in themselves; they take on importance when they are used to support interpretations that provide insight into human activity in the past.

MODELS OF THE PAST

This text uses models to discuss empires, feudalism, and various other recurrent phenomena in history. A **model** is simply a picture of how or why a general process works. As with any picture, its creator decides which elements are important and how they fit together. So that the picture will be simple enough to be comprehended easily, minor elements may be omitted. The result draws our eye to relationships that are central and critical, stripping away details that camouflage what the model-builder sees as the general pattern. Some models focus on how a process operates, and these are known as **descriptive models**; others focus on the motivations or underlying causes, and these are known as **explanatory models**. Both can be valuable in studying the past.

For example, we might construct a simple model to help us understand how recycling glass containers operates (Fig. 1.7). In our simple model, the collection of waste glass leads to recycling, which in turn leads to lowered cost of bottles and savings to consumers. Simultaneously, the collection of waste glass means that there is less litter on roadsides, and the costs of roadside trash collection are lowered. This simple version explains some of the benefits of glass recycling in general, but it certainly does not describe every case perfectly. In some communities, for example, roadside trash collection is carried out by volunteers, so there would be no appreciable savings; also, some container manufacturers might not pass the savings along to consumers. Still, the general pattern of the model can be expected to apply to most

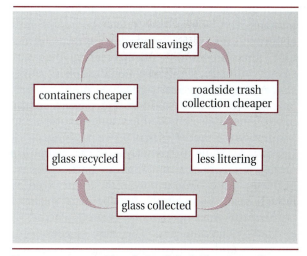

FIGURE 1.7 *Simple Model of Glass Recycling.*
A model is an ideal picture of a process, providing a way to conceptualize it, stripping away detail and reducing the process to simple relationships. This model of glass recycling shows how one action can be expected to lead to another, with causation indicated by arrows. However, not all the glass that is collected makes it to recycling, and a glass manufacturer may choose to increase profits rather than pass savings along to consumers. Recognizing such points where a model fails can help revise it.

cases, and exceptions can be used to refine the model further.

The model can be extended at will. For example, you might be interested in who receives the financial benefit of selling glass to recyclers. It may be that more well-to-do people tend to discard glass with trash, while poorer people might collect the glass and sell it. As with any good model, this leads you to consider new angles to the phenomenon under study.

It is easy to see why models are so useful in examining processes that have occurred repeatedly in history. Each process has its own unique history—the people, places, and events that are the cast, stage, and play in the real-life drama; underlying these unique and fascinating specifics, however, lies a set of basic relationships. A model is an attempt to recognize those basic relationships and draw attention to them.

One important value of models is their ability to suggest general patterns that characterize a process wherever it occurs. Is there a single path to the development of empires? Are certain factors always necessary to their development? Some scholars believe that the same process (such as the development of empires) will unfold in a similar manner every time it occurs and that good scholarship will reveal these common patterns of history. Others are more skeptical, believing that each case is so distinctive that generalization is pointless. A model suggests a universal pattern, challenging scholars to examine that pattern in the light of specific cases. That examination may lend support to the model or may prove it wrong.

This leads us to the second major value of a model. Rarely does a model fit any particular case perfectly and explain it fully. A model inspired by French cases, for example, may be incomplete or narrow and may need to be revised when it is applied to Nigerian cases. This process of examining cases and modifying the model in response often produces a refined, improved picture of the process under study.

Models are common in social science, and you will see several discussed in this text. Whenever you examine a model, remember what it is. It is a proposal to be tested, an idea to stimulate your thinking, a deliberate oversimplification to aid in understanding. It is a form of interpretation, not fact. It is not crystallized truth, and it always must be subservient to facts.

TIME AND PERIODS OF HISTORY

All societies have recognized the passage of time. Some have focused on the periodic repetition of nature, as when day and night alternate or the seasons pass through their annual progression. Those societies have conceived of **cyclical time**, where a sequence of stages is seen as repeating forever. Other societies have focused on the sequence of days, one following another throughout time in a long line. Those societies have conceived of **linear time**, where time passes inexorably forward with no repetition or cycles. Most societies have recognized both concepts of time, sometimes focusing on one or the other for different purposes. Western society, for example, uses linear time concepts in its use of numbered years; it also uses cyclical concepts in the repetition of months and days or seasons within a year.

Calendars

Linear time requires some means of keeping track of time. Sometimes this has been accomplished by simply counting years in a ruler's reign ("in the fifteenth year of the reign of Tiberius Caesar"), but more often people have constructed a system of dates and years that form a **calendar system**. A calendar can be very simple or very complex, but it has to reconcile itself with the facts of astronomy. The earth takes slightly more than 365 days to revolve around the sun, and every calendar has to have years that approximate that figure, if a date is to continue to occur in the expected season over a long period of time. The exact length of the solar year is important, and, if we reckoned each year to be finished when exactly 365 days had elapsed, the Fourth of July would occur in the middle of winter after only about 700 years!

Most calendars use the same approach to this problem: They add one or more extra days to the year at regular intervals to compensate for the fractional day by which the solar year exceeds the approximation of 365 days. In the Western calendars and in English, the year with the extra day is called "leap year" and it occurs every four years, with very few exceptions.

From the historian's point of view, the major problem with calendars is that different societies

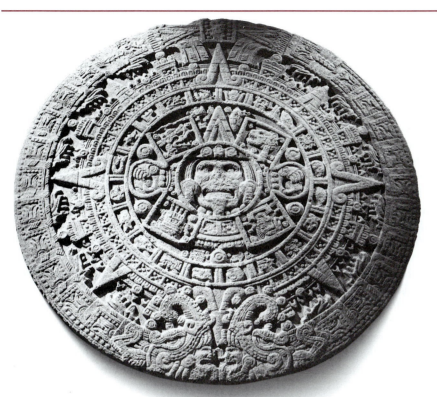

FIGURE 1.8 *Aztec Calendar Stone.* *Though not really a calendar in the modern sense, this artifact depicts the units that the Aztecs of Mexico used to keep track of time. The inner rings show the four previous cycles of the creation and destruction of the universe, as recorded in Aztec mythology. The next ring has twenty divisions, which could represent the twenty days of the Aztec month; since the Aztecs used base-twenty arithmetic, it probably had other symbolism as well. The calendar stone is made of volcanic rock and measures nearly fourteen feet across, weighing over twenty tons.* National Anthropological Museum, Mexico City. Paolo Koch/Rapho/Photo Researchers, Inc.

have used different ones. At least forty different historical calendars were adopted by civilizations around the world, and several calendars are still in use in the twentieth century. (Many of these contemporary calendars are used primarily for reckoning of religious rituals, as with the Hebrew and Chinese calendars. Others, such as the Islamic calendar, are used for everyday, secular timekeeping in several countries.) Local documents, of course, record events with the local calendar, and historians have to be careful to translate a date faithfully in order to see when an event fits into the broader world. An event might occur, for example, on 1 Hamal 1255 of the Borji calendar of Iran; that date might have to be translated into March 21, 1876 (Gregorian calendar, in use in most European countries), 25 Safar 1293 (Islamic calendar, in use throughout most of Southwest Asia), and March 8, 1876 (Julian calendar, in use in Russia), in order to place this event into the context of events in other countries. Most historians use the Gregorian calendar and convert dates to this standard.

Even in Europe, however, the use of a common calendar came late. The older Julian calendar had no leap years, and it was gradually supplanted by the more accurate Gregorian calendar, which incorporated leap years. Some places (such as Hungary, parts of Italy, and parts of Germany) adopted the more accurate Gregorian calendar in the sixteenth century, but others (including Russia, Lithuania, and parts of Greece) continued using the Julian calendar until the early years of the twentieth century. Different dates of adopting the Gregorian calendar led to confusing situations where adjacent cities might have dates that differed by up to two weeks. For example, the same instant of time was designated January 12, 1640 (London, England); January 4, 1640 (Dublin, Ireland); January 10, 1640 (Pisa, Italy); and November 28, 1639 (Moscow, Russia). Often, when a country decided to convert to the new system, it would adopt the date current in a neighboring country, sometimes necessitating that certain dates be skipped. For example, February 22, 1700, never existed in Norway, since this was in a skipped period.

Further complicating matters was the reckoning of the beginning of a new year. Traditionally,

England and its colonies considered the new year to begin on March 1, but in the eighteenth century, this was changed to the current January 1. George Washington, for example, was born on February 22, 1731; only in later years have we recalculated his birthdate by considering January 1 as the first of the year, moving his birthdate to 1732.

In the Western tradition, years are numbered. The starting point for this numbering is an approximation of the birth of Christ (Jesus of Nazareth), although the approximation probably is a couple of years off. All dates after that landmark are given in years since the birth of Jesus and are preceded by the letters "A.D." (*anno Domini*, Latin for "in the year of the Lord"). Some scholars prefer to distance themselves from the Christian implications of using "A.D.," and they use the letters "C.E." (common era) for the same meaning. Dates before the birth of Jesus are given in years before that event, as a number followed by "B.C." (before Christ); those who use "C.E." also will use "B.C.E." (before the common era) in place of "B.C." Finally, for convenience, dates with no letters following them are A.D./C.E. dates. So, A.D. 1371 is the same as 1371 C.E. or simply 1371; 551 B.C. is the same as 551 B.C.E. To simplify keeping chronological track, all dates in this textbook use the B.C./A.D. system.

Periodization

Historians and other scholars of the past typically use periods as basic units of analysis, so a few words about them are in order. A **period** is a span of time that scholars have defined for convenience. Ideally, conditions, events, and lifeways remained more or less similar during a period and were distinctive from preceding and succeeding periods. In reality, of course, the world has always been in a constant state of change, and no period has the kind of stability that such a description suggests. Nonetheless, a period sometimes is defined by momentous events that marked its beginning and end. The Cold War era, for example, may be defined as the period between the end of World War II (1945) and the collapse of the Soviet Empire (1989–1991). The period is marked by the political-military ascendancy of the Soviet Union and the United States as antagonistic superpowers, the absence of direct armed conflict between them, and the lack of a powerful common enemy.

Not all periods, however, are so easily defined. The European Renaissance, for example, has been defined by some scholars as the period after the Middle Ages when the arts and philosophy reoriented and great artists and thinkers developed.

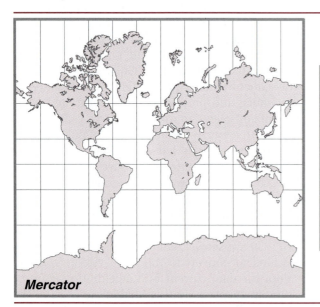

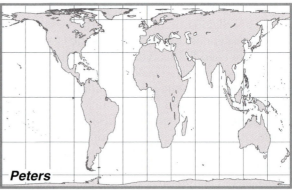

Map 1.1 *The Mercator and Peters Projections Compared.* *Translating the spherical earth into a two-dimensional map requires distorting the size, shape, or relative positions of land masses. The Mercator projection (left) retains the relative shapes and positions of land masses accurately but makes lands nearer the poles* *appear larger than they really are; Greenland is far smaller than Africa, though they are depicted as about the same size on this projection. The Peters projection (right) accurately indicates the sizes of land masses, but it distorts their shapes.*

UNDER THE LENS

Maps and Map Projections

Just as we use calendars to keep track of time, we use maps to keep track of space. Essentially, a map is a picture of a piece of the world, presented more or less as it would be seen from the air. Although most people think of maps as unambiguous reflections of objective reality, a single place can be rendered very dissimilarly on different maps.

The first cartographic variable arises because the earth is round and a map is flat. Consequently, it is impossible to produce a map that does not incorporate some distortion in terms of shape, size, or relative placement of landforms. The mapmaker needs to select a **projection**, a systematic mathematical formula that provides rules for drawing the two-dimensional map from three-dimensional data. When a map of a very small area, like a town or city, is drawn, what projection is chosen matters little, because all will produce very similar maps. When a larger area is mapped, though, the inherent features of each projection begin to emerge and can affect the reader's overall impression tremendously.

The Mercator projection, for example, was devised in the sixteenth century for navigation. Consequently, it retains directions accurately, so that a straight line on a map in the Mercator projection can be followed by plotting a straight course in the real world. Unfortunately, retaining accurate directions means distorting size and shape of land masses, and Mercator maps make areas near the poles seem unrealistically large. The Peters projection, used for the world maps in this book, solves the problem of relative size, but it distorts the shape and relative position of land masses and would be difficult to navigate by.

Cartographers have to make a series of other choices about the maps they make. What should be included or excluded? What should be emphasized or downplayed? What should appear in the center of the map? All of these choices translate into impressions on the users of the map, and cartographers can manipulate those impressions. Consider, for example, the Mercator map of the world so frequently used. The projection makes northern continents inordinately large; western Europe usually is at the center of the map; and typically several European countries are labeled, whereas no African countries are. The impression the map conveys—intended or not—is that Europe is a huge continent, geographically central to the world, and filled with important places. Africa, in contrast, appears inordinately small, peripheral, and empty. The choices made by the mapmaker have created an image that the map user may uncritically accept.

Understandably, there is little agreement on what dates should be associated with this vague definition. Many scholars argue that the European Renaissance began around 1400 and ended around 1600, but others would expand those dates, compress them, slide them forward in time, or slide them back. Some of the disagreement revolves around the part of Europe that a scholar is most interested in or familiar with, because events took place at different dates in different countries. Part of the disagreement also develops from the vagueness of the definition. After all, who decides who was "great"?

Other periods, especially earlier ones, cause even greater disagreement. The European Iron Age, for example, is defined as beginning with the development of iron technology and often is asso-ciated with increased militarism and the development of militaristic local governments ruled by chieftains. The Iron Age is usually thought to have ended with the spread of larger-scale government, often coming from major states, such as Rome. The dates for the Iron Age in Europe usually are considered to be around 1000 B.C. to A.D. 100, but some scholars, arguing largely on the basis of Scandinavian societies, readily extend the ending date to A.D. 1000.

The underlying reason there is so much dispute about the delineation of periods is that they are analytical tools subject to the same disagreements as other interpretations. Just as scholars can disagree over the causes of the American Revolution, they can disagree over the dates for the European Renaissance. One scholar may focus more on

FIGURE 1.9 *Old Sarum from the Air.* *This hill rises from the Salisbury Plain of southern England, but it is not exactly a natural landform. Rather, it has been modified and enlarged by human activity to produce an easily defended site for a settlement. Old Sarum was built during Britain's Iron Age, around 500 B.C. Chronological periods like the "Iron Age" must be referred to with caution, as the same term can apply to considerably different spans of time in various parts of the world.* University of Cambridge Collection of Air Photographs/Richard Muir.

literature than on painting, another more on sculpture than on philosophy; and all may dispute which artists they believe were "great." Such disagreement may cause only minor problems within the discipline, because scholars are aware of the differing interpretations and expect some variations in the dates assigned periods by various interpretations, but it can be a source of great confusion for beginning students.

Although periods serve a valuable purpose in organizing history, they should not be thought of as "real" in the usual sense; they are creations of scholars, not natural divisions of time. Periods can even obscure essential continuities. No one ever went to bed in the Bronze Age and woke up the next morning in the Iron Age. Rarely is there an event so earthshaking that it virtually transforms life overnight, and one should expect great similarities between the beginning of one period and the end of the preceding one.

A final point about historical periods is that they cannot always be extended to places other than where they were originally defined. The Iron Age, for example, was originally defined in Europe, then applied successively to Southwest Asia, Egypt, India, sub-Saharan Africa, and East Asia. As the definition was applied farther and farther afield, it became less and less appropriate. The dates associated with the Iron Age in much of sub-Saharan Africa, for instance, are about A.D. 500 to 1750, nearly two millennia later than in Southwest Asia; in addition, the militarism that was a hallmark of the Iron Age in Europe and Southwest Asia (and to a lesser extent in India) was virtually absent in the Iron Age of Africa. As the "Iron Age" has been extended around much of Europe, Asia, and Africa, the concept has lost much of its utility. Similar criticisms can be made of other extensions of periods, such as the medieval periods in China, Korea, and Japan.

THE GLOBAL PAST AND RELATIVISM

The title of this text, *The Global Past*, indicates its emphasis on a planet-wide approach. Rather than restrict its focus to one or two continents—typically Europe and North America—this text treats peoples and countries from all over the world. Literally, it spans the human past from its beginning to today and on all the inhabited continents, as well as many islands.

Of course, selections have had to be made. Some areas have been omitted and others have received less attention than they warrant, but these compromises were necessary in the interests of keeping the text to a manageable size. The basic outline of the history of all major regions has been maintained, along with more in-depth treatments of places and issues that have had major impacts on the shape of the modern world.

This approach highlights comparisons between different places and times. In some cases, the text will point these out, but the student also

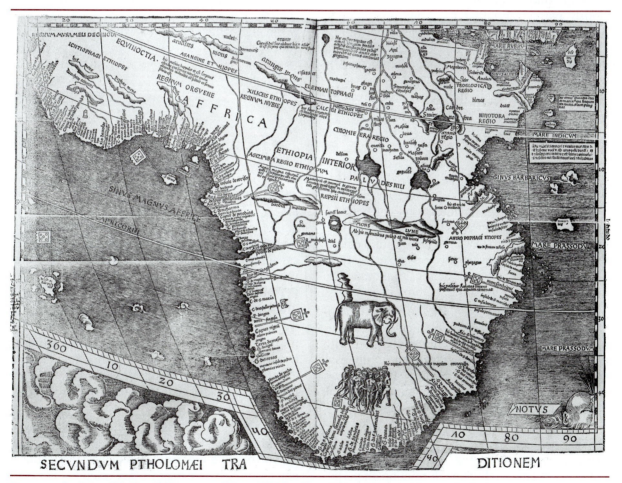

FIGURE 1.10 *Medieval European Map of Ethiopia. This map probably was drafted by John Ruysch in 1508, and it appeared in a republished edition of Ptolemy's* Geography. *The map depicts some recognizable features of northeastern Africa, but it incorporates errors and obsolete conventions that make it difficult for modern readers to use. Labels are in Latin and describe some fanciful places, such as "Troglodica regio" ("Region of cave-dwellers"). "Notus," or North, is in the lower right corner, not at the top as it would be on a modern map. Despite such difficulties and imaginative errors, maps like this one provide valuable information for scholars studying the past.* Waldburg-Wolfegg Princely Collection.

should be alert to thinking in these terms. Such comparisons are especially important in recognizing patterns of similar responses to similar conditions. Revolutions, resource shortages, incursions of aggressive neighbors, the spread of religious ideologies—all these classes of events and processes have common threads that unite them, and their analysis is one of the great opportunities of historical study.

But there also is a special responsibility that this approach demands. Human beings are particularly adept at **ethnocentrism**, the attitude that one's own ideas, values, culture, and cherished behavior patterns are socially, morally, or religiously correct and that all others are inferior. When learning about other people, ethnocentric attitudes can get in the way, leading to the condemnation of anything different or foreign. The whole point of studying a broad range of societies and countries is to learn from their diversity, to be able to see things a bit more through foreign eyes. Rejecting alien viewpoints out of hand defeats this purpose. **Cultural relativism**, the suspension of value judgments about other peoples and their ways, is important to the study of the past; it also is important to successful living in the modern, multicultural world. Certainly it is understandable to be shocked by genocide or social repression and to condemn it; but cultural relativism asks that we examine and understand the situation *before* we form our opinions. Cultural relativism does not require embracing the beliefs or value systems of foreigners or giving up one's own values. Rather, cultural relativism is the granting of respect to a society, people, or country, trying to see their world and behavior in their own terms, rather than simply rejecting all viewpoints but one's own. It is essential to the thoughtful consideration of the global past.

SUMMARY

1. Studying the past allows us to seek patterns of solutions to problems that may be parallel to modern problems, to learn the background of current world controversies, to recognize fictitious history tailored to support political policy, and to understand the diversity of the human condition.

2. Many disciplines study the past, particularly history (primarily concerned with documents), archaeology (primarily concerned with physical remains), and geography (primarily concerned with use of the land and spatial patterning). All provide valuable insights and should be used together to build a fuller understanding of the past.

3. Documents are subject to distortion and bias and must be evaluated before being accepted. Physical remains rarely give information on particular individuals yet frequently provide information on the everyday life of common people. Taken together, documents and physical remains form a stronger knowledge base than either alone.

4. Historical facts are generally accepted descriptions of what occurred in the past. Interpretations are arguments regarding the causes of, interrelationships among, or significance of several of those facts. Facts alone are of limited value to the study of history, because they say little about causes, motivations, or consequences; interpretations are valuable because they analyze that activity, but the same facts are subject to different interpretations.

5. A model is a simplified picture of a phenomenon or process that aids in understanding how or why it occurred. Models should be viewed as interpretations, not facts. Real cases that deviate from the model can point out its shortcomings, helping to refine it.

6. Calendars provide societies with a means of recording linear time. Although different calendars follow very different rules, a date in any one can be converted to a date in any other calendar. For convenience, historians divide the past into periods during which certain factors remain more or less consistent.

7. Cultural relativism is the notion that we should suspend our personal and moral judgments while trying to understand other peoples and their ideas.

SUGGESTED READINGS

Aveni, Anthony F. *Empires of Time: Calendars, Clocks, and Cultures*. New York: Basic Books, 1989. A detailed discussion of the variety of calendric and other time-keeping systems throughout history.

Brothwell, Don. *The Bog Man and the Archaeology of People*. London: British Museum of Natural History, 1986. An excellent, readable, and well-illustrated account of the analysis of Lindow Man and other bog bodies.

Rendell, Kenneth W. *Forging History: The Detection of Fake Letters and Documents*. Norman: University of Oklahoma Press, 1994. An entertaining and illuminating discussion of the methods used to detect fake documents.

Renfrew, Colin, and Paul Bahn. *Archaeology: Theories, Methods, and Practice*. London: Thames and Hudson, 1991. An excellent introduction to archaeological methods.

Shafer, Robert Jones, ed. *A Guide to Historical Method*. Third edition. Homewood, Ill.: Dorsey Press, 1980. A standard work on historiography (the methods of history).

Vansina, Jan. *Oral Tradition as History*. Madison: University of Wisconsin Press, 1985. A classic treatment of oral accounts; insightful, though not easy reading.

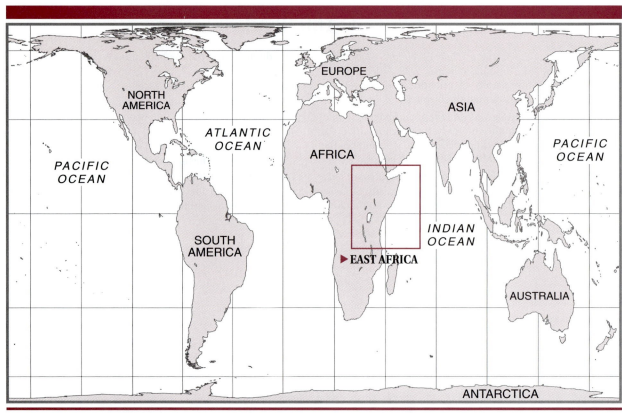

► EAST AFRICA

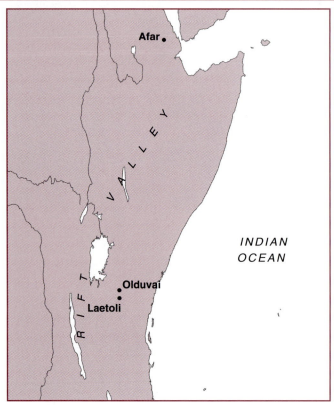

► EAST AFRICA

Beginnings

around 4,500,000–around 100,000 B.C.

On a hot summer day, Mary Leakey and other members of her archaeological expedition to the Laetoli[1] Beds of eastern Africa discovered footprints left by human ancestors who had died 3.5 million years before. A slight rain following a volcanic eruption had left damp ash that was the perfect medium for preserving tracks, and three of our forebears had trudged across the moist soil, one stepping in the prints of another and the third a bit off to the side. This is by no means the only evidence of these ancient ancestors, but it is perhaps the most dramatic.

As ancient as the Laetoli tracks are, they are comparatively recent in terms of the universe. Most astronomers place the beginning of the universe some 20 billion years ago. Geologists studying the earth date its beginning at 4.5 billion years ago, and paleontologists studying fossils conclude that life on earth began more than 3 billion years ago. Placed in this cosmic perspective, the human species is a newcomer to the scene, and the scant few thousand years of conventional history are merely a moment.

This chapter will trace the long journey from the earliest known human ancestors to today's human beings, focusing on the characteristics that make us distinctly human. It will also discuss the philosophical and technological developments that make it possible for scientists to investigate human evolution.

---

[1] **Laetoli:** ly eh TOH lee

FIGURE 2.1 **The Laetoli Footprints.** *Nearly 4 million years ago, a volcano in present-day Tanzania spewed out tons of dusty volcanic ash; within a few days, it rained slightly, turning the ash into a fine mud. Then, dozens of creatures—including three* Australopithecus afarensis—*wandered across this ash field, leaving tracks that subsequently were buried and protected by another layer of ash. These tracks are some of the earliest evidence of possible human ancestors.* John Reader/Photo Researchers, Inc.

THE SCIENTIFIC QUEST TO UNDERSTAND HUMAN ANCESTRY

Pondering human origins certainly is nothing new. People have been fascinated by the mystery of their own beginnings, and have created stories to explain them, probably for as long as they have had brains competent for the task. These stories became enshrined as myths, and every known religion and culture has at least one creation myth.

The scientific study of human ancestry began in Europe, where the Judeo-Christian tradition was dominant, so Judeo-Christian creation mythology, as recorded in the Book of Genesis in the Bible, was the starting place for scientific studies of human development. According to a myth recorded in Genesis, the earth and everything on it (including the first people, Adam and Eve) were created by God over the course of seven days. The Genesis myth certainly is explicit that human beings were created from clay, not modified from some other sort of organism, and it is explicit that only a week was required for the entire creation. Further, Archbishop James Ussher (1581–1656), a biblical scholar studying the chronology of the Bible, reasoned that creation took place in 4004 B.C. Though we now recognize this date to be in the very recent past, it was accepted as very ancient and therefore reasonable for the beginning of the universe by most Western scholars following its publication in 1654. Because Judeo-Christian myth was believed to be literally true by many European scholars, it seemed only sensible to use it as the basis for any scientific study.

The Great Shift in Worldview

Beginning in the eighteenth century, a succession of scientists began questioning the historical and scientific accuracy of the biblical creation myth. Geologists like James Hutton (1726–1797) and Charles Lyell (1797–1875) made convincing arguments that the earth was much older than Ussher's claim. Building on their conception of a long chronology, Charles Darwin (1809–1882) published *On the Origin of Species* in 1859. The central theme of this work is **biological evolution**, the concept that one species of plant or animal can (and did) change into another over long periods of time. Darwin argued that the great diversity of modern life all derived from a single, primitive, early species and that human beings evolved from ape-like ancestors.

Darwin's theory of evolution was grounded in the concept of **survival of the fittest**, the idea that individuals with traits that aid in their survival will live long enough to pass those traits on to their offspring. In contrast, individuals with maladaptive traits will be weeded out, because those traits will lead to their deaths before they have the opportunity to pass the traits on to offspring. In this man-

The Iroquois Creation Myth

Creation myths around the world often follow a common pattern: A god sees a void in the world and fills it with land, water, important plants and animals, and people, often creating them from some common material, such as dust or clay. Usually the mythically created world is familiar, with modern plants, animals, and cultural practices. One version of the creation myth of the Iroquois[a] Indians of northeastern North America has been perpetuated for centuries as an oral account. The version presented here was recorded by one of this book's authors in 1976 at the Tyendinaga[b] Reserve in eastern Canada.

The world sprang up miraculously to form a place for the Great Spirit to live. The Great Spirit had to have existed before this time, but we have no knowledge of this earlier period. In order to populate the world, the Great Spirit created the diversity of plants and animals with which the Iroquois later would become familiar, as well as the hills and rivers that filled their lands.

[a] **Iroquois:** EE roh kwah
[b] **Tyendinaga:** ty ehn dihn AY guh

On one side of the world, the side where the Iroquois eventually would live, was a lake, beside which lived a woman and her daughter. They may have been truly people or spirits, but it is clear that they lived before the Iroquois of today. The mother instructed her daughter never to bathe in the lake, but she did so on one occasion and became pregnant with twins. The twins competed with one another to be born first, since that ensured greater spiritual power. While one twin [later called "the Good Twin"] outmaneuvered the other and was in position to be born first, the other [later called "the Evil Twin"] forced his birth through the mother's arm pit, killing her but succeeding in being born at the same time as his brother. The Good Twin created good things for the use of the Iroquois, such as corn, deer, and water; the Evil Twin created demons, snakes, and droughts to harass the Iroquois.

Creation myths such as this one provide a society with an explanation of how things began, as well as a place in a divine plan. As such, they promote cultural unity.

---

ner, nature rewards individuals lucky enough to have adaptive traits, whereas it penalizes all others with reduced likelihood of survival. Although Darwin never knew the exact mechanism through which traits were inherited, we now realize that genes, which are passed from parents to offspring during reproduction, carry the information that leads to the development of biologically inherited traits.

In the years following Darwin, science was won over to his theory of evolution and the idea of survival of the fittest. By 1900, virtually all scientists agreed that all modern forms of life came about gradually as ancient species evolved through intermediate species on the way to their modern forms. Human beings were seen as simply animals, though very special ones, shaped by natural forces over a very long time.

The story of Darwin's ideas is a complex one, and this is not the place for its detailed consideration. Here, the important point is that the middle part of the nineteenth century saw a major shift in the way in which most educated people viewed human origins. For a century or two prior to the work of Darwin and his colleagues, most Western scholars accepted some version of the Genesis story. This acceptance was an article of faith, based on a literal interpretation of the Bible. After Darwin, human origins were viewed as a scientific question, subject to reasoned debate and revision in light of new evidence or interpretations; the Bible was no longer considered the final authority on this question. This was a major shift in worldview that signaled a great change in Western society and opened up the scientific search for human ancestors.

The Search for Human Ancestors

Hutton, Lyell, and Darwin opened the door for scientists looking for tangible remains of the prehuman species that Darwin had predicted. A few fossils of premodern, humanlike creatures had been found in Europe prior to the publication of Darwin's theory, most notably the Gibraltar skull found in 1848 and the original Neanderthal skull found in Germany in 1856. These finds originally had been dismissed as pathologically deformed—but fully modern—bones; after Darwin, scholars began considering the possibility that they represented ancient human ancestors. The term **"missing link,"** referring to a human-ape that could

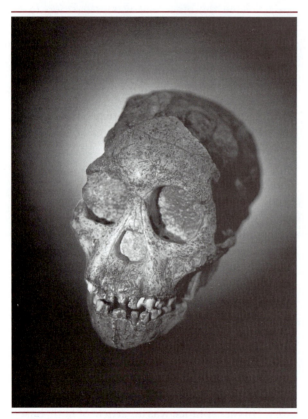

FIGURE 2.2 *The Taung Skull. Found in South Africa in 1924, this fossil turned scientists' eyes to Africa for possible human ancestors. The skull came from an* Australopithecus africanus *individual who died before reaching six years of age; babies and young children of all nonhuman primates resemble human beings more than older nonhuman primates do. Consequently, the Taung child skull misled scientists into expecting* Australopithecus *to be more humanlike than subsequent adult fossils indicated.* John Reader/Photo Researchers, Inc.

bridge the gap between modern human beings and our proposed apelike ancestors, first appeared in the popular literature in 1879; its commonness after that date is an indicator of the public interest in the search.

The remains found, however, were unsatisfying as missing links, because they were decidedly more humanlike than apelike. (This is not surprising, as they were forms now recognized as quite recent.) A series of remains from Java found in 1891 by Eugène Dubois now are recognized as early, but criticisms kept these finds controversial until the 1930s. Before that time, two competing sets of finds promised to provide the long-sought missing link.

The first set of finds came from England, an unlikely spot for the evolution of a species whose nearest nonhuman relatives were from Africa. (In fact, Darwin had targeted Africa as the likely cradle of human evolution for just this reason.) In 1911, a clerk and amateur paleontologist named Charles Dawson brought into the British Museum of Natural History some fossils he reported finding in a gravel pit near the small town of Piltdown. They were oddly intermediate between human being and ape, and they were heralded immediately by the press and many scholars as the missing link. The Piltdown remains, however, were a false lead, the result of a clever hoax that would not be exposed unequivocally as fraudulent until 1954.

In 1924, a second set of remains was found in South Africa by Raymond Dart, a biologist. These remains proved to be among the earliest of our prehuman relatives to be found for the next half century. Dart named the creature, discussed later in this chapter, *Australopithecus.*[2] Although few people today believe Dart's creature to be a direct ancestor of modern human beings, it clearly is a close relative, and Dart's discovery—once the false lead of Piltdown was disposed of—led the search for human ancestors into sub-Saharan Africa, where it remains today.

Many modern researchers, including such well-known figures as L. S. B. Leakey, Mary Leakey, Donald Johanson, Glynn Isaac, and others, have devoted their professional lives to trying to unravel the tangles of the human evolutionary story. Although the tale is far from complete and many details are still in question, their efforts have pro-

[2] **Australopithecus:** ah strahl oh PIHTH eh kuhs

Dating Our Fossil Ancestors

Many of the dates assigned to fossils of our prehuman ancestors are very early and would have staggered Archbishop Ussher, or even Lyell. There are dozens of means of calculating these dates, but four methods are most widely used.

The simplest method of dating a fossil is to date the deposit in which it is found by **faunal succession**. As evolution progresses, different species in a line develop, become common, then die off. If the dates for the different species are well known—as they are, for instance, with wild pigs and antelopes—then a deposit can be dated on the basis of these species. The date of the deposit is the date of the fossils within it.

Another common method of dating is **potassium-argon dating**. A radioactive form of potassium, present naturally in volcanic rocks, produces the gas argon at a regular and known rate. The clock begins when a rock or volcanic ash is formed, and it is a simple matter to measure the argon and calculate the material's age. Potassium-argon dating of the volcanic ash layer in which the Laetoli footprints appeared, as well as dating of layers immediately over and under it, provided the date for the prints.

Radiocarbon dating works in a similar way, although its use is restricted to materials that were once alive, and its clock begins with the death of the organism. Although radiocarbon dating is extremely valuable for dating recent archaeological deposits, it is unreliable earlier than 70,000 years ago and is not useful for dating early prehuman fossils.

Finally, **paleomagnetic dating** sometimes is useful for dating fossils. The earth's magnetic north pole is slowly but constantly migrating, producing changing magnetic fields over the earth. Because magnetic fields are preserved in either burnt clay (as with a cooking fire) or natural clay deposits (as with a dried-out mud puddle or lake), these deposits can be dated by reading their preserved magnetic fields and comparing them with known magnetic fields at different dates.

All of these techniques, with the possible exception of radiocarbon dating, focus on dating the deposit in which the fossil is found, not the fossil itself. Often the fossil itself cannot be dated by any known technique, but fortunately dating its surroundings does the job equally well. None of these techniques is perfect, but their results usually are within 5 percent of being correct.

duced a general picture that probably will survive the challenges of future research and discoveries. Many of their conclusions have been made possible by the battery of scientific tools and techniques developed in the past decades, and these will support their ongoing efforts to learn more about our ancient relatives.

THE PATTERN OF HUMAN EVOLUTION

Human beings are members of the **primates**, the order of animals that also includes apes (such as gorillas, chimpanzees, and orangutans) and monkeys. The earliest primates occur in the fossil record around 70 million years ago, just before the extinction of the dinosaurs, and were small, rodentlike creatures. It was not until about 25 million years ago that monkeylike primates appeared, and primates resembling apes appeared only around 18 million years ago. These creatures are of great interest to anthropologists, but our concern here is primarily with the forms that were ancestral, or at least closely related, to human beings.

Early Ancestors and a Tentative Family Tree

The study of human evolution requires that we use a few specialized terms. A **hominid** is any member of the family that includes human beings. The technical definition of hominids focuses on anatomy, particularly dental anatomy, but it is suf-

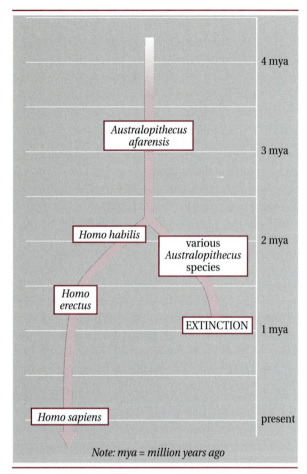

4 mya

Australopithecus afarensis

3 mya

Homo habilis

various *Australopithecus* species

2 mya

Homo erectus

EXTINCTION

1 mya

Homo sapiens

present

Note: mya = million years ago

FIGURE 2.3 *A Reconstruction of Hominid Evolution.* *From a single ancestral line, hominids branched into two lines. The various species of* Australopithecus *grew more robust and adapted to eating inefficient high-fiber foods like leaves, eventually becoming extinct. The species of* Homo, *in contrast, used their intelligence to take advantage of a wide range of circumstances.*

ficient here simply to note that all hominids share some anatomical similarities and are related to one another. Hominids are divided into two major groups, *Australopithecus* and *Homo.* Each of these groups is a **genus**, a category of moderately closely related species. Modern human beings are members of the genus *Homo—Homo sapiens,*[3] to be precise. *Australopithecus* means "southern ape-man" and is the genus of the earliest known human predecessors.

Prior to about 5 million years ago, we have few fossil remains of hominids. It is conjectured that

hominids developed around 15 million years ago, but preservation conditions for their fossils in the intervening 10 million years apparently were poor. Some anthropologists believe that during this period our ancestors were living and dying in forests, where acid soils rapidly decayed their bones. After 5 million B.C., the early hominid remains come from dry savannas, where bone preservation was better.

Figure 2.3 shows the relationships among hominids according to the most current reconstruction. Solid lines indicate an evolutionary line of descent, and blocked lines indicate extinctions. The evidence underlying this chart consists of several hundred fossils, most of them well or fairly well dated. Although there is disagreement among anthropologists about details of this family tree, the general picture has remained little changed for the past twenty years.

As the chart shows, there are two lines of hominids, sharing a common ancestor in *Australopithecus afarensis.* Just before 2 million years ago, the *Homo* line split off from the rest of the hominids and went on to become us; the *Australopithecus* line went on to produce several forms, all of which became extinct. Although there are occasional sensationalist reports that Bigfoot, a presumably mythical beast of northwestern North America, is a belated *Australopithecus,* there is no evidence that any of that line survived beyond 1 million years ago.

Lucy and the First Family

As the first clearly human ancestor, *Australopithecus afarensis* deserves special discussion. Fortunately, it is rather well known, thanks to a remarkable series of discoveries in Ethiopia by Donald Johanson in the mid-1970s. Johanson found and studied first a single well-preserved skeleton (nicknamed "Lucy"), then a group of well-preserved skeletons (nicknamed "The First Family"). These skeletons probably came from individuals who were killed and buried rapidly, perhaps by a mudslide, about 3.5 million years ago, preserving their skeletons.

The degree of completeness of the skeletons permits us to deduce a great deal about Lucy and her contemporaries. They were short, probably about four and a half feet tall, with bodies quite similar to our own. They walked upright with a nearly modern gait, not at all like modern apes.

[3] **Homo sapiens:** HOH moh SAY pee ehns

FIGURE 2.4 *Lucy's Portrait. Lucy—*Australo-pithecus afarensis—*was a short creature with a body similar to ours and a more rugged, more forward-projecting face. We can reconstruct the contours of her face quite accurately from fossil bones, but the details of skin and hair cannot be inferred from fossils. It is proba-ble, however, that she had dark skin and more body hair than modern human beings.* Illustration by John Richards. © by Weldon Owen Pty Ltd./Bra Bocker AB. Reproduced by permission of HarperCollins Publishers, Inc.

Their hands were very similar to our hands, with a thumb that could produce both delicate and pow-erful grips, though not exactly with the precision of modern human beings. Because only bones were found, no one knows about the skin color or hairi-ness of Lucy, but it is logical to assume that she was dark-skinned (because such coloring would have provided protection from ultraviolet poisoning in the sunny tropics) and may have had more hair than modern human beings (because that is the general pattern in primates).

Although the body of Lucy was more or less a scaled-down version of modern people, the head was quite different. The brain was much smaller, even when the body size is taken into account. The face also was very different, with a projecting mouth, a very flat nose, large ridges over the eyes, and a generally heavy cast. A useful oversimplifica-tion is that Lucy had the head of an ape and the body of a human being.

It is not easy to tell just how human Lucy was from the kind of evidence available, but some con-clusions are clear. Lucy and her cohorts used no tools (at least, none that have been preserved), built no houses, and had no fire. If Johanson's interpretation is correct, the First Family really is a kin group, traveling together at the time of their demise, but family groupings of different sorts are common among many modern nonhuman pri-mates. There is no way to know whether Lucy had language, but few if any anthropologists think that she did. Lucy appears to have been pretty nonhu-man in her lifestyle.

The Divergence of the *Australopithecus* and *Homo* Lines

Just before 2 million B.C., rapid evolution brought about an irrevocable split between the *Australo-pithecus* line and a new genus, *Homo*. At first, of course, the two lines showed only relatively minor differences from each other, but the two lines diverged radically as evolution proceeded.

Most of the *Australopithecus* line showed little major change, although some became more robust, particularly in their teeth and associated facial structure. At one time, it was thought that these changes meant that *Australopithecus* was getting larger or at least brawnier, but now it is clear that overall size remained more or less con-stant. The heavier teeth of some *Australopithecus* permitted a diet more specialized in leaves and

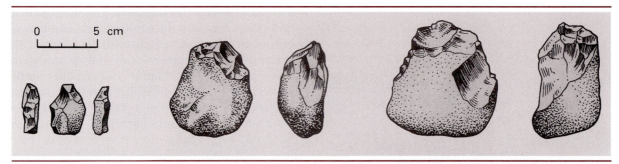

FIGURE 2.5 **Oldowan Tools.** *These simple stone tools, invented by* Homo habilis, *were a major step in technology. There may have been earlier tools made of perishable materials, but Oldowan tools were rugged and required many decisions by their makers: selecting the correct stone, predicting where a blow would detach a flake, and matching the final product to a task. Nonetheless, they were much less complex than the later, highly patterned tools of* Homo erectus. From Kevin Shillington, *History of Africa* (1989). Reproduced courtesy of Macmillan Press Ltd.

other vegetable matter that required extensive chewing. Brains remained about the same size.

The *Homo* line, on the other hand, was following a radically new direction. *Homo habilis*, the first of this line, was becoming slightly larger and developing a somewhat more delicate face—but the big changes were taking place inside the head, not outside it. *Homo habilis* was developing a larger brain.

A larger brain, in general, is disadvantageous. Large brains mean large heads, and a large-headed offspring and its mother are more likely to have serious difficulties during childbirth. In evolutionary terms, the gene that produces a large brain may be weeded out by the increased likelihood of death during childbirth. To outweigh this disadvantage, a large brain must confer some greater advantage. In the case of *Homo habilis*, that advantage presumably was intelligence.

Given the limited evidence regarding *Homo habilis*, we have few ways to infer its level of intelligence. Most scholars think that *Homo habilis* had no language, though solid evidence is lacking; we have no clear knowledge of home life or social activities. But, for the first time, we have evidence of technology.

Homo habilis made stone tools, known as **Oldowan tools**. Oldowan tools, named for the Olduvai[4] Gorge in Tanzania (eastern Africa), where they first were recognized, are moderately simple. They consist of a piece of stone with one to five

flakes removed from an edge by striking it with another stone, creating a sharp but irregular edge. Oldowan tools are revolutionary, because they are the first evidence of hominids' modifying the objects of nature to make them more useful; they show judgment in selecting a stone with the appropriate fracture and in being able to direct the blows so that the resulting sharp edge will be produced. One of the basic hallmarks of humanity—technology—was developing.

Homo erectus Becomes Human

By 1.6 million years ago, a new hominid had developed: *Homo erectus*. Although this form evolved out of *Homo habilis*, there appears to have been a period when both forms were in existence, just as Darwinian evolution would suggest, but *Homo erectus* outcompeted *Homo habilis*, which became extinct shortly thereafter.

Homo erectus was a natural outgrowth of its immediate ancestor. It was a bit larger (with modern or near-modern stature), less heavy in the face, and brainier. A *Homo erectus* on the subway or in the bus would be noticeable as unusual, but it probably would not be a cause for alarm.

Although *Homo habilis* showed sparks of intelligence, *Homo erectus* showed the full flame of intellect, developing several significant advances during its million-year existence. *Homo erectus* produced stone and other tools that improved on those of its predecessor in terms of effectiveness and ingenuity. Significantly, these were patterned:

[4] **Olduvai:** OHL doo vy

Tools of a similar kind were made to standardized, symmetrical shapes, showing a level of planning previously unknown. We also see the first use of fire, both for heating and for cooking. We see the first housing, both in caves and in constructed huts.

Another significant development of *Homo erectus* is cooperative behavior. For the first time, we have evidence that hominids coordinated their activities for their mutual benefit. At the archaeological sites of Torralba and Ambrona in Spain, *Homo erectus* hunted large game, including elephants. To do so must have required a number of hunters, and there is evidence that beaters, perhaps using fire, drove animals over cliffs and into swamps where they could be dispatched by hunters. Finally, there is evidence of butchering of the animals and removal of large quantities of meat, presumably for distribution to the families involved. Such a level of cooperation shows that *Homo erectus* recognized the benefits of sharing effort and rewards in a more profound way than other predators, and it shows the intellect necessary to communicate during complicated and coordinated activities, presumably through language.

Prior to *Homo erectus*, all hominids were found in Africa, the cradle of human evolution. With *Homo erectus*, however, hominids expanded out of Africa into diverse environments. By 500,000 B.C. or shortly thereafter, they were living in Africa, Asia as far north and east as northern China, Indonesia, Spain, England, and Germany. This spread certainly indicates that *Homo erectus* possessed the intellect necessary to solve the problems of new environments, particularly cold ones.

FIGURE 2.6 *Artist's Reconstruction of the Huts at Terra Amata.* *Some of the earliest constructed housing known is from this site in coastal southern France. Built by* Homo erectus *around 400,000 years ago, these huts were probably used over several years by a small group of individuals—perhaps fifteen people—during successive summers. Each hut was made of saplings lashed or woven together at their tops and wedged in place at their bases by rocks, resulting in a light oval structure with plenty of ventilation: perfect for summer on the coast.*
Illustration by David Bergen © Time Inc.

FIGURE 2.7 *A Cave Painting from Lascaux.* *Animals dominate the European cave art that blossomed around 23,000 B.C. The animal shown, probably a bison, has a spear driven into its body. The frequency of such depictions in this art has led many scholars to interpret it as part of a ritual designed to bring good fortune in the hunt. This painting from Lascaux Cave in France lies far underground and is accessible only after crawling through long tunnels and wading through an underground stream.* Sisse Brimberg and Norbert Aujoulat/NGS Image Collection. Photo by Norbert Aujoulat. Courtesy of Centre Nationale de Préhistoire, Périgueux.

Although they never have been found, clothing, needles for sewing it, and a host of other technological innovations must have been necessary for *Homo erectus* to have lived in the north.

Another implication of the spread of *Homo erectus* is that the species must have had a steady increase in population size. Normally a species with a stable population has little incentive to expand into less hospitable environments with which it is not familiar. The pressures of rising population levels, however, can encourage groups of intrepid individuals to set out in search of a less crowded locale. It also is possible that *Homo erectus* possessed the quintessentially human trait of curiosity.

Was *Homo erectus* human? There is no scientific definition of human, but *Homo erectus* certainly possessed many of the characteristics usually thought critical to humanity. At the very least, it represented a quantum leap toward humanity in the modern sense.

The Rise of *Homo sapiens*

Biologically modern human beings (*Homo sapiens*) evolved out of *Homo erectus* around or slightly before 100,000 years ago. The real question about the evolution of modern people is not when or from whom, but where.

One school of thought, known as the **trellis theory**, argues that modern *Homo sapiens* evolved locally from preexisting *Homo erectus* populations. This would mean that modern Chinese were descended from Chinese *Homo erectus*, that modern Africans were descended from African *Homo erectus*, and so forth. This theory was first put forth in the 1930s, supported primarily by similarities between the teeth from *Homo erectus* remains in China and the teeth of modern Chinese. It had fallen into disfavor until recent discoveries at Yunxian,[5] in China, resurrected it. There, *Homo erectus* bones have anatomical traits in common with modern Chinese, suggesting an unbroken ancestry.

The opposing school of thought, dubbed the **"out-of-Africa" theory**, argues that the transition to modern *Homo sapiens* took place only once and in Africa. From there, modern people spread to the rest of the world, outcompeting earlier local hominids, who became extinct. Proponents of this view cite controversial evidence based on molecular biology that suggests that all modern people are

[5] **Yunxian:** yuhn SHEE ahn

descended from a single woman who lived as recently as 100,000 years ago. At this point, both theories are viable, though current anthropological opinion appears to favor the trellis theory.

Aside from the relatively minor cosmetic differences, *Homo sapiens* differs from *Homo erectus* primarily in intellectual capacities. Modern people have a larger brain and presumably greater intelligence, which may be reflected in improvements in technology and such. It is difficult, however, to know whether these improvements are because people are smarter or because there are more of

F I G U R E   **2.8**   *Carved Venus.*   *Nearly one hundred carved-stone Venus figures like this European example have been found. They were made across much of Eurasia between 30,000 and 15,000 B.C., but most are from Central Europe. They typically show large breasts, thighs, and buttocks, featureless faces, and fancy braided hairstyles. Emphasis on these female sexual characteristics suggests that these figures were used in fertility rituals. The Venus figures are some of the earliest evidence for religious activity and art production.*   Jean Vertut.

them and they have been working at the problems longer. There are, however, two areas of endeavor in which modern human beings clearly outstrip *Homo erectus*: art and human burial.

Little or no art has survived from *Homo erectus*, consisting perhaps of a fossil shell with an **X** cut into it and a few similar items. In contrast, early *Homo sapiens* produced abundant expressions of art, including the famous cave paintings of Europe and the Sahara and the less famous—but equally impressive—Venus figurines of Europe and adjacent Asia.

Human burial is unknown for *Homo erectus*, yet early modern human beings practiced it regularly. At Shanidar Cave in Iraq, for instance, *Homo sapiens* skeletons from nearly 40,000 B.C. were found with clusters of pollen on them, indicating that flowers were interred with the dead. Tools and other artifacts occur sporadically in early *Homo sapiens* graves, probably offerings to assist the deceased in an afterlife. Early *Homo sapiens* burial practices suggest strong religious belief.

There is no evidence to prove that *Homo erectus* possessed the same capacity for abstract thinking as modern people. Both art and religion (and most early art probably was religious) demand considerable abstract thought, and *Homo erectus* might not have been mentally equipped for it.

HALLMARKS OF HUMANITY

Human evolution has produced a creature unlike any other on earth. Several features have contributed to this human uniqueness and have equipped human beings for their unparalleled accomplishments. These include:

—upright bipedalism;

—demographic potential;

—continuous sexual receptivity;

—intelligence;

—language; and

—technology.

Upright Bipedalism

Although human beings can crawl or climb, their most usual way of moving about is by walking on their legs. This stance, called **upright bipedalism**, characterized the earliest known hominids, as shown by the Laetoli footprints discussed at the beginning of this chapter. Bipedalism probably developed in response to the need to carry infants away from danger, but it also conferred the advantage of elevating the eyes to provide better vision on the savanna. Its greatest advantage, however, was realized only millions of years later, when tools were developed by *Homo habilis* and the hands were already free to use and carry them.

It is no accident that human hands are as flexible and versatile as they are. Freed from the need to carry the body around, they evolved toward other uses, particularly grasping and carrying of babies. This preadaptation made tools possible and practical immediately upon their invention. Without our hands, it is difficult to imagine any kind of developed human technology.

Upright bipedalism, however, brings its disadvantages. It has created considerable stresses in the lower back, often leading to injury, and human beings are slower and less efficient at walking and running than their four-legged competitors. Obviously, however, the adaptive advantages of upright bipedalism outweigh the disadvantages, because evolution favored the early bipedal hominids.

Demographic Potential

Compared with most animals, human beings have few young and invest a great deal in each one. Human beings mature much more slowly than most animals, so the learning period for each individual is long. This pattern of heavy investment in a few, slow-maturing young is called **k-selection**.

The implications of k-selection are several. First, a species with k-selection must be pretty successful to break even demographically. Given life expectancies and fertility in societies without modern medicine, a modern human being is unlikely to have more than five or six children. Some of these will die young, and others will survive but have no children. But to break even, an average of two children per family must survive to adulthood and reproduce; to have population growth, the average must be greater. These figures may sound unimpressive, but a cemetery from only a century ago will tell sad stories of infant deaths, epidemics, and other tragedies, underscoring the difficulties of maintaining human population levels.

Second, the long maturation period for children permits them to learn a great deal. Unlike some animals whose behavior is determined largely by instinct, human children learn most of their behavior. The system of learned behavior that is shared by a human group is called **culture**. Instincts are genetically programmed and take many generations to change through evolution, but culture can be changed quite rapidly, often over the course of a generation. The dominance of culture over instinct means that human societies are more flexible and able to adapt to changed circumstances faster and better than are creatures more ruled by instinct.

Finally, although many factors work against population growth in human beings, their fates are

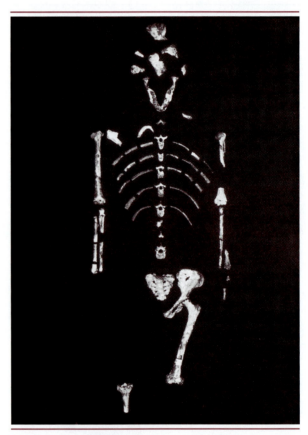

FIGURE 2.9 *Lucy's Skeleton.* *The skull of* Australopithecus afarensis *was attached to the spine underneath the brain case, the arms were too fragile for supporting weight continually, and the feet were specialized for the striding gait of bipedal walkers. These and other anatomical details confirm what was suggested by the Laetoli footprints: At this early date, nearly 4 million years ago, Lucy and her contemporaries were fully upright and bipedal. Modern human posture developed at an earlier period whose date we do not know.* Courtesy of the Human Origins Institute.

largely in their own hands. Unlike oysters, which simply spew their young into the ocean, human beings can use their culture to improve their success at survival. Paradoxically, while k-selection made it difficult for human beings to break even demographically, it also planted the seeds for the most dramatic population increases ever known, once the appropriate strategies of survival had been worked out.

Continuous Sexual Receptivity

Almost all animals have a limited breeding season during which all sexual activity takes place. Human beings, on the other hand, are continuously sexually receptive; that is, they can have sexual relations at any time and are inclined to do so. Consequently, the instinctual urge for sexual gratification probably encouraged early hominids to congregate into permanent groups—unlike most other animals, which gather together for the breeding season, then disperse again.

This distinctive characteristic, most anthropologists believe, is ultimately responsible for the prominence of the family among human beings. Although the specifics vary from society to society, every known human group has had some form of family. The family typically functions as a co-operative economic group, working for its communal survival, and is an important building block in most modern societies.

Intelligence

Intelligence is difficult to define and even more difficult to measure. The problems are considerable when the people being evaluated are sitting in front of you, but they become far greater when the subjects for evaluation are hominids who have been dead for millions of years.

Although there is no single, universally acceptable definition of **intelligence**, a working definition is the ability to learn, reason, and create. Given this definition, human beings clearly have greater intelligence than other animals. If we judge intelligence by its fruits, we also can rank hominid species. The *Australopithecus* species, with no tangible signs of intelligent behavior, would be at the bottom rung. *Homo habilis*, with crude tools and little else, would have ascended the first or second step of the ladder. *Homo erectus*, with its more complex technology, cooperative behavior, and

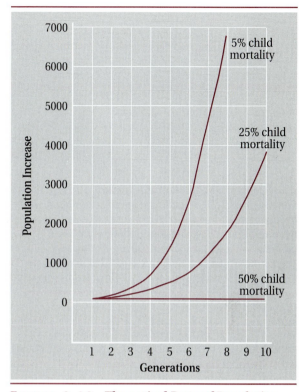

FIGURE 2.10 *Theoretical Rates of Population Increase.* *This graph shows the potential rate of population growth under differing estimates of the child mortality rate (the percentage of children who die before reaching maturity). Child mortality rates of 40 to 50 percent were common before 10,000 B.C.; modern world rates are around 5 percent.*

language, would be several rungs farther up, and *Homo sapiens*, with perhaps improved abstract thought, would be a couple of rungs above *Homo erectus*.

This ranking probably is adequate for our purposes, but there is an additional means of evaluating intelligence between species. Henry McHenry, an American anthropologist, has developed what he calls the **encephalization index**. Simply put, the encephalization index is a measure of the average brain size for a species, adjusted for its body size. (The latter adjustment is necessary because, all else being equal, larger animals have larger brains.) When the index is applied to living creatures, most animals measure in the 9 to 12 range, although chimpanzees and other apes have indexes in the low 30s; human beings measure in at 99.1—a huge increase over other animals. Table 2.1 (p. 40) shows that encephalization indexes produce about the same picture of relative intelli-

TABLE 2.1
Encephalization Indexes for Hominids

Hominid	Encephalization Index
Australopithecus afarensis	33.1
Other *Australopithecus* species	31–35
Homo habilis	51.1
Homo erectus	86.0
Homo sapiens	99.1

The encephalization index measures brain size in relation to body size. It provides a way to compare the intelligence of different species. Dogs, cats, mice, and most other mammals have indexes ranging from 9 to 12, and modern apes have indexes around 30 to 35. Comparing these figures to ones based on fossil hominids suggests that Australopithecus *had intellectual capabilities comparable to those of modern apes and that* Homo habilis *and* Homo erectus *had no modern analogue.*

gence for the hominids as did our ranking based on cultural accomplishments.

The importance of intelligence to human development cannot be overemphasized. By 100,000 years ago, all people throughout the world had developed intelligence comparable to that of modern human beings, and those abilities and skills were turned toward the development of survival strategies, the arts, mythology, social organization, and all the other aspects of culture. Intelligence is the key to language and technology, two other critical hallmarks of humanity.

Language

Language is the ability to communicate through the use of symbols; many linguists argue that the communication must be primarily verbal, although others disagree. The critical word in this definition is **symbol**, referring to an arbitrary marker that stands for something else. For example, "lemon" is a symbol for a yellow citrus fruit; there is no special reason why "bacon" isn't used to refer to that fruit, but it isn't—this is the nature of arbitrariness. On the other hand, a high-pitched scream in reaction to pain or a grunt while moving a piano is primarily instinctual, so these sounds fail the test of arbitrariness. By using symbols, human beings can create a limitless repertoire of messages, combining existing symbols in new ways or creating new symbols altogether.

As far as we know, no animals use language in nature. Their communication, instead, appears to be based entirely on **signs**, vocalizations that indicate meaning but are instinctual and therefore not arbitrary. When a chimpanzee, for example, hoots in a certain manner, it indicates danger. Because that hoot is instinctual, it is understood by chimpanzees who never have heard it before; all normal chimpanzees make the same hoot for the same meaning. The use of signs, in contrast to language, is limited to the relatively few messages that are part of the animal's instinctual repertoire. Chimpanzees, for example, have about thirty signs; rabbits have only about four. New or complicated messages, no matter how urgent or significant, simply cannot be communicated with signs.

Some captive gorillas and chimpanzees have been taught American Sign Language (ASL) by researchers and appear to communicate with hand gestures using grammar and other characteristics of language. There is disagreement over whether this is a true use of language or whether the animals are cleverly mimicking their teachers without any true understanding of the symbols. In any case, such possible use of language has never developed in nature and has resulted only from intensive and purposeful teaching on the part of human instructors.

The development and use of language permitted hominids to communicate a far wider range of messages than would have been possible before. This would have been highly useful in practical matters, such as the killing of elephants at Torralba and Ambrona and the distribution of their meat, and it also would have encouraged the development of personal interaction and friendships. Such relationships are characteristic of human beings and further strengthen family and group relationships, making the human social group more integrated and effective.

Technology

It is difficult to imagine human existence without technology. **Technology**, the production of material items, opens up avenues of human existence. Without it, human beings would be restricted to the relatively few parts of the world whose climate permits us to survive without clothes, fire, or other assistance. We would have to procure all our food from nature using only our hands and mouths, and these same hands and mouths would be our

FIGURE 2.11 *Koko Using Sign Language.* *Koko, the female gorilla in this photograph, has been taught to use American Sign Language, the language of hand symbols developed for the deaf. She has learned to express her wants, describe events, and inquire of her human custodians, but she has trouble dealing with topics in the future and with some abstract ideas. Without human intervention, no ape is known to have learned any language. Here, Koko does not read text; rather, she responds to the picture in the book.* Dr. Ronald H. Cohn/Gorilla Foundation.

only defense against wild animals and one another. Art and many other expressions of creativity would be out of the question.

Of course, technology has been part of the human heritage since the time of *Homo habilis.* Our intelligence permitted us to conceive of technological devices and techniques, and our upright posture and grasping hands permitted us to fashion and use them effectively. Since *Homo habilis,* we have continued to improve our technology and apply it to new problems. We shall see throughout this text that the relative advantage conferred by superior technology and the drive to secure resources to support this technology have been driving forces in the shaping of history.

AFTER BIOLOGICAL EVOLUTION

Biological evolution is an ongoing process with no goal or ending point, and we can be assured that human beings will continue to change. The rate of evolution slowed considerably, however, with the development of technology and social institutions. Lucy, for example, would not have lasted long on the dangerous African savanna if her vision had not been sharp. All three authors of this book, in contrast, would have suffered an unhappy fate

early if our survival had depended on our vision. Today we survive (and our genes are available for reproduction) because of eyeglass technology; 50,000 years ago we might have been supported by our community with the expectation that we would contribute to the group with activities that our limited vision would permit.

Nonetheless, biological evolution continues. A classic instance is **lactose intolerance**. Some adults develop cramps and diarrhea when they consume milk or milk products, whereas others can consume these foods with no ill effects. The difference is that those who develop problems have a genetic inability to produce the appropriate stomach enzymes to digest the sugar (lactose) in milk, which then passes to the intestines and wreaks havoc. This might seem like simply individual differences, but the distribution of lactose intolerance is closely related to where one's ancestors lived, and how long people there have kept cattle herds.

Prior to the development of **pastoralism**, the keeping of domesticated herd animals, milk was available to human beings only from one's mother, and that source was available only for the first few years of life. As a genetic encouragement to weaning, most children lose their ability to digest milk fully at about four years of age. The exceptions are lactose-tolerant children from societies with long traditions of dairy herds. The Fulani of western

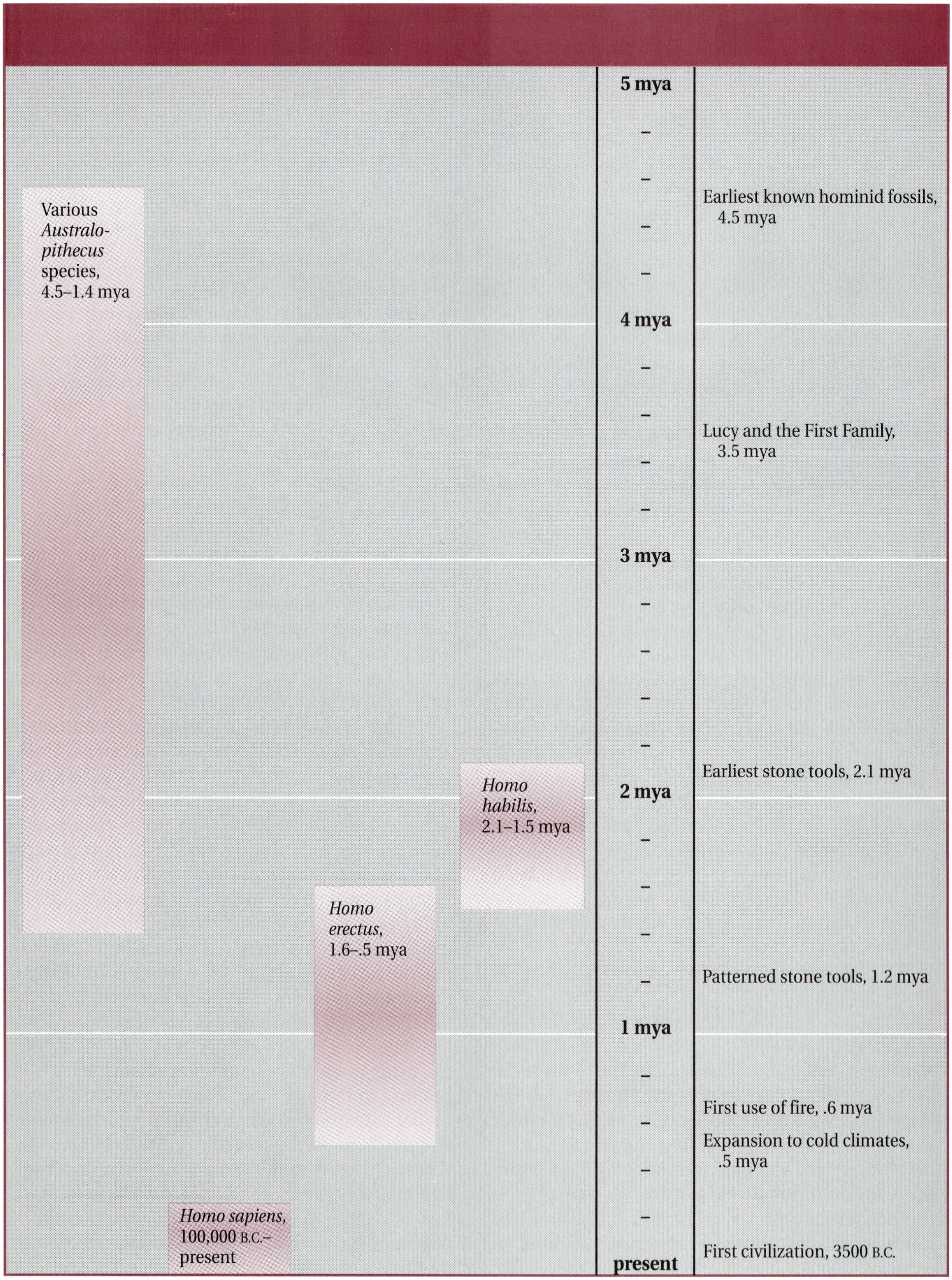

5 mya

–

–

Earliest known hominid fossils,
4.5 mya

–

–

Various
*Australo-
pithecus*
species,
4.5–1.4 mya

4 mya

–

–

Lucy and the First Family,
3.5 mya

–

–

3 mya

–

–

–

–

Earliest stone tools, 2.1 mya

*Homo
habilis,*
2.1–1.5 mya

2 mya

–

–

*Homo
erectus,*
1.6–.5 mya

–

Patterned stone tools, 1.2 mya

1 mya

–

First use of fire, .6 mya

Expansion to cold climates,
.5 mya

–

Homo sapiens,
100,000 B.C.–
present

present

First civilization, 3500 B.C.

Africa, for example, are pastoralists and have only 22 percent lactose intolerance; their neighbors, the nonpastoralist Ibo, have 95 percent lactose intolerance. Most people of Southwest Asian, South Asian, or European descent are lactose tolerant; most people of East Asian descent are lactose intolerant; and people of African descent can go either way, depending on their specific background. This patterning is all the more remarkable when one considers that lactose tolerance must have become common only in the past 6,000 or 8,000 years, the period after the development of dairy pastoralism.

Although biological evolution will continue, we should expect cultural change to be the primary way in which human beings of the future will adapt to their changing world. Since the attainment of modern capabilities around 100,000 B.C., human beings have changed primarily in their cultures. With the environmental improvement that accompanied the end of the glacial ages around 10,000 B.C., human beings began a steady and dramatic increase in their numbers, spreading to virtually all habitable niches. Within a few millennia of this change, developments that would lead to the rise of civilization were well under way.

SUMMARY

1. In the nineteenth century, scholars concerned with human origins shifted from a viewpoint based on scriptural revelation to one based on scientific philosophy. At this point, Darwin and others produced plausible theories and evidence to support human origins through evolutionary processes.

2. The earliest hominids are of the genus *Australopithecus* and existed in Africa by 5 million years ago. Although physically similar to human beings, they show no clear signs of culture.

3. The genus *Homo* developed around 2.1 million years ago in Africa, and its members show varying degrees of cultural behavior. *Homo habilis* used simple tools; *Homo erectus* used more advanced technology, fire, and cooperation to expand into cold climates; *Homo sapiens* may have greater ability for abstract thought than did *Homo erectus*.

4. There are two competing theories about the evolution of human beings. The trellis theory

argues that *Homo erectus* populations migrated to Asia around 500,000 B.C. and Europe a bit later, evolving locally into the modern races of *Homo sapiens*; the "out-of-Africa" theory argues that modern *Homo sapiens* developed only in Africa around 100,000 B.C. and migrated to the rest of the world.

5. As culture has become more prominent, human biological evolution has become less important. Most human adaptations in recent times have been cultural.

6. The hallmarks of humanity are upright bipedalism, demographic potential, continuous sexual receptivity, intelligence, language, and technology. These characteristics have permitted human beings to assume a unique position in their relation to the world and to one another. The biological potentials acquired through millions of years of evolution have left their mark on human events in the recent past and continue to do so.

SUGGESTED READINGS

Johanson, Donald, Lenora Johanson, and Blake Elgar. *Ancestors: In Search of Human Origins.* New York: Villard Books, 1993. A chatty discussion of one reconstruction of human evolution.

Leakey, Richard E., and L. Jan Slikkerveer. *Man-ape, Ape-man: The Quest for Human's Place in Nature and Dubois' "Missing Link."* Leiden, Netherlands: Netherlands Foundation/Kenya Wildlife Service, 1993. An enthralling account of the scholars who have built the modern picture of human evolution.

Rasmussen, D. Tab, ed. *The Origin and Evolution of Humans and Humanness.* Boston: Jones and Bartlett, 1993. A collection of *Scientific American* articles on various aspects of human evolution.

Walker, Alan, and Pat Shipman. *The Wisdom of the Bones: In Search of Human Origins.* New York: Knopf, 1996. An excellent and authoritative account; the best single work of its sort.

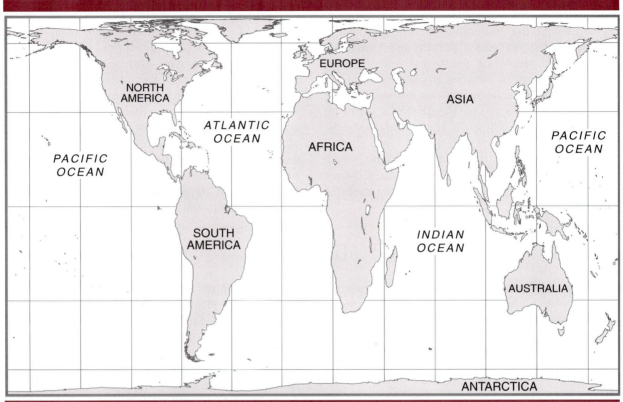

Three Diverse Forms of Writing. *Different writing systems use different principles, exemplified in the three scripts shown here. Ancient Egyptian writing (center) used pictures to represent words; early Korean calligraphy (left) used complex and arbitrary strings of symbols to form words; and nineteenth-century Cherokee writing (right) adapted European letters to reproduce sounds in the spoken Cherokee language.* Left: Courtesy of Yushin Yoo; *center:* British Museum/Michael Holford; *right:* Courtesy of the Georgia Historical Society.

Cultural Evolution, Complexity, and Civilization

A general definition of civilization: a civilized society is exhibiting the five qualities of truth, beauty, adventure, art, peace.

–ALFRED NORTH WHITEHEAD

This definition, by a British philosopher of the early twentieth century, equates civilization with all that is good; in common usage, the word carries a similarly positive meaning. An urbane sophisticate may be described as "very civilized," while an ill-behaved child may be urged to "act civilized."

In the study of the past, however, the term has a more neutral meaning, referring simply to societies that have developed a considerable degree of complexity. There is no implication that civilized people are any better or more moral or more intelligent than their noncivilized cousins. This chapter examines the general lifestyles of those who lived in the millennia before the development of civilization, which began around 3500 B.C. In addition, it explores the distinguishing characteristics of civilized societies and considers why it is useful to study these features.

THE IDEA OF CULTURAL EVOLUTION

Underlying the dichotomy between civilized and noncivilized peoples is the concept of **cultural evolution**, the idea that there is a general tendency over time for cultures to become more complex.

Increased complexity, of course, does not necessarily imply improvement or advancement, but simply a more tangled web of human interactions. This complexity is expressed in a wide variety of ways. More complex societies have a greater number of roles that their citizens can fill, with differences in occupations, wealth, social status, and political power. More complex societies settle in larger, more diverse groups that reflect the differences among the people that occupy them. More complex societies have advanced knowledge and skills, largely the result of the occupational specialization by members who have devoted great amounts of time to particular fields of endeavor.

Members of a simpler society, in contrast, are more like one another. Most or all have about the same degree of wealth and power, live in similar circumstances, and perform similar activities. An Amazonian rain forest farmer, isolated from any outside society, would live like most other Amazonian rain forest farmers in the essentials.

Stages of Cultural Evolution

Several models of cultural evolution are in use by social scientists, and most utilize **stages**, patterns of cultural characteristics that are common to societies of a similar level of complexity. Stages are artificial devices, created by scholars to help them catalogue and understand societies, and the model presented here uses four stages based primarily on political considerations: how a society allocates power.

The simplest stage of cultural evolution in this system is the **band**. Bands typically are small, with 30 to 200 people living together, deriving their food from hunting, fishing, and gathering of plant foods. Bands move with the seasons to take advantage of seasonally available foods. Although there may be division of labor according to gender, people of the same sex perform about the same range of activities. Men typically spend much of their time in hunting and making certain types of tools for their own use; women are more concerned with gathering plant materials for food and medicine and with domestic duties, such as preparing food and producing certain domestic implements. (These activities became women's work, probably because they were compatible with child care, itself a logical outgrowth of the biological function of breast-feeding infants.) Each family largely meets its own needs, although there are various communal tasks for which labor is pooled. Because everyone in a band is related, kinship links are very important. A family with plenty of food is likely to share with a family suffering a temporary shortage, because they can find some sort of kin relationship; a family that needs assistance in some task can expect to call on relatives for labor. Religion is personal, focused often on individual visions, but there is a shared body of belief. There often is no formal leader of a band, and no

TABLE 3.1
Typical Characteristics of Stages of Cultural Evolution

Stage	Size	Politics	Religion	Economics
Band	30–200	none	personal	hunter-gatherer; kin-sharing
Tribe	100–2,000	leader with persuasive power	kinship group–oriented	agricultural; kin-sharing
Chiefdom	1,000–10,000	leader with coercive power	priest-oriented	agricultural; class-oriented
Civilization	over 10,000	coercive leader with bureaucracy	state ideology	agricultural; class-oriented; occupational specialists

Most societies fit neatly into one or another of these stages, possessing all the defining characteristics. There are some exceptions, however, like the chiefdom-level hunting-gathering Native American groups of the northwest coast of North America. Similarly, the people of a region usually pass through the stages in sequence, beginning with bands, though there are exceptions to this generalization, too.

one has legitimate authority to compel obedience from another. War usually is rare for band-level peoples.

At the next level of complexity is the **tribe**. (This is a more technical usage than informally referring to an "Indian tribe," which may be at a band, tribe, or other stage.) The tribe typically is somewhat larger than the band, usually consisting of around 100 to 2,000 people. Tribes get most of their food through the growing of crops, although hunting and gathering may still be practiced. There are few or no occupations other than farmer, and everyone performs more or less the same activities. The need to tend their crops encourages them to settle in a single, permanent village—in other words, to be **sedentary**. There may be a formal leader, although he or she can lead only by example and persuasion; the leader has no power to enforce a policy. Societies at the tribe stage usually have limited involvement in warfare until population levels become high enough to create severe competition for agricultural land. Most religious responsibility is in the hands of kinship-based organizations that perform calendric ceremonies, many of which are to ensure good harvests.

More complex is the **chiefdom**. The chiefdom is somewhat larger than the tribe, consisting usually of 1,000 to 10,000 people, but it is distinguished by a radical shift in political power. The leader of a chiefdom, the chief, has true coercive power, the right to make a decision and forcibly implement it. In a band or tribe, a bad suggestion from a leader can be simply ignored; in a chiefdom, a chief's decision, good or bad, is enforced, sometimes against the will of the people. The chiefdom also has several layers of wealth, authority, and prestige, often with named classes. There frequently are many different occupations, although some people may continue the earlier path of the farmer who carries out a wide variety of activities. The trend toward the increasing importance of warfare in the tribe continues and intensifies with the chiefdom. Religion usually is in the hands of a priestly hierarchy, sometimes intimately linked with the government. Agriculture or pastoralism is almost always the economic base underwriting a chiefdom, although a few chiefdoms have been based on hunting and gathering.

The final stage of cultural evolution, **civilization**, further intensifies the occupational and sta-

FIGURE 3.1 *The King of Kuba.* *This photograph from the mid–twentieth century shows an African king in the splendor of his court. Even this late into the colonial period, the king retained great political, military, and economic power and paraded his status in his leopard skin, his expensive beaded ornaments, and his personal bulk. Such power and status are typical in chiefdoms such as Kuba.* Photo by Eliot Elisofon, 1947, neg. No. 22923. Eliot Elisofon Photographic Archives, National Museum of African Art, Smithsonian Institution, Washington, D.C.

tus differences among its members. It also possesses a number of distinctive characteristics, discussed at length later in this chapter. The concept of civilization, riddled as it is with connotations of superiority, is rejected outright by some modern scholars, but we will use it for reasons discussed at the end of this chapter.

If you examine one region, you usually will see a general trend that follows this band-tribe-chiefdom-civilization pattern over long periods of time. Sometimes, however, societies in a region skip over a stage, return to a stage previously abandoned, or stop at a stage before they reach civilization. These exceptions are fascinating and demand special attention, but they should not obscure the fact that the general model holds true most of the time. Most social scientists believe that population growth is at the root of cultural evolution.

The Population Trigger for the Agricultural Bomb

Human demographic potential was discussed in Chapter 2, where it was noted that human beings can increase their population levels through culture, adopting new lifeways to aid survival. In fact, they are so good at it that population pressures probably developed fairly early with the warming climates and improved conditions around 10,000 B.C. This meant that new ways of gaining food had to be found to support these increasing numbers of people.

Hunting and gathering was not a brutish or nasty way to procure food. Indeed, it required less labor and often provided a more reliable food supply than most forms of agriculture, and hunters and gatherers clearly had a more balanced diet that, given sufficient quantities of food, led to generally higher levels of health than most agriculturalists enjoyed.

The primary disadvantage of hunting and gathering, however, was that it could support only a limited number of people in a given area. Once people had reached the limit for their area, population levels would stabilize through increased mortality. On average, mothers bore about five children, yet only two could survive to replace their parents, if the limit of an area to provide food had been reached. Other children usually would die of diseases to which they were more susceptible because of hunger; in some societies, infanticide was practiced to ease the burden of providing for a larger family in hard times.

To put it in human terms, then, parents had to choose between the easier life of a hunter-gatherer and the more restrictive life of an agriculturalist. Hunters and gatherers realized that seeds germinate into plants, and there was no dramatic "discovery" of agriculture. Rather, parents decided that the increased efforts and lost freedoms of agriculture were an acceptable price for having more of their children survive.

Almost incidentally, choosing to become agriculturalists allowed their populations to grow to sizes and densities necessary for the development

FIGURE 3.2 *Aerial Photograph of Northern Mesopotamia Showing Irrigation Canals.* *This network of canals hints at how much effort is required to keep them operating and how they open land up to agriculture. Many of these canals are in identical positions to canals first constructed thousands of years ago.* Georg Gerster/Comstock.

of complex societies. Population pressure led to agriculture, which in turn released the brake on population levels, leading to greater numbers of people than ever before seen—and to greater cultural complexity. Once taken, the step to agriculture was normally irreversible, because the farmers had to settle in one place, and the wild food resources within traveling distance no longer would be sufficient to feed their increased numbers of mouths.

Irrigation agriculture warrants special attention. Agriculturalists in environments where water is scanty must use **irrigation**, the practice of bringing water to agricultural fields through canals or similar devices. Irrigation is very time consuming, with major labor investments in digging canals, as well as in repairing and cleaning them. Large-scale irrigation also requires special skills and organization for its effective operation. Efficient design of canals requires some engineering skill, because slopes must be steep enough to keep the water flowing yet shallow enough so that the canals will not be below the level of the fields by the time the water arrives. And irrigation always seems to lead to disputes over excessive drawing off of water upstream and the like; these disputes require adjudication by an individual or group.

The development of agriculture was fundamental to the development of complex society. Agriculture, sedentism, and population growth were partners in fostering the accumulation of goods, the development of different occupations and levels of wealth, and the need for stronger political leadership. The juggernaut of cultural evolution was gaining speed.

Why Some Cultures Never Developed Civilization

The previous paragraphs have discussed one possible trajectory of human evolution, where complexity continually increases; another possibility, of course, is that society in a region reaches a certain level of complexity and remains there. There are many reasons why this might happen. In the Kalahari Desert or along the Arctic coast, for examples, climate does not permit the development of agriculture, and populations large enough to lead to cultural complexity never developed locally. In some places, such as Panama and Costa Rica, local chiefdoms were conquered by the Spanish before they reached civilization. In still other places, such as the northwest coast of North America, chiefdoms were based on fishing in the exceptionally rich waters and were following a different track from those of most chiefdoms elsewhere.

It is important to recall that there is no reason why a society would want to evolve. Indeed, personal welfare was almost universally superior in the *less* complex societies. A member of a band traveled with the seasons, worked short hours, was healthy, and was not subject to the whim of a leader or government. Many personal freedoms were gradually surrendered on the road to civilization.

THE CORE ELEMENTS OF CIVILIZATION

Scholars, of course, vary somewhat in their ideas of which elements are essential to a definition of civilization. Nonetheless, there is consensus that some elements are crucial to the definition and always must be present, while others are sometimes important but more variable. This section discusses what we consider the six essential elements of civilization, and the section that follows discusses the variable ones.

The following are the core, invariable elements of civilization:

— dependence on agriculture;
— occupational specialization;
— class stratification;
— state government;
— long-distance trade; and
— urbanism.

Other characteristics (such as the presence of religion, art, tools, houses, and the like) could be included in this list, but, as discussed in Chapter 2, these really are characteristics of human existence, whether civilized or not.

Agricultural Dependence

To most people living today, getting food from the raising of plants and animals seems the normal thing to do, but this mode of food production has been in existence only for the past few thousand years, prior to which human beings got all their food from nature by hunting, fishing, and gathering.

The specifics of agriculture will vary from civilization to civilization. Civilizations of Africa, Europe, Asia, and the Pacific Islands, for example, had a wide variety of both plant crops and domesticated animals; in the Americas, on the other hand, civilizations had an equally broad range of plant foods but a more restricted range of domesticated animals. Pigs, cattle, sheep, goats, horses (originally food animals), chickens, ducks, geese, and other animals were common in civilizations in various parts of Asia, Africa, and Europe. In the Americas, far fewer animals were raised. The Maya, for example, had only dogs, ducks, and stingless bees, while the Inca had only dogs, guinea pigs (another food animal), and two domesticated animals of the camel family. Similarly, some civilizations have focused on grains, while others have gotten most of their calories from root crops.

Although the specifics of agriculture vary, all civilizations have developed some way of storing agricultural surplus. This is critical, of course, in seasonal environments, where crops grow poorly or not at all in the off season. It also is important elsewhere, because the amassing and control of agricultural surplus is one means that a government has of ensuring the loyalty—or at least control—of its people. For this reason, agriculture always has focused on crops that can be stored easily, usually in dried form.

Occupational Specialization

In early societies, each person was a generalist, shifting from one task to another in order to accomplish all or most of the jobs necessary for survival. Of course, certain members of a family or community would provide certain services for the whole group; this division of labor was especially common along sexual lines, with women's and men's tasks standardized within each society. But, in general, there was little specialization.

In civilizations, however, the situation was drastically different. Here, there was a great deal of **occupational specialization**, the division of labor into narrow jobs. In the precivilized Indus Valley of Pakistan in 4500 B.C., for example, a typical man produced stone tools, worked in the wheat and barley fields, built his own house, and butchered an animal for food when he was lucky enough to have meat; the typical woman raised children, prepared meals, and produced clothing. Two thousand years later, however, the development of civilization demanded much greater occupational specialization (at least for men) in the Indus Valley. By that time, a man might follow a career as a potter, a weaver, a butcher, a stone tool maker, or another specialist; he would ply his trade and hire other specialists to provide services at which he was unskilled. If he was a specialist farmer, he no longer made his own tools and perhaps did not even build his own house. In many societies, occupational specialization is far more marked for men than it is for women, many of whom have continued as generalists to the present day. Presumably,

the greater focus on the spectrum of domestic activities typical for women has demanded a greater breadth of activity for women than for men.

There is a certain efficiency to occupational specialization. A specialist typically is more skilled at a particular task than a generalist and may have specialized tools that would not be sensible investments for a generalist who performed that task only occasionally. Further, a specialist who devotes so much time to a task may, through practice, develop greater skill or new and more effective ways of performing that task.

From the point of view of the society as a whole, occupational specialization means that every specialist is dependent on every other specialist, because the generalist skills no longer are developed, especially in cities, where there are

FIGURE 3.3 *Chinese Capmaker. Civilizations spawn diverse and specialized occupations, such as the making of caps, shown here in an eighteenth-century depiction. Any society in which a person produces only a single type of ware has to rely on the cooperation and interaction of hundreds of specialists, each of whom produces and exchanges a single product.* From George Henry Mason, *The Costume of China* (London: W. Miller, 1800), Plate LI. Reproduced courtesy of the Harvard-Yenching Library.

An old vaudeville line, revived in Mel Brooks's film *History of the World—Part I*, says that "it's good to be the king." Certainly kings and emperors are at the top of the hierarchy of class stratification, and the rules surrounding their treatment point out their lofty position. The Aztecs ruled most of Mexico from 1300 to 1520, and their treatment of the emperor exemplifies this well.

The *Florentine Codex*, a book written by Aztecs just after the Spanish conquest, tells us how the ruler traveled.

When the ruler went forth, in his hand rested his reed stalk which he went moving in rhythm with his words. His chamberlains and his elders went before him; on both sides, on either hand, they proceeded as they went clearing the way for him. None might cross in front of him; none might come forth before him; none might look up at him; none might come face to face with him.

The same work gives a hint of the splendorous clothing in which the emperor was clad:

The cape with the serpent mask design, bordered with eyes; the cape with the conch shell design, bordered with eyes . . . the tawny colored breech cloth with the ocelot head; the ocelot breech cloth with a step design . . . the head band with two quetzal[a] feather tassels set off with gold, with which they bound their hair; a quetzal feather crest device set

[a] **quetzal:** KEHT zahl

IN THEIR OWN WORDS

It's Good to Be the Aztec Emperor

off with gold, which he wore upon his back . . . a golden arm band; golden ear plugs, which he inserted in his ear-lobes . . .

While the emperor was arrayed in gold, rare furs, and decorations incorporating feathers of the sacred quetzal bird, commoners were more likely to wear merely simple cotton breechcloths and capes.

Even the act of dining underscored the special nature of the emperor, as shown in this account by Bernal Díaz del Castillo,[b] a member of the Spanish conquering army:

The great Montezuma had more than three hundred dishes prepared for him. . . . Everyday they cooked for him hens, turkeys, pheasants, partridges, quails, venison, marsh birds, hares, and rabbits and many kinds of birds and things that are reared in these lands. There are so many things that I would not soon finish telling you of them. . . . When he began to eat, they put in front of him a kind of gilded door so that they would not see him eating, and the four women withdrew and four important old gentlemen stood at his side whom Montezuma talked to and asked questions from time to time and as a great favor he would give each one of these old men a dish of what he liked best. . . . [When he was done] the same four women removed the tablecloths and came back to wash his hands, and they did it with great deference.

[b] **Díaz del Castillo:** DEE ahth dehl cahth TEE yoh

plenty of customers. There may be an incentive for individuals to become specialists, because they may be able to charge enough for their services so that they raise their standard of living. Because the community as a whole needs specialists' services, they are able to increase their charges, providing these charges do not become exorbitant.

Class Stratification

At its simplest, **class stratification** means that there are rich and poor people within a society; a slightly more complete definition is the condition under which members of a society have differential access to resources and power. Each level of society is called a **class**, and many societies have names for the different classes. Among the Natchez Indians of Mississippi, for example, there were three named classes—the sun (the ruler), the nobles, and the stinkards (commoners)—each with its own set of rights and obligations. Once classes have been established, distinctive aspects of culture develop for the different classes; **elite culture** refers to the cultural elements distinctive to the upper classes, while **folk culture**, as used in this text, refers to the cultural elements embraced by the lower classes. Class stratification has been a part of most modern societies for so long that many students have difficulty imagining a classless society, one in which such distinctions did not exist.

Class stratification is usually seen as an outgrowth of occupational specialization. If individuals have different occupations, it is a short step to income disparities, because those with more critical or difficult tasks can demand and receive greater compensation for their services. Trade flourished in a class-stratified society, because traders often were able to make great fortunes by taking chances in investment; at the same time, members of the elite were seeking expensive and rare items to demonstrate their wealth and importance. The power vested in the hereditary rulers of state governments permitted them to set themselves up as the highest class and to accentuate class differences by granting privileges and economic favors to their favorites.

State Government

All people have a need for some method of decision making, both to determine domestic policy and to deal with outsiders. There is, however, a wide variety of ways to perform these tasks, ranging from simply discussing them around a campfire to having elaborate dynasties or election systems. Civilizations are characterized by **state governments** (also known as **polities**): governments with strong leadership, a supporting bureaucracy, and a supportive ideology. These state governments can take many forms, from kingdoms to dictatorships to democracies.

In particular, state governments have coercive powers. That is, the leaders of a state government have the legitimate right to force citizens to conform to the will of the state. For example, if a citizen of seventeenth-century France was commanded to donate an estate to the king, that citizen could be legally forced to do so or suffer the consequences of refusal. Similarly, if a citizen of the United States decides not to pay taxes, that person can be forced to do so by the government or can be imprisoned. Because almost everyone alive today lives under a state form of government, these powers often seem basic to all political systems, but they really are a relatively recent development of the past few thousand years. To people living in a tribe or band, this power of the state to

FIGURE 3.4 *King Kamehameha II.* *This portrait of the last king of Hawaii was painted by an unknown artist in the early years of the twentieth century. Shown in European-style clothing, Kamehameha was the last of a line of divine kings who were attributed special powers and obligations by their subjects. Kamehameha had to avoid contact with certain categories of people who could pollute him, including women, low-class persons, and criminals. Eating food prepared by them, being touched by them, or (in some cases) even being seen by them would be spiritually dangerous.* Bishop Museum, The State Museum of Natural and Cultural History.

enforce its own dictates would be unreasonable and unacceptable.

Yet the coercive nature of state government is absolutely essential to a civilization. The greater numbers of people involved make simpler (and less forceful) forms of government ineffective. In living with so many other people, the individual must surrender many personal choices and freedoms for the good of the group. Of course, selfish and corrupt leaders also can take advantage of such a government to subvert its power for their own personal benefit.

The second characteristic of a state government is **bureaucracy**, a hierarchy in which officials represent the state and its ruler in many interactions. This also is the result of the size of a civilization. A smaller government (such as that of a chiefdom) might be able to operate with a single leader who would make decisions and deal with all governmental problems, but a civilization is simply too large for this option. A civilization must have officials to assist the leader in dealing with regional government, and they, in turn, must have their assistants to deal with local government, and so on. Many state governments, including most today, can involve significant percentages of the population in governmental roles somewhere within their bureaucracy.

The third defining characteristic of a state government is a state ideology to support it. The state ideology usually is a religion, but it also can be a more secular idea system, such as Confucianism in earlier China or Marxism-Leninism in many twentieth-century communist states. Whatever form it takes, the state ideology is distinctive to a particular state, serving to unify the people behind a common cause and to legitimize the state. The notion of independence of church and state is a recent idea, developing largely in the American and French revolutions of the eighteenth century. In contrast, most earlier civilizations have had their own distinctive religions, each with its characteristic gods, rituals, and mythology.

Sometimes, the religious and governmental officials are one and the same. Such a system, called a **theocracy**, usually recognizes a deity as the head of the government and a high religious official as the interpreter of that deity's will. A high priest (or, less commonly, high priestess) becomes the supreme worldly ruler under such an arrangement, merging priest and monarch and forging a direct and major link between government and religion. Ancient Egypt is an excellent example of this kind of a theocracy, where the supreme leader (pharaoh) was not only the head priest or priestess but also was considered divine in his or her own right, an earthly manifestation of a deity.

In nontheocratic states, the link is less direct but no less important. In those cases, the state ideology legitimizes the rulers, who frequently cite divine will as their ultimate source of power. It is critical to leaders that their positions remain unquestioned, and no higher authority could be invoked than that of the deities. The coronation of royalty in medieval Europe was conducted by religious officials, this practice growing directly out of divine underwriting of this royal authority.

Looked at even more broadly, a state ideology provides another function for a state government.

Unlike smaller-scale governments, state governments are often quite heterogeneous, incorporating diverse local factions that previously had viewed themselves as distinct. A common religion is an important way of promoting a sense of unity in a state that might otherwise risk dissolution. The Inca found religion a potent way of controlling ethnic groups within their empire, forcing them to adopt the Inca religion while allowing them to incorporate some of their own gods into the Inca pantheon. In this manner, a common bond was forged throughout the empire at the same time that the divine status of the emperor was confirmed.

Long-Distance Trade

Every society trades goods with its neighbors, often as symbols of their mutual good will. Civilizations, however, typically conduct large-scale trading operations at great distances. In part, this is in response to their greater ability to devote labor and resources to the activities necessary for this kind of trade. The mounting of a trading expedition begins with the amassing of goods to trade (and possibly the securing of loans to purchase the goods), an operation that requires up-front investment. Next, a team of skilled specialists must be assembled. They must be able to navigate to the intended distant place, to translate from one language to another, to defend the trading party from raiders and robbers along the way, to make judgments about values of goods, and to organize the entire operation. Finally, the organizers of the trade must accept the possibility that they will have to absorb big losses, because the risks in long-distance trade are usually great; but so are the profits.

Civilizations typically have had not only the means to mount long-distance trading operations but also the incentive. Many items procured through long-distance trade are luxury items to be used by a privileged class. Not only are the upper classes the only ones that can afford such exotica, but they can gain prestige from their ownership. Rare gems have been the privilege of the rich in most societies, and a jewel could serve as a symbol of the owner's status.

Although there have been cases of nonroyal entrepreneurs who have successfully negotiated major long-distance trading, until the past few centuries it typically has been controlled by a royal

FIGURE 3.5 *The Aztec* Pochteca. *The Aztec Empire of Mexico accorded long-distance traders,* pochteca, *a high status. The* pochteca *carried out trade over vast distances and also served as spies and government representatives. The top frame of this Aztec painting shows them meeting with a noble (on the left); the middle frame shows porters carrying parcels for the* pochteca; *the bottom frame shows a* pochteca *bargaining at the market.* Biblioteca Medicea Laurenziana, Florence.

family. Among the Aztecs of Mexico around 1300 to 1500, for example, there were *pochteca*,[1] a class of specialist traders employed by the government. They sometimes traveled well over a thousand miles from the Aztec heartland of central Mexico, including regular trips to Central America and possibly to the Mississippi Valley and what is now Arizona. These *pochteca* were a hybrid of diplomat, trader, and spy; they were feared and respected by their trading partners, and this fear and respect undoubtedly aided them in negotiations. The silk traders of Eurasia, sometimes royal and sometimes private, also mounted caravans that crossed thousands of miles of inhospitable terrain to link China and Europe.

Urbanism

Urbanism, of course, refers to the presence of cities, but the definition of "city" is not so easy as it sounds. Certainly, a city must be large, but are all large settlements cities? Further, how large is "large"? If the Athens of Aristotle were to be placed in the modern United States, it would be merely a small town, yet its importance in classical Greece was far greater than its small population (in modern terms) might indicate. What is needed is a definition of urbanism that does not rely exclusively on size, and such a definition comes from the discipline of geography.

As used in this text, **urbanism** refers to the condition in which the settlement system in a region meets the following conditions:

— some settlements are relatively large;

— the larger settlements have internal diversity, with rich and poor neighborhoods, commercial districts, and perhaps other zones; and

— the larger settlements serve as **central places**, places where people from surrounding communities go to procure goods and services unavailable in smaller settlements.

This definition, although more complex than some, emphasizes what is really important about urbanism. It is not merely the size of a settlement that matters, but what its relationship is to the entire region. The fact that Ur, the capital of ancient Sumeria, had an estimated population of more than 100,000 persons in 2200 B.C. is impressive, but the real significance of Ur is that it served

[1] *pochteca:* pohch TEH kuh

FIGURE 3.6 *Present-Day Teotihuacán, from the Air.* *The ancient Mexican city of Teotihuacán, one of the world's largest at its height in* A.D. *700, had all the internal complexity of a modern city. Its central precinct was the most exclusive, with massive temples and palaces; nearby was a neighborhood of elite housing boasting courtyards and even fountains; farther away were industrial districts, warehouse districts, low-class neighborhoods, and slums. There were ethnic neighborhoods, too, such as "the Oaxaca barrio," where Oaxacan immigrants lived, practicing their religion and customs.* A. Moldvay/NGS Image Collection.

as an administrative, commercial, and religious center that controlled a vast area of what is now Iraq, with palaces for the rulers, great storehouses for grain, temples for worship, and craft centers for the manufacture of goods used over all of the Sumerian civilization.

Typically, **urbanization** (the development of cities) is a relatively rapid process. For example, at the ancient city of Teotihuacán[2] in central Mexico, the estimated population of 2,000 persons in 500 B.C. remained nearly constant until about 200 B.C. At that time, it swelled rapidly to 25,000 by 100 B.C., more than tenfold in a century; in the following 500 years, population increased another eightfold to nearly 200,000 by A.D. 400. This incredible rate of growth cannot be explained by the usual mechanism of **intrinsic growth**, the increase in popula-

tion as a result of families' having more than two children who survive to adulthood and become parents. To achieve this magnitude of population increase from intrinsic growth would require that every family more than double its size each generation, something that never has happened in recorded history. Instead, the growth of Teotihuacán must be attributed to the migration of people from the countryside into the city; indeed, during this period of intense growth at Teotihuacán, surrounding villages went into a population decline.

For many people, moving to the city meant abandoning their traditional kinship ties and support systems. Indeed, many left behind their families or disrupted their kin relationships, leaving themselves vulnerable to disaster with limited means of emergency help. Newly immigrated urbanites often found themselves among

[2] **Teotihuacán:** tay oh tee hwah KAHN

strangers, rather than among supportive family members who could help them through a lean time.

Why did country people wish to go to the city to live? Probably for reasons that are starkly similar to those of today. Life in the countryside was known to be hard, perhaps dull; for some people, rural farming had led to debt and even to loss of their land. The city, in contrast, was a vibrant place, full of good-paying jobs, excitement, and opportunities, especially in commercial and service occupations. Village farmers moving to Teotihuacán (or Ur or any other city) probably had visions of an improved life, perhaps a better job, and probably a higher standard of living. The fact that many were disappointed and found themselves trapped in the ancient equivalent of slums appears to have had little effect on the flood of immigrants into cities. The very factors at the heart of our definition of urbanism—the diversity of occupations, goods, and services in a city—probably have been directly responsible for the staggering growth of ancient and modern cities.

Although cities often develop as commercial centers, they usually gain other functions as well. State governments typically find them very handy as central places where administrative power can be concentrated, and religions usually find cities appropriate places to house their central hierarchies.

THE SECONDARY ELEMENTS OF CIVILIZATION

Although the six core elements discussed in the preceding section define civilization, many other elements often are present in civilization and are intimately linked to the core. Certain of these elements, called "secondary elements" in this text, are present in every civilization, but which ones are present will vary from case to case; relatively few civilizations will possess all the secondary elements.

There will be some disagreement among scholars about which elements belong in the set of secondary elements, but the following clearly are important:

— a developed transportation system;

— writing;

— standards of measurement (including currency);

— a formal legal system;

— a great art style;

— monumental architecture;

— mathematics;

— sophisticated metallurgy; and

— astronomy.

Developed Transportation System

The earliest human beings walked along trails blazed by animals, carrying their goods on their backs or in their hands. This mode of transportation proved adequate for millennia, and it is still important in many places. Civilizations, however, often have made improvements to facilitate the movement of people and goods. Without such transportation improvements, a civilization might experience difficulty moving troops to establish internal order or repel intrusion, moving commodities that were produced in one area for use elsewhere, or moving vital diplomatic information rapidly.

Many improvements have been in terms of vehicles. The development of boats is lost in prehistory, but early agriculturalists clearly used them. The ongoing technical improvement of boats has resulted in faster, more manageable, more stable, and larger vessels.

Much later than boats, wheeled vehicles were developed in Eurasia and Africa. The earliest evidence for such vehicles comes from the ox-drawn wagons of Sumeria and the later horse-drawn war chariots; human beings have drawn carts at most periods, too. In the Americas, the wheel was known in some areas but never was used for vehicles, and human or pack-animal labor was used for transportation.

In a sense, the animals that pulled vehicles were developed by human invention, because they were domesticated animals, modified from their wild forms by selective breeding. Although strength and stamina clearly were important considerations, docility must have been primary, especially in Africa and Eurasia, where many of the wild progenitors of draft animals were vicious and dangerous beasts. In the Americas, only a single draft animal was developed, the llama of Peru, and that was used for carrying bundles but never for drawing vehicles.

FIGURE 3.7 *Wheeled Toy from Ancient Mexico.*
This pottery toy from Veracruz is nearly 3,000 years old and still rolls on its tiny, axled wheels. While people in the Americas were well aware of how a wheel could work—as this toy shows—they chose not to utilize it. This choice may reflect the dense rain forests and steep mountains in which the earliest American civilizations developed, as well as the shortage of animals that could be domesticated for pulling carts. © Justin Kerr 1987.

A second approach to improving transportation is to improve the route over which a vehicle passes. Graded and paved roads, bridges, and causeways through wetlands can vastly improve the speed and ease with which goods and personnel can be moved. The Roman road system is particularly well known and admired, but the Incan, Chinese, and Persian road systems were equally sophisticated and perhaps more impressive because of the rugged nature of the lands traversed.

A final way to attack the problems of land transportation is through improved organization. The Inca, for example, employed a system of runners (*chaski*) and support facilities that permitted a message or light parcel to cross the empire rapidly. Each *chaski* would run only a few miles to the next way station, where his message or parcel would be passed on to the next *chaski*, covering hundreds of miles in just a few days.

Writing

The idea that spoken language could be converted into a written form and preserved is such a revolutionary idea that it took true genius to conceive of it. Some forms of writing are **alphabetic**, using a limited number of symbols to represent the component sounds of a language. English is alphabetic and uses just twenty-six letters (and a few punctuation marks) to produce all of its messages. In contrast, some other forms of writing are **ideographic**, wherein each symbol represents an idea, irrespective of the pronunciation of the spoken word. (Chinese and Mayan writing systems are largely ideographic, although each also incorporates some phonetic [pronunciation-based] elements.) Ideographic writing has many more symbols than alphabetic writing, often thousands of characters.

Writing has developed in many places around the world. In many cases, a preexisting written language that was developed in another place served as a model for imitation, but it appears that writing developed independently in at least three places in antiquity. Curiously, the motivations behind the development of writing in each of these places seem to have been different.

The earliest system of writing developed in Sumeria around 4500 B.C. This system apparently began as an ideographic system that soon was modified into **cuneiform**,[3] an ideographic system with some alphabetic (or syllabic) elements that is discussed in more depth in Chapter 4. It was developed primarily to keep track of business accounts among the traders of Sumeria.

Independently, writing developed in the Shang Dynasty of China around 1500 B.C. This writing was largely phonetic, though there also are pictographic (picture-writing) and ideographic elements. Our earliest evidence of this writing suggests that it developed as a medium for religious-divinatory expression. (Chinese writing is discussed further in Chapter 5.)

Again independently, the Maya of the third century and their immediate predecessors in eastern Mexico developed a system of glyphic writing that is neither alphabetic nor ideographic but a mixture of the two. Mayan writing's primary purpose was to glorify rulers and nobles on monuments dedicated to them, and it is discussed further in Chapter 6.

---

[3] **cuneiform:** koo NAY ih form

FIGURE 3.8 *Three Babylonian Recipes.* *Writing permits a society to commit its knowledge and ideas to a durable medium, passing it along to the future. This clay tablet from Babylon in Mesopotamia is in the Akkadian language, recorded with cuneiform script. It gives recipes for goat stew, bird stew, and braised turnips. All were heavily seasoned with leeks and onions.* Yale Babylonian Collection.

Once writing developed, regardless of the initial function, it proved useful for a wide spectrum of purposes. Curiously, some civilizations never developed writing, notably those of Peru.

Standards of Measurement

A traditional builder can estimate lengths by eye, just as a barter system may work perfectly well using no more sophisticated or standardized measure than "some." But a larger-scale society needs a more accurate and standardized system of weights and measures. An Aztec tax levy required a particular amount of corn or cotton, just as a Babylonian merchant expected to get a consistent amount of wheat for his *shekel*. Further, monumental architecture demands standardized units of measure, both for planning and construction.

Only disaster could have followed if several beam-cutters for a Chinese temple had measured the lengths of their beams in multiples of their own forearms or, worse yet, if they simply had guessed at length.

Most civilizations used standardized units of measure for length and volume, and many had standardized units of weight. Less common were units of time, the best known of which is the hour, ultimately based on Sumerian astronomy (filtered through Egypt) and the sundial.

A special case is the standardized unit of currency. Money usually derives its value from one of two characteristics: its natural rarity or the labor that goes into its production. The use of gold as a standard for currency in recent times and the use of cowrie shells as money in interior Africa (far from the ocean where the mollusk lives) are examples of rarity-based money. Examples of labor-based currency are the shell beads (*wampum*) used by the Iroquois and Algonquian[4] Indians of northeastern North America; the shells occurred locally in great abundance, but the value of *wampum* came from the great deal of work required to laboriously grind out the beads. Early civilizations typically used rarity-based currency, particularly metals. Later, however, they frequently switched to labor-based currency, possibly to permit the government to produce greater quantities of money to cover its debt.

Formal Legal System

Small-scale societies display a high degree of shared values and attitudes about what constitutes proper behavior and what should be done about departures from that standard. Larger-scale societies, on the other hand, have more diversity of opinion and greater possibilities of avoiding punishment for a transgression, because one can simply move to another community where no one knows of the wrongdoing. Under these circumstances, a formal legal system with a code of laws and sometimes with police and judges to enforce them emerges.

The most famous and one of the earlier of these formal legal systems was established by Hammurabi[5] of Babylonia in the eighteenth century B.C. Hammurabi actually revised the codes of

[4] **Algonquian:** al GOHN kee uhn
[5] **Hammurabi:** hawm oo RAH bee

Libit-Ishtar, Ibi-Sin, and Ur-Nammu, all earlier judges of Sumeria, making two contributions. First, he adapted the codes for the three-tiered social system of Babylonia, which differed from that of Sumeria, which had only two legal classes. Second, unlike earlier local codes, Hammurabi's code served as a model for judges throughout Babylonia. (See "In Their Own Words" in Chapter 4 for more discussion.)

Formal legal systems appear to never have been in force in the earliest civilizations of a region. Rather, they seem to have developed several centuries later, after the civilization has had sufficient time to identify its problems.

Great Art Style

The term **great art style** refers to an art style that occurs over a broad area and is the dominant style, often the only style other than family-based folk art. A great art style typically—though not always—occurs in public settings and is associated with a state government and state religion. Despite the way it sounds, the term conveys no value judgment of what is or is not "great" art.

A great art style can help unify a civilization by providing a commonality throughout the geographical extent of the civilization. At the same time, its grandeur often serves to enhance the prestige of the rulers, and its usual focus on religious and dynastic themes aids in legitimizing the government and its leaders.

In some cases, great art styles are very easy to appreciate, as with the socialist-realist poster art associated with the Russian Revolution. These images were realistic and powerful, evoking the strength and importance of workers. Such art styles provide a rallying point for sympathies. In contrast, some great art styles are obscure and mysterious to all but the initiated elite. An example of this latter type of great art style is the Chavín[6] style of Peru, around 1200 to 100 B.C., in which figures are formed of out-of-place body parts and intertwine with one another in a complex mass that is very difficult to interpret. This difficulty probably made the priests especially important, because only they were privy to the arcane truths and events represented by the art.

Some civilizations had no great art style, as was the case with the Inca and, according to some

scholars, the Roman Empire. These civilizations instead incorporated aspects of the styles of neighbors and conquered peoples into an eclectic and composite—though sometimes disharmonious—style.

Monumental Architecture

Monumental architecture simply refers to large and impressive buildings and similar structures erected at public expense. Although the concept is simple, the execution is not. The production of monumental architecture demands many technical and organizational skills usually available only in civilizations, and the costs for labor and materials could be extravagant and beyond the means of less complex societies.

Unlike simpler architecture that can be planned without extensive engineering skills, monumental architecture requires professional planning. The mechanical stresses involved in large buildings can be quite extreme, and small deviations from a plan can result in major problems for a large structure, sometimes affecting its stability.

No lesser a logistical problem is organizing the workforce. Assuming that sufficient funds have been allocated, the task of assembling and maintaining a workforce sufficient to build a monumental structure is daunting. Every worker must be fed; if workers are paid, someone must do the calculating of wages and distribution of pay; housing for the workers must be established; various other needs must be met, sometimes including such items as clothing, medical care, female companionship for male workers, and spiritual comfort. Organizing such an effort and keeping it organized over a period of years is no small task and requires a large force of administrators, accountants, quartermasters, and the like.

The materials for monumental architecture often were special, selected for their unusual appearance or their special structural characteristics. For example, many polished limestone blocks that faced the great pyramids of Egypt came from the Libyan and Arabian hills, hundreds of miles distant, because suitably beautiful stone was not available locally. The colossal stone heads of the Olmecs of eastern Mexico were rafted and hauled over 100 miles through jungle in order to provide a sufficiently hard stone for the preparation of huge portraits of the Olmec rulers.

[6] **Chavín:** chah VEEN

FIGURE 3.9 *The Bayon.* *Eight hundred years ago, the Khmer civilization flourished in what is now Cambodia. To proclaim the grandeur of their cities and their deities, Khmer rulers built massive temples, some so large that they are termed "temple-mountains." The one shown here, the Bayon, has fifty-four towers and a central spire, all rising majestically from the jungle. Such monumental architecture enhances the stature of a society, its rulers, and its deities.* Wilbur E. Garrett/NGS Image Collection.

Monumental architecture can serve many purposes. The pyramids of Egypt were primarily monuments to and resting places for dead royalty. In contrast, the Mayan pyramids of eastern Mexico, Guatemala, Belize, Honduras, and El Salvador were primarily raised platforms to support temples for worship. The massive temples that flanked the main streets of Teotihuacán were used for religious ceremonies, but many scholars feel that their main function was to impress visiting traders.

But these and other examples of monumental architecture had a common underlying purpose: They aggrandized the deities, the rulers who represented them, and the civilizations over which they ruled. As such, they were impressive reminders to the commoners, to internal political rivals, and to visiting representatives of foreign powers. They served as tangible proofs of the legitimacy of the state and its associated religion, as well as its awesome power.

Although monumental architecture was erected with public funds, the edifices were not necessarily open to the public. Many monuments were visited only by a select few of the elite classes. Mayan temples and their counterparts at Teotihuacán were forbidden to the commoners, and some were accessible only to the highest of the nobility and priestly classes. Indeed, massive Mayan temples that might have taken hundreds or thousands of workers many years to complete were designed for use only by the favored few, as evidenced by interior spaces that could accommodate no more than ten or twenty people at a time.

Mathematics

Many small-scale societies have had very limited mathematics, often merely counting of the one-two-three-many variety. Civilizations, on the other hand, have greater need for a developed mathe-

PATHS TO THE PAST

Building an Egyptian Pyramid

Egyptian pyramids are magnificent examples of monumental architecture, longstanding symbols of ancient engineering skills. They served as memorials to—and often burial places for—pharaohs and a few other important officials. These monuments were huge: The Great Pyramid is 754 feet along each side and 481 feet high, covering an area of 13.1 acres. All the pyramids had the familiar shape of four triangular sides tilted together to form a point at the top, and many had internal chambers and passages, mostly for the storage of treasures or of the bodies of the deceased. These are impressive monuments, but how difficult were they to build? Careful analysis of ancient Egyptian documents and artifacts, coupled with experimentation by archaeologists, has provided answers.

There are six basic steps to building an Egyptian pyramid. First, because such a massive structure requires bedrock to rest upon, workers—including slaves, hired laborers, and soldiers—had to remove the sand and loose rock on the surface and level the bedrock to receive the pyramid foundation. This, as well as other Egyptian stoneworking, was accomplished primarily with stone hammers, copper chisels, and a great deal of labor.

Second, the area had to be surveyed so that the pyramid could be laid out facing the cardinal points (north, south, east, and west), with equal sides. The surveying tools for this were known from canal building and consisted primarily of the *merkhet* (a bar and plumb line used for measuring the angle of a star or the sun above the horizon), the *bay* (a sighting rod with a notch in its top), and a calibrated measuring cord (for measuring distances). With these three instruments, some ingenuity, and some knowledge of arithmetic and elementary geometry, a surveyor could achieve the accuracy shown in the positioning and construction of the pyramids.

Third, while the first two steps were going on, crews were quarrying the limestone for construction and transporting it to the construction site. The transportation was primarily via the Nile River, which, during flood, was within a mile of the pyramid sites. After that, the stones were hauled along a temporary construction road by human labor, using sledges (heavy platforms with runners like those on modern sleds), ropes, perhaps rollers (wooden poles over which blocks were pulled), and a great deal of labor. Experiments have shown that these techniques are fully workable.

Fourth, at the site itself, the stones were cut into shape and smoothed. This was done primarily with copper chisels and stone hammers, although sand abrasives probably were used sometimes. Although some early scholars speculated that ancient Egypt had some "lost secret" for tempering copper to make harder tools, there is neither evidence nor need for this explanation: Experiments with copper tools have shown them equal to the task of working the soft limestone used for the pyramids.

Fifth, the shaped stones had to be raised to their proper positions and placed there. Fanciful ideas have been advanced of machines ranging from the quaint (a catapultlike wooden frame that would have swung a block into place) to the bizarre (spacecraft assisting the ancient Egyptians for reasons that presumably were known only to the space aliens). More likely, the blocks were hauled up earthen ramps that were laboriously built to where the stones were needed, then removed. Both the huge interior blocks and the smaller exterior blocks were apparently brought to their places in this way.

Sixth and finally, the pyramids may have been painted. Although we are accustomed to thinking of the pyramids as the gleaming white of their limestone facings, several analyses of materials on their surfaces have suggested the possibility that they may have been painted brightly as a final step. Scaffolds would have supported painters on the sloping and slippery pyramid faces.

How difficult was it to build an Egyptian pyramid? The principles and skills involved were not incredibly complex, at least in terms of modern standards, and we certainly need not resort to "lost secrets of the ancients" or to space aliens to understand how the construction took place. On the other hand, the scale of the task was daunting, and the construction was carried out within fine tolerances, as with the less than one-half-inch variation for the basal level of the Great Pyramid. We must admire the ancient builders who brought together skills, planning, organization, and labor to produce some of the greatest monuments of their day.

matics. Both commercial trade and tax collection for a state government require arithmetic as a means of calculating and recording figures. Monumental architecture demands enough sophistication in geometry and arithmetic to calculate angles and lengths and to accurately estimate amounts of materials needed. Astronomy requires skills in analyzing number series. For the most part, early civilizations focused on mathematical procedures that facilitated practical tasks, rather than on theoretical concerns. We have little idea of how sophisticated mathematics was in preliterate civilizations or in civilizations whose writing has not been deciphered, although the presence of monumental architecture may provide a clue that it was moderately well developed.

Sophisticated Metallurgy

The set of skills, practices, and knowledge that relate to the working of metals collectively is known as **metallurgy**. Metals have been in use in various parts of the world for the past 10,000 years, but early usage was based on very simple principles and limited understanding. For example, the most common early metal use consisted of taking native copper (copper found in pure form) and hammering it into shape without the use of heat. Although this practice produced a workable tool or attractive ornament, it was limited by the rarity of native metals, the restriction to soft metals like copper, the relative crudeness of the product, and the impossibility of mass production.

The sophisticated metallurgy of many civilizations goes beyond these simple practices. More advanced techniques include smelting (the rendering of ores to derive pure metals from compounds), alloying (the mixing of different metals to produce a metal with characteristics different from those of any of its components), casting (producing shaped objects by melting metal and pouring it into a mold, where it hardens), plating (the production of a thin layer of one metal on another, usually a precious metal on a less valuable one), annealing (heating and gradually cooling a metal to reduce internal stresses and make it harder and more durable), and other techniques.

In Europe, Africa, and Asia, metallurgy was considerably more developed than in the Americas. Much of the impetus for this greater development was military. The development of bronze in

what is now Turkey around 3000 B.C. was a turning point in Eurasian metallurgy. Bronze, an alloy of copper and tin, was harder than other available materials and could be formed easily into weaponry, giving its possessors an immediate edge over their enemies. From this time, Eurasian metallurgy focused largely on improving weapons, leading finally to iron and steel.

In the Americas, the range of known metallurgical techniques restricted artisans to using relatively soft metals, such as gold, silver, and copper. As a result, ornaments were the focus of metallurgical work, and metal tools had only limited importance in technology.

Astronomy

Early civilizations saw astronomy very differently from modern ones. Although modern scholars conceive of astronomy as a theoretical science, their earlier counterparts saw it as a craft that supported practical activities with major impacts on daily life. One of astronomy's greatest impacts in ancient civilizations was in terms of maintaining the calendar, a critical task for scheduling religious rituals. The other major impact was in the practice of **astrology**, the prediction of the future on the basis of the alignments of stars and planets. Both ritual scheduling and astrological prediction were important activities in most ancient civilizations.

Before the development of civilizations, small-scale societies used simple astronomy, largely to predict a few simple yearly events. Foremost among these were the equinoxes (when sunlight and darkness are of equal duration) and the solstices (the days with the shortest and longest duration of daylight). These "four corners" of the solar year mark the beginnings of the four seasons in the modern Western calendar, and their importance to changing seasons was not lost on other peoples.

But the astronomy of early civilizations went much further. Ancient Egyptians, basing their reasoning on the dates when the star Sirius rose above the horizon, realized that leap years were needed to adjust the calendar to account for the fractional part of a day exceeding 365 days per year. Zhou[7] Dynasty astronomers in China predicted solar eclipses, although not flawlessly, as shown by a document from 1311 B.C. that notes one such

[7] **Zhou:** JOH

FIGURE 3.10 *Stonehenge.* *Built on a grassy plain in southern England, Stonehenge was begun around 2800 B.C. and was finished by 1500 B.C. The structure was apparently a combination of temple for religious rituals and astronomical observatory for viewing (and perhaps predicting) celestial events. Lines of sight along stones' edges produce shadows and light shafts that shift with the seasons, permitting the recognition of the vernal equinox and other potentially significant astronomical events. These in turn triggered seasonal rituals and astrological predictions.* Christopher Chippindale.

eclipse occurring "on the wrong day." Assyrian astronomers compiled a list of rising times for the planet Venus and apparently could predict future risings. Further, ancient astronomers could apply some of their knowledge to building, as at Chichen Itzá,[8] a Mayan city in Mexico. There, at the spring and autumn equinoxes, the shadow of a railing falls on a stairway of a temple to form the undulating body of a snake that terminates at the bottom of the stairway with a sculpture of a snake's head.

These are impressive successes of ancient astronomers, but we should not ascribe more knowledge to them than is warranted. Much of their knowledge was gained by relentless observation and record keeping, rather than by scientific understanding. Babylonian astronomers had some knowledge of lunar eclipses and their recurrence, but they attributed them to the moon deity's doing battle with demons, not to the geometrical and physical explanations of modern science. Given the calendrical and astrological purposes of early astronomy, scientific explanation of the modern sort simply was irrelevant.

INTERRELATIONSHIPS OF THE ELEMENTS OF CIVILIZATION

As no doubt has been obvious in the reading of this chapter, the elements that characterize civilization are not independent of one another. Rather, they are intimately related to one another, with the development of one leading to the development of others. It is easy to create various models of how these elements interrelate, although there is no guarantee that such a plausible picture will be accurate.

One possible model for interrelating the elements of civilization begins with population pressures that lead to the agricultural dependence that kicks off the process. The increased food supply permits population increase, which in turn encourages urbanism and long-distance trade. Urbanism and trade lead to increased occupational specialization and class stratification; some scholars believe that it also leads directly to a state

[8] **Chichen Itzá:** CHEE chehn eet ZAH

government. The establishment of the state is followed by a state religion, a great art style, and a legal code; state support, in combination with occupational specialization, leads to monumental architecture, developed transportation systems, sophisticated metallurgy, mathematics, and astronomy. Writing develops out of some combination of occupational specialization, trade, and the aggrandizing of rulers.

Probably the best explanations of the development of civilization recognize that there are many processes taking place simultaneously and that there is no simple sequence of events or set of causes and effects. The best explanations also probably are directed toward specific cases, rather than toward discovering any single cause of the development of civilization in all places. The differences among Peru and China and Egypt and India are so great that no recognizable pattern may characterize them all.

UTILITY OF THE CONCEPT OF CIVILIZATION

The discussion earlier in this chapter noted that some scholars find the civilization concept so flawed that they reject it outright. Now that we have discussed the concept at some length, is it worth using?

We believe that it is, though it carries some liabilities. The concept of civilization grew out of a kind of judgmental and ethnocentric scholarship that few scholars of today would endorse. We hope history and related disciplines have matured to a stage where the term no longer will be used with these implications.

But the concept emphasizes a basic distinction that is useful in the study of the human past: There are fundamental differences between simple, small-scale societies and complex, large-scale societies. Those relatively complex societies, which we call "civilizations," have a different and faster pace of development and change; they are stimulated by economic and political competition; and a greater diversity of events and processes shapes their futures. The smaller-scale societies, in contrast, have a slower pace of change; they have fewer and less complicated factions; and the lifestyles and life histories of their members are more alike. All of these factors distinguish civilizations from other human societies.

We believe these differences to be basic and important, but the line between civilized and non-civilized societies should not be drawn too starkly. In reality, societies lie along a continuum of complexity. At one end of the continuum lie the small-scale, less complex societies, and at the other end lie the highly complex ones. Although there will be no controversies regarding the societies near the ends, some societies in the middle may pose difficulties in classification. The wise student will remember that it matters little how one categorizes those borderline cases; what really matters is an understanding of how that society was organized and developed. After all, the concept of civilization was invented by human beings as a convenience to help understand human diversity; it has no independent existence, and it is meaningless to search for the answer to whether or not a society is "truly" a civilization.

SUMMARY

1. Cultural evolution is the general pattern of change that has occurred over long periods of time in most places throughout the world, where societies become more complex, particularly in terms of different roles for their members and advanced knowledge and skills.

2. The underlying cause of most cultural evolution probably is population growth, which leads to agriculture, which in turn leads to a wide variety of developments.

3. One model of stages of cultural evolution defines bands (hunter-gatherers with little leadership), tribes (agriculturalists with leadership by example), chiefdoms (agriculturalists with coercive leadership), and civilization.

4. Civilization is defined by six core elements: agricultural dependence, occupational specialization, class stratification, state government, long-distance trade, and urbanism. Secondary elements are common but not universal among civiliza-

tions: a developed transportation system, writing, standardized measurement, a formal legal system, a great art style, monumental architecture, mathematics, sophisticated metallurgy, and astronomy.

5. The elements that characterize civilization are intimately interrelated, with one element encouraging the development of others.

6. Societies that are not civilizations are simply smaller-scale societies that have been able to survive successfully without resorting to the more complex strategies of civilizations, many of which place restrictions on their citizenry.

SUGGESTED READINGS

Lamberg-Karlovsky, C. C., and Jeremy A. Sabloff. *Ancient Civilizations: The Near East and Mesoamerica*. Second edition. Prospect Heights, Ill.: Waveland Press, 1995. An accessible comparison of the origins of civilization in Southwest Asia and Mesoamerica.

Renfrew, Colin. *Approaches to Social Archaeology*. Edinburgh, Scot.: Edinburgh University Press, 1984. An influential discussion of theories and models of cultural evolution.

Sabloff, Jeremy A., and C. C. Lamberg-Karlovsky, eds. *Ancient Civilization and Trade*. Albuquerque: University of New Mexico Press, 1975. A collection of classic scholarly articles on the role of trade in civilization.

Tainter, Joseph A. *The Collapse of Complex Societies*. Cambridge, Eng.: Cambridge University Press, 1988. A scholarly examination of the processes that bring about the collapse of civilizations, drawing on different world examples.

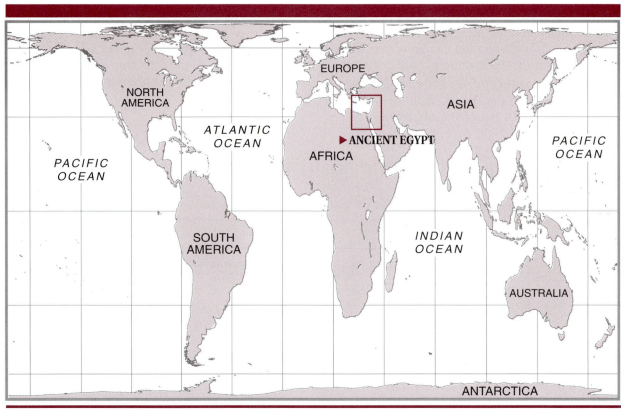

NORTH
AMERICA

EUROPE

ASIA

ATLANTIC
OCEAN

► ANCIENT EGYPT

PACIFIC
OCEAN

AFRICA

PACIFIC
OCEAN

SOUTH
AMERICA

INDIAN
OCEAN

AUSTRALIA

ANTARCTICA

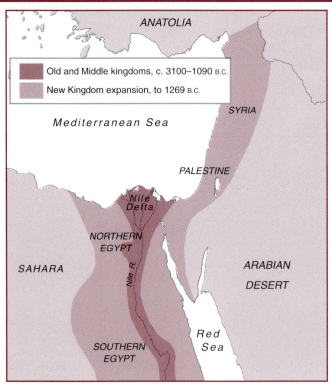

ANATOLIA

▮ Old and Middle kingdoms, c. 3100–1090 B.C.

▯ New Kingdom expansion, to 1269 B.C.

SYRIA

Mediterranean Sea

PALESTINE

Nile
Delta

NORTHERN
EGYPT

ARABIAN

SAHARA

DESERT

Nile R.

SOUTHERN
EGYPT

Red
Sea

► **ANCIENT EGYPT**

Southwest Asia, Egypt, and the Eastern Mediterranean

around 3500–331 B.C.

The young man stood up, rubbed his aching lower back with his hands, and kicked at the parched ground. Rain had been scarce, causing river levels to drop and irrigation ditches to dry up. If moisture didn't come soon to the shriveling plants, the entire crop would be dead. He made up his mind to spend the next day traveling with other farmers from his area to the nearby city, where they could pay the priests to offer a special sacrifice to Ishtar, the fertility goddess. He believed that her intervention with Enki, the water god, would appease whatever insult had caused the god to withhold the precious life fluid. Perhaps Enki would allow the water to flow again in the mighty rivers.

Approximately 8,500 years ago, agriculture developed in Southwest Asia and Egypt in the Tigris-Euphrates[1] and Nile river valleys. The turn from a hunter-gatherer society to an agriculturally based society produced the opportunity for the development of civilization, as discussed in Chapter 3. Growth toward urbanization first occurred in the river valley of southern Mesopotamia (roughly modern Iraq and Kuwait) and in Egypt. Some larger urban centers could support extensive long-distance trade, massive building projects, and armies to protect them. Scholars call these centers **city-states** and identify them by the cities' names. Eventually, several city-states negotiated treaties or conquered their neighbors, resulting in the development of kingdoms that placed several cities under central authorities. Several kingdoms divided Mesopotamia, but Egyptian city-states

[1] **Tigris:** TY grihs; **Euphrates:** yoo FRAY teez

merged into two large kingdoms (in the north and south). Egyptians eventually moved toward unification, finally encompassing the entire river valley civilization in one large kingdom. Unification was often a fleeting phenomenon in Mesopotamian history; a few kingdoms expanded into **empires** (states that control large areas that incorporate societies culturally different from themselves).

The impact of large-scale agricultural production and the growth of urban centers also influenced labor practices and gender roles. In sedentary agricultural societies, the rate of childbearing increased to as frequently as possible to ensure that enough surviving children could help with chores and tend fields. Women needed to be engaged in labor compatible with the needs of child rearing; their work had to be relatively safe and easily interruptible, like textile production and food preparation. Men's occupations remained outside the home as farmers, artisans, and merchants, who sometimes traveled long distances to sell their goods; while they were traveling with the caravans, however, their wives sometimes managed their business interests.

The religious practices of ancient peoples in Southwest Asia, Egypt, and the eastern Mediterranean also changed after the development of wide-scale agriculture. They developed formal ritualistic practices to manipulate the actions of nature deities who they believed controlled wind, rain, and agricultural cycles and war deities who defended their cities. Rituals became increasingly complex, necessitating a priestly class to memorize and perform them. In many areas of Southwest Asia, Egypt, and the Mediterranean, new deities were introduced through conquest and migration. When one city conquered another, the subjects often identified the conqueror's deities with existing ones, intertwining the myths until the divinities became indistinguishable.

Scholars call the worship of many deities **polytheism**; in some cities, hundreds of deities were worshiped. The worship of deities residing in natural forces and objects such as wind, groves of trees, and mountains is called **animism**. The practice of attributing to deities such human characteristics as human form or temperament is **anthropomorphism**. Agricultural communities focused their worship on fertility goddesses, while city populations predominantly worshiped male sky gods that were said to afford the city protection and guide warriors in battle.

FIGURE 4.1 *Pazuzu, the Assyrian Wind Demon.*
Pazuzu's fierce features (the body of a lion, snarling lips, a scorpion's tail, and wings) reflect the fear Mesopotamians had of the violent and destructive winds that came howling through their lands. High winds blew dirt and debris that damaged crops and buildings, causing great human distress and sometimes financial ruin. Mesopotamians believed Pazuzu's countenance to be so menacing that pregnant women wore his image around their necks to scare off demons that might threaten the unborn baby's health. Louvre © R.M.N.

MESOPOTAMIA: THE LAND BETWEEN THE RIVERS

Mesopotamia contained many city-states with long histories of independence. The city-states included the cities and the surrounding supportive villages and farms, united under a single government. Just like those who lived within the city walls, those who lived several miles away in smaller villages identified with the city—trading there, paying taxes, and attending religious functions. Farmers of the Mesopotamian city of Uruk, for example, lived within the city walls and walked an hour or so to their fields nearby. As the city grew in population and area, from approximately three and a half to ten miles in radius, outlying villages and fields were incorporated to supply the city's needs, and farmers participated in civic affairs.

The climate and unpredictable behavior of the Tigris and Euphrates rivers also figured in everyday life in Mesopotamia. The rivers' headwaters, located in mountainous regions of modern Turkey, swelled in periods of heavy rainfall, causing floods that ravaged irrigation systems and crops downstream. The Tigris, in particular, caused severe damage to buildings and populations, as well as to agriculture. The rivers, not easy to navigate, often hampered trade. Yet the spring floods also left replenishing deposits of nutrients, and people found it practical to cultivate near the rivers and their tributaries. As a result, the periodic devastation had to be endured.

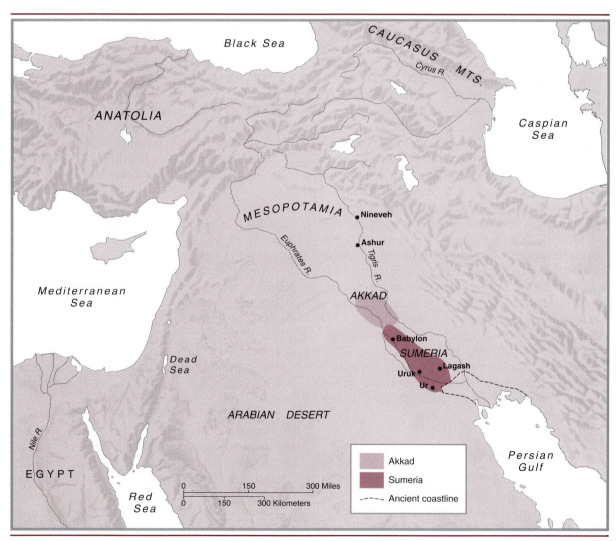

M A P 4 . 1 *Ancient Mesopotamia, around 3500– around 2100 B.C. The Mesopotamian civilization developed in Sumeria and its culture spread from the Tigris River to the eastern Mediterranean seaboard through conquest first by the Akkadians and then by other empires; Uruk, Ur, and Lagash were three of the first city-states. The flat topography of this area allowed for conquering peoples to move fairly rapidly through the region.*

Although kings are often portrayed in scenes of conquest and triumph, much of the surviving Mesopotamian great art depicts Mesopotamian kings' relationship with their deities. Reliefs on temple walls and in palaces featured mythological scenes. Statues and figurines of deities resided in each household to protect and give favor to the family within. Artisans shaped sacred vessels in gold and silver for priests to perform a variety of complex rituals. Musical instruments were highly decorated and used to perform sacred songs.

As Mesopotamian city-states grew and demand for greater public works increased, efficient political organization became essential. The growth of government, therefore, paralleled urban growth. Initially, cities were ruled by councils, usually composed of wealthy elders. Eventually the role of king developed, particularly because of increased hostilities between cities that encouraged people to look to a strong military leader. The king's authority grew out of three primary responsibilities: military, civic, and religious. The king's military responsibility gave him authority to lead the army against enemies and to defend the city against attack. The king's civic responsibility gave him authority to raise taxes, to care for the people's well-being through public works, and to keep the peace through the enforcement of customary and newly developing law codes. The king's religious responsibility gave him authority as high priest to oversee all religious practices. The king's role as high priest and lawgiver legitimized his rule.

The earliest city-state wars in Mesopotamia resulted from skirmishes over fertile land, water rights, and control of trade routes. The lack of naturally occurring barriers accommodated repeated attacks and raids, resulting in the loss of lives and property; captives became slaves, and the victors invested energy and wealth in the erection of walls for protection.

The Sumerians, around 3500–2350 B.C.

Civilization began in Sumeria, in southern Mesopotamia. Eventually, through long-distance trade, migration, and a series of later conquests of the area by larger kingdoms, Sumerian culture extended far beyond the borders of the Tigris and Euphrates rivers into major parts of Southwest Asia. A study of the Sumerians, then, serves as a good example of Mesopotamian civilization in general.

By 3500 B.C., Sumerian city-states had emerged. Three of the major cities, Uruk, Ur, and Lagash, constructed massive walls for protection. By 3000 B.C., Sumerian cities had an average of several thousand people; in 2700 B.C., Uruk housed around 50,000 people, not including those in its seventy-six satellite villages. The wall around the city measured more than six miles in circumference. The city of Ur had a population of about 30,000 people. A monumental structure called a **ziggurat**, a tiered temple near the center of the city, loomed over the entire area as a reminder of the divine presence and of the city's power. The ziggurat functioned as an administrative, religious, and market center. By 2500 B.C., approximately 500,000 people inhabited Sumeria, the majority of whom lived in cities.

Sumerians were agriculturalists and pastoralists. The fields yielded two annual harvests of wheat and barley (to make into bread, beer, or porridge). Women and children tended small household gardens of onions, leeks, cucumbers, and legumes. Sheep supplied wool for clothing, as well as milk, cheese, and mutton. The diet also included various fish from the rivers and dates from the palm trees that lined irrigation canals. Excess commodities could be traded at market, if anything was left after paying taxes; one Sumerian poet wrote, "You can have a lord, you can have a king, but the man to fear is the tax collector."

The Sumerian long-distance trade network included only neighboring cities at first but expanded eventually to include the Iranian Plateau, the Indus Valley, and the eastern Mediterranean. Traveling by rafts, sailboats, and overland caravans, merchants bartered grain and wool for scarce commodities such as lumber and stone, and for luxury items such as carved ivory combs from India and lapis lazuli from Iran.

Sumerian cities followed the pattern of most Mesopotamian cities in developing their polities. The open terrain of Sumeria left the cities vulnerable to raids and periodic conquests. Originally, council members governed each city-state, but during periods of emergency they elected a specific war leader called a *lugal*, meaning "great man." Because of accelerating hostilities in the region and the people's dissatisfaction with the council, the *lugal* remained in office for increasingly longer periods of time until the position finally became permanent. As his authority solidified, the *lugal*, now a king, gained the right to

FIGURE 4.2 *Ziggurat of Choga Zambil.* *Located in the southwestern part of modern-day Iran, the site contains structures that date back to around 1250 B.C. Close examination reveals a four-tiered ziggurat as well as the ruins of the city near its base and a portion of the city wall. In some ziggurats, the ground level was used as a market center and storage area for taxes paid in goods. The second level consisted of apartments for officials and meeting rooms, and the third level housed the royal family. The fourth and highest level was the temple area, where sacred rituals were performed. This massive monumental architecture demonstrates a complex government that could raise taxes to support the engineers, stone masons, and laborers needed to complete such a building project.* Georg Gerster/Comstock.

name his successor, usually his son. This was the origin of Mesopotamian **dynastic succession**, a succession of rulers from the same family.

Sumerians developed a bureaucracy to regulate and record the collection and distribution of tax monies and to keep records concerning trade. Scribes, an important part of this bureaucracy, originally came from aristocratic families that could afford to educate their sons. This record keeping spurred the development of cuneiform writing.

The Sumerian pantheon included more than 3,000 deities who had responsibility for every aspect of life, including plows, carts, and the production of beer (of which there were nineteen varieties). Sumerians believed that the deities created humans to be their servants; if humans did not perform their functions properly, the deities would destroy them. Two of the major deities of Mesopotamia were the goddess Ishtar and the god Enki. Through the centuries, Ishtar's myth changed and became associated with various other goddesses. She is primarily identified as a fertility goddess but is also a goddess of love and war. Enki's name in the ancient Sumerian language means "lord of the earth," but he was usually depicted as the god of the ever-precious life source: water. Sumerians fashioned a complex cosmology that viewed the heavenly bodies, air, earth, and water as the most important forces.

The deities required constant consultation and worship; consequently, the temple played a significant role in the life of the city. The priests and priestesses, in addition to performing rituals there, interpreted the deities' desires by reading animal entrails and observing natural phenomena

FIGURE 4.3 *Cylinder Seal.* *Cylinder seals (left) were an early form of writing in Meso-potamia, most designed with drawings of different commodities or scenes of deities that were then rolled over clay (right) to produce a record of a transaction or of a prayer against illness or calamity. Other seals endorsed such legal documents as contracts or tax records. The cylinder seal could be used over and over again. This seal depicts the Sumerian sun god, rising over a mountain, and the goddess Ishtar, shown with wings. In the center is Enki, the god of wisdom and water.* Courtesy of the Trustees of the British Museum.

for signs. The large tracts of land belonging to the temples supported the priestly class, and priests frequently rented tracts out. A portion of every farmer's harvest was a tax dedicated to the temple. The excess enabled the priests to distribute grain to widows, orphans, and needy families. Payments for special services, such as a private ritual or a visit to a temple prostitute (often a part of fertility rituals), also subsidized the temple economy.

Sumerian society consisted of a three-tiered class stratification: the elite, free subjects, and slaves. The elite included the king, his officials, the royal family, the high priests and priestesses, and the wealthiest landowners and merchants. Many elite estates outside of the urban center could become as large as small cities, with artisan work-shops that produced goods for trade, great fields for food production, and dormitories for the many servants, artisans, and slaves. A typical house of the elite in cities had multiple stories with numer-ous rooms, and the entire structure was white-washed.

The free subjects were farmers, artisans, scribes, and the lesser merchants, priests, and priestesses. For the most part, free subjects lived modestly in small one-story houses in the city or in rented houses on large estates. Clay pottery consti-tuted household crockery for the majority of sub-jects. Some farmers owned small pieces of property that barely supported a family.

People became slaves in various ways. War captives, subjects forced to sell themselves to pay their debts, and those convicted of crimes became slaves. Some men sold wives and children to keep themselves out of debt slavery. As in most ancient forms of slavery, **manumission** (freeing of a slave) occurred frequently. A Sumerian slave could engage in trade and business enterprises, borrow money, and marry a free subject.

Sumerians used cosmetics to beautify them-selves, which may have been a sign of status. Both elite men and women adorned their eyes with paints and used charcoal as an eyeliner. Most elite women and some men painted their faces white and their lips and fingernails red, and men wore highly stylized false beards. Oil was used for cleansing the body, and the body and hair were perfumed.

Clothing in Sumeria consisted of wool wraps for men, who went barefoot and bare-chested. Women wore a fitted dress or drape, with their hair in braids or pulled back with a headband or small hat. Women spun, wove, and sewed the clothing at home. On large estates throughout Mesopotamian history, owners organized servant or slave women into small cloth-manufacturing groups that produced enough cloth to export. Later in Mesopotamian history, different clothing styles spread through long-distance trade. Eventually men abandoned the wrap in favor of woven tunics.

FIGURE 4.4 *Sumerian Lyre.* *This Sumerian lyre depicts a sacred bull, symbolic of strength and fertility. The bull is fashioned from gold, and its beard from lapis lazuli, a deep blue gemstone. Musicians would wash their hands before performing ritual hymns; one such hymn to the Sumerian goddess Ishtar says, "They play songs for [Ishtar] to rejoice the heart."* Boltin Picture Library.

FIGURE 4.5 *Sumerian Priestess.* *This statue of a priestess shows the common practice of lining the eyes and eyebrows with a dark color. The woman's elaborate hairpiece includes a long woolen covering, typically worn by women of the nobility. She also wears a traditional woolen wrap, a skirtlike garment that was used by both sexes.* Courtesy of the National Museum, Damascus.

Women participated in the economies of Sumerian cities, although in limited ways. They could own property (but most land remained in the control of men, because property generally passed from father to son). In some cases women controlled the making of cloth and sent it with their merchant husbands to supplement the family income. There are later records of Mesopotamian women demanding that their husbands send them the money their cloth brought at market. Women also engaged in other businesses and exclusively produced the most popular drink, beer.

Gender roles became increasingly fixed as the civilization developed. Women's responsibilities remained primarily in the household; the majority of women spent hours gardening, weaving, or grinding on stone grinders. Specialization of labor led to mass production by male workers. Male artisans produced pottery, jewelry, and various wood products. Other male occupations included smithing, which produced bronze castings, and construction, which erected the first arches out of wedge-shaped bricks.

Formal legal codes were developed not only to assist in controlling crime and establishing order but also to clarify family relationships and property rights. A husband (with support from his family) paid a bride-price to the father of the bride. A man who broke his engagement forfeited his bride-price. If the engagement was broken off by the woman, the man received twice the worth of

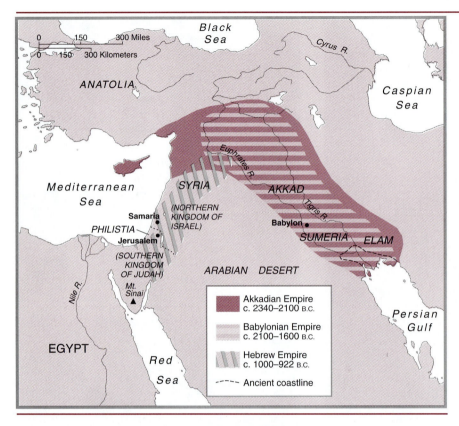

MAP 4.2 *The Akkadian (around 2340–around 2100 B.C.), Babylonian (around 2100–around 1600 B.C.), and Hebrew (around 1000–922 B.C.) Empires.* *The Babylonian Empire under King Hammurabi (reign dates 1792–1750 B.C.) stretched from the Persian Gulf to the borders of Syria. The Akkadian Empire encompassed Sumer, Elam, the various territories between the Tigris and Euphrates rivers, Syria, and Southeast Anatolia. The ancient Hebrews expanded this empire to the Euphrates River during the reign of King David, around 1000–961 B.C., but lost that territory by 922 B.C. The remaining lands were broken into two kingdoms: Israel and Judah.*

the bride-price. Whether or not they could read it, both the bride and the groom signed a marriage contract that enumerated conditions, such as the duties of each as husband and wife and the division of property in a divorce settlement. Women were subject to their husbands and fathers, and women who bore no children could be divorced.

Sumerian ingenuity also contributed to the advancement of technology. Farmers invented the plow, which initially demanded two people: one to push and one to pull. The adoption of bronze metallurgy revolutionized farming because the stronger, heavier bronze-tipped plows created deeper and straighter furrows in which to plant; this replaced the less-productive scattering technique (tossing the seed onto the ground). Eventually, ox-drawn plows increased productivity, because they could cut deeper into the soil and cultivate more land at a quicker pace. The discovery of the wheel allowed for greater amounts of goods to be transported in long-distance trade, because merchants could move significantly more material by cart than on pack animals. Cuneiform writing preserved myths and legends in early liter-

ature, such as the epic tale of King Gilgamesh, who set off on a journey to learn the secret of eternal life, and the story of the great flood.

Political Conquest, Migration, and Change in Southwest Asia

Sumerians warred among themselves for more than half a millennium until 2350 B.C., when they succumbed to their Akkadian[2] neighbors from central Mesopotamia, led by King Sargon. In a series of sweeping campaigns, the Akkadians united all of Mesopotamia into a large kingdom ruled through Akkadian governors. On several occasions of conquest in global history, the conquerors adopted the culture of those they conquered, and the Akkadians were among the first known to do so. After their adoption of Sumerian culture, the Akkadians spread it beyond southern Mesopotamia into all areas of their political and economic influence. After approximately a cen-

[2] **Akkadian:** ahk KAY dee an

tury, the Akkadians fell, inaugurating a period of upheaval during which the Sumerians regained political control over their cities. The resurgence soon ebbed, however, and Sumeria never regained political power, although its culture lived on in the lives of other Southwest Asian peoples.

FIGURE 4.6 *Hammurabi's Code. The top of this seven-foot stela shows King Hammurabi receiving the code of law from Shamash, the powerful sun god, seated on his heavenly throne. The first section of cuneiform writing describes Hammurabi as having been chosen by the deities to lead the peoples of Mesopotamia, thereby giving sacred justification to Hammurabi's conquests and legitimizing his reign. The rest of the stela is inscribed with the entire code of Hammurabi. Stelae like this were placed at major crossroads around the empire so that all people would see Hammurabi's relationship with the deities and accept his law.* Louvre © R.M.N.

It was not until the rise of another people, the Amorites, that a unified Mesopotamia again emerged. The migration of Amorites, out of the Arabian desert area, occurred sometime between 2000 and 1600 B.C. Most of these Amorites ended up in Mesopotamia, and one group established its capital at the ancient city of Babylon, from which they received another name—Babylonians. Another Amorite group may have been the tribal Hebrews, the religious ancestors of modern Jews.

The Babylonians conquered Sumeria during the kingship of Hammurabi (reign dates 1792–1750 B.C.). Under Hammurabi, Babylon became the seat of a mighty kingdom through a network of treaty alliances and opportunistic treaty breaking. Law codes had become increasingly complicated, reflecting the complexity of the growing Mesopotamian civilization. Hammurabi established a new law code that synthesized the various law codes of the peoples he ruled, helping to establish a uniformity of law in the area. He placed multiple large stones with engraved laws at important trade crossroads to attest to the legitimacy of his rule. Hammurabi legitimized his law code through the traditional declaration that law comes from the gods through their representative, the king. The law code reveals much about how the society operated. These ancient Mesopotamian laws form a legacy of jurisprudence that became the foundation of modern legal systems.

The Babylonians also contributed to the study of mathematics; working in arithmetic, geometry, and algebra, they used both base-ten and base-sixty number systems. Their mathematical contributions included calculation close to the true value of pi, the 360° circle, and methods for computing square roots. Today we continue to use their numerical system of twenty-four-hour days and sixty-minute hours. By 1590 B.C., however, the Babylonian kingdom suffered invasion by peoples east of Mesopotamia, reducing its influence and precipitating its decline.

The tribal Hebrews may have moved into Mesopotamia first, then relocated to Palestine, or migrated directly into Palestine. In any event, their culture was heavily influenced by Mesopotamia; their holy writings include a similar flood story to that found in the Sumerian legend of *The Epic of Gilgamesh*. Hebrew tradition professes a westward migration from Sumeria perhaps around 1900 B.C. or as late as 1600 B.C.; scholars are unsure of the

IN THEIR OWN WORDS

The Law Code of Hammurabi

King Hammurabi of Babylonia issued a law code in the eighteenth
century B.C. The stone panel on which
282 laws were carved stood nearly
eight feet high and shows Hammurabi
receiving the laws from a god. The laws
reflect the social and economic realities of Mesopotamian life. Many schol-
ars believe that several of the laws demonstrate an
attempt to curb abuses and injustices perpetuated
by the nobility, whose wealth gave them power. The
laws reveal a society divided into social groups, and
the code distributes justice by social status. Within the same social level, equal payment is exacted
on the pattern of "an eye for an eye and a tooth for
a tooth." A payment system is employed for retribution between the social levels. Many abuses existed
because victims of crimes could not always prove
their cases.

The following are examples of Hammurabi's
code. Review each selection, asking yourself what issues are being addressed, what status are the persons
involved, and what punishments are given.

l. If a man brings an accusation against another
man, charging him with murder, but cannot prove
it, the accuser shall be put to death.

4. If he bears [false] witness concerning grain or
money, he shall himself bear the penalty imposed
in that case.

5. If a judge pronounces a judgment, renders a decision, delivers a verdict duly signed and sealed,
and afterward alters his judgment, they shall call
that judge to account for the alteration of the judgment . . . and he shall pay twelvefold the penalty in
that judgment; and, in the assembly, they shall ex-
pel him from his seat of judgment . . .

22. If a man practices robbery and is captured, that
man shall be put to death.

23. If the robber is not captured, the
man who has been robbed shall, in
the presence of god, make an itemized
statement of his loss, and the city and
the governor . . . shall compensate him
for whatever was lost.

55. If a man opens his canal for irrigation and neglects it and the water carries away an adjacent field, he shall pay out grain
on the basis of the adjacent field [the field's yield].

129. If the wife of a man is caught lying with another man, they shall bind them and throw them
into the water. If the husband of the woman wishes
to spare his wife, then the king shall spare his
[subject].

142. If a woman hates her husband and says, "You
may not possess me" . . . and if she has been careful and without reproach . . . she may take her dowry
and go to her father's house.

195. If a son strikes his father, they shall cut off his
hand.

196. If a man destroys the eye of another man [of
equal status], they shall destroy his eye.

198. If he destroys the eye of a client [one of lesser
status] or breaks the bone of a client, he shall pay
one *mina* of silver.

199. If he destroys the eye of a man's slave or breaks
a bone . . . he shall pay one-half his [the slave's]
price [because the slave's worth is diminished].

221–223. If a physician sets a broken bone for a
man or cures a sprained tendon, the patient shall
[pay] five *shekels* of silver . . . a client pays three
shekels . . . a slave's owner pays two *shekels*.

229. If a builder builds a house for a man and does
not make . . . [it] sound, and the house . . . collapses
and causes the death of the owner . . . the builder
shall be put to death.

date. Portions of the Hebrew tribes may have
moved into Egypt, perhaps as a result of a famine.

Early Hebrew law demonstrates Mesopotamian roots and resembles Hammurabi's law
code in particular. These laws appear in the first
five books of Hebrew holy writings, the Torah, and
are comparable to the code of Hammurabi. Later

laws (including the Ten Commandments) were
developed after the exodus from Egypt and are less
specific, focusing on an ethical code of behavior,
such as "You shall not commit murder" and "You
shall not steal." These laws, unlike the more specific ones, usually did not spell out particular retributive punishments in the code but were open to

interpretation by judges. These later laws, usually called Mosaic law after the lawgiver Moses, do not wholly replace the earlier laws but demonstrate a general evolution toward abstract legal concepts, indicative of what was evolving throughout Southwest Asia.

Hebrew government experienced several stages of development. At first, the Hebrew tribes formed a confederacy loosely organized under tribal judges, who commanded during limited military crises and who provided arbitration in settling intertribal disputes. One of the judges was a woman named Deborah. The Hebrews turned to kingship around 1025 B.C., however, to provide skilled military leadership and to unify the tribes during their wars to conquer Palestine and to defeat the Philistines, who had migrated into the coastal area about 1175 B.C. Slowly, power passed from those chosen to lead by their merit to dynastic succession.

A treaty limiting the neighboring Philistines to the coastal strip, in combination with territorial expansion, brought the Hebrews a large kingdom during the reigns of David (reign dates around 1000–961 B.C.) and Solomon (reign dates 961–922 B.C.). The kingdom stretched from the Euphrates River to the Red Sea and played a significant part in the long-distance trade network of the region. The kingdom split under Solomon's sons into northern and southern kingdoms, both of which were then conquered by expansive empires. The northern kingdom fell in 722 B.C. to the Assyrians, and its population either relocated or assimilated into the invading culture. The southern kingdom succumbed to the New Babylonian Empire in 586 B.C., and many of its population were taken to Babylon as captives to ensure their obedience.

The king, his officials, and the priests were the traditional interpreters of divine will, but another figure in Hebrew society, the **prophet**, claimed great authority. A prophet was a person called by the god—regardless of station—to act as his representative. Prophets were not always accepted, but, nevertheless, they played a significant role in society, acting as a counterbalance to the king's authority and often challenging it.

Hebrews defined their relationship with the deity as a **covenant**: a contractual agreement between their god, Yahweh,[3] and themselves. Increasingly, city-states in Southwest Asia had

[3] **Yahweh:** YAH way

FIGURE 4.7 *The Torah.* *This painting depicts a Hebrew reading the Torah, or Jewish law, which was the expression of the covenant between the Hebrews and their god, Yahweh. Early Jews believed their laws came directly from Yahweh, just as Mesopotamians believed Hammurabi's code came from their deities. The individual books that made up the Torah were written on sheepskin scrolls that were read from right to left as the documents were unrolled. The priests in early Hebrew society were responsible for interpreting the Torah to the people, and when they failed to fulfill their responsibility, prophets denounced them. Over time, the Torah has come to include all of the Jewish sacred writings.* Yale University Art Gallery, Dura-Europos Collection.

chosen one particular god or goddess as its **patron deity**. The people believed this deity lived in the local temple and protected their city. They still practiced polytheism, but the patron deity became dominant locally, and the people believed they were the chosen people of that deity. The Hebrew covenant was similar to other cities' relationships to patron deities, but for the Hebrews "covenant" meant exclusive worship of their god. This attitude eventually developed from a belief of Yahweh's superiority over all other deities to **monotheism**, the belief that only one god exists. The idea of monotheism was not unique to the Hebrews; Egyptians, New Babylonians, and Persians experimented with monotheistic ideas, but only Hebrew practice of it has survived until the present. Hebrew monotheism also became the foundation for two later monotheistic religions, Christianity and Islam.

The covenantal relationship affected the Hebrew worldview. Hebrews believed that time was linear rather than cyclical (which was the prevailing Southwest Asian worldview) and that time would end when Yahweh's purpose for creation had been fulfilled. In addition, the covenant undergirded the egalitarianism inherited from their tribal past that assured the equal treatment of all free male Hebrews under the law. (The society was patriarchal, and law focused on male relationships.) This placed the king in a quite different position from that of kings like Sargon or Hammurabi. In Hammurabi's law code, social status frequently determined punishment or payment, but Hebrew society held every free male, even the king, equally subject to the laws of the covenant.

EGYPT: THE GIFT OF THE NILE

Egypt has been described as the gift of the Nile; the Nile River was the civilization's lifeblood. Its regular, mild flooding aided the development of an effective irrigation system and yielded rich deposits of silt. The Nile flooded between July and October (draining northward from the southern mountains) when spring rains swelled its East African tributaries. The peoples near the river exploited the waters and silt deposits for their agriculture. As farming intensified around 5200 B.C., the stable climate and relative geographical isola-

tion led to a civilization that lasted for thousands of years.

Early Egypt is usually divided by scholars into two major areas, northern and southern. In southern Egypt, natural reservoirs allowed villagers to plant grain and irrigate fields. The high agricultural yield soon led to urbanism, and, at about the same time Mesopotamian city-states were developing (around 3500 B.C.), Egyptian civilization emerged. The cooperative irrigation efforts between local villages led to trade agreements that became the basis of provincial areas called **nomes**, governed by **nomarchs**. Unification of the upper Nile culminated about 3300 B.C., when a single king ruled the entire upper area. In contrast to Mesopotamia, Egypt did not develop a competitive city-state system before unification.

FIGURE 4.8 *Egyptian Tomb Mural.* *This mural gives an idea of the abundance of foods available in the Nile River Valley. The servants prepare for a banquet that will include fresh grapes, pomegranates, lotus plants, cucumbers, and figs. The banqueters will also feast on eggs, fish, ducks, pigeons, and geese. Depictions of the variety of foods found in Egypt were common, often demonstrating the wealth of the individual in whose tomb the mural appeared.* Erich Lessing/Art Resource, N.Y.

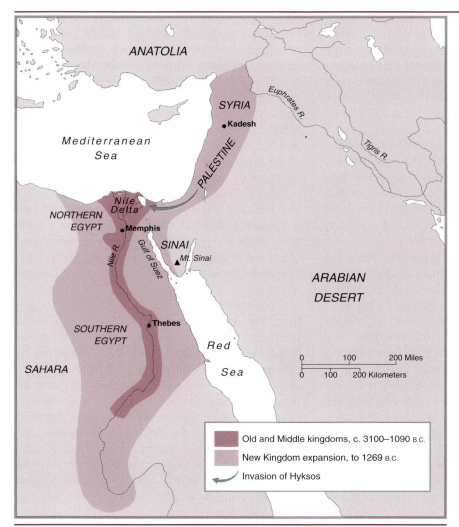

MAP 4.3 *Ancient Egypt, around 3100–1085 B.C.*
Egyptian civilization began along the Nile River Valley around 3500 B.C., eventually uniting into one polity by around 3100 B.C. During the New Kingdom Era, 1570– 1085 B.C., Egyptians established an empire, conquering territory as far north as Syria.

The delta area, or northern Egypt, experienced a slightly different development from that of its neighbor to the south because of different geographical conditions. Less urbanized, the area was marshy and pocked with swamps where crocodiles and hippopotami competed with human beings for limited habitable land. Early inhabitants consisted of herders and their cattle, as well as some persevering farmers.

The Egyptian diet was varied. As in Mesopotamia, grain crops became the mainstay of the Egyptian diet, providing the staples of bread, beer, and porridge. Fruit included grapes, dates, and pomegranates, from which wine could be produced. The Nile teemed with various kinds of fish that Egyptians enjoyed fresh, salted, or dried. Various animals supplied meat and milk products. The table of a wealthy Egyptian might be laden with various vegetables (like lentils, cucumbers, melons, and various gourds) flavored with herbs or honey. In later periods, trade brought in new foods, such as chickpeas. Egyptian agriculture usually produced more food than was needed for the population because of the favorable climatic conditions.

Labor in Egypt followed the seasonal rise and recession of the Nile waters. Between July and September, when the water rose, no work could be done in the fields. Many farmers, criminals working off punishment, and slaves provided labor for construction and maintenance of monumental building projects. When the flood waters crested, only the boundary stones could be seen across the fields. Occasionally they would dislodge, and the moving of a field marker to one's own advantage was considered a serious crime. After the flood waters receded in October, farmers broke up large clods of earth and began plowing with ox-drawn plows. Workers sowed seeds, and sheep and goats followed behind, trampling in the seeds. Poorer farmers received seed and the use of draft animals from the government to ensure a good crop.

During the growing season, October to February, irrigation canals continued to supply farmers with water as the ground dried out. The technology of a *shadouf*[4] (an upright support with a swinging lever to lift something) allowed a bucket to be lowered into the canal. The full bucket was then raised by a weight at the other end of a pole.

In February, the harvest began. Tending the crops was mostly a male occupation, but harvesting included women and children. Men cut wheat and barley with flint-bladed wooden sickles; later, the straw was collected to make mats or bricks. Draft animals carried the grain to a threshing area, and, after cattle loosened the grain by trampling on it, women tossed the material into the air to separate the grain from the chaff. Scribes recorded the amount harvested, and tax collectors took the government's portion to state granaries. Tax rates reflected the level of flooding; a good flood meant high yields. Canal repair occupied the farmer's time after the harvest until just a few weeks before the Nile's flood cycle began again.

Political unification of northern and southern Egypt resulted from the exportation of southern Egypt's political organization into the northern area. The process of unification is shrouded in legend. Traditional Egyptian folklore credits King Menes of southern Egypt with the political consolidation. (King Menes may be a composite of several heroic kings.) Whatever the process, unification came by about 3100 B.C. The Nile flowed northward, allowing its current to carry traders who had designed ships for long-distance trade into the northern area. The winds blew southward, allowing for sails to carry the traders homeward. This ease of movement on the river encouraged travel and trade between the two areas and encouraged unification.

Prior to unification, nomarchs claimed a semi-divine authority that evolved from their great houses resting in proximity to the temple of the patron god of the city. Traditionally the nomarch interpreted the will of the god. As unification occurred, the myths of the gods justified rule by one powerful king-nomarch: **pharaoh**.[5]

As Egypt united politically, so did it unite religiously. Egyptians worshiped over two thousand gods, and many deities and their myths amalgamated. The patron god of southern Egypt was Ra, and the nomarchs claimed to be the sons of Ra. The patron god of northern Egypt was Amon. With unification, the two deities eventually fused into the one high god, Amon-Ra,[6] whose incarnate son was pharaoh, ruler of all Egypt. The pharaoh, now a god-king, differed from Mesopotamian kings who merely represented the city's patron god. Upon the pharaoh's death, he became the ruler of the underworld, and his heir became the new pharaoh.

The rule of law developed differently in Egypt from the way it did in Mesopotamia. In Mesopotamia, law passed from the god to the king or, in the case of the early Hebrews, to a chosen representative. But the Egyptian pharaoh, as god incarnate, embodied all authority; everyone listened when the pharaoh said, "I have spoken it," for the pharaoh's words constituted law. Egyptian law was probably the first egalitarian law, and women could give testimony and bring suits. Unlike early Mesopotamian law, punishments did not reflect social status, and there seem to have been few complaints of bribery or favoritism. In a system similar to that of modern U.S. law, the accused was presumed innocent until proven guilty. The law demanded retribution for theft or property damage several times the original value. Other punishments included beatings, hard labor, exile, and mutilation. Tomb robbing, murder, or treason resulted in a death sentence.

The pharaoh dictated all policy and cared for the Egyptians as if they were children. The pharaoh instructed when to plant and when to harvest according to the Nile flooding pattern. Any disaster might call the pharaoh's legitimacy into question and, thereby, threaten the dynasty. The pharaoh, like the Mesopotamian kings, supervised the irrigation system, the granaries, and the temples. Yet, realistically, the pharaoh could not single-handedly rule the entire kingdom, and

---

[4] *shadouf*: shah DOOF

[5] **pharaoh**: FAIR oh
[6] **Amon-Ra**: AH muhn ray

so a hierarchy of authority emerged. The farther from the pharaoh's gaze, however, the greater the independence of the bureaucrats.

The chief administrators of the bureaucracy collected taxes, supervised public works, directed military campaigns and a police force, acted as chief justices, and managed artisans for the pharaoh's needs. Duties also included supervising the great royal estates and granaries. All officials in the bureaucracy lived well, often on large estates.

Egypt was divided into provinces run by the local nomarchs, who occasionally challenged centralized control through independent alliances or who emerged as powerful founders of new dynasties after the reign of a weak pharaoh. Among other duties, nomarchs levied and collected taxes assessed for the monumental architectural projects. They worked with the bureaucratic officials (who often carried large sticks as an inducement) sent to represent the pharaoh at tax time. The pharaoh controlled almost all the land and allocated its use to priests and nobility, but he occasionally gave land to temples and important officials. This land usage later developed into freeholding or private ownership that eventually hampered central authority.

The pharaohs were usually male, but a few women ruled during regencies. The pharaoh became divine upon marriage; the wife was a princess or queen and, therefore, a member of the royal family, often a sister or half-sister. In artwork, aristocratic women were often pictured equal in size to their husbands, showing their important social status in the community. A woman could not hold government offices but could take over duties while her husband was away on official business.

Women in Egypt owned property, which they could control and dispose of as they wished, and land often passed through the female line. Men brought a house and two-thirds of a marriage fund to the union. Women contributed a dowry, furnishings, and one-third of the marriage fund. In a divorce, the wife received one-third of the marriage fund and custody of the children (who received the other two-thirds of the fund for support). Her personal property and dowry remained in her control (as did any personal debts).

Gender roles in Egypt were similar to those in Mesopotamia. The most common labor for women consisted of food preparation, spinning,

F I G U R E 4.9 *Beer-brewing around 2500 B.C. This woman is in the process of forcing fermented grain through a sieve to make beer. Grain, a mainstay of the Egyptian diet, was used to make bread as well as beer, the most common drink. As in many early societies in Southwest Asia, Egyptian women were solely responsible for baking and brewing.* Egyptian Museum, Cairo.

weaving, and managing the household. Many women had careers, however, in various trades. Flax was grown for the production of linen, and some estates had servant women in workshops producing linen for market. Other trades included nursing, hairdressing, housekeeping, and performing (as musicians, dancers, and acrobats). As in Mesopotamia, brewing was exclusively done by women. Men worked as launderers, mat weavers, artisans, and in out-of-doors tasks like hunting, fishing, mining, building, and farming (the last of these being the most common occupation). The occupation of scribes allowed for the most social

PARALLELS AND DIVERGENCES

The Written Word: Cuneiform and Hieroglyphics

The impact of the written word in human history is immeasurable; writing enabled the preservation of ideas, values, and information beyond the memories and lifespans of individuals. Myths and epic tales were preserved for future populations, political and economic transactions were recorded, and laws were posted. The earliest known experimentation with writing occurred in Sumeria and Egypt. Both of these systems experienced a number of developmental stages, using increasingly more complex and abstract symbols.

Sumerian writing began about 3300 B.C. with pictorial representations primarily associated with financial record keeping by scribes. These first records consisted of numerical representations. As record keeping became more complex, pictographs, symbols for the actions and commodities involved—a shaft of wheat, a bundle of barley—were used. These pictographs were written vertically on clay tablets with sharp reeds.

Sumerian writing underwent several changes. For now-unknown reasons, the pictographs began to be recorded on their sides in about 3000 B.C. Perhaps it was discovered that fewer smudges occurred when writing horizontally from left to right and placing them on their sides somewhat preserved the vertical tradition. Whatever the reason, the pictographs, now less recognizable, became more stylistic. By about 2400 B.C., another significant change occurred: Scribes changed from using sharp reeds to wedge-shaped tips. This new style is called cuneiform by scholars after a Latin word meaning "wedge-shaped." The new cuneiform writing demanded even more abstract symbolism, and therefore the pictograph fell into obscurity.

Egyptian hieroglyphics developed by about 3300 B.C. Egyptian writing, however, took a somewhat different path from that of Sumerian writing. Some hieroglyphs, called **ideographs**, meant entire words or complex ideas, and some hieroglyphs came to represent phonetic sounds. The ideograph and phonetic styles began about 2900 B.C. and developed rather rapidly into a form that used only script. Many of the older hieroglyphs remained in use, so an Egyptian text, therefore, might contain both hieroglyphs and script. Egyptians developed a paperlike substance, perhaps as early as 3100 B.C., from the pulp of the papyrus plant, which grows plentifully along the Nile. The writing instrument was a reed, cut at an angle and dipped into black or red ink.

The uses for writing proliferated throughout Egyptian history. The earliest examples of writing correspond to the more mundane political and economic activities of urban living. Records of tax payments, king lists, and supply inventories head the list. As the use of writing increased, more diverse applications developed in religious and professional life. Individuals wrote prayers and left them in temples, and priests formalized rituals. Inscriptions of stories and myths adorned statues of individuals and deities. It became increasingly common to record and post legal codes, preserve medical records, and produce school texts for mathematical methods and scribal vocabulary. Great deeds of kings and pharaohs were recorded, biographical stories of important nobles written, and the various records of statecraft assembled. In addition, many explanations of the activities of deities and humans served as decoration and captions to beautiful paintings on household walls and tombs.

mobility; peasants who could afford to sent sons to school in hopes that they might find employment with a rich official. One royal scribe encouraged an apprentice to work hard by describing other, less desirable occupations: "The washerman's day is going up, going down. All his limbs are weak . . . the maker of pots is smeared with soil . . . the cobbler mingles with vats. His odor is penetrating. His hands

are red . . . ." Most scribes were men, but some women were court and temple scribes and officials.

The social structure of Egypt consisted of five basic classes. The three elite classes consisted of the royal family, who were officials and supporters at the court, the priests and priestesses, and the wealthy nobility. Scribes, lesser nobility, bureaucratic officials, and artisans filled the fourth class, and peasant farmers the fifth. By about 1570 B.C., two additions completed the social structure: professional soldiers and slaves (a consequence of military expansion). Wealthy nobles lived in beautiful houses with courtyards and many servants. No merchant class existed in the earliest period, because all trade was controlled by the pharaoh. Some social mobility persisted throughout Egyptian history, however.

Egyptian great art styles changed little over the centuries. The most popular painting style depicted daily scenes and myths on tomb and temple walls. These paintings portrayed dinner parties, hunting excursions (a favorite pastime of the wealthy), entertainments, and individuals, and were often accompanied by hieroglyphic texts explaining the art's content. Art also illustrated the complex rituals in texts of *The Book of the Dead*, a guide to the afterlife originally compiled around 2100 B.C. Egyptian artists crafted jewelry made from gold, gems, and glass beads. Other artists created statues, many depicting the pharaoh or Egyptian deities. The pharaohs' tombs were packed with beautiful gold and precious stone artifacts (which helps explain the attraction of tomb robbing over the centuries).

With unification and a relatively stable environment, the Egyptians perceived their existence as secure and harmonious and the idea of change as evil. Of course, change could be observed in Egyptian society, yet the stability of the Nile, unification, and isolation during the earliest centuries led to a worldview that life should be unchanging. Some major changes that did occur can best be recognized by a brief review of the three major eras in Egyptian history.

The Eras of Egypt, around 2700–1090 B.C.

Egypt has a long history of independence, and its noteworthy longevity is attributed to its stability and relative isolation. Scholars now know that thirty-one dynasties existed; they are grouped into four major divisions with intermediate periods during times of social and political upheaval. These divisions help us organize the long chronology of Egyptian history. Little documentary evidence survives from 3100 to around 2700 B.C., at which time records become more prolific and a clearer picture of Egyptian civilization emerges. For this reason, we will focus on the three eras

called the Old Kingdom, the Middle Kingdom, and the New Kingdom, spanning from around the year 2700 B.C. to 1090 B.C.

THE OLD KINGDOM, AROUND 2700–2200 B.C. The most striking phenomenon of the Old Kingdom period, besides unification and the growth of bureaucracy, was the construction of the pyramids. Whereas Mesopotamian ziggurats centered on economic, governmental, and religious activities, the pyramid served only as a tomb for early Egyptian pharaohs. The devotion of this architectural project to the eternal preservation of the remains of a single person demonstrates the power and religious authority of the Old Kingdom pharaohs. Only the pharaoh and those entombed with him to serve him in the underworld enjoyed an afterlife. Scholars estimate that roughly 2.5 million tons of limestone were hewn between 2700 B.C. and about 2600 B.C. to construct the tombs. Pyramid construction was abandoned after the Old Kingdom period in favor of smaller projects, however, because the pharaoh's authority waned under political and economic challenges. By about 2100 B.C., the afterlife became more egalitarian and eventually was extended to all social levels, in part due to the pharaohs' decreasing credibility.

The Old Kingdom ended with a series of devastating droughts that undermined the pharaoh's credibility. A later chronicler wrote, "Everything is filthy: There is no such thing as clean linen these days. The dead are thrown into the river. People abandon the city and live in tents. . . . Pharaoh is kidnapped by the mob." A series of pharaohs, all of whose legitimacy was thrown into doubt because of the continuing drought, took the throne. Twenty years saw twenty pharaohs. In 2200 B.C., a civil war among the nobility left Egypt open to intrusion by outside raiders and subject to local control.

THE MIDDLE KINGDOM, 2050–1800 B.C. Not until 2050 B.C. did a new dynasty regain control from the local nomarchs. The pharaohs of the Middle Kingdom forced recentralization and identified themselves as the saviors of the people. One pharaoh boasted that he gave charity to the destitute and to orphans and elevated the poor in status, which gave him broader political support. This political philosophy by pharaohs resulted in more local public reclamation projects, rather than the great pyramids of the Old Kingdom era.

Figure 4.10 *Pyramids. This aerial view attests to the immense size of the tomb and temple complex constructed at Giza. Built as tombs in the Old Kingdom Era 2700–2200 B.C., the pyramids stand as monuments to the power of Old Kingdom pharaohs. The ancient Greek historian Herodotus estimated that 100,000 workers labored for over twenty years to complete the tomb of Cheop (left). The tomb of Chephren (center) retains its original limestone cap. The pyramid on the right is the final resting place of Mycerinus; the three small structures to its right are probably the tombs of his immediate family. The Great Sphinx (lower right), with the body of a lion and the head of the pharaoh Chephren, is eighty yards long and twenty-two yards high but is dwarfed by the size of the pyramids. After 2200 B.C., monumental architecture changed to temple construction. This change reflects the religious shift in Egyptian society from a focus on pharaohs and their afterlife to a focus on the general population and its salvation.* John Ross.

The Middle Kingdom period experienced a surge in trade that linked the Nile with Southwest Asian trade routes. One dynasty engaged in commercial activity with Syria, Crete, and Nubia; this created a great network of long-distance trade and cultural exchange. The beginning of a merchant class developed in this period as trade expanded and the pharaoh's absolute control over the economy diminished.

Nomarch rivalries led to another civil war that heralded a second intermediate period. The final blow came with the invasion of the Hyksos[7] from the area of Palestine about 1700 B.C. Little is known about the Hyksos, who ruled Egypt until around 1570 B.C. They adopted Egyptian culture and political structure, ruling as pharaohs and continuing traditional political organization. The Hyksos also contributed to Egyptian culture, such as bronze technology that improved instruments of war and agriculture. Native Egyptians, however, resented Hyksos overlordship and retaliated with revolts and resistance. Eventually, a new dynasty (the eighteenth) defeated the Hyksos and established an empire in the New Kingdom era.

THE NEW KINGDOM, 1570–1090 B.C. The pharaohs of the eighteenth dynasty engaged in a policy of military expansion. No longer interested in the

[7] **Hyksos:** HIHKS ohs

FIGURE 4.11 *Egyptian Royal Family, Fourteenth Century B.C. This limestone carving of Akhenaton and Queen Nefertiti holding their children is in stark contrast to the earlier art of Figure 4.8. The warm, less idealized depiction of the royal family is indicative of the new art style that Akhenaton encouraged. The rays shine down to bring the breath of life from Aton, the new monotheistic deity introduced by Akhenaton. Although the worship of Aton did not survive, the use of realism continued in Egyptian art.* Bildarchiv Preussischer Kulturbesitz.

smaller trade network of earlier dynasties, the Egyptians pursued control of the lucrative trade routes of their former conquerors, the Hyksos. Having adopted Hyksos bronze weaponry and chariots, Egypt soon dominated the peoples of Palestine. In expanding beyond their cultural borders, Egypt had created an empire.

The fourth ruler of the eighteenth dynasty was a woman, Hatshepsut (reign dates 1496–1490 B.C.). At the death of her husband, a six-year-old son succeeded, and the queen became regent. The young prince could not resist Hatshepsut's authority, and she soon declared herself pharaoh, justifying her rule by claiming divine parentage from Amon-Ra. Palace priests supported her rise to power for their own political interests. Hatshepsut's reign focused on trade rather than on military expansion; she initiated a major trading expedition that met with almost universal success. But soon the adult prince deposed her and immediately tried to obliterate her name from all records and return her policies of commerce to policies of aggression.

Expansion that had hammered out an empire in the fifteenth and early fourteenth centuries B.C. halted under the pharaoh Amonhotep IV (reign dates 1367–1350 B.C.), who followed an isolationist foreign policy to allow internal political and religious reorganization. Amonhotep IV abandoned the traditional polytheism headed by Amon-Ra, whose chief priests located in Thebes[8] held great power and wealth. Amonhotep IV favored monotheistic worship of an obscure god, Aton. Neither animistic nor anthropomorphic, Aton represented an abstract concept of deity symbolized by the sun disk and its rays. By Amonhotep's sixth reigning year, he renounced his name and changed it to Akhen*aton*. Many ancient kings and pharaohs incorporated a god's name into theirs to demonstrate legitimacy, so *Amon*hotep became Akhen*aton* ("to be pleasing to Aton"). He built a new capital, which liberated him from the traditional political influence of the priests of Amon-Ra. This served both the spiritual and political agendas of Akhenaton.

During Akhenaton's reign, many changes took place. New art styles broke onto the traditional artistic stage. No longer was the pharaoh depicted in expressionless or disinterested remoteness. Akhenaton's body was reproduced in all its flabby

[8] **Thebes:** THEEBZ

glory, and one depiction shows the pharaoh affectionately kissing his child. Another change hit closer to Egyptian sensibilities; all Egyptians were instructed to worship only Aton, and Akhenaton was Aton's sole interpreter, thereby ensuring his control over all religious practice and the demise of priestly power. Akhenaton destroyed Amon-Ra's temples, but the outraged priests led many commoners in secret worship of the traditional deities; ill will toward the pharaoh boiled beneath the hot Egyptian sun. A corrupt bureaucracy capitalized on the pharaoh's decline in popularity by gaining control of the administration.

Monotheism proved too difficult to accept, and soon after Akhenaton's death his young heir, Tutankh*aton* (reign dates 1352–1344 B.C.), changed his name to Tutankh*amon*[9] (nicknamed by moderns "King Tut"). His name change signaled the restoration of polytheism, and the worship of Amon-Ra returned to the palace at Thebes. During his short reign, under the approving gaze of the priests, he tried to obliterate Akhenaton's name from the lists of pharaohs and to reverse his policies (similar to what had occurred after Hatshepsut). Isolationism gave way to renewed interest in foreign affairs.

Egypt's interests clashed with those of the Hittites, who conquered parts of Mesopotamia, Syria, and Palestine between 1400 and 1200 B.C. They intruded upon Egyptian territories during Akhenaton's isolationist rule. The reign of Ramses[10] II (reign dates 1290–1224 B.C.) heralded the decline of Egypt's military grandeur. Ramses failed to defeat the intrusive Hittites, but he managed to curb their invasion of Egypt. In 1269 B.C., the two kings signed "The Treaty of the Gods," which effectively halted expansion attempts. The protracted years of warfare and bloodshed had proved to be too costly for both aggressors.

After Ramses II, the authority of the pharaoh declined. Maintaining the military and engaging in grandiose temple projects depleted the treasury, and the priestly class increasingly opposed dynastic control. Egypt lost its empire by about 1085 B.C. and suffered through invasions, including conquest and temporary rule by the Nubians. Egypt finally fell to the Persian Empire in 525 B.C. after a series of invasions from the northeast.

EXPANSIVE EMPIRES

Throughout Southwest Asian history runs a checkerboard pattern of conquests and raids by expanding kingdoms. The Hittites, Assyrians, and Persians are representative examples of states that expanded into empires as they moved beyond their cultural borders. Each had its own history and important cultural contributions, but what brought these states into prominence were their innovations in military techniques, which permitted conquest and control of large areas, and in social and political structures, which maintained their vast holdings.

The Hittites, around 1700–around 1200 B.C.

The people called the Hittites had developed by about 1700 B.C. an empire in what is now modern Turkey. They were part of the large Indo-European migration that relocated peoples into India, Greece, and Southwest Asia around 2700 B.C. The king, chosen because of his military abilities, ruled as first among equals in the warrior society. A council of elders from among the nobility advised the king.

Expansion intensified in 1525 B.C. under the able chief Telepinush,[11] who led the evolution of Hittite kingship from a war leader of a chiefdom to a judicial and legislative monarch over an empire. He issued edicts similar to those of Hammurabi and established a clear path of succession and regulation of behavior to inhibit power struggles. The Hittites moved southward into northern Mesopotamia against the powerful kingdom of the Mitanni under the command of Suppiluliuma[12] (reign dates 1372–1334 B.C.). After conquering the Mitanni, Suppiluliuma turned toward Syria, taking several smaller kingdoms. The Hittite realm by 1353 B.C. had only one rival in size and power— Egypt. The recently widowed Egyptian queen offered an alliance with Suppiluliuma; the alliance was to be cemented by her marriage to one of his sons. Suppiluliuma distrusted the queen, and his diplomatic delays eventually lost him the chance

---

[9] **Tutankhamon:** toot ahngk AH muhn
[10] **Ramses:** RAM seez

[11] **Telepinush:** tehl eh PIHN oosh
[12] **Suppiluliuma:** SOOP ihl OO lee OO mah

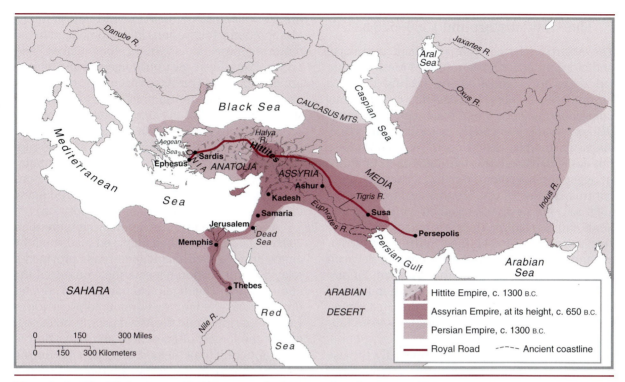

M A P 4 . 4 *The Hittite (around 1700–around 1200 B.C.), Assyrian (around 1300–626 B.C.), and Persian (559–331 B.C.) Empires.* *The Hittites migrated into Anatolia around 2700 B.C. and expanded into an empire by around 1700 B.C.; their expansion south was halted at Kadesh by the Egyptians. Assyrian expansion united Mesopotamian and Egyptian civilizations during the seventh century B.C. The Persian Empire controlled its vast territory with local governors called satraps, who ruled with semiautonomous authority. The Persian road system from Persepolis to Ephesus also served to unite the empire.*

to govern Egypt through his son. The Hittite Empire continued to expand, however, and grew to 260,000 square miles by 1334 B.C.

Hittite expansion relied heavily on iron weaponry and innovations in the use of chariots. Iron weapons were stronger and cheaper to make than those of bronze used by their enemies. Hittite chariots carried a driver and an archer, as did most chariots, but also one shield bearer, who could protect the other two in the heat of battle. Spoked wheels and an axle placed in the rear made the Hittite chariot more maneuverable, and specially trained horses gave it speed. Iron weaponry, chariots, and military use of horses revolutionized warfare in Southwest Asia.

The Hittites controlled their empire by setting up vassal kingdoms that allowed the local royal houses to rule in exchange for taxes and military support against Egypt. Their law extended to this web of vassal states, replacing the older Hammurabic law code; the newer laws focused less on retribution and more on restitution of property. Hittites often extended their interests through diplomacy, preferring negotiation and treaties to costly military conquest. These practices resulted in elite support in the local areas.

Overextension and preoccupation with fighting the Egyptians resulted in the weakening of Hittite control, however. Egypt's formidable resistance under Ramses II finally stopped Hittite aggression southward. Other Indo-Europeans who had been migrating into the area now known as Turkey caused disruption in the Hittite homeland. The Hittite Empire finally collapsed by about 1200 B.C., after devastating raids created political instability that left a vacuum of central authority throughout the region. The vacuum was soon filled by the Assyrians.

The Assyrians, around 1300–626 B.C.

The Assyrians' fertile lands, excellent pasturage, and cities on major trade routes in Mesopotamia led them to establish many trading colonies beyond their borders. The Assyrian city of Ashur enjoyed the prosperity of a major center for long-distance trade, particularly in textiles, limestone, alabaster, marble, and copper. Their lands were not easily defended; this left them open to attack by aggressive neighbors, and they fell under Hittite control. As the Hittite Empire declined around 1300 B.C., the Assyrians regained control of their lands and reorganized their aristocracy into a warrior society to protect their territory. Assyrian expansion soon created a large empire. Between about 1300 and 626 B.C., the Assyrian Empire gained some territories and lost others. In the seventh century B.C., the Assyrians defeated Egypt, and, for a short time, both civilizations were unified under Assyrian rule.

Assyrian military science, especially the use of iron, became the standard for later empires. Assyrians, like the Hittites, used iron weaponry, and it gave them a distinct advantage over the bronze weapons of their enemies in southern Mesopotamia. Innovations in equipment included battering rams, heavy bows, long lances, and armor. They effectively used horsemen and heavily armed infantry. The Assyrians used any means available to accomplish their goal of complete subjugation: Men of the cities were dismembered or burned alive, and even in those cities that surrendered to the approaching army, officials met the same fate. Assyrians often relocated populations as a punitive measure and as a means to control resistance. Assyrian methods convinced many cities to surrender with little or no opposition.

Assyrian armies, often numbering more than 200,000 soldiers, marched on paved roads built by engineers. The well-maintained roads provided a relay communication network that connected the entire empire. The roads also transported populations around the empire. Conquered populations were conscripted into the Assyrian army, making it one of the largest of its period, and relocation of various populations helped to maintain control. King Sargon II (reign dates 722–706 B.C.) built a new capital in 713 B.C. and wrote that he populated it with various "peoples of the four quarters, of

FIGURE 4.12 *Ashurnasirpal II at the Hunt.* *Hunting was a major pastime of kings and soldiers during periods of relative peace, as it honed fighting skills and used many of the same tactics as warfare. This relief carving is of Ashurnasirpal II, king of the Assyrians. Soldiers form an enclosure by interlocking their shield arms and drive the lions toward the king; the charioteer positions the chariot so that the king can take aim and kill the lion—a feat which bears witness to Ashurnasirpal's power and skill as a commander.* Courtesy of the Trustees of the British Museum.

strange tongues and different speech." It is estimated that as many as four million people may have been relocated.

The Assyrian great art style also reflected martial values. Reliefs depicted their kings in battle or hunting. Ashur, their patron deity, mandated that the king defeat Assyria's enemies, and the hunting scenes personified the warrior king, who, through the hunt, protected his people from the ravages of wild beasts. Hunting was also used as a means for military training during periods of peace. The Assyrian art style parallels Egyptian art and biography, in which pharaohs always defeated their enemies.

Like others before them, the Assyrians adopted cuneiform writing and compiled previous law codes and knowledge in order to assimilate the wisdom of their subjects. In the city of Nineveh, they built a great library that contained many tablets on such topics as religion, biography, and astronomy produced by the various peoples they ruled. They also developed a system of placing locations on maps that is similar to the modern system of longitude and latitude.

Although the Assyrians dispersed the conquered populations throughout the empire to weaken resistance, the empire eventually succumbed to a typical difficulty of overextended empires: the inability to perpetuate control over subject peoples. In 626 B.C., the last expansive Assyrian king died and Assyria's enemies united under the leadership of the New Babylonians and the Medes to defeat Assyria. After Assyria's defeat, the empire was devoured by the victors, especially New Babylon, which became a formidable empire itself.

The Persians, 559–331 B.C.

The ancestors of the Persians were part of the Aryan migration of around 2000 B.C. that wandered from the Eurasian steppes into India and Southwest Asia. They eventually settled in a land they called Parsa (Persia), next to the Persian Gulf in southern Iran. During the empires of the Hittites, of the Assyrians, and of their neighbors to the north, the New Babylonians and the Medes, the people of Persia remained in a tribal organization.

Persia rose to prominence against its Medean overlords under the growing power of Cyrus (reign dates 559–530 B.C.), who claimed the title of King of Kings (or emperor) and succeeded in uniting the various Persian groups into a political threat. Cyrus exploited the political unrest within the Medean bureaucracy and army through alliances with several key Medean leaders. On the day of battle, the leaders of the Medean army defected to the Persians, bringing the army with them, and Cyrus carried the day without the necessity of battle. The Medean army remained critical to Cyrus's successes. Diplomacy was a tactic Cyrus would use again.

Cyrus expanded northeastward onto the Iranian plateau, enveloping the kingdom of Lydia, and challenged Greek colonists on the coast of Ionia. Cyrus finally turned his attention to the last remaining empire in the area—New Babylon. The city of Babylon was the focus of a wealthy trade network that stretched through Syria into Palestine and the Mediterranean. The city boasted a population of more than 200,000 people. The city walls were so thick that two rows of houses and a street wide enough for a chariot rested comfortably at their tops. In 539 B.C., Cyrus was able to enter the city of Babylon without firing an arrow because he claimed he would reinstate the patron deity, Marduk. Marduk's worship had been prohibited when the New Babylonian king flirted with monotheism. As Cyrus approached Babylon, he professed himself the avenger of Marduk, and the great bronze doors of the Ishtar gate swung open. The people of the city threw garlands at Cyrus's feet, and the New Babylonian Empire was no more.

Cyrus based his administration upon the policy of using local authority and the relocation of displaced populations to their homelands, like the Jews from the southern Hebrew kingdom (Judah) who had been captives in Babylon. He divided the empire into twelve provinces called **satrapies**, with a ruling **satrap**,[13] or governor, appointed from the Persian aristocracy. Local administration fell under the satrap, who was encouraged by the presence of imperial troops to remain loyal. Codified laws and the standardization of taxes, 20 percent of the annual yield, gained Cyrus a reputation for fairness and consistency. Standardization of currency and weights and measures helped to stimulate long-distance trade. The collection of tariffs,

[13] **satrap:** SAY trap

commercial taxes, and tribute brought massive wealth to the royal treasury; Babylon supplied 33 tons of silver annually and India nearly 12 tons of gold. Cyrus's policies of diplomatic sensitivity tended to keep his subjects loyal, and this helps to explain the longevity of Persian rule over such a vast and diverse empire.

Conquest continued under Cyrus's son, Cambyses[14] (reign dates 529–522 B.C.). He conquered part of Egypt in 525 B.C., but expansion ended when he was unable to rule as effectively as his father. Persia was soon in rebellion and Cambyses died returning home. The Persian Empire returned to expansionist policies after the successful seizure of the imperial throne by Darius I (reign dates 521–486 B.C.), who conquered as far as the western bank of the Indus River. The Persian Empire now stretched from the Indus River to modern Turkey and southward, encompassing Egypt.

With secure borders in the eastern portion of his empire, Darius I turned his royal gaze westward toward the lucrative grain trade coming from the Black Sea into the Aegean Sea. Darius's plan to envelop these Greek commercial routes was thwarted by the Macedonians in 514 B.C. The Persian Empire, however, lasted another 200 years, until Alexander of Macedon conquered Persia in 331 B.C.

The vast highway network, inherited from the Assyrians and expanded by the Persians, enhanced both trade and communication among all the major cities in the Persian Empire. The caravans traveling the road system were protected in most areas, particularly on the 1,700-mile royal road between Susa and Sardis. The royal road had more than 100 inns located along its route, with about a day's journey between them. The Greek historian Herodotus[15] (whose words inspired a motto for the U.S. postal system) said of the royal messengers who traveled the road network, "Nothing stops these couriers from covering their allotted stage in the quickest possible time, neither snow, rain, heat, nor darkness."

Persian religion had a profound influence on the development of world religions. It is also a good example of a unifying ideology in an empire. Zoroastrianism, based upon the revelations of a visionary, Zoroaster,[16] was another experiment with monotheism. Ahuramazda, an all-powerful, wise creator-god, is locked in a cosmic battle with the forces of darkness. The dualistic nature of the contest between good and evil threatened the religion's monotheism, but Zoroastrians believe that Ahuramazda will eventually win this war. Humanity, which must choose to which side its allegiance is given, engages in a moral struggle that mirrors the cosmic battle. This religious perspective contributed to the age's ethical development in law and human behavior as it spread throughout the empire. It profoundly influenced the captive Hebrews in New Babylon, who were codifying Mosaic law, and inspired new concepts of heaven and hell that eventually were incorporated into Christianity and Islam. Zoroastrianism appealed to individuals rather than to particular polities or culture groups; anyone who followed the ethical tenets stated in the holy writings (Avesta) was given the rewards of righteousness from Ahuramazda.

SEAFARING PEOPLES OF THE EASTERN MEDITERRANEAN

The peoples of the Mediterranean were similar to those of many agricultural societies in Southwest Asia. Because of the topography of their regions, however, they harvested the seas and developed vast shipping networks that transported goods around the Mediterranean. Three of the most prominent of these peoples were the Minoans,[17] the Mycenaeans,[18] and the Phoenicians.[19]

Although the Mediterranean initially served as a barrier, discouraging invaders to the island, the people who occupied the island of Crete (called Minoans) perfected seafaring technologies as they exploited fishing beds in natural harbor areas and along the coast from around 2000 B.C. Minoans soon traversed the eastern Mediterranean and established trade colonies for business with the various island and coastal populations they encountered. The trading network brought wealth, which they invested in great palaces, aqueducts, and harbor improvements. Minoans created in their wall paintings some of the most beautiful

---

[14] **Cambyses:** kam BY seez
[15] **Herodotus:** hur RAHD uh tuhs
[16] **Zoroaster:** ZAWR oh ahs tur

[17] **Minoans:** my NOH uhnz
[18] **Mycenaeans:** my seh NEE uhnz
[19] **Phoenicians:** foh NEE shuhnz

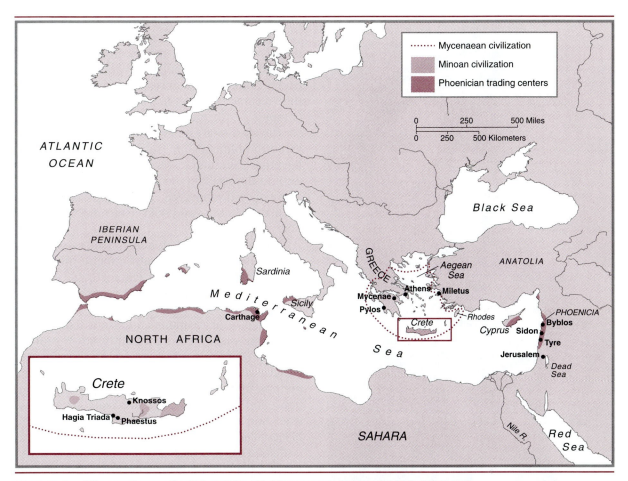

M A P 4 . 5 *Minoan (around 2200–1550 B.C.), Mycenaean (around 1600–1150 B.C.), and Phoenician (around 1000–146 B.C.) Civilizations.* *Minoan civilization developed on the island of Crete, where palace complexes housed goods at Knossos, Phaistos, and Hagia Triada for trade throughout the eastern Mediterranean. The Mycenaean civilization encircled much of Greece and the Aegean Islands by 1250 B.C. Mycenaeans often raided Minoan ships laden with goods bound for Aegean ports. The Phoenicians became a seafaring people, establishing colonies throughout the Mediterranean, disseminating their alphabet along with their trade goods.*

representations of sea and shore life of the Mediterranean world. Popular motifs included athletic games, picturesque landscapes, dolphins playing in the sea, and animals from much of the Mediterranean. Examples of Minoan artisans' handiwork have been found all over the eastern Mediterranean. Their jewelry, pottery, stone and ivory carvings, and other exports adorned the bodies and palaces of early kings and peoples.

Mycenaeans, northern neighbors in Greece, began to interlope in Minoan economic interests and seized many Minoan colonies in the Aegean. Their encroachment benefited from a great nat-

ural disaster, the volcanic eruption on the island of Thera (seventy miles north of Crete) in 1450 B.C. The resulting tidal wave hit the coastal area of Crete, destroyed harbor areas, killed thousands, and devastated the bulk of the Minoan fleet. Not long after, the island fell to the Mycenaeans.

The Mycenaeans had moved into the area of Greece during the Indo-European movement flowing from the area of the Black Sea and Central Asia in the second millennium B.C. They mingled with the local population, and, over the centuries, the two peoples became one. These invaders brought skills of horse handling and charioteering to the

FIGURE 4.13 *Minoan Priestess. The art of the Minoan civilization does not include portrayals of warfare. Instead, the walls at the palace at Knossos are covered with geometric designs, flora and fauna, and figures engaged in religious and everyday activities. This scene comes from a room that was probably used as a house shrine room. The woman wears a large earring and is dressed in brilliantly colored clothing similar to those depicted on fertility statues. Her face is made up with red lips and cheeks and outlined eyes and eyebrows. She moves toward a group that surrounds a seated goddess (not shown). Scholars believe that she may be a priestess performing a ritual; whatever was in her hand has been obscured.* Archaeological Receipts Fund (TAP Service).

area. Because of its topography, few places in Greece are more than a few miles from water, and the Mycenaeans soon turned to sea trade. They learned much from the great Minoan commercial centers, but the mentor relationship changed after the volcanic eruption at Thera. The Mycenaeans competed with the trade network of Egypt until shortly after 1400 B.C.; by 1350 B.C., they had subjugated the Minoans and interloped in the waning Egyptian commerce. Mycenaeans then became lords of the sea, and the distinction between trade and piracy disappeared. They often seized cargo from rivals' ships and sold it at non-Mycenaean ports.

Mycenaeans traded many goods, especially bronze items. The Minoans taught the Mycenaeans how to make and work bronze; farmers adopted it in agrarian technology, artisans used it for tools (hammers and carving knives), and warriors used it for weapons and armor. The king of Pylos controlled more than four hundred bronzesmiths in that one urban center. The Mycenaean pattern of trading and raiding worked well during periods of unimpeded commercial activity. But between 1300 and 1200 B.C., unrest in Egypt, Palestine, and the Anatolian Peninsula diminished Mycenaean wealth because of the interruption in trade and the shortage of cargos to confiscate.

The decline of the Mycenaeans has been hotly debated by historians because little archaeological evidence remains and almost nothing survives in Greek folklore. The Dorians (as they came to be called) probably migrated into southwest Anatolia, southern Greece, and Crete and mixed with or scattered their populations. They reintroduced pastoralism into the area, and their rural lifestyle replaced the urbanization of the Mycenaean period. Dorians populated much of the Greek mainland by about 1000 B.C. Other factors also influenced Mycenaean decline, such as interruption of long-distance trade during the Hittite Empire's collapse, overcultivation of lands for cash crops, and internal warfare.

The Phoenicians occupied the eastern coastal Mediterranean area now known as Lebanon, tending their sheep and crops as other Southwest Asian peoples had done. Many settled between the Mediterranean Sea and the mountains, turned to trade, and established port cities by about 1000 B.C. The mountain forests held the rich natural

EGYPT	MESOPOTAMIA	EASTERN MEDITERRANEAN		
			– 3500 B.C.	Copper tools used widely, c. 3500 B.C.
Ancient Egyptian Kingdom, c. 3500–1085 B.C.	Mesopotamian city-states, c. 3500–2350 B.C.		– – – – 3000 B.C.	Bronze technology spreads, c. 3000 B.C.
			– – – – 2500 B.C.	
	Akkadian Empire, c. 2340–2100 B.C.		– – –	
	Babylonian Empire, c. 2100–1600 B.C.	Minoan Civilization, c. 2200–1550 B.C.	2000 B.C. –	
			–	Hammurabi, king of Babylon, reign dates 1792–1750 B.C.
	Hittite Empire, c. 1700–1200 B.C.	Mycenaean Civilization, c. 1600–1150 B.C.	– 1500 B.C.	Iron technology in use, c. 1500 B.C.
	Assyrian Empire, c. 1300–626 B.C.	Dorians, c. 1200–800 B.C.	– –	Akhenaton, pharaoh of Egypt, reign dates 1367–1350 B.C.
	Hebrew Empire, c. 1025–922 B.C.	Phoenician seafaring, c. 1000–146 B.C.	1000 B.C. –	Carthage becomes center of Phoenician trade, c. 900 B.C.
			– –	

resource of cedar trees. These great cedars of Lebanon, prized throughout Southwest Asia and Egypt, often grew to 135 feet, making them ideal for masts and planking on shipping vessels and as building materials for wealthy kings and nobles in the sparsely forested interior areas.

Phoenicians soon dominated eastern Mediterranean trade by building a network of independent city-states at Tyre, Sidon, Byblos, and Arvad. They seized the opportunity to exploit the rest of the Mediterranean commercially and established a trade network that spread to Cyprus, North Africa, Sicily, Sardinia, and the Iberian Peninsula. By the seventh century B.C., Carthage (in North Africa), the most important Phoenician colony, dominated the Mediterranean. Phoenician commercial activities contributed to navigational and maritime technologies. They populated the sea with both merchant vessels and fast warships, which carried battering rams that could pierce the hulls of enemy ships with their bronze tips. Phoenicians could navigate by night using astronomy, yet they usually sailed in the safety of daylight. They used watchfires—an ancient form of lighthouse—at high points on shore during the night to help ships navigate safely into harbor.

Phoenician trade in the eastern Mediterranean eventually declined. By 900 B.C., Assyrians were threatening the eastern Mediterranean coastal areas, and Phoenician ships were confiscated for warships. As the Assyrians invaded the cities, the center of Phoenician trade shifted to Carthage, which dominated central Mediterranean trade until 146 B.C.

SUMMARY

1. Agriculture set the stage for the development of civilizations in Southwest Asia and Egypt. Polytheism was the prominent form of religion, but the Hebrews and Zoroastrians developed monotheism, which was long lasting.

2. The societies of Southwest Asia endured the ebb and flow of developing kingdoms and expanding empires whose religious ideology justified expansion under a divine mandate, while Egypt moved toward unification under relative isolation. Culture was often spread through conquest and during periods of migration.

3. In both Sumeria and Egypt, writing developed in response to political and economic needs.

4. In Southwest Asia and Egypt, women generally played minor parts in political history. Men worked in various professions and were the primary focus of law codes; women worked in the home and in some professions, and they were both property owners and property themselves.

5. The power of kingship varied: Southwest Asian kings' authority derived from their close relationship with the patron god, and the Egyptian pharaohs' authority derived from their divine nature. In Egypt, law came from the pharaoh's pronouncements. In Mesopotamia, law came from the deities through the authority of the king. The Hebrews perpetuated egalitarianism, placing even their king under the law of the covenant. Changes in Hebrew laws paralleled similar changes taking place in other legal codes, for example as abstract concepts like the Ten Commandments replaced more specific laws on retribution.

6. The introduction of iron and chariots revolutionized warfare. Hittites, Assyrians, and Persians made innovations in the governance of large territories that helped to establish and control extended empires.

7. Seafaring among the peoples of the eastern Mediterranean served as a conduit for the exchange of goods and ideas and as inspiration in the exploration of unknown coastal areas. Commercial activity inspired innovation in seafaring technologies.

SUGGESTED READINGS

Aldred, Cyril. *Egyptians*. Revised edition. London: Thames and Hudson, 1987. A cultural and political history of Egypt.

Gurney, O. R. *The Hittites*. Revised edition. New York: Penguin, 1990. A good overview of the history of the Hittites.

Harden, Donald B. *The Phoenicians*. Harmondsworth, Eng.: Penguin, 1971. A study of the Phoenicians and their colonization of the Mediterranean through archaeological and literary evidence.

Kramer, S. N. *The Sumerians: Their History, Culture, and Character*. Chicago: University of Chicago Press, 1971. A standard treatment of Sumerian civilization.

Oppenheim, A. Leo. *Ancient Mesopotamia*. Second edition. Chicago: University of Chicago Press, 1977. A review that centers on the Babylonian and Assyrian peoples.

Orlinsky, H. M. *Ancient Israel*. Second edition. Ithaca, N.Y.: Cornell University Press, 1960. A brief but thorough review of ancient Hebrew history.

Taylor, Lord William. *The Mycenaeans*. London: Thames and Hudson, 1983. A review of Mycenaean history and culture.

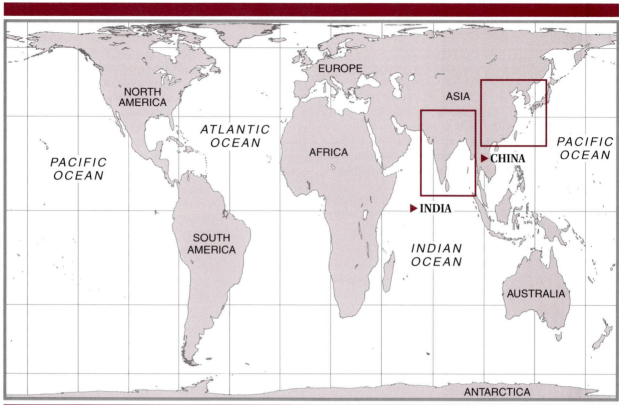

Shang Kingdom boundary
Zhou Realm

► CHINA

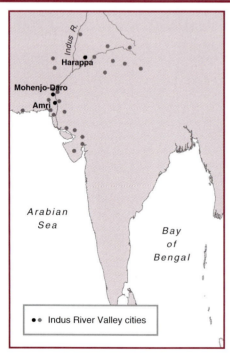

● ● Indus River Valley cities

► INDIA

Early River Valley Civilizations of South and East Asia

around 2500–around 700 B.C.

The Chinese king mused in the divining chamber. His army was to fight a great battle in three days, and he needed counsel from the spirit of his dead queen. What a splendid warrior she had been! Never once had she lost in battle, and many regarded her as the goddess of battle. What would she say to him? The solemn diviner readied the oracle bone to receive the answer to his question.

Near the end of the Shang Dynasty, religion featured prominently in the lives of the Chinese rulers. Religion became and remained important for the people of China and India, beginning in the early third millennium B.C.

Civilizations emerged in the river valleys of South and East Asia only shortly after the development of civilizations in Mesopotamia and Egypt. In South Asia, civilization arose in the Indus Valley; elements of that civilization fused with elements carried from immigrants from Central Asia, forming the first of a series of civilizations in the Ganges Valley.[1] In East Asia, civilization arose independently in the Yellow River Valley.

INDUS VALLEY CIVILIZATION, AROUND 2500–AROUND 1750 B.C.

Early nomads periodically inhabited the Indus floodplain during harsh winters. Around 5000 B.C., people in the lowlands began practicing settled forms of agriculture, and villages dotted the

[1] **Ganges:** GAN jeez

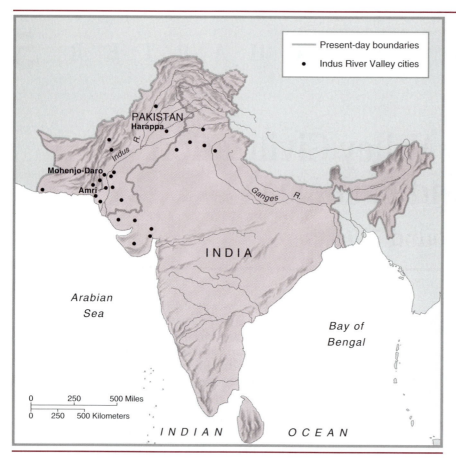

MAP 5.1 *Indus Valley Civilization, around 2500– around 1750 B.C.* *The earliest civilization in India lay in the northwestern part of the subcontinent. Although the major cities of Mohenjo-Daro and Harappa were three hundred miles apart, they were laid out in a similar plan. This suggests either overall political unity or a common cultural pattern of urban organization and development.*

Indus River banks. The excavated Amri Village archaeological site reveals a twenty-acre village with homes of mud brick. Amri villagers used a wheel to fashion pots decorated with geometric patterns. They hunted elephants, tigers, bears, boars, and deer. They also fished in the Indus River waters. Another excavation site reveals that the villagers grew wheat and barley, used flint blades, and raised domesticated sheep, goats, and cows.

Over the next two millennia, floodplain dwellers in larger villages or towns mass produced ceramics decorated with geometric patterns. These and other products were traded over long distances and brought modest prosperity to the larger communities. In the following centuries, many villages, like Amri Village, doubled in size. Houses were built from adobe brick with interior courtyards, often according to a common design. Archaeological remains from Amri Village and other sites demonstrate the continued evolution of villages, the development of intensive agriculture, the mass production of ceramic wares, and the improvement of metallurgical techniques to produce copper and, eventually, bronze vessels. Thus, many of the preconditions for civilization emerged in the Indus Valley.

From these and other sites we may conclude that the improving agricultural conditions caused the rapid growth of local populations and the development of civilization. Population densities in the Indus Valley reached a critical mass sometime after 3000 B.C., and urbanization emerged. In addition, the increasing grain yields supported these cities of people, like artisans, who engaged in specialized labor other than agriculture. The geographic expanse of the Indus Valley civilization covered areas from present-day eastern Iran to the western coast of India.

Mohenjo-Daro, a walled city of 35,000 to 40,000 people, rose according to a construction plan with a central citadel that towered nearly fifty feet. This wall measured about three and one-half miles along its perimeter. People in the

FIGURE 5.1 *The Great Bath at Mohenjo-Daro.*
The excavated ruins of the Great Bath at Mohenjo-Daro indicate the use of ritual cleansing in early Indian cultures. The bath's network of running water and covered drains also supported private bathing rooms. Today, Hindu temples use bathing steps built along the river banks for the purpose of ritual cleansing. Atop the brick structure of the Great Bath is a Buddhist ruin (upper right), built over 2,000 years later.
Josephine Powell.

Indus Valley used furnace-baked bricks for walls and major buildings, while sun-baked ones could be found in homes. These individual urban dwellings usually had interior courtyards around which families organized domestic life.

Because of Mohenjo-Daro's proximity to the Indus River, which tended to flood, the city was destroyed by the rampaging river, and, each time, a new city was built from the flood ruins. An extensive community sewer system that drained houses with indoor plumbing suggests a highly effective government. A major building in Mohenjo-Daro, perhaps a bathing complex, shows the value that Indians placed on water to clean and purify. Ritual bathing likely became a central part of religious life, as it remains in India today. Irrigation networks helped transform the Indus Valley civilization's agricultural base to yield even larger grain surpluses.

Indus Valley people harvested a wide variety of crops. They grew grains like wheat (the main grain staple), barley, millet, and sorghum and stored them in granaries on raised brick floors that permitted air circulation beneath and retarded mildew. They also ate dates, lentils, and peas.

Artisans lived and worked in special sections of the Indus Valley cities. Metallurgists forged copper and bronze implements, ranging from agricultural tools to weapons to ceremonial pieces. Bronze female figurines indicate that Indian artisans skillfully employed complex casting techniques. Potters also created ceramic utensils, such as drain pipes and terra cotta ornaments. They also fashioned miniature bullock carts and miniature ships for decorative purposes. Cotton appeared at this time in India, and the Indus people wove and dyed its fibers. These textiles became important trade items not only within the Indus Valley but also across Southwest Asia.

Long-distance trade, a major occupation of the Indus Valley people, transported commodities such as timber and cotton throughout the Indus region and as far as Mesopotamia and Central Asia. There was an especially robust trade with Sumer from around 2300 B.C. to around 2000 B.C., through which the Indians imported tin and precious stones. Local trade within the Indus floodplain flourished after the standardization of weights and measures, although some scholars argue that increasing trade volume created the need to standardize.

The organization underlying these activities suggests some kind of controlling political force or perhaps a common pattern of urban development throughout the Indus Valley. The regularity found in these cities indicates governments given to careful organization and planning. The massive citadels and other large buildings, including one in Mohenjo-Daro that may have been a palace, hint at centralized polity. Indus cities likely employed officials, including tax collectors, city planners, water control experts, and scribes, and they also supported merchants and artisans. Similarities among the dwellings and establishments of the merchants and artisans have caused most scholars of ancient India to argue for a **guild**, an organization of merchants and artisans based on specific trades and crafts that works for communal political, economic, and social interests. More should be learned about these elements of the Indus Valley civilization if its undeciphered language is decoded.

Recovered artifacts suggest that the Indus people worshiped animals and venerated a female deity, which may be seen in the large numbers of statues, jewelry pieces, and other relics. Many figurines are female with enlarged breasts and genitals prominently displayed, suggesting the worship of a fertility goddess. In Mohenjo-Daro, one unusual piece is a multifaced figure surrounded by animals and seated cross-legged in a yogi posture. These features have caused some to speculate that this represents an early form of Shiva, an Indian deity later associated with animals.

Among the most intriguing and elusive remnants of the Indus Valley civilization are small square seals. Merchants and others may have used these rectangular artifacts to mark and thereby identify their property. Seal surfaces might have been covered with ink and pressed on one's possessions, or perhaps a seal impression might have been left on a piece of soft clay or wax. The Indus Valley seals contain pictographic signs that may be the names of merchants.

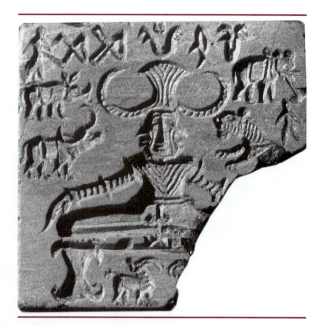

FIGURE 5.2 *Horned Figure of Mohenjo-Daro.*
The figure in this artifact is seated in a yoga position with arms resting on crossed legs, a meditation position still in use among Hindus and Buddhists today. Various creatures surround the figure, suggesting that this was a deity of animals, similar to Shiva in later centuries.
John C. Huntington.

The Indus Valley civilization flourished around 2500–1750 B.C., although some cities emerged earlier and others lasted a few centuries longer. Over time, the major cities declined. An imaginative interpretation of the archaeological evidence highlights catastrophic flooding induced by earth movements associated with earthquakes. Other scholars argue for a more gradual process as overfarming or overgrazing of the surrounding lands may have contributed to erosion, flooding, and decline. In areas where irrigation networks predominated, centuries of evaporating irrigation water may have left large amounts of salt or alkali residues, reducing the land's ability to sustain agriculture. Further, some have noted that accelerated cutting of trees for firewood removed a major energy source for brick makers and others. The continued clear-cutting of trees may have increased the amount of water runoff and overwhelmed the irrigation systems. Other scholars have argued that rainfall declined in the Indus region; one river in the northeastern Indus Valley ran dry, for example. Most likely some combination of these factors led to the civilization's decline.

Many of the Indus Valley civilization's cultural and social practices, like animal-centered worship and the yogic traditions of physical exercise and meditation, emerged in the Ganges Valley and other places. Water has been regarded as holy throughout Indian history, and the segregation of peoples along occupational and kinship lines persists in cities.

ARYAN MIGRATIONS AND EARLY SETTLEMENTS, AROUND 1400–AROUND 700 B.C.

Mountain barriers often limited extended contact and interactions between the peoples of India and other areas, while internal obstructions, like dense jungles, slowed the spread of groups across the Indian subcontinent. The Himalayan, the Hindu Kush, and the Pamir mountain ranges formed a kind of semipermeable alpine wall in the northeast and northwest of the Indian subcontinent. Although these ranges inhibited extensive interchanges between the Indian and Chinese civilizations, they did not act as impenetrable barricades. Mountain passes afforded access to determined peoples. Around 1400 B.C., an immigrant group called the Aryans crossed the mountains into India and migrated slowly across the region. After 1000 B.C., the Aryans reached the Ganges River Valley, an area of dense forest and jungles. Only with the mass production and use of iron tools, along with a climatic shift to less rainfall, did the Ganges region yield to widespread Aryan settlement. (See Map 5.2 on p. 102.)

The Aryan homeland was probably in the southern part of Central Asia. Some Aryans migrated toward Mesopotamia, and others moved through the Hindu Kush passes or across the Persian plateau into South Asia. In fact, the Aryans are part of a larger series of migrations of Indo-Europeans into broad areas of the vast Eurasian land mass; even today, most peoples in Europe and India speak languages that have evolved from a common tongue. The Aryans' warlike ways permeated their religious and poetic works, which were carefully transmitted by successive generations. Aryans herded cattle, sheep, goats, and

FIGURE 5.3 *Vedic Ritual of the Fire Altar.* Brahmans *have presided over many rituals during the last 3,000 years, one of the most important and enduring being the Fire Altar Ritual. The Vedas outlined the proper way to conduct the highly detailed, sometimes weeks-long ceremonies; as ritual experts, the* brahmans *directed such activities, thereby maintaining their elite social position.* Courtesy of Adelaide de Menil, 1975 © The Film Study Center, Harvard University.

horses. (The horse had been domesticated by pre-Aryan groups, but it had not been used in warfare.)

Because the Aryans gradually moved across India in a process that took centuries, Aryan social, religious, economic, and political practices changed through a process of cultural interaction and diffusion. The Aryan language, for example, borrowed many words from local peoples, and the Aryan religion adopted existing indigenous spiritual techniques, like yoga. Over the centuries, the resulting synthesis became Indian rather than Aryan or Gangetic.

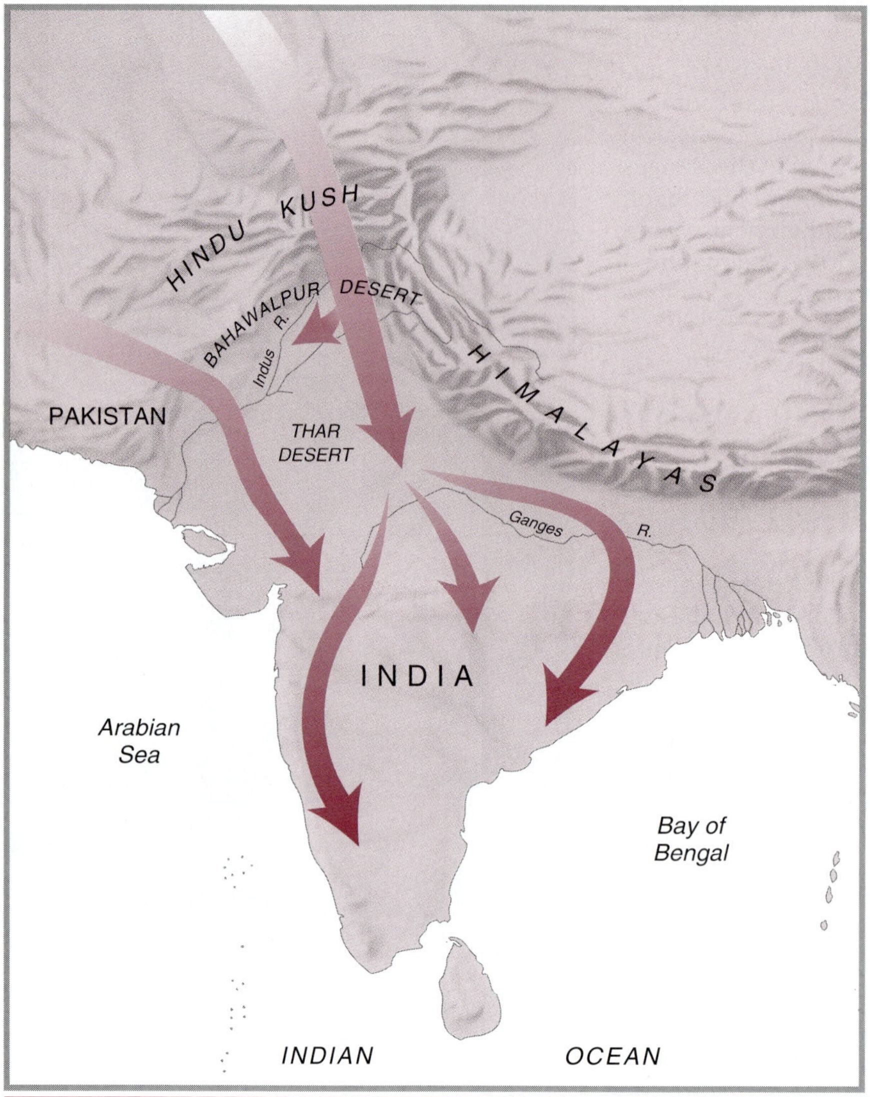

MAP 5.2 *Aryan Migration into India, around 1450–around 700 B.C.* *The Aryans migrated from Central Asia and from the Iranian plateau into the Indian subcontinent. They spread slowly over the subcontinent until about 700 B.C., mixing with the indigenous peoples.*

Knowledge of the Aryans comes largely from the four **Vedas**,[2] a series of religious and ceremonial writings transmitted orally until they were transcribed around 500 B.C. Rituals performed by the Aryan priests, the ***brahmans***, formed the core texts of the four main Vedas. The oldest and most venerable of the Vedas, the Rig Veda, consists of more than 1,000 poems. Rhyme facilitated memorization for the *brahmans*, the guardians of textual accuracy. These hymns praised deities like the bearded and powerful Indra, who loved to eat, drink, and fight. Often carrying a thunderbolt or wielding a great bow while riding in a chariot, Indra won all battles.

[2] **Vedas:** VAY duhs

Indeed, Indra may remind us of the Greek god Zeus or of the Norse deity Thor, both of whom hurled thunderbolts and were powerful among an anthropomorphic pantheon of deities.

Society

Although Aryan religion and society were strongly influenced by men, women sometimes played important roles. Men became the priests, and the dominant deities were male, some of whom had multiple wives. Men ruled hierarchies, including kingdoms and their own households. Women usually lived with husbands and were supposed to be subservient to them. Men worked in the fields, while women often wove textiles at home. After

1000 B.C., better harvests and population growth in the Ganges Valley spurred the need for more complicated political systems. A more rigid social and political organization developed, and this brought men even greater power.

Although society stacked the cards against women, there were exceptions. Women in the higher social groups accomplished many notable things. At least twenty women are listed as authors of parts of the Rig Veda, one of the holiest works in Indian literature. Some others received an education and became authorities on parts of the Vedas.

Many women in upper-class households could read and write. On occasion, a woman might even address an assembly of political leaders that advised the ruler on a variety of issues.

From 1000 to 700 B.C., women of elite groups enjoyed certain advantages usually denied to women of later times. A woman might choose a husband, and she was responsible for managing the household. She also could move relatively freely in the local society. Women at all social levels likely wove textiles, and the income from that endeavor often proved sufficient to

---

PARALLELS AND DIVERGENCES

Indo-European Connections

Students, teachers, and scholars are sometimes fascinated by the congruences between Indian and European languages, pre-Christian religions, and mythologies. Given the great distance between the two Eurasian civilization centers, the similarities are even more surprising. One factor in their relationship is the common origin of many Indo-European peoples. Around the beginning of the second millennium B.C., a movement of Central Asian tribal groups commenced. They spoke related dialects and had broadly similar social structures and religious systems. Some passed into the Indian subcontinent; others settled in Greece or other parts of Europe. Successive waves of tribes continued their expansion for the next millennium.

One clear similarity between Indians and Europeans is language. As long ago as the 1780s, Sir William Jones discovered significant linguistic bonds between the Persian, Indian Sanskrit, German (and its derivative language, English), and Latin (and its derivative language, Spanish), and he posited a single Indo-European language family. Different forms of the English word *father* illustrate Jones's discovery:

—German *vater*

—Sanskrit *pitar*

—Persian *pedar*

—Latin *pater*

—Spanish *padre*

Another congruence concerns religion. As noted in this chapter, the Aryan deity Indra resembles the Greek Zeus and the Norse Thor. All employ thunder-bolts as weapons and preside over other deities who have anthropomorphic attributes. These similarities suggest that early Indo-Europeans had common religious beliefs.

An additional similarity is the general likeness of the ancient Greek epic poem the *Iliad* and the Indian epic the *Mahabharata*. Both poems depict panoramic battles, warrior values, heroic acts, and interventions by impatient deities. The ancient Greek epic poem the *Odyssey* and its Indian counterpart the *Ramayana* depict the travels of their heroes, each of whom is an ideal ruler. Sita, Rama's abducted wife, is the ideal wife, loyal despite numerous temptations. Likewise, Penelope, Odysseus's wife, exemplifies loyalty to her husband, who has been absent from his homeland for two decades. Both husbands return when their wives are in the midst of being forced to decide among suitors. In each case, the disguised hero strings his bow, which only he has the strength to string, and dispatches the suitors with a volley of arrows.

Although the similarities are striking, a major point is that each epic, religion, or language is translated into a particular cultural context over time. The *Iliad* examines war, bravery, and honor, focusing on the battles themselves and the personal qualities of the warriors. The *Mahabharata* spends considerable time on political intrigues and combat, but it also contains lengthy passages that teach values like duty, honor, and courage. It further espouses important spiritual ideas. Yet both works have long provided examples for moral living to young and old alike.

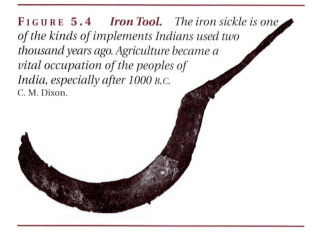

FIGURE 5.4   *Iron Tool.*   *The iron sickle is one of the kinds of implements Indians used two thousand years ago. Agriculture became a vital occupation of the peoples of India, especially after 1000 B.C.*
C. M. Dixon.

enhance their standing in the family or to support them if they lived alone.

Aryan society had strict regulations and hierarchical patterns. Atop the social pyramid were the priests (*brahmans*), followed by the warriors (*kshatriyas*[3]) and the merchants, farmers, and other commoners (*vaishyas*[4]); at the bottom were menial workers and indigenous peoples (*shudras*[5]). This ranking system was formulated in the time before the eighth century B.C. and may have developed out of a simple hierarchy based on skin color, with the lighter Aryans of the three highest categories holding higher status than the darker local people.

Politics and Iron

Early Aryan polities evolved into city-states and often were based on kinship ties, with the *raja*, the ruler who dominated the group's decision-making process, at the top. *Brahmans* acted as key advisors and officials. Additionally, the *raja* often consulted either with a council of elders or with household heads. These individuals and bodies limited the power of the *raja*. During the first half-millennium B.C., city-states appeared in the Ganges Valley, and they often fought one another. Gradually, however, a few kingdoms emerged from these wars, although no unified Gangetic state developed in this era.

Another key development was the mastery of iron metallurgy. Once the Aryans accomplished this sometime after 1000 B.C., they soon

mass produced weapons to arm the soldiers of the city-states. Aryans also tipped their plows with iron and made iron axes to clear the previously resistant forests in the Ganges Valley. This cluster of changes transformed agriculture, leading to larger grain supplies and a growing population density. At the same time, the conditions were ripe for the development of long-distance trade from the city-states and kingdoms to other parts of Asia.

The effort needed to make weapons and iron tools on a large scale taxed the resources of the city rulers. Iron had to be mined, and that process involved finding, organizing, and supplying a large number of people. The iron ore often needed processing, and the iron itself had to be fashioned into tools and weapons.

Elite Culture

Indian civilization boasts two preeminent literary works: the **Mahabharata**,[6] the world's longest poem, with nearly two hundred thousand lines, and the **Ramayana**,[7] an epic about the legendary hero Rama. The *Mahabharata* describes great tribal wars, including heroics and treachery amid ferocious battles. The Indian epics have long remained popular in India as well as in many Southeast Asian countries, including Indonesia, Cambodia, Vietnam, and Burma. The Thai monarchy still refers to itself as the Rama house.

YELLOW RIVER CIVILIZATION, AROUND 1500–771 B.C.

Mountains, jungles, and deserts usually inhibited human penetration into China. The South China Sea and the East China Sea also limited early contact with non-Chinese peoples. There was little contact in the northeast, because there were no significant invaders to trouble seriously the Chinese living there. The north, however, lacked natural obstacles to human ingress. There was, of course, the Gobi Desert, but it did not completely prevent various nomadic groups from invading China.

China's relative isolation from the rest of Asia may have meant that without the ability to directly

---

[3] *kshatriyas:* KSHAH tree ahs
[4] *vaishyas:* VAY shee ahs
[5] *shudras:* SHOO druhs

[6] *Mahabharata:* mah hah BAH rah tah
[7] *Ramayana:* RAH mah yah nah

ENCOUNTERS

Southeast Asian Food Contributions to Early Asian Civilizations

Early forms of agriculture appeared in Southeast Asia. Settled life was found in the areas of present-day Vietnam and Thailand. The people there were developing from a society based on hunting and gathering to one more settled and agricultural. Archaeological finds in the Spirit Cave in Thailand reveal a wide variety of food products like yams, rice, and domesticated chickens. During the period from around 4000 to around 2500 B.C., agriculture became more complex. New domesticated animals came into use, including the pig.

Over time, Southeast Asia played a vital role in the transmission of plants and animals to other parts of Eurasia. Rice is native to Southeast Asia and possibly to East Asia, and it spread to become the dominant grain harvested in much of East Asia and a major foodstuff in South Asia. Pigs and chickens were transported across the Eurasian land mass, and both became important food sources to the Chinese and other East Asian peoples. The pig especially has been a prized domesticated animal, not merely for its meat but also because it could be raised on the scraps and waste products of human consumption. A later Chinese writer noted that the pig was a miniature fertilizer factory. Pigs and chickens were transported west to India and then to Mesopotamia and beyond. The water buffalo originated in Southeast Asia and played a major role in China as a beast of burden and as a foodstuff. Taro, a tuber, was carried by people across Southeast Asia and then to the islands of the Pacific, where it became a major food source for the Polynesians, the Melanesians, and the Micronesians.

compare themselves with the peoples of other great civilizations, the Chinese viewed themselves as superior to all others. The Chinese name for China, Zhong Guo[8] ("the Central Kingdom"), reflected this self-perception. Although most peoples view themselves as superior to outsiders, China was unique in developing a long-sustained supreme self-confidence that lasted into recent times.

Mountains within China also had important consequences. The Qinling[9] Mountains were a watershed. South of these mountains, nearly forty inches of rain fell on average annually; north of the Qinling Mountains, average annual rainfall totaled in the ten-inch range, and aridity inhibited the development of agriculture in that part of the Yellow River Valley. Numerous mountain ranges slowed easy communication from one area to another; this promoted regional differences, for example in spoken dialects and cooking styles.

Ethnic diversity was a fact of ancient Chinese history, as in India. Despite the diversity, the unification of the Chinese written language in the third century B.C. gave successive governments an elite cultural base with common features. In addition, the relatively large number of Chinese aided their successful efforts to assimilate non-Chinese peoples. Those peoples who refused to be so assimilated were either destroyed or forced to live outside the Chinese settlements. These policies ensured the political and ethnic dominance of the Chinese.

Agriculture appeared in China by the sixth millennium B.C. For a long time, scholars believed the Yellow River to be the sole center of early agricultural life in China, but recent archaeological discoveries have altered this perspective. In Southeast China, one site dates the early cultivation of rice at around 5000 B.C., and archaeologists have found another major agricultural area along the coast.

We will focus, however, on the Yellow River area, especially on the area of Banpo Village near the present city of Xian.[10] Fishing and hunting dominated the early years of life in Banpo (around 4500–around 4000 B.C.), but farming and animal husbandry soon became major sources of food for the villagers. Millet, a grain that could weather long periods of little rainfall, was the primary foodstuff. Chinese in Banpo also knew how to spin, weave, and sew. Debris

[8] **Zhong Guo:** joong GWAH
[9] **Qinling:** CHIHN lihng

[10] **Xian:** shee YAHN

FIGURE 5.5 *Banpo Village Excavation Site.* *Banpo villagers made and used an assortment of clay pots. Some were used for grain and seed storage. Others were used to hold the remains of deceased children. A moat surrounded the village, probably for defense against wild animals and predatory humans.* China Pictorial Photo Service.

from several kiln sites reveal that the Banpo people fired pottery and decorated these pieces with images of animals and fish and geometric designs. Domesticated animals included the dog and the pig. The Banpo lifestyle was essentially peaceful, as discussed generally for early tribe-level peoples in Chapter 3.

By the third millennium B.C., a cluster of developments soon brought cities and centralized polities into being. Agriculture became more widespread and led to larger populations, as well as surpluses with which to feed the cities. Bronze metallurgy needed the organization of large numbers of people by a controlling force. City rulers, feeling the necessity to defend themselves against encroachment on their farmlands, organized armies and built huge earthen walls surrounding the urban centers. Unlike that of Banpo, this society was stratified with a ruling group, a pattern of Chinese civilization that began around 2000 B.C.

Two mythical cultural heroes indicate important Chinese ideals. Huangdi[11] ("Yellow Emperor"), an imaginary figure assigned to the early centuries of the third millennium (about 2700 B.C.), was said to have established monarchical rule, fought with non-Chinese peoples, and spread Chinese culture. In Chinese culture,

Huangdi holds a position akin to that of Rama in Indian culture. Both monarchs ruled fairly and lived heroically; they defined the ideal king for their respective peoples. Another moral exemplar, Yü (late third millennium B.C.), tamed the flood-prone Yellow River. He personifies the dedicated official. While directing a long-lasting water control effort, the digging of a channel for the Yellow River to reach the sea, not once did Yü take time out to return home. A popular Chinese saying noted that "We would be fish if it were not for Yü." Later, Yü supposedly founded China's first dynasty, Xia[12] (traditional dates 2205–1766 B.C.), but most scholars consider Xia to be mythical. Hence our attention will center on the successor Shang Dynasty, which began around 1500 B.C.

The Shang Dynasty, around 1500–around 1050 B.C.

Although traditional accounts have supported Shang's existence, material evidence supporting the actuality of the Shang came to light only around 1900. These remnants, along with other materials, confirmed the Shang's existence. Thirty Shang monarchs ruled, and succession passed from brother to brother or from father to son.

[11] **Huangdi:** HWANG dee

[12] **Xia:** shee YAH

POLITICS. Shang life revolved around walled cities. Inside one capital at Anyang (which may have covered an area of about ten square miles) lay the king's palace. In addition, about one dozen royal tomb complexes, residences of the aristocracy, government buildings, and dwellings of officials and artisans existed within the city. The planned city was laid out in a grid pattern along a north-south axis similar to that found in the Indus cities. The surrounding area included a religious center, an ancestral burial ground, and a hunting preserve.

Hunting provided sport, food for the royal table, and a means for training the armed forces. To surround game on large hunting preserves stretching over many square miles, the monarch and other members of the elite would have to coordinate the massed movement of mounted horsemen and perhaps charioteers. Subsequently, the hunted animals would be forced into a restricted area where they could be killed.

The Shang kingdom also included affiliated territories, the subordinate rulers of which received their titles and authority to rule from the Shang monarch in exchange for their recognition of his overlordship and promise to aid him when the realm came under attack. Such leaders usually came to the capital on a regular schedule, bearing tribute (often valuable products native to the affiliated area). On the other hand, the monarch recognized the affiliated lord's right to rule and aided him in times of conflict. Beyond the core area and affiliated lands lay the places where other ethnic peoples dwelled. The rulers of these places traded and sometimes warred with the Chinese.

SOCIETY. Shang society included an aristocracy, officials, merchants, artisans, peasants, and slaves (usually war prisoners, especially those who were non-Chinese). Some social mobility and mixing occurred. Women usually submitted to men in political, social, and economic matters, yet some aristocratic women transcended these social limitations. In the mid-1970s, an excavated Shang tomb revealed the remains of Fu Hao[13] (Lady Hao), who lived around 1300 B.C. She was a wife of King Wuding. Like her husband, Fu Hao acted as a diviner in the religious practice of seeking the spirits' views on various important matters. Hundreds of bronze pieces, bone artifacts, and

[13] **Fu Hao:** foo HOW

FIGURE 5.6 *Jade Figurine from the Fu Hao Tomb.* *This small carved piece demonstrates the sophisticated level of Shang artisanry. It also shows the sitting posture characteristic of early East Asian cultures and suggests the subordinate status of servants. The hooked portion at the rear may be an artistic extension of the figure's sash.* Institute of Archaeology, Beijing.

jade items were recovered from her tomb. Evidence suggests that Fu Hao commanded an army, garnered a reputation of military invincibility, and served as an official.

Some oracle bone inscriptions reveal that after Fu Hao's death, the king implored her spirit to aid in his battles. Although aristocratic women like Fu Hao were not commonly active, she was not unique. Fu Jing (Lady Jing), another wife of Wuding, led armies and played an active political role in government.

Other Shang tombs have provided social information about the aristocrats through lavish burial chambers with numerous grave goods. The scale of the funeral complexes suggests that the monarchs and other aristocrats could command large populations, including slaves, to work on these elaborate monuments. They also indicate a highly stratified society. Some tombs held the remains of people who had been killed and interred with the aristocrat, and there may have been a relationship between the numbers of people killed and the status of the aristocrat who was buried in the tomb. Chariots buried along with horses show a new and important weapon of the Shang era. The idea for these chariots came from Central Asia.

ECONOMY. Agriculture was the basis of the Shang economy. In the Yellow River Valley, millet was the key grain harvested; in the south, rice became the staple crop. Most Chinese worked in agriculture and produced enough of a crop surplus to support large cities and growing numbers of people.

Metallurgy reached sophisticated levels during the Shang era. Bronze pieces included not only tools and weapons but also ceremonial items that were exchanged between the monarch and the lords of the affiliated states during their ceremonies of pledging loyalty. Indeed, it seems likely that the ruling elite valued the ceremonial bronzes more highly than the bronze implements.

ELITE CULTURE. One glory of Shang China was the development of a sophisticated elite culture. Thanks to generations of dedicated archaeologists, a rich variety of artifacts has been recovered in the twentieth century. Most prized are the Shang ceremonial bronzes. Artisans perfected the techniques necessary to produce beautiful bronze items with surfaces so malleable that incisions carved on them could be made with remarkable ease. To achieve that result, the artisans experimented with alloys of copper, lead, tin, antimony, arsenic, and zinc. All bronze surfaces available for decoration were covered by intricate designs representing animals, birds, mythical creatures, gods, or human beings. Some weighed nearly one ton.

Shang religious practices are reflected in the monumental structures near the cities and in the practice of divination. Members of the Shang elite respected their dead ancestors and frequently called upon them for blessings and approval. Kings built impressive temples to their forebears and regularly visited these sites to perform ceremonial acts announcing victory in battle, a bumper harvest, or the birth of a son and heir. Other subjects of veneration included cultural heroes, celestial bodies, and natural objects, such as mountains.

Members of the Shang elite believed in a paramount diety, the Lord on High, and regularly requested its blessings or guidance on proposed actions. To divine the future, they used animal bones and turtle shells. The normal divining process began with preparing the shells or oracle bones by cleaning and drying them. Then the diviner scraped away the bone or shell until it was thin. After asking the Lord on High his question, the diviner placed a heated piece of metal on the thin surface. The high temperature would crack the bone or shell, and the diviner would interpret the cracks (the Lord on High's answer) and relay the message to the questioner. Diviners kept the divination artifact, often with the question, answer, and result written on the surface.

The oracle bones also tell us about the other key Shang contribution, the development of a written language. Since its development more than three millennia ago, the written word has become more important than the spoken word. The origins of the written characters predate by centuries the practice of divination. Crude markings, which may have reflected ownership or some form of record keeping, are found on artifacts recovered at the Banpo site. Certainly these efforts became more regularized and complex over succeeding centuries. In the Shang era, extant evidence associates writing with divination. From the 200,000 recovered oracle bones, scholars have reconstructed a written language containing 3,000 characters. Of these, about 800 have been deciphered. Many characters evolved from pictures (pictographs), others represented ideas (ideograms), and most combined a pronunciation indicator with a part that suggested the meaning of the character. Eventually 214 of these "parts" became key components of the written characters

Figure 5.7 *Bronze Mask of the Shang Dynasty.*
The stylized facial features of this piece demonstrate the skill of Shang metal workers. This bronze mask was apparently used for decorative purposes and probably was not worn. Asian Art and Archeology.

for literate Chinese. For the first thousand years, the characters developed regional and local variations. Only in the late third century B.C. did writing become standardized. Because regional variants of spoken Chinese became mutually unintelligible dialects over time, the unified characters gave a cultural cohesion that helped overcome the geographical and ethnic diversity.

THE LAST DAYS OF THE SHANG DYNASTY. According to historical documents, the last Shang monarch terrorized his subjects, and once he even drank wine from a cup made from the skull of an opponent. (This was a common practice in many parts of the world.) In what was a caricature of excess, hostile sources described him as a giant of a man who drank a lake of ale and ate a forest of meat. At the same time, evidence indicates that slaves revolted against the king and their other overlords.

Seeing an opportunity, successive leaders of Zhou,[14] a western affiliated state, carried out an extended campaign against Shang. At long last, around 1050 B.C, the Zhou state's army approached the Shang capital, where the Zhou captured and executed the hapless Shang king.

The Early Zhou, around 1050–771 B.C.

The Zhou Dynasty (around 1050–around 256 B.C.) arose in a strategic region that produced many of China's early dynasties. Although little is known about its first centuries, Zhou gained an honored reputation among later Chinese.

THE EARLY ZHOU GOVERNMENT. The dynastic founders included outstanding and revered figures, like the Cultured King (reigned before 1050 B.C.), who long pondered the overthrow of the Shang monarch. The motivation for his plans is hard to determine, given a paucity of documents, especially of those showing the Shang perspective. The Cultured King's eldest son, the Martial King (reign dates around 1050–around 1043 B.C.), defeated the Shang army and placed two of his brothers in charge of the Shang heartland. After a few years, the Martial King died and left a young son as his successor. The two brothers who ruled the Shang realm revolted against

FIGURE 5.8 *Shang Oracle Bone. Having been used to divine the future, this bone was etched with a record of the event, giving us an example of early Chinese writing. The inscription on the left begins, "On the day,* jia chen, *a great and violent wind struck, ... the moon was eclipsed. . . ." Diviners were important in Shang society and were usually members of the royal family.* From Joseph Needham, *Science and Civilization*, Vol. I, op. p. 84. Courtesy of Royal Asiatic Society.

their nephew, and former Shang officials joined the rebels. The boy monarch and government faced a serious crisis.

Members of the Zhou elite appointed another brother of the Martial King, the Duke of Zhou (lived in the eleventh century B.C.), as a regent, and he swiftly sent a force that crushed the uprising. To forestall future unrest, the Duke of Zhou resettled members of the Shang elite to places where they could be controlled. For his actions as well as for refusing to take power for himself, the Duke of Zhou has been revered by later philosophers.

To justify their conquest of Shang and to legitimize their own government, the Zhou rulers developed the idea of the **Mandate of**

[14] **Zhou:** JOH

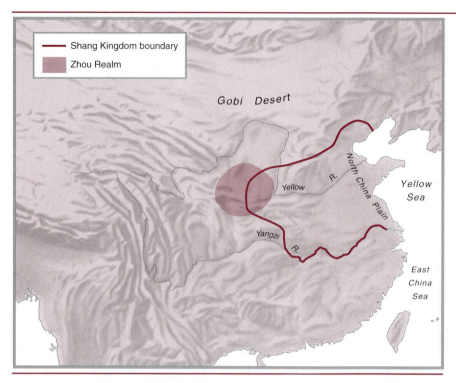

MAP 5.3   *Yellow River Civilizations, around 1500–771 B.C.*   The key Chinese civilizations developed in the Yellow River Valley of northern China, with the Shang in the east and the Zhou in the west. Zhou conquered Shang in the eleventh century B.C. by seizing and maintaining control of the mountain passes and rivers that served as natural defenses.

Heaven, a concept that justified rebellion in certain cases. "Heaven" was a name for a Zhou god who conferred upon a dynastic house the right to rule because of its virtuous behavior. Heaven could also assist a challenger, if the existing house had become corrupt and the new house was virtuous. Zhou claimed that Shang lost the Mandate and that this justified the change of regime. In fact, the Zhou god, Heaven, replaced the Shang deity, the Lord on High, and politics was henceforth equated with moral conduct.

The Martial King established a legal code to regulate the people. In addition, the monarch and many of his officials often traveled the realm to monitor lower officials.

THE DECLINE OF ZHOU: DECENTRALIZED POLITICS. The early years of Zhou saw effective government from the center, but gradually monarchs became less competent. One striking example of royal misrule came in 771 B.C., when threats from nomads north and northwest of the capital forced the creation of a warning-fire system. Lighted fires were a signal to bring armies from nearby garrisons. Enraptured by one of his wives, the frivolous king amused her by lighting the warning fires. The royal couple gleefully watched as the defensive forces arrived only to learn of the false

alarm. After a few false alarms, a legitimate nomadic attack came, but when the fires were lit, the rescuers refused to come and the capital fell. Whether or not this account reflected the whole story of the fall of the capital to outside forces, the remaining Zhou influence dissipated when the capital was moved a few hundred miles to the east.

Along with ineffective Zhou monarchs, geographical elements aided the decline of the central authority. The area of North and Central China was simply too large to administer effectively. Realizing this problem and following a general Shang political strategy, Zhou rulers created a series of states in their claimed territories and appointed rulers there. The appointments received confirmation in an elaborate ceremony during which the subordinate lord pledged loyalty to the king and obedience to his commands. They became his **vassals**, subordinate lords who loyally aided their king in exchange for lands and privileges. When the central polity lost its effectiveness, these territorial leaders gained some measure of independence.

Below the king was a hierarchical aristocratic order. The most important group comprised the blood relatives of the ruling house. Subordinate to this elite in social rank were vassal groups, which ruled smaller territories and had little royal blood. They often fought for the higher lords or served as officials.

Artisans and a few merchants worked in these urban centers but occupied a middle social rank. Those who worked the land were bound there for fixed periods. If they were mistreated, however, it was easy and common for them to flee elsewhere.

Agriculture grew more important with the rise of **manorialism**, a self-sufficient economic system centered on a lord's household and with some agricultural workers bound to the land. The growing trend was for local areas to produce as much as possible to meet their own needs. **Serfs**, rural folk who farmed the lord's land and who found themselves tied to it, worked their portions; collectively, all serfs tilled a central section for the lord's subsistence. Most of the harvest went to the lord, and the remainder was allocated to the serfs.

This system came to be known as the **well-field system** because the plots resembled the

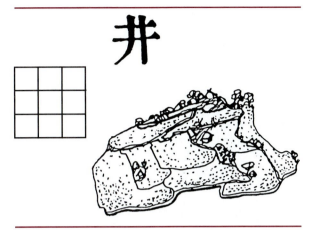

FIGURE 5.9 *Well-Field System.* *Based on* jing, *the Chinese word for "well" (top), this schematic (left) illustrates the gridlike farming system developed in Early Zhou China. All land belonged to the lord, who rented each outer section to a peasant family. The center plot was collectively farmed by all families and its harvest went to the lord. In practice, the well-field ideal was adapted to the natural topography of the land (right).* Left, right: From Ray Huang, *China: A Macro History* (Armonk, N.Y.: M. E. Sharpe, Inc.), an Eastgate Book © 1988. Reproduced with permission.

IN THEIR OWN WORDS

Daily Life as Seen in Chinese Poetry

Early Chinese poetry, the *Book of Songs*, reveals much about the lives of ordinary people. In that sense, it can serve as a source for the study of social history in ancient China. In one poem written more than 3,000 years ago, for example, the common folk ordered their lives about the calendar:

In the tenth month the cricket goes under my
    bed.
I stop up every hole to smoke out the rats,
Plugging the windows, burying the doors:
'Come, wife and children,
The change of the year is at hand.
Come and live in this house.'
. . . .

In the ninth month we make ready the stack-yards,
In the tenth month we bring in the harvest,
Millet for wine, millet for cooking, the early and the
    late,
Paddy and hemp, beans and wheat.
. . . .

My harvesting is over,

Go up and begin your work in the
    house. . . .

Gender issues were sometimes revealed in Chinese poetry of the same period:

Mat over mat, bamboo on rush
    so it be soft, to sleep, to wake in hush,
from dreams of bears and snakes?
. . . .
Bears be for boys; snakes, girls.
Boys shall have beds, hold scepters for their toys,
. . . .
bellow when they would cry
. . . .
Small girls shall sleep on floor and play with tiles,
wear simple clothes and do no act amiss,
cook, brew and seemly speak,
conducing so the family's quietness.

Boys slept on beds, while girls slept on the floor; this indicates the subordination of women in Chinese society. Girls were expected to behave and speak quietly, whereas boys might bellow when they cried.

SOUTH AND EAST ASIA

Indus Valley Civilization, c. 2500–c. 1750 B.C.		**2500 B.C.**	
		2000 B.C.	
Aryan migrations, c. 1750 B.C.			Fall of Mohenjo–Daro, c. 1750 B.C.
		1500 B.C.	Founding of Shang, c. 1500 B.C.
	Shang Dynasty, c. 1500–c. 1050 B.C.		
	Age of Vedas, c. 1200–c. 750 B.C.		Martial King conquers Shang, c. 1050 B.C.
Iron Age, c. 1000 B.C.	Early Zhou Dynasty, c. 1050–c. 771 B.C.	**1000 B.C.**	Duke of Zhou reconquers Shang, c. 1042 B.C.
			Fall of Early Zhou, 771 B.C.

Chinese character for "well" (*jing*), which looks similar to a tic-tac-toe schematic. Because this period of Chinese history saw the decline of larger cities that brought the widespread practice of subsistence farming, the population level likely stayed near that of the Shang era.

We know little about the women and children of this time. One source of our information about gender hierarchy is the *Book of Songs*, a diverse collection of music from all social groups. Each song provides a brief look at the lives and concerns of the Chinese people. The book shows a dominant male order with women clearly subordinated. Men worked in the fields, while women wove in the homes. This division of tasks based on gender lasted for centuries and extended even to traditional ceremonies in which the monarch plowed and his consorts wove.

Early Zhou elite culture continued some earlier traditions and added new practices as well. Shang divination practices, for example, vanished, but bronze making continued, although the Zhou pieces seemed to lose the complexity and malleability of their Shang predecessors. The Zhou rulers kept documents from the time of the dynasty's founding; these long resided in archives until their recovery and editing. Other glimpses of Zhou elite culture come from the popular *Book of Songs*.

SUMMARY

1. The Indus Valley civilization lasted for centuries and boasted cities with standardized patterns, including brick-built houses, effective drainage systems, and efficient grain-storage areas. A combination of factors brought about the civilization's decline, including excessive deforestation, recurrent flooding induced by earthquakes, salt accumulation, overgrazing, and a prolonged dry spell.

2. The Aryan peoples came into India and slowly moved across the northwest until they reached the Ganges River Valley. They brought chariot warfare. Their religious system, led by the *brahmans*, was described in the Vedas. The Aryans held themselves apart from and over the local peoples, yet a synthesis of Aryan and local culture gradually emerged.

3. Two key epic poems, the *Ramayana* and *Mahabharata*, reflected and influenced Indian political as well as religious ideas.

4. The Shang people built a civilization in the Yellow River Valley of China. It manifested elements of civilization, such as long-distance trade, cities, a writing system, and metallurgy.

5. The Shang polity, a loose confederation of aligned states, was a monarchy. Society was dominated by aristocrats, including a few women who fought in battles and ruled some areas. Elites developed a writing system and a process of predicting the future by using oracle bones. They also supported the production of sophisticated artifacts of bronze, bones, and precious stones.

6. The Shang fell to the Zhou, another Chinese group, who brought a new dynasty and a short-lived but more centralized government. After a few generations, however, political decline and the development of a manorial economic system led to Chinese decentralization.

SUGGESTED READINGS

Allchin, Bridget, and Raymond Allchin. *The Rise of Civilization in India and Pakistan.* Cambridge, Eng.: Cambridge University Press, 1982. A standard treatment of the Indus Valley civilization.

Chang, K. C., ed. *Shang Civilization.* New Haven, Conn.: Yale University Press, 1980. A classic examination of the archaeology of the Shang Dynasty.

Hsu Cho-yun and Katheryn Linduff. *Western Chou Civilization.* New Haven, Conn.: Yale University Press, 1988. A standard analysis and presentation of early Zhou history.

Thapar, Romila. *Ancient India.* Delhi: Oxford University Press, 1992. Interpretative essays about ancient India.

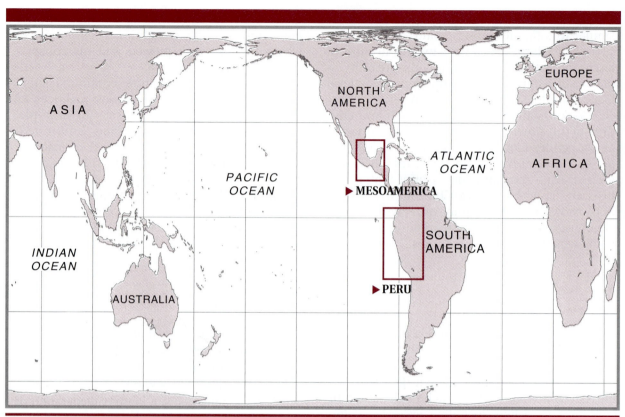

ASIA

PACIFIC
OCEAN

INDIAN
OCEAN

AUSTRALIA

NORTH
AMERICA

ATLANTIC
OCEAN

EUROPE

AFRICA

▶ MESOAMERICA

SOUTH
AMERICA

▶ PERU

Gulf of
Mexico

Valley
of
Mexico

Mayan
Lowland

Olmec
Heartland

Usumacinta R.

PACIFIC
OCEAN

▶ MESOAMERICA

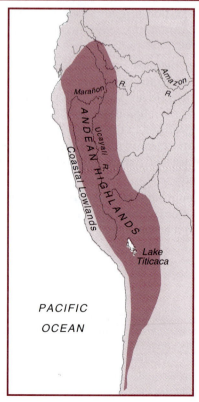

Marañón

Amazon
R.

R.

Ucayali R.

ANDEAN HIGHLANDS

Coastal Lowlands

Lake
Titicaca

PACIFIC
OCEAN

▶ PERU

The Development of Civilizations in the Americas

The earth's longest winter was ending. After five million years of cold weather, the climate finally was warming, and winters were getting shorter. Somewhere in northeastern Asia, people were going about their business — hunting game, sewing clothing, and preparing meals. They were unaware that they soon would become the first human colonists in a new world: the Americas.

When these immigrants, whose descendants became known as American Indians, came to the Americas sometime after 43,000 B.C., their arrival constituted the first population movement into the western hemisphere. Following this initial peopling, the Americas developed essentially independently of Africa, Asia, and Europe. Although there were a few sporadic contacts earlier, the voyage of Christopher Columbus in 1492 established the first sustained or significant contact between the two hemispheres. Despite their isolation from each other, the two halves of the world followed similar patterns of development that led to the development of civilization in various places. This chapter discusses that development in the Americas to about A.D. 1300, placing greatest emphasis on artifact-rich Mexico and adjacent areas; later developments are treated in Chapter 16.

In the period before 1300, few societies in the Americas had any system of written language. The major exceptions were the civilizations of Mexico and adjacent Central America, where writing began by 500 B.C. and perhaps a few centuries earlier. Even there, however, the vast majority of writings are lost to us. Although books were produced in much of this area, many of the older ones have been destroyed by natural processes over the centuries. More recent books, those still extant at the time of the Spanish conquest, often were searched out and destroyed by the Spanish as works of the devil; a reasonable guess is that the *conquistadores* burned or otherwise destroyed several thousand books (more than a thousand different titles) in Mexico alone.

One upshot of this paucity of documents is that most of the information we have about ancient American peoples has been derived from archaeology. The earlier peoples of the Americas had no writing, and the writing of some literate societies of later periods cannot be deciphered. When documents or inscriptions have survived and can be translated, however, their contributions have been incorporated into this chapter.

THE PEOPLING OF THE AMERICAS AND EARLY CULTURES

Separated from the rest of the world by the Atlantic and Pacific oceans, the American continents were not part of the spread of *Homo erectus* described in Chapter 2. Indeed, they were among the later parts of the earth to be colonized by human beings, and the only human remains that have been found in the Americas are of biologically modern *Homo sapiens*.

The Great Migration

Biological evolution is a slow process, and the time elapsed since the first immigrants came to the Americas is short. Consequently, one might expect the descendants of these immigrants—today's American Indians—to share many traits with people living in their old home, the source area for the migration to America. By far the closest similarity lies between American Indians and the inhabitants of Siberia in northeastern Asia. The two groups have literally hundreds of distinctive traits in common, including shovel-shaped incisors (an anatomical form of the front teeth, found only rarely among other human groups), characteristic

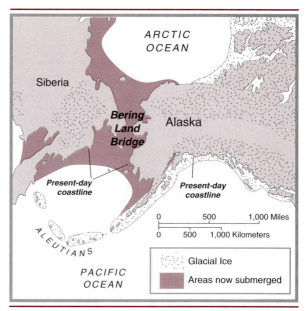

MAP 6.1 *The Bering Land Bridge.* *Lowered sea levels created a land link between Siberia and Alaska in the area that today is covered by the water of the Bering Strait. This land bridge appeared several times between 43,000 and 15,000 B.C. and was at times over one thousand miles wide. It provided the route for the first people to enter the Americas.*

blood proteins, and skeletal details. When dealing with genetics, it always is possible that a trait developed twice independently by chance, but the probability is billions to one against it. There is little doubt of the common ancestry of Asians and American Indians.

The Americas are separated from the other continents by water on all sides. However, the Bering Strait, which separates Alaska and Siberia, is only about 90 miles wide today. In some earlier periods, however, the colder climate caused huge amounts of water to freeze into glaciers, lowering the sea level and turning the Bering Strait into the **Bering Land Bridge**, a vast stretch of dry land connecting North America and Asia. We know that various animals crossed over the land bridge—mammoths (a now-extinct kind of northern elephant), for example, evolved in Eurasia and then migrated to the Americas—and people made the crossing, too. The Bering Land Bridge was an inviting place, offering milder winters and more resources than Siberia, and the immigrants probably moved gradually onto it, eventually crossing over into America without even realizing it. When the climate warmed again and the land submerged, they were stranded on the American side.

Modern scholars agree that the first human entry into the Americas took place via the Bering Land Bridge between about 43,000 and 10,000 B.C., but there is considerable controversy about the specific date of the crossing. This is not surprising, because the most crucial archaeological data for settling the issue lie under 120 feet of water in the Bering Sea, an area essentially inaccessible to archaeologists. It is clear that there were four major periods when the Bering Land Bridge was available, the earliest beginning at 43,000 B.C. and the most recent ending about 10,000 B.C. Correlating the possible crossing dates with the earliest known sites, most archaeologists believe that the first immigrants entered the Americas between 33,000 and 14,000 B.C.

Lifeways of the Earliest Americans

Unfortunately, we know less than we would like about the first Americans. The earliest archaeological sites are small and have a limited range of materials in them, principally because perishable items of wood, leather, and even bone usually have disappeared over the millennia. Most of what remains are stone tools, with occasional bones or seeds from food waste. On their basis, a general picture of these early Americans, called **Paleo-Indians**, has emerged.

The Paleo-Indians lived, for the most part, in small bands that consisted usually of about 30 to 100 people. At some seasons or for special activities, more than one band might come together, or the band might split into smaller family units. Paleo-Indians hunted, gathered, and fished for all their food, typically using a broad range of the foodstuffs available locally.

Paleo-Indians lived in a world in which many of the huge mammals of the glacial period had not yet become extinct. On the North American plains, for example, mammoths, prehistoric horses, and giant bison roamed, while mastodons (another extinct type of elephant) crashed about in swamps, and a wealth of other large animals occupied a variety of habitats. It is clear that Paleo-Indians hunted both mammoths and bison, sometimes killing them singly and sometimes driving bison herds over cliffs for mass killing. The hunting of game of this size with stone-tipped spears must have been dangerous in the extreme.

FIGURE 6.1 *Folsom Bison Excavation.* *In 1926, a local cowboy discovered a huge bison skeleton in a ravine in southwestern New Mexico. He recognized that the spearhead embedded in the bones meant that human beings must have been contemporary with this ancient beast. The archaeologists who later excavated the site found abundant evidence to confirm his conclusion. The left foreground of this photo is the area in which both bones and stone tools were found, confirming that American Indians had been in the Americas since ancient times.* Photo by Frank M. Figgins. Courtesy of the American Museum of National History.

In the past, archaeologists were very taken with the hunting of big game by Paleo-Indians, and some argued that these large animals formed the mainstay of the Paleo-Indian diet. This conclusion perhaps is understandable, given that many of the sites excavated early on were kill sites of these large prey, but recent evidence suggests that large game may have played a much smaller role in Paleo-Indian life than previously believed. Archaeological sites such as the Shawnee-Minisink site in New Jersey have re-vealed the other side of Paleo-Indian diet: squirrels, rabbits, fish, berries, and wild grain seeds. At sites like this one, prosaic foodstuffs formed the entire diet, and big game did not appear at all. Many archaeologists now believe that in most areas big game was an occasional element of Paleo-Indian meals but hardly everyday fare.

The big game, except for the smallest species of bison, became extinct mostly between 11,000 and 9000 B.C. Many archaeologists believe that human hunting may have played a part in those extinctions (although there is no evidence that Paleo-Indians ever hunted most of the species that became extinct), but there were other momentous processes going on at the same time. The world was becoming warmer, the glaciers were receding from the northern areas of North America, and vegetation all over the Americas was changing. These changes must have played a major role in the extinction of the big game, probably a greater role than human predation.

Around 8000 B.C., tool styles changed in the Americas, and archaeologists consider this date the end of the Paleo-Indian Period, which was replaced with a series of regional foraging traditions. With the exceptions of warmed climate, extinction of big game, and changed tool styles, however, lifeways continued much as in the preceding millennia.

NUCLEAR AMERICA

Two places in the Americas clearly developed civilization in antiquity: one in Mexico and adjacent Central America, and one in Peru and nearby areas. These areas are the ones that, throughout American prehistory, have been in the forefront of innovation and change. They were the earliest in the Americas to develop agriculture and the earliest to develop complex societies, and many would argue that they were the only areas where civilization emerged. Many ideas and practices that developed in these areas then diffused into other parts of the Americas. Because of this, these two areas collectively are termed **Nuclear America**, composed of Mesoamerica and Peru.

As a culture area, **Mesoamerica** is defined as the geographical area where certain distinctive cultural traits are or were present. Obviously, the boundaries of this area have varied over the centuries, but basically it consists of the area of the modern countries of Mexico, Guatemala, and Belize and adjacent portions of Honduras and El Salvador. In the past several thousand years, this area has shared a number of cultural characteristics, including corn-squash-beans agriculture, pyramids as bases for temples, a glyphic writing system, a similar calendric system, a distinctive ball game, and human sacrifice. The list could be elaborated; indeed, a recent compilation of defining characteristics of Mesoamerica listed seventy-eight cultural traits. What is important for our purposes is that the various regions of Mesoamerica shared knowledge and many ideas and practices, making the culture area as a whole a reasonable unit to examine.

Peru, when seen as a culture area, consists of the highland and coastal portions of modern Peru, as well as adjacent highland and coastal areas of Ecuador, Bolivia, and Chile. A few of the defining cultural characteristics of this culture area are corn-bean-potato agriculture, terraced fields, prominent sun gods, and mummification of the dead. As with Mesoamerica, Peru had its regional variations, but there was an overall pattern of similarity.

Although the area between Mesoamerica and Peru had some elements in common with these areas, the differences are great enough to warrant this intermediate area's being considered not part of Nuclear America. Indeed, the difficulties of travel in Panama and some other intermediate areas must have restricted direct land contact between the two parts of Nuclear America. Yet there is evidence that such contact occasionally occurred, presumably by coastal sea travel. The only linguistic relatives of the Tarascan language of western Mexico are found in South America, and several food plants domesticated in one area were transported to the other at various times in prehistory.

The chili pepper was one of the first plants to be domesticated in America, indeed in the world. Its use in the Americas spread to any place it would grow, and after Europeans brought it back to their homelands, its use spread rapidly in Europe, Africa, and Asia. Today, inhabitants of Ethiopia, Indonesia, western China, India, Thailand, and a host of other places have integrated chilis into their diet, sometimes with searing results. Indeed, the incorporation has been so complete that most of these people will tell you that chilis always have been part of their cuisine.

The initial attraction, doubtless, was the taste. Chilis vary tremendously, from the pungent bell pepper to the excruciatingly hot *habanero*.[a] Each adds its distinctive flavor, dominating or not at the discretion of the cook. Chilis can cover the flavor of food that is a bit spoiled, although this probably would have been of little advantage in the tropics, where spoiled food needs to be recognized and discarded, rather than consumed anyway. Chilis also have the ability to retard spoilage; capsaicin, the component that burns the mouth, has even direr effects on many bacteria,

[a]*habanero:* ah bah NAY roh

and a dish laced with chili is more likely to survive room temperature storage than one without.

An additional factor that may have favored the use of chili is conceptions of folk medicine. Most peoples in the world have some notion of heat balance in the body. Too much or too little heat can cause illness. (This concept is embedded in the English term "a cold," meaning a mild disease.) In these societies, foods that can restore balance by heating or cooling the body are valuable, and a strong chili certainly can restore body heat. We have no idea whether ancient Mexicans and Peruvians had this type of conception of disease, but it may be significant that virtually all of their modern descendants do.

Finally, chilis are good for you. They contain high concentrations of vitamin C, more than seven times that of oranges. Even small amounts of chili contain useful quantities of vitamin C, a nutrient that might have been difficult to get without chilis. Of course, ancient Americans had no way of knowing of this benefit, except possibly by the observation that chili eaters were less likely to contract scurvy, the vitamin C deficiency disease, than those who abstained.

THE RISE OF AGRICULTURE

The basic characteristics of agriculture and current explanations of why it has developed around the world were discussed in Chapter 3. To put it briefly, agriculture permits people to produce more food than do hunting and gathering, but it ties them to a single place and demands that they spend much more time working for their suppers.

The Chronology and General Nature of Agriculture in Mesoamerica

The process and details of agricultural development in Mesoamerica are much better known than are those in Peru, largely because more research has been directed toward Mesoamerica. Agricultural development in Mesoamerica followed two paths, one in the dry highlands of central Mexico and another in the moist coastal lowlands of eastern Mexico, Belize, Guatemala, and Honduras.

The earliest known domesticated plants in highland Mesoamerica appear about 6500 B.C. These include squash, chili peppers, avocados, and corn, with cobs only the size of a child's little finger. The wild progenitors from which these plants were developed came from a variety of zones and regions, but they are found together archaeologically, indicating that they had been brought together by the early agriculturalists. At this early stage of agriculture, people were expending little energy on cultivation; they planted the crops, then continued on their long-established seasonal movements for hunting and gathering. If the crops had done well when they returned to the area at harvest time, so much the better; if not, they could survive off wild foods.

From 6500 to 2300 B.C., Mesoamericans increased their reliance on agriculture. The variety of crops increased with the addition of various kinds of beans, new species of squash, and pumpkins. An import from Peru, cotton, also was grown in some quantity, and it is unclear whether it was used for its fiber in weaving, for its oily seeds as food, or (most probably) for both. Corn was being improved during this period and, by 3000 B.C., was nearly the size of an adult's thumb. Although agricultural produce had provided only about 5 percent of the diet in 6000 B.C., it had increased to about 40 percent by 4500 B.C. and to 85 percent by 3000 B.C. As agriculture's importance increased, farmers became sedentary, staying in one place to tend their crops.

From 2300 B.C. onward, virtually all peoples in central Mexico and many other portions of highland Mesoamerica were fully dependent on agriculture and lived sedentary lives in villages. Over time, new crops were domesticated and old domesticates were improved. By 700 B.C., experiments in irrigation were beginning, and sophisticated irrigation systems probably were in use by 300 B.C. By this time, agriculture had taken firm hold of highland Mesoamerican society.

The path to agriculture in lowland Mesoamerica was considerably different. There, year-round moisture and warmth created an endless growing season perfect for starchy root crops, especially **manioc** (widely known by its Spanish name, *yuca*[1]). Manioc roots cannot be stored very well after harvesting, but they can be kept in the ground until needed. They provide a delicious and calorie-rich starch similar to potatoes, but there is a catch. Until the development of recent forms, all manioc has had large quantities of oxalic acid, a poison, in its roots. This poison can be removed easily by grating the root, soaking it in water to leach out the oxalic acid, and cooking the grated manioc. Because manioc roots do not preserve well archaeologically, the earliest evidence of their use comes from small obsidian blades used for grating them. The blades are known from around 4000 B.C., but it is possible that earlier use of manioc has left behind no recognizable remains.

Around 1200 B.C., maize from the highlands first appeared in the lowlands. Although not terribly well adapted to the moist soils of the lowlands,

corn rapidly became popular and eclipsed manioc in importance. Other highland domesticates also came into the lowlands, and shortly after this date the lowland diet began to more closely resemble the highland diet.

The Chronology and General Nature of Agriculture in Peru

As noted previously, evidence on the development of agriculture is far less well known in Peru than in Mesoamerica. It is clear, however, that a fairly extensive set of plants was domesticated and cultivated by 5000 B.C., and many believe that the roots of Peruvian agriculture extend back earlier. Among the domesticated crops were some distinctive Peruvian species, including **quinoa**[2] (an important grain from the amaranth plant) and potatoes, a staple of the later Peruvian diet; there also were some crops domesticated independently in both Mesoamerica and Peru, including corn, beans, and chili peppers. The Peruvian versions of these latter crops, however, were different from their Mesoamerican cousins in subtle ways. Early Peruvian corn, for example, was sweet corn (the kind eaten on the cob in today's United States) and had a high sugar-to-starch ratio; early Mesoamerican corn, in contrast, was the popcorn type, with a low sugar-to-starch ratio.

Unlike Mesoamericans (who domesticated virtually no animals), early Peruvians domesticated a few animals, especially the llama and alpaca (camel-like animals raised for food, wool, and pack carrying) and the guinea pig (a food animal). Compared with Eurasia and Africa, however, Peru domesticated few animals, none of which affected the way of life to the extent livestock transformed most of Eurasia and Africa.

The Significance of Agricultural Development in the Americas

The primary significance of the development of agriculture in the Americas, of course, is that it provided a base for the development of larger, denser, sedentary populations, some of whom would launch the developments leading to civilization. There are, however, several other significant aspects.

---

[1] *yuca:* YOO kuh

[2] **quinoa:** KEE nwuh

FIGURE 6.2 *Ancient Inca Road.* *Segments of the massive Inca road network survive in many parts of modern Peru, Bolivia, Chile, and Ecuador. Here, a modern Aymara woman of Bolivia trudges along an Inca road, with its paved surface, raised curbs, and gentle slope. She leads one alpaca (a relative of the llama) and herds others. Alpacas provide soft, strong hair that is spun into thread and used in weaving textiles today, just as it has been since around 1500 B.C.* Hans Sylvester/Liaison International.

First, both in Mesoamerica and Peru, the early domesticated crops are derived from wild ancestors that came from widely scattered habitats. This means that agriculture, in a real sense, had no single point of origin, nor was it developed by a genius who first conceived the idea. Rather, different plants were experimented with in many areas, and the more successful experiments were passed from hand to hand, eventually becoming established as staples.

Second, there were some exchanges of crops between Mesoamerica and Peru. Common beans, popping corn, and perhaps chilis passed from Mesoamerica to Peru; cotton, lima beans, sweet corn, and probably jack beans came in return. This is significant, because although one society can, say, reinvent a similar pottery style by chance, plants with identical or near-identical genetic makeup cannot be developed independently. Consequently, we have unequivocal evidence of early contact between the two areas of Nuclear America, though we have no idea how it may have come about or how frequent it was. That these crops were unknown until much later in the area between the two halves of Nuclear America supports the idea of sea contact between Mesoamerica and Peru.

Third, both in Peru and Mesoamerica, domesticated foods were balanced and complementary. They were balanced in terms of agriculture, as corn, squash, and beans, planted in rotation in the same field, will replenish nutrients used by the others, keeping the soil fertile for long periods. Even more significant from the viewpoint of the development of civilization, the major staples of Nuclear America provided a nutritionally balanced diet that could support healthy life without major consumption of meat. This may help explain why American civilizations never developed the range of domesticated animals that their counterparts in Africa and Eurasia did. Also, because draft animals almost always have been first domesticated for food and then assigned labor duties, the dearth of domesticated food animals may account for the absence of draft animals and the concomitant lack of wheeled vehicles in the Americas.

Fourth and finally, the successful American staple foods were easily stored. Corn and beans dry easily, and the harder squashes keep well. Potatoes at first appear to be an exception, but ancient Peruvians preserved them by freeze-drying—exposing them to the frigid temperatures of glaciers in the high Andes peaks, producing a hard, nutty, and easily stored foodstuff through controlled freezer burn. This ability to store food is critical in seasonal environments, but it has an even more far-reaching implication. Stored food can be warehoused, and if a government controls that supply of food, it controls its people. It may be significant that in the Mesoamerican lowlands the advent of corn—the first storable staple there—corresponded exactly to the development of Olmec society, the first complex society in Mesoamerica.

ceremonial centers and the art and architecture within them. The centers were carved out of the jungle and apparently were used only seasonally, maintained the rest of the year by a small staff, perhaps composed of priests. We do not know what rituals went on there, but they must have been extravagant, if the scale of the centers themselves is an indication.

The ceremonial center at La Venta is the best known. The site is laid out with geometric regularity along a north-south axis, with an accuracy that suggests some skill at engineering and perhaps astronomy. At one end of the site, the Olmecs erected a huge pyramid of clay and earth, more than 300 feet high, with ridged sides. There are several rectangular clay-and-earth mounds, court-

THE GROWTH OF CIVILIZATION IN MESOAMERICA

As noted earlier, two major zones are particularly important in the study of Mesoamerica, because civilization developed there: the dry highlands of central Mexico and the moist lowlands of eastern Mexico and Central America. Each of the dozens of regions had its own complex developments and interactions with other regions, but we will restrict our treatment to four societies, two from the lowlands and two from the highlands.

The Olmecs, around 1200–around 400 B.C.

Olmec society developed around 1200 B.C. along the coast of the Gulf of Mexico, in the modern Mexican states of Veracruz and Tabasco. Of the four Mesoamerican societies discussed here, only the Olmec sometimes is considered not to be a civilization. Although the Olmecs possessed many of the elements of civilization, they may not have had the overall complexity that is implied by that concept. Theirs was, however, the first complex society in Mesoamerica, and they set the pattern for their successors. They made a deep and lasting impression on all Mesoamerican civilizations to follow them.

The primary Olmec characteristic that has earned them a place in history is their creation of

FIGURE 6.3 *Olmec Colossal Head.* *These enormous sculpted stone heads probably depict Olmec kings. All share certain characteristics, particularly flattened noses, broad faces, lips whose outline is more or less trapezoidal, and a leather helmet. Each has additional characteristics, however, such as scars, gapped teeth, big ears, or closely set eyes that make it unique. These individual traits suggest that the heads are portraits of real individuals rather than stylized monuments to a single individual or to a class of individuals.*
Richard H. Stewart/© National Geographic Society.

The Mesoamerican Ball Game

The Mesoamerican ball game, variously known as *pelota* or *pok-ta-pok*, was widespread in Mesoamerica and distinctive to the Mesoamerican culture area. Other versions of the game are known in the prehistoric Caribbean, in the North American Southwest, and in northeastern South America, where it probably originated.

The game was a team sport, as were many pre-Columbian sports. The rules, court, and equipment varied over time and from culture to culture, but the basics were similar. The ball was made of hard, solid rubber, about the consistency of a modern truck tire, and was the size of a modern softball or a little larger. The court was generally rectangular, I-shaped, or H-shaped; goals typically consisted of rings on the side walls, or of the area between two uprights in the "end zone." The object of the game was to propel the ball into the goal without the use of the hands or, apparently in some places, the feet. Art showing the game in progress often shows players, all male, knocking the ball with a hip. In some places, players wore padding or special guards; in others they were exposed directly to the battering effects of the ball. Needless to say, injuries were many and scores were low; in some places, the game ended with the first score.

The game, while clearly having a recreational function in some areas, was primarily a ritual. In some places, winning players were sacrificed; in others, losers were; in still others, all players lived to compete again. There are records of betting on ball games, and in some places successful players were able to claim the clothing of spectators, sometimes inducing spectators to flee the court at the scoring of the winning point.

The Mesoamerican ball game never became widely popular among Europeans, who widely adopted other Indian games like lacrosse. The Mesoamerican ball game, however, may have been the inspiration for the Spanish Basque *pelota*, a game that appeared in the seventeenth century, a few decades after *conquistadores* returned to Spain. The game was played with teams, and the object was to hurl a hard leather ball through a ring set high on a wall. Europeans had almost no team sports before the sixteenth century, and most of those they did have seem to have been borrowed from the American Indians.

---

yards between them, a fence made of stone pillars set into a mudbrick wall, and several series of pavements composed of colored stone blocks forming jaguar faces. Among these structures, all of which are related to one another in the strictest geometrical manner, are various pits containing offerings of jade axes and other precious materials; many mounds also contain offerings. Large statues, including the colossal heads discussed in the following paragraphs, were distributed through the site. La Venta had no ball courts for playing the ceremonial Mesoamerican ball game; other Olmec ceremonial centers, however, had ball courts, and ceramic figures of ball players have been found at La Venta and elsewhere. (Jade, jaguars, and the ball game all were associated with the gods in later Mesoamerica.)

The entirety of these ceremonial centers bespeaks a society that could marshal a good deal of labor to produce monumental architecture in honor of the gods. Not only was a huge amount of labor needed just to build La Venta, but the individual components sometimes required extra effort. The immense carved heads, for example, were made of basalt, a hard volcanic rock that does not occur naturally near La Venta. To obtain it, the Olmecs removed blocks from quarries 70 miles and farther away; the blocks, some weighing 12 to 15 tons, must have been floated down the Usumacinta River, then moved overland the half mile or so to their ultimate location. Only then could the long job of carving a hard stone with a stone chisel of equal hardness begin.

The **colossal heads**, as these sculptures are known, range in size from about 6 to 9 feet high. They probably represented Olmec rulers, and the twenty-five or so of them known may have represented the rulers of a single dynasty. The heads share common characteristics, particularly the baby face, the leather helmet, the broad nose, and the trapezoidal mouth. Yet each has an individuality, complete with scars, blemishes, or gapped teeth, that has led many scholars to believe they are portraits of individuals, not simply conventionalized images.

A later myth links jaguars and babies through a mating between a jaguar and a woman. The baby produced by this union devoured its mother while nursing, then went on to become the first ruler of the land. Are these baby-faced rulers the embodiment of that myth? Many scholars think so, especially because other Olmec art shows **were-babies**, babies with fangs, jaguar paws, and helmets, sometimes devouring their mothers while nursing.

Recent research has begun the decipherment of Olmec writing, which now appears to be ancestral to the better-known Mayan writing. Perhaps the translation of inscriptions on monuments will provide more information about this little-known people.

The Olmecs possessed many of the elements of civilization discussed in Chapter 3. They carried on long-distance trade and created monumental architecture and a great art style; they apparently had writing; they had class stratification, occupational specialists, and considerable technological skill. On the other hand, some important characteristics of civilizations were absent. They had no cities, and the vast majority of their population lived in small villages; they probably were not a state and were more likely governed through a chiefdom. In the spectrum of societies, they were at the very edge of civilization.

The end for the Olmecs came around 400 B.C. Most evidence suggests that the Olmecs quietly changed into the ancestors of the Mayan civilization that succeeded them in the lowlands, but there are disturbing hints that the end might not have been so gentle. A few colossal heads have broken noses and other damage that may suggest vandalism, and some scholars believe that a conquering people may have defaced the images of the previous rulers to underscore the change in rulership. There is, however, no other evidence of violence or conquest.

The Olmecs remain enigmatic, largely because of how little we know of their life beyond the ceremonial centers. It is clear, however, that many of their characteristics became embedded somehow in the traditions of Mesoamerica and kept cropping up in later civilizations. The ball game, the importance of the jaguar, the erection of pyramids, the use of glyphic writing—these and other traits have made many scholars view Olmec society as an ancestral culture that set the tone for all Mesoamerican civilizations to come.

The Maya, around 200 B.C.–around A.D. 800

After the disappearance of Olmec society, rapid changes took place for the Indians of the Guatemalan jungles. Around 200 B.C., these changes brought about the Mayan civilization, the successor of the Olmecs in lowland Mesoamerica. Mayan culture persisted through the Spanish conquest, but this discussion will focus on the civilization—formally known as "Classic Maya"—that flourished until around A.D. 800.

FIGURE 6.4 *Olmec Jade Sculpture of a Jaguar Baby.* *Much Olmec art focuses on babies, jaguars, and warriors, often showing a mixture of features. In this carving, for example, a mother holds a baby with a characteristic pudgy face and body, but with a nose shaped more like a jaguar's; the baby is also marked with a jaguar glyph. Other sculptures show babies with fangs or military helmets. It is believed that the dynasty of Olmec kings was linked to jaguars in mythology.* Lee Boltin Picture Library.

FIGURE 6.5 *Mayan Mural at Bonampak.* *This reconstruction of a wall painting from the Mayan city of Bonampak, painted by Antonia Tejeda, faithfully reproduces the detail originally recorded around* A.D. *800. The king stands in the center of a raised platform, flanked by counselors, high priests, and nobles. A war captive sprawls on the steps before him, stripped of regalia, his ear ornaments torn from his earlobes. Other captives are arrayed beside the central one, some bleeding and one shown only as a severed head. Victorious warriors of Bonampak are in full regalia below. These sacrifices (and the war to secure captives for sacrifice) were to confirm the designation of the heir to the throne at Bonampak.* Peabody Museum, Harvard University.

There can be little argument that the Maya were a civilization, possessing the core elements of civilization. They were agriculturally dependent, using sophisticated farming techniques; they focused on plant crops, but they also raised ducks and stingerless bees. They carried on long-distance trade over broad portions of Mesoamerica and into the Caribbean. They lived in cities ruled by state governments. They had a variety of specialized occupations and a rigid class system.

The Maya also possessed many of the secondary elements of civilization. A state religion, a great art style, and monumental architecture helped legitimize the government. A complex system of **sacbes**,[3] earthen roads raised above the surface of the jungle floor, connected major cities. A formal legal system governed the adjudication of disputes. The Maya had writing that seems to have been derived from an earlier Olmec writing system, moderately sophisticated astronomy, mathematics that permitted massive engineering projects, and standardized measures.

The Mayan civilization was not politically unified. Indeed, it consisted of a series of competing, often belligerent city-states, each ruled by its own monarch. True, there were alliances and several attempts at empire, but the single city and the villages surrounding it were the basic political entity. In the fourth century A.D., the Tikal[4] city-state conquered the neighboring city-state of Uaxactún[5] and held it for a few decades, but the captured

---

[3] *sacbes:* SAWK bayz

[4] **Tikal:** TEE kahl
[5] **Uaxactún:** wah shawk TOON

lands were lost within a generation; the Dos Pilas[6] city-state built a modest empire in the seventh century, though its conquests were lost within a century. The peace that archaeologists once thought reigned over the Maya was mythical; the Mayan city-states, like city-states elsewhere, were fighting with one another on a regular basis, sometimes nearly constantly.

Although Mayan rulers and diplomats usually were men, women played a crucial role in politics, because the political legitimacy of a ruler was based on the political station of both parents. By A.D. 645, for example, Dos Pilas was expanding and was threatened by neighboring city-states. Some years later, the king of Dos Pilas sent his daughter, Lady Wak-Chanil-Ahaw, to Naranjo,[7] another nearby city-state, to revive its royal house, creating an ally for Dos Pilas. Naranjo had been defeated in recent wars, and its royal house had little status until Lady Wak-Chanil-Ahaw married into it. She religiously revivified the city by spilling blood from her tongue, a sacrifice that was thought to open the spiritual channel between Naranjo and the gods. She ruled Naranjo until 693, when her son became king at the age of five, and in all likelihood remained a powerful regent over the child king. During her reign and that of her son, Naranjo effectively acted as an ally of Dos Pilas, facilitating its imperial ambitions.

The unity of Mayan civilization was cultural, not political. Although different city-states surely felt themselves quite distinct from one another, they really were very similar in ideology, technology, and way of life. Their mutual antagonism was rooted in both their competition for scarce resources and their religion, which demanded captives for sacrifice.

The environment of the Mayan lowlands is basically jungle with little variation from one spot to another. The soils, although moderately fertile, are easily exhausted by tillage, and the traditional method of clearing the jungle by fire only reduced their fertility. The corn-squash-beans agriculture of the Maya was reasonably productive, but there were many mouths to feed, and agricultural shortfalls may have contributed to the ultimate demise of the Maya.

The Maya, unlike their Olmec predecessors, were urban. The focal point of a city-state was a

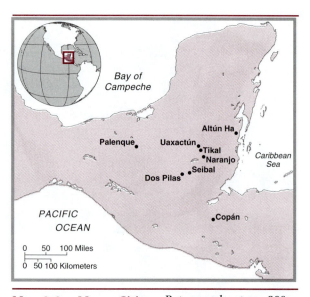

MAP 6.2 *Mayan Cities.* *Between about A.D. 300 and 700, a few dozen Mayan cities were distributed over the lowland rain forests of eastern Mexico and adjacent Guatemala and Honduras. Resources like good agricultural soils, water, and building materials were spread over the land quite evenly; consequently, these cities were located primarily with an eye to limiting territorial disputes with neighboring cities.*

city with large numbers of people, diverse urban zones, and the typical hierarchic relationship with its satellite villages. It once was thought that these cities were ceremonial centers, because they seemed to consist mostly of temples and palaces. Then it was recognized that the common people lived in the vast areas surrounding the grand stone buildings of the city centers in thatched huts that left only faint archaeological traces. Current estimates of the sizes of various Mayan cities range from around 10,000 to 60,000 people, with additional people in each city's hinterland (the villages served by and politically subservient to the city).

The central portion of a Mayan city was a splendid collection of monumental public architecture. Lining the streets were stone pyramids crowned with temples made of limestone, which was sometimes partially or entirely painted with bright colors. The king and his close relatives occupied a palace complex in the central area. A moderately sized city might have twenty-five temples and pyramids as well as several ball courts, some shrines to gods, **stelae** (large stones with low-relief carvings on their flat surfaces), and the palace. **Plazas** (flat open areas between buildings) and

---

[6] **Dos Pilas:** DOHS PEE lahs
[7] **Naranjo:** nah RAHN hoh

courtyards completed the typical roster of components for the central city.

While the king and his retinue lived in the palace, the commoners were relegated to simpler housing outside the central city. Common houses were wood-framed with grass or similar material forming a thatch for walls and roof; each usually was on a low mound to keep its floor dry in wet weather. This simple housing, though impoverished by royal standards, was well ventilated and easily cleaned. In fact, it seems to have produced more healthful conditions than the palaces—the skeletal remains of commoners show that their general level of health was higher than that of the elite.

The whole system and the splendor of the elite was supported, of course, by the commoners. The corn that fed commoner and king alike was grown by the commoners, the grand buildings were constructed by commoners (following the direction of engineers, of course), and the various industries were carried on by the commoners.

The king and the nobles formed one class, and the commoners formed the other. Commoners could not aspire to become nobles or rulers; a commoner would live as a commoner, marry another commoner, and die a commoner. But not all kinds of commoner were alike. Among the commoners, for example, feather workers had higher status than agricultural laborers. Although feather workers typically had somewhat greater wealth than farmers, the primary difference lay in social recognition by the community, which valued the production of feathered headgear for royalty more highly than the growing of corn.

Elite Mayan women shared the grand lifestyle of elite men, but they usually were less prominent in politics and trading. They were expected to propitiate the gods by participating in certain types of sacrifice, including piercing their tongues and other body parts. As elsewhere in Mesoamerica, the Maya regarded the act of weaving as the essence of being a woman, and elite women were expected to spend considerable amounts of time

FIGURE 6.6 *Palenque.* *The Mayan city of Palenque rises out of the rain forest on a hill in southeastern Mexico. The city center included the royal palace with its tower and subterranean rooms (center), the Temple of Inscriptions with the tomb of King Pacal (left), ball courts (just out of the picture to the right), and dozens of other temples. The road visible at the rear left is an ancient one that leads to the remains of agricultural fields and commoners' housing. Before clearing and reconstruction by archaeologists, Palenque appeared as a series of jungle-covered hummocks with only an occasional piece of masonry protruding.*
Charles M. Gordon/West Stock.

FIGURE 6.7 *Lady Xoc Offering a Sacrifice. The Mayan nobility were required to sacrifice to the gods in various ways, including the spilling of their own blood. This early eighth-century carving from a building facade at Yaxchilán shows Lady Xoc, the queen, running a rope through a slit cut in her tongue, part of a celebration for the birth of a son to the king by another wife. The bloody rope would then be placed in a bowl and burned or otherwise conveyed to the gods, while Lady Xoc would have a vision. Standing over her is her husband, King Shield-Jaguar, who carries a staff in the form of the Tree of Life; block writing at the top and left margins explains the scene. The faces have been eroded by natural processes but originally showed fine detail.* British Museum © Justin Kerr.

weaving. We currently know little about how involved women became in Mayan commerce.

Among the Mayan elite, at least the scribes and some of the nobility were fully literate. Their glyphic writing resembled a series of blocky pictures. Most surviving Mayan writing appears on stelae, the walls of monumental buildings, or painted pottery, often from royal tombs. These writings usually glorify the ruler and his dynasty, sometimes giving information about political

alliances. Information on the commoners, general histories, myths and religious rituals, and the like are not recorded in these sources. Paintings sometimes show scribes writing on paper or parchment, and a broader range of information doubtless was recorded on materials that have disintegrated over the centuries.

Extant Mayan archaeological remains proclaim the importance of religion. Temples, ball courts, godly representations, and ritual equipment are prominent at all the large sites. In part, of course, this reflects which segments of Mayan life produced durable and recognizable articles, but the conclusion is inescapable that a state religion dominated life, at least for the elite. Habitations of commoners housed small and simple female figurines, suggesting to many scholars that a female fertility cult was important to the nonelite.

Mayan religion recognized dozens of universal deities, plus dozens more of local gods and goddesses, including a patron for each city-state. The gods stood in a hierarchic relationship to the king that was similar to the relationship between the king and the nobles. Essentially, the deities rewarded the people of a city-state so long as the proper sacrifices were made to them. These sacrifices took several forms, including the sacrificing of prisoners of war, self-inflicted ritual bleeding on the part of members of the royal family or priests, the building of temples or other monumental architecture in honor of a deity, and the burial or destruction of precious items. All of these forms of sacrifice are depicted in Mayan art.

The moderately even distribution of similar economic resources throughout the Mayan lowlands made local trade less critical than in some places. Salt, scanty in the largely vegetarian diet of the Maya, was necessary for life but available only on the coast and constituted one of the few important items of trade within the Mayan lowlands. But the absence of essential resources—particularly obsidian and basalt—made trade with the outside imperative. **Obsidian**, the delicate volcanic glass required for the fancy and exquisitely sharp Mayan tools, occurred only in the highlands of Mesoamerica; basalt, the hard volcanic rock used for corn-grinding stones, also occurred only in the highlands. Salt, obsidian, and basalt, probably more than any other products, were responsible for long-distance trade among the Maya.

Mayan civilization lasted for nearly a millennium, although individual city-states came and

IN THEIR OWN WORDS

Mayan Glyphs

The Maya carved written messages on stone facings of buildings, painted them on pottery, drew them on the pages of books, and incised them on bone. Scholars had been unable to read these inscriptions until breakthroughs in the past few years. Recent translations have opened a new window on the Mayan world.

Mayan writing was a combination of pictographs (symbols that depicted the item being referred to), phonetic symbols representing syllables, and ideographs. Phrases were produced by combining these elements, and there often were several ways of writing the same word or phrase. These phrases were combined to produce sentences, usually in the following pattern: time of action, verb, direct object, subject. Sentences could merely describe the action of an associated picture or could present abstract religious and philosophical ideas.

The illustrations below are Mayan glyphs that show how words and phrases were formed. The first glyph shows the head of a big cat and could represent the jaguar, margay, ocelot, or any other large feline. The second glyph combines this basic element with a phonetic glyph to clarify that a jaguar is meant. The Mayan word for jaguar was *balam*, and the *ba* element to the left of the basic element indicates that the intended meaning begins with *ba*, eliminating all other big cats, as none of them was designated by a word beginning with *ba*. Similarly, the third glyph shows the basic glyph with a *ma* suffix (indicating a word ending with *ma* or *m*), and the fourth glyph shows phonetic glyphs preceding and following the basic element. The fifth glyph shows "jaguar" constructed entirely from phonetic glyphs. The symbolism could become very obscure, because the base element could be replaced with another whose pronunciation was similar.

The following text is an excerpt translated from the inscriptions at the Temple of the Foliated Cross in the Mayan city of Palenque.[a] The text links the ruler of Palenque to his mythical forebears, lending him legitimacy. It is presented in the order it was written by the Mayan carver, and editorial notes are in square brackets.

Thirty-four years, 14 months [20-day Mayan months] after God K had been born and then 2 *baktuns* [800 years] ended on February 16, 2325 B.C. On that day, Lady Beastie [First Mother of the Maya], Divine Lord of Matawil, manifested a divinity through bloodletting [i.e., created a god by spilling some of her own blood in self-sacrifice]. It had come to pass on Yax-Hal Witznal in the shell place at the Na-Te-Kan [places within the sacred precinct of the Palenque; "the shell place" refers to the feet of Pacal, the father of Lord Chan-Bahlum], on November 8, 2360 B.C. [this date was recorded wrong and should have been A.D. 622], 2947 years, 3 months, 16 days later. . . . On the next day, the Mah-Kina-Bahlum-Kuk Building [a temple at Palenque] was dedicated in the house of Lord Chan-Bahlum [the king of Palenque at the time the inscription was carved], Divine Palenque Lord. On the third day Lord Chan-Bahlum, Divine Palenque Lord, he let blood with an obsidian blade [spilling his own blood in self-sacrifice]; he took the bundle [received an offering] after it had come to pass at the Waterlily Place [the royal palace of Palenque]. . . . Forty-nine years, 6 months, 4 days after he had been born and then he crowned himself, Lord Chan-Bahlum, Divine Palenque Lord, on January 10, 692.

[a]**Palenque:** pah LEHN kay

balam

ba - balam

*balam - m*a

ba - balam - ma

ba - la - m(a)

From Linda Schele and David Friedel, *A Forest of Kings: The Untold Story of the Ancient Maya* (New York: William Morrow and Company, Inc., 1990), p. 52. Reproduced with permission.

went with time. Between 700 and 800, however, the civilization collapsed rapidly. The cities were abandoned; the state governments collapsed; monumental architecture and great art no longer were produced; knowledge of the calendar, writing, mathematics, and other fields of learning was lost. The Mayan did not simply exchange one government or art style for another: They radically changed their entire way of life, abandoning civilization altogether. At the same time, the population of the Mayan lowlands seems to have plummeted, eliminating the elite and drastically reducing the rest of the Maya. What was the cause of this catastrophe?

There is no shortage of suggestions. Earthquake, hurricane, and epidemic have been suggested, but no evidence supports the existence of any of these natural disasters. Invasions from the highlands, peasant revolts, and ecological failure all have their scholarly supporters, and all have some evidence to support them. Although the jury is still out on why the Maya collapsed, the possible explanation that follows incorporates several of the causes cited here.

Agriculture in the Mayan lowlands had certain intrinsic limitations, particularly the lowering of soil fertility with use. This problem is not amenable to a technological solution; the only answer is to increase fallowing periods and open more land, requiring greater labor expenditures. A people faced with a dwindling food supply brought on by steadily increasing population and perhaps a few bad harvests logically should devote increased labor to developing farmlands.

But, from the Mayan point of view, the appropriate response would have been different. Because the gods were unhappy, they had to be propitiated with sacrifices. Kingly sacrifices could be accomplished with relative ease (unless one was the king), requiring no major reallocation of labor; captives for sacrifice and temple building, however, meant the investment of commoner labor, either as soldiers or as construction workers. In short, most of the ways to meet a crisis required siphoning labor away from agriculture—precisely at the time that it required more labor. The diverting of labor from agriculture to warfare and the construction of monumental architecture can be seen in the last years of the Mayan cities. Again and again, the grandest and most numerous temples are from the period just before the collapse, and evidence of warfare is strongest for this period, too.

FIGURE 6.8   *Mayan Encountering Highland Mexican.*   *This detail from a scene decorating the rim of a Mayan pot shows a visit by a highland Mexican (perhaps from Teotihuacán) to the Mayan city of Tikal. Ethnic Maya are shown with distinctive features: sloping noses that descend from the forehead in an unbroken line, foreheads that slope backward markedly, and pendulous lower lips. Highland Mexicans, in contrast, are depicted with more vertical foreheads, noses that angle outward from the plane of the forehead, and thinner lips. Headdresses and other clothing styles differ, too. Such encounters appear increasingly in Mayan art just before the Mayan collapse.*   From Linda Schele and David Friedel, *A Forest of Kings: The Untold Story of the Ancient Maya* (New York: William Morrow and Company, Inc., 1990), p. 162. Reproduced with permission.

These practices would make the crisis more acute. As less and less food was available, the commoners would suffer the most, because the food redistribution system emanated from the king and the hierarchic system guaranteed that the nobility would be fed. Conditions would degenerate in a rapid spiral, and faith in the gods could be damaged severely. At this point, the commoners could be on the brink of violent uprising.

An additional factor has to be added to the mix. Around 650 to 700, Mayan art increasingly depicted highland Mexicans. This evidence, along with the increased presence of pottery and other goods from the highlands, suggests that trade or other contact was increasing. Outsiders could have actively supported the violent overthrow of governments, perhaps in hope of moving into the resulting power vacuum themselves; alternatively, they could have contributed inadvertently to the upheaval by undermining faith in the Mayan pantheon. The fact that the fall of Mayan cities traveled from west to east, with the earliest collapses nearest the highlands, suggests that highlanders were somehow involved.

Either way, the Mayan commoners eventually ousted their kings and nobles. Without the elite to operate the complex machinery of a Mayan city-state, it ground to a halt. Redistribution of food broke down, and the cities were abandoned in favor of villages that grew their own food locally. The call for engineers, scribes, and other occupational specialists disappeared. Despite its problems, the Mayan city-state had organized laborers for efficient agricultural production, and without that guidance, food supplies diminished, causing a drop in population. The delicate balance of the city-state, once upset, caused the disappearance of elite Mayan culture and major disruptions in commoner culture.

This plausible explanation is currently held by many archaeologists, but it is unlikely to be confirmed or rejected by the written Mayan record, which seems to be mute about the end of the Mayan civilization. In the northern parts of the Mayan lowlands, particularly the Yucatán Peninsula, Mayan culture persisted to the time of the Spanish conquest in the sixteenth century, albeit in a less complex form and minus many of the attributes of civilization.

Teotihuacán, around 100 B.C.–around A.D. 700

Perhaps the most dramatic case of urbanism in the Americas comes from Teotihuacán and its environs in the central Mexican highlands. Prior to about 200 B.C., only small villages existed in the area that would become Teotihuacán. In the next century, perhaps 25,000 people were attracted to the new city, and their numbers would swell to around 70,000 people by A.D. 150. By around A.D. 400, as many as 200,000 people lived there.

The growth of Teotihuacán, as with most cities, was at the expense of its neighbors and competitors. Not only were rural areas depleted of much of their population, but the rival city of Cuicuilco[8] was depopulated to the point of near-abandonment.

What was the attraction of Teotihuacán? Initially, there probably were two lures. The growth of the city itself was one, because huge numbers of laborers were required to build it. Second, the city was situated next to and controlled the Pachuca quarries, a rich source of fine obsidian, a stone that was traded throughout Mesoamerica. The quarrying and especially the flaking of that obsidian into tools and weapons was a specialized job that presumably would have brought financial reward with it. The volume of Pachuca obsidian found at great distances from the quarries suggests that the obsidian trade was a major boost to Teotihuacán's economy.

As the city was established, other attractants developed. Because the nearby villages had been nearly depopulated, an agricultural force of some size was drawn from Teotihuacán itself. Agriculture was based on sophisticated and massive irrigation systems that kept production levels high and may have stimulated the growth of a powerful government to administer them. The city became a trade center for a wide range of products, including pottery, stone tools, ceramic figurines, and shell beads; production areas within Teotihuacán have been identified archaeologically. All of these jobs would have attracted immigrants, even if not all of them were to find good jobs and actually better themselves.

Teotihuacán can be likened to Washington, D.C., and the comparison is apt in many ways. Traveling through Washington, the visitor sees the hustle and bustle of a major city. There is an abundance of monuments dedicated to important individuals, and the layout of the city is designed to awe the visitor. Although there is much beauty and elegance, there are poor sections of the city, and most of the inhabitants lead quite modest lives. Every one of these statements would have been true of Teotihuacán in its heyday, and a modern visitor might find Teotihuacán exotic yet strangely familiar.

Teotihuacán was laid out on a north-south grid, as were most Mesoamerican cities. At the city center, at the intersection of the two largest avenues, was the most imposing and ornate architecture. Here were dozens of stone pyramids topped with temples to the gods, dominated by the huge Temple of the Moon and the even larger Temple of the Sun. Nearby was the Ciudadela,[9]

[8] **Cuicuilco:** kwee KWEEL koh

[9] **Ciudadela:** see oo dah DAY luh

Figure 6.9 *Archaeological Map of Teotihuacán.* *This map shows the remains of the central precinct of Teotihuacán. Dominating the area is the massive Pyramid of the Sun, with the temple at its apex; it was one of the largest structures in the Americas before the twentieth century. Surrounded by various pyramids, temples, and palaces, the Pyramid of the Sun was located in an elite zone accessed via the Avenue of the Dead. This street, the largest and most important in the city, passed before dozens of examples of imposing monumental architecture.* From Rene Millon, *Urbanization at Teotihuacán, Mexico*, Vol. I, Part 2. Reproduced with permission.

probably a palace for rulers and certainly elite housing for someone. Across the street from the Ciudadela was the Great Market Place, a huge plaza flanked by buildings that may have been warehouses.

Farther from the center of town were the less prestigious areas. Commoner housing in the early days of the city was small and wood-framed, but beginning about 300, public housing projects were initiated. Large multifamily housing structures built of masonry—we would call them apartment buildings today—were constructed in this period. Many were low-cost housing, with small rooms and in poor neighborhoods; these tended to be the larger housing structures, one of which had 176 rooms. Middle- and upper-class housing also was erected, presumably for the growing ranks of suc-

cessful merchants, petty officials, and industrial specialists. This more elegant housing had fewer units per building and often was decorated with murals. Some such housing even had fountains in internal courtyards.

Building at this scale, of course, required careful attention to practical demands. Storm drain systems, sewage disposal, and trash removal all had to be planned and carried out by the central government.

The central government of Teotihuacán, unlike those of the Mayan city-states and many other Mesoamerican civilizations, is not portrayed prominently in art, unless in unrecognized symbolic representations. Coupled with the fact that the script at Teotihuacán has not been deciphered, this means that our knowledge about government there is limited. It is clear that Teotihuacán was a city-state and that it had no empire, although it apparently had considerable political influence in foreign lands throughout Mesoamerica. There may have been dual rulers, one primarily concerned with domestic affairs and business, the other (at least after 500) concerned with warfare. Although temples and religious art are everywhere in Teotihuacán, one is left with the impression that religion—like government—served as an organizational mechanism to promote commercial enterprise. In fact, it has been argued that the impressive religious architecture of Teotihuacán was designed to inspire admiration in visitors, in hopes of extracting better deals from awe-struck traders.

After about 300, Teotihuacán was the uncontested leader in trade in Mesoamerica. Goods produced there could be found throughout Mesoamerica, and foreign goods were common in Teotihuacán. Foreigners themselves were prominent in Teotihuacán, and there were neighborhoods whose goods, burial practices, and art reflected the tastes of their foreign occupants. These foreign enclaves may have been permanent trading stations, ghettos, or consulates.

Around 650, Teotihuacán was thriving. Business was good, there were no signs of internal strife, and the size and military power of the city discouraged attacks from outsiders. But disaster was about to strike. A huge fire in 716 enveloped the northern end of the city, destroying poor and middle-income neighborhoods, some industrial areas, and some commercial districts. There appears to have been some selective looting and perhaps arson, but it generally is believed that this was incidental to an accidental disaster. There are no signs of external attack, no signs of rioting or mass death, no signs of violence directed at the ruling elite. But the great fire marks the beginning of the decline of Teotihuacán as a city and the center of a vast trading network.

The city continued to be occupied for a few decades before it finally was abandoned, but abundant signs indicate that this was not the Teotihuacán of old. New construction nearly halted, and old buildings were not always well maintained. The trade of Teotihuacán's goods was drastically diminished, as evidenced both at home and abroad. The population plummeted; by 750, the population was so small that it may have consisted merely of squatters who had moved in to live on the ruins of the city.

With the demise of Teotihuacán there was no clearly dominant power in the highlands. There were several cities, each with its local sphere of power, but none that could consistently outcompete the others either in military or economic terms.

The Toltecs, around A.D. 900–around 1200

The Toltecs had their own unique writing system. Scholars today cannot decipher it, but as we move into this more recent period, we can consult oral tradition and other historical sources available at the time of the Spanish conquest and written down then. In this sense, the Toltecs may be considered the first "historical" civilization in the Mexican highlands about which we have a broad range of oral and written information.

The versions of Toltec history that have come down to us are sometimes conflicting and confusing. Some of this doubtless arises from the differing meanings of "Tollan,"[10] the name of the ancient Toltec capital. The word means "place of the reeds," but it was a common place-name, and several places have borne it, probably including Teotihuacán. Consequently, the oral traditions of the Toltecs probably are conflated with accounts of other peoples.

The Toltecs generally were mythologized by their descendants as a great people, taller than people of today and better-looking. They were said to excel in learning and the arts and even to possess lost arts, such as making cotton grow in colors or growing gigantic ears of corn. Small wonder that such wonderful people were always well fed, happy, and wealthy. This legacy of good press made claiming Toltec ancestry so desirable that versions of Toltec history clearly were manipulated by later peoples who created fictional kinship links to the Toltecs, legitimizing claims to land or political power.

The central series of events in Toltec oral tradition is the conflict between Quetzalcóatl[11] and Tezcatlipoca.[12] Both of these legendary gods and the

---

[10] **Tollan:** TOHL ahn
[11] **Quetzalcóatl:** keht zahl KOH aht
[12] **Tezcatlipoca:** tehz kawt lee POH kuh

events ascribed to them may refer to priests dedicated to their worship. The most popular version of the story has Quetzalcóatl, the feathered serpent, in conflict with Tezcatlipoca, the god of war. Quetzalcóatl abhors human sacrifice and favors the sacrifice of butterflies and flowers, but Tezcatlipoca, in keeping with his bloodthirsty patronage, demands human blood. After a series of conflicts, Tezcatlipoca defeats Quetzalcóatl by luring him into public drunkenness, a humiliating sin. Quetzalcóatl then leaves Tollan and goes eastward to the Gulf of Mexico, where he either sets himself on fire and ascends to the heavens as the Morning Star (Venus) or floats eastward on a raft of serpents, prophesying that he will return to conquer his people. In the meantime, Huémac,[13] a follower of Tezcatlipoca, has become king.

Clearly, this is not straightforward history, and gods and people have become intimately blended in a mythic account. Many interpreters feel it noteworthy that Quetzalcóatl is associated with the peoples to the north of the Valley of Mexico, while Huémac is associated with the peoples to the south. Allegorically, this may represent a struggle between dynasties or alliances, represented by gods. Alternatively, they may represent different religious factions or even the religious versus the secular factions of the government. Further complicating the interpretation is the suspicion that Quetzalcóatl's distaste for human sacrifice, a long-established institution in Mesoamerica, may have been a post-Spanish elaboration in the face of Christianity — placing words that condemned human sacrifice in the mouths of Mexican gods themselves. In any case, the interpretation of the account is anything but simple.

Historical accounts certainly have been kind to the Toltecs, granting them a favorable position and a great empire. Archaeological evidence, on the other hand, suggests that theirs was merely a modest state, perhaps a small empire. The town of Tollan was founded around 650 and was small until around 900. At that point, it appears to have gained some measure of control of the Pachuca obsidian deposits that had helped make Teotihuacán rich. It expanded to a city of 30,000 inhabitants at its peak, with another 30,000 persons in satellite towns and villages surrounding it. Although the city's buildings had a distinctive architectural style, the city was unplanned and not

nearly as impressive as Teotihuacán. Its political control appears never to have extended beyond the northern half of the Valley of Mexico and adjacent areas to the north. In fact, it can reasonably be considered merely one of two or three competing regional powers, none of which was successful at extending its influence broadly.

Were it not for the myths surrounding Tollan and the Toltecs, they would not stand out from their contemporaries very strongly. As we shall see in Chapter 16, however, later peoples found it politically imperative to trace themselves back to the Toltecs to legitimize their power.

THE GROWTH OF CIVILIZATION IN PERU, AROUND 4000 B.C.– AROUND A.D. 1300

The geography of Peru is dominated by the Andes Mountains, some of the highest and most rugged in the world. The highlands of Peru are cut by valleys, where human occupation is focused, and contact between valleys has always been limited by the difficulty of movement. On the coast lies one of the driest deserts in the world, and settlement was largely restricted to river valleys, where irrigation supported agriculture. These twin obstacles—dry desert and impassable mountains—have served to isolate Peruvian regions more strongly than in most areas, and the result has been a series of highly regional cultures. Only during exceptional periods have there been unifications, and they typically have been moderately brief, doubtless because of the difficulties of maintaining necessary transportation and communication systems.

Details of events that occurred in ancient Peru are far less well known than in Mesoamerica, largely because the Peruvians never developed a system of writing to record their own history. In the truest sense, ancient Peruvian civilizations were prehistoric.

Chavín

The first unification of Peru spans from about 1200 to 300 B.C. and is called Chavín. In many respects, Chavín archaeology is much like Olmec archaeology. It is known mostly from ceremonial centers

[13] **Huémac:** WAY mahk

FIGURE 6.10 *Chavín Sculpted Head. Chavín artists depicted the human form in various ways, one of the most striking being rows of large heads set into walls. About three feet in diameter and attached to the wall by projections in the rear, these heads from the site of Chavín de Hauntar in Peru bear a slight resemblance to Olmec colossal heads from Mexico. Archaeologists interpret pain, paralysis, or rapture in the lines of these Chavín faces, and the material in the nose may depict wads of hallucinogenic snuff. Such heads are found only at Chavín ceremonial centers.* Ric Ergenbright.

that exhibit a great art style incorporating monumental architecture. Some motifs and themes of the art are even similar, such as oversized portrait heads and prominent jaguars, prompting some scholars to speculate that there may have been some contact between Mesoamerica and Peru at this time. Finally, Chavín, like the Olmecs, demonstrates by its works that the society was stratified, with some form of elite that could command great amounts of labor.

But here the similarity ends. While the Olmecs formed a culture focused in a single region, Chavín had a discontinuous distribution that covered nearly all of Peru. To state it differently: Chavín seems to have been an overlay that bridged across various Peruvian cultures, not a culture itself.

Chavín is best conceived of as merely an art style and (probably) an associated religion that spread throughout Peru and was adopted by communities of very different cultures.

Perhaps the easiest way to conceive of Chavín is to compare it to modern-day Roman Catholicism. Catholic churches everywhere have similar statues, paintings, and architecture, reflecting generally similar (though not necessarily identical) beliefs and practices. Catholic churches in Brazil, Hong Kong, and Lithuania will be similar, especially in terms of the physical items that could survive for future archaeologists; but the everyday lives and cultures of people in Brazil, Hong Kong, and Lithuania are very different from one another. In essence, the Catholic Church can be seen as an

FIGURE 6.11 *Gate of the Sun at Tiahuanaco.* *Tiahuanaco, a major city of the Wari Empire, is believed by some scholars to have been the imperial capital. Today, this gate seems isolated on a windy Bolivian plain, but around A.D. 1000 it was part of the ceremonial complex of a thriving city. The gate stands nearly ten feet high, carved from a single slab of volcanic stone. At the top is the sun god, with radiating headdress and a staff in each hand; beside and below him are a series of bird-headed figures. Nearby are several religious buildings, including a subterranean temple with small sculptured heads set into its walls. The wall heads, staff god, and bird-people may derive from Chavín mythology.* Mireille Vautier/Woodfin Camp & Associates.

overlay onto different world cultures, just as Chavín can be seen as an overlay onto different ancient Peruvian cultures.

Conceiving of Chavín as a cultural overlay of this sort can explain how one region might have a strong Chavín presence, complete with a major ceremonial center, while a neighboring region might have virtually no Chavín presence. There is no evidence that there was a political wing of Chavín or any kind of central religious administration. Consequently, it is most reasonable to view Chavín as the result of a diffused idea, not a unification in the usual sense.

In the centuries following Chavín, regional societies continued following their several trajectories. Some quite complex societies developed, ones with massive irrigation systems and probably state-level governments; these were the first Peruvian civilizations. Technology, particularly metal-lurgy and civil engineering, saw a great deal of development, and several of these societies produced massive monumental architecture.

The Wari Empire

The first political unification of Peru came around A.D. 700 and lasted until about 1100. This is the Wari Empire, also known as the "Huari" or "Tiahuanaco"[14] Empire. There is disagreement about where the empire originated, with Peruvian and Bolivian archaeologists both claiming the heartland for their home countries. Regardless, in a few decades the empire came to control about two-thirds of the Peruvian area, including both highland and coastal areas. It is believed to have spread primarily by conquest.

---

[14] **Tiahuanaco:** tee uh wahn AH koh

PERU	MESOAMERICAN HIGHLANDS	MESOAMERICAN LOWLANDS		
Paleo-Indian Period, c. 43,000–c. 8000 B.C.			**14,000 B.C.**	Initial entry of people into the Americas, between 43,000 B.C. and 15,000 B.C.
			–	
			12,000 B.C.	
			–	
			10,000 B.C.	Rapid climatic warming, c. 10,000 B.C.
			–	
			8000 B.C.	Big game extinction complete, 8000 B.C.
Regional foraging traditions, c. 8000–c. 2300 B.C.			–	
			6000 B.C.	Beginnings of agricultural experimentation, c. 6500 B.C.
			–	
			4000 B.C.	Sedentary villages in Peru, c. 4000 B.C.
			–	Agricultural dependence, c. 3200 B.C.
			2000 B.C.	Sedentary villages in Mesoamerica, c. 2300 B.C.
			–	
Chavín, c. 1200–c. 400 B.C.	Teotihua-cán, c. 100 B.C.–c. A.D. 700	Olmecs, c. 1200–c. 400 B.C.		
Regional States, c. 1300 B.C.–c. A.D. 700		Maya, c. 200 B.C.–c. A.D. 800	**A.D. 1**	
Wari Empire, c. A.D. 700 –c. 1100	Toltecs, c. A.D. 900–c. 1200		–	Teotihuacán fire, A.D. 716 Maya collapse complete, A.D. 800

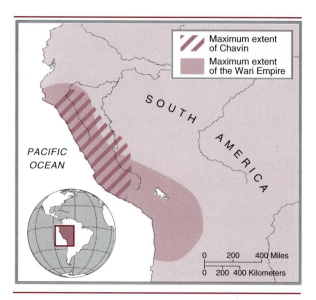

M A P 6 . 3 *Chavín and the Wari Empire.* *In the second millennium* B.C., *Chavín produced the first cultural unification of large parts of Peru. After the breakdown of Chavín, regional cultures dominated Peru for almost 2,000 years, until the Wari Empire achieved another unification in the first millennium* A.D. *While Chavín was largely limited to religion and art and was present only at some settlements within its range, the Wari Empire was comprehensive, controlling the political, economic, and social aspects of all communities within its territory.*

Wherever Wari extended its imperial hand, great changes took place. The empire was urban, and new planned cities sprang up across Peru, usually with the distinctive Wari style of architecture, emphasizing monumental buildings, closely packed structures, and carvings of the sun god. Great emphasis was placed on water control and on extending the range of cultivated lands through efficient irrigation systems, probably to support a growing population. The deities of Wari appeared everywhere the empire went, suggesting the existence of a state religion. The general similarity of Wari cities at this time has suggested to many scholars that the Wari central government was not only strong but also dedicated to imposing its stamp, perhaps forcibly, on subject peoples. Certainly the art reflects a concern with militarism that was rooted in earlier cultures but seems to have blossomed in the Wari Empire.

After the breakup of the Wari Empire, regional cultures again dominated. Many, but not all, of these had a state-level government, complex irrigation systems, and urban settlements. Some of the kingdoms known from historic Peru, such as the Chimú of the northern coast, were founded in this era. Only the Inca, treated in detail in Chapter 16, would unify these diverse polities into a single empire.

SUMMARY

1. The Americas were first peopled by immigrants from northeastern Asia who became American Indians. The exact date of the migration is unknown, but it probably took place between 33,000 and 14,000 B.C. via the Bering Land Bridge.

2. Agriculture developed independently in several areas of the Americas, particularly in Mesoamerica and Peru, which together make up Nuclear America. A variety of staple crops (especially maize, squash, and beans) provided a nutritional base that required little or no meat, and domesticated animals never were important in the Americas before Columbus.

3. Nuclear America preceded the rest of the Americas in the development of complex society.

4. In Mesoamerica, the Olmecs were the first complex society, though there is disagreement

over whether this society should properly be considered a civilization because it probably lacked both the state and urbanism. They were succeeded in the lowlands by the Maya civilization, with its city-states, monumental architecture, and developed writing.

5. In the Mesoamerican highlands, Teotihuacán established its vast commercial base in the largest city of the Americas in the first millennium. It was succeeded by the Toltecs, a group important in mythic history but modest in reality.

6. In Peru, geography encouraged regionalism that was punctuated only by unusual periods of unification. Chavín provided an ideological unification, and the Wari Empire provided the first political unification.

SUGGESTED READINGS

Coe, Michael D. *Breaking the Maya Code.* New York: Thames and Hudson, 1992. An account of Mayan writing for the nonspecialist.

Matos Moctezuma, Eduardo. *Teotihuacán, the City of the Gods.* New York: Rizzoli, 1990. A well-illustrated and accurate portrayal of Teotihuacán.

Miller, Virginia E., ed. *The Role of Gender in Precolumbian Art and Architecture.* Lanham, Md.: University Press of America, 1988. A collection of essays on gender and the arts in Mesoamerica and South America.

Moseley, Michael E. *The Incas and Their Ancestors: The Archaeology of Peru.* New York: Thames and Hudson, 1992. A textbook summary of ancient Peru.

Weaver, Muriel Porter. *The Aztecs, Maya, and Their Predecessors: Archaeology of Mesoamerica.* San Diego, Calif.: Academic Press, 1993. Widely used textbook on ancient Mesoamerica.

Trading in the Early United States. *Benjamin Hawkins, U.S. Indian Agent in South Carolina about 1800, trades iron agricultural tools with Creek Indians in return for agricultural produce.* Unidentified artist, *Benjamin Hawkins and the Creek Indians,* circa 1805. Oil on canvas, 35 7/8 x 49 7/8 inches. Greenville County Museum of Art, Greenville, S.C. Gift of The Museum Association, Inc., with funds donated by Corporate Partners.

Trade and Exchange

People have been trading items with one another for a very long time, possibly since before the biological evolution of fully modern human beings. The essential characteristic of trade is that two people agree to swap items, but there are many variations on how and why the exchange takes place.

For example, you may have a surplus of tomatoes in your garden, while a neighbor may have extra cucumbers. You can trade tomatoes for cucumbers to mutual benefit. This form of trade, where one useful commodity is exchanged for another, is known as **barter** and often is viewed as an early kind of trade. Although it is true that this kind of trade was among the earliest, it persists today, both in garden-level exchanges and in trade between major governments.

Alternatively, trade can take place with some unit of currency as its medium. When you buy cucumbers from a supermarket, for instance, you pay for them with paper money or coins (or some substitute, such as a credit card, debit card, or check). The use of currency lends convenience to the transaction, because you need not haul, say, a cartload of fish to the market to pay for your vegetables. Currency also permits a greater level of stability in pricing, because the currency maintains a generally constant value, while the value of tomatoes or apricots may fluctuate wildly, depending on the season, the weather, and other factors. Trade that uses currency usually is called **purchase**.

Purchase became a major mode of trade in most places as societies became more complex.

141

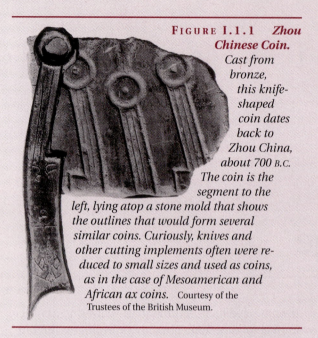

FIGURE I.1.1 *Zhou Chinese Coin. Cast from bronze, this knife-shaped coin dates back to Zhou China, about 700 B.C. The coin is the segment to the left, lying atop a stone mold that shows the outlines that would form several similar coins. Curiously, knives and other cutting implements often were reduced to small sizes and used as coins, as in the case of Mesoamerican and African ax coins.* Courtesy of the Trustees of the British Museum.

The nature of currency has varied greatly over space and time, including such diverse monetary units as cowrie shells (Africa, Asia, and elsewhere), blankets (North America and Central America), coins (Europe, India, China, and elsewhere), paper money (China and elsewhere), and cacao beans (Central America).

ECONOMIC AND NONECONOMIC TRADE

Just as modes of trade have varied, so have the motivations behind trade. The type of trade that most people think of first is **economic trade**, for which the underlying motivation is obtaining an otherwise unavailable item. Economic trade probably was practiced at least by 70,000 B.C. in Africa and Europe; we know this because large quantities of high-quality stone for tools are often found in archaeological sites at considerable distance from the origin of the stone, distances greater than people would be expected to have traveled under normal circumstances. Probably the stone passed through several hands before it reached its ultimate destination. Such economic trade became very important in later times, as with the obsidian trade in Bronze Age Europe and Mesoamerica and with the salt trade in China and Europe.

In contrast, some trade takes place not because the participants are anxious to obtain products from one other but because the act of trading serves to cement friendships and other ties. This kind of trade is known as **noneconomic trade**. For example, traditional Indians of the Amazon River Basin in Brazil who meet and wish to show friendly intentions will give one another arrows. The arrows from one group are scarcely different from those of the other, but the act of trading indicates the individuals' close and amicable feelings toward one another. Most people in modern North America exchange presents at holidays, and, although they rarely think of it as trade, it is another example of noneconomic trade. Although noneconomic trade is very important in small-scale societies, it has only a limited role in more complex societies.

THE CONSEQUENCES OF ECONOMIC TRADE

Some of the outcomes of trade are immediately apparent, but others are a bit less obvious. The most important of the consequences of trade fall into five categories:

—obtaining goods;

—obtaining ideas and information with the goods;

—carrying disease germs from one place to another;

—developing reciprocal political relationships with trading partners; and

—modifying the status of the traders.

Obtaining goods is the most obvious of the results of trade. Short-distance trade, whereby neighbors trade with neighbors, may help a community make it through a hard time. Over a series of good years, that community may have accumulated goods or currency that neighbors traded for surplus food when they were having poor harvests. Later, if the community has a bad harvest of its own, it has items to trade with its neighbors to obtain much-needed food. Over many years, the entire region benefits from the lessening of the impact of famine through trade.

Trade within a kingdom or empire often became enormous, permitting a state to provide most of its needs internally and thereby decrease its reliance on outsiders. The Maya, for example, required salt as a supplement to their overwhelmingly agricultural diet, and the easiest way to get it was by evaporating sea water on the coast. An extensive fleet of vessels carried this salt up and down the coast, and bearers carried it over the sacbe roads into the interior. Other routes brought from the highlands to the lowlands hard stone for grinding stones and obsidian for cutting tools. Those kingdoms that controlled all of these resources within their borders and could transport them throughout their domain were at a competitive advantage over their neighbors, not having to fear economic pressure.

Goods obtained through long-distance trade, until the dramatic transformation of transportation in the nineteenth century, could not be perishable, because the time required to import them was so long. As a result, long-distance trade focused primarily on nonfood products and a few durable foodstuffs, such as spices. Many of the items obtained by long-distance trade were of such rarity and cost at their destination that they were used only by the wealthy. Indeed, some were recognized status symbols, such as lapis lazuli, a blue gemstone imported into ancient Mesopotamia from Iran. The silks that were imported into India, Arab lands, and medieval Europe from East Asia were worn only by the rich.

Sometimes, however, items obtained by long-distance trade transformed a society, as in the case of basalt traded into the Mayan lowlands (discussed in Chapter 6). The Mayan lowlands have no hard stone to make grinding stones, and without grinding stones, dried corn could not be effectively processed for eating. The importation of basalt, a hard stone, permitted the production of grinding stones and the efficient milling of corn, in turn allowing the Maya to base their economy on the more efficient corn grain, rather than on roots.

But traders brought back more than merely the goods in their packs. As traders became familiar with the people they traded with, the traders came to know the people's way of life, their ideas, their culture. Often they had to live long periods among these foreign people, and sometimes they picked up new concepts, new ways of doing things, and new tastes. These they carried home, where the items sometimes became popular. Medieval European traders with the Arab world brought back styles of music, tastes for certain spicy dishes, new words and phrases, and new clothing styles.

Perhaps the most unexpected import to accompany long-distance trade was germs. No one until the last century or so had any understanding of germ theory, and traders did not fully comprehend the hazards they risked by traveling to foreign lands. A trading party often would consist of hundreds of people, and a few almost certainly would be infected with some contagious disease. Upon arriving at their destination, they would unwittingly spread germs to local people, few of whom were likely to have much natural

FIGURE I.1.2 *Peppercorn Harvest. Long-distance trade was restricted to nonperishable items of considerable value, such as spices. Here, fourteenth-century native workers in the Andaman Islands, off India, harvest the small berries that will become black pepper, while an Arab trader looks on and nibbles a berry to test its flavor.* Bibliothèque nationale, Paris.

FIGURE I.1.3 *Plague in Naples.* *Micco Spadero in 1656 painted this graphic portrayal of the horrors of being caught in a plague. Slaves with hooks are dragging bodies to mass graves, and litter bearers carry those stricken but not yet dead to hospitals. The germs that caused these plagues often were transmitted by trade or other long-distance interaction.* Museo Nazionale, Naples/Alinari/Art Resource, N.Y.

resistance. An epidemic might accompany the arrival of a trading company, and the company's return home could be equally disastrous, bringing back another set of exotic germs. The great plagues of Europe have been linked to increased trading contacts with Asia, and the devastation of Native American populations was largely the result of contact with diseased traders and others from Europe.

If countries have no trading relationships with one another, most of their dealings are likely to be hostile. Neighbors are in competition for borderlands, for resources, and for political or military superiority. But trade can change all that. The fortunes of your country may become linked to those of your trading partners, and anything that hurts them also hurts you indirectly. Consequently, the establishment of a trading relationship often leads to some form of political alliance. If trading is so crucial to the welfare of two countries that they cannot survive without it, political alliance is practically imperative.

On the other hand, trade can have a less benign aspect. If the trade is critical for your country yet not for your trading partner, your country is likely to find itself in a politically weak position and probably will become dependent on your partner. The ascendancy of Spain over Portugal in the scramble for colonial holdings in the sixteenth century was, in part, a result of their respective positions in trading relationships. One or more

countries also can use trade as a weapon against other countries.

Finally, the status of the traders as individuals often was changed by their success in commerce. Successful trading expeditions often brought great financial success to the traders or to those whose backing financed the expeditions. Sometimes these were individuals or companies, in which case the entrepreneurs often became very wealthy, such as with colonial fur-trading companies in North America. More often, the state controlled the trade, as in ancient Egypt and Mesopotamia, and the state or royal houses grew more wealthy and powerful. In general, successful trading has led to greater disparities between the wealth of the rich and the poor. In some cases, however, such as under the Roman Empire and in seventeenth-century Europe, trading has contributed to the growth of a middle class. In still other cases, as in China, merchants sometimes grew wealthy but maintained a low social status.

TRADE ROUTES

Successful trade requires efficient routes over which commodities can be transported. The ideal trade route provided rapid, safe, and inexpensive passage of goods between trading partners, but not all would-be traders were favored with such

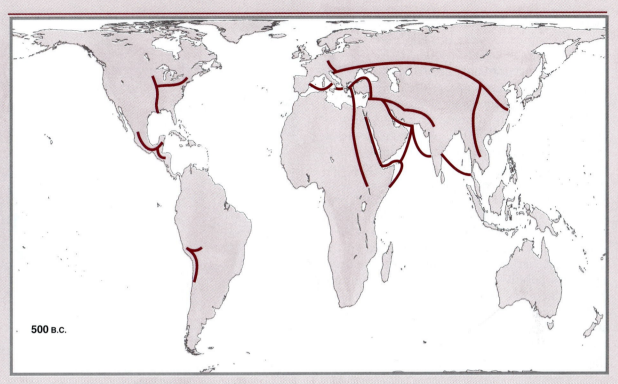

500 B.C.

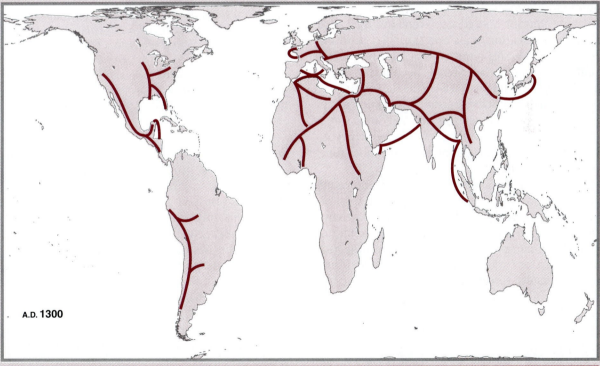

A.D. 1300

MAP I.1.1 *Major World Trade Routes of 500 B.C. and A.D. 1300.* Established trade routes avoided difficult terrain and especially dangerous areas, providing travelers with relatively safe passage and few surprises. People living along these trade routes supplied provisions and services to travelers, often prospering greatly.

From 500 B.C. to A.D. 1300 there is a great similarity of the major world trade routes, demonstrating how the benefits of a known trade route were not readily abandoned in favor of another. Many routes, however, became longer or added branches, reflecting an overall expansion of trade during this period.

routes. A good trade route was as much a valuable natural resource as were mineral ores, salt, or timber.

The optimal overland trade route should be as direct as possible, minimizing the distance traveled. In addition, it should avoid obstacles that will slow the passage or increase its danger, such as mountains or swamps. Similarly, human obstacles, such as notorious bandits and toll barriers, should be avoided. Technology available for land transportation, until quite recently, could carry only limited amounts of weight, so points for reprovisioning food and water were critical along a land trade route. Finally, because few traders were skilled at locating themselves in relation to the stars (and because few maps were accurate enough to permit this, anyway), it was important that a trade route be easy to follow. River valleys often fit many of these criteria, and trade frequently followed them when possible. Needless to say, once a good route was discovered, it was used repeatedly.

Sea routes became important with the development of substantial ships capable of oceanic voyages. Earlier sea routes were along coasts, because navigation skills and the need to reprovision small vessels required that land be in sight at all times. Later, when vessels became larger and more seaworthy and when celestial navigation and the magnetic compass became well known, sea trade routes cut across the oceans. Such routes usually followed prevailing winds and currents, though hazards to navigation, both real and imagined, were avoided.

Countries and peoples with good trade routes had great advantage over others and often prospered. Cities along trade routes often became wealthy by provisioning caravans or extracting tribute for safe passage, indirectly profiting from the trade; a city at the junction of two trade routes was especially fortunate. Wars were fought and empires built in part to control trade routes.

OTHER FORMS OF EXCHANGE

Although the term "trade" is reserved for cases of partners' mutually agreeing to swap items, other kinds of interaction share similarities with trade. These fall under the general category of **exchange**, any process whereby goods pass between part-

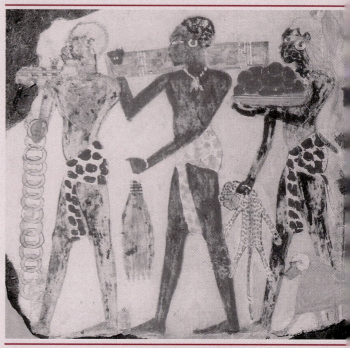

FIGURE I.1.4   *Nubians Rendering Tribute to Egypt.*   *This mural shows Nubian porters bringing a variety of goods to Egypt as tribute. A linked chain of gold rings, a leopard skin, and a live baboon are prominent in the scene, along with less easily identified food, feathers, and exotic wood. This painting comes from the tomb chapel of Sebekhotep, an Egyptian treasurer, and dates from about 1400 B.C.*   Courtesy of the Trustees of the British Museum.

ners, even if goods flow in one direction only. Trade, of course, is one kind of exchange, but there are many others. Piracy, raiding, and banditry, for example, result in goods circulating broadly, though certainly without the agreement of all partners. A Mycenaean pirate, for example, might seize goods from a Minoan vessel, then sell those goods at an Egyptian port. They then might be shipped aboard a Mycenaean vessel, which in turn might be captured by Minoan pirates, who sell the goods at a Minoan port, completing the circle.

An especially significant form of exchange is **tribute**, the rendering of goods to a powerful individual or state by a subordinate. Some governments in Mesoamerica, for example, received so much tribute from conquered states and subordinate allies that these goods became an expected part of the annual income of the state, one that was factored into the calculation of taxes and other revenue-raising programs. Although the subordinate state rarely received any material goods in exchange, it still benefited, because the powerful government to which it rendered tribute made a valuable ally against mutual enemies.

The flow of ideas has been prominent in some periods, also, and that often is considered exchange, as well. This textbook uses that extended meaning when discussing such periods of intense movement of ideas as the Roman imperial era and the spread of Islam.

Historians sometimes overlook the importance of these other forms of exchange, yet they can be quite significant. It has been estimated, for example, that as much as half of the exchange of goods in the seventeenth-century Caribbean took place through mechanisms other than trade, and certainly the exchange of ideas has been an important factor in many historic periods.

TRADE AS A CATALYST FOR CHANGE

Many scholars have seen long-distance trade as a major force in the development of civilization. In the past, several theories have discussed trade as the primary cause of increased complexity, but modern theorists prefer to be a bit more cautious, typically considering trade one of several factors that acted together to transform society.

Some of this caution grew out of a recognition that there are preconditions to long-distance trade. First, you need a product. Sometimes that product can be collected easily, but usually it needs to be manufactured or otherwise processed, and that requires certain technical skills and a workforce. Second, you need a society that is organized in such a manner that it can carry out trade expeditions. This means that personnel can be supported by specialist farmers while they are away on expeditions, producing no food for themselves. It also means that someone is in a position of sufficient authority to be able to organize the expedition and all that goes with it. Third, you need a society that has sufficient differences in wealth so that an individual, a company, or the government can invest the resources needed to mount the expedition, because the reward will be reaped only after the expedition is successfully completed. Goods need to be accumulated for trade, material wants during the expedition must be met, and some personnel may require compensation before the expedition is completed. The investor also has to be prepared for the possibility of a total loss and must have sufficient funds to be able to survive it.

The band-level societies described in Chapter 3 simply could not have engaged in long-distance trade of this sort, because they lacked the expertise and organization required. Rather, only societies that already were moving toward greater complexity (as a result of increasing population pressure and additional factors) could participate in long-distance trade. Once they engaged in such trade, however, they would be changed by it. Individuals with some wealth might become much wealthier; a political organization could become much stronger; occupational specialization and technical skills required in producing the commodity could develop further. Just as a catalyst facilitates a chemical reaction but does not cause it, trade was important in encouraging the ongoing process of evolving cultural complexity in early civilizations and their immediate predecessors.

SUGGESTED READINGS

Earle, Timothy K., and Jonathan E. Ericson, eds. *Exchange Systems in Prehistory.* New York: Academic Press, 1977. A set of provocative and timeless essays on models of trade.

Sabloff, Jeremy A., and C. C. Lamberg-Karlovsky, eds. *Ancient Civilization and Trade.* Albuquerque: University of New Mexico Press, 1975. A collection of classic essays on the role of trade in the origin of civilizations.

Torrence, Robin. *Production and Exchange of Stone Tools: Prehistoric Obsidian in the Aegean.* Cambridge, Eng.: Cambridge University Press, 1986. An excellent summary of extant models of trade, coupled with a thorough regional case study.

U P TO THIS POINT, *THE GLOBAL PAST* has emphasized primarily the earliest development of civilization around the world. Some of those civilizations adopted a type of government that brings several different peoples together under its aegis: an empire. Although empires existed in these early periods, they were relatively few and small. Part Two focuses on the several large empires that developed around the world in the first millennium B.C.

One of the great incentives to form an empire is economics. By controlling another people, a state can exact tribute or taxation, which can constitute a significant portion of its revenues. Perhaps even more important, an empire controls a wide range of environmental and production zones, giving it easy access to a broader variety of resources and commodities than any available to a smaller state. This may be why empires often expand along trade routes. Such factors allow an empire to rely less on foreign trade to support its needs, reducing the likelihood of its becoming politically subservient to a foreign power.

In most of the cases discussed in Part Two, empires were established through military action, meaning that the coalition formed in an empire is often fragile. If several peoples are united by the sword, they may simply wait until the sword wielder becomes weak, at which time they can defect from the empire and reestablish their independent governments. There seems to be a powerful tendency for

	GREECE	ROME	NUBIA	
2000 B.C.			Egyptian colonies	Kerma
1500 B.C.			Egyptian colonies	
1000 B.C.				
	Lyric Age		Kush	
500 B.C.	Classical Age	Etruscan Rome		
		Roman Republic	Meroë	
A.D. 1	Hellenistic Age	◄ Alexander's Empire	Early Roman Empire	
			Later Roman Empire	
A.D. 500				
A.D. 1000				

regional states to form out of the debris of a collapsed empire. In fact, one way of seeing history is as an alternation between vast interregional empires that unite many peoples and small, regional states, each dominated by a single people. Parts Three and Four will explore this pattern further.

A final consequence of an empire often is the establishment of a sphere of interchange, in which goods, foodstuffs, and ideas pass among the empire's component peoples. The impact of such an exchange typically far outlasts the political unity of the empire.

PART TWO

THE CONVERGENCE TOWARD EMPIRE

In Part Two, Chapters 7 and 8 discuss Greece and Rome, polities whose histories were linked by abundant cultural contact and which followed similar trajectories that led to expansive empires. Chapter 9 treats the Kush and Axum civilizations of Northeast Africa, each an empire for at least part of its span. Chapter 10 moves to India, discussing the Maurya and Gupta empires, and Chapter 11 treats the rise and fall of the Qin and Han empires, the first empires of China. Finally, Issue 2 discusses a general model of the formation, internal stresses, and collapse of empires.

ETHIOPIA	INDIA	CHINA	
			2000 B.C.
			1500 B.C.
			1000 B.C.
			500 B.C.
Pre-Axumite Period		Warring States Period	
	Maurya Empire		
	Regional states	Early Han Empire / ◄ Qin Empire	A.D. 1
Axum		Later Han Empire	
	Gupta Empire		A.D. 500
			A.D. 1000

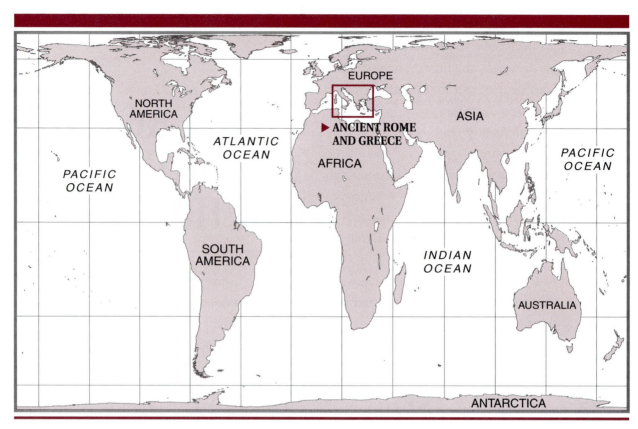

NORTH
AMERICA

ATLANTIC
OCEAN

EUROPE

ASIA

PACIFIC
OCEAN

▶ ANCIENT ROME
AND GREECE

AFRICA

PACIFIC
OCEAN

SOUTH
AMERICA

INDIAN
OCEAN

AUSTRALIA

ANTARCTICA

GAUL

ETRURIA

Adriatic Sea

Corsica

• Rome

Sardinia

Tyrrhenian
Sea

Mediterranean

Sicily

N. AFRICA

Sea

▶ ANCIENT ROME

MACEDONIA

Aegean
Sea

LYDIA

Ionian
Sea

Peloponnesus

• Athens

Crete

Mediterranean   Sea

▶ ANCIENT GREECE

The Greek Polis and the Roman Republic

around 800–31 B.C.

I sing of arms and of a man [Aeneas]: his fate had made him fugitive; he was the first to journey from the coasts of Troy as far as Italy. . . . Across the lands and waters he was battered . . . and many sufferings were his in war . . . until he brought a city into being and carried in his gods to Latium; from this have come the Latin race, the lords of Alba, and the ramparts of high Rome.

–VIRGIL, *The Aeneid*

The Aeneid, an epic by the Roman poet Virgil, is a story that demonstrates the great affinity Romans had for Greek culture, because they believed the founder of their city was Greek and that Greek culture was their own heritage. Greece and Rome faced similar challenges in their development and had many common characteristics. Chapters 7 and 8 discuss how each society governed itself and developed a definition of citizenship, how each responded to internal sociopolitical pressures, and how each dealt with expansion. It is important to pay attention to those instances where common challenges were met with different responses. This chapter will review Greek history from the ninth century to the fourth century B.C., covering what scholars call the Lyric and Classical periods. Roman history will be examined from early development under Etruscan control through the inception and demise of the Roman Republic, 509 to 31 B.C.

151

DEVELOPMENT OF THE GREEK CITY-STATE

Scholars know very little about Greece during the period between around 1200 and 800 B.C. because much of Greece experienced de-urbanization, and consequently minimal documentary evidence has survived. During this elusive historical period, Greek culture began to diffuse to the Aegean Basin, and, by about 800 B.C., the cultural unification of Greece was under way.

Early Greek communities supplied the population with shelter, defense, and a market for local trade. An **acropolis**, a higher area, served as a gathering place for safety against raids. People also came to an **agora**, a central market area similar to the Mesoamerican plaza, to barter goods and exchange news. The agora was a busy place, teeming with fixed and movable stalls. Sandal makers, potters, tanners, and bronzesmiths peddled their wares. A "fast food" meal could be purchased from one of the street vendors, as in large cities of today. Much like farm laborers today in the American Southwest, poor men met in a designated area hoping for a day's hire by a citizen who needed some extra workers. Slaves could be purchased in the agora, as well. The agora also housed courts, where aristocrats argued legal particulars and settled disputes.

In most cases, the rural areas and urban settlements that surrounded the acropolis and agora eventually evolved into city-states. The Greek city-state was called a **polis** (the plural is **poleis**[1]). Each polis jealously guarded its independence, and, ideally, every free male who belonged to a kin group and who owned land within the geographical area of the polis held citizenship there. A citizen's identity came from the polis. Generally, because the polis was originally populated by kin groups, Greeks resisted allowing outsiders to become citizens. When long-distance trade expanded, immigrant merchants paid higher taxes than citizen merchants. Later, laws often allowed the purchasing of citizenship, but the expense prohibited many from obtaining it. In any commercial center, however, citizens of many poleis might be seen selling their commodities and arranging future transactions.

At the same time as the development of the polis, a new style of warfare emerged that affected social and legal conditions. The older style of aristocratic warfare was no longer practical, and a citizen army developed under the leadership of local aristocrats. Each citizen-soldier, a **hoplite**, became a cog in a massive human machine called a **phalanx**,[2] a block of infantry soldiers consisting of as many as one hundred men lined up in rows as many as eight deep. As time passed, phalanx soldiers demanded better economic conditions, less arbitrary justice, and a vote in a citizen assembly in exchange for their invaluable defense of the polis and the personal wealth of the aristocrats. This change in warfare caused an important move toward the concept of citizens' rights.

Greek political history is a checkerboard of various government structures, such as monarchy, oligarchy, tyranny, and democracy. By about 750 to 600 B.C., monarchy gave way to **oligarchy**, rule by a few influential members of the elite in a council. Early oligarchy was usually based on a hereditary aristocracy rather than on wealth. Over the generations, the inherited influence of these aristocrats tended to support their own interests at the expense of citizens of the lower classes. With continued growth in trade, however, bloodlines offered less political influence and the oligarchy's membership shifted to the wealthy elite.

Tension between the oligarchy and other citizens remained common. Between 675 and 600 B.C., it was not unusual to see a polis develop a **tyranny**, originally meaning the usurpation of rule by an individual with widespread popular support. A tyrant was usually brought into power by citizens in opposition to oppressive oligarchical control. This individual promised reform to the hoplites or offices to the merchants. Several tyrants saved poleis from civil war and rebellion, often proving effective in steering the ship of state. Unfortunately, the outcome sometimes exchanged aristocratic oppression for tyrannical oppression after only a few months or years of reform; this is the condition that corresponds to the English meaning of the word "tyrant."

Other reformers replaced oligarchies or tyrants with democracies. A **democracy** is government in the hands of all its citizens or their elected representatives. In many poleis, two factions

---

[1] **poleis:** POH lee ihs

[2] **phalanx:** FAY langks

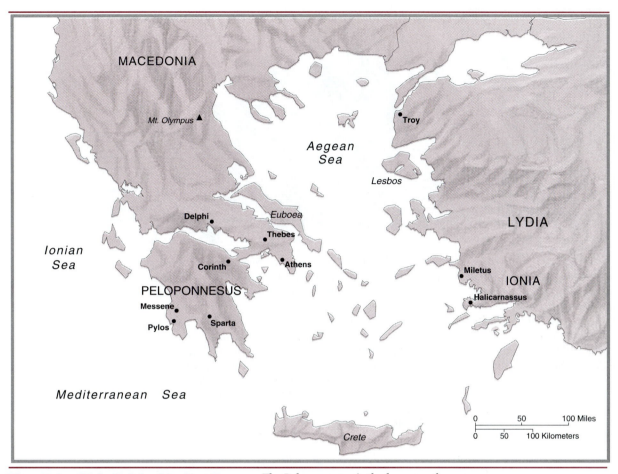

M A P 7 . 1   ***Major Poleis of Ancient Greece.***   *The Peloponnesus is the large southern area that was dominated by Sparta and was more rural than the area to the north of the isthmus, where the large poleis of Athens, Thebes, and Delphi were found. Lands north of Delphi were also more rural, in part because of the terrain, while Delphi, one of the most sacred sites in ancient Greece, was believed to be the center of the earth. Here the oracle temple of Apollo attracted many people from all over southwestern Asia and southeastern Europe, who came to consult the god on personal and political affairs through the young virgin who acted as a medium.*

developed: the oligarchs and the democrats, who constantly competed for control of the city.

Two examples of Greek political development are Athens and Sparta. Athens's history depicts the typical development spurred by the factors discussed, while Sparta's development demonstrates the exception.

Athens: The Typical Pattern

The polis of Athens dominated the surrounding countryside; as many as two hundred various-sized villages were incorporated into the city-state.

Athens's early government was an oligarchy, consisting of a council of aristocrats called the **Areopagite**,[3] a name derived from where they met—the Areopagus or "hill of Ares," the war god. This council met yearly and elected nine **archons**,[4] officials who ran the day-to-day government. The archons consisted of a chief judge and six lesser judges, an official in charge of priestly functions, and a war chief. In addition to the Areopagite Council and archons, the Citizens' Assembly met

[3] **Areopagite:** air ee OH pah gyt
[4] **archons:** AWR kahnz

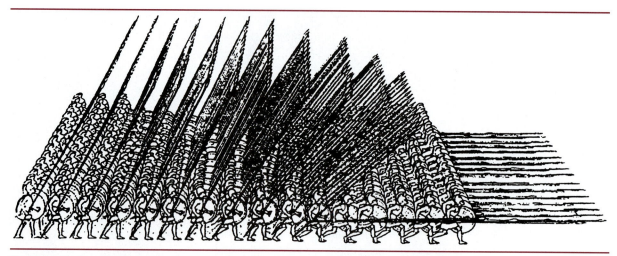

FIGURE 7.1 *Phalanx Warfare.* *Hoplites lined up in phalanx form, ready to fight, protected by helmets, and, later, by breastplates and shin guards. Each hoplite wore a sword strapped at the waist for hand-to-hand combat and held a shield in the left hand and a pike in the right. The left side of the shield covered the exposed right side of the man standing next to each hoplite. In battle, each phalanx moved as a unit, with pikes raised, as it tried to wedge its way through the enemy line. The phalanx that remained intact gained advantage and could fight as a block in hand-to-hand combat; this kind of warfare was much more effective than unorganized bands of men charging each other. The phalanx system required large numbers of hoplites, and because defense of the city depended upon these citizen-soldiers, they often demanded social and economic reforms and the right to redress oligarchical abuse of power before they would consent to fight. The hoplite threats to boycott battles eventually led to the concept of equal rights of citizens and to the world's first democracies.* Andromeda Oxford Limited.

when summoned by the archons on matters relating to diplomacy and warfare.

The move toward a democracy in Athens was actually the result of social unrest. Many Athenian citizens had fallen prey to aristocratic abuses, as when aristocratic interests were protected in the law courts to the detriment of other citizens. In 620 B.C., reform took shape through the efforts of a lawgiver named Draco, who was the first to write down Athenian law. Penalties under Draconian law were severe; even small offenses resulted in the death penalty. By the sixth century B.C., aristocratic abuses were common again. Both rich and poor agreed that peaceful reform was preferable to violence, and two lawgivers, Solon and Cleisthenes,[5] initiated reforms through the office of archon. The particulars of many of the reforms remain historically obscure, but scholars are aware of several economic and social innovations. Many poorer farmers had sold their property and, in extreme

cases, themselves into slavery because of repeated poor harvests brought on by droughts and decreasing yields from the exhausted soil. As a consequence, these farmers became ineligible to fight in the phalanx. In 594 B.C., Solon arranged for the purchase of many former citizens' freedom from slavery and enacted laws to cease the practice of using one's person as collateral for debts. Solon also made judicial and governmental policies less prone to aristocratic abuse by giving the poor redress in popular courts. In a one-time action, all free adult males living in Athens became members of the Citizens' Assembly, regardless of whether they owned land or were immigrants. To thwart the power of the hereditary oligarchy, Solon dissolved the old kinship groups and created four new fictive kinship groups determined by wealth. He then created a new ruling Council of One Hundred (made up of elected members from each new kinship group) to govern the city.

Solon's reforms broke the stranglehold of the old aristocracy in Athens, yet they did not yield

[5] **Cleisthenes:** KLYS thah neez

FIGURE 7.2 *Athenian Acropolis.* *The polis of Athens developed around the Acropolis, a high rocky area that afforded a good view of the surrounding terrain and was a defendable position against attacks. The ruins that crown the Acropolis date from building projects of the fifth-century B.C. period of Athenian dominance, and eventually became the models for Classical Greek architecture and sculpture. The most famous building, the Parthenon (seen here in the center of the Acropolis) was a temple dedicated to Athena, patron goddess of Athens. It measures about 228 feet by 101 feet and is constructed of marble, with eight columns on each end and seventeen on each side. The inner room that once housed a gold-and-marble statue of Athena had a two-tiered colonnade running along the sides and around the back of the statue. Other statues depicted scenes from the myths of Athena. (See also the close-up of a relief from the Parthenon in Figure 7.6.)* Robert Harding Picture Library.

long-lasting results. No land reforms accompanied the laws against debt slavery, and poverty soon led to the enslavement of poor citizens again, as the laws against using oneself as collateral increasingly were ignored. Additionally, Solon's establishment of wealth instead of heredity as the litmus test for power did not change oligarchical rule; it merely created a different ruling elite in the Council of One Hundred.

By 508 B.C., Athens was forced again to chose a reforming lawgiver, Cleisthenes, to settle social unrest. The ruling elite refused to allow new immigrants to participate in government, so many wealthy merchants living in the city had inferior legal status. Many poor farmers had sold them-

selves into slavery again. Cleisthenes created demes,[6] new political districts based on where one lived. Cleisthenes disbanded Solon's Council of One Hundred and created a new one. Its membership consisted of fifty elected members from each of ten newly formed fictive kinship groups composed of all economic and social levels from the demes. This created a Council of Five Hundred, whose members were elected on a yearly basis. An administrative subcouncil was then elected from the new Council of Five Hundred to do the daily work of the government. This was democracy in action, because even poorer farmers could be

[6] **demes:** DEEMZ

elected to the Council of Five Hundred and the subcouncil. Yet it did not take long for government's time-consuming work to become a low priority for the small farmers whose farms required their continued presence. Although elections continued, Athenian government again fell into the hands of the wealthiest citizens, who could afford to be absent from their estates or businesses.

Athenian democracy had occurred as a direct result of the need for social reform. Reforms were not long lasting, and, although Athens remained a democracy for most of its history, the wealthy were able to dominate it with patronage and the buying of votes.

Sparta: The Exception

Spartan history is singularly different from that of Athens and all other Greek poleis. During the seventh and sixth centuries B.C., Sparta engaged in a period of expansion and aggression. Most other Greek poleis sent out colonists or incorporated nearby territories that had space for expansion by making their inhabitants citizens. Sparta, however, conquered its western neighbor, Messenia, whose fertile lands could yield enough grain to feed the expanding Spartan population. The Messenians became **helots**, members of an inferior status, who were not slaves but were restricted in their rights and constantly guarded by Spartan soldiers.

Around 650 B.C., the helots revolted, and Sparta, greatly weakened by the uprising, almost lost its domination of them. This was a turning point in Spartan history; Sparta's fear of another helot revolt resulted in a complete reorganization into a rigid hierarchy. Helots remained at the bottom. Allies of Sparta were politically free but obligated to serve with the Spartan army when called. In Sparta, only males who had reached the age of thirty and had been born of two Spartan parents could be citizens. At any given time, there were approximately five to ten helots for every citizen, and defense became the driving force in Spartan society.

Sparta had a mixed government consisting of monarchical, oligarchical, and democratic elements that made it unique in Greek political history. Spartan governmental reforms retained monarchy in the two-king system, because it was believed that two kings met the need for a balance of power to thwart tyrannical abuse. The kings led the army in battle, policed the helots, performed rituals, and exercised judicial functions. The Council of Thirty, consisting of the two kings and twenty-eight retired soldiers, prepared legislation for the Citizens' Assembly and performed judicial functions. Five overseers, one elected to represent each of the five districts of Sparta, performed the daily work of government, oversaw the kings in their responsibilities, negotiated foreign policy, and presided over the Citizens' Assembly. The Citizens' Assembly included a gathering of all citizens (including the Council of Thirty and the overseers); its duties were to ratify council legislation, declare war, and impeach recalcitrant kings. This created a balance of political power in Sparta.

Harkening back to an ancient legendary lawgiver, Lycurgus, the Spartans justified their military society and their suppression of the helots through the enforcement of their idea of justice. They saw the helot revolt as a sign that they had abandoned the ancient traditions based upon good law, and they devoted their lives to the protection and promotion of their polis, making civic duty the mainstay of Spartan life. Consequently, Sparta, with no merchants of its own and no private ownership of land until the fourth century B.C., engaged in little commerce.

Spartans lived a regimented life wherein individualism was punished with exile or death to preserve the common good. Spartan babies were examined at birth to determine their strength and health; if they were sickly they were exposed to the elements and allowed to die. In Sparta, exposure was a state decision rather than a parental one. Female babies were less desirable, but those who were strong and might survive to produce more children were allowed to live. This practice of infanticide by exposure occurred throughout Greece as well as in some other cultures and served to limit the financial burden of unduly large families and to control sex ratios.

Young Spartan boys trained in athletics and military tactics when they were removed to barracks life at the age of seven. The military communal living limited personal freedoms. Spartans could marry at the age of eighteen years but had to continue living in the barracks; conjugal visits had to be made by stealth. Young men continued practical military training as hoplites in the army until they were granted full citizenship at thirty years of age, when they could live at home (though they continued to have meals at the barracks). Retirement finally came at age sixty, when the veteran became eligible for election to the Council.

Women were also trained in athletics and were given a mandate to serve the state by producing strong sons. Spartan women had a reputation for being outspoken and militaristic; they often lined the road as the hoplites marched out of the barracks on their way to war, and one mother is said to have challenged a son to "come back with your shield or on it!" The Spartan who dropped his shield and fled the battle disgraced his family and polis and probably would not make it home alive. But the Spartan who marched home or returned among the revered dead gave his mother and family great honor.

FIGURE 7.3 *Spartan Woman.* *This bronze statue represents a young Spartan woman performing gymnastics, in which both girls and boys were trained. Spartan women enjoyed more social freedoms than most other Greek women, because Spartans believed that outspoken and authoritative women challenged men to live up to their responsibilities. Stories circulated about Spartan women chastising weak or lazy men and hooting at the losers at competitive athletic events. Because hoplites were often called away into battle, women were expected to protect the polis from enemy attack. A story is told of a king invading in 275 B.C. from an area northwest of Greece and his reluctance to attack Sparta. He was aware that the city would be defended only by Spartan women, children, and old men, but the women's reputation for battle gave him pause.* National Archaeological Museum, Athens/Archaeological Receipts Fund (TAP Service).

LIFE IN ANCIENT GREECE

The geography of Greece and the entire Aegean area had a profound effect upon Greek society. Very few cities are more than a dozen miles from the coast, because most of the interior regions are mountainous. The earliest communities found themselves somewhat isolated by these natural barriers, resulting in a strong sense of self-sufficiency and local kinship identity that later inhibited Greek political unification. Coastal trade brought the various communities into contact with one another, but local citizens generally discouraged extension of citizenship to immigrants from other areas.

By 800 B.C., Greek farmers left their cities to work in the fields during the day and returned at night. This pattern lasted until the commuting time to newly cultivated and often remote fields became prohibitive, forcing those in the outlying areas to live on their land. Social structure then focused on the ***oikos***,[7] or household, which consisted of the family, land, slaves or tenants, buildings, and livestock of a single farmer. Each self-sufficient *oikos* produced and maintained most of what the family needed. As a matter of fact, the Greek word for the management of a household is *oikonomia*, from which our English word "economy" is derived.

Farmers produced many crops for the family's table and for exchange. The primary dietary crops were grain, grapes, and olives, from which bread, wine, and oil could be produced. Fruits and vegetables included grapes, figs, lentils, and leeks; honey was gathered to sweeten many dishes. Fish and shellfish were consumed fresh or dried. Goat milk was drunk or turned into milk products like cheese. Most meat came from wild game,

[7] ***oikos:*** OY kohs

including deer and boar, which adorned only holiday banquet tables. Farmers did not practice crop rotation for soil replenishment but let fields lie fallow to regenerate the soil. Oxen pulled the plows, designed merely to scratch into the limited topsoil of the region, and farmers followed, scattering the seed.

The Greek Social Structure

The social structure consisted of aristocrats, commoners (peasants, artisans, and laborers), and slaves. In early Greece, the wealthy aristocrats and peasant farmers lived in similar housing and engaged in the same types of employment. Housing was designed around a courtyard, giving maximum security with a surrounding wall (usually windowless). As a matter of fact, burglars were called "walldiggers" because of this construction, which forced them to tunnel through the outer wall to rob the occupants. Aristocrats tilled the soil in early Greek society; owning land and performing manual labor was the ideal. Odysseus, the hero of the Homeric epic *The Odyssey*, was known for being able to plow a straight furrow—a sign of a good farmer. As cities grew and political power became centralized, however, wealthy aristocrats participating in government or practicing law remained in the cities, leaving their estates in the hands of trusted servants.

Commoners and slaves comprised the largest percentage of the population. The peasant farmers tended to own land in hilly areas or in less fertile sections. Those farmers too poor to own land worked parcels of aristocratic lands as tenants for a portion of the yield. Urbanites worked as artisans or day laborers. Those who fell into debt or were captured in war became slaves. Most slaves were treated well as house servants or field laborers, but some slaves had to engage in dangerous work, like mining silver. Other slaves were highly educated doctors, teachers, and merchants. Manumission was frequent and often came in the form of a gift in a will or as the result of a slave's personal economic prowess; city slaves often engaged in commercial enterprises for their wealthy owners. A merchant class developed about the seventh century B.C., when increased long-distance trade brought greater wealth to the cities.

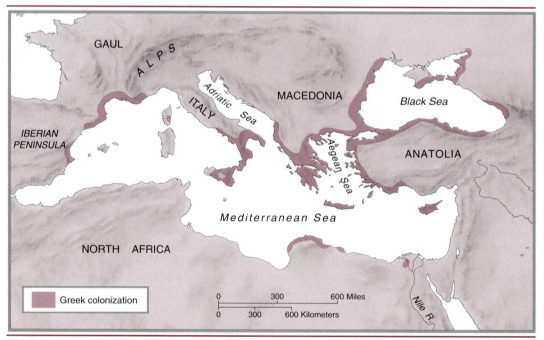

MAP 7.2 *Greek Colonization.* *This map shows the areas colonized by Greek poleis around the Mediterranean basin. The Greek trade network was based on ethnic ties between poleis and colonies; this alliance assured lower prices for all Greeks dealing with Greek traders. In addition, poleis with numerous colonies enjoyed a favored trade status with their colonies. Athens, for example, was able to support building programs and the fine arts and to employ some of the best educators in Greece for their children.*

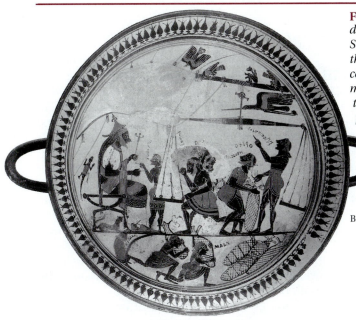

F IGURE 7.4 *Greek Colonial Trade.* *Greek colonies dotted the coastal areas of the eastern Mediterranean Sea, bringing great wealth to the poleis that originated them. Athens, Corinth, and Thebes established many colonies. This platter comes from a Greek colony in modern-day Libya. The large figure on the left checks the weight of a shipment of juice from the silphium plant, which was used for medicine and flavoring foods. A scribe makes notes on the transaction as the goods are assembled. The containers are stored under the flooring. The presence of weights and measures signifies their importance in the transaction; merchants often carried their own weights to ensure fairness.* Bibliothèque nationale, Paris.

Gender Roles

Gender roles developed in Greek society much as they had in other early civilizations. Women's contributions to family life focused on child rearing and household duties. Aristocratic women were often in charge of large households with a multitude of servants and sizeable budgets to manage. In the humblest hovel and the wealthiest villa, women wove cloth. As a matter of fact, some Greek myths associated the creative acts of procreation and weaving. Women also participated in society as priestesses or prostitutes, and the priestesses held a highly respected position in Greek religion. Greeks believed that women were more spiritual and less intellectual than men. The priestesses for the Oracle of Apollo at Delphi were selected from among the girls of local families and were chosen for their propensity toward erratic and ecstatic behavior. Aristocratic men engaged in political and legal professions, but most men worked as farmers, laborers, artisans, craftsmen, and merchants.

Children were welcomed into the family, but the father (except in Sparta) had the authority to choose life or death for any child deemed unsuitable or too expensive to raise. (Girls were considered more expendable.) Children were socialized in their gender roles from an early age, and wealthy families formally educated both young

boys and girls in reading, writing, singing, and playing instruments. In their teen years, girls continued their domestic educations, while boys progressed to studies in mathematics, poetry, philosophy, music, and gymnastics.

A favorite male pastime was frequenting a public gymnasium, consisting of pools, steam baths, and a sandy area for sports. Athletic activity was an important part of Greek society because Greeks admired a well-toned body as well as an educated mind. Formal games became sources of pride and honor for those cities whose athletes won prizes in competitions. Athletes were honored with tax exemptions, permission to wear purple (a sign of prestige), and often a statue. Besides creating a diversion, these competitive sports kept the citizen army in good physical condition; wars were frequent between the fiercely competitive and independent poleis.

Trade and Colonization

In the eighth century B.C., Greek trade and colonization expanded, profoundly affecting Greek society. The limited arable land and overcultivation were always problems for Greek farmers, forcing the importation of numerous goods, particularly grains from Egypt and the area of the Black Sea. Many cities sent out large groups of people to establish new colonies to relieve the

ENCOUNTERS

The Sicilian Caterer

By the fifth century B.C., Athens had achieved its status as the leader in Greek elite culture. While Athenians of earlier periods had focused on feasts dedicated to the gods, these now were eclipsed by more secular social dining. Dining at the earlier feasts to the gods had been a rigid affair, with diners seated at communal tables. Social dining in the later period, on the other hand, was more relaxed, with the diners typically reclining on couches in what was referred to as the "Sicilian style." This term is telling, because the Athenian banquet of this period owed much to Sicily, the island immediately to the south of the Italian peninsula.

Greek city-states had established colonies in Sicily beginning in the eighth century B.C.; the most famous was Syracuse. These essentially independent colonies had retained many aspects of Greek culture, but they also had absorbed certain Sicilian ways, especially in terms of food and dining. Sicilians, by all reports, enjoyed their meals and regarded them as an opportunity to delight the senses. Well-to-do Sicilians ate reclining, often with flowers arranged around them. Meals consisted of small amounts of many dishes, often prepared with exotic ingredients and served with sauces.

In part through connections with the Sicilian colonies, Athens imported this style of dining. The thick, unsauced slabs of roasted meat that had graced earlier Greek tables were replaced with daintier dishes that were prepared, not merely cooked, and dressed with sauces. Wealthy Athenian diners often festooned themselves with garlands of flowers while reclining "Sicilian style."

There was, however, another, more direct route by which Sicilian cuisine and dining habits made their way to Athens. Although everyday meals were prepared by a household's servants, special dinner parties with guests usually were catered, and the most sought-after caterers were Sicilians. Archestratus[a] was a famous wandering gastronome who would stoop to exercising his culinary skills when his funds were running short; Mithraicos[b] was so famous for his cooking skill that Plato discussed him in *Gorgias*; and there were two caterers named Heraclides.[c] All of these caterers were from Sicily, and there must have been many other less famous caterers whose names have been lost. Those mentioned here are known because they wrote cookbooks describing how dishes in the Sicilian style should be prepared; alas, none of the books has survived.

Hints at the Sicilian style of cuisine survive, however, and it seems to have contained a great many fish dishes. Combinations rare in today's cooking appear to have been common then, such as fish baked with cheese and vinegar. The Mediterranean was—and is—justly famous for its fresh fish, and the seasonings probably were to satisfy Sicilian tastes, not to disguise old fish.

Food historians have a saying that the French learned to cook from the Italians and that the Italians learned to cook from the Greeks. This is a convenient oversimplification, but it emphasizes the fact that there was a great deal of contact between regions and many influences that shaped the cooking of any single region. The Mediterranean was a small place, and people and ideas—like fish—circulated freely.

[a]**Archestratus:** ahr keh STRAY tuhs
[b]**Mithraicos:** mihth RAY cohs
[c]**Heraclides:** hair ah KLY deez

pressure of population growth and to improve trade. Colonies were sent eastward to the coast of modern Turkey (called Ionia), northeastward to the Black Sea, westward to Sicily and southern Italy, and even as far west as the coast of Spain. Greeks traded primarily olive oil and wine for staple foods and wood, along with luxury items. The colonists took Greek culture and attitudes with them, often displacing indigenous peoples through war. They did intermarry with local people, but they kept Greek lifeways dominant. The new colony usually had very close economic and religious ties to the originating polis, but like the polis at home, it remained politically independent.

Increased trade with colonies and other peoples of the Mediterranean shores brought wealth to many citizens. Conversely, catastrophic loss from poor business ventures or speculation could ruin a family economically and politically. Land remained the preferential basis of wealth, however, and many wealthy merchants purchased large tracts of land to legitimize themselves. Aristocrats disdained those who gained wealth through trade, but many provided financial backing to slaves to establish businesses, while themselves remaining silent partners.

A CENTURY OF GREEK CONFLICT

Greek poleis fought frequent wars of aggression and defense among themselves. Sometimes the oligarchy of one city supported the oligarchy of another city against tyrants or democratic reformers. Through all these conflicts, however, there remained the basic idea that all poleis should remain self-governing and independent of any non-Greek power. A series of events, however, threatened Greek society between 490 and 404 B.C., resulting in a century occupied mainly with war and conflict.

The Persian Wars, 490–479 B.C.

Greek poleis infrequently united in a common effort, but they did so to defend Greece from the Persians. By the sixth century B.C., the huge Persian Empire became interested in the lucrative Greek trade along the western coast of modern Turkey, threatening the Ionian cities there. After swallowing up the smaller nearby kingdom of Lydia in 546 B.C., Persia soon encroached on the Greeks in the region. The Ionian cities revolted against Persia in 499 B.C., with only nominal help from the European mainland Greeks. This conflict initiated long-term hostilities between Greece and Persia. When Persia's King Darius I invaded Thrace in 490 B.C., the Persian Wars (490–479 B.C.) began. Some Greek poleis had surrendered to the Persians, but others allied in a common effort to defeat Persian aggression. Athens soon emerged as the leader of the allied effort. After their defeat in 479 B.C., the Persians retreated from the Aegean, and a new era in Greek history unfolded as Athens exploited its leadership role.

Athenian Dominance, 479–431 B.C.

The city of Athens had established several colonies on the Ionian coast and had developed a fleet of merchant ships that became a significant factor in naval engagements with the Persian fleet. Naval victories during the Persian Wars proved the effectiveness of a standing fleet against Persian invasion. In the aftermath of the wars, Athens insisted on the continuance of a well-maintained fleet, which Athens would manage but the allies would fund. Athens soon dominated the **Delian League**, a coalition for the common defense and the liberation of any Greeks who remained under Persian control. A treasury, housed on the island of Delos, was established to accomplish this. Athens forced each polis to join the coalition on its liberation from Persia.

Athens's overlordship of other league members and financial control of the treasury soon threatened traditional Greek independence. Any threat of withdrawal from the coalition was met with force, and allies were treated as subjects. At the same time, because of its access to all ports, Athens enjoyed unprecedented commercial expansion and corresponding economic growth. Democratic Athens increasingly meddled in the political affairs of other poleis and dominated the Greek economy. The future of Athenian power seemed secure when the treasury was moved from Delos to Athens in 454 B.C. Athens had been severely damaged in the Persian Wars, and the money used to rebuild the city came from the league's funds.

The Peloponnesian Wars, 431–404 B.C.

Athens's dominance of the Delian League led to widespread unrest among the poleis. Hostilities with Persia came to an end in 449 B.C. with the signing of a peace treaty between the two antagonists. Athens continued to block secession from the Delian League, even though there was no longer a need for an organization for the common defense. The allies, realizing that they were actually subjects of Athenian interests, turned to rebellion. Sparta and its allies had resisted Athenian overlordship and had not joined the Delian League. Sparta took this opportunity to crush Athenian power and led the rebellion against Athens. The wars were fought in two major periods (431–421 B.C. and 415–404 B.C.), with an uneasy

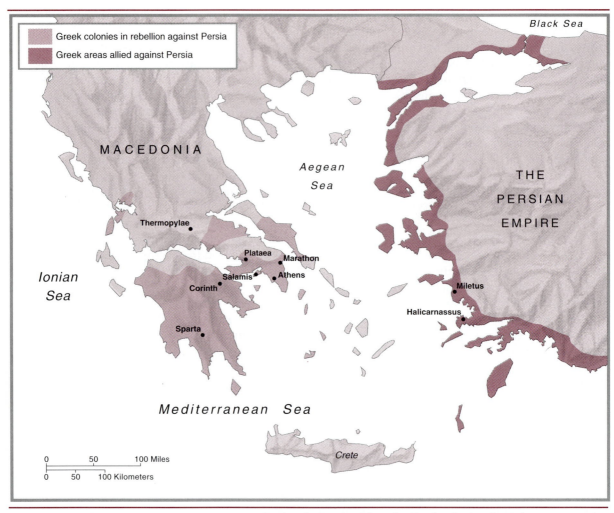

MAP 7.3 *The Persian Wars, 490–479 B.C. During the Persian Wars, the Greek colonies along the coast of modern Turkey were threatened by the encroachment of the Persians. Many of the poleis finally were taken over or were forced to accept pro-Persian governments. They soon rebelled, calling on aid from their Greek homeland. However, not all areas in Greece joined the alliance of poleis against Persia. Greeks rarely came together in political or military unity; each polis fiercely guarded its independence. During the Persian Wars, the powerful states of Athens and Sparta supplied commanders to lead the Greek alliance. The three major land battles of the Persian Wars occurred at Marathon, Thermopylae, and Plataea. The last and most significant naval battle, near Salamis, launched the Athenians into naval dominance.*

peace between them. By 404 B.C., Athens lay defeated, its walls demolished and its citizenry demoralized. Unconditional surrender placed the city in the hands of a tyrant backed by Sparta, but Athens overthrew the tyranny and regained its independence; democracy finally returned to Athens by the winter of 403–402 B.C.

The end of the Peloponnesian Wars did not mean peace for Greece. Skirmishes between poleis continued for a generation, which even saw the Persian emperor arbitrate local disputes. The tradition of polis independence discouraged Greece

from uniting politically, and the history of Greece from this point until the rise of Macedonia in the north is the history of each individual polis.

GREEK PHILOSOPHY AND THE ARTS

Ancient Greek history is often divided into several ages based upon periods in artistic and intellectual history. The Lyric, the Classical, and the Hellenistic

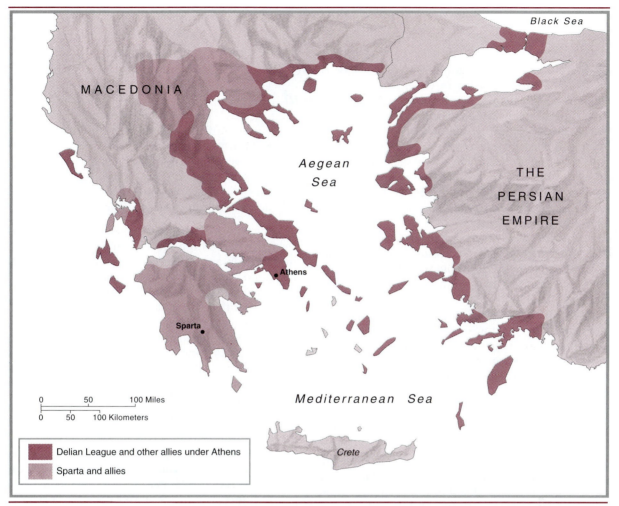

MAP 7.4 *The Peloponnesian Wars, 431–404 B.C. The two major antagonists in the Peloponnesian Wars were Sparta and Athens. Athens led the Delian League, which developed after the victory over Persia in 479 B.C., for the common defense of Greeks against any future Persian attack. Sparta and many of its allies had never joined the Delian League and resented Athenian overlordship in Greece. As the map demonstrates, most of Athens's strength rested on alliances developed along trade routes. Athens had used the Delian League as a means to further its dominance of shipping lanes; Sparta, on the other hand, gained allies from among the more rural areas.*

ages are periods of innovation in the arts and philosophy. We will discuss the Lyric and Classical ages in this chapter and the Hellenistic Age in Chapter 8.

The Lyric Age, around 800–around 500 B.C.

The Lyric Age includes some of the earliest literature of European civilization. The word "lyric" is used because early Greek poetry and epic stories were sung and often accompanied by musical instruments, usually the lyre. Through oral accounts, the Greeks kept alive many of the stories about the Mycenaean age that later emerged in the heroic epics *The Iliad* and *The Odyssey.* Their composition is attributed to Homer, but they are actually a compilation of legends by many storytellers of the eighth century B.C. These stories of heroic deeds and individualism became the foundation for Greek education. Greek boys, particularly aristocrats, were schooled in these two classics and committed long passages to memory. Each city-state claimed a heroic founder from *The Iliad,* and

Heroes played significant roles as models for behavior in Greek and Roman society. The Greek myths, reflecting on their Mycenaean forebears, recounted numerous adventures and deeds that inspired the youth of the Lyric and Classical ages. Roman myths also instructed many young, aspiring aristocratic boys to greatness as they heard or read about the deeds of the heroic past. Two such awe-inspiring heroes were Odysseus and Aeneas.

Odysseus was brave, astute, and enterprising. His cunning led to lies on occasion, but his prudent counsel and valor in battle made him the perfect mix of heroic ideals for Greek youth. Odysseus's life entertained as well as inspired; his experiences in *The Odyssey*, the story of his ten-year trek back to his homeland after fighting with other Mycenaeans at Troy, proved to be the most popular of Greek adventures. In this selection, his intellect liberates him and his men from the cave of the Cyclops.

The Cyclops [who had been blinded by Odysseus earlier] . . . sat down in the entrance himself, spreading his arms wide, to catch anyone who tried to get out with the sheep . . . but I was planning so that things would come out the best way . . . combining all my resource and treacheries . . . and as I thought, this was the plan that seemed best to me. There were some male sheep, rams, well nourished, thick, and fleecy. . . . Silently I caught these and lashed them together. . . . I had them in threes, and the one in the middle carried a man, while the other two went on each side, so guarding my friends. . . . There was one ram, far the finest of all the flock. This one I clasped around the back, snuggled under the wool of the belly, and stayed there still, and with a firm twist of the hands and enduring spirit clung fast to the glory of this

fleece, unrelenting. . . . [The Cyclops] felt over the backs of all his sheep . . . but . . . did not notice how my men were fastened under the breasts. . . . Last of all the flock the ram went out of the doorway . . . and when we had got a little way from the yard and the cavern, first I got myself loose . . . then set my companions free, and rapidly then, and with many a backward glance, we drove the long-striding sheep, rich with fat, until we reached our ship.

Romans believed that Aeneas, the founder of their city, came from the ancient Greek city of Troy. Aeneas had traits similar to Odysseus's, those of bravery, honor, and intelligence. Young Romans learned from Aeneas that duty to the state remained paramount and that honor came with loyalty. In the following selection from *The Aeneid*, Aeneas has traveled into a sacred cavern that leads to the underworld of spirits. Aeneas's dead father tries to convince Aeneas to do his duty and found the city by showing him the spirits of future Romans waiting to be born. The passage explains that it is Rome's destiny to conquer and rule the world.

Now turn your two eyes here, to look upon your Romans, your own people. Here is Caesar . . . and Pompey . . . who could leave to silence you, great Cato? . . . who can ignore the [Gracchus brothers]? . . . For other peoples will, I do not doubt, still cast their bronze to breathe with softer features, or draw out of the marble living lines, plead causes better, trace the ways of heaven with wands and tell the rising constellations; but yours will be the rulership of nations, remember, Roman, these will be your arts: to teach the ways of peace to those you conquer, to spare defeated peoples, [and to] tame the proud.

their nostalgic reverence for the heroic Mycenaean Age gave them a sense of unity, cultural superiority, and tradition.

The Lyric Age also produced prominent poets who wrote for the enjoyment of an increasingly sophisticated, literate clientele. One of these was Sappho (born about 612 B.C.), who lived on the island of Lesbos. Sappho grew up a typical Greek

girl from a wealthy family; when she was old enough, she married a husband suitable to her station, and they had a daughter. But Sappho's life changed following the untimely death of her husband. In ancient Greek society, most poets and intellectuals were male. Sappho overcame this masculine predominance and established a circle of women who were devoted to one another and to their love of poetry. The Greek philosopher Plato, normally uninterested in women's contributions, lauded Sappho's poetry, as did the scholars of following centuries, who named her one of the Nine Lyric Poets.

Many intellectuals from Greece traveled to participate in the artistic atmosphere of Lesbos. Sappho's poetry praises the feminine, and she

FIGURE 7.5 *Sappho. Sappho is depicted on a vase commemorating her fame as a lyric poet. Much of her work was viewed as depraved and was destroyed in later centuries by the early Christian Church. No complete poems of Sappho remain, but quotations from her poems, preserved in other writers' works, attest to her talents. During the Lyric Age, when Sappho wrote, Greeks came in contact with several other cultures from around the eastern Mediterranean and as far north as the Black Sea. It has been argued that interaction with these peoples led to a movement toward individualism in philosophy and literature and away from the older Homeric constructs. Sappho's lifestyle, portrayed in her poetry, was less tolerated than male homosexuality and demonstrates great individualism for this period.* Staatliche Antikensammlung, Berlin.

wrote love poetry about her relationships with many of the women who resided in her community at Lesbos (from which modern English derives the term "lesbian"). Homosexuality in ancient Greece was considered an appropriate expression of sexuality, and bisexuality was common. Although most Greeks thought a heterosexual relationship was the ideal (because it produced children to inherit property and prestige), they believed that experimentation made one a better partner. Elders were expected to teach younger partners of the same sex the sensual arts. Many selections of Greek poetry and plays treated sexuality as a driving force to be enjoyed, romanticized, and even joked about.

Philosophy, the pursuit of wisdom or knowledge, also blossomed in Greece's Lyric Age. Greek philosophy originated on the Ionian coast as a consequence of the interaction between Persians and the Ionian colonists; the intellectual challenge of meeting a new and different culture instigated Greek investigation into physics (the study of the natural world) and cosmology (the study of the origin and properties of the universe). The science and mathematics of southwestern Asia and Egypt challenged the older religious myths of these colonists. The Olympian deities had been associated with natural phenomena: The sun was Apollo's chariot; thunder and lightning were rages of Zeus. Now Greek intellectuals began asking different questions regarding how the universe functioned and how nature worked. They did not stop believing in their traditional anthropomorphic deities but removed them to a distant, uninterested role in the operation of the universe. The ancient cosmology of the Olympian myths gave way to such practical knowledge as recognition of tides and sea currents, greater understanding of weather patterns, and new techniques in agriculture.

The Classical Age, around 500–around 338 B.C.

The Classical Age was a period of warfare but also one of artistic and intellectual development. The wealth of Athenians attracted artisans and philosophers. Wealthy Athenians patronized the arts, and Classical Athens became a center for intellectual and artistic development.

Greek sculpture and architecture flourished under private and public patronage. Idealization

FIGURE 7.6 *Poseidon, Apollo, and Artemis.* *This relief from the eastern side of the Parthenon depicts three Olympian deities seated on their thrones. On the left is Poseidon, god of earthquakes and the sea, who was worshiped by sailors. The center figure is Apollo, the god associated with music, archery, prophecy, medicine, and philosophy. Many people traveled to the sacred city of Delphi, where Greeks believed Apollo spoke through the oracle of the temple. Seated at the right is Artemis, Apollo's sister, the goddess associated with uncultivated areas, like forests where wild beasts lived. She is described in myth as a lion among women and a hunter. Greeks worshiped her as a birth goddess, believing she brought fertility to men, women, and fruit trees and that she protected the unborn. She was particularly popular among the peoples living in the large rural areas of the Peloponnesus. This relief is a fine example of the style of sculpture during the productive period of fifth-century Athens.* Erich Lessing/Art Resource, N.Y.

of the human body became the focus of Greek sculpture in marble and bronze. Every city proudly displayed statues of anthropomorphic deities, prominent citizens, and favorite athletes. Building projects increased, and their architectural designs included multiple columns topped with different ornate designs. The buildings of the acropolis were constructed under the public works projects of Pericles (495–429 B.C.), the archon and most prominent political leader of Athens during its

period of dominance. The **Parthenon**, the temple of Athena on the acropolis, was decorated with painted relief sculpture.

In addition, Greeks wrote poetry, drama, and histories. Poetry continued to idealize love and war. Athenian dramatists, like Sophocles (496–406 B.C.), were producing plays concerning such notable topics as the mutual rights and responsibilities of the individual and the state, the powerful dilemma of good and evil, and the psychological struggles of human relationships. Such plays became vehicles with which to delve into the public and private lives of Greek citizens. The tragic and comic plays produced during the Classical Age have served as inspiration for dramatists of later centuries. There are few poets from Sparta; those who did write often penned stories about military life. Spartan virtues focused on bravery, duty to country, and self-denial. One Spartan poet glorified bravery with these words, "Let him [a Spartan hoplite] not stand beyond the range of the missiles, for he has a shield. Rather let him go near and slay his warrior foe, wounding him at close quarters with long spear or sword."

Herodotus[8] (484–425 B.C.) and Thucydides[9] (460–400 B.C.) wrote about the major conflicts of the age. Herodotus wrote a history of the Persian Wars but also digressed, filling pages with interesting mythic tales, customs, and events from various cultures. Thucydides, an Athenian commander and later exile from Athens during the Peloponnesian Wars, composed a more focused account of that conflict. His analysis, as well as details of battles and political rivalries, enlightens our understanding of Greek society during that period.

Sophists, itinerant paid instructors, developed a new style of teaching that was focused not upon the traditional values of the epics of Homer but upon the more practical instruction of how to advance in the professions of politics, law, teaching, and play writing. This was particularly true in the subjects of politics and law, where they taught the art of argument, **rhetoric**. Sophists focused upon winning the legal battle and supplied an argument for either side of an issue, regardless of the moral judgment of "right or wrong." By the mid–fifth century B.C., most sophists followed their fortunes to Athens, where their emphasis on rhetoric met with opportunities in the hire of young aristocrats primed for legal careers or with the commoner in the street who might be elected to the democratic council or argue for himself in a court of law.

Philosophy continued to challenge traditional thinking in the Classical Age. Socrates (469–399 B.C.) taught many students in Athens, but Socrates was not a sophist. He vehemently disagreed with the sophists' style of argumentation and situational morality and with their accepting payment for teaching. Like the sophists, however, Socrates did engage in dialogue with Athenian citizens, frequently questioning members of the Council, the archons, and other officials in public. This technique often infuriated and embarrassed those in leadership, as his probing questions demonstrated their ignorance. This behavior led his enemies to arrest him on charges of corruption and treason. After being convicted and sentenced to death, Socrates took poison (the usual means of execution for a citizen of his status) and died in 399 B.C. The Athenian democracy had executed a philosopher over the issue of freedom of speech.

Plato (427–347 B.C.) studied under Socrates and is the primary literary source for our knowledge of him. Like Socrates, Plato insisted upon clarity of thought and precise definition. He founded a school near Athens to teach his philosophy. Plato's political theory criticized democratic government; Plato believed that only the philosophically enlightened should have the responsibility of governing. Plato argued that government should be entrusted to individuals who have gone beyond the mere experiences of everyday life and who have achieved greater knowledge about the eternal principles of truth, beauty, and morality. These individuals' entire lives should be spent in the pursuit of higher knowledge and practical training. A leader, therefore, is not found among the wealthiest or most popular but is the one who despises wealth because of its baseness and who rejects pride because of its vanity. Such a leader would be a philosopher-king, a man incorruptible, truly indifferent to the usual accolades of the world.

Aristotle (384–322 B.C.) was Plato's most famous student and was the philosopher who invented formal **logic**, the methodology of systematic reasoning to discover truth. For Aristotle, no myth or revelation could produce as much knowledge as correct conclusions based upon accurate observation. Knowledge comes from the investigation of the causes of things, and Aristotle categorized four causes as a means to organize knowledge. Studying these causes leads to wisdom, which results in proper moral behavior. Aristotle's political philosophy led him to say that people are political animals. He saw human social

---

[8] **Herodotus:** hih RAHD uh tuhs
[9] **Thucydides:** thoo SIHD ih deez

evolution passing from birth and solitude to inter-action and learning in the family, to membership in the clan, to participation in the tribe, to the natural culmination of life in the polis. At the school that he founded, he studied more than 158 different constitutions, both Greek and foreign. Upon completing his analysis, Aristotle began to categorize the political systems into subgroups of monarchy, oligarchy, democracy, and others. Aristotle also studied biology and first arranged it into classifications. He applied his systematic use of observation and logic to order the particulars of nature and human experience.

Philosophers such as Plato and Aristotle are recognized for their persistence in trying to formulate moral political philosophies based upon ethics. Their contributions significantly influenced later political theory and philosophy, and their cosmologies laid the foundation for future speculation on the nature of the universe. Their cosmological theory of the earth as the center of the universe, for example, remained prominent in Western thought through the fifteenth century A.D.

THE EARLY HISTORY OF ROME

The Roman civilization developed from a small group of villages along the Tiber River by about 1000 B.C. and grew into an empire that enveloped much of the Mediterranean by 31 B.C. By about 600 B.C., the Etruscans, from lands just to the northwest, controlled the city of Rome and several of its neighboring cities. Rome rebelled against the Etruscans, finally winning its independence in 509 B.C. The study of Roman history is usually divided into three general eras: the Etruscan (around 600–509 B.C.), the Republic (509–31 B.C.), and the Empire (31 B.C.–A.D. 476). Chapter 7 covers the history of Etruscan Rome and the Republic, and the Roman Empire is discussed in Chapter 8.

Etruscan Rome, around 600–509 B.C.

The city of Rome gradually came under the political control of the Etruscans, whose twelve independent city-states flourished in the seventh and sixth centuries B.C. By around 600 B.C., an Etruscan monarch held the political reins of the city. Etruscan cities became important commercial centers for the Greek colonists from southern Italy, and the city of Rome continued to grow under Etruscan control. During Etruscan control, a restructuring of Roman society occurred.

The restructuring was similar to the changes made in Athens under Solon and Cleisthenes: The three original hereditary kin groups of the city were replaced with twenty-one regional fictive kinship groups, four urban and seventeen rural. The reason for the reorganization seems to have been for levying taxes and taking the census. As a result, old kinship loyalties were broken, and new Etruscan and immigrant families became influential.

The military probably reorganized under the Etruscans, although scholars still are unsure of the date when this occurred. Instead of fighting in clan blocks, soldiers mustered in **centuries**, groups of one hundred men. In times of emergency, the centuries would assemble together in a designated place. The assembly came to be called the Centurion Assembly. Membership in the centuries depended upon property ownership, paralleling development in Greece. Citizen-soldiers, like the hoplites of Greece, became the mainstay of the army.

Much of Etruscan culture influenced the Romans. The deities Jupiter and Juno were Etruscan and only later took on some characteristics of their Greek counterparts, Zeus and Hera. The Etruscans had used the Greek alphabet, which the Romans adopted and adapted, until it became the alphabet used by later European languages. Roman men also used the Etruscan toga, a white gown that became a symbol of citizenship status. Etruscans introduced Romans to long-distance trade with Greek colonists in southern Italy, a relationship that would eventually bring the Romans into the Mediterranean Sea trade network.

In the last years of the sixth century B.C., Etruscan monarchies outside of Etruria began to crumble. The customary date of the expulsion of the last Etruscan monarch from the city of Rome is 509 B.C., the traditional date for the founding of the Roman Republic.

The Republic, 509–31 B.C.

After the Etruscans were expelled, the Romans had to design a government. The political system was based upon the idea of government in public

FIGURE 7.7 *Etruscan Mural.* *This wall painting demonstrates the highly decorative art style of the Etruscans as found in the houses and tombs of the wealthy. Tomb painting usually depicted such events as banquets and funerals. Music was an important part of these Etruscan rites; lute and harp players accompany singers, and dancers perform the formal funeral dance for the occupant of the tomb. Etruscan wealth came from the cultivation of rich soils and from trade with Greek colonies, where Etruscan artists came into contact with and were influenced by Greek art. Etruscan art styles lived on in Roman art forms, particularly in Roman wall painting and architecture.* Scala/Art Resource, N.Y.

hands; Romans literally called the powers of government "public things." Romans hated the idea of monarchy and awarded leadership of the military to two army commanders, called **consuls**, who were elected yearly. Consuls held the power to command and coerce the troops and to execute the law. This division of power was similar to Sparta's choice of a two-king system to thwart the rise of a tyrant.

In addition, the elders of elite families within the city had acted as an advisory council, called the **Senate**, to the Etruscan king. Although the Senate had no formal legislative power, the consuls usually took its advice and sought its consent because elders were traditionally leaders in Roman society. The Senate emerged as a formidable body during the Republic because of the extension of this familial influence. Family lineage continued to play an important role in Roman political history.

A distinguished career gave the family prestige that translated into political opportunity; a respected family name could elevate a young politician into the heady circles of power politics.

The Centurion Assembly, mentioned earlier, met when called by the Senate. It elected the consuls and other officials from among candidates handpicked by the senators from their own families. As in Greece, the aristocrats continued to manipulate the outcome of elections. In times of emergency, the Centurion Assembly would be called to prepare for war.

As time passed, new offices and groups developed within the governmental structure, all controlled by powerful families. Although democratic elections were held, Rome was essentially governed by an oligarchy in the form of the Senate. Romans called their government *Senatus Populosque Romanus*, "the Senate and People of Rome."

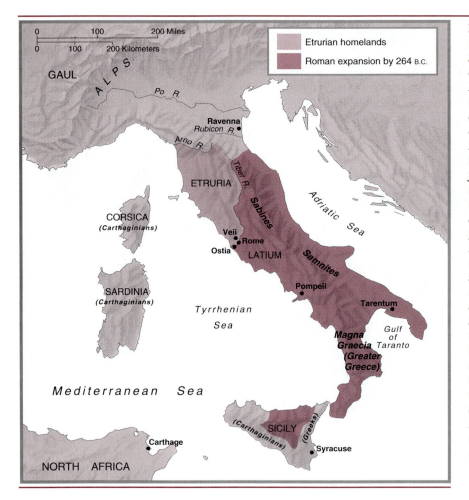

MAP 7.5 *Expansion of the Roman Republic, to 264 B.C.* *Roman conquest of central Italy brought Roman interests into conflict with established Greek colonies in southern Italy, called Magna Graecia. The Romans had drawn up treaties agreeing not to interfere in the politics or with the trade of southern Italian Greeks, provided they did not ally with any of the tribal peoples or cities falling to Roman expansion in the north. Once these areas were subdued, however, Roman interests turned to the south and Sicily. Roman ships were seen in the Gulf of Taranto near Tarentum in 282, a breach of the treaty that initiated hostilities with the Greeks. By 272 B.C., Magna Graecia was under Roman domination and soon Roman expansion into Sicily would spark the first war with Carthage.*

LIFE IN THE ROMAN REPUBLIC

Roman farming was little different from that of many civilizations. Oxen were raised and employed as draft animals. There was a variety of soil types in the area, so a variety of plows developed; some larger plows dug furrows in deep, rich soils, and other lighter plows scratched through the thinner layers of topsoil. Farmers rotated their crops and used animal dung or lentil crops to replenish the nutrients in their fields—unlike the Greeks, who replenished fields by leaving them fallow. These innovations led to higher annual production. Pigs, cattle, and sheep supplied meat; cattle and sheep supplied milk by-products. Olives were made into oil, grapes into wine, and grains into breads and porridges. The daily diet of the early Romans also included cabbages, turnips, and beans.

Family life and gender roles were also similar to those in Greece. Men were farmers, artisans, and laborers; wealthy men were occupied with the business of government. Only men were citizens. One of the most important roles for men was service in the Roman army. Every citizen between the ages of seventeen and forty-five spent a total of sixteen years in the Roman army, but service to the state could extend to twenty years in an emergency. These sixteen years were not usually served consecutively in the early Republic, and, because it was a citizen army, not everyone was called to fight at the same time. Usually armies consisted of about 20,000 troops. At first, fighting close to home did not significantly interfere with farming responsibilities. As the Republic expanded in later years, however, troops were forced to spend longer periods away from family and farms, and many became impoverished and lost their property. Because citizenship was a requirement for fighting in the army, loss of property resulted in ineligibil-

FIGURE 7.8 *Roman Family.* *This sarcophagus portrays a Roman family dining; the husband reclines and the wife plays music while the children romp with a pet dog. Slaves bring food, perhaps prepared with ingredients from as far away as the Black Sea or North Africa. Common dinners might include lamb, mackerel, or sowbelly cooked in salted tunafish brine. They might also feast on sliced eggs, leeks, ripe apples, or figs. As tomatoes were not imported into Italy until many centuries later, any dishes requiring a sauce used* liquamen, *made from the entrails and juice of cooked fish (which had a taste similar to anchovy paste). The normal drink was wine, usually watered down.* Vatican Museum.

ity to serve. Aristocrats, however, found that army service functioned as a ladder of opportunity for political advancement. Military offices were actually offices of state, and those with successful military careers garnered political power as well.

As in the Greek households, Roman women ran the business of the home. Women were engaged in the typical occupations of weaving and child rearing, and nonelite women attended wealthy women, serving as maids. A funerary inscription from Rome gives insight into the domestic lives of most women: "Here lies Amymone,[10] wife of Marcus, best and most beautiful, worker in wool, pious, chaste, thrifty, faithful, a stayer-at-home." Women also participated in Roman life as prostitutes and priestesses. Romans had fewer priestesses in their state cults than did the Greeks, but one of the most important religious functions of early Rome fell to the vestal virgins, who lived in the temple and tended the eternal hearth-flame of the goddess Vesta.

In the Republic, both women and children were literally under the hand of the husband or father, who had the power of life and death over them. Roman women did not even have personal names. A man usually had three names: a first or given name, a family name, and a clan name (Gaius Julius Caesar, for instance). Each woman bore the feminine form of her family name (such as "Julia" for the family of Julius). Women of the same name, living at the same time were designated by a number or the title of "the older" or "the younger."

Children were educated by their parents; there was no state-supported education, as there was in Greece. Most of the population remained illiterate, but wealthy parents saw to the formal education of their children. The mother had the responsibility of basic education until her children reached about seven years old, when a tutor (usually a slave) took over or the children were sent to small private schools, segregated by gender. Girls' formal education ended at about twelve or thirteen, after which they continued to be instructed in women's

[10] **Amymone:** ah MEE moh nay

UNDER THE LENS

Gods and Goddesses of Greece and Rome

Both Greeks and Romans were polytheistic. The primary deities tended to be anthropomorphic in both societies. Greeks often sculpted their gods and goddesses, but Romans less frequently portrayed their deities.

By the eighth century B.C., Greeks had developed the genealogy of deities. The origin of the deities, first written by a poet named Hesiod, was also a system of the origins of the universe. The entire system of deities is too complicated and contradictory to relate, but out of the copulation of these deities comes the pantheon of the twelve Olympian deities, named after their home on Mount Olympus. Each Greek polis had a particular deity as its patron and observed important religious ceremonies on that deity's behalf. Before the development of new cosmologies based on the four elements of air, water, fire, and earth in the sixth century B.C., belief in these anthropomorphic deities served to explain the origins of all things. People identified deities with particular functions, and with the personalities given in the myths, they emerged as topics of interesting and entertaining stories, as well as explanations for cosmic events. Zeus, the father of the deities, was associated with war, weather, and luck. Demeter was a goddess associated with agriculture and marriage. Apollo was the god of youth, music, poetry, and philosophy, and he was associated with the sun and enlightenment. Athena was goddess of wisdom and art as well as the patron deity of Athens.

After the introduction of formal philosophy in the sixth century B.C., belief in these deities often diminished among the intellectual elite, but the general population continued to worship them,

giving offerings and sacrifices at their temples. Old traditions are not easily given up. Little change in religious practice occurred until about the third century B.C.

The Roman religious experience was significantly different from that of the Greeks, who tended to be conservative in their beliefs. Instead of fearing the whims of their deities or ignoring them as many Greek philosophers did, the Romans viewed themselves as being in harmony with the will of their deities. Meticulous ritual kept them in a proper relationship with the myriad deities adopted throughout the years of expansion.

Roman religion, however, had less of a fixation on mythology, and few stories emerged. The deities were forces that wielded great power, but no priestly class developed to perform complicated rituals. Priestly functions were the business of the state and remained in the hands of political leaders; the chief priest, or *pontifex maximus,* was an elected position within the Roman government. Household deities also were piously revered after the example of Aeneas, who risked his life to bring the household deities out of burning Troy.

A major deity of Rome, Vesta, the goddess of the hearth, had no statue representing her in the city's temple. Vesta's hearth was the symbolic hearth of the city of Rome. A few girls between the ages of six and ten years were chosen to become vestal virgins, remaining in the temple's service until the age of thirty, at which time they could leave and marry. Each Roman household had a parallel responsibility, and the young girls and women of the household remained responsible for tending their home fires.

---

work. Boys continued their education to become participants in civic duties.

Romans originally worshiped animistic deities, but, after they came into contact with Etruscans (whose pantheon of anthropomorphic deities was similar to that of the Greeks), their religious attitudes changed. They adopted the Etruscan deities to their pantheon, and as they expanded throughout Italy and, eventually, into Mediterranean areas, they adopted conquered

peoples' religious practices as well. Over the centuries, Romans developed an ever-expanding list of officially acceptable deities to worship, believing that these deities would protect and strengthen the Republic if Roman citizens continued to worship them. The adoption of deities also aided in assimilating conquered peoples into the Republic.

The social structure initially featured three classes among Romans: the wealthy aristocratic class of **patricians**, the commoner class of **ple-**

beians, and slaves. In Roman society, you were born into the patrician or plebeian class and usually married within your class. The patricians acted as patrons to the client plebeians, who depended upon them for political favors, intercession in judicial matters, and help in times of emergency. Patronage in the Republic was similar to that of Greece. Plebeians supported their patrician patrons in elections to offices, while remaining ineligible themselves for influential positions because of their lower social status. As in many other societies, slaves were those who had fallen into debt and those who had been captured in war. The determination of aristocratic status and commoner status shifted from birth to wealth during the fourth century B.C., during a period of social reform.

EXPANSION DURING THE ROMAN REPUBLIC

Decades of upheaval followed the expulsion of Etruscan kings, as Rome and other city-states fought as allies to ensure that the Etruscan threat remained checked. Roman defense and trade interests led to warfare with their former Italian allies, and fragile alliances for mutual defense slowly deteriorated as the Romans expanded into neighboring territories. By the end of the third century B.C., with few exceptions, the Republic's military expansion caught all of Italy south of the Tiber in its political net.

Political control balanced upon a unique system of alliances that became the backbone of the

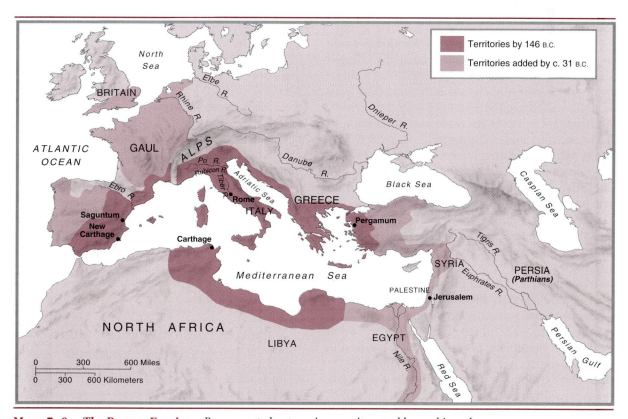

MAP 7.6 *The Roman Empire.* *Rome created an empire once it moved beyond its cultural area outside of Italy. By 146 B.C., Romans had acquired Carthaginian territories, including much of northern Africa, the southwestern coast of Europe, the coast of the eastern Adriatic, and Greece. By around 40 B.C., the Romans had conquered the interior of western Europe, most of modern Turkey, and the eastern coastal area of the Mediterranean Sea. Not long after, in 31 B.C., Egypt would also fall to Roman expansion. The Roman Empire then encircled the Mediterranean Sea, prompting them to call that body of water* Mare Nostrum, *"our sea." This encircling of the Mediterranean initiated a unified trade network that blossomed under the political unity of Rome.*

future Roman Empire, and the success of these alliances rested on new definitions of kinship as an element of citizenship. The award of citizenship was essentially the awarding of a Roman name, a holdover from the vestiges of clan membership prior to Etruscan restructuring. To have a Roman name meant that you were a member of a Roman family and deserved certain rights as a citizen. When Romans extended the rights of the Roman name to the people of a conquered city, the new citizens tended to remain loyal to the Republic because of the privileges attached. There were levels of citizenship, however, and those born of parents from the city of Rome enjoyed superior rights. Citizens of lesser status bore the majority of taxes and responsibilities but were better off than those without fictive kinship ties. The extension of the Roman name was significantly different from the Greek tendency to withhold citizenship from outsiders.

This expansion enriched the Republic's trade and created a military machine. Each city granted limited Roman citizenship also received special trade status with the city of Rome, but they were not allowed to negotiate treaties with other cities. All roads led to Rome for trade and diplomacy. In addition, the cities were required to send troops upon request, and this increase in the availability of thousands of citizen-soldiers to augment the centuries ensured that the Republic's army could win battles or wars by sheer numbers, regardless of skill. Enemies of Rome had difficulty defeating the Republic's army because an inexhaustible number of troops holding the Roman name were available from all over Italy.

Dominance also extended to independent allies of the Roman Republic with some differences; they did not receive citizenship, and their governments were allowed to continue ruling under the Republic's protection, as long as the local aristocrats remained loyal to Roman interests. The Republic's expansion into southern Italy was very different from Greek colonization. Greek colonies were populated by citizens who demanded political independence from the originating polis. They enjoyed a favored trade status but not compulsory political dependence. In Italy, cities had to submit to Roman political and economic supervision.

The Republic's trade interests moved beyond the Italian peninsula with three opportunistic wars fought with the city of Carthage, the Phoenician colony in northern Africa (264–146 B.C.). The Punic Wars, so called after the language of the Carthaginians, began when the Roman Republic challenged Carthage's dominance over commercial activities in the western Mediterranean. The battles that ensued demonstrated the tenacity of the Roman army. Three wars were fought (264–241 B.C., 218–202 B.C., and 150–146 B.C.) and, in the end, a siege by the Roman army ended in Carthage's complete destruction. The city was looted, then razed, the population killed or enslaved, and the territory annexed by the Roman Republic.

The Punic Wars actually brought the Roman Republic into an empire as it moved outside of its cultural base in Italy. The Romans took control of the western Mediterranean and continued expansion that took them northward into Gaul and eventually to England. Eastward expansion into Greece and Southwest Asia was initially a retaliation against the Macedonian monarch for aiding Carthage during the Punic Wars. Victory in the Macedonian Wars (215–146 B.C.) and the Syrian War (192–189 B.C.) brought Greece, most of modern Turkey, Syria, Palestine, and the Aegean Islands under Roman control. By the first century B.C., Egypt also fell to Roman rule, when Roman political rivalries drew the Egyptian queen into war. The Roman Empire then encircled the Mediterranean.

The new territories became Roman provinces and had a significant impact on Roman society. Land was available for economic exploitation and redistribution. The extension of the Roman name was awarded only selectively to peoples in the new provinces so that politicians in Rome could exploit the territories for higher taxes and personal investment opportunities.

Social, Political, and Economic Changes during Expansion

As in Greece, social conditions led to major tensions and reforms. Many plebeian soldiers who left their small farms for long periods to fight in foreign wars found themselves in financial distress when they returned. In addition, expansion had created an increase in wealthy plebeian traders, who wanted access to the privileges of the aristocratic patrician class. The first social conflict came in 494 B.C. after plebeian soldiers had experienced their first protracted absences from their farms while fighting against neighboring cities. Additionally, wealthy plebeian traders (many of them familiar with Greek democratic ideas through their trade contacts) aspired to participate in the governance of the Republic. The desperate plebeian farmers, spurred by the wealthy plebeians, marched out of the city and refused to fight in its defense. They organized themselves and demanded that the patricians recognize their elected representatives, **tribunes**. This plebeian boycott led to the formation of an assembly of plebeians called the Council of Plebeians, which enacted its own legislation. The Senate recognized the Council of Plebeians but maintained control through the process of giving advice to the council's members and consent to the council's actions before they could be recognized as law.

Reform came slowly, and, when grudgingly given by the patricians, its effects finally opened the door to power for wealthy plebeians and to occasional land reform for debtors. By 367 B.C., a law was enacted that each year at least one of the elected consuls must be a plebeian, breaking the exclusive hold of patricians on the consulship. Wealthy plebeians now could gain as much political prestige as patricians, and the traditional familial prestige could be inherited by plebeians, too. Henceforth, the distinction between wealthy plebeians and patricians diminished, and a new aristocracy based on wealth was formed that included both (much like the new ruling class in Athens under Solon's reforms).

The policy of expansion exacerbated the financial difficulties of the common farmers in the Republic. Because of the protracted wars fought in Spain, North Africa, and Gaul, many soldiers found themselves returning home after the campaigns to bankrupted farms. During the Second Punic War, Hannibal's soldiers fed off Italian farms and destroyed what they could not consume, leaving devastation in their wake. At the same time, increased trade from the new territories enriched the aristocrats, who bought these forfeited lands and used slave labor to farm them. The disenfranchised soldiers had little or no means of employment, and because many lost their property, their sons were no longer eligible for service in the army. In the second century B.C., while the Roman Republic was expanding geographically and trade was enriching many, the army was experiencing a manpower shortage, and the poor were becoming

FIGURE 7.9 *Voting in Republican Rome.* One of the significant changes in Roman politics was the initiation of the secret ballot in 137 B.C., which allowed lower-class Romans to vote without interference from the fiercely competitive Roman aristocracy. The aristocracy then moved from intimidation to bribery to ensure election to high office or passage of legislation. Later, when the optimate and populares parties emerged in Rome, each party spent large sums of money buying up votes among the poor and destitute. This coin shows the process of balloting. This citizen marked a piece of wood with a v, which represents an affirmative vote (v being the first letter of the Latin phrase meaning "as you propose"). Bibliothèque nationale, Paris.

destitute. Land reform came only sporadically through the Council of Plebeians, whose leadership was now part of the elite.

The poor found two brothers to champion social reform. Tiberius and Gaius Gracchus[11] challenged the ruling oligarchy by trying to force through reform legislation, like providing land for retiring soldiers so that their heirs would be eligible for military service. In 133 B.C., Tiberius, knowing that his initiation of reform could win him the gratitude of plebeian veterans and future success in elections, manipulated the vote in the Council of Plebeians to force land reform. Primarily concerned with how the reforms would affect their personal finances, the senators panicked, and violence broke out in the council meeting between

[11] **Gracchus:** GRAK uhs

Tiberius's supporters and those who were backed by senators. In the end, Tiberius was killed, along with many of his supporters. Using greater political sensitivity ten years later, his brother, Gaius, successfully introduced some reforms but eventually met the same end. Reforms came, but they only temporarily contained the discontentment. The oligarchy could not look beyond its own self-interest for long, and, consequently, the movement for reform initiated by the Gracchus brothers led to an atmosphere wherein new political parties emerged.

The **optimate**[12] party consisted of traditionalists who supported aristocratic control through old family alliances and senatorial contacts. The **populares**[13] party consisted of those who garnered the citizens' votes in exchange for reforms and grants. It was the same political game of patronage, but the old guard had competition from ambitious young politicians who saw that entitlements (giving away bread and arranging for circuses for entertainment of the urban poor) could buy them needed votes. The Gracchus brothers had inadvertently discovered a new political modus operandi: They could bypass the old oligarchy and use the mass vote of the poor to win elections and pass legislation. From now on, the optimate and populares factions rivaled for political control, creating a new ruling class of about two thousand wealthy, competitive politicians.

The Impact of Expansion on Roman Elite Culture

Expansion increased the trade and revenues flowing into the city of Rome and allowed many merchants and politicians to become extremely wealthy. Many used their buying power to purchase even more land, the traditional source of wealth. Large estates began to specialize in certain lucrative cash crops, such as grapes and olives. After Carthage's defeat, Italy became the major producer of wine and olive oil for Mediterranean trade. In addition, large estates also could support the grazing requirements of cattle, which provided leather, meat, and cheese. Slowly, as expansion continued around the Mediterranean, and, as cash crops became more popular in Italy, the Republic increased imports of basic commodities and

regional products. The economic result was a greater fiscal gap between the wealthy and the increasing number of poor, who were reduced to trading their votes for patronage and handouts.

Roman engineering developed massive building projects. A vast system of aqueducts carried water to thirsty citizens. It has been estimated that more than 220 million gallons of water per day came over the aqueducts into the city of Rome, furnishing fountains, public bathhouses, and households. Aqueducts employed the use of another engineering design, the arch. Romans had cut down most of the tall timber, and finding trees large enough for beams in large buildings proved difficult. The arch was a good engineering solution; it could support massive amounts of pressure, and Roman architects found it more stable than a flat beam in the new architectural styles of vaults and domes. The refining of arches and the development of concrete enabled some of the Republic's most memorable architectural accomplishments.

Romans linked their city and their newly won territories together with a system of roads built during the late Republic and continuing through the Empire period. The Via Appia[14] was built around 312 B.C. and, as a major thoroughfare into the city, brought thousands of ox-drawn carts loaded with harvests and goods into the city. Both slaves and soldiers worked on the massive road network; each road was first surveyed and then layered with sand, lime concrete and stone, more sand, and, finally, stone blocks set with concrete. Small gaps were filled with flint and pebbles to create a relatively smooth surface. These durable roads can still be seen in many places throughout Europe. They remained invaluable to trade, troop transport, communications, and travel.

Many members of the Roman elite enjoyed listening to political orations and reading the opinions of popular writers. Public speaking remained a means to fame, and successfully arguing legal cases often led to a promising political career. Cato the Elder (234–149 B.C.) argued in public addresses for preservation of traditional Roman values of austerity and patriotism in the face of newly imported foreign (particularly Greek) ideas infiltrating the Republic during its expansion. He complained of lax moral behavior, economic extravagance, and increased freedom of women.

---

[12] **optimate:** AHP tih mayt
[13] **populares:** pahp yoo LAHR es

[14] **Via Appia:** VEE yah AHP pee ah

FIGURE 7.10 *Ruins of the Roman Forum. Rome's forum was at the heart of the ancient city of Rome, in an area that developed into a government and market center with many buildings, temples, and shops. The architecture of the forum was duplicated in most of the areas that the Romans conquered. The phrase "all roads lead to Rome" came from the idea of the Golden Milestone in the center of the forum, where all roads to Rome converged. No chariot traffic was allowed in this bustling area, but hundreds of people, buying and selling goods and on their way to official business, crowded the lanes. It was in one of the buildings of the forum that the Senate presided and great speeches were delivered by Roman orators such as Cicero. This was also where Gaius Julius Caesar met his death at the hands of assassins in 44 B.C.* Dan Budnik / Woodfin Camp & Associates.

He was elected to a position that gave him the authority to enact reforms to improve moral behavior and curb economic excesses.

Cicero (106–43 B.C.) became the most famous of Rome's orators during the Republic. Although not born to wealth, he received support from a wealthy Roman entrepreneur who financed his career in politics. His individual talent for public speaking soon took him to the forefront of the Republic's elite. Fifty-eight out of more than one hundred of his speeches survive, as do eight hundred of his letters. These documents reveal to us the typical lifestyle of the successful politician of the Republic. Cicero's luxurious and cultured life included ownership of a mansion in the city of Rome and at least eight country houses. Several of the country houses were large villas, richly fur-

nished with wall paintings, floor mosaics, and Greek art. Like many of his day, he studied and followed the tenets of the school of Greek philosophy called **Stoicism** (the belief that knowledge and wisdom are virtuous and that a virtuous person lives in harmony with nature). Romans were not known for their own philosophical treatises but readily adopted Greek concepts. Cicero accepted the Stoic idea that no person should tyrannize another, and all should treat one another generously, because all humans have equal personal value. The reading of Stoic moral philosophy in Cicero's treatises influenced later Western thinkers down to the present day. The late Republic's politics were volatile, however, and Cicero found himself embroiled in the rivalries of a civil war; he died trying to escape execution in 43 B.C.

THE END OF THE ROMAN REPUBLIC

The Republic of the second century B.C. was essentially an empire, still governed by a political structure that was more in tune with the needs of a city-state. Rampant mismanagement of conquered territories persisted and was infrequently criticized by anyone with enough influence to change policies. Individuals desiring only to advance politically gained reputations that brought prestige and power. Eventually they retired into the Senate, where their personal accomplishments determined senatorial rank. Each retiring government official coveted the title "First Man of the Senate."

Power shifted from the Senate to consuls. Because of continuing battles in Gaul and in North Africa and a reluctance by the Senate to institute long-lasting debt relief, the property qualification for the army was dropped. This action opened the door for the creation of a professional standing army. Landless men could serve, and, upon retirement, their consuls requested that the Senate and Council of Plebeians award them severance pay in land, usually in one of the new territories. This innovation alleviated the habitual shortage of troops but also shifted troop allegiance to the consuls and away from the state, essentially making soldiers clients of the consuls. Consuls soon discovered that the army and not the Senate could dictate who would win elections and advance up the political ladder.

Ambitious consuls used foreign wars to satisfy their own appetites for greater prestige and wealth. Abuse of authority even led consuls to march their armies into Rome and place the city under dictatorial power. In 88 B.C., rivalry between two consuls, Marius (157–86 B.C.) and Sulla (138–78 B.C.), resulted in Sulla's marching his army into the city of Rome and declaring martial law. The majority of the Senate backed Sulla, an optimate, against Marius, a populares. Sulla received dictatorial power—full legislative, military, and financial control—and executed Marius's supporters. In 81 B.C., Sulla enacted legislation prohibiting any future commander from bringing troops into Rome. Although Sulla restored control to the Republic after he gave up his dictatorial powers and retired in 79 B.C., the precedent was set.

Figure 7.11 Caesar. *Statues like this figure of Gaius Julius Caesar were often used for propaganda in ancient Roman society. Shown in the carefully chosen dress and pose of a commander, this statue demonstrated the military authority of Caesar to all who viewed it. Each commander in Rome was given authority to lead his troops; this authority was called the* imperium *and the commander was called the* imperator. *The nature of the command determined the amount of* imperium. *Consuls held greater* imperium *than any other commander except a dictator, who held supreme* imperium. *When Gaius Julius Caesar became Perpetual Dictator, it meant he would hold supreme* imperium *for life. This is in part why his enemies assassinated him; they were fearful of this kind of military power because it reminded them of a king's power.* Alinari/Art Resource, N.Y.

In the middle of the first century B.C., the precedent was repeated during a rivalry between Gaius Julius Caesar (100–44 B.C.) and Pompey (106–48 B.C.). At first they formed an alliance with Crassus, another politician. The alliance was called the First Triumvirate and served as a means to gain mutual support. When Crassus died, however, the alliance disintegrated into rivalry because Julius Caesar was a populares and Pompey was an optimate. Civil war finally broke out in 49 B.C. Caesar began the war when he decided to illegally cross the Rubicon River, the border of the province of Gaul, and march his army to Rome. By the end of 45 B.C., Caesar held Rome and established himself as dictator. Pompey was dead and the Senate was cowed.

Caesar enacted many reforms for the betterment of the general population, including land grants for the resettlement of thousands of the impoverished to new territories. He remained unable to pacify the optimate party in the Senate, however, and he infuriated many of his populares supporters by enlarging the Senate from 600 to 900 members with Germanic representatives from the province of Gaul. In 44 B.C., he accepted the title of Perpetual Dictator, and his enemies interpreted this as a move toward monarchy. In secret meetings they conspired against him, and, on the Ides of March (March 15), 44 B.C., Caesar was assassinated on his way into the Senate.

Roman politics never reverted to the system of government of the early city-state. After the death of Caesar came another period of civil war and reorganization under the subtle brilliance of Caesar's nephew, Octavian. Like his uncle, Octavian gained singular control of the political structure. The formal end of the Republic came with the defeat of Octavian's last rival at the battle of Actium in 31 B.C., but, in a sense, the Republic died with Caesar's last gasp in 44 B.C.

GREECE AND ROME COMPARED

The histories of Greece and the Roman Republic demonstrate their unique experiences in global history, yet they exhibit some similar basic social and political developments. In the polis period of Greek history, roughly 800 to 338 B.C., and in the Roman Republican period, roughly 509 to 31 B.C., the peoples of Greece and Rome experienced social and political pressures that precipitated reorganization.

Greek and Roman cultures developed in strikingly similar ways.

—Both societies originated as city-states.

—Both societies viewed kinship (the family or clan structures) as the basis for political development.

—Both societies slowly moved away from a hereditary aristocracy toward one based on wealth.

— Changes in warfare and expansion resulted in social pressures that led to the development of limited citizens' rights and reforms.

—Both societies had a form of patron-client relationship, in which the wealthier citizens provided protection in exchange for political support.

—Both societies often had social unrest when the patron relationship was abused or ignored.

Although there were many similarities, there were also many differences between Greek and Roman development.

—As each society experienced growth, the Greeks usually sent out colonies that remained independent, with jealously guarded citizenship, while the Romans usually conquered and gave citizenship to foreign peoples.

—Greek political history usually moved through several styles of government, including monarchy, oligarchy, tyranny, and democracy, as social pressures dictated. Rome experienced monarchy under the Etruscans but rejected it in favor of oligarchy. Many aspects of the Republic's government were democratic, but its political history is really the history of the ruling class. Finally, the Republic succumbed to imperial control after years of civil war.

—The Athenian attempt at economic and political dominance led to Greek rebellion, while Roman control of neighboring areas of Italy led to empire.

ROME			GREECE		
				Lyric Age, c. 800–500 B.C.	800 B.C. — Cultural unification of Greece, c. 800 B.C.
					—
					—
					—
					700 B.C. — Greek colonization expands, c. 700 B.C.
			Age of Tyrants, c. 675–600 B.C.		— Greek Helots revolt, c. 650 B.C.
					— Sappho, Greek poet, born 612 B.C.
Etruscan control of Rome, 600–509 B.C.					600 B.C. —
					—
					—
					— Cleisthenes forms a democracy in Athens, 508 B.C.
Roman Republic, 509–31 B.C.	Roman expansion, c. 500–31 B.C.		Athenian domina-tion of the Delian League, c. 479–431 B.C.	Classical Age, c. 500–338 B.C.	500 B.C. — Roman council of Plebeians formed, 494 B.C.
					— Sophocles, Greek philosopher, 496–406 B.C.
					—
					400 B.C. —
					— Plebeians eligible Roman for consulship, 367 B.C.
					— Romans build Via Appia, c. 312 B.C.
					300 B.C. —
					—
					— Cato the Elder, Roman statesman, 234–149 B.C.
					200 B.C. —
					—
					—
					— Cicero, Roman statesman, 106–43 B.C.
					100 B.C. —
					—
					— Battle of Actium, 31 B.C.

SUMMARY

1. The geography of Greece contributed to attitudes of exclusiveness and independence. Citizenship was originally based on kinship. Oppressive aristocracies had to yield to demands for citizens' rights in order to get hoplites to fight for their cities and defend the wealth of aristocrats.

2. There was a variety of governing forms, including oligarchy, tyranny, and democracy. Athenian democracy is an example of political reformers' restructuring government to meet the citizens' needs. Sparta is a singular example of reorganization into a military state that employed elements of monarchy, oligarchy, and democracy, creating a mixed government.

3. Greek society originally consisted of three classes: aristocrats, commoners, and slaves. A merchant class developed as long-distance trade expanded. By about 800 B.C., the polis developed around the agora.

4. Greek gender roles mirror those of many early civilizations: Men were primarily farmers, and women were weavers and caretakers for children.

5. Many Greek poleis sent out colonies that were associated with the originating polis through trade and religious observance. The expansion of long-distance trade brought new wealth to many families.

6. The fifth century B.C. was a century of conflict marked by the Persian Wars, Athenian dominance, and the Peloponnesian Wars.

7. The Lyric and Classical ages of Greek history were fertile artistic periods. Sappho was an important poet from the Lyric Age, and new styles in sculpture and literature flourished under increased patronage in the Classical Age. Philosophers of both periods challenged old ways of thinking.

8. The city of Rome fell to the political control of the Etruscans. A rebellion expelled the Etruscan king and established the Roman Republic in 509 B.C. The Republic's government was basically oligarchical, ruled by the Senate, with consuls in charge of the army.

9. Roman society had three classes: aristocratic patrician, commoner plebeian, and slave. Social reform in the fourth century B.C. made the distinction between patrician and plebeian less significant. A new class system emerged based on wealth rather than birth.

10. The Republic was a period of great geographical expansion. The Punic Wars resulted in empire, and the Republic continued to expand into western Europe, southeastern Europe, Palestine, and Egypt.

11. Expansion and constant warfare brought about plebeian boycotts for land reform and increased opportunities for political advancement. Sociopolitical pressures created a two-party system of optimates and populares.

12. Romans built roads to connect their territories and aqueducts to bring water from long distances. The elite took advantage of the increased wealth resulting from the Republic's expansion and patronized the arts.

13. Roman governance disintegrated into competitions between rivals that finally ended in civil wars and assassination. The Republic ended in 31 B.C.

SUGGESTED READINGS

Boardman, John, Jasper Griffen, and Oswyn Murray, eds. *Greece and the Hellenistic World.* Oxford History of the Classical World Series. New York: Oxford University Press, 1988. Good coverage of social history, philosophy and the arts, and political history.

Boren, Henry C. *Roman Society.* Second edition. Lexington, Mass.: D. C. Heath, 1992. A general cultural history of Rome.

Frost, Frank. *Greek Society.* Third edition. Lexington, Mass.: D. C. Heath, 1987. A short but informative history of Greece, with special sections on the Greek people.

Grant, Michael. *The History of Rome.* New York: Charles Scribner's Sons, 1978. A standard history of Rome.

Green, Peter. *Ancient Greece.* New York: Thames and Hudson, 1979; reprint, 1989. A well-illustrated history of Greece for the general reader.

Lefkowitz, Mary R., and Maureen B. Fant. *Women's Life in Greece and Rome.* Second edition. Baltimore: Johns Hopkins University Press, 1992. A primary sourcebook, full of insights into women's lives in ancient Greece and Rome.

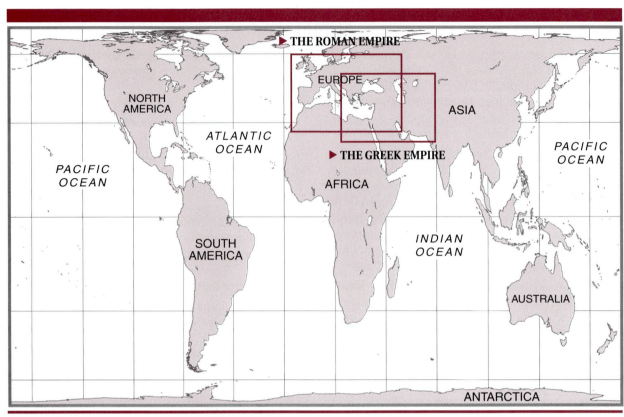

THE ROMAN EMPIRE

THE GREEK EMPIRE

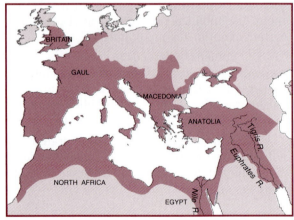

▶ THE ROMAN EMPIRE

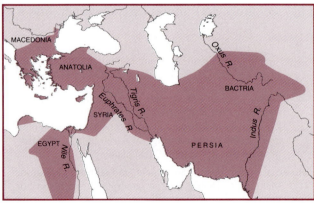

▶ THE GREEK EMPIRE

The Greek Empire, the Hellenistic Age, and the Roman Empire

359 B.C.–A.D. 476

You must now at last perceive of what kind of a universe you are a part, and the true nature of the lord of the universe of which your being is a part, and how a limit of time is fixed for you, which if you do not use for clearing away the clouds from your mind, it will go and you will go, and it will never return.
—MARCUS AURELIUS

This quotation from the writings of Marcus Aurelius (reign dates 161–180), a Roman emperor, shows us the blending of the Greek and Roman cultures. Marcus Aurelius followed Stoicism, a Greek philosophy popular in the Roman Empire. This chapter examines Greek expansion and empire, the Hellenistic Age, and the Roman Empire, with an emphasis on the cultural interaction between conquerors and indigenous peoples.

THE GREEK EMPIRE, 359–323 B.C.

After 479 B.C., Greeks were always mindful of the potential for another Persian war, and their fear of Persian attack led them to discussions on reorganizing a coalition for common defense. A leader in this movement spoke eloquently in favor of Philip of Macedon (reign dates 359–336 B.C.) as the natural military commander of the coalition. The opposition, however, warned against what they viewed as Philip's imperialist intentions. The poleis remained indecisive, with frequent eruptions of violence over the issue. Soon Philip held all of Greece, and, after his untimely death, his son Alexander conquered Persia.

Macedonian Greece, 359–336 B.C.

Macedonia, located in southeastern Europe, developed politically differently from the rest of Greece. The peoples of the area formed a patchwork of independent tribal principalities with strong kings instead of the poleis common in the rest of Greece. Macedonians were less urbanized than their southern neighbors, and other Greeks considered them barbarous and uncouth cousins. While the rest of Greece evolved toward urbanization, Macedonia did not develop the central administration necessary to support urban economic development. Macedonian tribes spent a considerable amount of time on border security. During a period of relative peace, unification was finally achieved under Philip II, whose exploits earned him a reputation for military skill and leadership far beyond Macedonia.

Philip II had forged a strong, loyal, professional army during his political career, and through diplomacy and warfare he gained a foothold in northern Greece. A war over the governance of the polis of Delphi, which housed the very popular and lucrative Oracle of Apollo, brought Philip and his army into central Greece. The poleis of Athens and Thebes united against his invasion, but the union crumbled when confronted by his superior military expertise. After his victory, Philip offered generous terms for peace, particularly to Athens, and managed to set up a coalition that united all Greek poleis into one uneasy confederacy under his authority. Shortly after the establishment of the confederacy and on the eve of beginning a campaign against Persia, Philip of Macedon was assassinated.

Philip's young son Alexander (reign dates 336–323 B.C.) took the helm of government. Although only nineteen years old, Alexander already was known as a brilliant commander of Philip's cavalry. Alexander soon redrew the map of Greece and Southwest Asia and thus received the accolade "the Great." Alexander's attentions first focused on crushing Greek uprisings against Macedonian rule. By the spring of 334 B.C., Alexander was ready to pursue his father's plan to liberate the Greek poleis in the Turkish Peninsula from Persian control. He left a trusted friend and troops behind to maintain his interests in Greece and Macedonia and attacked Persia. He never returned; his conquests kept him occupied until his death in 323 B.C.

Alexander's Conquests, 334–323 B.C.

Alexander engaged the Persian army in the northern Turkish Peninsula and then moved southward in a series of victorious campaigns. In 333 B.C., he fought the Persian king Darius III, who retreated from the battlefield when he realized that the

FIGURE 8.1 *Alexander as Egyptian Pharaoh.*
This Egyptian coin depicts Alexander wearing ram's horns, a symbol of power and authority throughout Southwest Asia, including Egypt. Alexander took the title of pharaoh, the incarnate son of Amon-Ra and the religious and political leader of all Egyptians. Egyptian subjects transferred their loyalty to Alexander and helped support his defeat of the Persian king, Darius. This coin was minted as a propaganda aid to demonstrate Alexander's authority as the conqueror and new king of Egypt. Ptolemy, one of Alexander's generals, seized Egypt as his own kingdom after Alexander's death in 323 B.C., setting up the Ptolemaic dynasty that reigned until 31 B.C. The Ptolemies also used coinage to depict their authority. Gift of Mrs. George M. Brett. Museum of Fine Arts, Boston.

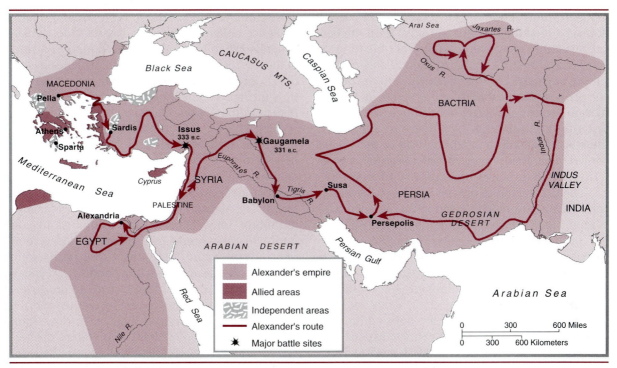

M A P 8 . 1 *Alexander's Empire.* *Between 333 B.C. and 323 B.C., Alexander had conquered most of Southwest Asia. Because of the rapidity of his conquests, Alexander was given the accolade of "the Great." Throughout European history, Alexander remained a hero to military leaders.*

Greeks were winning the day. This victory allowed Alexander to move southwestward along the Mediterranean coast, subduing cities in Palestine and liberating Egypt from Persian control. The Egyptians, already in a state of rebellion against Persia, hailed Alexander as a liberator and acclaimed him pharaoh. While in Egypt, he designed the city of Alexandria on the Mediterranean coast, one of several cities Alexander founded that bore his name.

By 331 B.C., Alexander left Egypt in pursuit of Darius. Going into the interior of Persia, Alexander systematically subdued numerous Persian cities, where vast treasures were stored. Darius was defeated again in 331 at the battle of Gaugamela[1] and fled a second time, only to be assassinated by his second in command, Bessus. When Bessus engaged Alexander in 330 B.C., he fared no better than his predecessor. Upon Bessus's capture, Alexander had him brutally killed in retaliation for assassinating his king.

With this victory, Alexander pressed on from the coast of the Caspian Sea and finally reached the Indus River Valley. Alexander forged ahead, penetrating the Punjab region, but his troops, exhausted, homesick, and fearful they might never return, demanded he halt the advance. For three days Alexander sulked in his tent, but then accepted the will of his army and began the return to Persia. The travail on the retreat route down the Indus River and then along the Indian Ocean and the Persian Gulf nearly caused Alexander's first defeat, as sickness and difficult terrain impeded the army's progress. Returning to Babylon after traveling more than 20,000 miles, his soldiers were fewer in number but full of stories about their conquests and the exotic Indian subcontinent.

The Problem of Governance in the Greek Empire

As of 330 B.C., Alexander was the king of kings, an emperor over a vast domain stretching from Greece and Egypt to the edge of the Indus River. The conqueror made few structural changes in the old Persian government; its subjects were used to changes of rulers and hardly noticed the minimal

[1] **Gaugamela:** gow geh MEHL ah

reorganization at the top. The only major innovation separated the military authority from the fiscal structure in western territories, creating a centralized financial administration to ensure that tribute payments did not disappear into the pockets of local commanders and troops. In Egypt, Alexander basically governed through traditional systems as pharaoh, and in Greece he remained the king of Macedonia and the head of the Greek confederacy. Maintaining control over such a vast territory with diverse peoples proved difficult.

The Greek Empire did not survive Alexander's early demise from an infection in old wounds complicated by heavy drinking, but even Alexander probably could not have held the empire together. The problems went beyond the mere governance of a vast territory; the greatest obstacles lay in very basic traditions of Greek culture. Macedonian troops viewed their kings as first among equals, and other Greek troops continued to resist the concept of empire at the expense of their poleis' independence. Finally, Greeks continued to view their culture as superior to all others and socially segregated themselves from indigenous peoples. Alexander's attempts to unite all the peoples of his empire failed to overcome these deeply rooted beliefs.

Alexander had initiated a campaign of integration between the Greek military and local peoples within the empire. This was done with various levels of success. He brought Persian cavalry into his army and began to train young Persians in the Macedonian style of warfare. Alexander also encouraged social integration; he married into the Persian nobility and forced his highest officers to marry Persians as well. One story tells of Alexander at a mass wedding banquet; as he mixed water and wine for drinking (dilution was a common practice), he announced that just as the wine and water mixed, so did the blood of the peoples. Although the marriages produced children, the families tended to perpetuate Greek lifestyles over indigenous customs because the fathers were Greek.

Alexander adopted both the Persian and Egyptian styles of kingship, with their ceremonies and royal costumes. He insisted that his commanders prostrate themselves before addressing him in court, as the Persian subjects traditionally did. Adoption of such ceremonies angered and alienated his Macedonian officers, who had enjoyed his close camaraderie and trust. He increasingly gave audience to Persian advisors over his Macedonian generals. When Alexander declared himself divine, in the tradition of all pharaohs of Egypt, he insisted that even his Greek troops accept him as deified, thus further distancing him from them and from his Macedonian heritage.

These cultural innovations were too much for the Greek sense of superiority over the other peoples of the empire and Greek attitudes toward kingship; troops reacted with disdain and rebellion at Alexander's promotion of a divine emperorship. By 324 B.C., Alexander again found himself facing a mutinous army. Many of the troops wanted to return to their homelands or demanded greater rights. At the same time, the Greek poleis were straining to regain their independence. Persian subjects also had reservations; many of the governors chosen from Persian nobility resisted reorganization and mismanaged their territories. Upon Alexander's death in 323 B.C., the empire disintegrated into rival territories. A successor had not been named, and the ambitious, battle-hardened veteran officers of his campaigns engaged in a geographical tug of war for the next fifty years.

THE SUCCESSOR STATES, 323–31 B.C.

By 272 B.C., three commanders emerged as the inheritors of most of the Greek Empire. Ptolemy,[2] a trusted friend of Alexander since boyhood, established a dynasty that held Egypt until it fell to the Romans in 31 B.C. Another commander, Seleucus,[3] successfully took Babylon in 311 B.C. and established himself as the dynastic ruler of the heartland of the old Persian Empire. He added Syria, Palestine, and Mesopotamia to his holdings, and his successors governed a Seleucid[4] Empire until Rome conquered much of the area in 62 B.C.

Macedonia and Greece were another matter. The third commander, Antigonus, returned to Greece and established the Antigonid dynasty, which tried to control the constantly rebelling

---

[2] **Ptolemy:** TAHL uh mee
[3] **Seleucus:** sih LOO kuhs
[4] **Seleucid:** sih LOO sihd

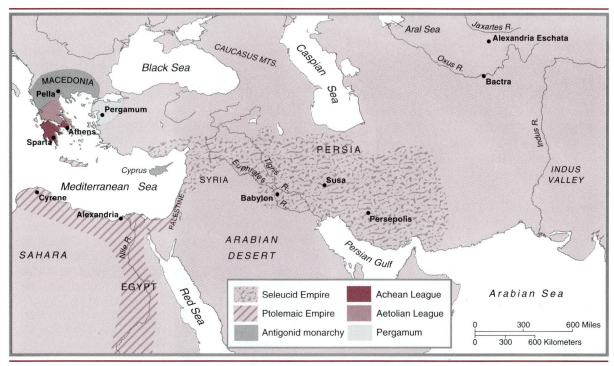

MAP 8.2 *Successor States.* *The Greek Empire did not survive Alexander's death in 323 B.C. Although his generals fought for control of various areas, no one was able to unite these territories again until the rise of Islam in the seventh century A.D. In the end, three successor states survived and two Greek defensive leagues developed.*

poleis. A philosopher of the period, Diogenes, requested that he be buried face down because, "in a little while, what is down will be up." This sentiment reflects the upheaval during the struggle to retain Macedonian overlordship of Greece. Defensive leagues were established against the Antigonids, with the innovation of multi-polis citizenship to strengthen the alliance. Nevertheless, many rivalries and the continued promotion of polis independence led to conflict. By 200 B.C., Greek embassies had appeared in the Roman Senate begging for help against Macedonian aggression. The Romans, who harbored a grudge against the Macedonian king for aiding Carthage during the Second Punic War, mounted a campaign against Macedonia that finally concluded with a peace settlement. The Greek poleis were declared free at the Isthmian Games in 196 B.C., and the thunderous response of the spectators is said to have killed a flock of birds flying overhead. Little did the Greeks realize that their continued requests for assistance to intervene between feuding poleis would bring

Romans permanently into Greece. By the first century B.C., most of the territory of the three Hellenistic successor states had succumbed to Roman occupation, and the history of Greece became entwined with the history of the Roman Empire.

THE HELLENISTIC AGE, 323–31 B.C.

Greeks had been calling themselves **Hellenes** since about the seventh century B.C., and scholars have named the era from 323 to 31 B.C. the Hellenistic Age because of the spread of Greek culture, **Hellenization**, across Southwest Asia and the Mediterranean basin. To a large degree, the process of Hellenization remained an urban phenomenon, because most Greeks who populated the cities remained culturally separated from the surrounding rural countryside. In a sense, Hellenization was a veneer.

FIGURE 8.2 *Hellenistic Theater.* *This Greek theater was constructed on a hillside in Pergamum, a city on the coast of the Anatolian peninsula. It demonstrates the importing of Classical Greek architecture into Hellenized areas. Drama was a significant part of social life in all Greek cities, much like the cinema in American culture today. The hillside construction provided acoustical advantages: As the players spoke their lines, the sound would rise up to even those seated at the very top of the theater. This theater shared the acropolis of Pergamum with a temple to Zeus and the royal palace of the kingdom of Pergamum.* Elizabeth Steiner/German Archaeological Institute, Istanbul. Courtesy of National Geographic Society Image Collection.

Hellenistic Cities

In most of the successor states, the rural areas absorbed little of Greek culture, and the Greeks of the urban centers remained aloof from many local customs, preferring their Greek heritage. It was the cities that were the conduits of intellectual and social interaction. In the cities, members of the ethnic elites often adopted Greek culture, including dress, mannerisms, and education. Local peoples tended to become bilingual, while most Greeks spoke only their own language. No common calendar prevailed, and no common body of law governed the cities until after the Hellenistic Age. The larger, more integrated Hellenistic cities, like Alexandria, eventually overcame Greek prejudices, and the indigenous elite found equal opportunities for advancement and political power.

The city of Alexandria, in Egypt, is perhaps the best example of a Hellenistic city. Alexander the Great laid out the city on a grid pattern, and the new city became the capital of Egypt. It grew into an unusually large city and became a regional administrative center, with residents from Palestine, Syria, Arabia, Babylon, and elsewhere in southwestern Asia. The most famous structures of Hellenistic Alexandria were the lighthouse and the museum-library. Temples, gymnasia, and theaters in the city were constructed in the Greek style.

In the Hellenistic Age, life changed significantly for elite women but little for those in other classes. Elite Hellenistic women had more access to wealth than their Classical Greek predecessors, as Greeks amassed fortunes from increased trade and power over new territories. More and more of the wives of statesmen participated in political intrigues. Some women became monarchs in two of the Hellenistic kingdoms that emerged after Alexander's death, becoming role models for other elite women. The most famous was probably Cleopatra VII, queen of Egypt. The Hellenistic Age opened formal education to elite women, who participated in intellectual movements of the day.

Wealth was the friend of opportunity; conversely, poverty was the companion of failure. Large slums surrounded the city centers. The feeling of belonging, so paramount in the kinship ties of the polis, gave way to feelings of displacement and disorientation. As a result, people tended to band into groups for personal identity. These groups were professional guilds and religious cults that gave a sense of security in an increasingly alienating social environment.

The Hellenistic Exchange

Although perhaps not as significant as later exchanges, like the Islamic, Mongol, and American exchanges, many kinds of cultural exchange occurred during the Hellenistic Age. For example, both plants and animals were part of the exchange. Greeks transplanted their olive trees and grapevines into new areas. One of Ptolemy's officials transplanted 300 fir trees onto his Egyptian estate, and, in another instance, palm trees were sent to Greece for planting. In addition, local spices were added to Greek perfumes. Parks and zoos housed animals exotic to Greeks but common to local peoples. Ideas also formed a part of the Hellenistic exchange, as philosophies and religions found new audiences. Mystery cults, for example, were a new expression of the powers of ancient deities, and religions like Judaism and Zoroastrianism found new adherents among various Hellenistic populations.

Food was a significant part of the exchange. Veterans of Alexander's campaigns returned to Greece with a variety of new foods they had encountered. Foremost among these, in the eyes of Greeks, were onions from Egypt and shallots from Phoenicia. The heatlike sensation these vegetables produced in the mouth was believed to spur the "martial ardor" of soldiers, making them more valiant in battle. These vegetables, therefore, were used as a kind of strategic weapon. Another import brought to Greece through Alexander's campaigns was sugar from India, known at that time as "solid honey" or "Indian salt"; it was very rare in Greece and used only for medicine. More commonly used was the lemon, introduced from Persia or India, also by the Alexandrian veterans.

Ease of travel helped the exchange of goods. The Persian road system was improved, with more inns and water supplies available to weary, thirsty travelers. The Persian road system was linked to the extensive silk-road trade, bringing silk (in both raw form and as finished cloth), skins, and spices westward and taking wines, linen, horses, and pomegranates eastward. Trade increased through-out Southwest Asia, and, although there were few technological innovations in shipping, larger ships carried greater amounts of goods. Larger port facilities, breakwaters to protect ships, and more warehouses were constructed. In some cases, improving port facilities was necessary for the increase in numbers and size of the ships.

The foods coming into Greece through trade were numerous. *Foie gras*, the enlarged liver of a force-fed goose, was an Egyptian delicacy that was introduced to Greece in this period, just as cumin seed was introduced as a seasoning from Syria. Cheesecakes were popular among Greeks, and various regional styles from all over the eastern Mediterranean were available at urban Greek bakeries, often prepared by bakers from the city where the recipe originated.

Hellenistic Arts and Sciences

Education of elite Greek men in Hellenistic cities continued, consisting of the teaching of basic grammar, math, music, and traditional mythologies from age seven to about fourteen years. From fourteen to about eighteen years, more sophisticated language studies began and were augmented with geography and the study of Homeric epics. At eighteen, schooling centered on the gymnasium, where athletics and advanced literature were the focus. Many of the larger cities' gymnasia had their own libraries and provided lectures on literature for their members. Finally, the wealthiest individuals were tutored in philosophy and rhetoric. In part, the extensive schooling in traditional Greek culture preserved Greek tradition for Greeks living far from the poleis. These young aristocrats then became the officials of the royal courts. Anyone who wanted access to the Greek elite had to become Hellenized.

Hellenistic literature focused on new interests and developed new styles. In each of the successor areas Greek historians wrote local histories. For example, several histories of Egypt and Babylonia were produced. Many literary works attest to the amount of travel during the Hellenistic Age. Megasthenes, a Seleucid diplomat, journeyed to the court of the emperor of India and returned with a journal of his impressions.

Several Greek philosophical systems flourished and spread throughout southwestern Asia and the Mediterranean. Many of the new schools were influenced by the exchange of ideas prevalent in Hellenized cities. The new ideas challenged older beliefs and systems, resulting in major reorientations in philosophy. To a certain extent, philosophical exposition focused on ethics and the art of living in the increasingly complex, cosmopolitan societies.

Many philosophers focused on finding the best way to live happily in "these trying times" and then taught it. The philosophy of **Epicureanism**, based on the philosophy of Epicurus, had begun in the fourth century B.C. Epicureans argued that human pleasure was the purpose of life but not in excess, for excess brings about an imbalance that in turn produces unhappiness. In the later Hellenistic and Roman Empire periods, however, the Epicureans withdrew into indifference, finding balance and tranquility in their image of life as a garden. The philosophy's tenet, "eat, drink, and be merry, for tomorrow we die," did not originally encourage irresponsibility, only the enjoyment of life. **Stoicism**, which also began in the fourth century B.C., concluded that human happiness lay in adhering to the laws of nature. These laws led

ENCOUNTERS
Mystery Cults

Mystery cults were part of the Hellenistic exchange, spread by merchants and soldiers as they traveled the expansive empires. The more intimate identity with the city-state had disappeared in the vast, impersonal empires, leading to feelings of isolation, helplessness, and abandonment. Individuals often asked for personal intervention from a traditional deity, but deities seemed indifferent to the sufferings of humans. The state required only that the rituals be performed; belief in the deity was not mandatory. Because of this political and religious detachment, personal devotion soon found expression in the private mystery cults of Southwest Asia.

The name "mystery cult" comes from the initiation ceremonies of the cults. Often thrilling, sensual, and dramatic, they represented the mysteries of the universe, and, as a consequence, the initiation rituals were kept secret by cult members. The mystery-cult deities were amalgamations of older deities from Southwest Asia, and their theologies presented them as more receptive than traditional Greek deities' myths to the personal needs of the population. Archaeological evidence, literature, and architecture help scholars to interpret some of the practices of mystery cults, such as baptismal rites and sacred meals. Mystery cults often provided for their widows and orphans and gave charity, but only to their own membership. Some cults were too expensive to participate in or were gender-exclusive. Two very popular cults were those of Isis from Egypt and Mithras from Persia.

The mystery cult of Isis evolved from the ancient Egyptian state cult of Isis and Osiris. By the Roman Empire period, the cult was highly Hellenized, with statues and temples of Greek design. Isis was increasingly identified with the powers of all deities and was named "O Thou of Countless Names." Worshipers came to her for miracles, advice, and the promise of eternal happiness. The cult had secret initiation rites and purification bathing in waters from the Nile. The more public rituals included the reenactment of Osiris's resurrection, with its dances, music, and processions. The cult was very popular, although rather expensive, and it attracted many wealthy women.

Another example is the cult of Mithras. Its ancient antecedents were in Persian religion, in which Mithras represented light, truth, and salvation. In the Roman Empire, Mithras was associated with the Roman sun god and had the additional identity of a victorious warrior over the forces of evil, which made the cult popular among Roman soldiers. Mithraism spread throughout the Roman Empire, particularly from the second century, and shrines have been found in Syria, Asia Minor, Spain, central Italy, western North Africa, and Gaul, as well as along the Rhine and Danube rivers.

Mystery cults that promised eternal life were extremely popular; if this life were a trial, the next might be a reward. While intellectuals tended to turn to ethical philosophies for purpose in life, the general population worshiped the deities who demanded moral behavior and who rewarded that behavior with salvation and resurrection.

FIGURE 8.3 *Realism in Hellenistic Art. A move toward portraying figures more realistically in Hellenistic sculpting is evidenced in this depiction of a young jockey on a racehorse. Absent is the idealized formality of the Classical Greek style, abandoned in favor of demonstrating the drama of the race. The young boy grimaces as he struggles to retain his balance on a horse straining to its full stride.* National Archaeological Museum, Athens/ Archaeological Receipts Fund (TAP Service).

humanity to self-control and performance of duty rather than to the mere pursuit of pleasure. According to Stoicism, wisdom is the goal of life, and a wise individual conforms to the natural laws instituted by the god of reason. True happiness, Stoics believe, can be found in distinguishing between what you can and what you cannot control.

Older schools, such as **Skepticism** and **Cynicism**, continued to find followers in Greece and elsewhere. Skeptics believed that nothing could really be known. They advocated that there is no ultimate pattern by which to order one's life; therefore, nothing really matters. In order to maintain peaceful coexistence, however, they maintained that moral behavior is based on the normal conventions of the polis. Most Skeptics argued against the luxury and material wealth that long-distance trade brought to Greece. Cynics often wandered around Greece calling for a return to the simple life of the early polis. They idealized the life of poverty, wearing only rags and eating only what was given to them.

Science and mathematics advanced during the Hellenistic Age. Archimedes[5] calculated the approximate value of pi, and Euclid[6] presented theorems on plane and solid geometry. Astronomy is a kindred discipline to mathematics, and many individuals contributed to both fields. One Greek developed the hypothesis that the stars and the sun were fixed bodies and that the earth revolved around the sun. There were also advances in stargazing; optical aids were invented that resulted in the production of star maps, for example. Eratosthenes,[7] a geographer, produced near-accurate calculations of the circumference of the earth and, with less accuracy, the size of the sun and moon and their distance from earth. Many of these ancient scholars were also inventors, creating ingenious mechanical devices, such as steam-driven toys, water clocks, water pumps, and war machines.

THE EARLY ROMAN EMPIRE, 31 B.C.–AROUND A.D. 200

Scholars have associated the beginning of the Roman Empire not only with geographical expansion but also with the political career of Gaius Octavian Caesar (reign dates 31 B.C.–A.D. 14), who transformed the political structure of Rome essentially into an imperial dynasty. Like Alexander, the nineteen-year-old Octavian was a prodigy; unlike Alexander, his expertise lay not with his military

---

[5]**Archimedes:** ahr kuh MEE deez
[6]**Euclid:** YOO klihd

[7]**Eratosthenes:** ehr uh TAHS theh neez

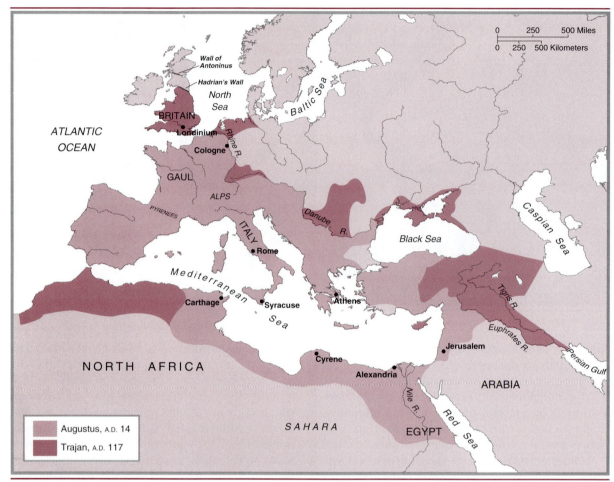

MAP 8.3 *The Roman Empire,* A.D. 14–117. *The Roman Empire covered a vast area that encircled the Mediterranean Sea. Augustus warned his successors not to expand the size of the empire, cautioning that it would become too difficult to defend. The expansion that followed Augustus's death brought the empire to its greatest size under Trajan in* A.D. 117. *Augustus's fears had been well founded; the northern borders in particular became difficult to defend when migrations began at the end of the second century.*

skill but in his keen administrative talent. Octavian created a system of governance, called the principate system, that ran the Roman Empire until about A.D. 200.

The Principate System

Octavian was the nephew and adopted heir of Julius Caesar. His inheritance included the wealth, clients, military loyalty to the name of Caesar, and family prestige garnered by his illustrious uncle. Marc Antony, Caesar's trusted colleague and a consul, described the young Octavian as that boy "who owes everything to his name." Octavian, who had been educated and resided in Greece, traveled to Rome to collect his inheritance. The young Octavian began his political career as a minor player, but history was to write a different chapter for the inexperienced but talented junior statesman.

After Julius Caesar was assassinated, government once again dissolved into party politics and military rivalry. Octavian (having inherited Caesar's influence with the army and his wealth) immediately realized that he could not defeat the popular Marc Antony, who had joined forces with another of Caesar's commanders, Lepidus. Octavian agreed to an alliance with them, called the Second Triumvirate, and the Senate commissioned the Triumvirate to rewrite the constitution and to restore the Republic through dictatorial powers. After a purge of 300 senators and as many as 2,000 of their enemies' supporters, Octavian and Antony forced Lepidus into retirement and soon revived their rivalry.

When Octavian's forces defeated Antony and his ally, Queen Cleopatra of Ptolemaic Egypt, in 31 B.C., the dictatorial powers fell solely into the hands of Octavian. Octavian reduced the size of the army from about 300,000 to about 140,000 troops, what he considered a manageable and affordable size. To help ensure peace in the provinces, imperial soldiers serving there received land, and indigenous troops were awarded citizenship on retirement. Octavian diminished the official membership of the Senate from 1,000 to 600 members, whom he alone chose by means of his dictatorial powers. By 27 B.C., Octavian's political grip was secure enough for him to declare the Republic restored. Not wishing to make the same mistake as his uncle Julius Caesar in appearing to want to be king, Octavian returned the dictatorial powers the Senate had bestowed earlier. A hand-picked and cowering Senate, however, clamored for his continued service to the state. The Senate awarded him the honorific title of Augustus, "Venerable One," which gave Octavian significant moral credibility and religious prestige. Thereafter, he abandoned his family name and chose to use Augustus only.

Although no longer holding dictatorial authority, Octavian nevertheless retained power through amassing traditional offices and honorific titles. He eventually secured superior authority over the consulships, tribunate power over the Council of Plebeians, and governing authority over lucrative provinces. He continued as *pontifex maximus*, the head of Roman religion, and received the honorific title of "Father of the Country." Augustus consolidated the legislative, military, financial, and religious powers into one-man rule, under the title of emperor. Because of the efficiency of the forty-four year rule of Augustus and the reluctance of both the Senate and Roman citizens to return to the chaos of highly competitive military rivals, the emperorship became a traditional hereditary position within the Roman state. With all direct descendants dead, Augustus placed his son-in-

FIGURE 8.4 *Roman Statue of Augustus. This statue depicts the emperor as* pontifex maximus, *chief priest of Roman religion. The style is reminiscent of Classical Greek statuary; Romans copied many famous Greek sculptors and many of the Greek statues in museums today are Roman copies of Greek originals. This particular statue is important for two reasons. First, its depiction of Augustus demonstrates his role in Roman religion. The Romans believed that proper worship through the state cults kept the empire safe under what they called "the peace of the gods"; the emperor was accountable for maintaining the "peace of the gods" because he was* pontifex maximus. *Second, Augustus gained politically by having himself portrayed in this manner because it gave the aura of religious legitimacy to his rule.* Alinari/Art Resource, N.Y.

law, Tiberius, as consul and adopted him as his legal heir to what essentially was a dynastic throne.

Augustus's political astuteness essentially established an imperial monarchy in Rome based on traditional titles and offices. Scholars call this structure the **principate system**. At the death of Augustus in A.D. 14, Rome encircled the Mediterranean, holding northern territories from England to the Rhine and Danube rivers, eastern territories from the Balkans and Greece to the Turkish Peninsula and Palestine, and southern territories from Egypt to Libya and Numidia on the coast of North Africa.

The Principate after Augustus, A.D. 14–211

After the death of Augustus, the principate system continued under Augustus's heirs, the Julio-Claudians. The dynasty ended with the death of Nero because he had no heir. From 68 to 69, Rome was thrown into a year of civil war as military rivals fought to gain the emperorship. The Senate did not try to regain its Republican-era power; because governance operated through the well-established bureaucracy, there was little impetus to change the system as it had evolved. The military supported effective emperors and assassinated ones whom they believed to be incompetent, often hailing popular commanders as new emperors. Consequently, the power and loyalty of the army slowly became a linchpin in the machinery of emperor selection and succession.

Emperors of the late first and second centuries continued to rule the vast empire through an effective administration, a comprehensive legal system, and competent people. In later years of turmoil and emperor assassinations, the business of empire continued to be conducted efficiently by the vast bureaucracy because purges were restricted to only the highest levels of government. Across the empire, the administration tolerated as much local autonomy as possible to discourage resentment and resistance. As long as peace was maintained, there was little interference in daily lives.

The second century once was called the "Golden Age" of Rome because of the relative peace and political stability between 96 and 192. During the second century, emperors were chosen and adopted by their predecessors on the advice of the Senate and with the support of the army. Edward Gibbon, an eighteenth-century English historian, wrote that second-century Rome was the ideal century and place in which to live in all of human history because of the Senate's role in the selection of emperors, the vast wealth of the empire, the relative peace, and the expanded bureaucracy.

Some scholars today hesitate to call the second century a "Golden Age," however, because its wealth and peace basically were enjoyed by only

FIGURE 8.5 *Triumphal Arch. This arch was constructed to honor the major accomplishments of Emperor Trajan during his reign; it was built around A.D. 117. Such arches were often constructed to demonstrate the great deeds of rulers and generals. They also served as imperial propaganda. Most people could not read, so men of power would pay artists and sculptors to depict heroic deeds on coins or in reliefs on arches. This particular view is the side of the arch that faces the city of Benevento, in southern Italy.* Alinari/Art Resource, N.Y.

UNDER THE LENS

Roman Law

The history of the Roman legal tradition is a long one, and Romans recognized law as an extraordinarily important development in their society. Virgil wrote *The Aeneid* in the first century B.C. In it, he clearly demonstrates the Roman attitude toward law when he writes that other societies have their arts and great learning, but the Roman contribution to humanity is justice and protection of the weak. Romans believed their destiny was to rule other peoples.

As early as the third century B.C., Roman professional jurists (not jury members, but teachers of Roman law) had attended Roman courts as qualified specialists, giving counsel to the elected officials and judges, who usually were not well versed in legal tradition. This innovation limited the arbitrariness of jurisprudence, and a tradition of consistency in law developed. Because the jurists were not advocates for either side in disputes, their competent interpretations usually were trusted by both parties.

Roman citizenship and law were complementary elements in Roman society. By the first century B.C., Rome was an empire with the ideology that Roman law was preferable to local legal traditions, and, as many groups in the provinces gradually gained citizenship rights, they held a vested interest in the success of the state. The benefits provincials received when enfranchised helped to curtail resistance and rebellion. In the first century, the Judean Christian missionary Paul chose to be transported to Rome for trial, as was his right as a Roman citizen. All in all, Roman law was an effective social organizer.

An important development for noncitizens arose in 242 B.C. with the establishment of a special office for cases involving at least one foreigner or noncitizen subject. With this alteration, Roman law moved from a civic legal structure, in which only citizens were addressed, to a universal legal structure that included all inhabitants of the ever-growing Roman state. The commercial, political, and social structures evolving during expansion brought about the need for this special office, and a new tradition of "the law of the nations" emerged. Romans were not entirely unique in this development; other polities (such as China) had created special legal definitions for noncitizen merchants and other foreign peoples living within their borders, but the Roman experience continued beyond merely defining specific commercial relationships. The "law of the nations" evolved into a legal system based on principles believed by Roman jurists to be universally applicable and universally acceptable. This universalist approach to dealing with the various peoples of the empire has been identified as the basis for the concept of international law in Western civilization.

The Roman legal system, however, did not establish a consistently fair and just legal structure. Ideally, jurists would be impartial, judges would come to fair decisions, and justice would prevail. But Roman courts fared no better than the legal courts of the twentieth century. Some professional jurists remained blinded by their own sympathies to oligarchical interests, and political circumstance frequently created an atmosphere tolerant of either apathetic neglect or extreme prejudice on the part of the officials who adjudicated.

---

the elite. Although the bureaucracy was efficient, many local bureaucrats were corrupt. Most of the provinces' lower classes suffered from having to pay more taxes than they owed and from little, if any, protection from bands of thieves. The empire's borders were extended during the second century (something that Augustus had warned against), an effort that proved expensive and yielded little political or military advantage. It increased the length of the defensive line, creating too sparse a military presence for effective protection. In fact, the **pax Romana**, the Roman peace established during Augustus's reign, had begun to crumble as early as 161, when the borders began to collapse. In 170, a military defeat in Venice saw that city burned, and it was not alone in this experience. Defensive walls had to be constructed to help impede the progress of enemy raids across northern borders. A civil service was employed that allowed nonmilitary personnel to work in the bureaucracy, freeing military officers for empire defense but raising the cost of administration. As the end of the second century approached, the added costs of defending the borders and the reorganization of the bureaucracy created a heavy tax burden for the lower classes.

THE LATE ROMAN EMPIRE, AROUND 200–476

As the third century dawned, the Roman Empire faced military and economic crisis. A military monarchy replaced the principate system by 211 in response to threats to the borders. The empire recovered in the fourth century under a political and military reorganization that stabilized its borders. Although the reorganization was not long lasting, it set the stage for the future division of the empire into two areas, the Western Roman Empire and the Eastern Roman Empire or Byzantium.

The Third-Century Crisis

Economic instability fed the flames of destruction in the third century. Coins were minted with debased metal, taxes were increased and collected from fewer and fewer farmers able to pay them, spiraling inflation ate away at those least able to maintain themselves, and the poor continued to file into the cities, expecting the state to support them as it had in the past. In order to keep the urban poor under control, the state had to distribute grain and bread at enormous cost. Much of the land near Rome had been turned into large aristocratic estates that grazed sheep and produced cash crops for trade. Aristocratic landowners remained wealthy and refused to offer land redistribution to ease the crisis. The small farmers persisted, as they had during the Republic, but their numbers diminished and they produced less. Consequently, greater amounts of grain had to be imported from Egypt and the Black Sea area than ever before.

In addition, the dispossessed, desperate, and unemployed population was riddled with crime and demanded reform. Emperors often appeased the Roman citizens with various entertainments, including gladiatorial games and the ever-popular chariot races. As entertaining as these events must have been, they were expensive to maintain on a regular basis. They became less frequent and ultimately were unsuccessful in pacifying the increasingly desperate population.

Rome previously had held its borders secure with troops and alliances with friendly Germanic tribes to the north. As early as the first century, many Germans had integrated into the Roman Empire through acculturation and service in auxil-iary units within the army. But in the third century, Germans amassed in the borderlands were too numerous to assimilate, and the rise of the Persians again in the east threatened the security of the eastern border defenses. In 212, the emperor issued a decree that awarded citizenship to every free male living within the empire, permitting a conscription to increase the numbers available for military defense. The Persian Empire attacked and captured thirty-seven Roman cities. In 244, the Roman emperor was captured while fighting against Persia and was forced to act as a footstool when the Persian king mounted his horse. With the increase in German migration and raids and with the attacks on the eastern borders, the empire faced the serious crisis of a two-front war. Troops had to be transported and serviced, so the military crisis inflated the economic crisis.

The military and economic crises paved the way to political chaos. As the armies panicked because of emperors' failures to gain victory in the field, assassination and rebellion broke out. A clear military monarchy arose during the Severi dynasty (193–235), replacing the ineffectual principate system and its semblance of titles and senatorial power. The Senate was reduced to a toothless, ineffectual body. An emperor who marched with his army in the field, however, could hardly keep the peace in the cities through the necessary hands-on administration of economic reforms. Within forty-two years, the Severi dynasty fell to anarchy; the next forty-nine years saw twenty-two emperors. The empire had to reform or collapse.

The Empire's Revival

The reform came with the able leadership of Diocletian (reign dates 284–305), who was proclaimed emperor by the army in 284. The key to stability resided in the army's loyalty. Diocletian retained the troops' loyalty by securing the Roman Empire's borders through administrative and military reforms. In addition, the savior motif of the mystery cults was popular, and Diocletian offered himself as a savior figure to the people.

REFORMS. The emperor could not be everywhere at once; he could not be in the cities working on bureaucratic and administrative reform and, at the same time, out in the field leading the troops against Germanic or Persian invaders. Because it

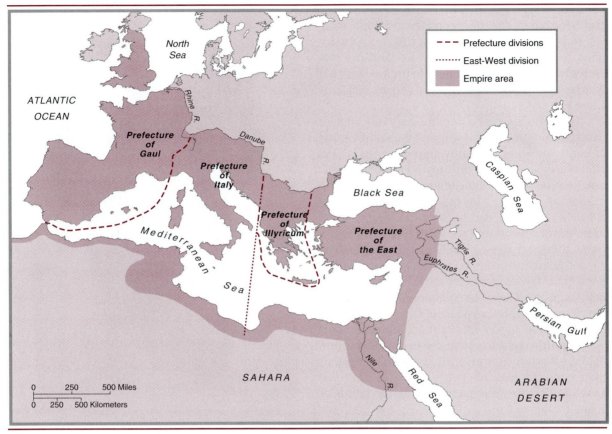

MAP 8.4 *Diocletian's Division of the Empire, A.D. 284–305.* *Diocletian divided the Roman Empire into two administrative territories and four prefectures (military areas defended by one of the four armies). Each of the rulers of the empire, two Augusti and two Caesars, was responsible for a prefecture's defense. This division saved the empire from border collapse during a two-front war.*

was apparent that power had to be shared, in 286 Diocletian split the empire into two administrative units in order to govern more efficiently. The division was basically between the eastern and western parts of the empire. Diocletian chose a colleague, who remained subordinate to him, to rule the west, while he remained in the east. Each of the two administrators took the title of Augustus, but Diocletian retained ultimate authority.

The military reform included another innovation in the hierarchy of authority. Under each Augustus would be a commander called a Caesar. The result was two Augusti and two Caesars, each of the four with control over an army that could mobilize quickly and move swiftly to areas of hostility. The sharing of authority among four confederates also allowed for a balance of power that temporarily impeded rebellion.

Diocletian also instituted economic and social reforms to reverse the effects of the second and third centuries. In 301, he introduced an edict on prices and wages that tried to curb the rate of **inflation**, the rapid increase in prices that causes a decline in purchasing power. Diocletian legislated against raising prices during times of crisis, considering it treason to do so. He also encouraged military officials to requisition supplies as a portion of the soldiers' pay to reduce the need to distribute coin.

Tax reforms were also introduced in an attempt to make taxation uniform and to increase revenues. A head tax, initiated on everyone living in the empire, raised badly needed revenues. The traditional land tax levied a tax on each tax district, which included several individual fields. More and more people were fleeing the rural areas for the protection of the cities or of a neighboring aristo-crat. This meant that fewer and fewer people were left to pay the tax owed for that district. Diocletian's response was to stabilize the land-tax revenues by forcing people to remain on the land. (Of course, many still ran away when the tax collector came.)

The administrative and military reforms of Diocletian shored up the empire for a short period of time. Dividing the army into four parts was effective in slowing the disintegration of the Western Empire. By 305, Diocletian assessed that the immediate danger on the borders had been checked, so he decided to force the new system's order of succession to work. Each Augustus was to retire, then each Caesar would be promoted to the vacant Augustus position, opening up the Caesar level for a new commander to be chosen by each new Augustus. The system had merit and, in a different time, might have worked. Diocletian underestimated the power of tradition, however, and civil war broke out again. In the end, Constantine held the Western Empire (in 312) and soon invaded the Eastern Empire, where his victory in 324 once again unified the Roman Empire into the hands of a single ruler.

CONSTANTINE. Like Diocletian before him, Constantine (reign dates 312–337) had to deal with a two-front war and economic problems. Diocletian's system, with its four armies, was very costly, essentially creating two bureaucracies and four military budgets. Constantine decided to pull the bureaucracy under one administration again. He credited all his victories to the Christian god, and, in a bold move to unify the population and to settle internal disputes, Constantine made Christianity one of the state religions. Appearances remained important, however, and Constantine carefully continued to use the symbol for the sun god on his coinage. By maintaining a dual relationship, Constantine demonstrated his alliance with a traditional god of Rome, while also endearing himself to a growing population of Christian subjects. Scholars still debate the sincerity of Constantine's conversion, but the sociopolitical impact remains significant.

With Constantine's patronage of Christianity, persecution of Christians ceased, and many members of the elite converted in order to gain political advantage. Christians, who saw Constantine's conversion as a sign from their god to support the

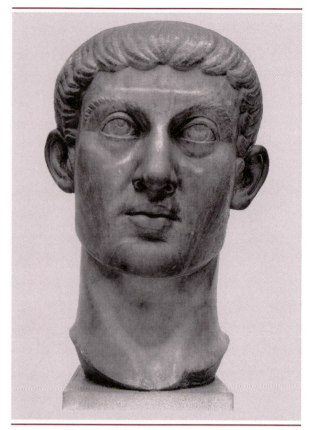

FIGURE 8.6 *Bust of Constantine.* *The heavenward gaze on this bust of the emperor Constantine has a propaganda purpose similar to that of the statue of Augustus as* pontifex maximus *(Figure 8.4). After the assassinations during the third century, it was politically even more important for an emperor to be perceived by the army as having spiritual authority and divine right to rule. Beginning with Diocletian, emperors claimed a new status as special friend to a Roman deity that protected them and guided their policies. Diocletian professed Jupiter as his friend and Constantine claimed both Sol Invictus (the Unconquerable Sun God) and the Christian God as his friends, which can be seen in much of the imperial art produced during his reign. This bust demonstrates Constantine's spirituality as he gazes heavenward for direction from one of the deities, a posture not lost on the army or the general population.* The Metropolitan Museum of Art. Bequest of Mrs. F. F. Thompson, 1926. 26.229.

empire, could now enthusiastically participate in the army. Some Christians had been in the army prior to this, but now patriotism became popular, as they fought and prayed for their Christian emperor alongside non-Christians. A common ideological motivation to protect and preserve the empire produced stability.

Constantine abandoned the western capital of Rome for a well-defended city, which he named Constantinople (modern Istanbul). Like Alexandria in Egypt, Constantinople became an intellectual, religious, and economic center, as well as the eastern capital. The city's walls and geographical location formed an imposing defensive system. Situated on a promontory, the city was bordered by water on three sides, making siege almost futile.

Diocletian's division of eastern and western administration was revived after Constantine's death in 337. One-man rule returned for the last time under Emperor Theodosius, who died in 395. By the dawn of the fifth century, Diocletian's east-west division had become permanent.

The Fall of Rome

"The fall of Rome" is a commonly used phrase describing the decline of Imperial Roman culture in the Western Empire. The Eastern Empire continued and evolved into a new state, called Byzantium (which will be discussed in Chapter 17). Scholars today recognize that the fall of Rome was a process that took centuries and had several causes.

Germanic migration into the Western Empire was a significant cause of change. By the fourth and fifth centuries, Germanic migrations occurred so rapidly and in such large numbers that both Germanic and Roman cultures changed; there was not enough time for the Germans to be absorbed. Other Germans raided or conquered large portions of the Western Empire.

As time passed, Roman aristocrats increasingly fled the overcrowded, chaotic cities for the countryside, where they could live in relative safety on their self-sufficient estates. Many displaced people also fled to these large estates, where aristocratic landlords protected them against tax collection, conscription into the Roman army, and invasion by hostile Germans. These people then worked the land for a portion of what they produced. Other small farmers exchanged a portion of their yields to the same aristocratic neighbors in return for protection against tax collection. Slowly, in the west, political and social disintegration continued under German migration, and eventually the Western administration collapsed entirely. Germanic tribal kings filled the administrative void by extorting yearly payments in exchange for protection and peace. In later centuries, the large aristocratic holdings became the manors of the Middle Ages, with the descendants of the small farmers attached to the land as serfs.

When a German king, Odovacar,[8] finally deposed the last Western emperor in 476, hardly anyone noticed or cared. Yet even this German king wanted to be identified with Roman culture; he sent the imperial insignia to Constantinople and informed the Eastern emperor that he would rule the west under Eastern overlordship. In actuality, Odovacar ruled the west as he did any Germanic territory, independent of Eastern control or interest.

Those areas that tried to remain independent of Germanic control were the cities and the surrounding countrysides that supported them. Rome had experienced devastating raids. Cities' populations decreased, with many officials abandoning the ship of state. With no imperial or local administration, citizens (often the poorest) turned for guidance to the only surviving urban authority, the Christian bishop. The Christian Church had in place a bureaucracy that could assume the secular duties. Consequently, many bishops, including Rome's, became secular as well as religious leaders, thereby filling the political vacuum.

By the late fifth century, the once-vast Roman Empire was essentially gone. Byzantium, which encircled the eastern Mediterranean territories until the Islamic invasions of the seventh century, prospered until Constantinople fell to the Ottoman Turks in 1453. The Western territories lay either in the hands of Germanic kings or were islands of independence.

LIFE IN THE ROMAN EMPIRE

Augustus had secured the borders of the empire, consolidated Roman administration, and established throughout the Mediterranean a cohesive trade network that had brought peace and stability in the first century A.D. The Roman road network behind the ramparts not only allowed troops to move swiftly into areas of hostilities but also provided trade routes linking the smaller towns to the economic activity of the growing empire. The vast empire became a conduit for the exchange of commodities and culture between provincial peoples and Romans.

[8] **Odovacar:** OH doh vah cawr

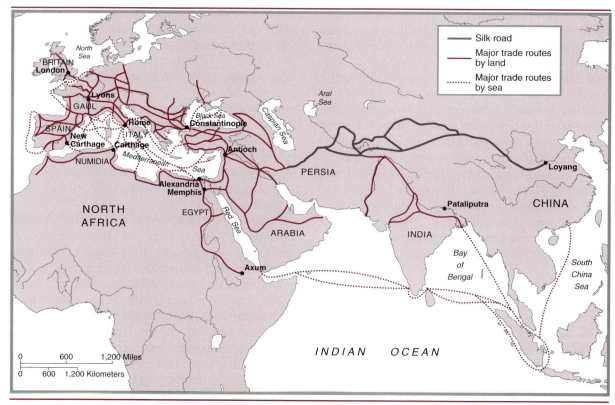

MAP 8.5 *Major Trade Routes around A.D. 200.* *The Roman Empire encircled the Mediterranean Sea and exploited it as a highway for the exchange of goods. Outside the Mediterranean basin, Roman ships sailed from Africa to India, then to Malaya and Java and, by the second century, to China. During the Han period, the silk road was opened and connected empires in China, India, and Central Asia with the Roman Empire. Goods were carried from one end of the empire to the other—for example, hides, tin, and wool from Britain might be exchanged at the same market as glass, carpets, and ivory from India and spices and silk from China.*

The Roman Exchange

Traditional commercial products, previously unavailable commodities, styles, and ideas coursed through the Roman Empire and its trading partners in great volumes, forming the **Roman exchange**. The Roman exchange was a significant aspect of life in the Roman Empire, developing rapidly as a result of the pax Romana.

The vast trade network and relative ease of travel linked the eastern caravans and southern shipping up the Nile to the northern and western Mediterranean all the way to the Black Sea settlements in the northeast and England in the northwest. Trade traveled overland in wheeled carts and by mule. In some cities, especially Rome, wheeled traffic had to be limited or restricted to nighttime because of the volume of traffic. (Still, the noise in the streets must have disturbed many a sleepy citizen.) Most trade, however, moved by riverboat or ship, because water transport was quicker and accommodated larger loads. In addition, commerce within the Roman Empire was facilitated by a common currency and low customs duties for goods moving between provinces.

The founding of new towns and the occupation of established cities in provinces enhanced stability and helped cultural exchange throughout the empire. Often beginning as military outposts, small market towns arose around the safety of the Roman forts and legion headquarters, and many of these eventually developed into urban centers that traded with local populations. Stationing troops away from their homelands was a policy that tended to keep rebellions down and assured that local soldiers would not have to fight their kinsmen. This policy exposed them to new ideas and lifeways; many soldiers married local women (who had their own languages and styles of cooking and clothing). On retirement, soldiers most often remained on the lands awarded them in the provinces where they had spent much of their careers. Soldiers who returned to their homelands brought back a patchwork of novel ideas, ranging from mystery cults to foreign words to new ways of making rope.

The love of exotica and a prosperous Roman elite stimulated trade with places outside the empire, too. Ivory from Axum, aromatic silphium gum from Hungary, perfumes and incense from India, silk from China, and rare foods made their way to the homes of wealthy Romans in Italy and abroad. In return, trading partners received Roman goods, as exemplified by a Roman silver goblet that made its way through the Egyptian trade route all the way to Meroë, in Africa.

Not all aspects of exchange resulted in benefit. Germs often traveled with those journeying from one part of the empire to another. In the second century, troops on campaign in Persia with Marcus Aurelius returned to the Italian peninsula carrying deadly contagion. The resulting epidemic devastated parts of the Italian population.

Life in the Roman Provinces

Of the approximately 100 million people within the empire at the time of Augustus, at least 75 percent lived in the provincial territories. Life in provincial towns consisted of a mixture between local customs and Roman practices, contributing to Roman exchange. For example, **Romanization**, the emulation of Roman ways, occurred among many local people, especially elites who desired social, political, or legal advantages. Sometimes Romans awarded citizenship (which included the right to wear the Roman toga, a sign of citizenship) to members of the local elite who supported Roman occupation. Romanization in Britain, for example, meant that local Britons adopted such aspects of Roman-style cooking as using the newly imported Roman bread oven, cooking hard-boiled eggs, seasoning their dishes with fish sauce, and relishing dainty pastries. The Germanic peoples who migrated into the Roman Empire in the first century came south for peace and opportunity. They became Romanized over the centuries and lost most of their Germanic culture. These Germans became citizens, wore Roman dress, and spoke Latin, and their descendants even became emperors.

Many provincial cities adopted the Roman recreation of bathing. Bathers would oil themselves and then clean away the sweat and dirt by running special scrapers across their skin. The water was heated by furnaces or naturally by hot springs, then pumped under the rooms and into the baths. These bathhouses served as centers for rest and relaxation, as well as conduits for gossip and news from abroad. A courtyard for games and exercise served patrons' needs as well. The baths were very popular, being inexpensive and free for children. Men and women often shared the same bath areas, but some public bathhouses limited women to morning hours, with men attending in the afternoons.

Roman entertainments also made their way to the provincial areas. Citizens and townspeople enjoyed plays, poetry readings, gladiatorial fights, animal hunts, and acrobatic displays. Exotic wild animals for the arenas included crocodiles from Egypt, lions from Mesopotamia, leopards from northern Africa, and bears from Scotland. Large arenas for racing and major sports were called **circuses**. Entertainments in circuses included boxing and chariot racing. In Rome, the Circus Maximus could accommodate 25,000 spectators. In provincial areas, circus patrons were fewer but just as enthusiastic. Chariot races were attended by hundreds of excited fans, many of whom lost great amounts of money betting on the outcome. Chariot racing was an expensive but significant business, run by private entrepreneurs, similar to major-league team owners today. Racers became heroic figures, often being memorialized in mosaics and statues, and the competition between rival cities' teams often resulted in riotous violence.

Similar to the Hellenistic rural areas, the rural provincial areas at first felt little impact from Roman occupation, because administration and trade occurred in either forts or urban centers. As time passed, however, the retired Roman soldiers farming their lands brought Roman ideas to rural households, particularly in the western parts of the empire. Wealthy Romans often purchased large amounts of land and built Roman villas, where

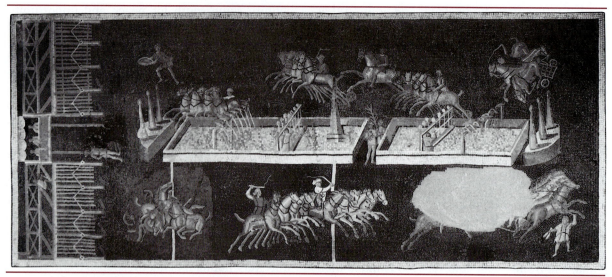

FIGURE 8.7 *Chariot Race.* *The action and excitement of the popular chariot races is shown in this mosaic; many mosaics immortalize the names of the talented charioteers who achieved fame and fortune. Chariot racing was extremely dangerous, and thousands of drivers lost their lives competing for a share of the considerable bets placed on them and their horses. The track was an elongated circular surface; terraced seating was built of stone or cut into a hillside that surrounded the track. Around the center of the track ran a small wall to ensure that head-on collisions were avoided, with a break in the wall for attendants to run onto the track and remove crashed chariots and mangled men and horses before another chariot collided with the wreckage. Inside the center area, counters moved stakes with color-coded balls to keep track of the completed laps of each charioteer, who wore the corresponding colors.* Cliche Ch. Thioc, Musée de la Civilisation Gallo-Romaine, Lyon.

they lived an idyllic lifestyle that held little resemblance to that of the hardworking farmer who eked out a living to pay Roman taxes. Many of the wealthiest villas had hypocaust heating (hot air pumped under a raised floor), tiled roofs, multiple rooms, glazed windows, plastered and painted walls, and mosaic-tiled floors. Villa living became a sign of wealth and power throughout the empire.

Many temples were erected in the provinces, and, in the usual manner of Roman religious inclusiveness, local deities were adopted into the official list of Roman religions. Among the state cultic practices that were exported from Rome was that of Roma, the patron goddess of the Roman state. Augustus encouraged his own veneration in a state cult, particularly in the eastern part of the empire, where there was a tradition of divine kingship. Augustus imitated Alexander by encouraging subjects to see him as divine. Mystery cults from the eastern provinces found their way into the city of Rome and into the western provinces, brought by tourists, merchants, and military personnel.

Life in the City of Rome

Citizens in the capital city became inundated with new ideas and goods, and the population swelled with artisans and merchants from around the empire. Roman city life improved somewhat during the empire period, but living in any city presents certain problems. Augustus had divided the city into fourteen districts, each with minimal self-governance and personnel who doubled as police and firefighters. Augustus and Agrippa (one of his commanders) had buildings inspected and repaired, initiated public works projects, and established a board of works to enforce building codes. Crime and fire always caused concern in the densely populated city, which had been mostly destroyed by a catastrophic fire in A.D. 64. Consequently, large portions of the city were rebuilt in stone.

Most citizens lived in overcrowded apartment complexes. It was common to throw waste into the streets below, often with devastating results. The satirist Juvenal complained, "See what a height it is to that towering roof from which a potsherd comes crack upon my head every time that some broken or leaky vessel is pitched out of the window!" Others complained about the poor living conditions. One slum landlord confessed that two of his buildings had collapsed, and in another the walls were all cracked. Not only the tenants but even the mice had left.

Buildings snuggled against one another, and windows, opened for a breath of air, invited in all the bustling noise of the city's streets. One poet bewailed the racket: "There's nowhere a poor man can get any quiet in Rome. . . . The laughter of the passing throng wakes me and Rome is at my bed's head." The city streets bulged with stalls, whose merchants each tried to outsell the competition. Vendors sold food to wide-eyed tourists, and street entertainers, many of them women, performed for enough money to buy their daily bread.

The elite of the city fared somewhat better than the apartment dwellers. Their houses, which were built around a courtyard, placed bedrooms in quieter areas off the street. Wealthy men and women were very style-conscious, wanting to demonstrate their status by wearing the newest imports from around the empire. As hairstyles became increasingly elaborate, many depended on wigs to give their hair height. Slaves attended the elite women, helping them with their elaborate hairstyles, dressing them in the newest fashions, and adorning them with layers of jewelry. Those who criticized the opulence of Rome's wealthy citizens often complained that servants and slaves wasted too much time grooming their masters and mistresses.

Some of the elite women had indirect political influence. Numerous wives and mothers throughout Roman history influenced the political careers of their husbands and sons, but few were able to hold power themselves. Emperor Claudius's wife, Agrippina the Younger, ran the empire as Claudius (reign dates 41–54) became increasingly incapacitated by infirmities. Agrippina maneuvered her thirteen-year-old son by a previous husband into the line of succession over Claudius's own younger son. In 54, when the young Nero became emperor, her image was placed on coins with his.

By the first century B.C., elite women had gained control over lands through inheritance or, sometimes, through private investment from

FIGURE 8.8 *Nero and Agrippina. Coinage was an important tool in Roman society; not only was it used as commercial exchange but its decoration served as a means for propaganda. This coin's obverse side shows Emperor Nero and his mother, Agrippina, who married Emperor Claudius after Nero was born. Although her husband was in line for the imperial crown, it is rumored that Agrippina poisoned him and married her uncle Claudius to make Nero his heir. Her influence is demonstrated in her appearance on this coin, minted soon after Nero's ascension to the throne in A.D. 54. Other women had been placed on coins but Agrippina is depicted on this coin as Nero's equal, demonstrating her desire to be empress and co-ruler. The writing around the edge of the coin identifies her as the emperor's mother. Nero arranged her death in 59.* Museo Nazionale, Naples.

funds under their own control. Augustus enacted restrictive laws to limit fiscal independence of women. In addition, harsh laws were passed against the promiscuity of elite women, whose sexual liberation surpassed even that of the prostitutes. Augustus's daughter, Julia, had created such a public spectacle of herself by entertaining multiple lovers that he banished her from Rome. Augustus was concerned also with elite women who were refusing to marry or who chose to abort pregnancies because their condition limited participation in social functions.

ROMAN ARTS AND IDEOLOGIES

The people of the Roman Empire adopted many of the Hellenistic arts, religions, and philosophies, contributing their own styles and intellectual speculation to them. There were many people traveling around the empire on business and for pleasure. Multiple belief systems, like peoples, rubbed elbows in the bustling Hellenistic cities of the eastern Mediterranean and soon found their way into the western territories. Not everyone thought that Roman occupation had a positive effect, as identity with their ancestral heritage was submerged in the vast, impersonal bureaucratic society. Many individuals frequented astrologers to reassure them or sought miraculous cures and interventions to ease their physical and emotional suffering. Others searched for meaning in life by pursuing personal enlightenment and salvation in the varied philosophies and mystery cults available.

Roman Arts

It is difficult to categorize art during the Roman Empire into one great art style, because a variety of local expressions continued. Certain decorative styles (such as mosaic floors and mural wall paintings) did become widespread, as the Roman elite decorated their provincial homes in Roman styles. Romans continued the use of arches in public works, such as the aqueducts, temples, and amphitheaters throughout the entire breadth and width of the empire.

Roman art, in turn, was heavily influenced by local styles; for instance, Romans adopted Greek techniques and forms in architecture and sculpture. In Egypt in the late second century A.D., painting mummy portraits became common. The portraits were painted on wooden boards and then wrapped and placed with the mummy at the time of burial. In addition, it became popular to paint murals or panels of scenes from epics and myths on walls in elite homes.

As with many governments, art served the propaganda purposes of the emperors. Many of the reliefs on columns and arches commemorated military or political themes. Emperors and high officials used sculpture to portray their power or benevolence. Roman coins are another example of art propaganda. Almost all emperors commemorated events or advanced policies on the coins that passed through their subjects' hands.

Literature during the Roman Empire was as eclectic as the various cultural areas of the empire. The most prolific writers were rhetoricians, philosophers, and historians, many of whom were Greek educators. One significant contributor to Roman history was the late-first-century historian Tacitus, who wrote several histories. The Jewish historian Josephus wrote a history of a Jewish revolt (A.D. 66–73) and a twenty-book history of the Jews from the Creation to A.D. 66, immediately before the outbreak of the revolt. Later Roman historians included many Christians who wrote about the relationship between the empire and the new religion. The most productive author may have been Plutarch (42–126), whose writings were widely read works in the empire. His *Parallel Lives of the Famous Greeks and Romans* brought not only Greek history to interested Romans but also Roman history to Greek readers. Roman biography enjoyed great popularity in the second century through the scandalous pen of Suetonius, whose biographies of the emperors exposed every rumored tidbit about their behavior. Many incorrect perceptions persist today because his work has been uncritically accepted as fact.

Ovid (43 B.C.–A.D. 17) was one of the few Roman poets who received wide acclaim in their own time. He abandoned the Roman profession of politics to write poetry. By A.D. 8, he became the leading poet of Rome, although he was later banished for some unknown reason by Augustus. His poetry included such topics as the art of love, cosmetics, the art of seduction, and intrigue. He also wrote a fifteen-book collection of Classical Greek stories and Southwest Asian legends.

Other Roman literary works include the satires of Juvenal and Petronius from the first and early second century. Juvenal detested the Hellenization of Rome and attacked what he considered to be depraved behavior among the elite. Petronius, a novelist, wrote one of the most popular and scandalous novels of the Roman Empire period, *The Satyricon*. In it, he mocked the lavish lifestyle prevalent among the elite in Rome and ridiculed popular Greek love romances of the day.

Roman Philosophies

Older philosophies (such as Stoicism and Platonism) took on newer applications and had revivals. Seneca (4–65) was a Stoic philosopher who wrote several plays that included maxims for moral behavior according to the Stoic virtues of patience and duty. Stoicism took on a religious tone under the able pen of the freed slave Epictetus (55–135). In his works, Epictetus stressed that all men were brothers (he didn't include women) and that human nature contained some of the divine nature of god. Plotinus (205–270) initiated a revival of Platonism called Neoplatonism in the third century. Plotinus brought the contemporary interest in salvation to the philosophy, making it analogous to the popular mystery cults of the period. Plotinus argued that the Ineffable One first created the Mind, where all the ideas resided. The Mind then created the World Soul, which in turn created individual souls who fell into material existence in bodies. Neoplatonism's development coincided with the development of Christian theology, and many Christian thinkers adopted Neoplatonic vocabulary and imagery. Some equated the Ineffable One, Mind, and World Soul with the Father, Son, and Holy Spirit of the Christian Trinity.

Religions in the Roman Empire

Romans were polytheistic and adopted into their pantheon conquered peoples' deities, the most powerful of which were officially listed as state deities. Usually Romans demanded that the state deities be worshiped in order to preserve "the peace of the gods." Romans were very religious and did not want to offend their deities with neglect. When famine or disease ravished local areas, citizens stoned or jailed nonworshipers, believing that the deities were punishing everyone because these individuals were being lax in worship. Mystery cults became popular in the empire and

FIGURE 8.9 *Domestic Scene.* *The walls of Roman aristocratic houses were often decorated with colorful murals depicting Roman architectural styles and scenes of flora and fauna, myths, and everyday life. In this mural from Pompeii, three women and a child are shown in a household scene.* Alinari/Art Resource, N.Y.

In the long history of the globe, many natural disasters have proven deadly to plant and animal life. Floods, earthquakes, and volcanic eruptions continue to demonstrate nature's power over humanity today. The eruption of the volcano on Mount Vesuvius, southeast of Naples, is an example of such devastation. On August 24, A.D. 79, the life of one young man named Pliny[a] changed forever. Although Pliny was across the bay of Naples and watched the eruption from afar, he and his mother experienced the accompanying earthquakes and gagged on the pumice and ash. The following excerpts from his letters to the historian Tacitus are a lasting historical record of the horrors of that day:

> It was not clear at that distance from which mountain the cloud was rising . . . its general appearance can best be expressed as being like an umbrella pine, for it rose to a great height on a sort of trunk and then split off into branches. . . . Sometimes it looked white, sometimes blotched and dirty, according to the amount of soil and ashes it carried with it.

Pliny's uncle quickly boarded a ship and accompanied the local fleet across the bay to aid in the rescue of those in danger from the eruption, an act of heroism from which he never returned. During the rest of the day and into the night, Pliny and his mother huddled together as the earthquakes continued and as Vesuvius belched flames and ash into the air. As buildings came tumbling down, they tried to evacuate the town to safety.

> Once beyond the buildings we stopped, and there we had some extraordinary experiences which

[a]**Pliny:** PLIH nee

IN THEIR OWN WORDS

The Eruption of Mount Vesuvius

> thoroughly alarmed us. We also saw the sea sucked away and apparently forced back by the earthquake: at any rate it receded from the shore [a tidal wave] so that quantities of sea creatures were left stranded on dry sand. On the landward side a fearful black cloud was rent by forked and quivering bursts of flame, and parted to reveal great tongues of fire, like flashes of lightning magnified in size.

Pliny then describes the panic of the citizens.

> You could hear the shrieks of women, the wailing of infants, and the shouting of men; some were calling their parents, others their children or their wives, trying to recognize them by their voices . . . then darkness came on once more and ashes began to fall again, this time in heavy showers. We rose from time to time and shook them off, otherwise we should have been buried and crushed beneath their weight. . . . At last the darkness thinned and dispersed into smoke or cloud; then there was genuine daylight, and the sun actually shone out, but yellowish as it is during an eclipse. We were terrified to see everything changed, buried deep in ashes like snowdrifts.

Pliny and his mother later learned the fate of his uncle.

> My uncle decided to go down to the shore and investigate on the spot the possibility of any escape by sea, but he found the waves still wild and dangerous. . . . He stood leaning on two slaves and then suddenly collapsed, I imagine because the dense fumes choked his breathing by blocking his windpipe. . . . When daylight returned on the 26th . . . his body was found intact and uninjured, still fully clothed and looking more like sleep than death.

spread from the eastern Mediterranean area to England. In addition, the emperor's cult demanded that citizens pour out a libation to the emperor's image, an offering of drink comparable to a national pledge of allegiance. Failure to respect the emperor in this way resulted in treason charges.

JUDAISM. The basic tenets of Judaism were discussed in Chapter 4. Judaism was a very old religion by the time of the Roman Empire and was tolerated by Romans because of its ancient heritage. Romans believed that the Jewish god deserved respect because of the numerous victories recorded in ancient Hebrew histories. Romans did not want to anger such a powerful god. Jews, however, were monotheistic and refused to worship the Roman state deities. Jews also demanded that the Romans not violate the sanctity of their temple by polluting it with the presence of unbelievers. Most of the time Romans did not enter the temple area, and the **Sanhedrin**,[9] the religious council and highest seat of Jewish justice, was allowed to run the temple without Roman interference. The Jews were given an exemption from worshiping all state deities, including the practice of pouring out the libation to the emperor. During the Roman occupation, some Romans converted to Judaism, but most of the time the Roman soldiers and officials lived in an uneasy peace with the Jewish population.

Jews came under attack by the Romans for political reasons in the mid–first century A.D. Many Jews resisted Roman occupation of Palestine and continually harassed the provincial governor and his troops. In 66, a group of Jewish freedom fighters took a fortress on the plateau of Masada from the Roman garrison stationed there. By 70, the Romans decided that the continuous unrest and rebellion had to be quelled or they might lose Palestine to the rebels; the Romans could not allow an independent state to control a portion of the Mediterranean's lucrative coastal trade network. Finally, after a six-month siege in 73, the Romans took the fortress back. When they breached the wall, they found the fortress burned and all but one woman and five children dead. The Jews of Masada had chosen suicide to mar a Roman victory. During this uprising, Jews endured the destruction of the temple in Jerusalem, the confiscation of holy articles (including the Ark of the Covenant), and the dispersion of many of their people to other provincial areas.

CHRISTIANITY. During Tiberius's reign, the new religion of Christianity emerged out of Judaism in Palestine. Christians were followers of Joshua ben Joseph of Nazareth (whose Hellenized name was Jesus, which is the common name used today), who they believed was the Jewish messiah, or savior. Jesus' followers claimed that he was crucified by the Roman governor of Judea to placate some of the Jewish religious leaders. They also believed that Jesus was resurrected from the dead after

three days. The movement gained popularity in the first century, inspired by the preaching of Jesus' closest followers, the twelve apostles.

The twelve apostles were men, but Christian tradition attests to several women as loyal followers of Jesus and leaders in the early movement. Many women, like Phoebe and Olympia, achieved official status in the Christian Church as deaconesses, although their role usually remained limited to the instruction of women and the care of the sick. There is evidence to suggest that Christian widows, who were supported by charitable funds, formally organized into a group that had certain responsibilities during the liturgy. Many wealthy women became patronesses of important theologians, like Jerome and John Chrysostom.[10] Several women became prominent theologians in what later became heretical movements, but other women were recognized as martyrs, saints, and ascetics to be emulated by both men and women.

Christianity's message of salvation and loving one's neighbor soon spread to many cities within the empire, becoming more and more popular. Christians came to believe in a Trinity, with the Jewish god as Father, Jesus as the incarnate Son, and the love expressed between the two as the Holy Spirit. In following centuries, Christians philosophically argued that the three entities constituted not three gods but one god with three personalities.

The Christian religious structure gradually developed into a formal hierarchy. Deacons and deaconesses helped the priests and administered communal funds. The priests presided over local house churches, performing religious rites such as baptism and the sacred sacrificial meal. The bishop remained responsible for teaching, preaching, and correctly interpreting the developing doctrine. As time passed, each urban center retained only one bishop, who supervised all priests and deacons. Bishops gathered in councils and debated correct interpretations of scriptures and philosophical constructs, eventually determining correct doctrine for all Christians.

At first, Christians considered themselves Jews; they claimed the same right as the Jews of exemption from practicing the rituals of the Roman state cults. Christians and Jews, however, had a serious dispute over monotheism. Because

---

[9] **Sanhedrin:** san HE drihn

[10] **Chrysostom:** KRIH saws tuhm

FIGURE 8.10 *Political Graffiti in Ancient Rome.*
Romans often used graffiti to communicate their
opinions of current events. A popular second-century
novel, The Golden Ass, *told of a hapless young man*
who was magically turned into an ass because of his
bad attitude and disrespect of religion. Through his
experiences he learned the value of religion and was
returned to human form, after which he joined the
mystery cult of Isis. Soon "ass" became a popular slur
for people considered unethical or impious. Romans
believed that both Jews and Christians were asinine in
their refusal to worship the traditional Roman deities or
participate in mystery cults. In this picture the scrawled
message reads "Alexamenos adores his god." It is the
earliest known rendering of the crucifixion of Jesus. In
this instance, both the crucified Jesus and his devotee
are the objects of ridicule. Alinari/Art Resource, N.Y.

Christians were soon barred from worshiping in the Jewish temple or synagogues, the Romans demanded that Christians participate in the state cults, particularly that of the emperor. Most Christians refused to recant their beliefs, and most Romans refused to recognize a mere mortal who had died a criminal's death as a deity worth worshiping. Thus began the persecution of Christians within the empire; their deaths, from the Roman point of view, were justified through the Christian failure to observe religious obligations. As a result, Christians were forced to worship their god in secret or face persecution and martyrdom.

As time passed, Romans learned that they had little to fear from the Christians; many citizens realized that family members, neighbors, and even wealthy aristocrats were Christians. Part of the new religion's appeal was its similarity to many of the mystery cults that had become popular during the Hellenistic Age. When Constantine became the first Christian emperor of the Roman Empire, he made Christianity an official state religion. Constantine's conversion, edicts of tolerance, and favorable tax laws for Christians made the new religion politically and economically popular. The religion also became popular in part because someone of any class or station could join, and anyone, whether a member or not, could receive charity during times of crisis. In addition, many of the intellectual elite had previously rejected the low social status and assumed illiteracy of Jesus and most of his followers. Christian theologians, however, soon were able to overcome these intellectual objections when they adopted Greek philosophical constructs and vocabularies. Christian theological development focused increasingly on philosophical issues and less and less on the stories and miracles of Jesus.

Christian leaders also adopted organizational structures from Roman culture. For example, Christian churches were grouped into dioceses, sectors that paralleled the Roman tax districts of the same name. In addition, many titles and offices of the Roman government eventually fell to bishops, who defended their cities and dioceses as the empire disintegrated in the late fifth century A.D. For example, the bishop of Rome became "duke," "defender of the city," and "pontiff" (high priest).

By the end of the fourth century, Emperor Theodosius made Christianity the only legal religion in the empire, but non-Christian religious practices persisted. Christianity's popularity continued to grow, however, and, by about the fifth century, approximately 60 percent of the population of the empire was Christian.

A COMPARISON OF THE GREEK AND ROMAN EMPIRES

The peoples of the Greek Empire and the Hellenistic Age (359–31 B.C.) and the Roman Empire (31 B.C.–A.D. 476) shared analogous problems and challenges. In some cases, both Greeks and

ROME	GREECE		
Roman Republic, 509–31 B.C.		**400 B.C.**	
	Greece unified by Philip of Macedon, 359–336 B.C.		
	Alexander's Empire, c. 334–323 B.C.		
	Hellenistic Age, c. 323–31 B.C. / Antigonid Macedonia, 272–196 B.C. / Seleucid Empire, c. 308–62 B.C. / Ptolemaic Egypt, c. 323–31 B.C.	**300 B.C.**	Alexander completes conquest of Persian Empire, 330 B.C.
		200 B.C.	Greek ambassadors to Rome, c. 200 B.C.
		100 B.C.	
Early Roman Empire, 31 B.C.–A.D. 200		**A.D. 1**	Ovid, leading poet of Rome, dies A.D. 8 / Christianity begins, c. 33
		A.D. 100	
			Marcus Aurelius, Roman emperor, dies 180
		A.D. 200	
Later Roman Empire, c. 200–476			
		A.D. 300	Diocletian divides the Roman Empire, 286
			Constantine makes Christianity a legal religion, 312
		A.D. 400	
			Last Roman emperor in the west deposed, 476
		A.D. 500	

Romans responded similarly to them, and at other times they pursued very different paths.

Many of the similarities involved citizenship and styles of governance.

— Greeks slowly abandoned the idea of single-polis citizenship and adopted multiple-polis citizenships, while Romans awarded citizenship to many conquered peoples that formed a unitary polity.

— Alexander's conquests swallowed up the entire Persian Empire, and his empire included the diverse cultures of the Greeks, Egyptians, Persians, and others. Roman expansion devoured the Italian peninsula, most of northern Europe and England, and the entire Mediterranean basin, including the cultures of the Greeks, Egyptians, North Africans, and Germans.

— Alexander and Roman emperors used existing governmental structures to help administer their empires.

— Alexander and Roman emperors adopted the eastern style of divine monarchy. (Alexander's Greek subjects rebelled, but Augustus's emperor cult set a precedent for succeeding emperors, like Diocletian.)

Many of the contrasting elements reveal the realities of trying to rule an empire.

— Expansion under Alexander was swift, and the empire's life was short, in part because of Alexander's death and because of the traditions of Greek culture. Augustus's long reign helped to solidify the Roman Empire.

— Alexander's military expansion was successful, but the empire lacked a universal ideology necessary for survival. Roman expansion into empire began under the Republic, as Rome conquered its Italian neighbors. After conquest, the granting of Roman citizenship, good administration, Roman law, and access to wealth by indigenous elites encouraged internal stability.

— Hellenistic culture tended to remain dominant in urban areas of Alexander's empire and the successor states, but Romans tended to adapt other cultures to their own.

SUMMARY

1. Macedonia united under Philip II, who then conquered Greece. Upon his death, Alexander overthrew Persia and created a vast, short-lived empire. After Alexander's death in 323 B.C., his commanders competed for portions of the empire. Three emerged victorious and established the successor states of Ptolemaic Egypt, Seleucid Persia, and Antigonid Greece.

2. Alexander's conquests ushered in the Hellenistic Age. Cultural interaction was somewhat limited because Greeks tended to retain Greek ways, but Hellenistic exchange brought many new commodities and ideas from eastern lands into Greek areas. The Hellenistic cities were centers of intellectual life. In larger Hellenistic cities, prejudices gave way to equal opportunities for Hellenized local elites.

3. Hellenistic arts and sciences contributed important works, like new mathematics, literature styles, and scientific knowledge regarding movements of the stars and the earth. New philosophies tended to reflect the uncertainty and concern over living in multicultural cities.

4. Octavian emerged from civil war as the sole ruler of the Roman Empire. Through cunning political maneuvering, he created the principate system. The Roman Empire after Augustus became embroiled in political rivalries among the emperors, the military, and the Senate. The military became the driving political force through assassination and promotion of emperors as early as 68. The pax Romana began to crumble, and eventually a military monarchy replaced the principate system by 211.

5. The third-century border hostilities did not result in the collapse of the Roman Empire because of the reorganization of the empire into two administrative areas by Diocletian. Although reunification existed temporarily under Constantine and Theodosius, the division eventually

became permanent in 395. This division foreshadowed the end of the Roman Empire and the evolution of two autonomous societies, the Western Roman Empire and the Eastern Roman Empire; the latter developed into the Byzantine culture.

6. The Roman exchange saw massive amounts of commodities and various ideas move across the vast empire, affecting both Romans and indigenous populations. Many individuals became Romanized, and many Romans adopted lifestyles of the indigenous populations among whom they lived. Life in the Roman provinces reflected the Roman exchange. Many soldiers retired in the provincial areas, where they influenced and were influenced by local peoples and customs. Rome became a bustling city, full of immigrants, tourists, and merchants.

7. Roman arts and philosophies adopted many Hellenistic styles. Although there was no single great art style, many works of art and literature were produced. Older philosophies enjoyed revivals in the Roman Empire.

8. Roman religious ideas respected the ancient Jewish god, but political hostilities eventually led the Roman government to destroy the Jewish temple and disperse large numbers of Jews throughout the empire. Christianity emerged from Judaism, and Constantine became the first Christian Roman emperor and moved Christianity onto the official list of tolerated Roman religions.

SUGGESTED READINGS

Adkins, Lesley, and Roy Adkins. *Introduction to the Romans.* Secaucus, N.J.: Quintet Publishing Limited, 1991. A short, beautifully illustrated review of Roman culture.

Bury, J. B., and Russell Meiggs. *A History of Greece to the Death of Alexander the Great.* Fourth edition. New York: St. Martin's Press, 1975; reprint with revisions and corrections, 1991. A standard history of Greece.

Ferguson, John. *The Heritage of Hellenism: The Greek World from 323 B.C. to 31 B.C.* In Geoffrey Barraclough, general ed., *History of European Civilization Library.* London: Thames and Hudson, 1973. A good review of Hellenistic culture.

Fox, Robin Lane. *The Search for Alexander.* Boston: Little, Brown, 1980. A study of the life and the impact of Alexander.

Grant, Michael. *History of Rome.* Englewood Cliffs, N.J.: Prentice Hall, 1978. An older but still valuable standard history of Rome.

Jones, A. H. M. *The Decline of the Ancient World.* New York: Longman, 1996. A review of the fragmentation of the late Roman Empire.

Koester, Helmut. *Introduction to the New Testament.* Vol. 1: *History, Culture and Religion of the Hellenistic Age.* Philadelphia: Fortress Press, 1982. A study that examines religious concepts in the Hellenistic Age.

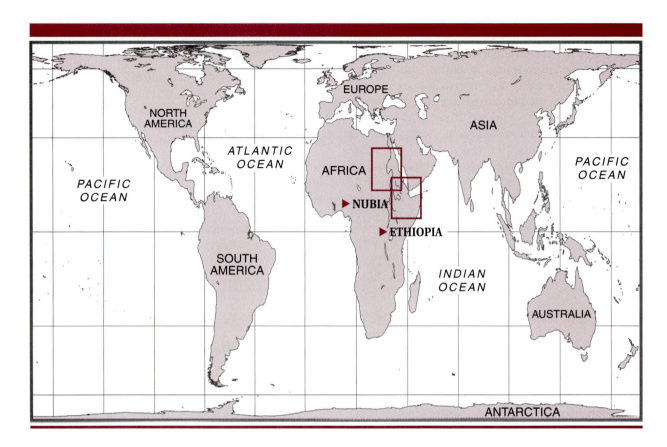

NORTH
AMERICA

ATLANTIC
OCEAN

EUROPE

ASIA

PACIFIC
OCEAN

AFRICA

► NUBIA

► ETHIOPIA

PACIFIC
OCEAN

SOUTH
AMERICA

INDIAN
OCEAN

AUSTRALIA

ANTARCTICA

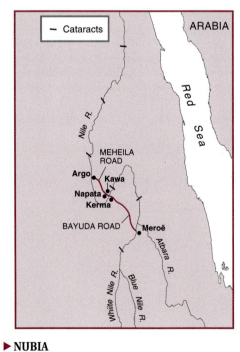

— Cataracts

ARABIA

Nile R.

Red Sea

MEHEILA
ROAD

Argo ● ● Kawa

Napata ●
Kerma ●

BAYUDA ROAD

Meroë ●

Atbara R.

White Nile R.

Blue Nile R.

► NUBIA

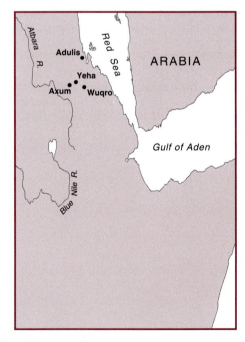

Atbara R.

Red Sea

Adulis ●

ARABIA

Yeha ●
Axum ● ● Wuqro

Gulf of Aden

Blue Nile R.

► ETHIOPIA

Early Civilizations in Nubia and Ethiopia

around 800 B.C.–A.D. 650

Around 2200 B.C., a group of Egyptian explorers scratched their names at the highest point they ascended the Nile. Whether they returned to Egypt and reported to the pharaoh is unknown, but no record of their expedition other than these fragile graffiti has survived. Within a few hundred years, a civilization would develop in the land these Egyptians visited, a civilization that briefly would eclipse and rule Egypt itself. This was one of three great early civilizations of northeastern Africa.

In northeastern Africa, to the south and southeast of Egypt, lay the regions of Nubia and Ethiopia, where the earliest African civilizations outside of Egypt arose. From early times, the people of Nubia and Ethiopia had had contacts with civilizations to the north, and long-distance trade led to the creation of local Nubian and Ethiopian elites, which in turn led to full-blown civilizations. The development of complex societies in other parts of Africa took place somewhat later and is treated in Chapter 15.

EARLY CIVILIZATION IN NUBIA: KUSH AND MEROË, AROUND 800 B.C.–AROUND A.D. 400

The Nubian region lies due south of Egypt, upriver along the Nile River in what today is the Sudan. During the period approximately between 800 B.C. and A.D. 400, this region was dominated by local

213

civilization in the form of states called Kush and Meroë.[1] These states developed largely because of Nubia's favorable location for trade.

Nubia's great virtue was its location along the only reliable route between Egypt and tropical Africa before the development of the domesticated camel and caravan routes across the Sahara. The hostility of the land away from the river made this corridor very narrow indeed, and all trade had to pass through the region's riverside communities, placing the people along it in a prime position to become brokers in trade between Egypt and resource-rich areas to the south. That position was strengthened by the cataracts of the Nile, six series of rapids that were difficult and dangerous to navigate with a boat, forcing traders to carry goods by land.

Although Nubia grew prominent as an intermediary in trade between sub-Saharan Africa and Egypt, Nubia itself was not blessed with great material resources. The Nile's banks supported only a narrow strip of lush vegetation, while areas away from the river were predominantly hot and dry desert. The only land with agricultural potential lay directly along the Nile, and irrigation was necessary to grow crops there. Modest amounts of gold, iron, and other minerals constituted Nubia's only notable natural resources.

Evidence for early civilization in Nubia comes from both documents and archaeology. Unfortunately, many of the documents are written in a locally developed alphabet and language that modern scholars have not yet deciphered. Consequently, most of our knowledge comes from archaeology and Egyptian writings about Nubia. The domination of documentary evidence by Egyptian sources may engender a bias toward stressing the connection between Egypt and Nubia.

Kerma: A Rehearsal for Civilization, around 1800–around 1600 B.C.

Twice Egypt extended its political sway over parts of Nubia, controlling them as colonies. From around 1900 to 1700 B.C., Middle Kingdom rulers held northern Nubia; again from about 1600 to 1100 B.C., New Kingdom rulers extended their rule over northern and central Nubia. While some scholars believe that these colonies were meant to be buffers protecting Egypt's southern frontier, most believe they were designed to control the lucrative Nile trade.

Near the end of the earlier period of Egyptian control, around 1800 B.C., a local society developed in central Nubia. Named "Kerma" after the major city in its territory, this society distinguished itself in terms of trade for the next two hundred years. The city of Kerma itself was walled and had a variety of large structures associated with it. Near the city were two (or more) **deffufas**,[2] massive towers constructed of mud bricks with fired brick facings. Within these structures, archaeologists have found abundant evidence of the manufacture and storage of goods. They also have found many Egyptian-style seals, placed on containers during shipment to ensure that they were not tampered with, and fragments of various goods manufactured in Egypt. The evidence seems clear that the largest structures in Kerma were devoted to the trade of goods and—to a lesser extent—their manufacture, probably an indication of the importance of these activities to the city.

Unfortunately, little else is known about Kerma. A major cemetery has been excavated, and one tomb has yielded what appear to be at least 322 sacrificial victims interred with several elite persons. This suggests that there was substantial class stratification at this date. It also underscores the local element in Kerma, because human sacrifice was not practiced in Egypt at this period.

At one time it was thought that Kerma was really an Egyptian colony, and scholars even wrote about a hypothetical "viceroy of Egypt." Now it is known that the viceroy never existed and that Kerma was an independent Nubian development that traded with Egypt and borrowed freely from its culture. Kerma developed during a weakening in Egypt's hold on the area around 1800 B.C.; and as soon as Egypt reasserted its control around 1600 B.C., Kerma was unable to withstand the hostile attentions of a powerful foreign civilization and yielded to Egypt its control of the Nile trade. Kerma dissolved as a political entity.

According to our limited current knowledge, we probably should not consider Kerma a civilization. Although it possessed the agricultural dependence, class stratification, and long-distance trade

---

[1] **Meroë:** MAYR oh eh

[2] **deffufas:** duh FOO fuhz

FIGURE 9.1 *The Western Deffufa at Kerma. Begun around 1800 B.C., this structure was used for many centuries and was the most important religious building in Kerma. The deffufa (temple) was massive but had very little space inside, most of its volume being composed of masonry. It was remodeled dozens of times, and in its final form the only open interior area was composed of a narrow passage with a sanctuary and a stair to the roof, where rituals presumably were conducted. Virtually nothing is known of the nature of these rituals.* T. Kendall.

that are core characteristics of civilization, it apparently operated with a chiefdom-level government and may have had little occupational specialization. But Kerma remains significant as the first Nubian experiment in complex society and the control of trade, a rehearsal of sorts for what was to follow with the Kush and Meroë kingdoms.

Kush: Nubia Asserts Itself, around 800–around 400 B.C.

Around 1100 B.C., Egypt's internal politics weakened its political situation so much that colonial control of the Nubian region collapsed. The power vacuum initially was filled by a series of local chiefs, each with a territory. Nubia had been under Egyptian control for most of the previous 800 years, and the power of Egyptian culture was demonstrated when the installation of chiefs required the approval of the Egyptian priests of Amun.

By around 800 B.C., the divided power of the chiefs came to be vested in a single king, establish-ing the Kush kingdom, the first indigenous state government in the region. The capital and principal city of Kush was Napata,[3] a colonial town of the old Egyptian regime. Kush's kings were crowned in Napata, at a major temple there. Although evidence is largely lacking, most scholars also suspect that Napata was the focus of Kush's trade, because it lies at the intersection of the Bayuda[4] Road (the land route to the city of Meroë, a major population center) and the Meheila[5] Road (the land route to Kawa and Argo, two more large population centers). In addition, Napata lay just downstream of the Fourth Cataract, at an ideal spot for the reloading of boats with goods that had been carried around the rapids.

During the Kush period, gold mining probably developed in Nubia, and some scholars believe that this was the underpinning of Kushite development. Gold is of little value, however, unless there

[3] **Napata:** nah PAH tah
[4] **Bayuda:** by OO duh
[5] **Meheila:** mah HAY luh

FIGURE 9.2 *King Shebaka of Kush. Identified by the Egyptian writing on his belt, King Shebaka reigned over Kush in the late eighth century B.C. He is shown in a posture distinctive to Egyptian art: rigidly symmetrical and frontal, kneeling in offering to the gods. The eyes, face, and garments show a strong Egyptian cast. The statue is about six inches high and cast in bronze.* National Archaeological Museum, Athens.

is someone to buy it, and presumably trade with Egypt would have been critical to the development of a gold industry.

The state government that ruled Kush was headed by an Egyptian-style divine king who claimed descent from Egyptian gods, particularly Amon. The kings were absolute monarchs with great power over their subjects and in death were memorialized with opulent tombs. King lists trace rulership for most of the Kush period, though there are some inconsistencies within them.

The king and related nobles formed the elite and lived in major cities. Most of the rest of Kush society consisted of commoners who either tilled fields and lived in modest villages or performed manual labor in the cities. An intermediate class in Kush is ill documented, but presumably there was at least a small class of skilled artisans who made luxury goods consumed by the elite and engineers who produced monumental architecture.

The major cities of Kush consisted of monumental temples, palaces, and government buildings (especially warehouses) within a central precinct, surrounded by densely packed houses, which in turn were encircled by a defensive wall. In a style that incorporated both Egyptian and local Nubian characteristics, the monumental buildings were made of both mud bricks and large stone blocks, requiring considerable engineering expertise. The simpler housing consisted mostly of single-room dwellings made of mud bricks with a porch to the rear where cooking and other household activities took place. Because the city walls were limited in diameter, population growth led to more and more commoners living outside the walls.

For a brief period, Kush conquered and ruled Egypt, establishing a short-lived empire. In 712 B.C., Kushite forces installed Shebaka,[6] the king of Kush, as the first pharaoh of Egypt's twenty-fifth dynasty. During the twenty-fifth dynasty, there was a return to Egyptian styles of architecture and art that had been current 1,500 years earlier, and some old temples were copied precisely in new locations. This turning to ancient models extended into the copying of ancient texts, and Kushite copies of some Old Kingdom Egyptian records provide our only copies of ancient documents. Historians have developed no satisfactory explanation for why a Kushite government would emphasize ancient Egyptian forms so strongly, but it may relate to an attempt to legitimize its rule.

Weakened by internal conflict and external assault, Egypt had been easy prey for its Kushite conquerors. But the Kushite military was not sufficiently powerful to protect Egypt from invasion by foreign conquerors; indeed, their weapons were primarily of bronze and no match for the iron weapons of contemporary Southwest Asian militaries. The first of the conquests of this period was

[6]**Shebaka:** sheh BAH kah

by the Assyrians in 667 B.C., and this dispossessed the twenty-fifth dynasty, ending Kush's brief rule outside Nubia. The Assyrians made no effort to penetrate Nubia, however, and the Kush state continued to rule there.

Meroë: Nubia Consolidates Its Position through Trade, around 400 B.C.–around A.D. 400

Around 400 B.C., Meroë began to supplant Napata as the first city of Kush. Though kings continued to be crowned at Napata, their palaces and courts were about 100 miles south in Meroë. Governmental administration was focused in Meroë, and burgeoning trade was controlled from there. In part, this shift may have been to place the capital in a position less vulnerable to military incursions that were constantly threatening the northern parts of Kush in this period; it may also have been in response to river fluctuations that threatened agricultural productivity in the north. Some scholars continue to call this kingdom "Kush," while others designate it as a separate kingdom called "Meroë," a policy we follow here. Our inability to read Meroitic writing prevents us from knowing whether contemporary Nubian writers recognized a distinction.

In general outline, Meroë was much like Kush. Divine kings continued to trace ancestry to Egyptian gods and rule absolutely; governmental hierarchies still carried out the king's wishes throughout the kingdom; the pattern of settlement persisted, with walled cities housing many people, while others lived in villages and produced food by farming and raising animals. There were, however, significant changes in Meroë.

In the forefront of change was the increased volume of trade and diversity of products traded. The Nubian region was now a major conduit of gold, ivory, slaves, and other goods going to Egypt. In return, manufactured goods came from Egypt. Many of these were luxury goods for the elite, including a Roman goblet of silver and a gold ring inscribed in Greek, both found at Meroë. Everyday goods for commoners also came into Nubia through this trade, including wine, pottery, and clothing. Most evidence indicates that goods flowing from Meroë were predominantly raw materials, while goods returning were mostly manu-

factured items. This pattern has become common in modern times, as developing countries supply resources for developed countries to process and return to them.

A second major change was the expansion of iron working. Although iron working in Nubia dates back at least to Kerma, the output was greatly expanded in the Meroë kingdom. Meroë itself, as well as other cities, accumulated high mounds of slag around its edges, testimony to the quantities of iron that must have been produced. There are no signs of technological breakthroughs or greater usage of iron in Meroë of this period, so presumably the increase in output was in response to expanded exportation. Traditional views of Meroë see large quantities of iron traded to the south of Nubia, although some scholars cite the lack of evidence for this and are skeptical. If Meroë had been a major exporter of iron implements, this

FIGURE 9.3 *Hinged Armlet of Queen Amanisha-kheto of Meroë.* *This jewelry, designed to be worn on the upper arm, is made of gold inset with bits of fused glass (at that time a rare and precious material). The central figure on the armlet is a winged goddess reminiscent of Egypt, but the surrounding geometric ornamentation is distinctly Meroitic. This and other gold jewelry overlooked by looters in Queen Amanishakheto's tomb suggest that she was a wealthy and powerful queen.*
Victor R. Boswell Jr. / NGS Image Collection.

would have increased the amount of exported finished goods, improving its balance of trade.

Another significant change is unequivocal evidence for an expanded middle class. Cemeteries consisted of graves with elaborate monuments for the elite and simple graves for the commoners, but for the first time there are graves intermediate in complexity and cost. This probably means the beginnings of a middle class, perhaps emerging from the more skilled artisans, scribes, and petty government officials.

Elite women also improved their status in Meroë. Women began taking increasingly important roles in government; some women, such as Queen Amanitere,[7] served as ruling monarchs. Our evidence is limited to the elite, and there is no evidence revealing whether middle-class and commoner women also had expanded roles in society.

Finally, population was growing rapidly. One result was that the limited agricultural land of Nubia was insufficient to support the number of farmers. As a result, many sought jobs in the cities, leading to a major increase in urbanization. Cities were becoming more numerous, larger, and more densely settled.

Meroë itself was typical of the larger Meroitic cities. In earlier Kush times, the city wall had enclosed most of the city; by the time of Meroë, the wall encircled merely the central precinct, with its monumental palaces and temples made of mud brick, a bath, and servants' quarters. All other development was outside the wall, including a densely packed mass of houses for all but the small elite. The huge iron slag piles at the edges of many cities took up space needed for housing, polluted water supplies, and increased problems of flooding and erosion.

Some population pressure was relieved by the development of the *saqia*,[8] an ox-powered water wheel to lift water from the Nile to agricultural fields. The northern parts of Nubia had been only scantily populated since around 700 B.C., because a long-term fluctuation of river level appears to have made previous irrigation technology ineffective there. With the invention of the *saqia* around A.D. 100, these areas were opened up, and their rapid resettlement between A.D. 100 and 300 suggests that good land was hard to find elsewhere.

[7]**Amanitere:** ah mahn ih TAY ree
[8]*saqia:* SAH kee uh

The Nile's banks in northern Nubia were lined with striplike agricultural villages in later Meroë times, around A.D. 200 to around 400, and a few fortified towns on hilltops administered the area.

Despite the development in northern Nubia, the Meroë kingdom crumbled by around A.D. 400. The reasons are not entirely clear, but the camel may be, in part, implicated. About 100 B.C. seminomadic desert peoples adopted the domesticated camel (camels had been domesticated earlier in southern Asia), and from this time onward, their raids on Meroë settlements became more frequent and intensive. There also are hints, discussed later in this chapter, that the Axum state may have invaded parts of Meroë. Either of these explanations could account for diminishing trade and fortified hilltop towns in northern Nubia in the later years of the Meroë kingdom.

Another intriguing possibility may relate to the demise of Meroë. The pattern of fortified administrative towns and prosperous villages in northern Nubia is in marked contrast to the pattern of rich cities and poor agricultural villages seen in the south. Although no documentary evidence supports the idea, some archaeologists have suggested that the northern pattern is out of keeping with a divine kingship, where commoners are expected to accept their poverty so that the king or his representatives can live in the opulence they warrant. Instead, they suggest, northern Nubia may have effectively seceded from Meroë and been ruled by a series of local warlords. Although this suggestion might explain certain aspects of the evidence, it is difficult to accept this interpretation without further support.

In any case, about A.D. 400 various poorly known local kingdoms, not unlike the domains of warlords discussed in the preceding paragraph, supplanted Meroë. By the sixth century, these were consolidated into the Christian Nubian kingdoms.

Kush and Meroë as a Civilization

Kush and Meroë form a cultural continuum, and, unlike Kerma, they clearly fit the core criteria for civilization. They inherited Kerma's agricultural dependence, long-distance trade, and class stratification, and they developed unambiguous occupational specialization, a state government powerful enough to establish a brief empire, and urbanism.

FIGURE 9.4 Saqia. *The ox-driven water wheel that permitted the expansion of Meroë into northern Nubia continues in use today. This photograph shows a man goading oxen into turning an axle, which transmits its power through gears to lift irrigation water from wells.* Michael S. Yamashita.

In addition, they possessed many of the secondary elements of civilization. Noteworthy among these are their metallurgy (especially as it related to iron), writing, monumental architecture, state religion, great art style, and sophisticated transportation system based largely on the Nile River. The monumental architecture suggests mathematical and engineering skills, and the prominence of trade suggests standardized units of measure, although only limited archaeological evidence supports this suggestion. Many of these elements seem to have been outgrowths of the long-distance trade on which Nubian civilization was based or the aggrandizement of the elite who controlled the trade.

The Relationship of Egypt to Kush and Meroë

The Egyptian heritage of Kush and Meroë is obvious, particularly in the arena of religion. Most of the gods and goddesses to whom temples were dedicated were Egyptian, including Amon, Isis, and Apis. Some temples, such as the temple at Jebel Barkal, were built by Egyptians themselves during their occupations of Nubia, while others were built along similar lines by Nubians after the end of the Egyptian occupations. Much of the painted and low-relief sculpted art that adorned the walls of the temples and other monumental buildings was similar to Egyptian art, with its emphasis on static images, limited perspective, and frontal or silhouette depictions of persons.

The debt to Egypt also was evident in the conceptions and treatment of Nubian royalty. The rulers of Kush and Meroë were divine kings and queens; their leadership was legitimized by their descent from Egyptian deities, and their claim to power was indisputable. In life, rulers assumed Egyptian names and trappings, and many of the luxury goods in their palaces were designed and manufactured in Egypt. In death, monarchs were buried in elaborate tombs, sometimes patterned after the pyramids and mastabas of Egypt, and were accompanied by goods of Egyptian pattern.

FIGURE 9.5 *The Royal Cemetery at the City of Meroë.* *The large pyramids in the final resting place of the kings and queens of Meroë reflect Egyptian influence. This cemetery was in use through most of the span of the kingdom of Meroë. In recent times, some of the small pyramids have been restored and new shrines have been built by Nubian Muslims out of reverence for what they consider as a holy place.* Michael S. Yamashita.

Kush and Meroë, of course, exercised selection in their adoption of Egyptian models for religion and royalty, rejecting or modifying them in some cases. The Egyptian pantheon was augmented with local Nubian gods, particularly Apedemak,[9] the lion god. Many Nubian temples incorporated features unknown in classic Egyptian architecture, including mazelike corridors with ramps connecting different stories. The paintings and sculptures decorating monumental buildings were largely Egyptian in style, yet somewhat different in content. For example, in the Temple at Naqa, Queen Amanitere is depicted wearing a Nubian-style wrapped skirt and brandishing a sword over her head in a very un-Egyptian manner. Ruling queens of Nubia apparently exercised more power than most female Egyptian pharaohs and were not required to wear false beards, as were their counterparts in Egypt. Despite such differences, it is clear that elite culture was heavily influenced by Egypt.

[9]**Apedemak:** ah PEH deh mak

Why did the elite of these early Nubian civilizations take on so many Egyptian characteristics? There probably were many reasons. Part of the answer lies in the political legitimation to be gained by adopting divine kingship on the Egyptian model, especially given the cultural and political links between Nubia and Egypt before 1000 B.C. Another part lies in the Kush rule of Egypt under Shebaka, a period when those links were strengthened greatly. But much of the answer probably lies in the trade relationship between Egypt and Nubia. Large-scale trade between Egypt and Nubia began with Kerma, and, at this time, Nubia was Egypt's untutored country cousin. Settlements in Kerma were smaller, governments were less powerful, the gap between the elite and the commoners was narrower, and the trappings of wealth and power were less grand. It is little wonder that the emerging elite of Kerma looked to a neighbor for a model of how a sophisticated elite should conduct itself. (This pattern has repeated itself in many times and places around the world, as one society emulates another that it believes to be more worldly or sophisticated; a good example is the emulation of French manners and cooking by eighteenth-century North Americans.) It probably is this self-conscious creation of an elite culture in early Nubian civilization that made Egypt's stamp so prominent.

FIGURE 9.6 *Queen Amanitere of Kush. This low-relief sculpture from the Lion Temple in the city of Naqa depicts Queen Amanitere of Kush as a warrior queen, carrying swords and flanked by a fierce lion. The style of depiction draws heavily on Egyptian art, with its profile view, conventions of facial depiction (especially the shape of the eyes), the queen's jewelry (including a snake ornament on her forehead), and the Egyptian hieroglyphics above her right forearm. Her attire and martial attitude, however, are distinctly Kushite.* From Graham Connah, *African Civilizations*, p. 44, fig. 9.6. Reproduced by permission of Cambridge University Press.

EARLY CIVILIZATION IN ETHIOPIA: AXUM, AROUND A.D. 50–650

To the east of Nubia lies the region of Ethiopia consisting of the modern countries of Ethiopia and Eritrea. Beginning around A.D. 50, the kingdom of Axum[10] was the first civilization of Ethiopia.

The region of Ethiopia is dominated by its highlands. Rising thousands of feet above the near-equatorial desert, the highlands provide rich environments with adequate rain and pleasant temperatures. To the northeast, they slant rapidly down to the Red Sea. Soils in many parts of Ethiopia are rich, but there is limited mineral wealth. This environment molded the Axum kingdom.

Information about Axum comes from a wide variety of sources. The Axumites developed a written language, **Ge'ez**,[11] that can be read by modern scholars, and they also wrote in Greek and in a form of Arabic. Although paper documents from Ethiopia are not known until the thirteenth century, earlier coins and stone buildings yield many valuable inscriptions written by Axumites. Also, foreign writers discussed Axum at length. Finally, archaeologists have excavated at several of the major sites.

The Pre-Axumite Period, around 500–around 100 B.C.

Long before the rise of the Axum kingdom, Ethiopians had become sophisticated agriculturalists, adopting crops domesticated elsewhere and domesticating some of their own, including coffee, **tef** (a milletlike grain), okra, and perhaps one kind of eggplant. From this base the Ethiopian population grew, protected from outside attack by mountain barriers.

The Pre-Axumite Period developed around 500 B.C., but there is little solid information about how it came into being. The use of southern Arabian writing is an indication that ties to southern Arabia were strong. Some scholars believe that South Arabians crossed the Red Sea and ascended the highlands, thus spurring the development of

[10] **Axum:** AKS oom
[11] **Ge'ez:** ghee ehz

UNDER THE LENS

The Afrocentric Interpretation

Beginning in the 1970s, some scholars have argued for an **Afrocentric** interpretation of history, wherein Africa is seen as the primary location of important innovations that subsequently spread, coalesced into Western civilization, and were adopted around the world. This interpretation challenges the more widely held view that Western civilization developed primarily through southwestern Asian and European inputs, with contributions from Africa, eastern Asia, the Americas, and elsewhere.

Some Afrocentric ideas are nearly universally rejected among scholars. These include claims that steel and birth control were invented in Africa and spread to the rest of the world, that Africans discovered the Americas, and that Ludwig von Beethoven was an African. Our concern in this box is not with unlikely suggestions such as these, which we see as obscuring the argument of Afrocentrism.

A far stronger argument for Afrocentric interpretation is presented by Martin Bernal. In his *Black Athena*, he developed a complicated argument that derives Greek civilization—and ultimately Western civilization—from black Africa. Reduced to its basics, his argument is that Egypt was "essentially African," relating more to sub-Saharan African cultures than to its neighbors in the Mediterranean and southwestern Asia; further, he argues that Egypt colonized Greece, taking it from its barbaric past into civilization and founding Western civilization, which later would spread around the world. Hence, Africa was the seat of the development of world civilization. He calls this model of development the "Revised Ancient Model," emphasizing his claim that it was accepted by the ancients; the alternative explanation, seeing ancient Greece as a melting pot of eastern Mediterranean and local influences, is called the "Aryan model," emphasizing its purported racist overtones.

Why have traditional scholars come to such radically different interpretations from Bernal and the other Afrocentrists? According to many Afrocentrists, it is because the traditional scholars either are racists or are captive to racist ideas that they learned in traditional history. The critics of Afrocentrism suggest that the reason lies in the weaknesses of the Afrocentric argument.

Many of the facts accepted by Afrocentrists are in question. Bernal, for example, states that he has determined 20 to 25 percent of all Greek words to be of Egyptian origin; linguists see almost no Egyptian origins in Greek, which is of the Indo-European family, not the Hamitic family of Egyptian. Bernal also argues that Greek art resembles Egyptian art; art historians see few such similarities.

Although these facts may or may not be in error, a deeper criticism of Afrocentrism is that it searches for *the* place from which Western civilization spread. The authors of this text argue that Western civilization was woven out of diverse threads from many places, including Africa, Asia, and Europe, and that no single homeland can be found. Because of this, we reject Afrocentrism, Eurocentrism, or any other "centrism" that argues for focusing undue attention on the contributions of one people and (by implication) paying less attention to the contributions of the rest of the world.

---

the Pre-Axumite kingdom; others argue that the link to southern Arabia was based on trade and stimulated a local development. In the southern Arabian writing the Pre-Axumites used, they referred to themselves as the "kingdom of D'MT." (In common with ancient Hebrew, this writing omitted vowels, so the true name might have been something like "D'Meta.")

The Pre-Axumite kingdom was urban, with a major city at Yeha.[12] There, archaeologists have found a temple to Almouqah[13] (the local moon god), elite tombs, and a stepped pyramid of unknown function. All of these were made of masonry and, though by no means so massive as the later Axumite architecture, qualify as monumental. The people used iron and bronze and may have obtained the bronze through trade. The Pre-Axumites of Yeha may have had a state, although many scholars believe the "kingdom of D'MT" was really a sophisticated chiefdom. Pre-Axumite soci-

[12]**Yeha:** YAY hah

[13]**Almouqah:** ahl MOO kah

FIGURE 9.7 *Early Axumite Writing.* *This stone altar from the first century A.D. shows a man on a camel, identified by the writing beneath as Ha'anum, son of Du-zu'd. The inscription is written in the Ge'ez script and bears similarities to writing from South Arabia.* British Museum/Michael Holford.

and the *nagashi* became the king. From this beginning, the Axum kingdom expanded to become the Axum Empire, absorbing (sometimes forcibly) smaller polities at the fringes of its realm. These groups often maintained their distinct ethnic status, although, as the Axum state expanded, those near the center were likely to become assimilated into generalized Axumite culture.

Throughout its span, the Axum Empire was primarily agricultural, in that the majority of its people lived in villages and towns, farming or raising livestock for a living. The variety of altitudes in the highlands provided many microclimates, so a great variety of crops could be grown within walking distance of most communities. The only major limitation to agriculture was scarcity of water in some places, and terracing and irrigation solved that. Although there are records of occasional famines, the Axum Empire seems to have suffered hunger less frequently than most of its neighbors.

The Axum Empire was built on a strong agricultural base, but long-distance trade was what made it an important civilization. Land trade through the rugged highlands of Ethiopia was difficult and costly, though it was carried on to some extent. The Red Sea coast of Ethiopia (now Eritrea), which provided an economical link to major sea routes, was much more widely used. By A.D. 65, the Axum Empire had extended its domain to include portions of the coast, notably the city of Adulis. Adulis had been developed by the Ptolemaic Egyptians, but the Axum Empire expanded the harbor and improved its facilities in the last years of the first century A.D. With its sheltered harbor at Gabaza and its fine facilities, Adulis was an excellent place for vessels to stop; equally important, it lay along the Red Sea route that connected Egypt and the Mediterranean with Arabia, Persia, and India. From this point onward, Axum's fate was tied to foreign trade.

There was something of a power void in Red Sea trading following the fall of Egypt to the Roman Empire in 31 B.C., and Axum was one of the states that took advantage of the situation. Its excellent harbor, government-supported trade, and keen interest in trading made it a strong competitor in the field, and the profits from this trade are what permitted the Axum Empire to develop.

The city of Axum apparently was the first capital of the Axum state. Like Yeha before it, the city of Axum had been a religious center before it became a major political center. A divine king

ety, in many ways, was analogous to Kerma in Nubia, because each had many of the primary elements of civilization but probably did not have state-level government. Each also paved the way for the emergence of the civilization that followed.

Around 100 B.C., the Pre-Axumite kingdom disappeared under unknown circumstances. Shortly thereafter it was replaced by a more extensive, powerful, and important polity: Axum.

The Rise of Axum

After the fall of the Pre-Axumite kingdom, Ethiopia was ruled by a multitude of small, local chiefdoms. Around A.D. 50, several of these welded together under the ***nagashi***, an individual who led several clans. This group was the core of the Axum state,

FIGURE 9.8 *Ethiopian Meal.* *There are few known pictures of everyday Axumite life, and none that show people eating. It is clear, however, that many modern Ethiopian eating habits developed in the Axum Empire. This eighteenth-century Ethiopian illustration depicts table manners that probably extend unbroken from Axum to contemporary Ethiopia. At the right, a woman is shown making* injera, *a spongy and flexible bread, from a millet-flour batter. In the center, men use the* injera *to grasp bits of a stewlike dish from their bowls, eating wrapper and stew together.* British Library Orient 723/Courtesy of the Harvard University Library.

serves in both the religious and political worlds, and a religious center brings an aura of authority that makes it an appropriate secular capital.

Axum as a Functioning State

The Axum state was ruled from at least the second century A.D. by an absolute monarch called "the king of kings." This was more than merely a colorful title, because the administration of provinces was delegated to local kings who owed allegiance and tribute to the king of kings in the city of Axum. Axum was an empire.

In pre-Christian times, the king was considered divine: the son of Mahrem, the god of war. After the fourth-century official conversion of the Axum Empire to Christianity, the king's legendary parentage was shifted to King Solomon and Queen Balkis of Sheba (modern Yemen in southern Arabia). Within the Christian setting, this was as close to divinity as possible, and it underscored Axum's special relationship to southern Arabia, discussed in the following paragraphs. King lists exist for the Axum Empire, though they have gaps.

Beneath Axum's emperor and other members of the royal house were at least two classes. By 300 or so, a middle class had developed, consisting of artisans, government officers, and skilled workers. Below them were commoners—mostly rural peasants and urban laborers. There also apparently were slaves, though we know little of the details of their status.

Although there were many cities in the state of Axum, the city of Axum was the largest and probably the most complex. Like almost all Axumite cities, it had no fortifications surrounding it, but it had a unique feature: a central precinct devoted to the royal family and their retainers. In this area were the palace, governmental administration buildings, military garrisons, and a religious center. Outside of town, two **stela parks**, elite cemeteries with tall stones as markers, housed royal tombs. Surrounding the central precinct were industrial areas and houses. The population of the city of Axum at its height is estimated at between 10,000 and 20,000 people.

Trade ranged far and wide, by both land routes and sea routes. The Axum Empire is known to have had extensive trading relations with Rome and its eastern provinces (including Egypt), southern Arabia, India, and Sri Lanka. Trade was highly regulated to benefit the royal house. There were royal taxes on imports into the Axum Empire, as well as on goods that passed through its port on the way to other destinations; these were collected at a posh customs house at Gabaza, the port installation for Adulis. Certain goods were under royal monopoly, and although their nature is unknown, it is almost certain that they were items that returned high profits.

Documented imports into the Axum Empire include iron, other metals, fabrics (including silk), clothing, perfumes, glass, and ceramics. The Axumite elite seasoned their foods with imported spices, cooked it in imported vegetable oils, and washed it down with imported wine; they used sugarcane from Southwest Asia, though it is unknown whether it was used as a food or as a medicine. Documented exports include a variety of materials for jewelry and art, including ivory, gold, obsidian, emeralds, and tortoise shell. Other exports include exotic medicinal items, such as rhinoceros horn and hippopotamus teeth; spices, perfumes, and slaves were other important exports. The Roman Empire was a market for certain popular "African exotica" that were funneled through Axum: monkeys for pets, other live animals for fighting in the arenas, and exotic foods for Roman tables. The Axum Empire had a healthier balance of trade than Kush and Meroë, with a mix of raw materials and finished products among both imports and exports.

The Axum Empire apparently was always alert to an opportunity to expand its trade. According to Procopius, a contemporary Roman writer, ambassadors from the Eastern Roman Empire had little trouble convincing King Kaleb of Axum to attempt wresting the silk trade away from Persia around 520. The Axum Empire's geographical location, however, was at the edge of the silk trade network, putting it at a disadvantage and dooming its attempt to failure.

In return for the rewards it reaped for its elite, the Axum Empire guaranteed traders safe passage. This required a significant military, which probably already existed, since the origin of the Axum state may have involved military action, and certainly its maintenance did. Rebellions of subject polities sometimes occurred, particularly during the confusion at the succession of a new king, and coin inscriptions inform us of the zeal with which the military put them down. Military garrisons guarded the city of Axum and other settlements. The general lack of archaeological evidence of warfare throughout the Axum Empire is impressive, and walled settlements were rare, suggesting that the capable Axumite army served as a successful deterrent to internal warfare. The importance of the military, particularly in the establishment of the Axum state, probably was symbolized by the descent of the pre-Christian king from the god of war.

Although Axum and Meroë were rivals, the Axum Empire's military might probably was not directly responsible for the fall of Meroë in Nubia. In an inscription dating to around 340, King Ezana[14] of Axum claimed that he had conquered lands to the west along the Nile, and some historians have interpreted this statement as referring to Meroë. The date may be a little early but is approximately appropriate. The problem with this interpretation is that there is little or no evidence for it in Meroë. Ethiopian goods appear with no greater frequency there after this date (they actually drop off somewhat), and there are no evidences of conquering invaders. There are at least five major branches of the Nile to the west of Ethiopia, and Ezana's claim, if true, probably refers to the conquest of some local polity along one of those branches.

Military action in southern Arabia is less ambiguous. Axumite troops occupied Sheba in the sixth century. In 570 they made an unsuccessful attack on Mecca in Arabia. This was the year of Muhammad's birth, and the failure of a Christian army to take the holy city would later take on great symbolic significance in the Islamic world.

The conversion of the Axum Empire to Christianity began around 330. At this date, Frumentius (an Axumite leader known by this Latinized name) was ordained first bishop of Axum, and King Ezana's well-orchestrated conversion followed shortly thereafter. A public baptism, initiating Ezana into Christianity, was advertised in advance and attended by throngs. The conversion of the elite was rapid, and pre-Christian state and royal symbols were replaced. Coins formerly had a disk and crescent on them, representing the sun god and moon god; these motifs were replaced with a cross. The pre-Christian royalty were buried in

[14] **Ezana:** eh ZAHN uh

IN THEIR OWN WORDS

Ezana's Account of His Nubian Victories

This account, written by Emperor Ezana of Axum around 340, describes his victories beyond the western edge of his empire. Clearly, this was in the Nile region, but was it Meroë? Some scholars consider the Seda River of this document to be the White Nile branch of the Nile and the Takkaze River to be the Atbara River, in which case the conquests would be in Meroë; others, however, suggest that the Seda may be the Blue Nile branch, in which case these conquests probably were to the east of the kingdom of Meroë.

Through the might of the Lord of All[a] I took the field against the Noba,[b] when the people of Noba revolted, when they boasted, and the Noba said, "He will not cross over the Takkaze," when they did violence to the peoples Mangurto and Hasa and Barya,[c] and the Blacks[d] waged war on the Red[e] Peoples and a second and a third time broke their oath and without consideration slew their neighbors and plundered our envoys and our messengers whom I had sent to interrogate them, robbing them of their possessions and seizing their lances. When I sent again and they did not hear me and reviled me and made off, I took the field against them. And I armed

myself with the power of the Lord of the Land and fought on the Takkaze at the ford of Kemalke. And thereupon they fled and stood not still, and I pursued the fugitives twenty-three days, slaying some of them and capturing others and taking booty from them, where I came, while prisoners and booty were brought back by my people who marched out, while I burnt their towns, those of masonry and those of straw, and seized their grain and their bronze and their dried meat and the images in their temples and destroyed the stocks of grain and cotton, and the enemy plunged into the river Seda, and there were many who perished in the water, the number I know not, and as their vessels foundered, a multitude of people, men and women, were drowned. . . . And I arrived at the Kasu,[f] slaying some and taking others prisoner at the junction of the rivers Seda and Takkaze. And on the day after my arrival, I dispatched into the field the troops of Mahaza and the Dawawa and Falha and Sera[g] up the Seda against the towns of masonry and straw. . . . My people returned safe and sound after they had taken some prisoners and slain others and had seized their booty through the power of the Lord of Heaven. And I erected a throne at the junction of the rivers Seda and Takkaze, opposite the town of masonry which is on the peninsula.

[a] **Lord of All:** the Christian God
[b] **Noba:** Nubians
[c] **Barya:** tribal peoples within the Axum Empire
[d] **Blacks:** dark-skinned people
[e] **Red:** light-skinned

[f] **Kasu:** a Nubian people
[g] **Sera:** more tribal peoples within the Axum Empire

---

subterranean tombs with tall stone stelae over them in special cemeteries in the city of Axum; Christian royalty were placed in above-ground tombs on a hill outside the city. The legendary ancestry of the king, already discussed, shifted from pre-Christian gods to biblical figures.

The rapid conversion of Axumite leadership, many historians believe, was prompted by political and economic reasons. As will be discussed later, the Axum Empire had strong ties with the Roman Empire, which had recently become a Christian empire. Axumite leaders well may have felt that sharing religion would assist the formation of alliances with Roman traders. Whatever the motivation, Axum was one of the earliest states to adopt Christianity.

As was usual in many places that adopted Christianity in this era, conversion of commoners, especially in the more rural provinces, went more slowly. Despite royal encouragement, conversion went so slowly that the king found it necessary to sponsor activities by Syrian Christian missionaries in rural Axum as late as the early fifth century.

Axumite Christianity was **monophysite**. That is, it held that Jesus Christ had a single, unitary nature, not the dual natures of man and god that mainstream Christianity claimed. Monophysite churches were common in this period, centered on the eastern Mediterranean and northeastern Africa. A council of Christian bishops declared this view heretical in 451, creating a rift between Ethiopian and mainstream Christianity.

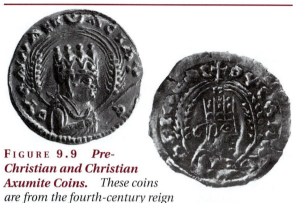

FIGURE 9.9 *Pre-Christian and Christian Axumite Coins.* *These coins are from the fourth-century reign of King Ezana; both bear his image. The pre-Christian coin (left) is from the early part of his reign and displays the disk and crescent that symbolize the sun god and the moon goddess respectively. The coin on the right was minted after Ezana's conversion to Christianity and replaces the earlier symbols with the Christian cross. Ezana's religious conversion was a major event in the history of the Axum Empire, and it was commemorated in literature, songs, and art.* Left: Courtesy of the Trustees of the British Museum. *Right:* Courtesy of the Institute of Addis Ababa, Ethiopia.

Axum as a Civilization

Axum possessed all the core elements of civilization. Its agricultural base supported a state government that developed into an empire; long-distance trade financed the government and the elite of the class structure. Occupational specialists produced items to fuel trade and provided services for other specialists. The city of Axum dominated an urban hierarchy that extended throughout the Axum Empire.

In addition, most of the secondary elements of civilization, many of which have been touched upon in the preceding pages, also were present in Axum. These include metallurgy, a state religion, a well-developed transportation system, and writing. Monumental architecture and coinage warrant a bit more discussion here.

Axumites designed and erected many works of monumental architecture. Reflecting cosmopolitan influences in the Axum Empire, designers gave some buildings Greek or Arabian elements, while others have such distinctively Axumite elements as wall recesses and low-relief geometric designs carved into stone faces. The Axum Empire primarily derived its great art style, symbols, and trappings for the elite from within, borrowing only occasional elements from neighboring countries.

Perhaps most unusual of the Axumite monuments are the immense stelae that mark royal tombs in the stela parks. Some of these are the largest single-piece sculptures ever made. They are tall, slender stones, carved to imitate windows and doors and conventionally described by the number of "stories" the carving makes them appear to have. The tallest known is 13 stories, measuring more than 108 feet high yet only about 9 feet wide. The stone for these stelae was quarried locally, reducing the hazards of long-distance transport of such long and narrow pieces of stone. Nonetheless, the engineering skills and organization needed to transport, work, and raise these enormous and unwieldy stelae were considerable.

FIGURE 9.10 *Stela from Axum.* *The death of a member of the Axumite royalty was an event of great importance, and the deceased was interred in a special royal cemetery that included many stelae. These stelae were tall and narrow, with carved surfaces that resembled the doors and windows of a house. Carved from a single stone, the stela shown rises seventy feet and is carved to depict ten "floors." Dating to about* A.D. *600, this stela is the only one that is still upright.* Werner Forman/Art Resource, N.Y.

Axumite coins have been mentioned as sources for inscriptions, but their place in Axumite civilization is important, too. Axum was the first African state other than Egypt to mint coins, doing so from about 270 onward. Presumably the Axum Empire's mercantile orientation made coinage an important item, and Axumite metallurgical skills made it practical. Axumite emperors took the opportunity to place political slogans and symbols on coins, fortifying their position. Axumite coins were used regularly in southern Arabia, Syria, Meroë, and the Roman Empire.

Unlike Kush and Meroë, Axum was a vibrant part of the Greco-Roman world. Far from a provincial backwater, it took a significant role in political relationships between major countries. Indeed, in the late third century, Mani, the noted Persian historian and theologian, placed Axum in powerful company as one of the four great empires of the world, along with Rome, Persia, and China.

The Decline of Axum, around A.D. 600–650

From the beginning it was clear that the Axum Empire would rise or fall with its trade. In good times the Axumites had profited from their membership in a commercial network that linked countries on three continents, but they were trapped in that network when new networks developed, excluding the Axum Empire.

Between around 600 and 650, the Axum Empire went into a rapid decline from which it never recovered. Imports dwindled, the port languished, and royal coffers were depleted. Even the long-time capital city may have shifted. In 630, King Ashama ibn Abjar[15] was buried not in the city of Axum as had been all of his predecessors but at Wuqro,[16] to the southeast. This may indicate that the religious glue holding together the Axum Empire was coming undone. Finally, in 650, the Axum state was conquered by Gudit, a woman chief of the Agau tribe, and the old Axumite territory was divided into local rulerships.

During the rise of Axum, the Roman Empire had been politically ascendant. Its powerful military had claimed a huge empire, and its efficient political machinery had administered it. On the eastern side of the Red Sea, the Roman Empire and

the Axum Empire had come to an alliance of sorts, based on common economic interests. Axum exported certain goods to Rome, particularly the so-called African exotica: rare animals, unusual foods, and strange medicines. The effort by ambassadors from the Eastern Roman Empire to channel the silk trade through Axum was merely an attempt to expand an existing trade link.

But Persia and its Arab allies were on the opposite bank of the Red Sea, poised to challenge the Roman-Axumite alliance. In the early seventh century, the Axum Empire sent troops to southern Arabia, probably in an unsuccessful attempt to thwart the efforts of Persian troops there. In the meantime, Persian assaults were weakening the Eastern Roman Empire, and Arabs allied with Persia finished the conquest in 642. At this point, a critical market for Axum's goods closed and military rivals were strengthened. Concurrent with its commercial woes, the environment of Axum was suffering from misuses. Environmental degradation depleted critical resources, creating problems in supplying luxury goods for trade as well as food for local consumption. The upshot was the destruction of Axum's commercial power and the rapid end of the state.

THE COMMERCIAL BASIS FOR THE EARLY CIVILIZATIONS OF NUBIA AND ETHIOPIA

Kush, Meroë, and Axum shared a commercial basis for their prosperity. They were situated in favorable locations along transportation routes, and their agricultural bases were strong enough to support economies focused on trade. To a certain extent, their fortunes were linked. Many scholars believe that the opening of Adulis as an Axumite port hurt Meroë's economic welfare, and some believe that this was an important contributing factor to the breakup of Meroë.

It may have been inevitable that the Axum Empire would dominate the trading competition. Its position gave it access to the sea and areas beyond sub-Saharan Africa, such as Arabia and India. Meroë, on the other hand, was restricted to the sub-Saharan trade that made its way down the Nile. Axum's stronger economy also made it more

[15] **Ashama ibn Abjar:** ah SHAH mah ihb uhn AB jahr
[16] **Wuqro:** WOO kroh

PATHS TO THE PAST

Environmental Degradation at the City of Axum

Smog and acid rain may be recent problems, but the actions of ancient peoples also damaged their environments. A study by the geographer Karl Butzer has examined some of the unanticipated and negative effects that resulted from use of the environment at the city of Axum.

Soils record amazing detail about the environment during their formation, and their careful analysis can reveal details of climate, vegetation, and human land use. Butzer looked at soils around the city of Axum and teased out their story through careful analysis. The chronology of Axum has been revised since his study, and this summary adjusts his dates in light of more recent findings.

At around 100 B.C., a marked climatic change took place in the Ethiopian highlands. The rainy season, formerly three to four months long, nearly doubled to about six months. The total amount of rain falling per year increased considerably, meaning that more water was available in and on the surface of the ground. This resulted in a near doubling of the growing season, so that two crops—rather than one—could be harvested in a normal year. It also meant that most locales could accomplish this result without irrigation. The result of this change was an increase in the food supply, followed by steady population growth.

This climatic pattern persisted for several centuries, during which time the city of Axum reached its peak population. By about 500, however, problems began to set in. Catastrophic erosion began occurring, sometimes denuding entire hillsides to the bedrock. Most of this erosion was in the form of sediments washing gently down a slope, but some of it was in mudslides, occasionally burying parts of the outskirts of the city of Axum.

The erosion was only a symptom of the greater problem: overuse of the land. Even at only 14 degrees above the equator, the city of Axum's elevation of about 6,700 feet above sea level kept the climate cool, and firewood must have been a critical commodity. Add to this the need for wood to build houses and to cook food, and the city's 10,000 or more inhabitants must have used a good deal of wood. In so doing, they cut too many trees from their forests, opening up soils to erosion.

The consequences were several. First, of course, wood had to be cut at increasing distances from the city of Axum, increasing the cost of procuring it. Also, forest-dwelling animals were driven farther away. The cost to the ecosystem undoubtedly was much broader, but two species were very important to the Axumites. The civet cat, a forest-dwelling carnivore, has strong scent glands that produce **civet**, a musky substance used in perfumes. This was one of Axum's exports, but it would have been increasingly difficult to procure after 500. Similarly, elephants would have retreated from these cleared areas, making ivory harder to obtain for export.

Finally, around 600, the climate changed again, decreasing the reliability of rainfall. After this date, total amounts of rainfall diminished, though rain increasingly fell in a few big storms that spawned flooding and erosion. The forest had difficulty reestablishing itself under these conditions, and the decrease in usable farm land meant that people had difficulty producing enough food for themselves.

These problems were not the cause of the Axum Empire's fall, but they were significant problems that the empire would have had to face if it had survived long enough. As it was, the successors to Axum were left with scars that have not yet entirely healed. Human beings are naturally intrusive to environments, building cities and establishing high concentrations of people. Only with the greatest care can they avoid degrading the environment that supports them.

of an equal trading partner with countries to the north, dealing in both raw materials and finished products.

Kush and Meroë were shaped by a complex interplay of local factors and external contact with civilizations that served as models. Although they derived some inspiration from Egypt and southern Arabia, they were not mere copies of those civilizations. No amount of instruction about urbanism, for example, will induce a society to live in cities unless it has the population levels, economic development, and political organization to permit it.

NUBIA	ETHIOPIA		
		2000 B.C.	
Kerma, c. 1800–1600 B.C.	Egyptian colonies, c. 1900–1700 B.C.		
	Egyptian colonies, c. 1600–1100 B.C.	1500 B.C.	
		1000 B.C.	
Kush, c. 800–400 B.C.			Shebaka installed as Kushite pharaoh of Egypt, 712 B.C.
			Kushites ejected from Egypt by Assyrians, 667 B.C.
		500 B.C.	
Meroë, c. 400 B.C.–A.D. 400	Pre-Axumite Period, c. 500–100 B.C.		
			Adoption of domesticated camel, c. 100 B.C.
		A.D. 1	
	Axum, A.D. 50–650		Axum expands to coast, 65
Rapid settlement of northern Nubia, A.D. 100–300			*Saqia* invented, c. 100
			Axum begins minting coins, 270
	Conversion to Christianity, A.D. 330–450		Ezana converts to Christianity, 331
			Ezana conquers lands to west, 340
		A.D. 500	
			Unsuccessful Axumite attack on Mecca, 570
			Conquest and dissolution of Axum, 650

SUMMARY

1. Trade between Egypt and sub-Saharan Africa encouraged the development of the Kush and Meroë kingdoms in Nubia. They were preceded by the Kerma culture, which may have been a sophisticated chiefdom and apparently was not a civilization. Kush and Meroë meet the criteria for civilization.

2. Around 800 B.C., about three centuries after Egyptian withdrawal from its Nubian colony, the Kush kingdom developed; Meroë developed out of Kush. Trade intensified throughout the span of Kush and Meroë.

3. Kush and Meroë were states with divine kings who traced their ancestry to the Egyptian gods. Many of the elite symbols of these kingdoms were adopted from the Egyptians whose colonies had ruled much of the area for nearly 800 years and who formed their most important trading partners. In addition, Kush's conquest and half-century rule of Egypt cemented the Egypt-Nubia ties.

4. The Meroë kingdom disintegrated, perhaps under military pressure from camel-mounted desert raiders or from Axum. It was replaced by local chiefdoms. The rise of Axum may have sped the fall of Meroë—either directly, through military action or, more likely, through superior geographical position and the luring away of trade.

5. The Pre-Axumite kingdom probably was an urban chiefdom, though little is known about it.

6. The Axum kingdom developed in Ethiopia, also under the stimulus of trade; it rapidly developed into the Axum Empire. The Axum Empire focused its commercial attentions on the Red Sea trade and had a strong partner in the Roman Empire.

7. The Axum Empire was ruled by a divine monarch, an emperor who delegated power to subordinate local kings, who in turn rendered him tribute. Regulations ensured that the divine monarch would profit greatly by trade.

8. The Axum state had a strong military that ensured domestic peace and safety to traders and conquered new areas to become part of the Axum Empire.

9. The Axum Empire officially became a Christian state around 330. The elite converted rapidly, though rural peasants took much longer. Conversion probably aided the Axum Empire's economic alliance with the Roman Empire.

10. Axum was a society meeting the criteria for civilization. It was a major power and exerted considerable influence in politics beyond its borders.

11. The Axum Empire declined and disintegrated as changes in political relationships between countries destroyed its commercial basis. The alliance between Persia and some Arab groups was successful at overcoming the Roman-Axumite alliance. Supply problems created by environmental deterioration aggravated Axum's commercial problems.

SUGGESTED READINGS

Adams, William Y. *Nubia: Corridor to Africa*. London: Allen Lane, 1977. (The 1984 reprint has an updated introduction.) Classic treatment of the Kush and Meroë civilizations.

Bernal, Martin. *Black Athena: The Afroasiatic Roots of Classical Civilization*. Two vols. New Brunswick, N.J.: Rutgers University Press, 1987, 1991. Presentation of Bernal's Afrocentric interpretation.

Butzer, Karl. "Rise and Fall of Axum, Ethiopia: A Geo-Archaeological Interpretation." *American Antiquity* 46(3) (1981):471–95. Technical treatment of Axum's historic environmental degradation.

Connah, Graham. *African Civilizations: Precolonial Cities and States in Tropical Africa: An Archaeological Perspective*. Cambridge, Eng.: Cambridge University Press, 1987. A good general treatment of African civilizations other than Egypt.

Munro-Hay, S. C. *Aksum: An African Civilisation of Late Antiquity*. Edinburgh: University of Edinburgh Press, 1991. A popular account of Axum and the author's excavations there.

Trigger, Bruce. *Nubia Under the Pharaohs*. London: Thames and Hudson, 1976. General treatment of Egyptian colonies in Nubia and their possible successors.

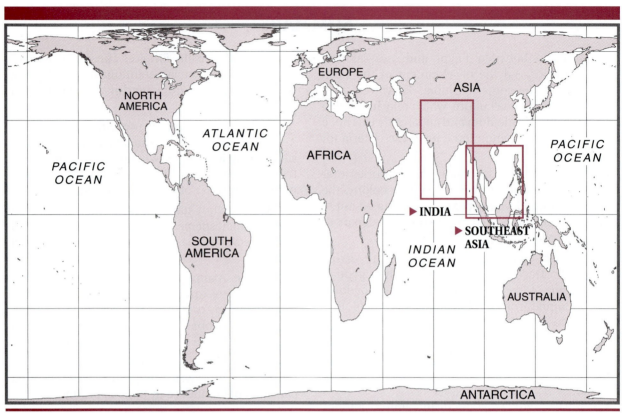

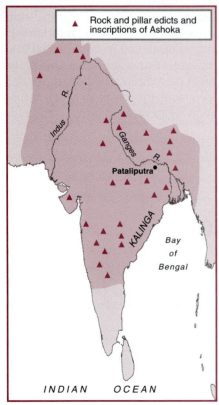

▲ Rock and pillar edicts and inscriptions of Ashoka

Indus R.

Ganges R.

Pataliputra

KALINGA

Bay of Bengal

INDIAN OCEAN

▶ **INDIA**

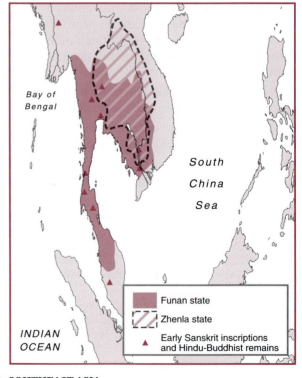

Bay of Bengal

South China Sea

INDIAN OCEAN

Funan state

Zhenla state

▲ Early Sanskrit inscriptions and Hindu-Buddhist remains

▶ **SOUTHEAST ASIA**

NORTH AMERICA

ATLANTIC OCEAN

EUROPE

ASIA

PACIFIC OCEAN

PACIFIC OCEAN

AFRICA

▶ INDIA

▶ **SOUTHEAST ASIA**

INDIAN OCEAN

SOUTH AMERICA

AUSTRALIA

ANTARCTICA

Indian Empires, Society, Ideology, and Regional Influence

around 500 B.C.–around A.D. 600

The Indian emperor had wielded enormous power for years. His stooped shoulders testified to the heavy burden he had borne, and he wished to retire to a life of ascetic discipline far away from the burdensome world. His son could rule effectively, expanding the vast realm already conquered. Yes, it was time. The Jain priest smiled and offered the white robe, and the two men set off to join their fellows on a journey to the south.

This Jain story recounts the fate of Chandragupta, a mighty Indian emperor who abandoned his throne for spiritual treasures. In this chapter, we will examine the interplay of politics, society, ideology, and international influence in the early imperial age.

In this era, Indians fashioned two major empires, the Maurya and the Gupta, that united significant regions of the subcontinent. Each used religion to govern culturally diverse subjects. Buddhism spread throughout Central, East, and Southeast Asia, while many Southeast Asians adopted aspects of Hindu culture.

At the same time, Indian society grew more complex, and a caste system developed that was largely based on occupation and strictly regulated group interaction. Indian rulers regarded agriculture as an essential part of the economy and also encouraged trade. Both were important revenue sources for Indian governments.

THE MAURYA EMPIRE, AROUND 320–AROUND 180 B.C.

Over the centuries after 1000 B.C., small states began to appear in the Ganges River Valley. By the sixth and fifth centuries B.C., regional kingdoms with complex bureaucracies appeared and lasted for decades. In the late fourth century B.C., the first empire emerged, united the Ganges region, and used it as a base from which to expand westward and southward. At its height, the Maurya[1] Empire united and ruled much of the Indian subcontinent.

Origins and Early Empire

Significant economic and social developments underlay the founding of the Maurya Empire. The introduction and spread of iron axes and plows in the Ganges River Valley during the first half-millennium B.C. helped develop an agricultural economy. By the sixth century B.C., agricultural villages became key sources of tax revenue for states. Over time, villages also became socially stratified, and artisans began producing wares for urban markets. As cities grew, artisans and merchants organized themselves into guilds that managed trade and other matters. By the fifth century B.C., coinage, letters of credit, and promissory notes reflected widespread economic activity and stimulated further growth.

The founder of the Maurya Empire, Chandragupta Maurya (reign dates around 320–around 301 B.C.), came from an elite family of the warrior caste. He founded a dynasty that ruled for nearly 150 years. Specifically, Chandragupta ruled for decades after usurping power from an earlier monarch, and that state in the central Ganges region provided a base for conquering the entire river valley and expanding west to the Indus region. A key aim of these policies was to gain control over important trade routes. Indeed, the prosperity of Maurya rule lay in the lucrative trade taxes.

Bureaucracy had been a feature of earlier political life, and the system Chandragupta inherited was complicated. Most government bureaus dealt with financial matters or control of the people and the lands. Manufacturing enterprises were supervised by a board of officials. Tax collection was a vital state concern, and the tax on agricultural land usually averaged between one-quarter and one-half of the annual harvest. Commercial activities also received the attention of a bureau. A census and statistics bureau kept the state informed about the population and the yields of mines and other government properties. Another board oversaw the upkeep of public lands and facilities. A separate governmental unit handled military affairs. The infantry numbered in the tens of thousands. Thousands more served in the cavalry or worked in the elephant force.

Pataliputra,[2] the imperial capital, possessed a palisade with nearly 600 towers and was several times larger than Rome in the second century A.D. The circumference of the city wall measured 21 miles, and a wide and deep moat further protected the capital.

Security matters became an obsessive concern for the Maurya emperor and went far beyond the physical defense measures of the palisade and moat. A vast network of spies and informers also provided security in the capital and a check on the bureaucracy. These informers included clerics, students, merchants, ordinary subjects, and prostitutes.

The empire was subdivided into districts approximating the earlier tribal and regional boundaries. Significant areas received the close attention of government officials, including trusted military commanders and kin of the monarch. Often, if a region handed over its tax revenues, the central government left it alone.

Though published long after the fall of the Maurya state, the *Treatise on Financial Gain* presents a political philosophy that probably originated in Chandragupta's era. Largely written by Kautilya, one of Chandragupta's most effective officials, it underwent many revisions. Begun around 300 B.C., the *Treatise* opens with a section on the education and training of a monarch, who was to be ever watchful and trust no one. The ruler had to be attentive to messengers and listen to the advice of his officials, who represented the will of his subjects. Finally, the emperor was warned to control his desires, like greed and lust, because these "enemies" could lead to trouble.

[1] **Maurya:** MOH ree ah

[2] **Pataliputra:** pah TAH lee put rah

One section urged that officials be carefully selected and supervised. Only trusted and capable people should be given the top positions. Because humans are subject to changeable moods and bad habits, they must be closely and continually monitored. The emperor should also see that his officials do not form cliques, because they would form alternate power centers.

The *Treatise* stressed the protection of the monarch's subjects. The monarch had to control crime by implementing and maintaining an effective police force. Furthermore, he had to see that the legal codes either deterred criminals or punished them; thus, crime prevention rested with the ruler, who enforced the laws through harsh penalties.

Some of our information about the government and society of Mauryan times comes from the diary of a Greek ambassador, Megasthenes. It indicated the hierarchical nature of Indian society. The royal family members formed the top social group, with the *brahman* priests beneath them in the social scale. Farmers came next, then herders and soldiers.

Chandragupta ruled ably; he established the empire and left a stable system for his successor. The tradition recounted at the start of this chapter has Chandragupta abandoning his throne and dying in the south. Little is known about Bindusara[3] (reign dates around 301–around 273 B.C.), the second emperor, who expanded the empire's borders southward. Bindusara left the throne to one of his elder sons, who did not reign for long.

The Age of Ashoka

The youngest of Bindusara's sons, Ashoka[4] (reign dates around 269–around 232 B.C.), was not heir to the throne. He revolted against his ruling brother, causing a civil war that killed many, including all but one of Ashoka's brothers. After coming to power, Ashoka started a war with Kalinga, a southeastern state, for control of its land and sea trade routes. The carnage from the campaign brought much death, injury, and imprisonment. Remorseful, Ashoka attempted to rule more humanely, employing Buddhist ideas.

[3] **Bindusara:** bihn doo SAH rah
[4] **Ashoka:** ah SHOH kah

FIGURE 10.1 *Carved Pillar from Ashoka's Era.*
Ashoka had carved pillars like this one placed around his empire. They contained accounts of his reign and gave his subjects commands regarding proper behavior. Today, they are important primary sources of information about the Maurya Empire. Archaeological Survey of India. Courtesy of the India Office Library, London.

Ashoka is a significant figure in Indian history, because he established a Buddhist-inspired humanistic philosophy to guide his government and his subjects. He changed his grandfather's harsh ideology of conquest to one more appropriate to ruling humanely. Ashoka modified the traditional concept of **dharma**—the cosmic law of truth and proper conduct. He emphasized the ethical content of *dharma*, turning it into an idea of morally guided living. Because Ashoka ruled a vast empire of culturally diverse subjects and believed that they must be united in service to the state and one another, he also promoted *dharma* as a policy of social responsibility. People were exhorted to be truthful, compassionate, and morally upright. The village leader collected taxes, and the household head properly ordered the family. All were to help others, especially the less fortunate.

Ashoka created a cohort of trusted officials (Dharma Officers) who traveled the empire investigating the conduct of local officials. These officials had the authority to rectify injustices and punish errant bureaucrats. This effort extended the monarch's hand into his realm and gave people a sense that the state could correct its own mistakes. Of course, it also reflected Ashoka's centralized control of his empire. In another effort to humanize his rule, Ashoka ordered a general revision of the legal code to weed out poorly conceived, unjust, and harsh laws. Attention was given to prisoners to see that they were not treated too harshly. Laborers and slaves received special consideration from Ashoka, who protected their interests. Behind these efforts lay the conviction that taking care of the social welfare of all people brought social stability.

Ashoka established an extensive public works system. There were public treatment centers for the sick and establishments for the care of animals. Medicines were free. Travelers rested in the shade

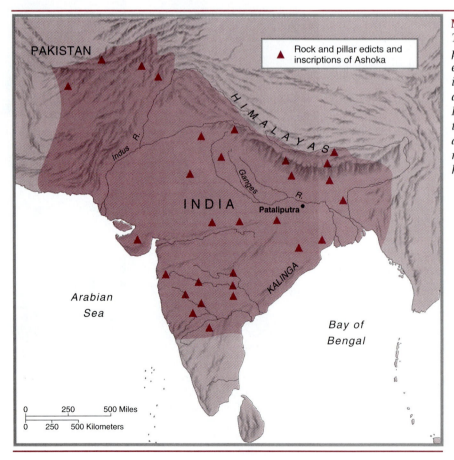

MAP 10.1 *India in 240 B.C.* *This map shows the vast empire ruled by Ashoka near the end of his reign. The territory includes much of present-day India, Bangladesh, and Pakistan. Only in the eighteenth century would India again be so united. Ashoka's rock edicts are found all over his empire.*

Soon after Ashoka came to power, he ordered the carving of stones to provide permanent messages to his subjects, including his own descendants. A major theme within these stelae relates to *dharma*, the concept modified by Ashoka to mean correct behavior and helpfulness to others. The edict here also notes Indian relations to other states along and beyond its borders.

IN THEIR OWN WORDS

A Carved-Rock Edict of Ashoka

> When he had been consecrated eight years, the Beloved of the Gods . . . [Ashoka] conquered Kalinga. A hundred and fifty thousand people were deported, a hundred thousand were killed, and many times that number perished. Afterwards . . . the Beloved of the Gods very earnestly practiced *dharma*, desired *dharma*, and taught *dharma*. On conquering Kalinga, the Beloved of the Gods felt remorse, for when an independent country is conquered, the slaughter, death, and deportation of the people is extremely grievous. . . . What is even more deplorable to the Beloved of the Gods, is that those who dwell there whether . . . householders who show obedience to their superiors, obedience to mother and father, obedience to their teachers and behave well and devotedly toward their friends, acquaintances, colleagues, relatives, slaves, servants—all suffer violence, murder, and separations from their loved ones.

The Beloved of the Gods believes that one who does wrong should be forgiven. . . . And the Beloved of the Gods conciliates the forest tribes of his empire, but he warns them that he has power even in his remorse, and he asks them to repent, lest they be killed. . . .

The Beloved of the Gods considers victory by *dharma* to be the foremost victory. And . . . [he] has gained this victory on all his frontiers . . . where reigns the Greek king named Antiochus, and beyond the realm of that Antiochus in the lands of the four kings named Ptolemy, Antigonus, Magas, and Alexander; and in the south over the Cholas and Pandyas as far as Sri Lanka. . . .

What is obtained by this is victory everywhere, and everywhere victory is pleasant. This pleasure has been obtained through victory by *dharma*, yet it is but a slight pleasure, for the Beloved of the Gods only looks upon that as important in its results which pertains to the next world.

This inscription of *dharma* has been engraved so that any sons or great grandsons that I may have should not think of gaining new conquests. . . . They should only consider conquest by *dharma* to be a true conquest, and delight in the *dharma* should be their whole delight. . . .

---

of banyan trees planted by the state along the major roads, and they ate mangos from other state-planted trees. Wells for public use were dug.

Ashoka had come to power as a mature adult who shrewdly created a public relations bureau that interpreted celestial apparitions to enhance his august image. Ashoka had edicts announcing his ruling philosophy carved in rock, some of which survive. (They cover a vast area from Afghanistan to South India.) Ashoka enjoined his subjects to obey their parents and to be truthful and compassionate with others. People were instructed to avoid killing animals; to set an example, the number of meat dishes on the royal dining table was sharply limited. The policy of not killing animals severely curtailed the animal sacrifices

prescribed by the Vedas, thereby reducing the income of the brahmans who relied on these sacrifices for their livelihoods.

Apart from the blossoming of Buddhism through Ashoka's patronage, elite culture flourished. Sculptures decorated the capital's Buddhist temples and shrines. Architecture prospered under a monarch who knew that monumental art powerfully advertised his imperial image.

Around 232 B.C., Ashoka died after decades in power, and rivalries and conflicts erupted among many claimants to the throne. At the same time, distant regions began to assert their independence; like the Roman Empire, the Maurya Empire split into eastern and western parts. The great national expenditures for the government, the army, and the building ventures also declined with the continued warfare. Divisive tendencies overwhelmed the state, and, for the next half-millennium, India fell prey to invaders and to a time of regionalism (around 180 B.C.–A.D. 320), as will be seen in Chapter 14.

THE GUPTA EMPIRE, A.D. 320–550

After this period of disunity, India's next empire, the Gupta, united the two northern river valleys and much of North India, beginning in the fourth century A.D. Gupta monarchs based themselves in the Ganges River Valley because of its significant economic base and association with the heartland of the Maurya Empire. As the Mauryas favored Buddhism, the Guptas supported Hinduism. Because of this royal patronage, Hindu arts, literature, and architecture flourished. In addition, Hindu priests benefited from this support and their own commitment to their religion's growth.

Origins and Early Empire

Agriculture and trade formed the Gupta economic base. The first rulers built irrigation systems, including canals fed by rivers and lakes, to promote and maintain high agricultural yields. Because the Gupta tax on agricultural land was a percentage of annual harvests, increasing the crop yields also expanded state revenues. Farmers who worked on fields irrigated by these waterworks also paid additional taxes. Internal and long-distance trade increased.

Like Chandragupta Maurya, Chandra Gupta I (reign dates 320–335) used a policy of marriage alliances and military conquest to forge an empire of long duration and relative prosperity. Control of land and sea trade routes in the north gave added financial resources to support a large bureaucracy and army. Additionally, the Guptas permitted significant local autonomy as long as taxes were paid. This reduced the financial burden at the imperial level, although the widespread practice of **tax farming**, the selling of tax-collecting authority by the state, led to abuses. Chandra Gupta I's heir, Samudra Gupta, ruled from 335 to 375. During that

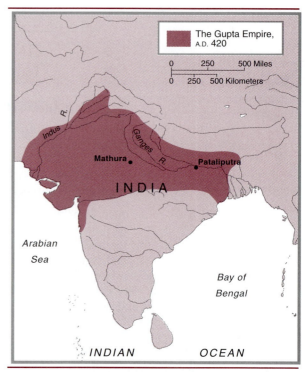

MAP 10.2 *The Gupta Empire in A.D. 420.* *Gupta rule was largely confined to northern India and included the Indus and Ganges river valleys. The area was smaller than that controlled by Ashoka, but it provided great wealth to the Gupta treasury by helping to support artisans and artists who worked for the state.*

forty-year span, he brought northern India under the Gupta sway and expanded his empire's borders southward.

The Age of Chandra Gupta II

The forty-year reign (375–415) of Emperor Chandra Gupta II was a time of political stability and artistic growth. Some of our knowledge of the court life and general society of this era comes from the diary of a Chinese traveler, Faxian,[5] who came to India on a six-year Buddhist pilgrimage (405–411).

According to Faxian, Chandra Gupta II's capital was a place of wealth and peaceful policies. Neither capital nor corporal punishment existed there. Faxian also praised the harmonious living of the people, who enjoyed freedom and practiced

[5] **Faxian:** fahs YEHN

religious tolerance. In addition, the state provided hospital care for all.

The state's ability to provide significant social services for the urban populations came not only from taxes on agriculture and commerce but also from other sources. Chandra Gupta II relied on substantial income from royal monopolies on salt and minerals, on gold and silver workshops, and on mills that produced prized textiles.

Artisans and merchants organized into guilds; and apart from economic benefit, these organizations provided significant means of controlling their members. Each had its own regulations, banner, dues, ranking hierarchy, and profit-sharing methods. Guild rules had the force of law for members. Marriage opportunities for artisans, disputes between guild members, work rules, and funeral arrangements occupied guild leadership. Looking after the interests of orphans and widows of members also became a major guild concern. Thus, from the Gupta perspective, guilds controlled significant numbers of people and provided welfare benefits.

During the Gupta era, the imperial court fostered achievements in the arts, especially in literature. Sanskrit became the dominant literary language in northern India and remained so for centuries. Many commentaries were written on ancient Indian classics, like the Vedas, and a major collection of folk tales, *Panchatantra*,[6] depicted talking animals, charming its Indian readers. Audiences in Southwest Asia, Africa, and Europe also delighted in these tales, thus demonstrating the primacy of Indian arts in other countries. Writing poetry was a major preoccupation at the court of Chandra Gupta II, himself a poet and dramatist. Poetic competitions awarded prizes for all kinds of word play, including puns and epigrams.

The most significant literary form of the Gupta era was drama. Many playwrights composed Sanskrit plays, and imperial attitudes fostered a positive image of court life and insisted that tragic endings and themes be omitted. Kalidasa[7] (lived in the fifth century), one of India's great writers at this time, was a court dramatist. His position in Indian literature has been favorably compared with that of England's William Shakespeare. Kalidasa's extant seven plays, all written in Sanskrit, reveal a dramatist of great craft. The play *Shakuntala*[8] shows the writer's skill in creating characters of humane manners or courtliness; these reflected the values of the Gupta court. Kalidasa also eloquently described the beauty of both humans and nature in his plays and poems.

Architecture and sculpture, especially that associated with Hindu and Buddhist temples, flourished. Hindu temples began to be built around the time of the Gupta Empire, partly to counteract the religious influence of Buddhist communities. Each Hindu temple was dedicated to a single deity such as the popular Vishnu or Shiva, who were represented by sculptures with human features as well as by more abstract symbols. Buddhist sculpture reached high levels of realism, and Buddhist temples were decorated with colorful frescoes and intricate, highly detailed wood carvings.

Intellectual life also flourished in universities across northern India. Students came from all over Asia to study in schools like Nalanda University, where Indian astronomers and mathematicians made discoveries that spread across Eurasia. One astronomer posited a round earth that rotated on

FIGURE 10.2 *Gold Coin of the Gupta Empire.*
This coin represents the only known portrait of Emperor Chandra Gupta II. Depicted as an archer, he wears a halo that suggests divine status. This coin is also a fine example of Indian artisanship of the Gupta era.
Los Angeles County Museum of Art, gift of Anna Bing Arnold and Justin Dart.

---

[6] ***Panchatantra:*** PAHN chah TAHN trah
[7] **Kalidasa:** KAH lee DAH sah
[8] ***Shakuntala:*** shah KUN tah lah

FIGURE 10.3 *Relief Carving of Vishnu. This colossal sculpture of the Gupta era depicts Vishnu in one of his forms, the boar. He has just rescued the Goddess of the Earth from the Serpent King of the Sea. This is one of the earliest major Hindu relief carvings, and shows many carved devotees of the Hindu deity.* Archaeological Survey of India.

an axis; this individual also solved problems using quadratic equations and negative numbers. Others discovered zero, developed place value ordering of numbers, and calculated the value of pi with accuracy.

Able rulers kept the Guptas in power for another century after Chandra Gupta II's death, but the huge cost of defending the ever-vulnerable northwest frontier depleted the treasury. Although the Gupta Empire collapsed in 550, the development of Hindu arts continued.

INDIAN SOCIETY

The Indian subcontinent is home to diverse social groups, and Indian history has seen a wide range of solutions to the ordering of its peoples. Caste, class, and gender are three significant groupings of Indians in the period under consideration.

Caste in the Imperial Age

Two social classification systems existed in India during the imperial age. One system was the traditional **varna** structure of the Aryans (the four-group model discussed in Chapter 5). Another was the **jati**, a system defined by one's birth and pollution. One aspect of pollution is one's job and another is one's birth. We will treat both as caste systems. A **caste** is a hierarchical system of categories that determine one's status, occupation, rights, and duties. Usually, little mobility among castes occurs, because physical characteristics, such as darkness of skin, were different for each caste. Although some historians use caste in a specific way to mean only the *jati* system, we will apply caste to both the *varna* and *jati* systems.

The *varna* castes achieved a general acceptance among the elite early in the imperial age. The *brahmans, kshatriyas,* and *vaishyas* generally were the Aryans, and the *shudras* were the darker-skinned indigenous peoples. Another group was the outcastes, or pariahs; its members were conceived of as being outside the caste system and beneath the lowest caste member—consequently, they were shunned even by *shudras*. This status stemmed from the outcastes' willingness to work at menial and polluting tasks, such as waste removal. According to this reasoning, the outcastes were unclean and therefore unworthy of incorporation into the *varna* system.

UNDER THE LENS

Nalanda: An Important Indian University

During the Gupta era, a Buddhist university was established in the city of Nalanda. One of many universities in India at that time, Nalanda University boasted at its peak three separate libraries and eight colleges. Several thousand students attended Nalanda at a time, some of whom came from states in other parts of Asia, including Sri Lanka, Indonesia, Korea, and China. Perhaps only 30 percent of those who applied were admitted after taking rigorous entrance examinations. The university was funded by various endowments (some from foreign countries), grants, and the assigned revenues of 200 villages.

Students studied a variety of subjects, including religion, philosophy, logic, and grammar. More than 1,000 teachers lectured to students or led discussions at Nalanda University. Many teachers were Buddhist monks; others were Hindus, indicating the tolerant religious atmosphere of the Gupta era. Nagarjuna, one of the great Buddhist scholars, taught at Nalanda.

At Nalanda and other places, Indian mathematicians built on earlier mathematical work and developed the rudiments of algebra. They worked out a number system of nine digits and zero, all of which we use today and which is mistakenly called the arabic numeral system. Indian mathematicians also calculated the value of pi to nine decimal places, solved quadratic equations, explored trigonometry, and approached the discovery of calculus.

Indian scientists affiliated with Nalanda University proposed an atomic theory of matter, and Indian physicians knew the workings of the nervous system and its relation to the spinal cord. The medical course, which originally took eight years to complete, was reduced to six years. It included both theoretical and practical subjects, including operating on patients to set bones and deliver babies. Indian doctors also treated ailments with a large variety of drugs.

Many Indian discoveries passed to Southwest Asia and Africa through the Muslims, who referred to mathematics as *Hindisat* or the Indian art. Islamic mathematicians regularly employed the Indian system of numeration in their calculations. Muslim astronomers relied on Indian conceptions of the universe in developing Islamic astronomy. In the eighth century, Muslim rulers invited Indian physicians to organize hospitals in Persia, indicating the international prestige accorded Indian medicine.

Nalanda University played a significant role in the development of science and the humanities in India. It inspired the foundation of other centers of higher education, producing some of India's greatest scholars, who perpetuated a tradition of independence of thought and freedom of criticism. Nalanda University was in decline by the thirteenth century, when its libraries and educational facilities perished in the fighting caused by invaders.

FIGURE 10.4 *Ruins of Nalanda University. This picture of Nalanda University conveys a sense of its immense size. Nalanda was an international university and monastery with several libraries and colleges. For centuries, Nalanda faculty instructed students from all over Asia in mathematics, medicine, astronomy, and the humanities.* Martin Hürlimann.

The *jati* classification system of castes seems to have developed in the Ganges River Valley and slowly spread across India. Over time, thousands of *jati* (occupational groups similar to guilds) formed. Occupations that involved the taking of life, such as hunting, fishing, and butchering, polluted an individual. Similarly, dealing in the necessary removal of dead bodies brought pollution. Thus, social interaction among *jati* was strictly limited so that less-polluted castes were not contaminated. Marriage, for example, was limited to partners from one's own *jati*. Both the *varna* and *jati* systems became increasingly rigid over time, prohibiting nearly all movement from one caste to another.

Class in the Imperial Age

Imperial society revolved around three groups: an upper class, an intermediary class, and a lower class. The top class included the royal family members and their kin, plus various courtiers, high officials, and their families. The intermediary class contained middle and lower officials, as well as merchants and financiers. At the bottom were artisans, peasants, and others, including slaves.

The imperial government brought forth a ruling class of larger numbers and social diversity. Preimperial rulers generally came from the *kshatriyas* and were supported by the *brahmans*. As governing became more complex, *kshatriya* and *brahman varna* members ruled together. In addition, clerks and tax collectors were two new groups that joined the ruling class. Political influence depended on one's special talents, for example in the ability to complete administrative tasks.

Money lenders and prosperous landlords became a significant social and economic force in the imperial age. With the rise of trade and the expansion of agriculture, financiers often made fortunes lending money. Over time, some of these wealthy people helped imperial governments manage their own financial issues; a few even loaned money to monarchs. Landlords also gained economic prestige in the communities, and some parlayed their influence into tax-farming ventures by the Gupta age. They purchased the right to collect tax revenues and often used devious means to amass far more than the prescribed amount, keeping the excess for themselves.

Lower social classes represented the largest segment of India's population in the imperial age.

FIGURE 10.5 *The Sacred Thread of Caste.* *This thirteenth-century sculpture shows the sacred thread of the upper caste draped over the left shoulder of the figure, and under the right arm. Such emblems marked upper-caste members, keeping them distinct from other castes.* Courtesy of Robert Fisher.

The peasant village spread throughout the Ganges area and from there, with government prodding, to frontiers. As peasants grew in number, tax revenues based on their labor became vital to state finances. Although Kautilya warned against excessive taxes in his *Treatise*, the number and amount of taxes in Maurya times heavily burdened peasants. Later, under the Guptas, the picture of urban prosperity depicted by Faxian gave way to a harsher reality for peasants, who paid heavy taxes and labored for the state during the non-agricultural season. Corrupt and ravenous tax collectors often brought added misery for peasants in late Gupta times, many of whom responded by either revolting or fleeing.

Gender Matters

Men and women had distinct social identities and economic functions in the imperial age. Men generally dominated, while women remained subordinate to men. During the imperial age, however, gender practices sometimes changed significantly.

Indian men began the imperial age at the top of various social groups. They headed households, ruled and administered *varna* and *jati* castes, performed most of the work outside the home, and created most elements of elite culture. Exceptional women might exert social influence, but most did not.

Women of the social and political elites experienced a declining array of choices regarding their lives during the imperial era. At the time of the Maurya Empire, some elite women not only read and wrote but also commented on important religious works like the Vedas. Part of the reason for this was that the accepted marriage age for young Maurya women was in their late teen years, and women had time to be formally educated. By the time of the Gupta Empire, the marriage age dropped to the low teens for women, and this meant that their educations under the supervision of their parents ceased, reducing opportunities for young women.

Women sometimes enjoyed better treatment in religious institutions than in other social groups. In some lower social classes, female deities, including mother goddesses, were popularly worshiped, and women usually served as priestesses for these religions. Buddhism's rejection of the existing social system meant that many women became nuns, and the great majority came from the social elite. Individual women were prominent, as in early Buddhism, but ceased to wield influence after a few centuries. In other countries where Buddhism spread, nuns enjoyed a high status.

INDIAN IDEOLOGIES

All three major Indian religions—Jainism, Buddhism, and Hinduism—began before the imperial age. All three became deeply embedded in Indian society and contributed greatly to Indian history. Buddhism and Hinduism were patronized by emperors and benefited from these associations. The **Upanishads** (discourses speculating about the

F I G U R E 1 0 . 6 *Mother Goddess Figure of the Imperial Age.* *This striking figure is evidence of worship of female deities during the imperial era. While much attention was given to Hindu and other deities, many commoners were comfortable worshiping local deities. This figure was discovered in North India.* Courtesy of the Government Museum, Mathura.

nature of reality and appended to the Vedas) were also composed before the imperial age, but these texts never formed the basis for a religion.

Common to these religions are the concepts of *karma* and reincarnation. Indians believed that **karma** is the residue of actions by an individual, and it attaches to one's soul. Some actions leave good *karma* and others leave bad *karma*. Taking of life and dealing in human waste, for example, are considered polluting, which provides a rationale for low caste rankings. Once *karma* is removed by spiritual enlightenment, the soul reaches an ideal state and ceases to be reborn after the death of the body. **Reincarnation** is the belief that people have past lives and will have future lives, each time the soul of the dead person is reborn. The soul's reincarnated form is determined by the amount and nature of the *karma* the soul accumulated in its previous lives.

Spiritual Unrest in the Sixth Century B.C.

During the sixth century B.C., intellectual questioning brought a significant transformation of the ideological landscape. Domination by *brahmans* had long been established through the priestly *varna*, yet many people were dissatisfied with the power and wealth of these priests and with the rigid rituals they espoused. Within several decades, a group of thinkers created the elements of Jainism, the basis of Buddhism, and the foundation of the Upanishads. What brought forth this dynamic intellectual ferment?

Scholars have offered many reasons for the serious questioning in India and in many other parts of the world during the sixth century B.C. Some have pointed to the breakup of tribal loyalties and the development of settled urban life. Change occurred in the appearance of more complex and less personal governmental agencies. People seemed less likely to know their local officials personally.

In India, a variety of factors may have led to the acceptance and spread of new religious ideas. Newly prosperous merchants, for example, felt discriminated against by the *brahmans*. Some historians have emphasized a growing disenchantment by *kshatriyas* and others with *brahmans*, who demanded large fees for performing the Vedic rites. Some scholars have suggested that the extension of the caste system triggered local resistance and prompted questioning of institutions and their underlying assumptions. Many religious leaders responded to the basic perception of impermanence and illusion, giving different solutions. In fact, no one reason has proved acceptable, and a combination of explanations seems reasonable.

The Upanishadic Tradition

Scholars generally accept the view that commentaries on the Vedas began around 1000 B.C. The first group of writings, the Brahmanas, expounded upon ideas in the Vedas and stressed the impor-

tance of the kings and priests for political and social stability. Brahmana commentaries developed over the succeeding three centuries.

As noted previously, in the seventh and sixth centuries B.C. spiritual seekers left their homes and sought solitude as well as answers to questions about the nature of the universe and the place of human beings within it. From these came the poetic and religious dialogues known as the Upanishads.

The authors of the Upanishads accepted the Vedas, including their sacrifices and special religious chants. In fact, the 108 Upanishads are included as a part of the Vedas. The Upanishads constitute late additions to the nearly 1,000 years of Vedic religious development.

The Upanishads greatly extend the spiritual thinking of the Indians. One major tenet of these works is that each human has a soul, a spiritual entity seeking union with the omnipresent spirit essence. This union is hampered because the senses serve the body by seeing and interpreting a world that is an illusion.

How does one realize that such illusions blind the soul? One learns through the guidance of a spiritual teacher or by reading the Upanishads. Thereafter, the seeker must begin an arduous process of meditation and spiritual discipline.

Assuming that one approaches the goal of knowing the two realities, what then? The final knowing of the Upanishadic teachers is that the soul and the omnipresent spirit essence are one. This spiritual realization means that one's remaining task is to shed the bodily form so that upon death the individual soul merges into the cosmic soul.

Mahavira and the Jain Response to the Life of the Senses

One sixth-century spiritual seeker, Vardhamana Mahavira (around 540–around 468 B.C.), ardently followed a path toward release from the bonds of the sensate world. Born into a politically elite family in the Ganges River Valley, Mahavira lived an ordinary upper-class life for his first thirty years. Then he experienced a personal crisis that caused him to abandon his worldly life and seek a different meaning of existence. This path occupied the next twelve years; during that time, Mahavira became less encumbered by social convention and

FIGURE 10.7 *Bahubali, a Jain Saint.* *This example of Jain sculpture is over fifty feet tall and depicts one of the first Jains to reach enlightenment. Bahubali was so long immersed in meditation that plants grew around him, encircling his legs and arms. This art clearly depicts the Jain value of being in harmony with nature.*
S. Nagaraj/Dinodia Picture Agency.

material needs. He threw off his clothes and practiced acts of self-denial, such as fasting or eating the barest minimum of food necessary for survival. Ultimately, Mahavira determined that death by starvation would bring release of the soul and its passage into the perfect peace of paradise, a place of no karmic activity. He believed that any action, including eating, would kill other beings and cause bad *karma*. Mahavira became the founder of Jainism.

Jains (from *jina*, meaning spiritual warrior or self-conqueror) practice determined self-mortifi-

cation (acts of fasting, enduring pain), because Mahavira believed the senses and the body imprison the soul. Because life's ultimate quest is liberation from pain, suffering, and ignorance, the body and the sensate world hinder success. In fact, Jains believe that suffering, willingly undertaken, eliminates existing karma that binds the soul from release.

One unique aspect of the Jain worldview offers a vision of a universe fully alive in its manifestations. This perspective sees souls everywhere as part of a spiritual nomenclature. The first category of creatures has six senses: sight, taste, touch, smell, hearing, and intelligence (mind). Included are humans, gods, monkeys, horses, pigeons, and snakes. Another category has four senses (touch, taste, smell, and sight) and lacks intelligence and hearing. Some representative beings are flies, wasps, and butterflies. A fourth category, two-sense creatures (those of touch and taste), includes worms and leeches. One-sense beings (those that have touch) are vegetable bodies (trees), earth bodies (stones, minerals, jewels), water bodies (rivers, seas, rain), fire bodies (lights, flames, lightning), and wind bodies (gases and winds of all kinds). For Jains, life is in all matter and all things are revered.

Ahimsa (causing no harm to and revering living souls) developed at the time of Mahavira. It may have originated with Jains or with Buddhists; our sources do not offer definite proof. Nevertheless, Jains became ardent adherents of the *ahimsa* lifestyle. *Ahimsa* means not merely avoiding physical injury to all creatures—for example, turning the other cheek when struck—it means not verbally abusing creatures. In fact, *ahimsa* covers even intended actions: A person's having violent thoughts is the same as his or her doing violence toward another creature. Jains believed that one must guard against one's thoughts and live a carefully circumscribed life or face eternal soul bondage.

Some Jain monks followed Mahavira's path of nudism and self-mortification in keeping with the tenets of *ahimsa*. If any clothing were permitted, it was a cloth covering the mouth to prevent unwary beings from entering the mouth and being killed. Jains might also be seen stepping carefully or carrying brooms to gently sweep the path before them. These Jains did not light fires at night, because moths or other beings might perish in the

PARALLELS AND DIVERGENCES
Eating Implements

Throughout traditional India and many other places around the globe, food usually was eaten with the hands. In other places, implements of one sort or another were used. People raised to use eating implements often view the eating of food with the hands as distasteful and potentially unclean, though there always is a developed code of etiquette that rules the use of the hands, as fully as in the traditions with implements. Conversely, those accustomed to using their hands often find eating with implements dangerous-looking and barbaric.

There are four main modes of transporting food to one's mouth. The oldest and most widespread is the use of the hands. All peoples use the hands to some extent, but Indian, Arab, and most African traditions employ this primary mode of eating. Second, some people modify hand eating by adding an edible sheet, pieces of which are torn off and used to envelop loose food. Examples are in Ethiopia, where a supple bread called *injera* is used, and Mexico, where corn tortillas serve the same purpose. Third, some peoples use chopsticks, slender rods serving as extensions of the fingers to grasp chunks of food; their traditional use is in East Asia. Finally, the knife-fork-spoon toolkit of Europe can be used to cut, spear, and scoop food. The spoon has been used by most societies, although sometimes only as a serving implement.

At one level, any approach serves the desired end: The food finds its way to one's mouth. In addition, each allows a way to distinguish sophisticated from rustic diners. A refined Indian diner, for example, eats only with the right hand, because the left is ritually unclean and is used for defiling but necessary hygienic functions. The hand should be held palm downward in eating, and one mouthful should be chewed and swallowed before the next is eaten. Failure to follow this etiquette labels the eater a boor.

At another level, however, the mode of eating reflects a delicate balance among ecology, values, and tastes. Under Jainism, foods were primarily vegetables cut into small pieces. They could be eaten without additional implements, and, because they were prepared lukewarm, the hand would not be burned. Traditional Jains did not have reusable plates because of the implied lack of cleanliness; instead they placed their food on leaves, which could be disposed of after each meal.

Chopsticks, on the other hand, developed partly from a fuel shortage in China. Cooking with fast-burning grasses, the most readily available fuel, required that food be cut into small pieces and stir-fried briefly at high temperatures. Implements were needed because of the extreme heat. Rice was cooked into a sticky mass that could be easily grasped with chopsticks, while smaller morsels could be transferred from bowl to mouth with a scooping motion.

Finally, the knife and fork developed as eating implements in Europe, because that region favored heavy meat consumption, and meat tended to be roasted in large chunks. Rather than cutting up a slab of meat before serving and risking its cooling, the diner carved it one slice at a time. The fork appeared in medieval times, but it frequently was replaced by the hand or a knife.

---

flames. They begged for their daily food and water so that they would not take life in preparing food. They also preferred to eat vegetables, and a few, like Mahavira, starved themselves to death.

Other Jain monks wore clothes, and, although they accepted Jain doctrines, they did not go to the lengths of the other group. All Jains rejected Hindu texts, like the Vedas, as sole sources of the truth. By rejecting the Vedas as the authoritative texts governing one's life, Jains made each individual responsible for personal spiritual development. In this way, Jains appealed to urban groups like the merchants, who rejected their low *varna* status. In fact, many Jains became merchants and bankers, and some grew wealthy. Others promoted learning by collecting and disseminating books, including non-Jain works, because Jains practiced toleration of diverse ideas and practices. Because they appreciated education, Jains contributed to India's mathematical discoveries, to developments in astronomy, and to the study of languages. Mahavira encouraged storytelling, and some Jains wrote in the local vernacular languages. They helped develop India's rich regional languages.

Siddhartha and Buddhism in the Imperial Age

Like Jainism, Buddhism rejected the authority of the Vedas. Unlike Jainism, Buddhism has many sects and three major subdivisions. For a variety of reasons, however, Buddhism ultimately disappeared in India, its homeland.

Prince Siddhartha Gautama (around 563–around 480 B.C.) lived a life similar to that of Mahavira, his contemporary. Both came from the warrior *varna*, and both lived without experiencing significant suffering until around the age of thirty years. Stories about Siddhartha were not written until after his death; therefore, knowledge about his life has remained suspect. Buddhist tradition claims that Siddhartha Gautama, who resided only within his father's royal domain, took a series of trips on which he saw seriously ill people, dead people, and an ascetic who followed the path of spiritual seeking. The combined experiences are said to have shaken Prince Siddhartha to the foundation of his being and offered him a path to spiritual insight. He spent nights of sleepless questioning and decided to abandon his wife, son, and father, the king. Like Mahavira, Siddhartha began a quest for the meaning of existence.

Within six years, Siddhartha tried varied spiritual disciplines, including self-mortification practices. Siddhartha ate the bare caloric minimum to sustain life and briefly followed the starvation way. Near death, he suddenly halted this regimen and resumed a life-nurturing diet. Moreover, he announced that he would follow a path of moderation, which he called the "middle way"—not indulgent and not ascetic.

Apart from a moderate asceticism, meditation became the way by which Siddhartha became enlightened. Meditation had been long practiced by Indian ascetics and became a key discipline in Buddhism. Basically, meditation quiets the chattering mind. Buddhists believe that when one becomes skilled at meditation, spiritual knowledge may erupt into the consciousness, including the basic perception of the world's impermanence. Siddhartha meditated and saw his past lives and their connection to his present life; he then knew the meaning of existence. At that time, he became enlightened, seeing life as it truly was, in all of its interconnectedness. Siddhartha became the **Buddha**, the one who is enlightened.

After this experience, the Buddha walked to a nearby park and preached a sermon that presented the famous **Four Noble Truths**, a key basis of Buddhism:

—First Truth: Life is suffering.

—Second Truth: Suffering has a cause.

—Third Truth: The cause is desire.

—Fourth Truth: Desire and suffering may be eliminated by following the **Eightfold Path**, composed of correct views, correct aspirations, correct speech, correct conduct, correct livelihood, correct effort, correct mindfulness, and correct meditation.

FIGURE 10.8 *Fasting Siddhartha Gautama. This sculpture from northwestern India shows Siddhartha Gautama following the extreme asceticism of some spiritual traditions. He eventually abandoned this path and sought moderation in all things. This ethic became the cornerstone of most Buddhist sects and earned Siddhartha the title Buddha, meaning "enlightened one." The sculpture vividly captures the results of disciplined food deprivation.* Courtesy of the Central Museum, Lahore.

The Four Noble Truths provide a perspective with which to view life and a way to eliminate suffering. "Life is suffering" means that the universe is in constant flux or change, but people fail to recognize its essential nature. Instead, they seek permanence by desiring attachments, like spouses, children, and material things. These, however, give only a temporary sense of permanence. Humans may become ill, they die, or they may not follow the path we wish them to. In other words, all relationships have pain and will ultimately be severed by time and death. By eliminating these attachments and the desire for permanence that underlies them, one is freed to completely adhere to the Eightfold Path, becoming a monk or a nun.

The preliminary step to the Buddhist goal is enlightenment, seeing the world as impermanent. After that, one must live an exemplary life like that of the Buddha, who preached for the more than four remaining decades in his life. Finally, when death comes to the enlightened, correct-living person, one enters *nirvana*. Literally meaning "blowing out," like the flame of a candle, *nirvana* signified the state at which existence ceases. In other words, one is no longer reborn; one has been extinguished, and that is all. Centuries later, *nirvana* became heaven, especially in Mahayana Buddhism.

Buddhism remained a small sect of traveling ascetics who performed spiritual disciplines and accepted food and drink from people. In the monsoon season, they lived in sheltered dwellings, and soon permanent residences, monasteries, appeared. This community of monks followed a lifestyle that included chastity, *ahimsa*, and poverty, thus eliminating the worldly attachments. Soon, these monasteries, among the first in history, became centers of learning and discipline.

Nearing death, the Buddha left a final message for his disciples: He told them to be their own lamps, to be their own refuges. The Buddha implied that adherents should rely on themselves rather than on external sources. They should strive vigilantly and hold firmly to truth. After the Buddha died, sectarian differences emerged among his followers. Buddhism remained a modest movement in India until the time of Emperor Ashoka, who promoted Buddhist missionary activity.

The history of Buddhism in India centers on thinkers who elaborated on the already sophisti-

cated Buddhistic treatment of psychology. Nagarjuna[9] and Vashubandhu[10] developed treatises on reality and how the mind perceives it. They wrote *sutras,* prose or poetic treatises about some issues in Buddhism.

Buddhism ultimately disappeared in India as it spread across Asia. One reason may be that Buddhism regarded all humans as capable of being enlightened in a single lifetime. This perspective went against the Indian belief that members of the lowest caste would have to live an exemplary life merely to be reincarnated into a higher caste. Buddhism tolerated Hinduism and had no ritual specialists of its own. It stressed a monastic life and detachment from society. It gradually waned as a religion.

Beginning in the fourth century A.D., Hinduism experienced a revival. Hindus borrowed from other ideologies; Shankara, a key Hindu thinker of the ninth century, used Buddhist ideas in his own system of belief. Incorporation of borrowed ideas blurred the distinctions between Hinduism and Buddhism and aided in Buddhism's extinction in India. Shankara also founded many Hindu monasteries. Finally, Hindu temples competed with Buddhist and Jain monasteries that were involved in trade, especially trade with Central Asia. Often with the aid of local governments, Hindus attacked and destroyed Buddhist monasteries. Jainism was strong enough to withstand the persecutions; Buddhism was not.

The Development of Hinduism

Hinduism developed in India over a long period from around 500 B.C. to around A.D. 500. It was closely associated with *brahmans*, ritual specialists who relied on the Vedas for their ritualistic knowledge. *Brahmans* wandered across India spreading their beliefs and gaining converts. In addition, Hindu temples and monasteries became tightly connected with society. Hindus were also accepting of local deities.

Many deities formed the Hindu pantheon. One early god, Indra, represented the warring nature of the Indo-Europeans but lost his importance as Aryan society evolved. When ruling

[9] **Nagarjuna:** nah GAHR juh nah
[10] **Vashubandhu:** VAH shuh BAHN dhuh

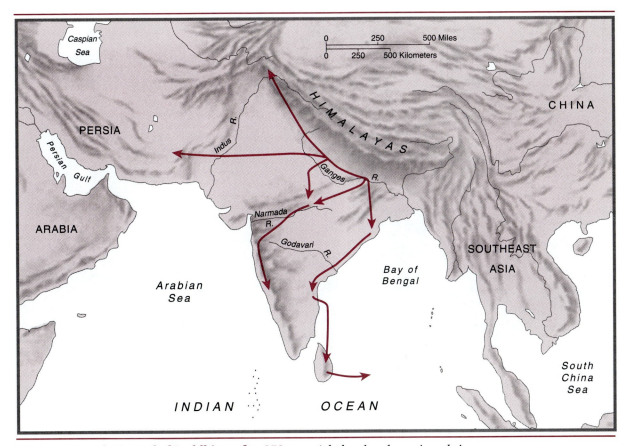

MAP 10.3 *The Spread of Buddhism after 250 B.C.* *Ashoka played a major role in spreading Buddhism in India and surrounding areas. Tamraparni (modern-day Sri Lanka) became an important Buddhist center. From there, Buddhism was spread throughout Southeast Asia by missionaries and merchants.*

became more important, Varuna, a deity associated with order and justice, assumed a larger role. A stable political order grew more attractive to the rajas (rulers). During the imperial era, two other deities, Shiva and Vishnu, assumed prominent places in Hinduism. Shiva was probably an indigenous, non-Aryan deity, while Vishnu was originally an unimportant Aryan god.

Hindus, who believe that Shiva, the Mighty Lord, in his manifestation as a fierce destroyer controls life and death, represent him wearing a necklace of skulls. He also is seen as a naked ascetic, typically depicted with a third eye in the middle of his forehead. This is the mystic eye or the eye of wisdom, important to the yogis and other spiritual adepts. One common symbol representing Shiva is the phallus, which stands for his fertility aspect. In another guise, Shiva is lord of the animals and is associated with the Indus deity mentioned in Chapter 5.

Vishnu represents the supreme being from whom the universe emanates. In addition, he is the preserver of life. Two of his incarnations are Rama and Krishna. The Krishna form is one of the most popular avatars in Hinduism. According to Hindu lore, Vishnu, in his preserver role, saved the world from destruction numerous times. Hindus also believe that Buddha was an incarnation of Vishnu.

A cluster of developments, including the establishment of temples and the worship of local and regional deities, fused into Hinduism during

FIGURE 10.9 *A Carved Hindu Temple.* *This eighth-century Kailasha Temple was carved 100 feet down into the rock at Ellura in South-Central India. It shows the skilled artisanry and massive resources available to Hindu monarchs, even after the imperial era.*
Victor Kennet/Reproduced courtesy of Thames and Hudson Ltd.

the first millennium A.D. Some national and regional governments granted land and other resources to *brahmans* in exchange for political support. Gupta emperors were especially favorable to the *brahmans*, and many temple complexes were founded in the capital region as well as in the empire.

Hindu temple priests interacted with local leaders and their communities. Deities of these settlements, for example, became more firmly tied into the Hindu pantheon, and, because of the linkages of exchange between villages and clusters of villages in a region, a popular local deity might become venerated throughout the region. Krishna, a regional god, evolved into his paramount identity in this way. Thus, deities were woven into a religious tapestry of great complexity and diversity.

Vishnu, Shiva, and Krishna became three significant Hindu deities. Krishna's main temple at Mathura in northern India attracted devotees from all over the region. Temple priests demanded that adherents be loyal to the deity; thus, religious devotion meant faith in and salvation from a god. Hinduism became India's most important religion.

IMPERIAL INDIA'S REGIONAL IMPACT

India long enjoyed trade relations with Eurasia and Africa. The origins of economic ties date at least to the third millennium B.C. In later periods, products from India were popular in the Seleucid, Roman, and Axum empires. The influence of India, however, went beyond trade goods. Mathematics and astronomy strongly attracted attention in many lands, and Buddhism and Hinduism exerted a great amount of influence far beyond India's borders. Southeast Asian countries particularly enjoyed close relations with Indian governments and used Indian ideas and religions to bolster their political systems.

Trade and Other Relations with Regions West and North of India

Since the third millennium B.C., Indians traded extensively with peoples of Asia and Africa, and Indian products remained popular with Persians,

Egyptians, Greeks, and Romans. Later, when Arabs reached the borders of India and even briefly settled in the Indus Valley, Indian products contributed to the Islamic exchange that will be discussed in Chapter 12.

Diplomatic contacts also flourished from the imperial era. Chandragupta Maurya enjoyed peaceful relations with the Seleucids, after he stopped their eastward advance. Ashoka sent ambassadors to parts of Asia in the third century B.C., and diplomacy aided peaceful relations in the Maurya and Gupta eras.

Buddhism slowly spread to the north and northwest beginning with Ashoka, who sent Buddhist missionaries to other Asian lands. The conversion process advanced partly through missionary and merchant contacts into Central Asia. In the first century A.D., Central Asian rulers in India played a key role in the spread of Buddhism into Central Asia and China. As will be seen in Chapter 14, Buddhism slowly took root in China,

and many monks and Buddhist students came to India, the home of Buddhism, in later decades and centuries.

India's Impact on Southeast Asia

More than trade linked the peoples and governments of Indian and Southeast Asia (Indochina). Certainly, ships and merchants plied the coastal waters of South and Southeast Asia. We have even seen in Chapter 5 that rice and various animals (particularly chickens) came from Southeast Asia into the Indian subcontinent during prehistoric and early historic times. In later centuries, the flow of trade continued in both directions.

Large Indian ships bearing cargo reached Southeast Asian ports by the time of the Maurya Empire. They used the seasonal winds to sail to the Isthmus of Kra on the Malay Peninsula, transported the trade items across the narrow land strip, and loaded their wares on waiting ships.

FIGURE 10.10 *Relief of an Indian Ship.* *This carving attests to the maritime skills of Indians who ranged far across the Indian Ocean. During the imperial era, many sailors, merchants, and priests brought goods and ideas from India to Southeast Asia.* Courtesy of Robert Fisher.

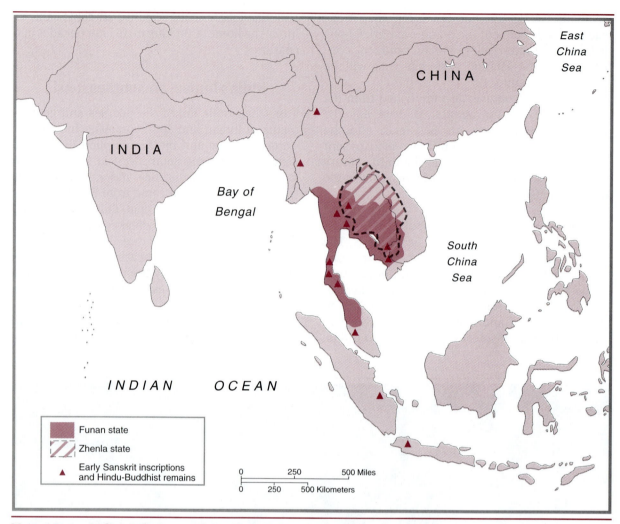

MAP 10.4 *India's Relations with Southeast Asia.* *Both mainlanders and islanders in Southeast Asia had extensive trade contacts with Indians. Nearly all such trade occurred through maritime activity. Cultural influence came slowly and may be seen in the Sanskrit inscriptions on Hindu-Buddhist artifacts.*

Then, they made landfall near the Mekong River Valley. The return trip needed the shift of the winds that usually took months to occur. During the interim, the Indian merchants and others lived in the Mekong River region. Even though the Maurya Empire fell in the second century B.C., trade with the Southeast Asians continued.

During the first and second centuries A.D., two things caused a heightened Indian commercial interest in Southeast Asia. The Roman emperor Vespasian banned the export of gold coins from the Roman Empire, and this forced Indian rulers, who needed gold for various purposes, to seek new

supplies. At the same time, chiefdoms in the Mekong River Valley united under a single rule that the Chinese called Funan. This kingdom commanded the Mekong trade route, a major one between India and China.

Two popular stories, perhaps historically inaccurate, symbolize the growing Indian and Southeast Asian relationship. The first tale concerns a traveler, Kaudinya, who arrives in the Mekong River Valley by sea. He marries a local princess, then establishes a dynasty. A later account gives the same name, Kaudinya, to an Indian *brahman* who marries a princess and begins ruling with her.

INDIA

Spiritual unrest leads to founding of Upanishadic tradition, Buddhism, and Jainism, sixth and fifth centuries		**500 B.C.** — Birth of Buddha, c. 563 B.C. Birth of Mahavira, c. 540 B.C.
		400 B.C.
	Maurya Empire, c. 320– c. 180 B.C.	**300 B.C.** Chandragupta founds Maurya Empire, c. 320 B.C. Ashoka ascends throne, c. 269 B.C. Kalinga War ends, 261 B.C. Beginning of Buddhist missionizing, c. 250 B.C.
Regional Indian states, 180 B.C.–A.D. 320		**200 B.C.** Fall of Maurya Empire, c. 180 B.C.
		100 B.C.
		A.D. 1
		A.D. 100
		A.D. 200
		A.D. 300
Expanded patronage of Indian elite arts, 320–650	Gupta Empire, 320–550	Nalanda University founded, c. 320 Chandra Gupta II begins reign, 375 **A.D. 400** Faxian travels in India, c. 405–411 Kalidasa writes plays, c. 450 **A.D. 500** Fall of Gupta Empire, c. 550 **A.D. 600**

This story notes that he changed local rules to be in accord with Indian practices. What the tales show is the influence of Indians on Southeast Asian governments.

Archaeologists also know that in the early part of the first millennium A.D., Funan rulers welcomed Indian trade and *brahman* advisors. The monarchs adopted the Indian title "Varman" (meaning armor or protection by a deity) as a part of their dynastic names. They followed the Indian calendar system, they used parts of the Indian legal system, and they worshiped the Hindu deities Shiva and Vishnu. Thus, local people, likely Khmers,[11] incorporated elements of Indian culture into their own. In that sense, India's impact on Southeast Asians parallels China's impact on East Asians.

Material evidence shows that there was extensive trade between countries around the Indian Ocean in the first millennium. In one manufacturing center controlled by Funan, for example, scholars have found Roman medallions and Iranian coins. Much jewelry was fashioned there from diamonds, gold, sapphires, rubies, jade, and opals. Many raw materials had to be brought from other parts of Asia.

When Funan declined, a second state also known by a Chinese name, Zhenla,[12] rose in the same area. The elite of this successor state regularly used Sanskrit to write their names. The Zhenla monarch worshiped Shiva, and the elite built temples to Shiva to curry favor with their sovereign. Thus, Indian religious practices helped bind the ruling elite. Indian *brahmans* advised Zhenla rulers, and eventually a school for the study of the *Treatise*, the Indian manual of politics, was founded in the capital. Gupta architectural styles graced the large buildings of Zhenla. Although Sanskrit was used for rituals, Khmer remained the vernacular language.

Buddhism spread across Southeast Asia. In Ashoka's age, it crossed the strait into Sri Lanka, the teardrop-shaped island off India's southern tip. Gradually, the Sri Lankans began sending missionaries into the parts of Southeast Asia today known as Burma (Myanmar), Thailand, Cambodia, Laos, and the islands of Indonesia. Then, mainland peoples like the Mon-Khmer group that settled in the river valleys of Southeast Asia often converted to Buddhism; many of their descendants still follow this faith today. Tolerant embrace of Buddhism permitted the enfolding of the older animistic practices into the Buddhist fabric. Other states in Southeast Asia experienced strong influences from Indian culture. Dancers in modern Java and Bali still perform versions of the Indian epics, and temples in the Hindu style are found on both islands.

SUMMARY

1. Chandragupta Maurya seized control of a state and used its bureaucracy and army to fashion an empire. The imperial ideology is reflected in a later text, the *Treatise on Financial Gain*.

2. Ashoka, the third Maurya emperor, seized power in a bloody civil war and fought another war. Thereafter, Ashoka changed state policy from conquest to rule and humanized his polity by modifying *dharma*, a Buddhist and Indian religious concept, to mean ethical and social responsibility. People lived more easily, but Ashoka failed to provide long-term stability.

3. After a five-century interim the Guptas imitated the Mauryas and built a prosperous state. Hinduism flourished.

4. The *varna* system of the Vedas declined during Ashoka's age and largely gave way to the *jati* caste system of kinship communities tied by economic benefit. Merchants and peasants contributed greatly to the economic well-being of imperial states.

5. In the sixth century B.C., spiritual and social unrest led some to found major Indian ideologies: Jainism, Buddhism, and the Upanishadic tradition.

6. Upanishadic thinkers explored the nature of the universe and the place of humans within it.

[11] **Khmers:** kuh MAIRZ
[12] **Zhenla:** JEHN lah

7. Mahavira developed Jainism to seek release from life. Jains rejected the Vedas and embraced *ahimsa*, a way of life revering living souls and causing no harm to them.

8. Siddhartha Gautama founded Buddhism on the Four Noble Truths. Buddhism became a religion that stressed meditation and *ahimsa.*

9. Hinduism developed from ideas and practices associated with the Vedas, from devotion to Shiva and Vishnu, and from the building of temples by Gupta monarchs.

10. India influenced many peoples through trade, ideas, and religions. Southeast Asians welcomed Indian goods, as well as *brahmans* and Buddhist monks, who advised their rulers. Law codes, calendars, and rituals followed in their wake. Shiva, Vishnu, and the Buddha were venerated by some Southeast Asians.

SUGGESTED READINGS

Auboyer, Jeannine. *Daily Life in Ancient India.* London: Morrison and Gibb Limited, 1965. A description of life in the early imperial era of Indian history.

Embree, Ainsley, ed. *Sources of Indian Tradition.* New York: Columbia University Press, 1988. A significant selection of Jain, Buddhist, Upanishadic, and Hindu sources and commentaries upon them.

Thapar, Romila. *Asoka and the Decline of the Mauryas.* Oxford, Eng.: Oxford University Press, 1961. A classic treatment of the reign of one of India's greatest rulers.

Wolpert, Stanley. *A New History of India.* New York: Oxford University Press, 1993. A standard history of India.

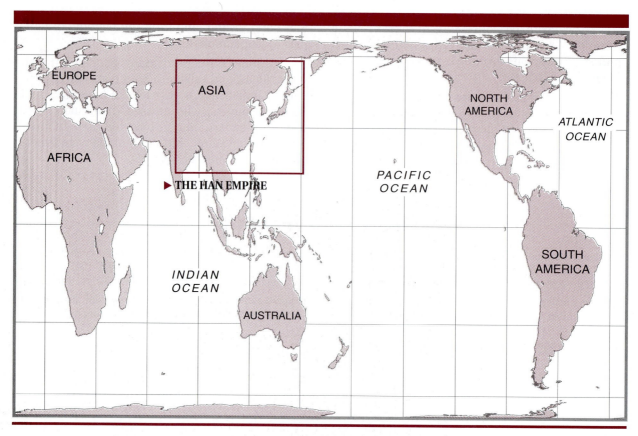

EUROPE

ASIA

AFRICA

► THE HAN EMPIRE

NORTH
AMERICA

ATLANTIC
OCEAN

PACIFIC
OCEAN

INDIAN
OCEAN

AUSTRALIA

SOUTH
AMERICA

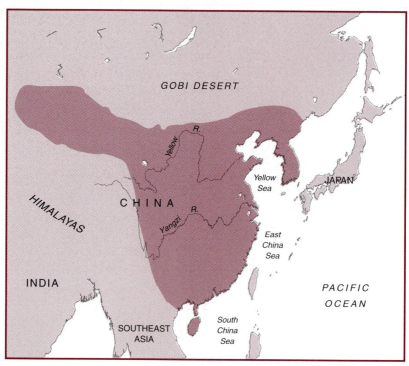

GOBI DESERT

Yellow R.

CHINA

HIMALAYAS

Yangzi R.

Yellow
Sea

JAPAN

East
China
Sea

INDIA

SOUTHEAST
ASIA

South
China
Sea

PACIFIC
OCEAN

► THE HAN EMPIRE

China: From Feudalism to Empire

770 B.C.–A.D. 220

A Chinese philosopher once dreamed he was a butterfly. In that dream, the butterfly flitted from place to place, doing butterfly things. When he woke, the philosopher did not know whether he was himself or whether he was a butterfly, dreaming he was a philosopher.

This story from the Warring States Period, an age when iron helped transform life in China, has charmed readers and inspired poets, artists, and movie directors. In this chapter, we shall see how the appearance of iron and the consequences of its widespread use in the seventh century B.C. improved agricultural production, stimulated population growth, and brought about the rise of large cities. Feudalism faded before the metal plows and iron weapons. Gone too were the chariot-driven aristocratic warriors, made obsolete by peasant-conscript armies. To support these large military forces, governments mobilized their human and material resources as quickly and as efficiently as possible. Leaders adopted a centralized political system with a chain of command emphasizing strict obedience. Failure to adopt this effective but harsh political method meant defeat and annexation by larger states. Eventually, China was united by emperors who ruled empires, dominating East Asia.

LATE ZHOU: THE DECLINE AND FALL OF FEUDALISM, 770–221 B.C.

The loss of the western capital in 771 B.C. symbolized the impotence of the Zhou ruling house. Although nearly all other rulers paid lip service to the Zhou kings, royal commands were ignored. Many states, both powerful and weak, were ruled by dukes. In respect for tradition, the Zhou title of king remained solely for the Zhou sovereign's use until around 300 B.C. During the succeeding decades (770–670 B.C.) the existing local governments warred with one another with increasing ferocity. Of perhaps two hundred or more states, fewer than a dozen survived by the seventh century B.C. Because the Zhou state had no political might with which to bring stability, the more powerful states tried to impose peace. But power shifts among states threatened stability.

In the late fifth century B.C., a major state (Jin) in the central Yellow River Valley broke into three parts. This event began an era (403–221 B.C.) known as the Warring States Period, when a few mighty governments engaged in warfare on a massive scale. Decentralized feudal polities had long since fallen to more centralized regimes.

Economic and Social Change in the Warring States Period

A cluster of developments transformed Chinese agriculture and led to widespread social and economic change. The making of bronze and iron agricultural tools, the use of manure as fertilizer, the employment of cattle as draft animals, and the introduction of plows permitted farming of new lands and better use of existing fields. Grain yields per land unit increased significantly and brought the surpluses to support larger populations and larger cities. As the urban centers grew, merchants

FIGURE 11.1 *Early Chinese Plow. The plow shown in this stone relief from southwestern China of the Late Han era is similar to plows used centuries earlier. The draft animal is probably a water buffalo, although humans sometimes provided the labor. Iron-tipped plowshares transformed Chinese agriculture and life throughout the imperial age.* Werner Forman/Art Resource, N.Y.

and artisans became more numerous. Social mobility, upward and downward, became commonplace.

As seen in Chapter 5, the Chinese developed the techniques of bronze metallurgy in their earliest cities. Yet the overwhelming use for bronze was only in ceremonial pieces and weapons. By the fifth century B.C., employment of bronze and iron agricultural tools had spread from the Yellow River Valley to other regions of China. Around the same time, the Chinese began replacing some human labor with cattle used as draft animals. These changes enabled farmers to work a wide variety of soils, thus increasing the amount of land under cultivation. Scholars do not know exactly when the Chinese developed techniques of iron metallurgy, although some archaeological finds suggest its appearance as early as the seventh century B.C. By about 500 B.C., the Chinese made iron agricultural tools and, over the next centuries, began mass producing iron implements that helped transform agriculture. Farmers either purchased iron plow tips or rented them from the state governments.

New techniques of political control also permitted officials to gather and direct large numbers of people in public works projects. One effort was a canal in the state of Qin.[1] The monarch of a rival state sent his hydraulic engineer, Zheng Guo,[2] who promised the Qin ruler bountiful harvests from the irrigated lands. They schemed to entice the Qin monarch to waste his state's human and material resources on the extravagant water control effort. Qin laborers using iron shovels and other tools began digging the hundred-mile-long canal. Later, Qin spies learned of the deception. Summoned before the Qin ruler, Zheng Guo noted how the Qin state efficiently absorbed the expenditures of resources. He reiterated his promise of immense wealth, and the king kept him. After eight years the canal was completed and irrigated large tracts of land. The Zheng Guo Canal, along with a second major hydraulic project in the southern Qin territory, reduced fears of drought-induced famines.

Water projects like these brought even larger agricultural reserves, which fed the burgeoning cities. Trade grew and some merchants became wealthy, though most peasants struggled to produce enough to pay their taxes and to provide for their families.

[1] **Qin:** CHIN
[2] **Zheng Guo:** JUNG gwaw

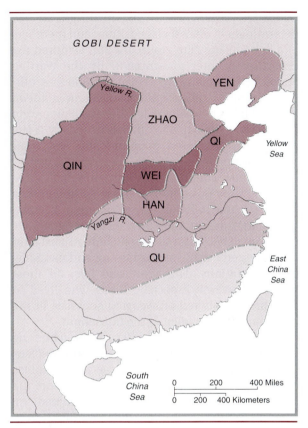

MAP 11.1 *China in 250 B.C.: The Warring States.* *Around 250 B.C., China was divided into seven warring states. They ruled much of northern and north central China (the Yellow and Yangzi river valleys). The Qin state in the northwest conquered the other states in a unification war lasting from 230 to 221 B.C. It also conquered additional territory in the south, extending China's boundaries farther than ever before. China's southward expansion continued for centuries.*

The Chinese also built road systems linking the cities. Peasants made the roads, constructed hydraulic works, erected city walls, and put up the barrier walls at the borders. As the flow of goods increased, one major problem limited the growth of trade. Because China lacked a system of standard axle lengths, the ruts of one warring state's roads often stopped the movement of another state's carts. Consequently, merchants spent much time reloading their trade goods at a state's border.

Many factors undermined the traditional social structure. The old aristocracy failed to meet the challenges of new political systems that needed the services of the best-qualified people.

Education began challenging birthright as the determinant of one's social position, and members of a low-ranking elite group, the *shi*, acquired the expertise to enter government. By the Warring States Period, many *shi* replaced nobles as officials. Artisans, especially the leaders among them, attained a high social and legal status. Some were considered to be equal to officials in society. A few merchants prospered economically, yet their social position remained low.

The new conditions in the cities had some impact on the position of women. Although they never became officials, some women became skilled artisans with their own social designations. One woman became a successful industrialist after she inherited her husband's mining and metallurgical operations. The economic lives of most women, however, especially those who lived in rural areas, centered on weaving activities in the home and management of the household.

Feudalism could not withstand the withering demands of all-out warfare, and decentralized feudal polities succumbed to the large states. Nobles could not effectively raise and long support the small personal armies that had dominated the campaigns of earlier eras. The manor system described in Chapter 5 could not compete with the newly emerging individual landholding system. Furthermore, large centralized states could control the labor armies that built the massive irrigation networks.

Chinese Intellectual Culture

The transformation of society and the economy created the material prosperity to support larger numbers of scholars, including writers and philosophers. Monarchs and officials, for example, sponsored scholars who published literary anthologies.

During this age (around 500–230 B.C.), two poetry collections appeared. Although the *Classic of Songs* was compiled in the sixth century, its songs had been sung for centuries. Poignant love songs of simple yet vibrant verses inspired later poets. Another collection, the *Songs of the South*, contained poems attributed to Qu Yuan,[3] an exiled official of the third century B.C. During travels across luxuriant southern lands, Qu Yuan com-

[3] **Qu Yuan:** CHOO ywahn

posed songs lamenting his misfortune. He tired of his exile and drowned himself, and Chinese annually remember him in Dragon Boat Festivals.

Prose blossomed. The *Classic of Documents*, a collection of early Zhou writings, appeared along with a basic chronicle of the Lu state (*Spring and Autumn Annals*). Both were associated with **Confucianism**. Perhaps the most significant development in prose, the essay, expanded into a sophisticated genre.

Confucianism representative of *shi* aspirations has been the most significant philosophy in Chinese history. Founded by Confucius (551–479 B.C.), the son of an aristocratic warrior, Confucianism stressed a human-centered, moral-based life. Orphaned at an early age, Confucius acquired an education and a profound love of learning. Nurturing a lifelong ambition to transform the corrupt political culture of his state, Confucius joined the government but fell from power before he could effect significant change. In his remaining years, Confucius taught disciples how to govern subjects, families, and themselves. Although Confucius considered himself a failure, generations of Chinese have been profoundly influenced by his writings.

A vital part of Confucius's teachings concerned ritual. He came from a group of aristocrats who mastered various rituals used in government. These experts were sometimes called upon by political leaders to advise them about the correct procedures of enthronement. Confucius took that sense of ritual and broadened it to include the rituals of one's daily life. Eating, sleeping, walking, conversing, parenting, and other daily activities were assigned proper ritual forms. By wholeheartedly following these mannered ways, one would live morally. Confucius believed that monarchs, officials, husbands, wives, parents, and children all must do the right things in their lives. For Confucius, ritual showed a way to social harmony and stability.

Although Confucius taught practical military subjects like archery and chariot driving, he believed that education should teach people to be good. He not only developed a teacher-student relationship but also defined the content of education. Students studied and practiced loyalty, humaneness, sincerity, and **filial piety** (honoring one's parents).

The Confucian ideal type, the **gentleman**, embodied all of these traits. The Chinese charac-

FIGURE 11.2 *Illustration of Filial Piety.* *Made in Sichuan, this painted lacquer basket was discovered at the site of a Chinese city in Korea. The Chinese conquered and ruled Korea for centuries, beginning in the second century B.C. The figure on the extreme left is a parent receiving homage from children. The closed sleeves and slight bow of the first child show respect and obedience. A similar scene may be seen with the fifth and sixth figures from the left. Chinese and East Asians regarded filial piety as a person's most important obligation.* R. B. Fleming.

ters for "gentleman" originally meant "son of a lord" in the feudal period. In that sense it connoted a birthright. Confucius, to be in accord with the social changes taking place and to meet the needs of his students, transformed the gentleman into one of noble character, not necessarily noble birth. The gentleman treated people humanely, and the Confucians encapsulated this sentiment with the saying, "Do not do unto others as you would not have them do unto you." This maxim is similar to Christianity's Golden Rule: Do unto others as you would have them do unto you. The gentleman aided weak and poor people. Ideally, the gentleman reviewed and criticized his daily actions. Finally, he radiated moral force. In the company of others, his personality compelled imitation of his actions. Thus Confucius hoped to change the political culture of his state, and later Confucians hoped that a few good men could transform any ailing government.

The gentleman showed loyalty to superiors, friends, and family. Confucians believed that people had to be loyal: Subjects had to obey their rulers, children their parents, and subordinates their superiors. Over time, the Confucians elaborated the concept of loyalty and its corollary, obedience, into a hierarchical system of five relationships:

— ruler-subject,

— parent-child,

— husband-wife,

— elder sibling–younger sibling, and

— elder friend–younger friend.

The person on the left side of the relationship dominated the one on the right, and superiors had to care for subordinates. The person on the right side of the relationship obeyed or showed loyalty to the one on the left.

Filial behavior impressed the Confucians, who saw the family as the basic social unit. A well-ordered family meant social and political stability. If a parent died, the children mourned their loss, usually for twenty-seven months. Every dutiful son had to produce a son to carry on the family name. Through a cohesive family structure, Confucians offered rulers social stability.

The hierarchical social order also gave each person a place and an identity. One consequence was the elaboration of an ideology that reinforced the subordination of women. Indeed, it was said that a woman's father, husband, and son dominated her sequentially in her life stages. When she married, she moved to her husband's house, which usually meant living with her in-laws. Filial piety required that she obey her parents-in-law. The most difficult relationship involved mother-in-law and daughter-in-law, because both competed for the affection of the son/husband. Wives who enjoyed their husbands' open attentions often faced the ire of their mothers-in-law.

The tough-minded side of the Warring States politics is seen in the **Legalists**, philosophers and bureaucrats who espoused a statist political theory. Legalist thinkers and officials believed that government must be powerful militarily and economically. In the Warring States Period, survival demanded harsh laws enforced by the toughest punishments. Therefore, the Legalists believed that people often behaved badly and needed to be kept under the most strict control. The all-powerful Legalist state had to suppress all who undermined its interests, including scholars, who lived off the production of others and who carped incessantly against government. Confucian scholars took a different view of the state. Most agreed that some laws were necessary, but only for the uneducated. They vehemently opposed restrictions on morally upright scholars. Confucians also believed that government should nurture the people, while Legalists insisted that subjects obediently serve the state.

Daoism was another Chinese philosophy that became popular in the Warring States era. Daoism has a mystical, intuitive component, unlike either Confucianism or Legalism. In addition, Confucianism developed near the original heartland of Chinese civilization, preserving many of its elements. Legalism developed in the northern frontier, reflecting the harshness of border life. Daoism flourished in the south, harmonizing with the lush landscapes there. The two main Daoist thinkers are Lao Zi[4] (around the sixth century B.C.), who wrote the *Dao De Jing*, and Zhuang Zi[5] (around 340–around 280 B.C.), who wrote *Zhuang Zi*.

Daoists employ symbols to help explain their way. **Dao** literally means a path or way; metaphorically, it signifies the totality of everything or the

[4] **Lao Zi:** LOW dzuh
[5] **Zhuang Zi:** joo AHNG dzuh

FIGURE 11.3 *Lao Zi Riding an Ox.* *Legend says that late in his life, Lao Zi became tired of the human world and traveled west. As he left China, a gatekeeper implored Lao Zi to leave behind something of value. In response, Lao Zi wrote the* Dao De Jing; *the scroll shown here may be this work. Riding effortlessly on the animal without using reins illustrates the Daoist ideal of acting in harmony with nature.* National Palace Museum, Taipei, Taiwan, Republic of China.

universe. On another level Dao is the origin of all things; it is, however, unknowable. One Daoist passage states that "The Dao that can be spoken about is not the true Dao." It can be ascertained only in nonrational ways, and to give it a name—even Dao—is to limit it. Thus, we come to the ultimate human paradox: talking about something about which we cannot speak. The third level of Dao is a path or way of life that one travels to a higher plane of being.

Daoists ridiculed the Confucian education and behavior codes, which Daoists believed hindered people from living naturally. Daoists hated offensive warfare and fought only when given no other choice.

Some scholars divide Daoism into **Contemplative Daoism** and **Purposive Daoism**. Contemplative Daoism, the most mystical and anarchistic philosophy in China's intellectual culture, asserts that the best government is no government and that the best social conventions are no social conventions. This form, not unlike the mystical tradi-

tions of India, stresses looking within oneself and seeing the natural world in a holistic way. For example, in looking at a tree one sees the leaves, branches, trunk, and roots; the Daoists would say that the person misses the totality of the tree. When we analyze the tree into its component parts, we miss the essence of the tree. The ideal type in Contemplative Daoism, the **immortal**, possesses magical attributes, subsists on simple foods (no meat), drinks dew from plants, flies, and cannot be destroyed.

The Purposive Daoists, unlike the Contemplative Daoists, believe in limited government. They also differ from the Contemplative Daoists in that

---

UNDER THE LENS

Chinese Perspectives on Yin/Yang *and the Five Elements*

The Classical Age's concepts of *yin/yang* and of the Five Elements merit focused attention. Although ancient texts from the first half of the first millennium B.C. mention *yin* (dark) and *yang* (light), their appearance as part of an interpretative perspective occurs only late in the third century B.C. The same may be said of the Five Elements system. We will examine each perspective and see the resulting integrated view of the human world.

Ancient Chinese saw certain alternating symmetrical patterns in natural cycles like the day and the year. Days had dark (*yin*) and light (*yang*) times. The years also had times when the daylight periods were more lengthy and times when the night grew longer. Each increase of light brought a decrease by dark and vice versa. Other polarities like cold/hot and wet/dry were added to the *yin/yang* analytical framework.

By the third century B.C., societal components were included in the *yin/yang* schema. *Yin* became viewed as passive, and the vagina was *yin*'s sexual symbol. *Yang* became seen as active, and the penis was its sexual symbol. In a broad sense, men were linked with more active traits, while women were labeled with passive aspects. All of this reflected the perspective of the dominant patriarchal culture.

Yin/yang analysis may be applied to medicine. If one has a fever (too much heat or *yang*), medicine with a *yin* nature must be ingested to bring the body back into balance. Other illnesses may be diagnosed

as reflecting too much bodily *yin*, so *yang* medicines will be prescribed.

The Five Elements system also became an elaborated perspective in the third century B.C. The Five Elements are Earth, Fire, Water, Metal, and Wood. In general, one element overcomes another, but no unilinear hierarchy is determined. In addition, the Chinese associated each element with a dynasty, a color, and other things. During the Zhou era, Fire dominated, and its corresponding color was red. Later, the Five Elements system was further elaborated to correspond to things such as a major organ, a season, a cardinal point on the compass, a note on the musical scale, and so forth. One scholar has noted that this organizing scheme paralleled the growth of the imperial bureaucracy and its organization of the empire.

China's Five Elements perspective resembles the system of correspondences of the Hopi Indian tribe of Arizona. The Hopi base their system on the four directions. Each direction has a specific, corresponding color, cloud pattern, lightning formation, tree species, type of obligation, and so forth. When the Hopi construct their religious altars, they combine materials like corn and colored sand, each of which stands for a specific concept. A whole panoply of concepts, therefore, can be visually arrayed and connected to give thanks to the spirits and to request future favors. Both the Chinese and Hopi ways signify attempts to understand and interpret the natural world.

they favor minimal social regulation. Purposive Daoists shun combat situations, but if forced to fight, they will employ all available means to win. Some martial arts employ Daoist ways. Purposive Daoists believe that aggressive people cause resentment in others, so they counsel quietude and patience in one's relationships.

Another condition of the intellectuals' creative lives stemmed from the leisure time they enjoyed to formulate their ideas. Indeed, they lived off the manual labor of others. This material prosperity enabled the support of a large leisured class that created elite culture, a class that the Legalists despised.

THE QIN EMPIRE, 221–207 B.C.

During the eighth and seventh centuries B.C., the Qin state appeared in western China. Natural defenses helped protect the Qin region, but intensified large-scale warfare threatened ruin. Soon a traveling strategist, Wei Yang[6] (around 390–338 B.C.), gained the confidence of the Qin ruler and launched a program that transformed his government into a great power.

Wei Yang developed a centralized Qin polity. He implemented a series of laws enforced by punishments and rewards, and then he imposed these regulations on all except the ruler. Wei Yang divided the state into **commandaries** (large administrative districts similar to provinces) and appointed officials, accountable to the monarch, over them. This system of central authority permitted Qin rulers efficiently to raise and supply large armies that regularly defeated enemy forces.

Wei Yang's successors added techniques of statecraft to improve Qin's government. They gathered statistics about demographics, agriculture, mines, tax revenues, and expenditures. Job descriptions were written in order to find the best-qualified people, and a merit-rating system evaluated their performance. The Qin bureaucracy effectively ruled a powerful state that awed its rivals.

Agriculture received favored treatment in economic planning. Wei Yang believed that farming was the foundation of political and military power, and he promoted individual landowning, as well as

the abolition of the manorial feudal system. The government lent or rented iron farm tools to peasant farmers. Wei Yang lauded the peasants as hardworking, loyal subjects and denounced aristocrats and other groups (like scholars) as lazy, disloyal idlers. During the Warring States Period, Qin officials harassed scholars and killed many aristocrats who unsuccessfully challenged the government.

Wei Yang's reforms contributed to the Qin state's growing power. In a campaign against the powerful state of Zhao,[7] during the Battle of Changping (260 B.C.), the Qin army trapped a large opposing army. After receiving assurances of good treatment, the Zhao commander surrendered. Nevertheless, the Qin force annihilated the unarmed enemy troops. The Qin state gained a reputation for ruthlessness.

King Jeng (259–210 B.C.) of the Qin state gathered talented advisors who devised stratagems such as bribing officials in the enemy states. The unification wars began in 230 B.C. and lasted for nine years. In one campaign, a river was diverted against a state capital's wall and destroyed it. The last warring state fell in 221 B.C., and King Jeng ordered national celebrations to inaugurate a peaceful era. He also commanded his advisors to choose a new royal title, because "king" seemed unworthy. These men, along with their ruler, settled on "emperor." King Jeng became the First Emperor of the Qin Empire.

Below the emperor, three officials presided over the bureaucracy, supervising record keeping, military affairs, and lower officials. Next came nine bureau chiefs who handled the key decisions and directives of their agencies. All received orders directly from the emperor, who monitored their labors.

The Qin government imposed a unified, centralized rule and an administrative system of commandaries on the conquered territories. Three officials ran a commandary: a military commander, a civil official, and an inspector who watched all. Subcommandary officials toiled in this chain of command and passed their reports to the appropriate commandary officials. All obeyed the central government, which hired and fired them.

Officials standardized weights and measures, money, written characters, axle lengths, and laws. Laws in particular extended everywhere in a mas-

---

[6]**Wei Yang:** WAY yahng

[7]**Zhao:** JOW

FIGURE 11.4 *The Great Wall.* *This view of the Great Wall shows it snaking across the mountains of northern China. Technically called the Long Wall, the edifice shown here was built in the fifteenth century by laborers of the Ming Empire. During the Qin era, it deterred the Huns; in the Ming era, it deterred the Mongols. The wall was also meant to hinder Chinese from traveling and carrying Chinese technology away with them.* Henri Cartier-Bresson/ Magnum Photos.

sive social engineering experiment that outlawed local customs and unnecessarily angered the newly conquered peoples. An early Zhou official once noted, "Never change local customs of conquered peoples, or they will resent it and you." As we have seen elsewhere, the Romans, Mauryas, and Guptas permitted a great deal of local autonomy in their empires. But the strong militarist orientation of Qin rulers led them to demand that local customs conform to Qin practices.

Large-scale public works projects began before the final unification in 221 B.C. China's northern frontiers were vulnerable to incursions by nomads. In preimperial times, various northern states erected walls to protect themselves. The Qin Empire built a 2,000-mile-long barrier, using the surviving walls and adding new sections. This effort took much labor and resources, but it defined the border between nomads and agriculturists. The wall system was intended to slow, rather than stop, attacks. Once warned, the Qin army could mobilize and repel invaders. The Great Wall as it exists today was built in the fifteenth century. The emperor also built scaled-down replicas of palaces and mansions from the states conquered by his armies. He ordered architects and engineers to defeated states, and they returned with drawings of prominent dwellings. A road network also linked the new regions with the capital.

Many Qin policies reflected a concerted effort to bring security both to the state and to adversely affected social groups. During the unification wars, the Qin regime moved rich and powerful families to the capital region. One historian claimed that 120,000 families were forcibly shifted there. The Qin government uprooted more of its subjects by forcing them to settle frontier areas. The great Qin highways may have carried as many as a million of these forced settlers. Another security matter came with the disarmament of the people. All had to turn in their weapons, some of which were recast into statues or bells.

Peasant farmers received good treatment, for the emperor decreed that landless people could acquire previously vacated or virgin land. Apparently the supply of labor available to the Qin state greatly increased, because the monarch abolished the labor tax of thirty days' labor owed to the state. About the same time, plentiful grain supplies enabled him to give a tax rebate. Each village

FIGURE 11.5 *The First Qin Emperor.* *This painting shows the Qin ruler presiding over the burning of the books and the execution of scholars. Completed late in the imperial era, it mistakenly assumes that both events happened at the same time. The earliest account records these events as happening a year apart. The marring of the ruler's face shows the hatred with which he was regarded by scholars of later generations.* ET Archive.

received an amount of grain and a few animals. This action is one of the few tax rebates in world history.

To advise him about key policies and other matters, the emperor gathered a brain trust. Earlier kings had assembled large numbers of intellectuals, and the First Emperor emulated these forerunners. In 213 B.C., the monarch invited his imperial academicians to a banquet during which a Confucian criticized the centralized rule. He argued for a return to the Zhou feudal system with kingdoms established in frontier areas and ruled by blood relatives who could aid the government in troubled times. The emperor ordered officials to deliberate on the proposal and approved a chief minister's petition recommending that privately owned books, except those concerned with medicine, agriculture, and divination, be burned. Most of China's classics disappeared in flames. Unfortunately, the copies of all banned and permitted works stored in the Imperial Library also burned a few years later.

The year following the book-burning, the emperor learned of a treasonous speech by two academicians. Suspecting similar sentiments by others, he ordered the interrogation of court scholars. As a result, 460 academicians died, and a like number were forced to toil on the Great Wall project. For these two transgressions, scholars have long reviled this monarch.

Because he lived in fear of assassination, the First Emperor led a secretive life. He never slept in the same room on successive nights. When he walked on the palace grounds, walled pathways hid him, and he traveled in covered carriages. Although the First Emperor feared for his life, he often traveled around his beloved realm. On imperial tours, he ascended sacred peaks to sacrifice animals to local deities. A downpour interrupted one such ascent, and, grateful to a sheltering tree, the monarch ennobled it. On another sortie, he punished a mountain spirit that thwarted his progress by denuding the mountain, painting some of its rocks red, the color that convicts wore.

The First Emperor's last trip took place in 210 B.C. Accompanied by Hu Hai[8]—his favorite son—and by key officials, the imperial party meandered through southeast and coastal China. When the entourage stopped by the sea, the emperor con-

---

[8] **Hu Hai:** HOO hy

PATHS TO THE PAST

Did the Qin Empire Burn Books and Bury Scholars?

We saw in Chapter 1 how historians analyze and interpret sources in order to understand an event. Here, we will examine accounts in *The Historical Records*, written by Sima Qian around 100 B.C. In recent years doubt has been cast on the infamous events of 213–212 B.C., when the Qin Empire supposedly burned books and executed 460 imperial academicians.

The 213 B.C. event centered on an imperial banquet, at which an academician criticized the government. The First Emperor commanded his officials to debate the speech, and a top official proposed burning most books in private hands.

But not all historians accept this account. They note that although Sima Qian lamented the loss of literature, there is no condemnation in his biography of the official who urged the emperor to burn the books and who should have been denounced for that destruction. In fact, this minister is ranked at a level of the greatest officials. Another discrepancy in the record concerns the lack of punishment for the offending academician, who should have been a logical target for reprisal. The same account alleged that the Qin state permitted people to keep possession of works on divination. Because divining could have been used to predict the fall of a government, works of divination would presumably have been burned.

A skeptical view has been taken of the alleged punishment of nearly 1,000 academicians. *The Historical Records* offers a conversation between two academicians who slandered the emperor, then fled. The ruler learned of the verbal attacks and launched an investigation of all academicians. Eventually, the history alleges, 460 scholars perished and more were punished by being sent north to work on the Great Wall. How would Sima Qian have been able to reconstruct a conversation between two academicians who lived more than a century earlier? They would have taken great pains to speak in guarded ways. It is difficult to imagine that a plot encompassing more than 900 scholars could have existed. These officials had advised their sovereign on various matters. In short, they rendered the Qin Empire invaluable service long after the 212 B.C. date.

One modern scholar using this kind of textual analysis has concluded that some of Sima Qian's negative accounts of the Qin Empire are later additions by scholars who hated the First Emperor of the Qin Empire. If true, this perspective shows *The Historical Records* in a different light. It also suggests that understanding of the Qin Empire has been obscured by the smoke of deliberate intent.

Whether or not one agrees with a particular scholar's interpretation of an event, new ideas or perspectives may be uncovered by subjecting a document to rigorous analysis, including focused questions. This constant probing and examining opens historians to exciting vistas of discovery.

---

tracted a fatal disease and succumbed. Far from the capital and in unfriendly territory, the top officials, Hu Hai, and the dead monarch's servants conspired to hide the death and plotted to elevate Hu Hai, instead of the presumed heir apparent, to the throne. This plot commenced a significant political struggle that eventually toppled the Qin Empire. To maintain the ruse that the emperor lived, trusted servants brought food, clothing, and other necessities to the covered imperial carriage. The hot weather intensified the death stench, so the plotters masked it by placing a cartload of dead fish nearby. Upon reaching the capital, the conspirators commanded in the emperor's name that his heir apparent commit suicide. The young man dutifully obeyed "his father's orders." Only then did the plotters announce the emperor's death and Hu Hai's immediate ascension to the throne.

Preliminary work on the First Emperor's tomb had commenced when that monarch had assumed power in 246 B.C. When he finally died in 210 B.C., tens of thousands of people hastily completed the tomb complex. A detachment of clay soldiers, horses, and vehicles symbolically guarded the First Emperor's burial place. More than seven thousand life-size soldiers modeled on an elite-guard detachment lay buried there until their discovery and excavation in the mid-1970s. Bronze soldiers, horses, and a carriage have also been recovered. The central tomb lies beneath a large artificial hill. Inside the mound rests a palace with a gigantic relief map of China and river channels through which mercury once coursed. (Mercury rivers flowed into a mercury sea upon which floated the First Emperor's sarcophagus.)

The collapse of the Qin government came rapidly. Hu Hai resumed work on dormant construction projects and commissioned a special guard of 50,000 soldiers. Discontent with the government, resentment about the labor projects, and anger about the changing of local customs caused the unrest. Deteriorating weather contributed to the Qin state's demise. Recent scholarship suggests that a volcanic eruption in Iceland thrust a massive amount of volcanic material into the atmosphere and altered weather patterns in the northern hemisphere. Extant Chinese texts note heavy and prolonged rainfalls. Not only would the deluge have provoked floods, it would have destroyed crops and brought famine.

Whatever the circumstances, uprisings began. Although Qin armies defeated the early rebels, more successful anti-Qin efforts proliferated. One imperial messenger brought news of additional challenges to an irritated Hu Hai, who had the messenger killed. Subsequent "positive" reports meant that the Second Emperor had lost touch with his realm. At the same time, a general purge crippled the top government levels as Hu Hai's former teacher and trusted advisor eliminated political rivals. The tutor assassinated the Second Emperor and elevated a grandson of the First Emperor. The new monarch soon killed his "patron." While these sordid events consumed elite figures, a rebel force broke through the capital region's southern defenses and captured the hapless grandson.

The Qin state's collapse should not mask its achievements. An administrative structure like that of the Qin Empire, with top officials each supervising a clearly delineated area of government, served successive imperial polities. The Qin

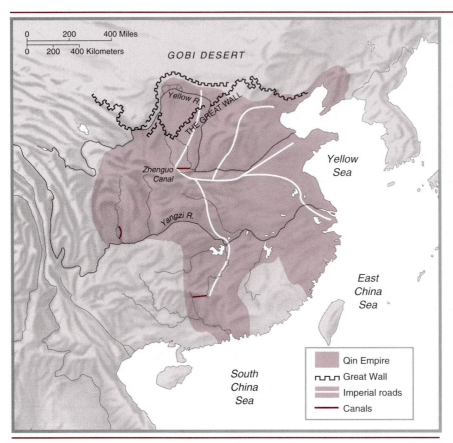

MAP 11.2 *The Qin Empire in 210 B.C.* *The Qin road system linked many far-flung parts of the empire with the capital. The Great Wall is also indicated, as well as three major canals: the two northernmost were used primarily for irrigation and the southernmost was used primarily for transportation. Effective communication and transportation were essential to the empire's well-being.*

FIGURE 11.6 *Figures from the Qin Emperor's Tomb.* *Excavations in the 1970s uncovered part of the vast remains of the First Qin Emperor's burial site. Construction of this complex began more than thirty years before the emperor died. Terra-cotta figures of warriors are arranged in rows, and each has an individual face. A few smaller bronze figures, like this horse-drawn cart, have also been found. The artisanry testifies to the cultural splendor of China's first imperial age.* Cultural Relics Publishing House.

legacy of standardization provided cultural and political cohesiveness. By erecting the Great Wall, the Qin government finished delineating the boundaries between the northern nomads and the Chinese agriculturalists.

THE HAN EMPIRE, 202 B.C.–A.D. 220

The Han Empire has been regarded as a defining era in Chinese history, and the Chinese people during this time often called themselves the "People of Han." During that time, Chinese power dominated many parts of East Asia, and Chinese influence held sway over Koreans, Vietnamese, and other Asians. In addition, some of China's most important historical works were written in the Han imperial period.

The Early Han Empire, 202 B.C.–A.D. 9

Although Early Han emperors adhered to the Qin political structure, they lessened its tax and service burdens on the people. This permitted society to recover from the disastrous wars and famine of the

Qin era. Around 120 B.C., however, the Martial Emperor revived costly public works projects and expansionist military campaigns. His successors contented themselves with ruling more humanely and seeking pleasure.

POLITICAL DEVELOPMENTS. In the last years of the Qin Empire, some peasants ignited the first unsuccessful challenge to the empire. Although it failed, an aristocrat and a commoner led new rebellions. The aristocrat regularly defeated the Qin forces and proclaimed himself dictator, naming the commoner as the King of Han. Within months, Liu Bang,[9] who was the king of Han, seized the former Qin capital and declared war on the dictator. During the years of civil war (206–202 B.C.), Liu Bang selected outstanding people to command his armies and to run his government. He held the strategic center and ultimately won, founding one of China's great empires, which lasted for four centuries. Therefore, Liu Bang became the First Emperor of Han.

Liu Bang softened the Qin laws, lowered taxes, and lightened the people's burdens, because, as a commoner, he knew their travails. He controlled

[9] **Liu Bang:** LYOH BONG

the Qin heartland and other populated areas while installing his top military commanders as kings of distant realms. By 195 B.C., the First Han Emperor replaced these kings with his kin to secure the dynasty. Gradually the military nature of the new government assumed a more civilian character, something that the Qin monarchs failed to do. The First Han Emperor needed the Confucians' ritual expertise for the enthronement rites that gave him legitimacy, and some Confucians entered government service.

Succession worried the new emperor. At one point he favored a son by a concubine over his empress's son, the acknowledged heir apparent. Because Empress Lu frequently gave sage advice to her husband and often acted courageously, she earned the ruling elite's support. When the emperor tried to replace the heir apparent, their opposition dissuaded him. Before he died in 195 B.C., the emperor named Empress Lu as regent for their son, who was still a minor.

Empress Lu (reign dates 195–180 B.C.) ruled through minors and followed her husband's policies of relaxed rule and mild laws to give the common people relief from years of war, disease, and suffering. Fearful that the population might not recover from its terrible losses, she decreed that single women of childbearing age be taxed five times more heavily than other adults. Empress Lu provided a steady ruling hand, and when she died, another son of the First Han Emperor succeeded.

Some Chinese historians have reviled Empress Lu by exaggerating her negative traits and de-emphasizing her significant contributions. If she had been politically inept, the Han state would have collapsed. Because most of these historians adhered to Confucian ideals, they may have reflected the Confucian bias against females. Nearly every woman who ruled endured negative assessments by these historians.

Like the Qin capital, Changan, the capital of the early Han state, became a vibrant city for tens of thousands of Chinese. The city was laid out on a grid pattern according to the four cardinal directions; the streets inside the city ran along north-south or east-west lines. Palaces took up a significant fraction of land inside the city, and an armory was built between the two main palaces located in the southern part of Changan. The city walls, which were built after the two palaces, were constructed using the conscript and convict labor of both men and women. These walls of rammed earth were about 40 feet high and 40 to 50 feet wide at the base. Nine markets served the city, and records of the day describe various activities in Changan, including the existence of city youth gangs, each with its own distinctive color of clothing. Most of Changan was in place by 180 B.C.

The next two reigns (180–141 B.C.) continued the policies of low state expenses and minimal taxes. Some scholars have asserted that the light government hand reflects a commitment by monarchs to Contemplative Daoist beliefs that the best government rests easily on the people. Frequent decrees solicited nominations of honorable people to be officials. One problem—the peripheral kingdoms that had been created in the early years of the empire—exploded around 155 B.C., when kings who nursed personal grudges or ambitions to rule the empire revolted. After a few worrisome weeks, the Han armies prevailed, and the central government reduced or abolished the larger and more dangerous kingdoms.

Because Liu Che,[10] the Martial Emperor (reign dates 141–87 B.C.), succeeded to the throne as a minor, others made decisions for him early in his reign. His grandmother, for example, promoted Daoist ideas that were prominent at this time. Another early decree favored Confucian scholars, because it asserted that people who espoused other philosophies could not hold high positions. By the first century A.D., Confucianism had become the orthodox ideology of the empire.

The reign of Liu Che is significant because during this time Han power dominated Central and East Asia. Interest in distant lands grew. Zhang Qian,[11] a diplomat, went west to gather knowledge and to seek alliances with friendly states. After many years, Zhang Qian returned—without diplomatic treaties, but with much knowledge. His mission set the foundation for Chinese trade and intercourse with other peoples. Han armies invaded the western lands of what came to be called Chinese Turkestan, and, despite heavy casualties, Chinese influence prevailed. Other armies conquered Korea and Vietnam. The costs of these campaigns demanded new resources.

The Han state took a variety of measures to cope with the rising costs of its expansive foreign policy. Iron and salt monopolies began when the

[10] **Liu Che:** LYOH CHUH
[11] **Zhang Qian:** JONG chee YAHN

IN THEIR OWN WORDS

Peasant Life in Early Imperial China

Life for the common folk was often quite difficult, as may be seen in a memorandum sent by Chao Cuo,[a] an official, to his emperor around 160 B.C. Perhaps a bit of rhetorical emphasis may be found in the document, but the sometimes horrible living conditions are, in fact, vividly portrayed.

> If the people are poor, then depravity follows. Poverty originates in insufficiency; insufficiency originates in not farming. If the people do not engage in farming, they will not be attached to the land. If they do not become attached to the land, they will leave their native places and regard their families lightly. . . .
>
> A wise ruler says that this is so. Therefore he urges people to devote themselves to farming and mulberry culture. He lowers taxes and enlarges stores in order to fill the granaries against [the time of] floods and droughts. . . .
>
> Pearls, jade, gold, and silver cannot be eaten in case of hunger, nor can they be worn in case of cold. Yet people value them because of the emperor's use of them.
>
> They [peasants] till the land in spring, hoe in summer, harvest in autumn, and store in winter. [Besides,] they have to cut wood for fuel, work in the government buildings and render labor service. In the spring, they cannot escape the wind and dust; in the summer, they cannot escape the heat; in the autumn, they cannot escape the chilling rain; and in the winter, they cannot escape the cold. Throughout the four seasons, they do not have a single day of rest. Furthermore, their private expenditures for parting with those who are leaving and for welcoming those who are coming, for consoling the bereaved, visiting the sick, caring for the orphans, and bringing up the young, all have to be defrayed from that income. . . . Collections are urgent, taxation exorbitant; and the taxes are collected at no fixed date. Orders issued in the morning have to be executed in the evening. Those who have something sell it at half price, those who have nothing have to borrow at 100 percent interest. Hence there are people who have sold their land, their houses, their wives and children in order to pay their debts [taxes]. . . .

The picture, of course, details a life of desperate poverty, and the monarch took measures to help the poor. A few decades later, however, taxes rose to levels where people became so impoverished that some revolted against the state.

[a]**Chao Cuo:** CHOW swohw

---

government licensed the production, distribution, and sale of salt and iron to a few people. Liu Che imposed burdensome taxes on commerce, and the peasants suffered from additional levies. Frontier soldiers farmed to defray garrison expenses, and this military colonist system became a regular policy of successor states.

Despite the glories of Liu Che's reign, his expansionist and statist policies impoverished merchants and peasants alike. Great unrest troubled the empire, and it took harsh measures to crush incipient uprisings. Court maneuvers, including charges of witchcraft leveled at the empress, compelled her adult son, the heir apparent, to attack those who influenced his father. Both mother and son perished in the ensuing struggle. On his deathbed, a saddened Liu Che created a Regency Council of trusted advisors to supervise his infant son and successor.

Although limited prosperity and stable rule continued for a few decades after Liu Che's reign, serious decline set in after 49 B.C. A major problem of reduced revenues developed because Liu Che had rewarded outstanding officials with tax-free estates. As these estates expanded, key revenue sectors disappeared and increased the burden on peasants, many of whom fled to the tax-exempt estates. A vicious cycle of rising taxes shrank the tax base and caused tax revenues to decline. The financial crisis precipitated a political crisis.

Despite the many problems facing the political elite, members of the Wang[12] clan benefited

[12]**Wang:** WONG

from the long life of Empress Wang (reign dates 49–33 B.C.). When her husband died, she became empress dowager and regent for her young son and outlived several reigning emperors. She never dominated the government in the manner of Empress Lu. Each new monarch under Empress Dowager Wang had to act like an obedient, filial child to this matriarch. Through successive reigns she appointed her clan's members to key posts. One, Wang Mang, amassed power, usurped the throne, and proclaimed a new dynasty (A.D. 9–23).

Wang Mang limited landholding, abolished tax-free lands, lowered taxes, reinstituted the monopolies, pushed currency reforms, and mounted aggressive campaigns against the northern nomads. The tax reforms alienated elite groups. A massive rupture in the Yellow River dike system killed many and made beggars of others, who turned to banditry and rebellion. One rebel group, the Red Eyebrows, named for distinctive red markings they painted over their eyes, overwhelmed Wang Mang's armies, took the capital, and assassinated him. After a civil war, a Han relative ascended the throne in A.D. 25.

SOCIAL AND ECONOMIC DEVELOPMENTS. Han society developed in the relatively relaxed atmosphere of the Early Han period. Social mobility took place, as demonstrated by several top officials who came from the commoner ranks. By the first century B.C., ennobled aristocrats had passed their titles and property to their heirs. As we have noted, these tax-free estates unduly burdened governments. Han society included many social gradations: aristocrats of royal blood, ennobled aristocrats, officials, commoners, and slaves who served the government and private citizens alike.

Agriculture was recognized by the state as the dominant economic form. Not only did the state resume the practice of lending or renting iron agri-

FIGURE 11.7 *State Burdens on the Peasants.* *This stamped brick illustrates a familiar scene: paying taxes. The bowed peasant pours his grain before the tax collector, who is seated with accounting slips in his hands. The subservient posture of the peasant suggests that he is bowed under the weight of his obligation. His simple clothes also contrast with the official's finery.* Courtesy of the Chinese Cultural Center of San Francisco.

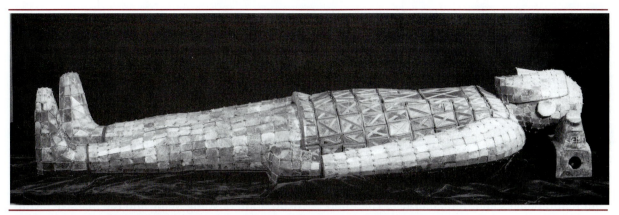

FIGURE 11.8 *The Han Jade Princess.* *This burial suit for royalty of the Early Han Period was discovered in the 1970s. Jade was believed to inhibit bodily decay, and for this reason jade pieces were sewn into an enclosing suit for the body. Princess Dou Wan died in the second century B.C. Her headrest is similar to ones used as pillows for sleeping.* Robert Harding Picture Library.

cultural tools, but some officials also identified farming experts who were sent at public expense through areas to disseminate their expertise and to increase production. By the second century of Han rule, monarchs had established large public granaries to be filled in times of surplus and drawn upon in times of shortage.

Manufacture and commerce prospered. Iron foundries proliferated in Han times, and, although many establishments were privately owned, the state also supported these works. The monopolies of iron and salt during the time of the Martial Emperor were highly unpopular, because they drove up prices. Later the state abolished the monopolies only to reestablish them a short time after. Trade grew dramatically after 120 B.C. with the opening of western trade routes to Chinese merchants, and many Chinese goods circulated through most of Eurasia. Although merchants traded lacquerware, iron products, precious jewels, and other items, silk provided the greatest profits. In fact, the two western routes across the formidable deserts (the Gobi Desert and the Tarim Basin) were appropriately named the silk roads.

ELITE CULTURE. Many different forms of literature developed in the Early Han period. The dominant literary genre was the prose poem, a form that combined lengthy prose and poetic passages. The Han era saw the perfection of the prose poem in the hands of a succession of capable writers.

Another Han literary development came in the area of bibliography under the leadership of a Han prince who categorized the imperial holdings.

History writing set a pattern of excellence that was imitated for centuries. Sima Tan,[13] the Grand Historian of Han, began a general history of China. The project passed to his son, Sima Qian,[14] who chose castration over death when punished for angering the Martial Emperor. The son lived to fulfill his father's dying wish that the history be completed. The work, *The Historical Records*, is a masterful, comprehensive treatment of two thousand years. Written in a graceful, elegant style, it contains a half-million written characters. It accurately dates events and long-deceased rulers. Although Sima Qian sometimes embellished things for dramatic effect, scholars have admired his methods of weighing evidence.

Confucianism survived the Qin oppression to become the favored ideology of Han. We have seen the promotion of Confucian books and scholars during the Martial Emperor's reign. Successive monarchs gathered Confucian worthies and excluded followers of other traditions. Wang Mang, the usurper, even based his reforms on an ancient Confucian work. A key Confucian thinker, Dong Zhongshu[15] (179–104 B.C.), reworked Confucian

[13] **Sima Tan:** SEE mah TAHN
[14] **Sima Qian:** SEE mah chee AHN
[15] **Dong Zhongshu:** DOONG joong shoo

ideas into a framework suitable to an empire. He posited the existence of three interrelated levels of the universe: the realm of Heaven, the realm of Humanity, and the realm of Earth. These realms joined in the monarch. If the state governed well and people prospered, Heaven and Earth gave favorable signs. Conversely, when a ruler became tyrannical, negative portents occurred: An earthquake might devour a city (such an event is recorded) or a comet might light the sky. (Chinese first recorded Halley's Comet during the Han Empire.) Thus, "bad" rulers felt admonishment from natural forces and human critics. The interpretation of portents gained favor across East Asia.

The Late Han Empire, A.D. 25–220

For about a century after the Han emperor ascended the throne, peace and prosperity were the norm for most Chinese. After A.D. 120, corruption began to become widespread, and factional politics weakened the imperial court. Large-scale uprisings weakened the imperial system, bringing warlords into power in many parts of China.

POLITICAL DEVELOPMENTS. Political control slowly returned to the Han Empire after the usurpation of Wang Mang and the massive revolts that toppled him. Korea remained under Chinese

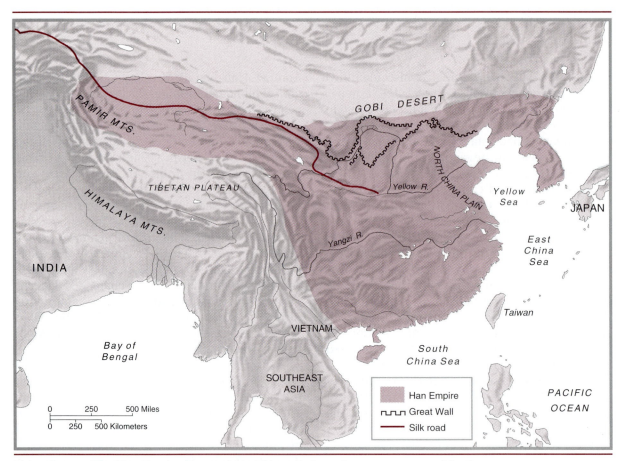

MAP 11.3 *The Han Empire in A.D. 120.* *This map shows the greatest extent of the Han Empire, which controlled parts of Korea, Vietnam, and Central Asia. The silk roads came under Chinese jurisdiction and carried Chinese wares westward, some eventually arriving in Rome to the delight of wealthy Romans, who prized Chinese silk. Land trade was a major revenue source for Chinese rulers, who paid much attention and wealth to keeping land routes under their control.*

FIGURE 11.9 *Flying Horse of Late Han.* *This bronze sculpture captures the great speed and pride of the horse. To emphasize the flying ideal, the horse's hoof rests on a soaring bird. Power and grace are combined in this excellent example of Chinese artisanry from centuries ago.* Robert Harding Picture Library.

domination, but Vietnam rebelled under the Trung sisters, whose fragile government fell to a new Chinese campaign around A.D. 50. The Chinese armies also returned to Central Asia and remained there until nomads pushed them back.

The first monarchs of the Later Han Empire ruled effectively. They selected able officials and presided over stable and prosperous times. Over time, the decline of the monarchs permitted the interaction of three key political groups: the empresses and their families, the court officials, and the **eunuchs** (castrated boys and men). Eunuchs influenced politics in Chinese history. Men were needed to guard the women's quarters of the inner palace, but the monarch did not wish to have virile males there because they might impregnate his empress. Yet, eunuchs did gain influence by supporting strong-willed empresses or by befriending heirs apparent.

The last effective ruler was Empress Deng[16] (reign dates 106–121), who ruled as regent for her infant son and who relied on the significant political influence of her family. When the child died, she kept power as regent, ruling for another child

[16] **Deng:** DUHNG

successor, and during her tenure the country enjoyed general tranquility. Several of her family members held key political posts. After her death, power came into the hands of other prominent families that produced empresses. Eunuchs also gained prominence through their close ties to monarchs and their control of key government and military posts. Officials opposed the other groups. Despite continual friction among the factions, a customary practice of balancing alliances kept each group from becoming too powerful.

Stability was shattered when warlords gained control late in the second century. These military figures rose during the Yellow Turban Revolt of 184. The Yellow Turbans lived in communities with healers or "miracle workers." These peaceful centers sprang up in the 170s and 180s, but the Han government saw the Yellow Turbans as subversive because they were tightly organized groups of thousands, some of which carried weapons for self-defense. In 184, a Han military campaign against the Yellow Turbans triggered a major uprising. The corruption-ridden Han forces disintegrated before the fierce attacks of the enemy. Military power soon shifted to regional armies and their commanders, who defeated the rebels.

FIGURE 11.10 *Zhang Heng's Seismoscope.* *This cutaway view of an adaptation of Zhang Heng's seismoscope shows how the mechanism was designed to work: The central weight shifted with any movement and caused the dragon's jaws to release a ball, which fell into the frog's mouth and thus indicated the line of an earthquake's seismic wave. Placement of several of these devices would allow the scientist to plot the quake's epicenter. The piece is an example of Chinese technological development nearly two thousand years ago.* Science and Society Picture Library.

Eventually, the commanders became warlords who challenged the central government. One warlord seized the capital and destroyed the political system. His successor captured the last hapless Han monarch and terminated the dynasty in 220.

ELITE CULTURE AND SOCIETY. Daoism changed during the Han era from a philosophy accessible to a tiny elite into a popular religion. This metamorphosis began in the Early Han when Lao Zi became a Daoist divinity. Soon a myriad of divine beings, including the Stove God, who symbolizes Daoist experimentation with alchemy to discover elixirs of immortality, were recognized.

Religious Daoists became interested in health issues, seeking to prolong their lives by a variety of practices. Cinnabar was the preferred elixir of longevity because its bright red color seemed to connote health, vitality, heat, and happiness. Ingested cinnabar was a poison, however, and shortened life. Daoists also experimented with diet, exercise, and breathing techniques to prolong life.

Many patterns and trends described for the Early Han era continued after A.D. 25. Although aristocratic families perished in the wars that toppled Wang Mang, the new government created an aristocracy that dominated society and politics. In fact, some great clans persisted into an era of division (220–589) that followed the Han period. One's education, especially when tied to government service, afforded privileges and honors. Individual elite women, some of whom were educated, played important political and cultural roles, although females generally were subordinated to men.

SOUTH AND EAST ASIA

	Chinese feudalism, to 403 B.C.	— **700 B.C.** — Zhou king moves capital, 770 B.C.
		— **600 B.C.** Iron used in China, c. 620 B.C.
Origins of Con-fucianism, Daoism, Legalism		— **500 B.C.** Confucius begins teaching, c. 500 B.C.
		— **400 B.C.** Wei Yang starts reforms in Qin state, 356 B.C.
Qin ► Empire, 221–267 B.C.		— **300 B.C.** — Founding of Qin Empire, 221 B.C.
	Early Han Empire, 202 B.C.–A.D. 9	**200 B.C.** Founding of Early Han Empire, 202 B.C. — Conquest of Korea, Vietnam, and Central Asia, 111–100 B.C.
		100 B.C.
Wang ► Mang's rule, A.D. 9–23	Late Han Empire, A.D. 9 – 220	**A.D. 1** End of Early Han, 9 — Founding of Late Han, 25
		A.D. 100 Invention of paper, 105 — Yellow Turban Revolt, 184
		A.D. 200 Fall of Han Empire, 220

The Han era was a dynamic time for economic development. Agriculture continued to dominate the Chinese economy, and agricultural specialists were employed by the state to share their expertise with other farmers. In essays, they discussed planting techniques, new tools, and new seed varieties. Manufacturing continued, and the mass-production techniques for iron and steel greatly improved. Chinese trade grew, especially in Chinese silks, which were in demand all across Eurasia. The famed silk roads were conquered by the Martial Emperor and remained in Chinese hands through much of the era.

Zhang Heng[17] (78–139), a prose poem master and a noted scientist, designed instruments to facilitate the observation and display of heavenly bodies. He invented the first seismograph and mastered diverse mathematical branches. Cai Lun,[18] a eunuch and member of the inner court around A.D. 100, invented paper. The method he employed yielded a writing surface that could be inexpensively fashioned and widely distributed. Not only did it transform state business, but books became lighter, easier to handle, cheaper, and more widely read.

Imperial veneration of Confucius grew, and the sage's family home became a national shrine. Little original thought characterized Confucianism at this time. The most significant work came from a skeptical rationalist, Wang Chung[19] (27–97), who debunked myths and superstitions. He ridiculed the art of divining the future. Wang Chung pioneered in the effort to base arguments on observation and reasoned discourse.

SUMMARY

1. The Zhou state entered 770 B.C. in a weak condition and remained so until the mid–third century B.C., when it was conquered.

2. The Late Zhou era, 770–256 B.C., is overlapped by the Warring States Period, 403–221 B.C. The Qin Empire united and ruled China from 221–207 B.C. The Han Empire endured for four centuries but also saw a failed attempt at usurpation by Wang Mang.

3. China experienced a transformation from the seventh to the third centuries B.C. The two major forces of prolonged warfare and iron technology drove this change and brought the demise of Chinese feudalism.

4. Warfare on an increasing scale forced states to mobilize their economic and human resources. Most successful states moved to a centralized political system.

5. Bronze and iron plow tips, along with manure fertilizing, led to more plentiful grain supplies and larger populations. Iron weapons changed the nature of warfare. Central governments employed armies of workers to build massive hydraulic projects to improve crop yields.

6. Aristocrats failed to adapt to the profound changes and lapsed into insignificance or disappeared. Peasants became individual landowners, and merchants became more prosperous. A few successfully entered politics.

7. Confucianism developed an ethically based educational system along with a way to rule an empire. Legalism offered a path to military success through central rule and merit-based office holding. Daoism appealed to people who devalued social conventions and sought spiritual solace in private.

8. In the fourth century B.C., the Qin state used the Legalist system to conquer its rival states and forged an empire. It standardized laws, money, weights and measures, and written characters. It also built a road system linking key regions with the capital and the Great Wall. The founder's death and hapless rule of his successor coupled with widespread discontent toppled the Qin Empire.

[17] **Zhang Heng:** JONG huhng

[18] **Cai Lun:** SY lwuhn
[19] **Wang Chung:** WONG chee UHNG

9. The Han Empire emerged from the civil wars, and able monarchs ruled lightly and permitted the people to recover. Decades later, Liu Che conquered parts of Korea, Vietnam, and Central Asia, but the costly wars nearly toppled his rule.

10. Decline weakened the monarchy and precipitated a usurpation by Wang Mang, who failed to reform the Han system. New uprisings enabled a Han family member to reclaim the throne. The Late Han lasted for two centuries.

11. Many elements of elite Chinese culture developed in the Han era. Two historians wrote major works. Prose poems reached an apex of development. Science and technology also flourished.

SUGGESTED READINGS

Bode, Derk, ed. *The Cambridge History of China*. Vol. 1. Cambridge, Eng.: Cambridge University Press, 1986. A synthesis of scholarship on early imperial Chinese history.

DeBary, William, ed. *Sources of Chinese Tradition*. New York: Columbia University Press, 1960. A standard collection of sources and commentary for Chinese history.

Durrant, Stephen. *The Cloudy Mirror*. Albany: State University of New York Press, 1995. A recent study of the philosophy of Sima Qian, the Grand Historian of the Han Empire.

Hsu Cho-yun. *Han Agriculture*. Seattle: University of Washington Press, 1980. A study of Chinese agriculture.

Riches from a Han Emperor's Tomb.   Rows of life-sized ceramic soldiers from the tomb of
the first Han Chinese emperor underscore the military might and orientation of the empire.
China Pictorial Service.

Empire

All thys were of hys anpyre.

–Robert of Gloucester

In this first known written usage of "empire" in English, Robert used the term in 1297 to indicate an extensive territory made up of formerly independent states. The word also carried the connotation of supreme power, reflecting its genesis in *imperare*, the Latin verb meaning "to command."

Our modern usage of "empire" is similar to Robert's: a state that controls a large area, incorporating into itself previously independent societies that view themselves as culturally different from the controlling society. Stated differently, an empire is a politically unified state in which one people dominates its neighbors. This domination usually is by military force, but a number of other means of control can come into play, including religion, diplomacy, and trade. **Imperial** simply refers to an empire. The core idea of empire—the domination and political control of its neighbors by a single state—has occurred to would-be emperors in many places and times around the world.

Why do empires develop in some places and not in others? What are the consequences for states that become imperial? Why do empires eventually crumble? This chapter presents a model that tries to answer these questions. In thinking about this model, remember that models are not necessarily "true" in every detail but that they are interpretations created by scholars. Models serve as simplified versions of reality, helping us see a general pattern. The details that don't fit the model can help us refine it for future use, pointing out shortcomings and additional factors of importance.

THE CONRAD-DEMAREST MODEL OF EMPIRE

In an attempt to understand better the development and fall of empires, Geoffrey Conrad and Arthur Demarest recently have produced a model. Both Conrad and Demarest are specialists in Latin American civilizations, and their examples and inspiration came primarily from the last of the major pre-Columbian American civilizations, the Aztec of Mexico and the Inca of Peru. Nonetheless, their model is designed to apply to empires in all places and all times.

The Rise of Empires

Many earlier models of the imperial process proposed a single cause for the development of empires; greedy leaders, stressful environmental circumstances, and population pressure have been common suggestions. The Conrad-Demarest model takes a different approach. Rather than claiming that all empires developed in response to the same singular condition, Conrad and Demarest argue that empires arose out of many causes, working together and intimately linked with one another. They draw a distinction between the preconditions of empire (conditions that are necessary to support an empire but not sufficient to bring empire about) and critical causes (factors that, in the presence of the preconditions, will spark the development of empire). The preconditions are factors that might permit or encourage the development of empire as an effective solution to societal problems, but not every society that is characterized by these preconditions will develop an empire. The critical causes, according to the model, are those that actually bring about empire and are distinctive to the few societies that become imperial.

As Conrad and Demarest see it, the primary preconditions of empire are six: high agricultural potential, an environmental mosaic, state-level

government, several states with none clearly dominant, mutual antagonism among those states, and adequate military resources.

Environmental factors, according to the Conrad-Demarest model, are preconditions. Good agricultural potential, for example, is critical, because an expansionistic society without good land probably will be unable to support the initial conquests necessary to begin building an empire. In addition, a region with a mosaic of different environmental zones will be more conducive to the birth of empire than one with more or less even resource distribution. Each zone in an environmental mosaic has distinctive resources and potentials, and they are wedged in among one another. A society whose control extends over only one of these zones must trade with its neighbors or in some similar manner obtain the materials that come from other zones. The empire, on the other hand, gains great advantage by controlling many of those zones, reducing dependence on trade, increasing self-sufficiency, and increasing the ability to weather a bad year when some (but not all) of the zones have limited production of food or other necessities. In pre-Columbian Mexico, for example, major empires developed in the central highlands, where there is a marked environmental mosaic; in the eastern lowlands, where the environment is more uniform, successful empires never developed.

Conrad and Demarest also consider aspects of demography in relation to the development of empire. They reject the simple argument that empires develop when population becomes too great in an area and its inhabitants are forced to expand. (This argument, incidentally, often has been used as a justification for expansion by would-be conquerors, as with Adolf Hitler's doctrine of *lebensraum* ["living space"] during World War II.) Instead, Conrad and Demarest argue that population levels typically are manageable before the establishment of empires. Indeed, empires often institute programs designed specifically to promote population increase, often to produce soldiers to fuel the military engine that runs the state. The Aztecs, for example, actively encouraged women to have large families, and women who died in childbirth were promised deification as *mociuaquetzque*[1] goddesses and an afterlife in the

---

[1] *mociuaquetzque:* moh see yoo KEHTZ kay

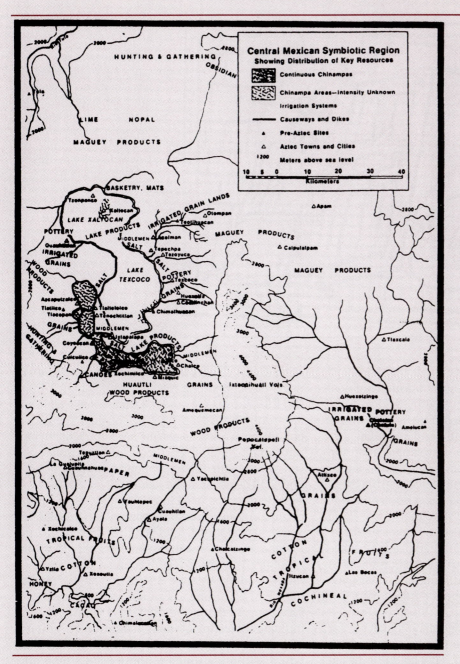

FIGURE 1.2.1 *Central Mexican Environmental Mosaic.* *Central Mexico, the heartland of the Aztec Empire, was composed of various environmental zones, each with different resources and potentials. By controlling several such zones, the Aztec rulers enhanced the developing empire's wealth and access to vital resources.* From Geoffrey W. Conrad and Arthur A. Demarest, *Religion and Empire: The Dynamics of Aztec and Inca Expansionism* (New York: Cambridge University Press), 1984. Reproduced with permission.

supreme heaven normally reserved for warriors who died in battle. Indeed, mothers were perceived as special warriors in the struggles for empire. Ironically, gross overpopulation appears to be a result of empire, not a cause.

The Conrad-Demarest model also considers economic motivation as a precondition to the development of empire. Once a state is successful at conquest, booty or tribute will follow, and those can be very major contributions to that state's economy. The leaders, of course, receive the bulk of this windfall, but wise rulers will redistribute some of this wealth to others immediately below them in the hierarchy, who in turn will distribute some of it to those below them, and so forth. This redistribution can be in the form of rewards for meritorious service, outright gifts, public works, or tax rebates. The redistribution of wealth helps

FIGURE I.2.2 *Death of an Aztec Woman. This Aztec drawing shows a woman who has died in childbirth and become a* mociuaquetzque *goddess. Her body is locked up and protected for four days by her family to prevent the removal of body parts for use as charms to give warriors courage in battle. A link between childbirth and warfare is also seen in the belief that spirits of women who died in childbirth shared the heaven otherwise reserved for warriors killed in battle.* Detail from the *Codex Florentino.* Courtesy of Biblioteca Medicea Laurenziana, Florence.

involve everyone, regardless of rank, in the fruits of conquest and empire, assuring continued political support. And, because the wealth trickles down through the established hierarchy, it helps reinforce the system of social and political ranking.

Conrad and Demarest also argue that the absence of a dominating competing state is a precondition to the rise of empire. Such a strong state would be in a position to quash the aspirations (and the soldiers) of a small state that was seeking empire, and it would be in its best interest to do so. The power vacuum that Conrad and Demarest see as critical to the nurturing of a fledgling imperial power ensures that a state with imperial intentions can develop without interference from a superior military power.

Finally, out of this antagonistic jockeying for power a successful imperial power must develop considerable military might. This could be based on large armies, superior equipment (including new weapons, such as iron spears or jet fighters), sophisticated strategy, or improved organization. A combination of these factors would be most effective.

The model has accumulated a substantial number of preconditions, many of which seem important. Why are they only preconditions? Because one can find plenty of examples of soci-

eties that met all of these preconditions and yet never developed empires, including Shang China, Old Kingdom Egypt, and the Greek poleis. This has led Conrad and Demarest to consider these preconditions as necessary but not sufficient to support empire building. They wanted to isolate the spark that lights the fires of empire and conquest, and they believe it to be ideology.

Ideology, as used in this model, refers to that complex of ideas and philosophy that directs one's goals, expectations, and actions. It can include religion, but it also can be secularly based, as with a political theory like communism. The ideology that will make a state successful at the empire business, according to Conrad and Demarest, will focus on glorifying the military and fostering the individual's feeling of identification with the state.

The ideology of some preimperial states, no doubt, is more attuned to these factors than others, but the Conrad-Demarest model suggests that a nascent imperial power can rework its ideology to emphasize these features. The Aztecs, for instance, elevated one god in their pantheon to the status of the most important: Huitzilopochtli,[2] the god of war. The cult of Huitzilopochtli glorified warriors, encouraging young nobles to participate

[2] **Huitzilopochtli:** hweet zee loh POHCH tlee

FIGURE I.2.3 *Human Sacrifice to Huitzilopochtli. This reproduction of an Aztec drawing shows a priest, at the top of the temple stairs, grasping and tearing out the heart of a person whose chest has been slashed open. At the base of the stairs, relatives collect the body of an earlier sacrifice whose remains have been hurled down the stairs. These sacrifices were to Huitzilopochtli, the war god, to ensure continued imperial success in battle. Being sacrificed was a great honor, often actively sought by Aztecs.* British Museum/Fotomas Index.

in the winning of empire. The Aztecs also expanded the existing institution of human sacrifice, bringing it to a scale previously unknown. The world would cease to exist if the sacrifices were not made in sufficient numbers, and the major way to procure sacrificial victims was through warfare; therefore, warfare, the fulcrum of Aztec empire building, was necessary as an ongoing institution. The Aztec people were inundated with propaganda, a technique in use by many societies, both ancient and modern, urging them to do their share in the noble cause of the furtherance of the empire. In short, by manipulating ideologies, the leaders of the successful Aztec imperial state produced a population that felt a duty and a desire to support the drive for empire.

According to the Conrad-Demarest model, therefore, many small states may have the preconditions of empire. They may have good agricultural land that is part of a larger environmental mosaic; they may covet the wealth of their neighbors; there may be a power vacuum that has created a panoply of antagonistic, belligerent states; and they may have considerable military power. But all this will not be enough if a state's ideology does not endorse and justify warfare and expansion. Many states might profit from an empire, but few are able effectively to establish it.

The Conrad-Demarest model is attractive in its ability to integrate several factors into an explanation of the rise of empires. Unlike explanations based on simple assertions—for instance, that a state's leaders were greedy or that the military establishment was strong—the Conrad-Demarest model, although it does not quarrel with those assertions, goes further. It tries to explain why some states that had greedy rulers and strong armies became the seats of great empires, while others were absorbed into someone else's empire.

There are, however, limitations to the Conrad-Demarest model. Although it recognizes the importance of environmental differences in resource endowment, other models place the role of trade more centrally. Further, probably because their model was inspired by American examples, Conrad and Demarest do not consider certain factors that were important in Eurasia and Africa but not in the Americas. Particularly, they do not consider the development of superior iron weaponry and subsequent domination of neighbors by one people, such as the example of the Hittites and Assyrians. Nor do they address **pastoralism** (specialized livestock herding) and its implications for some Eurasian and African empires, such as the Mongol and Songhai.

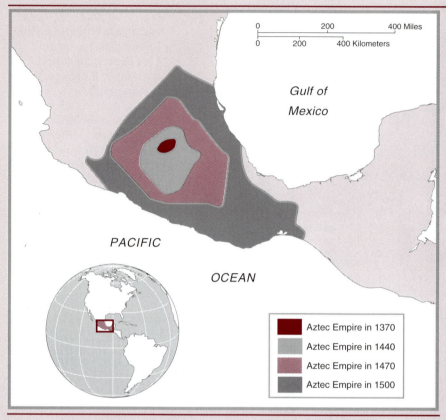

MAP I.2.1 *Growth of the Aztec Empire.* The Aztec Empire expanded rapidly through conquest, threat, and diplomacy. From 1440 onward, the size of the empire approximately doubled every generation. Such rapid growth is predicted by the Conrad-Demarest model of empire formation, but it is unsustainable for long periods.

Map labels:
- Gulf of Mexico
- PACIFIC OCEAN

Scale: 0 200 400 Miles / 0 200 400 Kilometers

Legend:
- Aztec Empire in 1370
- Aztec Empire in 1440
- Aztec Empire in 1470
- Aztec Empire in 1500

The Fall of Empires

If the factors discussed earlier produce empires, what do Conrad and Demarest believe causes the downfall of empires? Exactly the same factors. As they see it, the ideological and other conditions that are necessary for the establishment of an effective empire will eventually consume that empire.

An ideology that supports warfare and conquest will drive an imperial power farther and farther from its homeland and central power base. The need for captives to sacrifice, for heathens to convert, or for peoples to dominate persists long after the empire has expanded to a point where further conquest is economically counterproductive. As imperial armies travel farther from home, they face a host of difficulties: unfamiliar terrain (where conventional tactics might be ineffective), long and fragile supply lines, difficulties of reinforcement, and communication problems. Distant states that are incorporated into the empire become especially difficult to govern, because distance from the imperial heartland increases the costs and problems of controlling local rulers. As the cost of conquest goes up, the profits often go down: The richest states near home already have been conquered, and states farther removed may be less wealthy. In addition, the difficulties of transporting booty back to the capital become overwhelming. Alexander's Greek empire presents a classic example of expansion beyond the point of practicality. In such a case the pragmatic reasons for conquest are gone, but the ideology that demands it remains.

In the meantime, other aspects of imperial expansion also are souring. State-supported efforts to increase population, if successful, now may be creating a real problem. Just at a time when more effort is needed to increase production of food and other necessities in order to support the domestic front, warfare becomes more expensive, draining resources. If this situation continues, domestic shortages might erode faith in the ideology, which in turn might lead to class or regional conflicts, perhaps even to revolt.

The only hope for the survival of the empire, according to the Conrad-Demarest model, lies in an ideological change. The ideology that underlies empire building, once the erosion of faith begins, must be modified so that continued expansion is unnecessary. A less militaristic, less aggressive ideology might allow the empire to redirect its energies toward domestic problems. The establishment of such a new ideology, however, would be no easy matter, especially given that subject states would notice the change and might interpret it as weakness, perhaps staging uprisings at inopportune moments. According to this analysis, empires are inherently unstable, a conclusion supported by their generally short duration.

The Conrad-Demarest Model in Brief

Models are simplifications, and they can be summarized as a few principles. The Conrad-Demarest model can be reduced to the following principles:

1. Necessary preconditions for the rise of empire are:
   a. state-level government;
   b. high agricultural potential of the environment;
   c. an environmental mosaic;
   d. several small states with no clearly dominant state (a "power vacuum");
   e. mutual antagonism among those states; and
   f. adequate military resources.

2. The primary reason a state succeeds in empire building is an ideology supporting personal identification with the state, empire, conquest, and militarism.

3. The major results of empire are:
   a. economic rewards, reaped especially in the early years and redistributed to the elite and often to all levels of the citizenry; and
   b. population increase, often supported by the government and its ideology.

4. Empires fall because:
   a. the ideology of expansion and conquest fuels attempts at conquest beyond practical limits;
   b. failure to continue conquest indefinitely and to continue to bring its economic fruits home erodes faith in the ideology that supports the empire; and
   c. rebellions topple the empire.

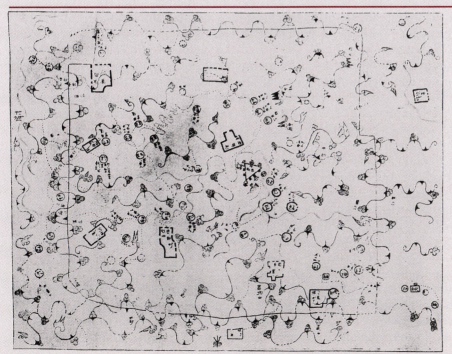

FIGURE I.2.4 *Han Chinese Map.* *This second century B.C. map, one of the earliest surviving from China, shows mountains (circles), rivers (wiggly lines), and military defenses (angular boxes). Chinese maps of this period may have been devoted exclusively to military functions, since contemporary documents mention them only in that context.* Wen-wu, Beijing.

APPLYING THE CONRAD-DEMAREST MODEL

As with most models, the Conrad-Demarest model sounds appealing when presented in the abstract or when applied to a case that was used as inspiration for the model. The examples presented here are mostly from the Aztecs, and they support the model. The real test, of course, is whether the model can help us understand a new case.

The Qin and Han empires, as discussed in Chapter 11, unified central China for the first time. Out of the power vacuum produced by centuries of turmoil and disunity during the Warring States Period, the Qin state and its successor, the Han state, emerged as powers that could forge an empire by conquering previously independent states. The two empires formed a continuum sometimes called the Qin-Han Empire, which will be examined here in light of the Conrad-Demarest model.

The core states of the Qin-Han Empire possessed all the necessary preconditions suggested by the Conrad-Demarest model. The preimperial Qin state was in a region of great agricultural potential, yet the environmental mosaic of China left it lacking resources found in neighboring regions. The Warring States Period established a series of mutually antagonistic states, several of which had considerable military power yet none of which was clearly dominant. With these preconditions met, the spark necessary to ignite imperial expansion, according to Conrad and Demarest's model, was ideology.

During the short-lived Qin Empire and the early years of the Han Empire, emperors predominantly followed Legalist philosophy, advocating militarism, conquest, and unification. The emperor whose warriors carved out much of the early Han Empire by conquest was not nicknamed "the Martial Emperor" because of pacifist inclinations. This ideology glorifying the military fits well with the predictions of the model.

The Qin-Han Empire reacted to imperial success much as predicted by the Conrad-Demarest model. This empire took advantage of its control of various zones in the environmental mosaic through the **ever-normal granary system**, a system whereby the government collected grain from all over the empire into warehouses and redistributed it to the people as it was required. This system pooled the produce of various regions, creating a more or less constant total supply, regardless of the agricultural success of any zone in the mosaic.

The emperor received massive material benefit in tribute, spoils of war, and commerce, once the sources for goods were controlled. The emperor then distributed some portion of that wealth. Much of that redistribution was directed through the official hierarchy, from the emperor through officials and eventually to the people. Public works, for example, normally were announced to the people by local officials, who took care to be sure it was clear that the emperor ultimately was the source of this munificence. There also were general gifts to the people on special occasions, such as the reaching of adulthood for a royal heir; these gifts usually consisted of wine, meat, or (more rarely) money. All these gifts, as well as the more ostentatious rewards reserved for top advisors and officials, helped cement the Han people together with the emperor in whatever endeavors he undertook.

Although Legalist philosophy was dominant at the Qin-Han court during the period of initial expansion of the empire, Confucianism gradually arose as a competitor. There was a period when the two vied for the emperor's support, but Confucianism eventually became the dominant philosophy of the Han Empire.

Confucian philosophy, in Han hands, evolved in a manner that elevated the emperor. Han scholars, such as Dong Zhongshu, extended Confucian thought to incorporate the concept of emperor (a notion invented in China centuries after Confucius's death). Dong developed the formula that was to characterize the Han version of Confucian political philosophy: "to subject the people to the emperor, and the emperor to heaven." This fit nicely with the Han conception of the emperor as the "son of Heaven," an official title: As a divine-right ruler, his will was inspired, perhaps informed, by the gods. The only sensible course for a devout mortal was total obedience to the emperor.

The Legalist philosophy of the Qin Empire is exactly the militaristic type of ideology that the Conrad-Demarest model predicts for the rise of empire. Elements of that philosophy were dominant during the period of greatest expansion of the early Han Empire. After that, the Confucian philosophy, although not militaristic, provided a different kind of ideological underpinning for the empire. Confucians stressed ritual and persuasion over might to maintain imperial rule; they often spoke out against expansionist military campaigns. A glorification of militarism was unnecessary in the later Han Empire, because the glorification of the emperor superseded it: If the emperor decreed military action, it was, by definition, the will of the gods and therefore appropriate.

In short, the Qin-Han Empire fits Conrad and Demarest's suggestion that a long-lived empire will modify its ideology to reduce dependence on militarism. The Qin Empire failed to make an ideological transition and fell within fourteen years. The Han Empire successfully made the transition to an appropriate ideology and lasted four centuries.

Has the Conrad-Demarest model improved our understanding of the Qin-Han Empire? Certainly it has drawn attention to factors that probably were important in the formation and functioning of the empire. It has helped us see how diverse practices, such as the ever-normal granary system, fit into the imperial system. Finally, it has drawn attention to a potentially significant factor for future research: the role of imperial government in Qin-Han population increase. The frustratingly fragmentary evidence could be seen as supporting a state-sponsored population increase, but more research will be necessary in order for us to see whether that conclusion is justified.

SUGGESTED READINGS

Carneiro, Robert L. "Political Expansion as an Expression of the Principle of Competitive Exclusion." In Robert Cohen and Elman R. Service, eds. *Origins of the State: The Anthropology of Political Evolution.* Philadelphia: Institute for the Study of Human Issues, 1978, pp. 205–23. Presents an alternative model for the development of empires, based on ecological and economic factors.

Conrad, Geoffrey W., and Arthur A. Demarest. *Religion and Empire: The Dynamics of Aztec and Inca Expansionism.* New York: Cambridge University Press, 1984. The book-length origin of the model discussed here.

REGIONAL STATES HAVE BEEN PERHAPS the most common political form in history. It is easier to rule a small territory than a large one, especially if the larger entity includes more than one ethnic group. Because of this, empires have traditionally been inherently unstable, and their declines can lead to regionalism. Often, regional and local states preceded large kingdoms and empires, and occasionally they succeeded empires that collapsed.

To explore these aspects of regionalism, we have devoted Part Three to times when regional states flourished. We will examine the evidence in Asia, Africa, and Europe as we formulate answers to various questions. What is the relationship between trade and the development of regionalism? How do people reorganize their political structures when imperial bureaucracies weaken?

Chapter 12 examines the rise of Islam from Muhammad's visions in a desert town to a religion commanding the allegiance of people on three continents. The Islamic Empire expanded so far and so rapidly that its initial political unity broke down, although sociocultural unity persisted and grew. Chapter 13 explores

	ISLAM		EUROPE
200 B.C.			
A.D. 1			
A.D. 200			
A.D. 400			
A.D. 600			Early Middle Ages
A.D. 800	Umayyad Caliphate	Abbasid Caliphate	
A.D. 1000	Islamic regionalism		
A.D. 1200			Central Middle Ages
A.D. 1400			Late Middle Ages
A.D. 1600			

PART THREE

THE RISE OF REGIONAL STATES

European history from the collapse of the Western Roman Empire to around 1450. Despite serious challenges from outside and within, regional states created political stability, economic prosperity, and artistic development. Chapter 14 discusses regional states of South, Southeast, and East Asia and shows how their governments were increasingly linked by maritime trade. Chapter 15 probes the histories of sub-Saharan African states and finds both diversity and similarity of political forms there. Once again, trade seems to have been an impetus to the rise and fall of larger states. Issue 3 develops the concept of feudalism, a sociopolitical structure common during times of regional states. Feudalism was a response to collapsing empires or governments in many parts of Eurasia.

ASIA				AFRICA			
Indian regionalism							200 B.C.
							A.D. 1
				Regionalism in West and Central Africa			A.D. 200
	Chinese regionalism	Japanese regionalism					A.D. 400
	Regionalism in Southeast Asia				Regionalism in East Africa		A.D. 600
Indian regionalism							A.D. 800
						Regionalism in Southwest Africa	A.D. 1000
							A.D. 1200
							A.D. 1400
							A.D. 1600

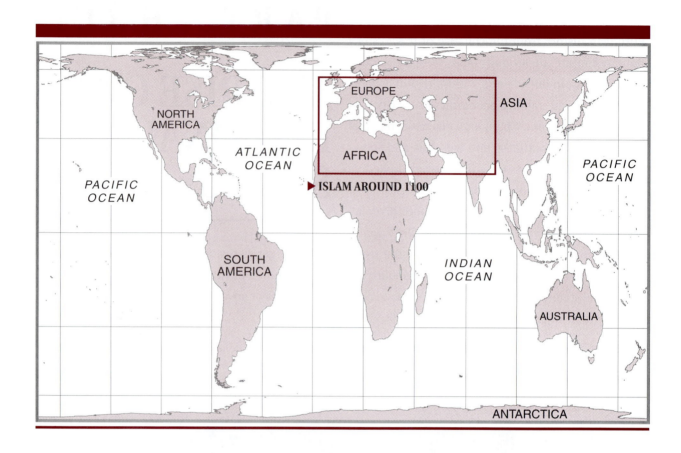

ISLAM AROUND 1100

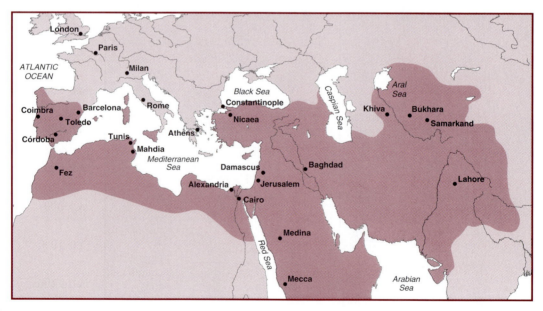

▶ ISLAM AROUND 1100

Islamic Expansion and Regionalism

622–1258

Rumi was dead. People from all over central Turkey came to the funeral of this scholar and mystic, who for decades had danced and sung in praise of Allah. His joyous enthusiasm infected many in and around the mountain town where he lived. Now they came to mourn and celebrate Rumi's passing and his reunion with Allah. Muslims, Jews, and Christians attended, because Rumi spoke to everyone.

This anecdote about a thirteenth-century Islamic thinker and poet shows the respect and affection with which he and many like him were held. In the seventh century, Islam developed as a religion, expanding through parts of Asia, Africa, and Europe, and Islam's success also sowed the seeds of regionalism. Although some of Islam's spread came through military conquest, much resulted from peaceful conversion by Islamic mystics (Sufis) and traders. "Muslim" is the name for a follower of Islam. For two centuries, the vast realm of Islam was politically tied together rather loosely. Centralized rule weakened, and regional patterns asserted themselves. Nonetheless, common religious adherence and general social practices, including a legal system, held Muslims together.

In this chapter, we will examine the rise, expansion, and regionalism of the peoples who were united by Islam. We will discuss the various factors that propelled these processes and explore the consequences of the Islamic Empire's early development. **Dar al-Islam**, or the Islamic world, connected Asia with Africa and Europe. People of diverse ethnic groups and occupational backgrounds embraced Islam and shared certain beliefs and practices, like daily prayers while facing toward Mecca, the home of the most sacred Muslim shrines. Muslim travelers visited places like Ghana in western Africa, Samarkand in Central Asia, and Canton in southern China, where they usually were welcomed warmly by their fellow believers. Foodstuffs and ideas also traveled to most areas of Eurasia and Africa, where they enriched people's lives.

THE EARLY DECADES OF ISLAM: MUHAMMAD AND THE FOUR CALIPHS, 622–661

At the center of Islam's beliefs are the revelations received from the god **Allah** by Muhammad ibn Abdullah (around 570–632). Muhammad grew up as an orphan, eventually marrying a wealthy widow with connections to merchant families of Mecca, an oasis-city at the western edge of the Arabian Desert. Around the age of forty years, Muhammad began having a series of religious experiences that changed not only his life but also those of millions around the globe. He became the prophet for a religion that developed into a political system.

Before addressing the rise and expansion of Islam, we should examine the environment into which it came.

Pre-Islamic Society

Mecca straddled key trade routes that ran between Africa and Asia; consequently, merchant families of Mecca gained extensive knowledge about the outside world. They remained independent of the imperial power struggles of the Byzantine Empire with the Sassanian[1] Empire and negotiated a working arrangement with tribal groups to permit Meccan caravans to travel peacefully through their territories.

Pastoral tribes lived in Arabia's harsh desert terrains, which were punctuated here and there by oases or by the occasional city, like Mecca. Tribal politics included consultative decision making at

councils where men and (more rarely) women were able to express themselves; in this way, people were made to feel a part of the system. Thus, tribal leaders could count on the loyalty of their members. Tribes traded with settled peoples or sometimes raided wealthy merchant caravans by employing swift cavalry attacks. Occasionally, women fought alongside men.

Although Muslims view Islam as the universal religion, they believe that Judaism and Christianity also had prophets. Adam, Moses, and Jesus, for example, were prophets of God, stating or restating the first tenets of Islam in the eyes of Muslims. Thus, Jews and Christians were "Peoples of the Book" even though from the Muslim perspective they had strayed from Muhammad's true teachings. In addition, some Christians and Jews who converted to Islam did so because they felt that Muhammad's teachings were natural outgrowths of Christianity or Judaism.

Muhammad's Role and Legacy

The visions and voices that provided the essential message of Islam began to come to Muhammad in a cave to which he retreated from time to time. A pious man, Muhammad often took solitary retreats into the nearby mountains to receive, Muslims believe, messages from Allah through Gabriel, the messenger angel. One central theme of these revelations was that Allah had chosen Muhammad as his prophet and desired him to preach the message of submission to Allah. The word "Islam" means submission.

Gradually, Muhammad gathered followers and enemies. His disciples adopted his message of social justice and charity, especially to orphans and widows. As the message spread, merchant oligarchs who ruled Mecca vehemently opposed the new religion, which challenged their political and financial well-being. They threatened Muhammad and his tiny band. At the same time, people in Medina, around 250 miles to the north, invited Muhammad, who had gained a reputation for honesty, to mediate internal disputes there. Muhammad and his followers fled Mecca and arrived in Medina, where they spread Allah's message. This move, known as the *hijra*[2] (migration), took place in 622 and is the beginning date of the

[1] **Sassanian:** sah SAHN ee ehn

[2] *hijra:* HEEJ rah

Muslim calendar, which is still followed in many parts of the world. By mediating disputes in Medina, rendering judgments, and receiving delegations, Muhammad served as both administrator and prophet of Islam.

Muhammad ruled Medina, using it as a base from which to unite the tribes and peoples of Arabia. The prophet's charismatic manner attracted a wide following, and his evolving political statecraft brought him great personal respect. Several caravans from Mecca were attacked by the Muslims, and the Meccan merchants retaliated; Muhammad won many of the battles against the armed forces from Mecca. Eventually, the leaders of Mecca could not stem the growth of Islam and the consequent undermining of their own power. When Muhammad returned to Mecca, the city capitulated. Mecca became the religion's spiritual center, while Medina became a political and administrative capital of the new Islamic state. By 632, Muhammad had united the Arabs, exercising both political and religious influence over them.

Central to Islam are its five pillars or basic tenets:

— belief in the oneness of Allah and Muhammad as Allah's prophet,

— prayer five times each day,

— the giving of charitable contributions,

— fasting from sunrise to sunset during the holy month of Ramadan, and

— pilgrimage to Mecca at least once.

Muslims were thought to go to paradise if they followed these tenets or to suffer punishments if they failed to uphold them.

Muhammad also forged an alliance between urban merchants and tribal leaders. He used networks already established by Meccan merchant families, expanding them to include important tribes. Both tribal leaders and merchants played a role in the planning of Islam's initial expansion and contributed to evolving social egalitarianism.

Islam's First Crisis and Expansion

The religion of Islam and its government faced a serious crisis after Muhammad died in 632, but Islam continued to expand dynamically. Some Muslims who had submitted because of Muhammad's charismatic personality abandoned their new faith. Other figures, jealous of Muhammad's success, claimed to be prophets, hoping to wrest some followers from Islam.

Responding to these challenges, the close, early followers of Muhammad selected one of their own, Abu Bakr,[3] as **caliph**, the religious and political successor of Muhammad. Abu Bakr declared that none could leave the religious community. Military force gave strength to the caliph's words; the divisions soon closed, and the threatening prophetic challenges faded.

At the same time, the caliph ordered that the spiritual messages of Allah to Muhammad be gathered into the **Qur'an**,[4] the Holy Book of Islam. The Qur'an, written in Arabic, reached its final form around the middle of the seventh century and has remained unchanged over the succeeding centuries, although various commentaries on it have appeared.

The next three caliphs followed the direction of the first caliph and presided over a rapid expansion of the Islamic state, spreading the religion as Muslims went throughout Southwest Asia and into North Africa. The remarkable early growth of Islam resulted from the able direction of experienced urban leaders, combined with the formidable mobility of the nomads. For example, the use of cavalry forces meant that the Muslims rode far into the territory of the enemy before effective resistance could be mounted. Often these Arabs were aided by the large number of other Arabs living in Palestine, Iraq, and Syria; they collaborated in taking control of various governments. Once the Sassanian Empire fell to the Muslims, vast resources commanded by that agrarian state came under their control. Thus, a combination of military factors, organizational skills, and resources proved formidable.

Another driving force behind the Arabs' success was the desire to take wealth from the conquered peoples and redistribute it to members of the Islamic community. This process was designed to create the de facto economic equality promised by the Qur'an and Muhammad, yet some of the distributions were deemed unfair and triggered opposition movements. The **Shi'a**,[5] one of the most prominent of the dissident groups, fought for

---

[3] **Abu Bakr:** ah BOO BAH kur
[4] **Qur'an:** KOOR ahn
[5] **Shi'a:** SHEE ah

FIGURE 12.1   *Early Qur'an with Kufic Script.*   *Calligraphy is considered the earliest and among the most important of the Muslim visual arts. An accomplished calligrapher exemplified discipline of mind and hand, as well as the idea of the cultured individual. The Kufic style of calligraphy is most associated with the Qur'an, since Kufic was the first form of Arabic used to write the words of Allah. The Kufic text here dates from the mid–seventh century.*   Courtesy of Biblioteca Ambrosiana, Milan.

power in the name of Ali (the fourth caliph) and his descendants. Ali had been assassinated in a succession crisis, and most Shi'ites claimed that his killing had interrupted the clear succession from Muhammad.

A major factor in the Islamic state's early success was the unity it forged. A tribe's primary loyalty was directed to the caliph, the head of the religion and of the state. A general loyalty superseded tribal allegiances and brought widespread unity. At the same time, the early caliphs' charge to reconquer those Arabs who had abandoned the faith brought coalitions of Islamic forces drawn from various tribes.

A major alliance of Syrian tribes soon joined forces with the Muslims and played a vital part in the Islamic state's expansion. Syrians long had preyed on the caravans plying the trade routes of their region, and they had religious and economic motives for converting to Islam. With Syrian assistance, much of the early Islamic expansion followed the trade routes of the entire region. These confederations brought conflict with the Sassanian and Byzantine empires. Soon, the Sassanian Empire fell to the Muslims, and the Byzantine Empire was severely weakened.

As with all wars, loss of life resulted. Zealous Muslims took to heart the Qur'anic injunctions of

jihad,[6] or struggle to make the world Islamic. Some interpreted *jihad* to mean military struggle, but many others took *jihad* to mean persuasion. Both were important in the spread of Islam. Early Muslim warriors sought booty. They sometimes slaughtered urban peoples, who were despised by nomadic warriors. Women and children might be carried off as slaves.

Thus, the first four caliphs also presided over a military expansion of Muslims far beyond the borders of Arabia, creating an Islamic empire. This growth transformed Islam into a transregional religion, one that united diverse peoples across a wide section of Southwest Asia and North Africa.

THE UMAYYAD AND ABBASID CALIPHATES, 661–1258

During the nearly six centuries of the Umayyad[7] and Abbasid[8] caliphates, expansion continued along with the development of artistic pursuits. Islam spread across Africa and into Europe and deep into India and reached the borders of China.

[6] *jihad:* jee HAHD
[7] **Umayyad:** OOM ee yahd
[8] **Abbasid:** ahb BAH sihd

The blending of Arab, Persian, and Indian ideas, literary forms, and art styles enriched courtier and commoner throughout the Dar al-Islam.

The Umayyad Caliphate, 661–750

Damascus became the Islamic Empire's capital. The ruling Umayyad clan had been an important Meccan merchant group specializing in trade with Damascus. Although Mecca and Medina remained religiously important to Muslims, Damascus, a major urban center and the nexus of vital trade routes from Asia and Europe, dominated Dar al-Islam's political and economic affairs. From Damascus, Umayyad caliphs directed operations in Africa, Europe, and Asia.

The rise of Damascus as the political center of the Islamic Empire brought a challenge from factions in Medina and Mecca, who resented the shift away from Arabia and their own loss of influence in shaping policy. Fighting erupted and finally ended with victory for the Umayyads and their supporters. Dynastic succession became a regular feature of the Damascus and successor empires. Damascus's strategic location facilitated its role as nerve center of the Umayyad Empire.

Early eighth-century Umayyad caliphs or emperors attempted a series of reforms in order to secure long-lasting political and fiscal stability, but their efforts were undermined by continuing sectarian social unrest. Centralizing policies kept the caliphate's control of officials at all government levels, and the caliphs gave income from state lands to military leaders who promised to use the funds to support and equip themselves and an agreed-upon number of soldiers. The incessant need for trained military personnel forced succeeding Muslim rulers to extend this land policy

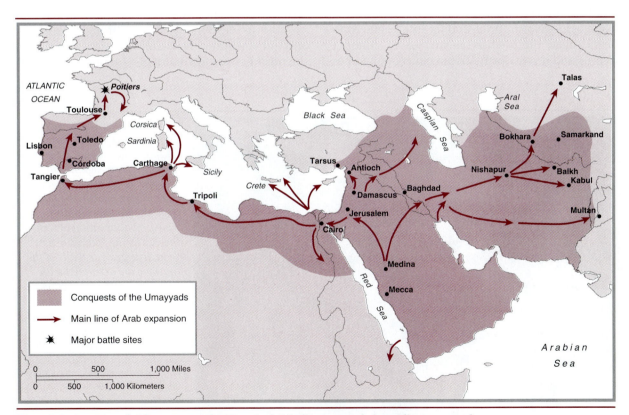

MAP 12.1 *Dar al-Islam around 750.* *Arab Muslims expanded rapidly across trade routes in Asia, Africa, and Europe, reaching the Atlantic and Indian Oceans in less than a century after Muhammad's death. Cities usually fell to conquest while the rural folk were converted, generally by peaceful means. Much of the southern Mediterranean Sea became a place of commerce for Muslim merchants. These early Islamic centers often became bases for later expansion across Africa, Europe, and Asia.*

over widespread areas. Gradually, state control lagged, and revenue from these state lands came under the complete charge of military officers. This reduced the amount of tax revenues and made the warriors semiautonomous, leading to decentralized rule in later eras.

Although Umayyad caliphs borrowed from Byzantine traditions and practices, they also put an Islamic stamp on their rule. Byzantine political institutions, like absolute monarchy, were used by the Umayyad caliphs, who adopted and adapted court rituals and bureaucratic institutions as necessary. Another Byzantine pattern adopted by the Umayyad caliphs was the patronage of artists. During the time of Abd al-Malik (reign dates 685–705), Arabic was introduced as the administrative language. The caliph also introduced a new style of coinage that replaced human figures with words proclaiming in Arabic the oneness of Allah and Muhammad as the prophet. Islam forbade pictorial representations of Muhammad.

The Umayyad rulers directed the expansion of Islam across North Africa and far into Spain. Arab fleets sailed the Mediterranean Sea to conquer Cyprus and many North African cities. Arab forces that conquered the Nile River Valley pushed westward and soon came into contact with Berbers, nomadic peoples of North Africa, many of whom converted to Islam. In part because of the strong nomadic component in the Arab forces, an Arab-Berber alliance emerged. By 710, Muslims crossed the Strait of Gibraltar into Spain. Within five years, much of Spain had fallen to the combined forces, who were increasingly referred to as **Moors**, North Africans of mixed Berber and Arab parentage. Parts of Spain remained under Muslim control until the fifteenth century, and Spanish Muslims traded extensively with Christian Europeans.

Arab military forces also moved eastward into India and northeastward into Central Asia. By 711, an Arab fleet had taken several cities in the Indus River Valley, and an army marched overland to extend the conquests up the valley. Although Muslim control of the Indus Valley was weak, it provided trade links with the core region of the Islamic Empire and gave important benefits to Muslims in terms of trade goods and ideas.

Just as eastern expansion brought Persians and Indians under the Islamic Empire's control, so the northeastern push brought Turkic peoples into

FIGURE 12.2 *Mosaics of the Great Mosque of Damascus.* *These mosaics from the early eighth century are part of an artistic tradition dating back to the Roman period, showing the absorption and adaptation of techniques by the Islamic artists and artisans. The walls of the mosque are decorated with architectural motifs, while the arcade (the supporting column arches) are decorated with trees. The trees are realistically portrayed, reflecting a careful study of nature.* Photo by J. E. Dayton/Reproduced courtesy of Thames and Hudson, Ltd.

FIGURE 12.3 *Great Mosque at Kairouan, Tunisia.* *This seventh-century mosque was a site of pilgrimage and the first major Islamic monument built in North Africa. Shown are the prayer hall, domes, and facade, lined with columns taken from other, pre-Islamic structures. The use of columned interiors may have been both structurally necessary and a borrowing from other architectural traditions, but Muslim architects used them in religiously and artistically unique combinations. This mosque was rebuilt in the ninth and tenth centuries.* George Rogers/Magnum Photos.

the Muslim realm. Persian and Turkish joined Arabic to become major languages in Dar al-Islam.

Muslim monarchs frequently ruled the Islamic realms with mild policies. They basically left the existing social systems intact when indigenous customs did not interfere with Islamic practices. Muslims retained the tax rates of former monarchs or sometimes reduced them. In some cases, therefore, peasants found their tax obligations less under Muslim rulers. One assessment levied by most Islamic monarchs was a head tax on nonbelievers, and its rate was generally assessed according to the nonbeliever's wealth. The tax provided an economic incentive for non-Muslims to convert, while favorable treatment for Muslim merchants brought additional conversions among the

traders. Because merchants and artisans were respected and taxed moderately, trade generally improved, benefiting rulers and subjects alike. Islamic stress on works of charity resulted in government and private monies for helping organizations like foundling homes.

Ineffective rule by later Umayyad caliphs and widespread tribal unrest undermined the caliphate. Corruption by the caliphs provoked unrest among the Shi'ites and others, while ambitious tribal groups plotted to overthrow the Umayyads. A coalition of opposition forces led by the Abbasids claimed the caliphate position and launched a serious revolt in Mesopotamia. Within a short time, the Abbasid rebels ousted the Umayyads from power. The Abbasid Caliphate

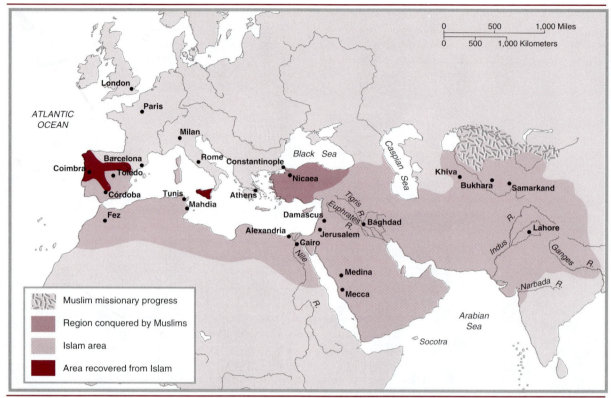

MAP 12.2 *Islam around 1100.* *Although military conquest continued to add new territory to Dar al-Islam, much of the religion's spread came from missionary activity. Sufi mystics were especially effective in spreading the teachings of Muhammad. The great expanse of Dar al-Islam, however, proved difficult to rule from a single center. Eventually regional centers emerged and vied for political dominance.*

rose in Mesopotamia, farther east and nearer the geographic center of Dar al-Islam. Eventually, the Abbasids located their capital in Baghdad, near the heart of their support base.

The Abbasid Caliphate, 749–1258

Early Abbasid caliphs enjoyed the varied pleasures of a lavish urban lifestyle. Baghdad, even more than Damascus, became a vibrant intellectual center where ideas from ancient Greece were treasured and developed and where scholars from Persia, India, and Egypt interacted with one another. Finally, Baghdad symbolized a widespread urbanization that saw the appearance of cities like Cairo, Basra,[9] and Toledo in diverse parts of Dar al-Islam. An unintended consequence of the shift of the Islamic Empire's capital farther east

[9]**Basra:** BAHZ rah

was the growing difficulty of maintaining control of the western regions in North Africa and Spain. Indeed, some Umayyads fled to Spain, established an independent caliphate there, and ruled into the eleventh century.

The growth of cities in Mesopotamia, of course, increased the demand for agricultural produce and spurred improvements of yields per land unit, largely through more intensive cultivation of the land. At the same time, a massive land reclamation project in southern Mesopotamia took most of the ninth century to complete. In order to have labor resources to clear the land and work on sugarcane plantations, landowners imported hundreds of thousands of sub-Saharan African slaves. Abuses of these workers provoked an uprising that lasted from 869 to 884.

Although the Abbasid caliphs ruled effectively until the tenth century, their far-flung empire eventually proved too difficult to govern, both at the core and at the periphery. Political challenges came from formerly conquered groups, like the Persians and Turks, who maintained and manipulated the existing political structure for their own purposes. The great expanse of Dar al-Islam challenged centralization, with the result that the decline of the Abbasid caliphs mirrored increasing local rule. Regionalism gradually replaced centralization in the Islamic world. Tax revenues declined as many private estates were taken off the tax rolls. Economic weakness accelerated political decay, and the last Abbasid caliph succumbed to a Mongol army in 1258 (see Chapter 19). Regionalism had fully replaced control from Baghdad or from any other major city.

THE BIRTH OF ISLAMIC CULTURE

The Islamic religion inspired many artists to create works of art, and Muslim rulers patronized artisans and architects to develop works of beauty and majesty. As the immense wealth of the realm poured into the Abbasid coffers and trade flourished, Baghdad prospered. **Mosques**, the Muslim places of worship, were built in monumental style with large buildings and great courtyards to encompass the faithful. The minaret tower also made its appearance in Baghdad and became a major element of the mosque complexes. Stucco decoration reached a high level and adorned official buildings. These stylistic patterns were soon replicated throughout the Islamic world.

Knowledge was sought by the Abbasid caliphs and their officials. Works in Sanskrit, Greek, Persian, and other languages were translated into Arabic and furthered rational inquiry. Mathematicians built on the fundamental work of Indians and Greeks to explore the field of algebra. The Indian numeration system and concept of zero passed to Muslims and from them to the Christian Europeans. Medicine was diligently studied by scholars who translated the Classical Greek studies.

Astronomy and astrology occupied the attention of some Islamic thinkers. Many astronomical texts from India and the Mediterranean were translated and carefully studied. Al-Khwarizmi[10] (died around 850) synthesized Greek, Iranian, and

[10] **Al-Khwarizmi:** ahl KWAR ihz mee

FIGURE 12.4 *Chess Piece from the Abbasid Caliphate.* *Chess originated in India as a game of strategy and warfare. This ivory piece with an official atop an elephant reflects Indian chess pieces of similar design. Instead of kings and queens typical of European chess figures, Asian chess pieces usually portrayed kings and chief ministers.* Bibliothèque nationale, Paris.

Indian astronomical knowledge with his own discoveries and helped establish the reputation of Islamic astronomy. Chinese rulers, for example, invited Muslim astronomers to their courts.

Arabic language and literature benefited from the patronage of the Abbasid caliphs. Qur'anic Arabic became the vehicle for new forms of poetry and prose, including essays, didactic writings, and historical writing. Grammar was a field of diligent study because the interpretation of Qur'anic passages depended on an accurate understanding of word order, usage, and meaning. In addition, with the spread of Islam among the subject peoples through religious conversion, Arabic became the language of rulers and ruled alike.

Written Persian evolved into a significant literary language during the Abbasid era. Often called "New Persian," the language developed from the

In 1244, Shams Tabrizi and Rumi forged a friendship that transformed Persian mystical poetry into direct, erotic idioms. Both men, the former a wanderer who took any job and the latter a scholar and teacher, sought union with the divine. In the famous story that follows, we can see how Shams was a disciple to a basket maker and worked as a mason, two occupations associated with Sufism. We can see how artisan networks supported Sufis. Rumi's disciples founded the Mevlana Order of Dervishes, a Sufi group devoted to dancing as a mystical practice. Whirling dervishes and Sufis played a significant role in the peaceful spread of Islam.

IN THEIR OWN WORDS

Shams and Rumi: Two Sufi Mystics

Shams wandered the world looking for a companion, a friend on his level of attainment. Sometimes, for three or four days he would be lost in mystical awareness. Then he would take work as a mason, or a mason's helper, to balance his visionary bewilderment with hard physical labor. When he was paid, he would always contrive to slip the wages into another worker's jacket before he left. He never stayed anywhere long. Whenever students began to assemble around him, as they inevitably did, he would excuse himself for a drink of water, wrap his black cloak around [himself], and be gone. . . .

Shams arrived in Konya sometime in the fall of 1244. He took lodging at an inn, pretending to be a successful merchant, a seller of sugar, though in his room there was only a broken water pot, a ragged mat, and a headrest of unbaked clay. He fasted continually, breaking it once every ten or twelve days with bread soaked in mutton broth.

Shams was a disciple of a certain basket maker in Tabriz, Ruknaddin Sanjabi, but he traveled all over the region to find and hear the deepest teachers. . . . One day as Shams sat at the gate of an inn, Rumi came riding by on a donkey, surrounded by a crowd of students. Shams rose and took hold of the bridle, . . . "Tell me! Who was greater, Muhammad or Bestami?" "Muhammad was incomparable among the prophets and saints." "Then how is it he [Muhammad] said, 'We have not known You [Allah] as You should be known,' while Bestami cried out, 'How great is my glory!'" Rumi fainted when he heard the depth the question came from and fell to the ground. When he revived, he answered, "For Muhammad the mystery was always unfolding, while Bestami took one gulp and was satisfied." The two tottered off together and were closeted for weeks and months at a time in that mystical conversation called *sohbet*.

Rumi's disciples feared the fascination of their teacher with Shams, and, eventually, they forced Shams to leave. Rumi, however, sent his son to bring the mystic back. Later, Shams disappeared a second time and for good, and Rumi wrote poems expressing his abject grief at his friend's departure. Rumi also wore mourning clothes, including a hat and black cloak that are now customary among modern followers of the dervish sect.

---

ninth to the eleventh centuries from Middle Persian, and came to include words from other languages, including Arabic. New Persian began as a means to disseminate popular poetry and evolved into an elite vehicle to express more subtle and complex ideas. Rudaki[11] (died around 940) built on existing Arab and Persian poetic traditions and is seen as the first New Persian poet. His poetic style is regarded as combining freedom and simplicity of expression with nobility of theme.

Hadith,[12] a collection of accounts of Muhammad and early Islamic personalities, became a treasured source of information. Preachers mined it for stirring tales with which to delight people, and scholars interested in legal matters used it as a basis to develop legal theories.

Although the Abbasid Empire fell into decline and eventual destruction at the hands of the Mongols in 1258, Islam continued to flourish. Sufi mystics traveled alone or in company to rural areas

[11] **Rudaki:** ruh DAKH ee

[12] *Hadith:* HAH deeth

and new lands, spreading the message of Islam. Sufis played a major role in Islamizing the countryside by performing attention-getting feats of mental and physical control. They often built mosques in the towns or communities where they resided, and these places of worship were also used for other activities. Many Sufi tombs became venerated places of pilgrimage for Muslims.

In parts of Africa, wandering scholars, judges, and saints carried Islam from place to place, establishing educational centers and mosques in places where they resided. People in the community often converted to Islam and enjoyed the varied benefits they believed this faith bestowed.

ISLAMIC SOCIETY

Muhammad and the Islamic religion significantly affected Islamic society. Muhammad established the norms and traditions of Islamic law, using them as a means to regulate society by delineating the standards of accepted behavior. Although social hierarchies existed within the Islamic Empire, all people were equal before Allah, and all were to be given status according to law. Through Muhammad, Allah also decreed that orphans and poor people be given good treatment and charity when necessary. Islam also provided for the favored treatment of women, especially in comparison with other religions and social traditions.

Islamic Law

Muhammad himself played a significant role in rendering verdicts in legal matters, and, because of his reputation for integrity, fairness came to be an important matter in law. Judges and lawyers attempted to tie their decisions to the injunctions given in the Qur'an. Four main schools of law emerged in the first Islamic centuries, and judges usually had to claim adherence to one school's avowed perspective on legal interpretations. In addition, a legal opinion was often formulated by connecting it with a previous ruling. General acceptance of the new decision by one or more schools depended on the persuasiveness of the legal reasoning and its being written in Arabic. There was no system of appeals for legal decisions, and only a mistake made by a judge was grounds for another judge to reverse a decision. Within the mainstream of legal thought, this tradition and process allowed for stability but permitted some adaptation to changing conditions. At the same time, other legal traditions grew up in the far reaches of the Islamic world.

Many early legal scholars came from merchant families, and they attempted to represent their business interests in the face of officials who asserted absolute state power to order and run society. Merchant judges and scholars created Islamic law as an expression of the responsibility of people for their own lives and for the ordering of society. Thus, the community as a whole gained an

FIGURE 12.5 *Islamic Law and the Family.* *Law in Dar al-Islam had a significant impact on political, economic, and social life. This manuscript illustration shows a judge settling a dispute between father and daughter. Often a father had a higher standing in law, but women, in fact, generally received fairer treatment under Islamic law than they did under most other legal systems in the world at the time of early Islam.*
Bibliothèque nationale, Paris.

FIGURE 12.6 *Mamluk Hunting Scene.* *From their origins as slaves, the Mamluks became the rulers of parts of Africa and Syria for centuries, beginning in the mid–thirteenth century. This basin, inlaid with silver and gold, shows Mamluk emirs and their servants in a detailed hunting scene.* Louvre © R.M.N.

autonomous standing that over time undermined the legitimacy of imperial authority. This legal tradition strengthened the religious community and weakened strong monarchies, often causing them to negotiate rather than dictate.

Merchant influence on Islamic law also may be seen in its emphasis on contractual matters. Great respect for contracts gained currency in legal cases, and people were held to the letter of a contract in business or in social affairs like marriage. When a case involved general principles, tradition usually prevailed, except when a contrary point emerged from a contract between two parties. Then, the contract usually prevailed. This gave stability to economic relationships and facilitated trade.

Social Classes

Islamic society was organized in a hierarchical manner, with members of the royal family and aristocracy at the top. In addition, officials and merchants formed an intermediate class, and urban laborers and peasants constituted the lower classes. Slaves usually languished at the bottom of Islamic society. We will consider merchants, artisans, and slaves.

One of the most significant contributions of the merchant class was to help develop and preserve a degree of flexibility in Islamic society. Islamic government had its share of officials from various social levels, and merchants played vital political roles from Islam's inception. Furthermore, by helping to create an autonomous legal system that recognized contracts as significant, merchants permitted a variety of social groups to be free from arbitrary administrative rulings. This process allowed for legal flexibility and forestalled a bureaucratically imposed social structure.

Artisans also played a vital social role beyond their economic contributions. Certainly, artisans organized themselves into guilds to provide social stability and regular work. Later Sufi brotherhoods formed around artisan guilds. These organizations also provided for social interaction among spiritual seekers who lived in communities of likeminded mystics. Sufi missionaries who were connected to a specific brotherhood often helped spread Islam by peaceful means.

Slaves played significant roles in Islam's history, and they were used primarily as soldiers, agricultural workers, house servants, and concubines. Because Islam forbade the enslaving of Muslims, the great majority of slaves came from outside the

Islamic realm. Many male slaves served in Islamic armies, and a few gained political power. The Mamluks, for example, were slave-warriors who ruled Egypt from the mid–thirteenth until the early nineteenth century.

Family and Gender Issues

As with nearly all societies we have studied, men were socially dominant; yet women in Muslim society had certain rights and a position somewhat different from their counterparts elsewhere. Marriage was recognized in Islamic law as a contract between the husband and wife. Although a husband was permitted to have four wives, each was legally regarded as equal to the others. All children of these unions were considered legitimate. Birth control measures were accepted in marital relations, but the husband could not interrupt the sexual act because doing so denied his wife her own pleasure. Judges recognized the equal participa-tion of male and female in the creation of a child. The wife was regarded as more than a mere vessel for male seed, as was believed in many societies before 1500. Usually, unless another arrangement was spelled out in a marriage contract, the husband had legal guardianship of children.

Concubines were a class of slaves that had a special position in Islamic society, and, although they were treated as property, these women had certain rights. Once impregnated by her owner, a concubine could not be sold to another, and she was freed when he died. One concubine married a caliph, and two of their sons became caliphs. Some concubines had property, and any child of a slave-master union was legally recognized and free. Many concubines became educated and were accomplished dancers, poets, and storytellers.

Social forces permitted some women to assert themselves, especially in Islam's early history. Because of the more egalitarian nature of early Islamic society, some women played active roles.

FIGURE 12.7 *Harem Wall Painting.* *This reconstruc- tion of a ninth-century wall painting depicts the intricate and precise harem dance, one of the entertainments avail- able to the political elite in early Dar al-Islam. The orig- inal painting, with its Eastern- style figures, decorated the harem quarters of Jausaq Palace in Samarra.* Staatliche Museen zu Berlin—Preussischer Kulturbesitz, Museum fur Islamische Kunst.

Kahdijah,[13] Muhammad's first wife, also assumed a vital position in Islam's founding, choosing him as her husband and becoming his first convert and strongest supporter. After Kahdijah's death, A'isha,[14] another wife of Muhammad, became a significant political figure. Because she came from a powerful family, A'isha's opinion carried great weight. She supported various factions in succession disputes, helping her candidate to gain power. She also was the source for many stories about Muhammad. As Islamic political control spread to Damascus and Baghdad, however, older traditions of covering and secluding women began to dominate social life. A'isha, for example, donned the veil in her later years.

THE ISLAMIC EXCHANGE

The hemispheric nature of Islam with its spread to India, the borders of China, the civilizations of Africa, and the Iberian Peninsula of Europe brought a dramatic exchange of goods, technologies, foodstuffs, and ideas. Trade usually flourished in Dar al-Islam as Muslim merchants traveled the trade routes of Eurasia and Africa. Muhammad himself appreciated the value of commerce to a society and government, and his orientation characterized most of his political successors.

Mechanisms of Exchange

People took goods and ideas across Dar al-Islam by a variety of ways, including proselytizing, traveling, and trading. We have seen how Sufis took Islam to areas over much of the eastern hemisphere, and they carried other ideas along with their religion. Many Muslims faithfully made the **hajj**, the pilgrimage to Mecca, at least once in their lifetimes, and this resulted in a large number of people who traveled. In addition, the *hajji*, the Muslim pilgrim, met and associated with others who had made the journey to Arabia. This resulted in exchanges of ideas and information across Dar al-Islam from West Africa to India. Itinerant scholars and judges also frequently traveled not only for the *hajj* but also for adventure and the spreading of their religion. Some ended up at the courts of

[13] **Kahdijah:** kah DEE jah
[14] **A'isha:** AYH shah

caliphs, and others found employment at schools or translation centers, like the one at Toledo in Spain. These intellectuals played a major role in the spread of ideas in the eastern hemisphere.

Trade provided the greatest vehicle for the transmission of goods and ideas. For centuries, Muslims dominated the land routes across Central Asia, and only in the thirteenth century did the Mongols seize these avenues from the Muslims. The Mongols admired the Muslims' financial skills and placed them in charge of commerce in Central Asia. Water routes in the Mediterranean Sea, the Red Sea, and the Arabian Sea were filled with Arab ships. In fact, there was a large amount of commerce on water between Muslims and Chinese.

Paper

One of the things the Chinese passed on to the Muslims was the knowledge of making paper. Paper making played a variety of roles throughout the Islamic world. In the mid–eighth century, Chinese artisans who knew how to make paper were captured by Muslims in Central Asia, and, by the end of that century, paper-manufacturing works could be found in Baghdad. Knowledge of paper making reached Spain by the beginning of the tenth century, and with paper came a greater appreciation for the written word and a spread of literacy among the higher classes. At the same time, the ease of manufacture and relative inexpensiveness of the process guaranteed a larger reading audience and a spur to learning.

In West Africa, the spread of paper making and the use of paper often paralleled the movement of Islam. Oral tradition played a major role in African religion, but, because the Qur'an was written, Islam had seemingly limitless longevity. When paper making spread from North Africa into West Africa, along with it came authorities on the written word, scholars who included judges, teachers, and students. They formed the core of believers and founded institutions that firmly anchored Islam into society. In the thirteenth and fourteenth centuries, Islamic schools appeared all across western Africa and across much of central Africa.

During the thirteenth century, Muslim Turks brought paper-making technology and paper when they invaded northern India. After the establishment of a Muslim government over parts of the north, the use of paper spread across the subcon-

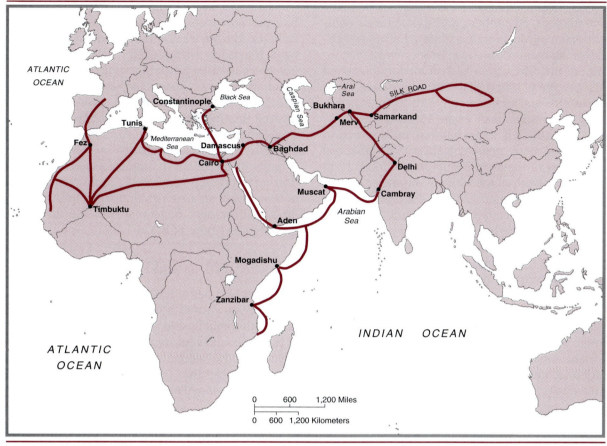

MAP 12.3 *Islamic Trade Routes around 1200.* Muslims controlled many of the major trade arteries in Central and Southwest Asia by 1200. Peoples, products, and ideas went by these and other routes across Asia and Africa. Merchants played an important role in the spread of Islam in Africa and around the Indian Ocean. Europeans eagerly traded with Muslim merchants, especially in Spain and the Mediterranean basin.

tinent. There the diffusion came by choice rather than through forced acceptance, because people preferred the cheaper and easier-to-use paper to the palm leaf, which previously had served the same function. At the same time, the widespread availability of paper meant that Indian and other governments could increase the number of reports and information about their jurisdictions. Control often increased with the amount of accountability demanded.

Foodstuffs

From the eighth through the thirteenth centuries, there was a rapid diffusion of agricultural products, especially from India to other parts of Asia, Africa, and Europe. Dar al-Islam, which bordered on or controlled parts of these areas, helped bring about the spread of these items, some of which greatly affected local and regional economies.

Grain staples, including new varieties of wheat and rice, came into Southwest Asia and Africa. Because these crops could grow in the hot months, when the agricultural fields would otherwise lie dormant, planting them facilitated double-cropping agriculture. This spread economic prosperity and supported larger populations, promoting the growth of cities. Certain foodstuffs needed large amounts of water, and Muslim farmers were forced to develop or improve irrigation techniques. Cisterns and underground canals reduced water evaporation and improved supplies, while water-lifting devices and techniques improved the delivery of water to the fields.

Sugarcane, bananas, sour oranges, lemons, watermelons, cucumbers, and spinach were regularly eaten by Muslims. In addition, European Crusaders, many of whom lived in Southwest Asia for most of their lives, grew accustomed to the varied cuisines there. When they returned home, some ingredients and recipes came with them. Norman Sicily was another place where Muslims and Christians interacted; it was a gateway on the road to Europe for many new vegetables that enhanced diets. Most of the people who ate the foods from the south came from wealthy or otherwise prominent families; common folk seldom could afford the expense of incorporating almonds or spinach into fare for their tables.

Cane sugar became a major elite foodstuff and preservative. Although employed in small quantities for flavoring, sugar was also used in the preserving of fruits, especially oranges and lemons. Preservation of other foods or seasoning dishes was helped by the addition of spices like cumin, coriander, and cinnamon. Color became an important enhancement to a feast, and saffron was added to many preparations to give a yellowish-golden hue.

The Islamic exchange also extended beyond Europe. Rosewater came into Christian Europe from the Muslim areas and was used in a variety of ways. It not only enchanted the palate of the diner but also gave off a pleasant aroma to charm a discriminating nose. Rosewater served both Arabs and Europeans as a medicine, prescribed as a favored treatment for fevers. Once the Europeans established colonies in the Americas, they took along those southern foodstuffs that were difficult to grow in the relatively inhospitable climates of northern Europe. Sugar found a comfortable home in the Caribbean area, rice flourished in the Carolinas, and oranges benefited from the favorable growing conditions of Brazil.

Ideas and Practices

The great number of travelers on the highways of Dar al-Islam carried a variety of ideas and practices with them. Rashid al-Din, a Persian historian of the thirteenth century, spent time in China as an advisor to the Mongols. As a physician, he was impressed by the specialized knowledge of anatomy developed over the centuries by Chinese

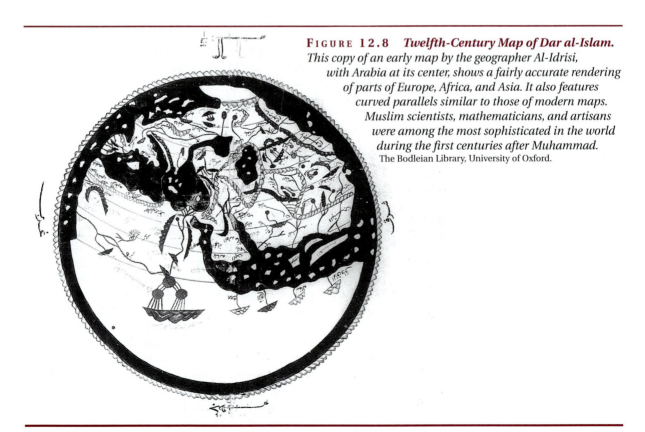

FIGURE 12.8 *Twelfth-Century Map of Dar al-Islam.* *This copy of an early map by the geographer Al-Idrisi, with Arabia at its center, shows a fairly accurate rendering of parts of Europe, Africa, and Asia. It also features curved parallels similar to those of modern maps. Muslim scientists, mathematicians, and artisans were among the most sophisticated in the world during the first centuries after Muhammad.* The Bodleian Library, University of Oxford.

medical practitioners. During his visit, Rashid al-Din had a major Chinese anatomy text translated into Arabic, and he carried it home, from where it eventually reached Christian Europe.

Muslim Spain also benefited from ideas and practices that came from other parts of the Islamic world. Use of the water-wheel arrived from Syria, while the information on how to build underground canals passed from Persia.

THE INTELLECTUAL HERITAGE OF ISLAM

Early in the rise and spread of Islam, Muslim rulers supported artists, writers, scientists, and other intellectuals. Education was highly prized, and generations of scholars and students benefited from the growing body of knowledge transmitted from other parts of the hemisphere, as well as from the synthesis of Muslim-discovered ideas and technologies with those from Greece, Persia, and India. Libraries were founded in most large cities, and some became scholarly research centers. During the ninth century, for example, Muslims founded Al-Azhar, a university in Cairo that became famed for its scholarly endeavors. When Europeans began establishing universities, Al-Azhar was one model for some of their institutions.

Mathematics was a subject of intellectual pursuit for many Muslims. Because they inherited much of Greek and Hellenistic mathematics and because they came into contact with Indian mathematicians, Muslims were able to synthesize and develop old and new branches of mathematics. We have already seen that the Muslims adopted and adapted the Hindu numeration system for their own purposes, and we know that this fundamental way of presenting mathematical ideas enriched European thought. Al-Khwarizmi, an outstanding Muslim mathematician, made discoveries in geometry and arithmetic by improving on the discoveries of his predecessors. He developed the field of algebra by combining Greek geometry with Indian arithmetical discoveries. Al-Khwarizmi's translated writings were used by European thinkers in their own mathematical studies.

Ibn Sina,[15] also known as Avicenna (died around 1037), came from Bukhara in Central Asia.

[15] **Sina:** SEE nah

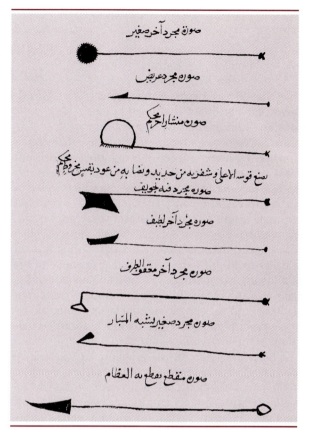

FIGURE 12.9 *Surgical Instruments of Islamic Spain.* *These illustrations are from an encyclopedia of medicine written in the tenth or eleventh century by Abu az-Zahrawi, a Spanish physician. Az-Zahrawi designed and drew his own surgical instruments, including the scrapers, scalpels, hooks, and forceps shown here. Some of these implements were used in Az-Zahrawi's obstetrical practice. His work was translated into Latin in the twelfth century and gained great attention in other parts of Europe.* The Bodleian Library, University of Oxford.

He mastered several intellectual disciplines and traveled to Baghdad to further his education. In the realm of philosophy, he helped establish the foundation of Persian philosophical inquiry by writing a short encyclopedia in Persian. Ibn Sina prided himself on his successful synthesis of the universal insights of philosophy with the discoveries and interpretations of Islamic prophecy. In addition, Ibn Sina's medical knowledge drew the attention of physicians because he and other Muslim physicians incorporated the discoveries of Galen and other Greeks in their own medical writings. Ibn Sina wrote a medical encyclopedia used throughout Dar al-Islam and published in Europe in the sixteenth century. Other medical texts by Ibn

ENCOUNTERS
Ibn Battuta: World Traveler

Abu Abdallah ibn Battuta[a] (1304–1368), who lived in an era later than that covered by this chapter, journeyed farther afield than any other Muslim of his era. Ibn Battuta left his home in Morocco and went to Mecca, like many Muslims. Yet he also ventured throughout Dar al-Islam from extreme northwestern Africa and southwestern Europe to India and Central Asia. Once he traveled to the southeastern coast of China and wandered through many islands of present-day Indonesia. Scholars have estimated that he logged around 73,000 miles, a distance far greater than any other known traveler until the sixteenth century. Because of his significant "wanderings," an official account of his trips was ordered by Ibn Battuta's monarch, and that document forms almost the sole basis of our knowledge about him. It also tells us much about Dar al-Islam in the fourteenth century.

Born in North Africa, probably to moderately wealthy parents, Ibn Battuta studied law, a subject that made him welcome in nearly all parts of the Islamic realm. Because lawyers and judges were in constant demand, Ibn Battuta found employment readily enough. Having such a background and training also meant that Ibn Battuta consorted with members of the social elite on his journeys, and because most of the places he visited had long been under Islamic rule, Ibn Battuta's ideas, customs, and moral outlook found a resonant echo in the people and groups with which he interacted. Faces and clothing may have differed greatly, but the intellectual discourse and values underlying the social interaction showed a remarkable similarity. Ibn Battuta traveled among his peers, who were often friendly familiars rather than exotic aliens.

Central to his journeys were pilgrimages to Mecca, the holy city of Islam, and Ibn Battuta made several *hajjs* in his lifetime. In Mecca, Ibn Battuta met and socialized with a great variety of people, most of whom enjoyed elite status in their homelands. One individual contact afforded Ibn Battuta a chance to work in India, because at that time a Muslim government ruled over part of North India. Ibn Battuta took up the offer and ventured to India, where he worked for some years. Additional travel in India convinced Ibn Battuta that he must visit China, a place spoken of in glowing terms. Resigning from his post, the restless traveler made his way to the eastern coast of India and booked private passage to China, where he stayed for some months. Leaving East Asia in the mid-1340s, he eventually returned to Mecca and finally home.

Ibn Battuta's remaining years were spent in travels to West Africa and Spain. Finally, the last days of this remarkable adventurer were spent as an official in a regional administrative post, while a younger scholar was assigned to write a travel journal in collaboration with Ibn Battuta. It took two years and flowed in the style of travel literature that was common for that day in the western part of Dar al-Islam.

Ibn Battuta had much in common with Marco Polo, the famed European traveler. Indeed, both men journeyed far and served as officials in distant lands. Yet Marco Polo moved as a stranger among unfamiliar peoples, while Ibn Battuta usually felt intellectually and socially at ease with his peers. Ibn Battuta, who traveled much farther than Marco Polo, was a valued member of the global Islamic elite, and his extensive journeys show the elite cultural unity of Dar al-Islam.

[a] **ibn Battuta:** IH buhn bah TUH tah

Sina and his fellow physicians were translated into Latin as early as the twelfth century and remained valuable resources for Europeans for half a millennium. Muslims established pharmacies and medical schools, and rulers required that prospective doctors pass state medical examinations before they could be certified to practice medicine.

Muslims played a significant role in the transmission of many Greek manuscripts of which Europeans were ignorant. In the twelfth century, for example, European scholars who visited Muslim cities, like Toledo in Spain, returned with several texts of Aristotle. They learned about Aristotle's writings on physics and metaphysics. Because Aristotle's ideas had long been admired in Europe, these manuscripts created a sensation in various intellectual circles and enriched the discussions and writings of European thinkers.

ISLAM

		Date	Events
			Muhammad's birth, c. 570
		600	
	First four caliphs, 622–661		*Hijra* to Medina, 622
	Umayyad Caliphate, 661–750		Assassination of Ali, fourth caliph and head of Shi'a, 661
		700	
			Arab fleet captures Indus Valley cities and Arab forces enter Spain, c. 710
			Paper making in Baghdad, c. 752
Abbasid Caliphate, 749–1258		**800**	
			Death of Al-Khwarizmi, mathematician and astronomer, c. 850
			African slave uprising begins in Southern Mesopotamia, 869
		900	
	Islamic regionalism c. 900– c. 1600		Al-Azhar Mosque and School founded, c. 910
		1000	
			Death of Ibn Sina, philosopher and humanist, c. 1037
		1100	
		1200	
			Rumi and Shams meet, 1244
			Fall of Abbasid Caliphate to Mongols, 1258

UNITY AND DIVERSITY

Although Dar al-Islam encompassed a vast realm by the thirteenth century, it was fragmented politically. The rapid conquests during the early decades after Muhammad's death could not be held together over the following centuries.

The unity of Dar al-Islam stemmed from Muslims' adherence to a range of common religious and social practices. Believers prayed to Allah five times a day, knew that Muhammad was Allah's prophet, and practiced charitable acts whenever possible. They submitted to Islamic law and were judged when they failed to follow it. After the first centuries of Islam's appearance, travelers, including pilgrims, could go from place to place in Dar al-Islam and feel comfortable talking with their Muslim brothers and sisters who lived thousands of miles away.

Despite these similarities, great diversity could be found in the Islamic world. Political differences were perhaps most apparent. Factional infighting characterized Islam from the beginning and continued to plague various caliphates. Another problem stemmed from the great distances between areas over which Islam held political sway. Communication necessary to run a centralized polity soon broke down, fragmenting administrative control. Thus, the unity of Islamic states was sundered, leading to regionalism. The destruction of the Baghdad Caliphate in 1258 by the Mongols caused the few remaining allegiances to a universal polity to dissolve.

SUMMARY

1. Muhammad, a merchant, experienced a series of spiritual messages telling him to convey Allah's message to all people. His religion of Islam began in Arabia, and his death sparked a drive to carry Islam's message to distant places. The subsequent fusion of religious and political elements transformed Islam into an empire.

2. Within half a century, Damascus fell to the Islamic advance. It became the center of the Umayyad Caliphate and directed further expansion. The Umayyads, a Meccan merchant family, illustrate one dimension of Islam's debt to merchants.

3. By the mid–eighth century, the Abbasid caliphs took over leadership and built Baghdad as their capital. Ideas and practices from the Greeks and Persians enriched Arab thought and brought about the first of many intellectual syntheses.

4. Islamic society developed a more flexible social structure, because merchants were determined to remain independent of autocratic domination. Merchants played a vital role in the development of Islamic law and society unencumbered by political manipulation. Artisan organizations sometimes served as centers where Sufi mystics interacted. Slaves became a vital part of Islamic society.

5. Families were subject to Islamic law, and the equal rights of a husband's wives were recognized. Individual elite women sometimes became politically important, although the seclusion of women became widespread when traditional patterns asserted themselves.

6. Islam was spread primarily by Sufi spiritual leaders who converted millions by their ardor, ethical living, and amazing feats. Eventually Dar al-Islam stretched from the Atlantic Ocean eastward to the Pacific Ocean and included Indonesia, part of the Philippines, and India.

7. The expanse of dominion that touched most of the eastern hemisphere's great civilizations, along with Muslim receptivity, brought an Islamic exchange of goods, foods, and ideas that benefited hundreds of millions of people.

8. Islam's intellectual impact stimulated thinkers and practitioners in Africa, Europe, and Asia. It set the basis for additional discoveries across continents and centuries.

9. Despite many factors favoring unity within Dar al-Islam, the vast political realm proved impossible to govern. Unified rule broke down, leading to regionalism and localism.

SUGGESTED READINGS

Adas, Michael, ed. *Islamic and European Expansion.* Philadelphia: Temple University Press, 1993. Interpretative essays on Dar al-Islam, especially after the tenth century.

Donner, F. M. *The Early Islamic Conquests.* Princeton, N.J.: Princeton University Press, 1981. A classic treatment of the early decades of Islam.

Hodgson, Marshall. *Rethinking World History.* Ed. Edmund Burke III. Cambridge, Eng.: Cambridge University Press, 1993. A collection of important essays by a major scholar of Islam.

Hourani, Albert. *A History of the Arab Peoples.* Cambridge, Mass.: Harvard University Press, 1991. A standard history of the Arab peoples before and after Islam.

Shah, Idries. *Sufi Studies.* New York: Dutton, 1973. Essays on the development of Sufism.

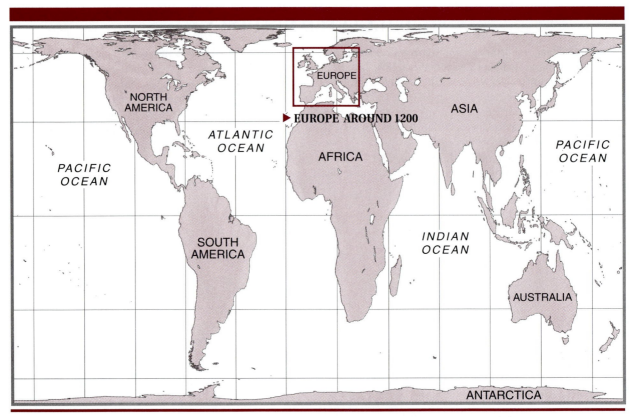

▶ **EUROPE AROUND 1200**

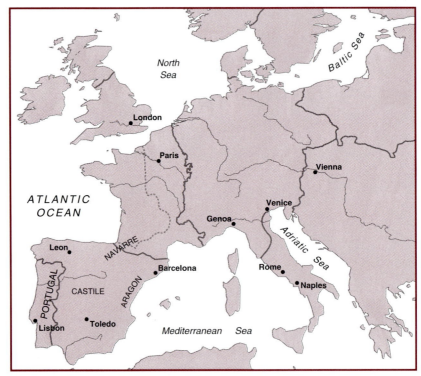

▶ **EUROPE AROUND 1200**

The European Middle Ages

around 500–around 1450

Many people have heard of the fearless King Arthur and his Knights of the Round Table. Arthur was probably a sixth-century British king, and oral tradition has preserved little more than his name. A twelfth-century poet created the imaginary kingdom of Camelot and cast Arthur as a tragic hero to entertain the courts of Europe. Although the knightly adventures are entertaining, little of the King Arthur story—or much of popular belief about the Middle Ages today—is real history.

Scholars call the era in Europe from around 500 to around 1450 the medieval period, or the Middle Ages. The geographic area that most scholars identify as medieval Europe encompasses roughly central, western, and northwestern Europe. The various peoples that populated medieval Europe synthesized a new culture around 500, as a result of the Roman exchange discussed in Chapter 8. This new European culture consisted of Greco-Roman, Germanic, and Christian elements. Europe coalesced only briefly into an empire, during the reign of Charlemagne. Christianity was fostered by kings in their areas, and the papacy during the Central Middle Ages tried, with little lasting success, to develop a universal sovereignty over all of Europe. Medieval contributions to art, architecture, literature, economics, statecraft, religion, and agrarian technology had a profound impact on later European civilization.

THE EARLY MIDDLE AGES, AROUND 500–AROUND 1050

Slowly, Germanic kings who had migrated into the disintegrating Western Roman Empire conquered and unified large territories into regional kingdoms across Europe. In each kingdom, the Germans settled on farms and estates, where their warrior-elite intermingled with the ecclesiastical and Roman aristocrats. This blending of Roman, Christian, and Germanic societies under regional Germanic kings created the basis for a new European culture.

The Rise of the Franks and the Carolingian Empire

The history of early medieval culture is dominated by the rise of the Franks, a Germanic people who eventually turned the regional kingdoms of central Europe into a unified empire. When King Clovis converted to Christianity and was baptized in 496, the Franks became closely allied with the pope in Rome. Other central European peoples at this time were either non-Christian or had converted to a sect of Christianity called Arianism, which defined Jesus as more human than divine. Clovis supported Roman missionary efforts within his expanding territory. As the subject peoples converted, they acknowledged the legitimacy of the Christian Frankish king's rule. Competition between Roman and Arian Christianity added to the Germanic political rivalries, as adherents tried to conquer and convert one another.

MAP 13.1 *Germanic States of the Early Middle Ages around 500. Germanic peoples migrated into the Western Roman Empire's territories during the fourth and fifth centuries. This map shows where the major folk movements ended by around 500. With these migrations came the opportunity for Germanic, Greco-Roman Classical, and Christian elements to synthesize into a new medieval culture in Europe.*

The kingdom of the Franks grew in size and influence. The Frankish Merovingian[1] dynasty kept control of the expanding territories through a loose network of regional bureaucrats. The Merovingian kings, however, slowly weakened as expansion ceased in the seventh century. The royal family was soon impoverished because of the customs of dividing inheritance equally among sons and awarding land gifts to loyal warriors. Royal impoverishment undermined royal authority over the kingdom. The Carolingians,[2] one regional bureaucratic family, emerged as rivals to the Merovingians through careful land management and through territorial expansion that brought in new wealth. In 732, a Carolingian named Charles Martel led the Franks to victory against invading Muslims from Spain. This victory essentially ended Muslim expansion farther into Europe and gained the gratitude and loyalty of many Franks to the Carolingian family. Charles's son, Pepin[3] the Short (reign dates 751–768), challenged the right of the weak Merovingians to rule the Franks. After gaining papal approval for his actions, Pepin deposed the Merovingian king, and a papal emissary anointed him the new king of the Franks.

Pepin soon traveled to Rome to defend the papacy against threats of Lombard invaders. While Pepin was there, the pope again crowned him king of the Franks to solidify their alliance and to reiterate Pepin's legitimacy as a Christian king and not a usurper. The pope, fearing that Pepin would establish himself in Italy as king of the newly conquered territory, narrated the folk story of Emperor Constantine's having given this western territory to the papacy. In imitation of Constantine, Pepin granted the pope political jurisdiction over much of central Italy, forming the Papal States. The alliance between the Franks and the papacy initiated a new missionary surge during the reign of Pepin's son, Charlemagne.

It was during the reign of Charlemagne[4] (reign dates 768–814) that the Franks extended their holdings over most of Europe. The Carolingian Empire, which was established by Charlemagne, took decades to achieve and was won at the cost of much bloodshed. Charlemagne ruled his empire through a network of warriors in the tradition of Germanic culture. In earlier Germanic chiefdoms there had been a close relationship between the king, who had been seen as a gift giver, and his warriors, those who had fought for him and who had received his gifts in exchange for their loyalty, advice, and political support. This loyalty was based upon a Germanic friendship structure, the **comitatus**,[5] which compelled kings to rule in consultation with their warriors.

Charlemagne allowed his most trusted warriors to govern large regions of the empire and, using the comitatus structure as justification, demanded a personal oath of allegiance from them. The warrior-governors accepted Charlemagne's rule because it resulted in the acquisition of lands and treasures, and governors often needed the military support of other elite warriors in times of regional rebellion.

In addition, Charlemagne kept administrative control through bureaucratic envoys who usually traveled in pairs. One secular person (to consult with Charlemagne's warriors) and one person from a religious order (to consult with church officials) assured that revenue was raised, military support was garnered, and Christianity was established. They also reminded the distant and sometimes reluctant warrior-elite not to waver in their allegiance, lest they face the revenge of Charlemagne's loyal warriors. Because many of these envoys lived in their assigned regions for long periods of time, there was always a tendency for the envoys to fall under the influence of the regional governor.

Charlemagne also extended royal law to territories he conquered beyond the Frankish homeland, using both Germanic and Roman structures. These laws regulated interpersonal relationships and defined responsibilities to the crown and to the Christian Church. In a law of 802, Charlemagne states:

> Let no one, through his cleverness or astuteness, dare to oppose or thwart the written law, as many are wont to do, or the judicial sentence passed upon him, or to do injury to the churches of God . . . but all shall live entirely in accordance with God's precept, justly and under a just rule. . . . And let the [envoys] themselves make a diligent investigation whenever any man claims that an injustice has been done to him by anyone. . . .

[1] **Merovingian:** mair oh VIHN jee an
[2] **Carolingians:** cair oh LIHN jee anz
[3] **Pepin:** PEH pihn
[4] **Charlemagne:** SHAHR leh mayn

[5] **comitatus:** koh mee TAH toos

FIGURE 13.1 *Fall of Pampelona.* *This scene on Charlemagne's tomb in Aachen depicts him defeating the Saracens (a term used for any Muslim or Arab in the Middle Ages) who held the city of Pampelona, in northern Spain, in 778. The hand of the Christian God, at the top of the picture, is seen striking down the defensive walls of the city. Charlemagne's defensive wars against the Saracens set up a buffer zone, called the Spanish March, between Muslim Spain and his empire. Throughout the Middle Ages, Charlemagne was hailed as a hero and model for good kingship because of his military prowess and his administrative talents.* Bildarchiv Foto Marburg/Art Resource, N.Y.

Charlemagne modeled his reign on the tradition of Christian emperors. For example, he followed Pepin's policy of supporting missionary activity throughout the empire. At Charlemagne's request, the papacy had sent him copies of church liturgies and practices so that he could initiate uniform practices and establish schools for the education of clergy within the realm. He encouraged Christian intellectuals from diverse areas to reside at his court, and their presence inspired cultural innovation and renewed interest in education and Greco-Roman ideas.

At the end of Charlemagne's reign, western and central Europe were part of a single empire. Charlemagne employed Christianity to help unify the empire ideologically and used the services of scholars to help educate his bureaucracy. As long as he continued expansion, the empire prospered economically and politically; new territories brought wealth and lands to distribute to his loyal warriors.

Charlemagne came to the aid of the papacy during a dispute in Rome between the pope and rival political factions within the city, adjudicating the dispute and ruling in favor of the pope. In doing so, he judged the pope and returned him to the papal throne. Later, on a return visit to Rome, Charlemagne was crowned Western Roman Emperor by a grateful pope on Christmas Day, 800, during holy services. With this action, the pope resurrected the imperial crown and set a new precedent of popes making emperors. Charlemagne accepted the title but also retained the title of "King of the Franks and Lombards." Charlemagne's action of judging the pope and reinstating him and the pope's action of crowning Charlemagne set the precedent for the controversies over authority between popes and monarchs in later medieval history.

By 804, the Carolingian Empire ceased expansion, causing economic and political instability reminiscent of the Merovingian period. With the end of military expansion came the end of large land grants, both of which not only threatened the king's control but also lessened the acquisition of wealth. Although Charlemagne enforced some unity through the strength of his own personality and expertise, and his control of the comitatus, the empire was at best a loosely aligned network of territories bound by loyalty and land gifts. The long-term consequence was the disintegration of the empire. Louis (reign dates 814–840) was not the warrior or administrator that his father, Charlemagne, had been. He had great difficulty controlling the warrior-elite of his realm, some of whom were his sons.

The rivalries between Louis's sons plunged Europe into decades of violent warfare. The sons rebelled in the last years of Louis's reign, fighting over territories and titles, and a settlement was not made until three years after Louis died. In the Treaty of Verdun of 843, Europe was essentially divided into three regional kingdoms: the old western lands of Francia[6] (which for the sake of clarity we will call France), eastern Francia (which again for clarity we will call Germany), and a long narrow strip between the two that also extended to include Italy, whose king also held the imperial crown. Eventually, the imperial title and the territory of Italy fell into the hands of the king of Germany. The kingdom division of this period foreshadowed the early modern map of Europe, and the battles of Louis's sons over territory between France and Germany were inherited by generations of French and German peoples.

The Eighth-, Ninth-, and Tenth-Century Invasions

In the eighth, ninth, and tenth centuries, Europe experienced invasions and migrations that contributed to political fragmentation within the embryonic kingdoms. Magyars[7] from eastern Europe, Muslims from Spain and North Africa, and Vikings from Scandinavia invaded into the disintegrating empire with such ferocity that the newly formed kingdoms were unable successfully to resist the multidirectional onslaught.

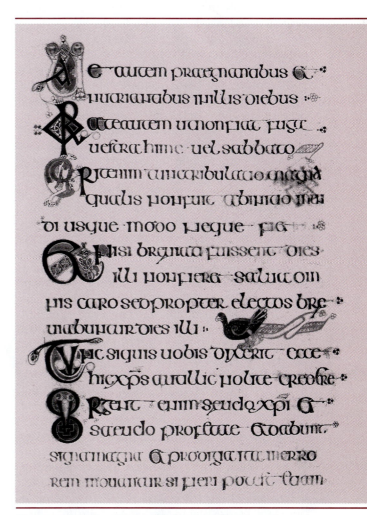

FIGURE 13.2 **Book of Kells.** *An illuminated manuscript of the Christian gospels produced by Northumbrian Celtic monks around 800, the* Book of Kells *is highly decorated with geometric figures, fanciful beasts, and human portraiture. This page shows some of these decorative features, in particular the script developed by these monks. After the Northumbrian writing style was imported to the Carolingian court of Charlemagne, it became known as Carolingian miniscule. Prior to this time, Latin was written in all capital letters with no spaces between words, making it very difficult to read. The innovation of lowercase letters spread throughout Europe and is still in use today, including in the English language.* Trinity College Library, Dublin.

---

[6] **Francia:** FRANK ee uh
[7] **Magyars:** MAG yahrz

UNDER THE LENS
Medieval Renaissances

Scholars today recognize that medieval Europe saw a series of **renaissances**, which were artistic periods when Greco-Roman styles were emulated and synthesized with local techniques to create new styles. Five major periods of renaissance have been recognized in the medieval period: the Northumbrian Renaissance of the seventh century, the Carolingian Renaissance of the ninth century, the Ottonian Renaissance of the tenth century, the more widespread Twelfth-Century Renaissance, and the Italian Renaissance of the fourteenth century. The Twelfth-Century Renaissance is examined more fully in the context of the Central Middle Ages in this chapter.

The renaissance in Northumbria (a region in northern England) was occasioned by the importation of Greco-Roman arts to northern English monasteries in the seventh century. Artistic innovation produced a style of manuscript illumination (the decorating of a manuscript) of geometric design, a new script style, vernacular epic poetry, and a new style of architecture. One of the Northumbrian intellectuals of the day, Bede (died 735), wrote on a variety of subjects, including textbooks for monks. His best-known literary work is the *Ecclesiastical History of the English Church and People*. He also wrote a book on natural philosophy. Bede used the astronomical knowledge of the day to develop principles of timekeeping and dating, most specifically the A.D. system explained in Chapter 1.

Many ideas from Northumbria were exported by Alcuin[a] (735–804) and other monks to the Carolingian Empire, which was experiencing its own period of artistic innovation under Charlemagne. Charlemagne and Alcuin set on a course of education that raised the literacy standards of the empire, for members of both the clergy and the Carolingian nobility. Einhart, one of Charlemagne's biographers, wrote *The Life of Charlemagne* in the tradition of Roman biography. The new Northumbrian script evolved into Carolingian minuscule, a script that employed both upper- and lowercase letters that allowed for easier reading. Perhaps the most notable Carolingian scholar was John Scotus Eriugena[b] (810–877), who translated numerous philosophical texts from Greek and who was also an original thinker and scholar. Eriugena wrote a successful synthesis of Neoplatonism and Christian theology in the work *On Nature*, which was essentially a natural philosophy. Architecture also blossomed at Charlemagne's court. Carolingian architects built the palace in Aachen[c] on the model of Hagia Sophia,[d] the famous church in Constantinople. Under Charlemagne, schools were opened to address the illiteracy of the clergy and monks, and scholars focused on correcting translations and preserving traditional Christian theology. The educational foundation of this period directly facilitated the later development of the major schools and universities that became the intellectual centers of Europe in the twelfth to the fourteenth centuries.

The Ottonian Renaissance climaxed in the last three decades of the tenth century in Germany under the emperors Otto II (reign dates 973–983) and Otto III (reign dates 983–1002). Many scholars and artists flocked to the Ottonian court. Monasteries received significant endowments that supported theologians, teachers, and writers. Gerbert (940–1003), a monk who later became Pope Sylvester II, journeyed to Spain and returned with books and ideas on Islamic science. He also studied astronomy, Greco-Roman literature, logic, and mathematics. Gerbert was perhaps the first medieval European to import Arab knowledge into medieval intellectual circles.

[b]**Eriugena:** AIR ih yoo GAY nah
[c]**Aachen:** AWK awn
[d]**Hagia Sophia:** HAW jee uh soh FEE uh

[a]**Alcuin:** AL koo ihn

Kings were unable to defend against raids in several places at once because of the invaders' mobility. This created the need for local responses to attack. Consequently, regional lords were given or took over many royal responsibilities and usurped royal rights; this was particularly true in France, where the king was unable to stem the tide of Viking raids in the north and Muslim raids in the south. One story tells of a monastery in France that moved from the mouth of a river farther inland, only to be attacked again the following year. The monastery relocated several times, but each time

Vikings found and attacked it. Finally, the monastery moved hundreds of miles into eastern territories and the following year was wiped out by a Magyar raid coming from the east.

In Germany, invasions resulted in periods of decentralization but also periods of centralization under strong monarchs. Weak monarchs in the ninth century prompted the rise of five prominent nobles from the five traditional tribal areas, who reinstated the Germanic custom of kings ruling with a council of warriors. These five nobles eventually became rival princes, and whenever the monarch was weak, they threatened to usurp royal authority, sometimes even forcing an imperial election that placed one of them on the throne. Stronger monarchs, however, forced centralization policies on the five princes. One example of effective centralization occurred under the leadership of Otto I (reign dates 936–973), who instituted a period of monarchical control that witnessed the defeat of invading Magyars in 955.

As emperors, German kings were also responsible for the protection of Italy, and many emper-ors, including Otto I, crossed the Alps to defend Italy and the papacy against various threats. Italy remained under imperial rule, but because of the geographical obstacle of the Alps, succeeding emperors found it difficult to maintain Germany and Italy in a tight alliance. Whenever the emperor was in Italy, the German nobles tended to usurp authority, and whenever the emperor was in Germany, the papacy and the Italian cities pushed for independence. The empire of Germany and Italy, which in the twelfth century became known as the Holy Roman Empire, endured more in name than in reality. Italian coastal cities built fortifications against Muslim raids and employed naval power to check Muslim dominance of the western Mediter-ranean. The Papal States continued under the power of the pope, but the political governance of Italy was increasingly under the influence of local families within powerful, fortified cities.

Muslims and Vikings were not just raiders but also settlers in Europe. Muslims had been in Spain as early as the seventh century and had traded with their neighbors to the north long before they

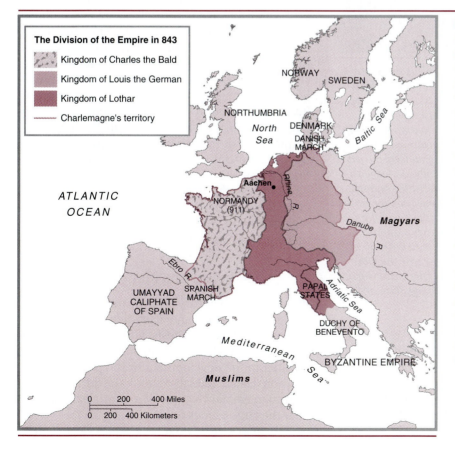

MAP 13.2 *The Carolingian Empire and Its Division in 843.* *This map shows the extent of the Carolingian Empire under Charlemagne and his son, Louis. Louis lost control of the empire to three of his sons, who continued to wage war after his death, until a treaty was established in 843. The Treaty of Verdun split the empire into three kingdoms under a tenuous imperial title held by Lothar. Eventually Lothar's kingdom collapsed, a result of Viking invasions as well as the intermittent fighting between the kingdoms. Its territories were divided between Charles the Bald and Louis the German's successors, and the imperial title fell to the king of the Germans.*

FIGURE 13.3 *Viking Carving. This stone was found in Sweden and is carved with the symbols for a memorial to a Viking warrior. From carvings like this, scholars have learned about Viking attitudes toward death and afterlife. In the center of the carving is a ship on its journey to Valhalla, the Viking heaven, with the souls of brave warriors. Viking kings often were buried or burned in their ships, which were fully loaded with their possessions for use in the afterlife. At the bottom of the carving is the dead warriors' homeland, including the village they are leaving behind. At the top of the carving, two warriors fight another warrior approaching Valhalla on horseback. At the entrance the rider is met by a Valkyrie, a handmaiden of the war god Odin. The duty of the handmaiden is to lead the brave warrior into Valhalla and to Odin, the chief Viking deity.* ATA, Sweden.

fought with Charles Martel in 732. Goods acquired through piracy and raiding were traded downstream or across the sea. Vikings moved down the Dnieper and Volga rivers into the Black Sea area. They set up a trading center in Kiev and exchanged

goods with traders from Europe and Southwest Asia. Vikings or Muslims, after raiding one coastal city, often sailed farther down the coast to exchange goods with merchants in the next city. It was through these two groups that Europe was able to exchange many goods and ideas with traders from the eastern Mediterranean.

Eventually, the Vikings were able to establish a settlement in France at the mouth of the Seine River. The Vikings had used the area as a wintering base, typically raiding upriver during milder weather. The French king, Charles the Simple, struck an agreement with the Vikings to refrain from further raids in exchange for governance of the territory as a vassal of the king. The Viking chief, Rolf, agreed, and Normandy was established.

Vikings successfully conquered and settled in the northern and central sections of England and soon held Ireland as well. Heretofore, England had been a loose confederation of small Anglo-Saxon kingdoms that cooperated under the ambiguous authority of a commander-in-chief. Four of the kingdoms dominated England before the Viking raids, but, with the Viking invasion in the ninth century, all the major areas fell except the southern kingdom of Wessex, which emerged as the home base for English consolidation and resistance. Although England recovered independence for a short time under the able leadership of Wessex's King Alfred (reign dates 871–899), a second wave of invasion resulted in the establishment of a Viking empire of Norway, Denmark, and England. The empire did not endure beyond the first ruler, and by 1042 a descendant of Alfred had taken back the English throne. The result of Viking invasions in England was the opposite from Europe's experience; instead of decentralization and political regionalization, England experienced unification under a single monarchy.

Feudalism and Manorialism

By the tenth century, the synthesis of Greco-Roman, Germanic, and Christian elements was completed. This synthesis and the regionalism resulting from three centuries of invasions contributed to the development of the political organization called feudalism and the jurisdictional land-management system of manorialism, named after the large estates or manors.

Feudalism in Europe was the political system by which kings tried to rule, without bureaucracies, through regional leaders who gave military support and loyalty in exchange for **fiefs** (gifts of land that included manors) to use for their own support and enrichment. Upon taking the oath of loyalty to the king, the leader became a vassal and assumed legal authority over the lands and the people living on them. The relationship between the vassal and lord was contractual and developed into a pattern of rights and obligations of vassals. Charlemagne had laid the foundation for feudal relationships in Europe through his policies of land granting and oath taking. The level of feudalism varied throughout Europe.

Vassals were responsible for local governance, the collection of taxes, the establishment of courts, and the maintenance of the peace. Many powerful vassals received or usurped royal rights, such as the building of castles, the minting of coins, and the collecting of taxes and fees. As long as the vassal remained loyal to the king, there was little monarchical intervention in regional affairs. Strong kings occasionally attempted to reassert central dominance, but when an ineffectual king came to the throne royal power was usually weakened again.

Manorialism was most common in northern France and parts of England but was rare in Scandinavia, northern Germany, the southern coastal areas of France, and Italy. The lands of medieval manors were farmed by peasants or serfs. A peasant was merely a farmer who worked family-owned land or worked for the lord of a manor; a **serf** was a farmer who lived on the fief and was not free to leave. Serfs owed a variety of manorial obligations, such as a certain number of hours per week laboring for the lord directly. Peasants sometimes worked on manors for wages but were free to leave the manor and travel to towns or other manors for work. Usually they did not move because social conditions were such that travel and relocation were very difficult.

Although feudalism and manorialism began in the Early Middle Ages, their structures continued into the thirteenth century in many areas of medieval Europe. Remnants of feudal society persisted into the fifteenth century and beyond in social mannerisms and class attitudes, in part because poets and other writers of the Central Middle Ages idealized the lives of knights in literature.

THE CENTRAL MIDDLE AGES, AROUND 1050–AROUND 1350

By 1050, Europe was engaged in economic expansion, political recentralization, and new artistic creativity. Political centralization under monarchies also supported growing bureaucracies, and more individuals within the population gained access to political power. The economic prosperity brought new patronage of the arts and another medieval renaissance period.

Commercial Expansion and Its Consequences

Commercial activity expanded rapidly in the years between 1050 and 1300, as towns and cities grew in size and population and as trade further developed commercial exchange. Trade with Byzantine and Muslim areas increased in Italy, where Italian merchants soon challenged the dominance of Muslim traders in the Mediterranean and opened central and western Europe to luxuries such as pepper, sugar, cinnamon, and silk. In northern Europe, areas like Flanders were developing into mercantile centers. The Flanders wool trade with England, the Rhineland, and the Baltic Sea area supported the largest European textile production in the twelfth century, supplying most of Europe and beyond. Many areas specialized in particular commodities for export under commercial alliances and consequently increased the importation of goods they no longer locally produced.

Long-distance trade increased the need for capital, and early banking developed and investments accelerated as profit margins soared. Risks were tremendous, but a commercial venture could return as much as a 100 percent profit. Kings generally encouraged the commercial activities of the cities, seeing the opportunity for taxes and revenues independent of feudal lords' claims.

As a result of the increased commercial activity, several fundamental changes took place within European society. A middle class of merchants and artisans emerged, creating new social and political pressures. A monied economy developed, and the right to mint coins became a closely guarded prerogative of kings and great lords. Peasants who remained on manors increasingly received wages

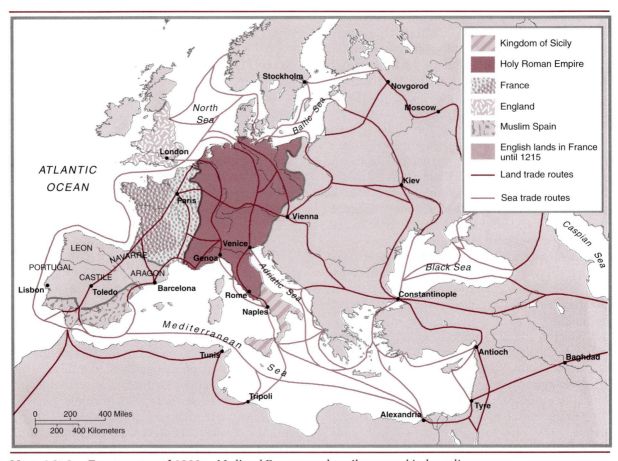

MAP 13.3 *Europe around 1200.* *Medieval Europe was heavily engaged in long distance trade by 1200, as shown in this map. Tin and wool from England and citrus, leather, and honey from Portugal and Spain were traded for dried fruits and almonds from North Africa. Slaves, timber, grain, honey, and furs came to markets from territories north of the Black Sea. Central European furs, metals, and wine were traded in Italian markets for olive oil and goods imported from Southeast Asia, such as carpets, glassware, and spices. At the same time goods traveled the trade networks, ideas were exchanged among merchants and travelers throughout the Mediterranean area.*

for their labor or paid rents for their fields. During the twelfth century, kings gradually replaced the vassalage military obligation with money payments called "shield money," hiring mercenary soldiers instead of calling up retainers. Kings also employed paid professionals in ever-growing bureaucracies.

The Twelfth-Century Renaissance

More commercial wealth created opportunity for greater patronage of the arts in the twelfth century, creating what scholars describe as the Twelfth-Century Renaissance. Schools and universities

developed, new literary styles became popular, philosophers and theologians argued fine points of law and physics, and innovations in art and architecture appeared.

In the twelfth century, education became increasingly important. Most students had traditionally come from the aristocracy, but education was a path to social mobility. Students from the various social levels attended monastic schools, where talent and skill determined opportunity. In addition, wealthy merchants sent younger sons to schools, some of whom returned to the family businesses and others of whom became bureaucrats or entered teaching. The growing bureaucracies of both royal and ecclesiastical administrations called for talented, educated individuals who could produce deeds and wills, conduct government surveys, keep financial records, and record legal proceedings. Europe moved from an oral, memory-based society of oaths to a society of paper, pen, and ink. Many who could not read or write chose to employ the educated to record their legal transactions.

Both secular and religious schools gave students a liberal arts education. Such an education was identified as the seven subjects of astronomy, geometry, arithmetic, music, grammar, rhetoric, and logic. Each student also chose one specialty area in church or civil law, medicine, or theology. Many universities became associated with particular disciplines because of their faculties' reputations; the University of Bologna (in Italy), for example, specialized in law.

Student life in the Central Middle Ages had many commonalities with student life today; one student pleaded in a letter home:

> The city is expensive and makes many demands: I have to rent lodgings, buy necessities, and provide for many other things that I cannot specify. Therefore, I beg you, [father], that by the prompting of divine pity you may assist me, so that I may be able to complete what I have so well begun.

The father replied to his wayward son:

> I have recently learned that you live dissolutely, preferring play to work and strumming your guitar while others are at their studies.

Increasing literacy among aristocratic men and women led to the production and patronage of secular and devotional literature. Lyric poetry, epic stories, romance poetry (inspired by the

IN THEIR OWN WORDS
Hildegard of Bingen

Hildegard of Bingen (1098–1179) was a poet, dramatist, musician, composer, scientist, mystic, biographer, counselor to the famous, and abbess. In her own day, she was well known and revered. Numbered among her many correspondents were various kings and ecclesiastical authorities, including Frederick I, the Holy Roman Emperor. In one treatise on physics, Hildegard describes medicinal properties of more than three hundred herbs, metals, stones, and minerals. In another treatise on causes and cures, she delves into nutrition and metabolism. Her advice to individuals was to engage always in balance in life, just as (in her view) the cosmos is perfectly balanced. In her visionary literature, she focused on cosmology and the centrality of humanity in creation; as she saw it, each individual is a microcosm of the created world and is intricately bound to nature.

The following selection is taken from one of her works in which she describes a vision of God, the creator, as a divine flame. Her poetic prose is a good example of the beauty of medieval literature.

> I am the highest fiery power, who has enkindled every spark that lives and breathes. . . . I distinguish all things as they are, surrounding the circle of the world with my superior wings; that is, flying about it with wisdom, I have ordered it rightly. And I, flaming life of the divine substance, flare up above the beauty of the plains, I shine in the waters and blaze in the sun, the moon, and the stars, and with an airy wind, as if by an invisible life which sustains the whole, I arouse all things to life. For air lives in freshness and flowers, the waters flow as if they were alive. The sun, too, lives in its light, and when the moon wanes it is fired anew by the light of the sun, just as if it lived again; the stars also grow clear in their light as if [they] were living. . . . And so I, the fiery power, lie hidden in these things, and they themselves burn by me, as the breath unceasingly moves the man, like a windy flame in a fire. All these things live in their essence and were not devised in death, for I am Life. And I am Reason, and have the wind of the resounding Word through which every creature has been made, and I have given my breath to all these things so that none of them is mortal in its kind, for I am Life. I am Life whole and entire, not cut from stone, not sprouted from twigs, not rooted in the powers of a man's sex; rather all that is living is rooted in me. For Reason is the root, and in it blossoms the resounding Word.

FIGURE 13.4 *Twelfth-Century University.* *Universities became more numerous during the Central Middle Ages. A university education consisted of the seven liberal arts, with opportunities for graduate work in theology, philosophy, medicine, and law. This twelfth-century Italian woodcarving shows a variety of students; some wear religious garb while others are dressed in the popular secular clothing of the day. The fact that they all have books suggests that this is a graduate class—probably a class on law.* Alinari/Art Resource, N.Y.

ideals of courtly love), personal letters, autobiographies, and genealogies became increasingly popular. Many aristocratic women became patrons of the troubadour poets in the courts of the twelfth century. French lyric poetry crossed the channel from France to England through the patronage of Eleanor of Aquitaine (1122–1204). Eleanor had supported troubadour poetry at the court of her first husband, King Louis VII of France. Upon her marriage to King Henry II of England, Eleanor became a significant patron of poets and musicians in England. A few women produced lyric poetry themselves, such as the twelfth-century countess Beatriz, who wrote about an unrequited love in this poem:

> I've lately been in great distress
> over a knight who once was mine,
> and I want it known for all eternity
> how I love him to excess.
> Now I see I've been betrayed
> because I wouldn't sleep with him;
> night and day my mind won't rest
> to think of the mistake I made . . .

William IX, Count of Poitou (1071–1127), teased his peers with this little gem that parodied the popular lyric poetic style:

> I'll make some verses just for fun
> Not about me nor any one,
> Nor deed that noble knights have done
> Nor love's ado:—
> I made them riding in the sun
> (My horse helped, too) . . .

The growing middle class enjoyed stories that bawdily poked fun at social mores and tales of clever, humanlike animal characters who outwitted opponents. These genres became increasingly popular among the general population. Geoffrey Chaucer (1340–1400), a famous English poet, amused many English with the delightful parodies of personalities in his *Canterbury Tales.*

Philosophy, theology, and medieval science were intertwined in the entire Middle Ages. Religion supported investigation into the rational order of the universe, and theologians populated the ranks of early scientists. Medieval science was called natural philosophy, and for most natural philosophers, faith and reason were inseparable, because God was seen as the divine architect of the universe. This use of one's reason to develop faith and an understanding of the created universe during the twelfth century was called **scholasticism**. Astronomy, mathematics, medicine, biology, and botany were several of the areas of medieval intellectual pursuit that laid the foundations for modern science.

Throughout the Twelfth-Century Renaissance, many scholars consulted Greek and Roman works and embraced Muslim knowledge. New thought was not threatening to theology but opened up the cosmos to closer scrutiny and better understanding of how the Christian God was thought to order the natural world. In the twelfth century, some Greco-Roman philosophical and scientific works were brought into medieval Europe through contact with Muslim traders and intellectuals. This access to Greco-Roman and Muslim works on physics, mathematics, astronomy, astrology, and medicine led to a surge of intellectual activity that created a deluge of writings.

Scholastic thought continued into the thirteenth century. The monk-scholastic Thomas Aquinas[8] (1225–1274) had an immense effect on the development of European physics as well as that of Christian theology. Aquinas was a natural philosopher who accepted the scholastic principle that reason enhanced the revelation found in Christian theology. He argued that a proposition is valid only if it is argued from the facts found in the natural world. One famous argument is his "proofs for the existence of God," in which he rationally argued that all things must have a cause. He observed that in nature everything that moves does so because of some action upon it. If one logically moves backward through each movement and action, one will eventually get to the first mover, or the uncaused cause. Aquinas concluded that the first mover must be the creator of the universe.

Perhaps the most visual representation of the Twelfth-Century Renaissance is the parallel development of Gothic architecture and the realistic style of sculptural decoration that became popular in twelfth-century cathedral building. One scholar has noted that more stone was quarried for building churches, abbeys, castles, hospitals, and town halls in medieval France than for the pyramid and temple building of ancient Egypt. The structural engineering of these stone edifices remains remarkable even in light of today's standards. The curved arches and thicker walls of Romanesque architecture in the eleventh and early twelfth centuries gave way to the ever-increasing height and delicacy of the Gothic style in the twelfth and thirteenth centuries. Rib-vaulted ceilings and pointed arches allowed ever-narrowing pillars to support greater and greater heights. The Gothic style permitted multistoried walls with stained-glass windows that bathed the immense interior in light. The incentive was to attract the eye to move from ground level heavenward; and even today most people, upon entering a cathedral for the first time, look up.

The building boom was, in part, a result of increased commercial wealth. The cathedrals were funded through donations and increased taxes,

FIGURE 13.5 *Gothic Church.* *This example of Gothic architecture is Westminster Abbey in London, England, built in the early thirteenth century in the French style. Most churches were built in a cruciform shape with chapels at the end of each transept; at the far end of this church is a typical chapel area with a large stained-glass window. The high altar was usually placed where the cross intersects. This view is a good example of a long nave, bordered by huge interior columns that support the rib-vaulted ceiling, common to Gothic architecture. The large windows of the exterior walls bathe the nave with light, as seen here reflecting on the floor.* Edwin Smith.

and many guilds donated labor or money for special projects, like windows that featured typical guild scenes. The likenesses of wealthy merchants and aristocrats often could be recognized in the faces of stained-glass figures. These edifices were

[8] **Aquinas:** uh KWY nihs

viewed with great pride; any city that supported a cathedral saw an increase in the local economy when pious pilgrims spent money on food, lodging, and souvenirs. Sometimes the masses of people inside the cathedrals were so great that the clergy could hardly go about the business of daily services.

Regional Monarchies

The trend in centralization during the eleventh century resulted in the growing power of the monarchy within England and France. After a brief revival of imperial power in the twelfth century, thirteenth-century Germany experienced a resurgence of the authority of the five princedoms at the expense of imperial power, and the imperial crown was increasingly subject to the older tradition of election. In Spain, Christians expelled Muslims and established the Christian kingdom of Castile.[9]

Generally, increased royal administrative responsibilities gave rise to bureaucratic governments. Royal law and **canon law**, church laws regulated by church officials, continued to develop in opposition to local feudal customs of law, giving greater uniformity and control of judicial practices. Conflict shifted from the battlefield to the courtroom. Chanceries (secretarial offices) grew in size and output, creating the need for larger numbers of highly educated personnel.

England had developed somewhat differently from Europe after 1066, when Duke William of Normandy conquered England. William brought French feudal customs of vassalage with him to England, but regionalism did not occur. William retained many Anglo-Saxon political traditions that reserved significant monarchical influence in local areas. In England, all levels of vassals owed direct allegiance to the new king over their loyalty to their immediate lords. William carefully awarded noncontiguous lands to his vassals in order to frustrate independence and regionalism. Thus, the concept of the community of the realm (similar to Charlemagne's comitatus) developed, perpetuating the idea of king and great vassals ruling the kingdom for mutual benefit. Denied regional independence, vassals developed a vested interest in cooperating with the crown to assure the safety and success of the entire realm. Because

of this, England moved toward a centralized system of government.

When King John (reign dates 1199–1216) lost his French holdings during a war with the French king in 1215, his English vassals forced him to sign the **Magna Carta**, or Great Charter, which reiterated traditional English aristocratic rights to participate in the rule of England. Many of John's English vassals also had lost their French properties, and they wanted to limit John's ability to act without their approval. In the vassals' opinion, John had abused his monarchical authority by taxing his subjects without their consultation, by challenging the papacy over selection of a new archbishop of Canterbury, and by developing policy without the consent of his great vassals. Because of these actions, the Great Council of the Realm (the traditional English council of great vassals who advised the king) was able to knot up the purse strings of the English monarch. John could not raise taxes without the council's consent. English political history is essentially the history of the tension between monarchical interests and the interests of the great lords of the realm.

The French experience was somewhat different. Although French kings traditionally had been weak from the ninth to around the twelfth century, the monarchy gradually recovered its authority in the following centuries. Effective governance under several talented kings led the French crown toward centralization and soon placed royal rights over those of aristocrats. The Estates General (consisting of clergy, the first estate; nobles, the second estate; and townspeople, the third estate) was called to meet only at the king's desire. The capture of the English king's French territories made the French crown exceedingly wealthy and powerful again. For the first time in centuries, the French king was wealthier than the major vassals of France. The monarch continued centralization policies, and, unlike the English Council of the Realm, the French Estates General had no control over taxation.

In Spain, the European defeat of Muslims who had held parts of that country since the early eighth century resulted in the establishment of the Christian kingdom of Castile. By 1085, the Muslim city of Toledo fell to the Christians and remained an important center for the exchange of goods and ideas. During the twelfth century, several Christian kingdoms in northern and central Spain estab-

[9] **Castile:** KAH steel

FIGURE 13.6 *French Illuminated Manuscript.*
Illuminated manuscripts were often used for portraiture in the Middle Ages. These portraits are of Blanche of Castile, regent of France from 1226 to 1234, and her young son, Louis. The two figures below probably represent the abbot who had this manuscript prepared and the scribe who did much of the work—it was typical to portray important individuals who had commissioned a work as well as those who had prepared it. The scribe on the lower right writes with a quill pen in his right hand, while his left hand holds a knifelike instrument used to scrape off dried ink when a mistake was made. The scraping often caused abrasions on the vellum, and sometimes even holes that obscured the text. The Pierpont Morgan Library/Art Resource, N.Y.

lished themselves and pushed the Muslims farther south. At times, Muslims and Christians allied against other Spanish Christians in the competition for territory. In 1212, the papacy declared a crusade against all Muslims in Spain, and a united, multinational Christian army invaded the south, expanding Castile and the Christian kingdoms of Aragon and Portugal. By 1300, the only Muslim presence was the small kingdom of Granada, which was eventually taken over by Castile. Former Spanish Muslim territories were populated quickly with relocated Christian peasants. The two kingdoms of Castile and Aragon eventually united into the single kingdom of Spain, and Portugal remained a separate kingdom.

Women were not traditionally rulers in the Central Middle Ages, but several exercised significant political influence. Mothers of young kings served as regents during their sons' infancies. Blanche of Castile (1188–1252) married a French king and reigned as regent for eight years after his death. During her regency, Blanche defeated a vassal rebellion. Many years later King Louis IX left for Southwest Asia on crusade, again leaving France in the able hands of his mother, Blanche. Many daughters of kings were given in marriage to princes to solidify alliances or, as inheritors of large estates, to consolidate territories. Eleanor of Aquitaine, the patroness of medieval literature and music, controlled wealthy lands that were coveted by her second husband, Henry II of England.

THE LATE MIDDLE AGES, AROUND 1350–AROUND 1450

By the Late Middle Ages, many changes had taken place across Europe. Monarchs were developing strong central authority within their realms, and economic and artistic growth persisted. But new problems soon forced additional changes in the map of medieval Europe and engendered new religious attitudes.

Late Medieval Politics

Late medieval monarchs continued to challenge regional lords for control of their realms and engaged in war with their neighbors as they tried to expand their territories. In Spain, the marriage of Ferdinand of Aragon to Isabella of Castile in 1469 effectively united most of the Iberian Peninsula under one monarchy. By 1492, the small Muslim state of Granada fell to the Spanish kingdom, leaving only Portugal independent.

In England, the continuing tension between royal and aristocratic rights pitted the elite against a king in need of funds to fight the French. The Hundred Years War (1337–1453) between France and England was the result of years of English claims to French territories. To finance the war the king was forced to grant concessions of legislative rights for fiscal support of his policies. The English king was still unable to untie the purse strings of England.

In France, the Hundred Years War created economic and political instability. The war was fought on French soil, and the devastation to property and life was enormous. Political instability threatened the monarchy; for a short time in 1356, the Estates General came under the control of a cloth merchant from Paris, after the king had been captured by the English. Royal rights were usurped, as the Estates General took over the royal privileges of legislation, taxation, and administration in regular meetings. Within another year, the French peasantry rebelled for two weeks until an aristocratic

and urban coalition put down the rebellion. This chaotic dissolution of law and order led to renewed support of royalism, and the long-term result of the rebellion was the loss of an opportunity for cooperative governance between the crown and the Estates General. French monarchs compromised with the aristocracy and the middle class by appointing leaders from these classes to its growing bureaucracy.

French kings were unable to stem the tide of the English onslaught and devastation of French lands. Finally, with the aid of a pious young Joan of Arc, the king was able to rout the English and turn the tide in favor of France. Joan was captured and stood trial on trumped-up charges of heresy and witchcraft. She was subsequently burned at the stake by the English. But because of Joan's successes and inspiring example, the Hundred Years War came to an end with a French victory in 1453.

Italy and Germany experienced the same kinds of internal struggles that England and France had endured, but no central, unifying political entity emerged. The Holy Roman Empire endured under regional disputes. Italy remained dominated by regional jurisdictions, and rival factions vied for regional leadership. Many cities retained their independence and grew wealthy in the lucrative Mediterranean trade.

Death and Disillusionment

As the Middle Ages came to an end around 1450, the European population had been profoundly affected by demographic, social, and economic changes. Wars and plagues disillusioned and devastated the population. Many of these changes gave way to economic recovery that spurred new commercial and intellectual activity.

Several wars marred the peace during the Late Middle Ages, including wars between rival Italian city-states, wars between Christians and Muslims in Spain, and the Hundred Years War. The Hundred Years War had held northwestern Europe hostage; the social, economic, and human toll left a mark that was not soon erased from memory. The devastation to the English and French economies was incalculable. The war also interrupted commerce to and from most other areas of medieval Europe, affecting the local economies.

As a consequence of simultaneous plagues from 1347 to 1349, the European population was ravaged, trade and commerce were virtually stopped in many areas, and whole towns and villages effectively disappeared forever. Europeans named the plagues the "Black Death." A series of intermittent plagues followed the Black Death in the years from 1361 to 1407, and, when the diseases had run their course, more than 20 million people had died. Occasionally plagues returned from the fifteenth to the nineteenth centuries. The Black Death influenced artistic styles; many graphic scenes of plague victims, mass burials, skeletons, and the "Grim Reaper" (death personified) became common in artists' work. There was a spectrum of reactions, from religious fanaticism to atheism. The horrors of disease and destruction psychologically crippled much of western Europe.

War and plagues created a shortage of labor, which, ironically, benefited many who survived in the form of higher wages. In some areas, serfs were relieved of obligations in order to entice them to stay and work; in other areas, serfdom became even more oppressive. Many landowners changed to commercial enterprises (like wool production) because they were more lucrative. This dislocated some people whose families had farmed the acreage for generations. Although the plagues devastated urban populations, they had a greater impact on rural peoples because entire village populations were ravaged. Many cities saw an increase in population as the rural dispossessed relocated in urban centers. Many remained unemployed because of a lack of special skills or because guild members and town leaders reserved jobs for their own members. During the second half of the fourteenth century, there were various outbreaks of violence as social tensions exploded.

Recovery

Several pockets of medieval Europe had not suffered the devastation of intermittent warfare, and a few isolated rural populations had escaped the worst onslaught of the plagues. Some commercial centers, particularly in the far north, continued to prosper at the expense of rival centers that had not fared so well. By the mid–fifteenth century, as the Hundred Years War came to a close, many of the

FIGURE 13.7 *Grim Reaper. The Late Middle Ages were fraught with death and disease. Many popular apocalyptic texts were illustrated with depictions of the Grim Reaper, or Death. Death was often shown as a triumphant warrior, striking down the innocent, the heedless, and the sinful without regard for social station or age. Many responded to their uncertain futures either by losing their faith entirely or by becoming more religious.* Giraudon/Art Resource, N.Y.

areas that had suffered the most were also recovering from their recessions.

Many innovations of the Late Middle Ages had profound effects on European recovery. New technologies in ship building helped to open up the New World to Europeans in need of funds to reinvigorate their economies. A by-product of increasing literacy was the demand for more books. New technologies produced better paper, and woodblock carvings were perfected and used to stamp artwork on the numerous and more cheaply produced devotional books. The manuscript illumination of the Early and Central Middle Ages was too expensive for mass production, and wood-block printing inspired the adoption of the Asian technology of movable-type printing, which soon revolutionized society. Gunpowder, developed in China, was a new technology in the Late Middle Ages. In the later era of the Hundred Years War, its use with cannon led to new architectural advances in wall defenses. Soon, individual foot soldiers were carrying guns into battle.

While much of western Europe was still experiencing a slow recovery, Italy was in the beginning of an economic expansion and cultural revival of Greco-Roman styles called the Italian Renaissance. Less affected by war, disease, and the resulting economic devastation, Italian cities continued to take advantage of commercial opportunity throughout the Mediterranean Sea. The new wealth and new ideas that inspired the Italian Renaissance would soon cross the Alps and help stimulate the recovery of late medieval Europe.

EVERYDAY LIFE

The general population of medieval Europe continued to rise until around the middle of the fourteenth century. City populations of 25,000 to 50,000 were not uncommon, and a few major centers, like Paris, could boast of populations around 100,000. Scholars estimate the entire European population by 1300 to have been about 70 to 80 million, an increase from the approximate total of around 26 million in 600. Although urbanization and commercialism grew at a rapid pace from 1050 to 1300, most Europeans, like most peoples of the world, lived in rural areas. The mean family size in cities was 3.9 and in the country 4.8.

Rural Life

Each manor consisted of the lord's manor-house, a village, fields, an orchard, and buildings for special tasks. Each farmer worked his own strips in the various fields as well as a portion of the lord's strips (see Figure 13.8). The produce from each strip was divided between the farmer and the lord according to each farmer's obligation. All produce from the lord's strips was retained by the lord. As time passed, occupational specialization increased on the manors; smiths, bakers, shepherds, and other artisan specialists worked full time at their occupations for the benefit of the entire manor population in exchange for other farmers tilling their strips.

The lords of the manor were also the lords of manorial law. Each lord held a manorial court where villagers could make complaints against their neighbors or where the lord could pronounce punishments or exact payments. Usual proceedings included complaints of negligence of required duties, charges of petty theft, and typical lord-villager transactions, as the following notations from a manor court demonstrate:

> Hugh Free appeared asking for clemency because his beast was caught in the lord's garden; Roger Pleader appeared with a suit against Nicholas Croke explaining that neither he nor his [kin] killed Nicholas's peacock; Gilbert Richard's son paid five shillings for a license to marry.

Some farmers lived as peasants in nonmanorial communal villages. The villages were small agrarian communities of several huts surrounded by fields not subject to feudal control. These villages often developed around secure locations, like castles, or in ecclesiastical districts where stone churches offered protection. Many such villages came under manorial jurisdiction during times of crisis. As in the manorial system, nonmanorial farming was a cooperative effort; tools, draft animals, and plows were too expensive for a single peasant to own. Law was established by a village council, and the necessity of mutual dependence gave incentive for quick settlement of disputes.

Many agricultural innovations and new technologies led to increased productivity and improved quality of life. The three-field system divided the land into three major field areas, where planting was done by rotation. Each season, farm-

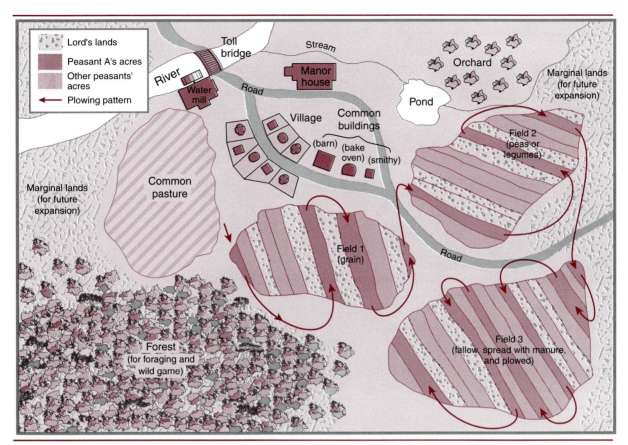

FIGURE 13.8 *Medieval Manor.* *Serf and peasant farmers tilled fields divided into long, alternating strips that made plowing easier by eliminating the need for tight turns with plow and oxen. Individual farmers often owned some animals and equipment, but more typically, almost everything on the manor belonged to the lord: the common bakery, the orchard, the pond or stream and the fish in it, the forage area, and everything else needed to work a self-sufficient farm. The marginal lands near the manor held wild game, but those who hunted without permission were charged with poaching. Each farmer had to pay the lord, in goods or in labor, for the use of any equipment or special service—even for picking apples from the orchard.*

ers planted crops in two fields and let the other lie fallow, allowing nature to replenish the nutrients in its depleted soil. Careful planning and the spreading of manure helped to bolster the yield per acre, which in turn yielded surpluses. In addition, the introduction of new harnessing techniques, the heavy-wheeled plow, and iron plow tips resulted in increased cultivation in the heavy, rich soils of Europe. Water mills and windmills led to increased productivity. All of these factors increased the food supply and resulted in a healthier and growing population.

Villages and manors were successful only when families worked together for the benefit of all. Women and older children toiled alongside their husbands and fathers on the farms, and in their spare time children played with their toys: tops, play swords, wooden tricycles, and dolls. Everyday life consisted of rising early and laboring long hours tilling in the fields, tending animals, or working at any of the other myriad chores associated with farm life. Next to their huts, most farmers had small vegetable plots that required their attention after their village or manor obligations were complete.

Medieval women had varied employment. In order to supplement income, peasant women often hired out to other manors if laborers or

FIGURE 13.9 *Feudal Agriculture.* These miniatures from a fourteenth-century manual on agriculture depict the seasonal chores of feudal life. Each scene features a monthly task associated with different crops, animals, and regions. Giraudon/Art Resource, N.Y.

maids were needed. Women, whether aristocratic or poor, were responsible for the preparation of food in the household. They also managed the household and cared for children, servants, and many of the family-owned animals. They frequently were the healers and midwives. Aristocratic women often ran the manors when their husbands and sons were absent because of feudal obligations. These women instructed the overseers on how to run the manors and kept the financial records, collecting rents and payments and procuring supplies not produced on the manor.

By the end of the Early Middle Ages in the eleventh century, many marginal lands were coming under development, trade towns were growing into cities, and most local economies were thriving. Economic growth was the result of new technologies that led to greater production on village communes and manors, and the surpluses for trade benefited both farmer and lord. The growing village and manorial populations often meant relocation for some peasants, because many villages and manors were landlocked by their neighbors and could not expand to accommodate the increasing numbers. Cultivation of marginal lands

drew excess population from settled areas, and lords of new manors enticed laborers by establishing more liberal manorial conditions. Some lords had to ease their control to keep peasants and serfs from running away in search of better opportunities elsewhere.

Urban Life

From around the twelfth to the fifteenth centuries, opportunities for employment proliferated. Many artisans from the village communities and manors relocated to the growing towns, particularly smiths, bakers, tanners, and others who could sell their goods or services. They joined merchants, who traded goods from as near as the manor down the lane to as far away as China.

Towns and cities that developed and prospered on feudal lands were given charters from the lords who held jurisdictional authority. The charters were essentially contracts of operation that spelled out the obligations of the towns and cities to the lord and the lord's responsibility to the town. Eventually, many towns extracted charters that gave them greater freedom. Usually the town was awarded the right of self-governance in exchange for yearly payments.

Town governance was organized around the guild system. Each profession, artisan or merchant, had a guild. The shoemaker guild, for instance, licensed, set prices, and generally regulated all shoemakers in the town. Shoemakers (like all artisans, bankers, and merchants) were located on the same streets: Shoemaker Street, Baker Street, and so on. Every shoemaker had to be a member of the guild, paying dues and performing guild responsibilities. Guilds permeated all aspects of urban life, from the workplace to recreation. They gave donations to churches, often paying for chapels, stained-glass windows, and upkeep. The building of a cathedral was usually a boon to a town, giving carpenters, stonemasons, cloth makers, candle makers, and many others employment for centuries. Guilds helped with funeral expenses and supported widows and orphans. Elected representatives, almost always the wealthy and influential from each guild, formed an urban council responsible for justice, trade laws, and negotiations with the lord. Towns and cities gained these freedoms sometimes in cooperation with investment-hungry lords and, at other times, through violent riots or with the help of mercenaries hired to fight for the town's cause.

Many women played important roles in the towns and cities. As mentioned earlier, some were artisans themselves. Some women found employment as goldsmiths, cloth makers, and various other professions that required periods of training and apprenticeship. Many a wife worked with her husband and continued the family business after his death, directing apprentices just as the husbands, the mastercraftsmen, had. These women inherited membership in the guilds. Single women also had the right to own property and establish businesses. By the thirteenth century, many aristocratic women and wealthy merchant women were engaged in long-distance trade ventures. One English woman lost her cargo to Spanish pirates; upon learning of her loss, she filed a lawsuit and gained royal permission to seize Spanish cargo at English ports until the loss was repaid.

MEDIEVAL CHRISTIANITY

During the Christianization of medieval Europe, the Christian Church extended its bureaucracy, focusing on uniformity. Monastic houses served as spiritual retreats and educational centers. Liturgical practices became universal, the parish system was fully developed, the seven sacraments were regularized, and sacred law was codified. The papacy in the early eleventh century was still primarily a regional power with little political influence beyond Italy. This slowly changed from the eleventh through the thirteenth centuries as popes

FIGURE 13.10 *Florentine Guilds.* *On the feast day of Saint John the Baptist, the citizens of medieval Florence proceeded to the cathedral to honor the saint and to display their civic pride. This scene on a painted chest shows thirty-nine-foot-high banners, embroidered with the symbols of numerous guilds and hung from houses along the processional route. Among those represented by such associations were wool makers, furriers, doctors, druggists, and sword makers; in all, about seventy-three guilds functioned in the city. Some of the more prominent groups were highly political, controlling commercial regulations as well as magisterial concerns.* Scala/Art Resource, N.Y.

who were trained as lawyers brought the bureaucracy under closer papal scrutiny. These popes organized and instituted reform within the ecclesiastical hierarchy.

Although medieval Europe was predominantly Christian, various religious minorities were present throughout the period. The largest group of non-Christians consisted of Jews, who had been present in western Europe since the first century. Christian theology forbade persecution of Jews, but most of them found living in Christian Europe dangerous, if not deadly. Periodically, many Jews were attacked and beaten, killed, or expelled from territories because angry mobs believing that Jews had murdered Jesus wanted to retaliate. In some cases, kings and bishops protected Jews and gave them sanctuary; in other cases they instigated the attacks for personal gain. Often, Jewish businesses were bankrupted, confiscated, or destroyed.

Some areas of medieval Europe were more accepting of religious and intellectual differences. The Norman kingdom of Sicily and southern Italy was well known for its religious tolerance of and openmindedness to non-Christian ideas. The kingdom was a playing field of artistic, intellectual, and social exchange. For most of medieval Europe, however, the Christian worldview dominated, and there was no concept of the separation of church and state.

Monasticism

Monastic houses played a key role in medieval society. Men and women took vows of poverty and chastity in their personal lives and pledged obedience to the abbots and abbesses, who headed the monasteries and nunneries. Most lived lives of prayer and hard work. Many monasteries and nunneries supported the poor in their local areas through donations and alms. Monks divided their days between farm labor and prayer. As some monasteries became centers for learning and monks spent less time in the fields, the need for agricultural laborers increased. These monasteries often hired day laborers or housed peasants who agreed to live a semimonastic lifestyle without taking the formal vows.

Nuns also lived lives of prayer and work. Nunneries hired laborers or produced sewn or woven items. Some nuns served as nurses in aristocratic households or in monastic infirmaries. Many nunneries were endowed by the families of wealthy aristocratic women or by retired aristocratic widows who donated their own wealth to the nunnery. Most early monasteries and nunneries were constructed in close proximity, with the abbot as the joint head, but some abbesses wielded great power too; Saint Hilda governed the joint nunnery and monastery at Whitby (in northern England) in the seventh century. Because women could not be priests, some nunneries maintained a priest to officiate at the liturgical services. The priest, in these circumstances, came under the authority of the abbess (except in judicial matters concerning church law). The number of double houses (consisting of a monastery and a nunnery) headed by abbesses was greatly reduced in the twelfth century under the reform movement.

Education had traditionally been reserved for members of religious orders and the aristocracy. Many monasteries became centers for learning; in the Early Middle Ages they had been the preservers of Greco-Roman literature. Because of monastic education, many monks were advisors or administrators in the kings' bureaucracies. Nuns were also highly educated and contributed to manuscript copying and illumination. Some nunneries became famous for their expertise in illumination and calligraphy. Nuns were expected to read the scriptures, the works of early theologians, biographies of saints and founders of their order, and the rules of their order.

Feudalization of the Church

The Christian Church was not immune to the feudal development of Europe. Many church lands fell into the hands of kings and great lords, who then made bishops vassals and granted the church properties as fiefs. Many of these fiefs were cathedral towns, some of which were great centers of trade. Scholars call this process the **feudalization of the church**. Because bishops were lords, they held feudal rights within their own fiefs and executed justice in their own religious law courts. When kings had regained control over the judicial practices within their realms, these ecclesiastical courts retained their independence. Criminal clergy were not to be tried in the king's court because the clergy were under the authority of their religious superiors. Kings bristled at this independence, and they increasingly took over the appointing of bishops and abbots rather than allow a traditional local election. This allowed kings to regain jurisdiction over the church properties within their realms. Bishops often married and they fathered children, but these offspring did not have legal rights to inherit church lands. Therefore, on bishops' deaths the lands reverted to kings, who could keep tight control over the wealth. Many younger relatives of kings and great lords became bishops to ensure a close allegiance and to keep control and wealth in the family.

Monasteries also became feudalized under abbots who were also vassals. During the invasions of the Early Middle Ages, monastery lands gained protection from kings or powerful lords. Abbots soon were granted the monastery as a fief and became feudal lords, with the same feudal obligations as any knight: support, loyalty, and military service (which was filled by hiring mercenary knights). Every monastery was a self-sufficient enterprise, often bustling with activity. Most had large agricultural lands that were cultivated to support the monastery. Many monastic grounds became the sites for local or regional fairs for the exchange of goods and gossip, and some towns developed around monastic grounds. Because individual monks took vows of personal poverty, all the income of highly productive monastic lands went into the communal wealth of the monastery, making it a desirable fief. Many younger sons of aristocratic families were groomed to become abbots.

Reform Movements

By the mid–eleventh century, concerns over the abuses within monasticism and the feudalization of the church spurred reform movements. Reform was not a new phenomenon; particular reforms of liturgies and practices had been supported by early medieval popes. Apprehension over the buying and selling of ecclesiastical offices, the common practice of marriage among clergy, and feudal obligations by ecclesiastical officials led many lay people and clergy alike to support reforms to eliminate such activities.

In monasteries and nunneries, reformers called for withdrawal from worldly affairs and the return to the spiritual discipline of poverty, chastity, and obedience. Within monasticism, those who had chosen the spiritual life as adults often desired a more austere, devoted religious life than those who had matured within the walls of the monastery. Many aristocrats had placed young

children in monasteries and nunneries for education and religious training that someday might benefit the family. Aristocratic women often retired into nunneries after their husbands died—this was to escape having to remarry, and not for religious reasons. Laxity and, sometimes, outright antimonastic behaviors permeated many of the monasteries and nunneries. To accomplish monastic reform, several reformers turned to secular benefactors.

LAY REFORM. Lay reform included land grants to churches, monasteries, and nunneries that were free of feudal obligations and statutes against lax practices. As early as 909, Duke William of Aquitaine gave lands for a new monastery at Cluny, which led to the establishment of many monasteries free of feudal obligations. Other reform monasteries sprang up across Europe on donated marginal lands or in areas where devout laity supported reform. Reform ideas spread throughout medieval society at large. Pious individuals read devotional literature, helped erect magnificent cathedrals, and joined pilgrimages. Lay reform gave birth to an entire movement of lay piety, discussed in the following section.

MONASTIC REFORM. In addition to the Cluniac monks, the Cistercian and Carthusian monastic reformers focused on austere lives, limiting the comforts of the monasteries. In some cases, the austerity became so severe that monks and nuns died of poor diet and the cold. The reformers focused on a return to a life of devout prayer and tried to stem the corrupting tide of monastic wealth that caused laxity. Many great reform monasteries and nunneries, however, became communally wealthy as a result of their early austerity, because more people donated lands and wealth to them and the economic successes of their lands brought in revenues. Others refocused their attention from a devotion to prayer to a devotion to intellectualism and became known as great theological centers and libraries. There was a constant trend toward reform because of the countertrend toward permissiveness and disillusionment.

Toward the end of the Central Middle Ages, a new monasticlike movement created a different avenue for spiritual life. The Franciscans and Dominicans, for examples, lived communally but did not take the vows of the monastic orders.

FIGURE 13.11 *Saint Francis and Saint Dominic.* *This sculpture depicts an imaginary meeting of Saint Francis (left) and Saint Dominic (right). Saint Francis was famous for his work among the poor and sick, representing the embodiment of Christian charity and love. Saint Dominic was known for his intellect and his work among heretics, representing the embodiment of Christian faith and doctrine. Both figures had a profound effect on medieval Christianity as founders of major religious movements who participated in the reforms of the late medieval period.* Mansell Collection © Time Inc.

Instead of separating themselves from the world, they served it by caring for the sick and the destitute and by preaching against heresy. Franciscans were particularly associated with the ministries to the sick and the poor, Dominicans with education and preaching. Women's houses remained closely associated with men's. Saint Francis himself supervised the women's counterpart to the Franciscans—the Poor Clares, established by Saint Clare, a devoted follower of Francis.

PAPAL REFORM. Papal reform centered on the concept of ecclesiastical jurisdiction and the independence of church officials within kings' realms. The issue of independence was primarily played out in the confrontation of the pope with the Holy Roman Emperor and kings who tried to resist the reformation of feudal relationships within the church. Papal reformers established decrees that challenged the tradition of **investiture**, the proce-

dure whereby secular lords chose ecclesiastical successors and awarded them the symbols of holy office. The papal view held that secular lords should not control church lands through choosing friends or relatives as ecclesiastical officials, nor should they invest spiritual authority. The imperial and monarchical views held that the divine right of royal authority allowed for investiture. Because most bishops were feudal lords over vast church lands, the king wanted to retain control over them. At this time, from one-quarter to one-third of Europe's lands were church lands, and kings' loss of control over these territories would have had serious economic and political ramifications for the realms.

The issue came to a head during the Gregorian Reform, led by Pope Gregory VII (reign dates 1073–1085), and the imperial reign of Henry IV (reign dates 1056–1106). Each man insisted that he held authority over the other. Gregory excommunicated Henry and deposed him. Henry ignored Gregory's decrees to stop investiture and deposed Gregory. The issue of supremacy that had been introduced by the pope's crowning Charlemagne in 800 was fought out between the two men with no real resolution during their lives. Eventually (between 1107 and 1122), several compromises were reached between popes and monarchs. Bishops were elected and then invested by other bishops, but the king or emperor retained the right to veto any candidate up for election. In reality, the king's veto power permitted a series of choices until his candidate was chosen.

Tension between secular and religious authority continued to plague medieval culture. Many reforming bishops and popes tried to eliminate monarchical encroachment on church properties, church tithes, tax monies, and judicial responsibilities. As a result of the Gregorian Reform, the papacy entered into European political affairs as popes tried to gain control of church properties and religious functions within the kingdoms and regional boundaries of medieval Europe.

Popular Piety

Reform movements helped incite a widespread religious revivalism among medieval commoners that is usually termed popular piety. Popular piety reflected an atmosphere of devotion and emotionalism that led to a focus on spirituality. Pilgrimages became more common, interest in the healing powers of holy relics became widespread, and a faith in miraculous intervention became a bastion against the harsh realities of earthly life. None of these was new, but they became intensified.

Another result of popular piety was the change in attitude toward Jesus and Mary. Earlier representations primarily pictured Jesus as the second person of the Trinity, the divine Christ, judge of the world. In this atmosphere, there was more focus on the humanity of Jesus, the lover, comforter, and healer. The representations of Christ the king gave way to the suffering, bleeding Jesus with whom humanity could empathize. A focus on the Virgin Mary (mother of Jesus) also became popular, giving women a more positive image. As men saw themselves redeemed by Jesus from the sins of Adam, women gained a model in Mary that liberated them from the sins of Eve. Chastity became the idealized state for women, inspiring more women to become nuns. One legend circulated

FIGURE 13.12 *Fourteenth-Century Crucifix.*
During the Late Middle Ages in Europe, popular piety helped to spur emotionalism in the practice of Christianity. One result of the increased emotionalism was a tendency to portray Christ less as the king of heaven and more as a suffering servant. While earlier crucifixes tended to show Jesus in a triumphal pose with a golden crown, this fourteenth-century crucifix demonstrates the Passion of a suffering Jesus on the cross. People seemed to relate better to a god that could share the heartaches and travails of human life, and scenes of Jesus' life and death became more common in religious art. This is also the period during which artists designed works to commemorate the fourteen stages of Christ's Passion and death, later known as the stations of the cross. Like the suffering Jesus shown here, the stations were designed for devotional purposes, particularly for those who could not read devotional literature.
Bildarchiv Foto Marburg/Art Resource, N.Y.

ENCOUNTERS

The Crusades

The Crusades of medieval Europe were Christian holy wars against Muslims in the western and eastern Mediterranean and against heretics within the interior of Europe. Crusades were a product of pilgrimage mentality, personal greed, and feudal knighthood. Liberating early Christian holy lands in Southwest Asia from nonbelievers or Christian territory from heretics inspired crusaders—knights, peasants, and even children—to take up the cross and sword and go on a pilgrimage to save souls and lands for Christ. The promise of land and wealth inflamed many Europeans, from kings to lowly squires, to strike out on the long and arduous journeys toward hostilities that they believed would result in immeasurable rewards.

The initial endorsement by the pope to attack Muslims in Palestine was in response to pleas from the Byzantine emperor, whose territory Muslims had conquered, and from the general European population to control fighting between groups of knights. Trained for fighting, and in the absence of wars to occupy them, knights often broke the peace. Efforts to restrain them from pillaging and plundering Europe were unsuccessful, until the call from the Byzantine emperor in 1095 to aid against the Muslim invasions of Byzantine lands gave a focus for knightly energies. Pope Urban II seized the opportunity and preached in support of the first crusade.

There were many crusades, some successful in their outcome, most devastating to crusader and enemy alike. Some crusaders never reached their goal; thousands died along the way or finally dispersed. Several European kings—including Henry II and Richard I from England, Philip II from France, and Emperor Frederick I (who died on the way while taking a bath in a river)—set out on crusades. One crusade was sidetracked to Constantinople, where the crusaders became embroiled in local politics. Crusaders who arrived in Palestine fought bloody battles against Muslims that horrified even the combatants. In some cases, the Roman Christians could not distinguish Muslims from Jews or eastern Christians, and they tended to kill everyone indiscriminately. Crusader states were established and governed by European lords. Although continuously defended by knights, the area could not withstand reconquest by Muslim forces. By 1291, the crusader states were abandoned.

The crusades in Europe and in Southwest Asia had a significant economic impact. Towns and cities on the crusader routes enjoyed economic booms as crusaders and pilgrims traveled through. The crusaders returned home with stories of the various peoples they had encountered and with many relics and sacred art objects that soon adorned the cathedrals of Europe. There were enough pieces of the "true cross" of Jesus purchased to build an entire cathedral. The crusader states established travel routes that brought nonmilitary pilgrims from Europe. Pilgrims returning home introduced new foods, new ideas, and technology, all of which helped to stimulate exchange between the eastern and western Mediterranean.

The military orders of the Teutonic Knights, the Knights Templar, and the Hospitalers attacked heretics in Europe and non-Christians on the border of eastern Europe. In some areas, particularly in parts of Germany, the military orders received vast estates and became very wealthy, powerful forces challenging royal authority. Crusades against heretics were fought in a variety of ways—by military orders fulfilling their vows against heresy, by kings and aristocrats feeding their hunger for lands by confiscating territories, and by Dominicans acting as papal inquisitors.

that told of God's receiving complaints from the Devil because Mary's merciful tenderness was allowing too many of the damned into heaven. Intense personal piety and devotion also led to larger numbers of men and women entering the monastic life. The strength of these new devotees' faith was matched by the increasing frequency of mystical experiences.

Popular piety often veered from the formal theological introspection of the church hierarchy and intellectuals. The bishops were responsible for the spiritual care of all souls, the supervision and education of all priests, and the eradication of all heresies within the diocese. Because of their responsibilities these bishops tended to be less tolerant of new ideas than the Christian intellectuals. Many bishops, however, allowed lay preachers (not ordained) within their dioceses but closely scrutinized what was being preached. Lay preachers were encouraged to enter the church schools and to adhere to established church doctrine; some agreed, and some refused. The tension between official doctrinal belief and individual inspiration sparked many disagreements between the institutional church and the popular pietists.

Medieval popular piety sometimes led lay preachers to espouse ideas that had no basis in medieval science or theology. An example is the Cathar belief that Jesus did not have a real physical body or that the creator God of the Old Testament was evil for trapping souls in physical bodies. Many lay preachers attacked ecclesiastical abuses that they thought should have been reformed, while some bishops exposed major theological errors in popular preaching. Sometimes because of arrogance on the part of ecclesiastical officials and sometimes because of obstinacy on the part of lay preachers, disagreements became violent.

The rise in popularity of lay preachers led to a concern by church officials over the issue of religious dissent. Many tolerant bishops encouraged lay preachers' efforts to reach the poor and the displaced. When a question of competency arose, however, ecclesiastical officials usually performed an inquiry, or **inquisition**, into what was being taught or preached. These were usually minor investigations limited to local interests. By the 1230s, however, the papacy saw a need to establish consistency in questioning and punishment and formed the formal papal inquisitional system. Most medieval inquisitions resulted in dismissal of charges or a few years of imprisonment.

Papal Monarchy

The monarchical paradigm of centralization in the Central Middle Ages was used by the papacy as a model for its own organizational development. The closest thing to papal dominance was the period of papal authority from roughly the end of the twelfth century to the end of the thirteenth. Scholars refer to this development as the **papal monarchy** because the papacy had established a central administrative bureaucracy that rivaled those of kings. The papal chancery more than doubled its output almost yearly; thousands of letters passed from Rome to various cities within Europe. Taxes from church lands and donations increased papal wealth, which helped to support the growing papal bureaucracy and the papal missionary activities. The papal court was established as the last court of appeal for the courts of Europe, increasing

the number of visitors to the holy city of Rome. The pope had been elevated from a regional ruler and general spiritual advisor to a universal political authority competing with monarchs for the loyalty of Christian subjects. The height of papal power came during the reign of Innocent III (reign dates 1198–1216). Innocent III intruded on the election of a Holy Roman Emperor, challenged a French king's divorce, and forced King John of England to become a papal vassal.

Continued papal intervention in secular affairs after Innocent III gradually led to disillusionment with papal spiritual leadership. Popular piety and reform movements continued to examine practices of Christianity, which included the actions of the papacy. During the pontificate of Boniface VIII (reign dates 1293–1300), the English and French kings actively resisted papal interference in their affairs. Pope Boniface pressed papal claims farther than ever, but the more pressure he exerted, the more resistance he encountered. After a period of papal residence in Avignon, under the protective eye of the French crown, the papacy never again achieved the political influence of Innocent III's day. From the fourteenth century, the papacy gradually became a political puppet of rival factions in Italian politics. Increasingly, trust was placed in the hands of ecclesiastical councils and assemblies under strong monarchical influence. Christian governance was becoming regional.

New Theologies

The devastation of war and plagues in the Late Middle Ages led to religious questioning and sparked new intellectual speculation. The fourteenth century produced numerous mystics, both men and women, who argued that to know God one must turn away from natural philosophy and toward purely spiritual exercises. Theology continued to be systematized, and rational explanations of the universe increasingly gave way to theories of the incomprehensibility of God. The new theology of nominalism taught that any knowledge of the divine was so minute and limited that rational inquiry was ineffectual in its ability to fathom the universe. Intellectual speculation tended toward a separation between inquiry concerning the natural world and inquiry concerning the divine realm. This philosophical split foreshadowed the divergent paths of early modern science and theology.

EUROPE

Early Middle Ages, 500–1050

Northumbrian Renaissance, seventh century

Carolingian Renaissance, ninth century

Viking, Magyar, and Muslim invasions, ninth and tenth centuries

Central Middle Ages, 1050–1350

Twelfth-Century Renaissance

Black Death, 1361–1407

Hundred Years War, 1337–1453

Late Middle Ages, 1350–1450

600

Bede dies, 735

800   Charlemagne crowned Western Roman Emperor, 800

Cluny, reform monastery, founded, 909

1000

Pope Gregory VII issues decree against lay investiture, 1075

Hildegard of Bingen dies, 1179

1200   Eleanor of Aquitaine dies, 1204
King John of England signs Magna Carta, 1215

1400   Geoffrey Chaucer dies, 1400

SUMMARY

1. The Early Middle Ages was a synthesis of Greco-Roman, Germanic, and Christian societies. The Franks eventually conquered most of medieval Europe and established the Carolingian Empire, ruled by Charlemagne.

2. After the eighth-, ninth-, and tenth-century invasions by Muslims, Vikings, and Magyars, Europe developed regional kingdoms. As areas experienced further regionalization, feudalism and manorialism became more common. The entire medieval period saw the ebb and flow between localization under vassal authority and centralization under royal authority.

3. The people in the Central Middle Ages experienced commercial expansion and economic growth. During the Twelfth-Century Renaissance, literacy increased and intellectual speculation spurred new ideas. New styles of literature and architecture reflected economic growth as urban centers patronized the arts. National monarchies developed bureaucracies that challenged vassal localism.

4. In the Late Middle Ages, Europe experienced both destruction and innovation. Several kings gained greater control of their realms and expanded their territories. Those who survived plagues and wars often found greater economic opportunity. Recovery came with a reinvigorated European economy.

5. Rural life was centered on the manor. New technologies resulted in surplus production and occupational specialization, which in turn led to better health, longer life, and increased opportunities in rural and urban life. Towns took on self-governance through representative guilds.

6. Monasticism was a significant part of medieval European society; many monasteries were houses of learning. Religious and secular leaders led reform movements, and popular piety inspired religious revivalism but sometimes led to heresy. The papal monarchy emerged out of papal reform against investiture but could not sustain universal authority over the Christian society. Wars and plagues led to religious questioning and new theologies.

SUGGESTED READINGS

Epstein, Steven A. *Wage, Labor, and Guilds in Medieval Europe.* Chapel Hill: University of North Carolina Press, 1991. A fresh examination of labor and associated themes in the Middle Ages.

Hanawalt, Barbara A. *Growing Up in Medieval London.* Oxford, Eng.: Oxford University Press, 1993. A highly readable study of what childhood and parenting were like in medieval England.

Hollister, C. Warren. *Medieval Europe.* Seventh edition. New York: McGraw-Hill, 1994. A very informative and entertaining review of medieval Europe.

Russell, Jeffrey Burton. *A History of Medieval Christianity.* Arlington Heights, Ill.: Harlan Davidson, 1968. A standard history of medieval Christianity, with emphasis on the tension between established order and spiritual reform.

Shahar, Shulamith. *The Fourth Estate: A History of Women in the Middle Ages.* Translated by Chaya Galai. New York: Methuen, 1983; reprint, New York: Routledge, 1994. A study of the various roles of women in medieval Europe.

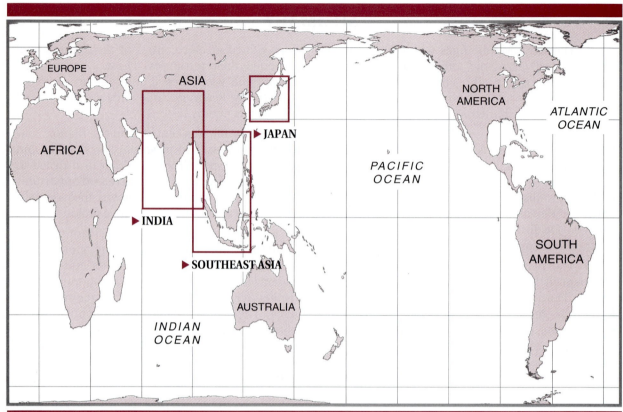

EUROPE

ASIA

▶ JAPAN

AFRICA

NORTH
AMERICA

ATLANTIC
OCEAN

PACIFIC
OCEAN

▶ INDIA

▶ SOUTHEAST ASIA

AUSTRALIA

SOUTH
AMERICA

INDIAN
OCEAN

INDIA

CHINA

Pagan

VIETNAM

PAGAN

Bay
of
Bengal

KHMER
EMPIRE

CHAMPA

Indrapura

Angkor

South
China
Sea

SRIVIJAYA

Palembang

INDIAN
OCEAN

MATARAM

Borobudur

▶ SOUTHEAST ASIA

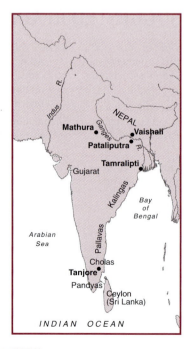

Indus R.

Mathura

Ganges

NEPAL

Vaishali

Pataliputra

R.

Tamralipti

Gujarat

Kalingas

Arabian
Sea

Pallavas

Bay
of
Bengal

Cholas

Tanjore

Pandyas

Ceylon
(Sri Lanka)

INDIAN OCEAN

▶ INDIA

Hokkaido

Sea
of
Japan

KOREA

Honshu

Kyoto

Kamakura

Nara

Ise Shrine

Shikoku

Kyushu

PACIFIC
OCEAN

▶ JAPAN

Regionalism in South, Southeast, and East Asia

around 180 B.C.– around A.D. 1450

The Japanese warrior grew nervous. To whom should he give his loyalty? Many of his friends supported the regional lord, Minamoto Yoritomo, but others supported leaders elsewhere. It was confusing to have so many different great warlords. The breakdown of imperial power had caused problems for simple folk like himself.

Regionalism was a common development in Asia, and regional governments frequently emerged with the decline or collapse of imperial governments. In Japan, an emerging feudal system demanded the allegiance and subordination of local warriors to a regional military lord.

In previous chapters pertaining to Asia, we focused on empires and the factors that led to their unification and decline. Here we will examine the appearance of regional states in southern, southeastern, and eastern Asia to probe elements that promoted regionalism and localism. Two additional themes, the spread of religion (Buddhism, Hinduism, and Islam) and the role of maritime trade in state building, will be explored.

REGIONALISM IN INDIA, AROUND 180 B.C.– AROUND A.D. 1100

Northern states dominated coverage of India in Chapters 5 and 10; in the period under consideration here, the south became politically significant. Not only did southern states raid northward, but they also controlled much of the maritime trade along the Indian coastline and fostered their own elite culture.

Northwestern India

After the collapse of the Maurya Empire, invaders from Central Asia and Persia created instability in the Indus region. Some conquered and ruled Gandhara, in a part of the Indus Valley where Buddhism had long been established. By the second century B.C., artists in Gandhara produced a new art style, most notably represented in sculpture. The Gandhara sculptures of Buddhas and Bodhisattvas displayed elements of Greek artistic realism that contrasted with the more "Indian" figures from Mathura, a major artistic center farther east. Greek influence came from descendants of Greeks who had settled in the Indus Valley in the fourth century B.C. Mathura works show Buddhas with non-Greek features dressed in *dhotis*, traditional Indian loincloths.

Invaders—like the Kushanas, a Central Asian people—fought to control a key trade route that snaked across northern India. The Kushanas settled in western India, where they adopted Indian names and practices of the warrior caste. The Kushanas forged a government that controlled some of northern India but were unable to extend their control to the south.

By the first century A.D., the Kushanas adopted Buddhism and patronized artists and artisans who continued to develop impressive sculptural and other art forms. The Kushanas also maintained close links to their Central Asian homeland. In the third century, the Kushana state suffered a fatal defeat at the hands of the invading Persians and disappeared.

From the fifth to the eighth centuries, other groups invaded India from the north and west. Tribes of Huns, peoples from Central Asia, invaded northwestern India in the fifth and sixth centuries, causing great political instability. Beginning in the eighth century, Arab fleets and armies also conquered parts of the Indus Valley. These events set in motion a long process of the introduction and slow spread of Islam throughout much of India in succeeding centuries.

The northwestern and western parts of India also experienced social change caused by invasions from Central Asia. As new invaders displaced

FIGURE 14.1 *Standing Buddha from Mathura.* *Mathura, in northern India, became a major center of Buddhist sculpture in the era of regionalism (around 180 B.C.–around A.D. 1450). This standing figure portrays the serenity of the Enlightened One, dressed in the traditional Indian robe. The circular array behind the figure represents the aura of light emanating from the Buddha, not unlike the halos around holy figures in Christian art.* National Museum, Delhi.

an existing government, they absorbed the ruling groups or pushed them south. Continual infusions of peoples enriched the regional societies, showing the continued social flexibility of the Indian caste system.

Northeastern India

After Gupta rule collapsed, the next major ruler, Harsha (reign dates 606–647), used the Ganges Valley as a base. Harsha conquered a vast territory and brought changes that perpetuated Indian regionalism.

Harsha never controlled the trade routes in the northwest and consequently ruled with fewer financial resources than the Guptas, who had controlled the Indus Valley. Instead of paying his officials with money, Harsha often gave them land. Like the Gupta emperors, Harsha was obliged annually to donate land or other forms of wealth to Hindu temples, according to customary practice.

Because these church lands were untaxed, they deprived the state of essential revenues.

At the same time, Harsha expanded the *samanta* **system,** the granting of semiautonomous rule to recently conquered territories and their rulers. The Guptas had permitted some local control, but Harsha could not afford a large central bureaucracy. Consequently, he maintained local political elites, providing that they swore loyalty to him.

Harsha's shift of his capital from Pataliputra to Kanauj, farther west in the Ganges Valley, had the unintended consequence of promoting regionalism in the long term. This move permitted the eventual growth of autonomous kingdoms in and around the Ganges Delta during times of political weakness of the central government. Successors to Harsha maintained Kanauj as the capital and permanently lost control of the east.

Although Harsha adhered to Buddhism, he tolerated Hinduism, including practices that he

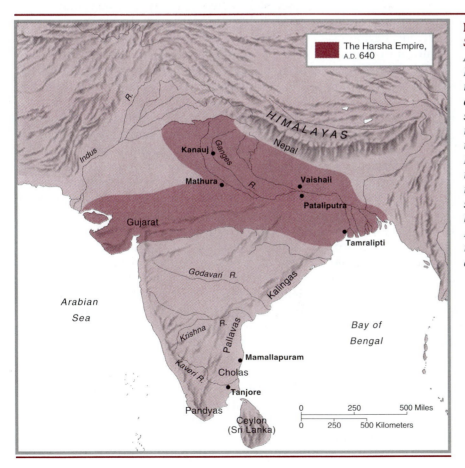

MAP 14.1 *Regional States in India around 640. Although much of northern India was united under the rule of Harsha, the rest of India was divided into regional states. For the remaining centuries until 1500, regionalism was the dominant theme in Indian history. The Pallavas, the Cholas, and the Pandyas ruled parts of the south in succeeding centuries, each being temporarily dominant. Intraregional trade continued to flourish despite political division.*

personally disliked. Harsha supported Buddhist priests and Buddhist art, and he also supported Hindu temples and their *brahmans*. The practice of **suttee**, the suicide of widows on the funeral pyres of their husbands, had appeared among members of the Hindu elite. When Harsha's widowed sister faced this ordeal, the monarch intervened to spare her a fiery death. He spoke against *suttee* but did not legislate against it, unwilling to antagonize powerful Hindu leaders.

Many features of Harsha's administration remind one of the system of Charlemagne in Europe. Neither ruler could afford large bureaucracies and so resorted to the expediency of permitting local rulers much autonomous control over their domains. Harsha and Charlemagne also granted land to subordinates in exchange for oaths and acts of loyalty. In addition, Harsha and Charlemagne aided religions by generous donations and other pious acts. Many of these actions eventually undermined the central government and led to regional rule in the decades after the deaths of Harsha and Charlemagne.

Muslim raiders and conquerors from Central Asia drove deep into northeastern India beginning in the eleventh century. By the thirteenth century, one group established the Delhi Sultanate in north-central India and used it as a base from which to expand southward.

Southern India

Southern Indians usually stopped invasions by northern states. Geography played a key role in that resistance, as mountain ranges blocked easy access inland and along the coast.

From the second century A.D., many states rose in the south and vied for political dominance. Three of these states, Pandya, Pallava, and Chola, developed long-lived polities, although at times one of these three dominated the others. Indeed, much of the time, decentralized rule followed feudal patterns similar to those in Zhou China and medieval Europe: Land was granted to subordinates in exchange for loyal service, and the manor or landed estate became a system for managing agriculture. One similarity with Europe but difference from Zhou China was the practice of donating tax-free land to religious institutions. In both Europe and India, these practices reduced state revenues.

People in southern India added a third kind of caste system to the other two caste structures, and all became fully established in the south. The latest division of castes in the south was based on geographical factors: the hill-people caste, the plains-people caste, the desert-people caste, the forest-people caste, and the coastal-people caste. Each of these five divisions comprised various occupational groupings, among them farmers, boat makers, and hunters.

Another feature in the south was the place of women in politics, elite culture, and the economy. Female rulers were not uncommon in the south, and succession occasionally passed from one woman to another. Princesses often received excellent educations, and some served as diplomatic emissaries. Elite women wrote poems; Vijavanka,[1] for example, was favorably compared to Kalidasa, the great poet and dramatist of the Gupta court. Women also worked alongside their husbands as artisans and merchants, although their individual contributions often went unrecognized. Some planted, weeded, and harvested grains in the paddy fields, too.

Arts and scholarship in southern India reflected a variety of factors, including patronage from monarchs, merchants, and devout believers. Many Hindu temples in the south had universities attached to them, and students not only learned Sanskrit grammar and Hindu philosophy, but they also studied law, medicine, and astronomy. Others wrote major poems, plays, and essays. Indeed, the corpus of writings in the many southern languages is vast. Tamil, an indigenous language unrelated to the Indo-European language family, developed into a major literary language of southern India.

Religious art, especially sculptures depicting Hindu deities, thrived in the south. Monarchs there sponsored exceptional pieces in the eleventh and twelfth centuries. One of the most famous sculptures is a bronze cast of Shiva dancing. This dance of life represents the dual nature of Shiva, the creator and destroyer, two necessary elements of universal existence. Hindus believe that destruction of the old is necessary before the creation of the new, which in turn must be destroyed to be created anew. The piece combines a dynamic sense of movement with delicate beauty and is a splendid example of southern art.

[1] **Vijavanka:** vee jah VAHN kah

FIGURE 14.2 *Shiva as Lord of the Dance.* *Produced in southern India during the eleventh century, this copper sculpture shows the major Hindu deity, Shiva, performing the dance of creation and destruction. In one hand he holds a drum, symbolizing sound, or creation, and in another he holds the fire that will destroy that which was created. Shiva dances within a circle of fire, reflecting the cyclical and never-ending nature of the processes of creation and destruction. The figure crushed beneath his foot is a demon representing ignorance.* Nataraja: Siva as King of Dance, South India, Chola period, 11th century. Bronze, H. 111.5 cm. © The Cleveland Museum of Art, 1996, Purchased from the J. H. Wade Fund, 1939. 331.

Temple building became a major form of religious devotion in the south, and many places boasted major temple complexes. In the eighth century, Pallava rulers and merchants patronized construction of numerous temples, and Pallava artists and architects set the pattern for temple building not only in southern India but also in Southeast Asia.

The affluence of the merchants testifies to the importance of trade among cities in southern India. India's maritime trade also grew through the entire first millennium A.D. Merchant guilds formed in the manner we have seen elsewhere and controlled their members' lives. Monarchs appreciated the significant revenues from trade that flowed into their coffers, and they undertook a variety of measures to promote trade.

The Chola government's growing dominance in the tenth and eleventh centuries reflected its participation in Indian Ocean trade. Two monarchs, Rajaraja I (reign dates 985–1014) and Rajendra I (reign dates 1014–1044), built the foundation of Chola power by taking control of trade routes, especially those along the two Indian coasts. In addition, Rajaraja I began a major raid on Sri Lanka, and Rajendra I completed its conquest. They also took control of the major islands off the eastern coast of India. In the eleventh century, maritime rivalries between the Indians and Malays of Southeast Asia led to a major naval campaign launched by the Chola state. The Indians devastated the Malay kingdom that controlled most of the shipping between India and China.

Despite the significant revenues emanating from trade, the bulk of Chola financial resources came from the land. The core area of Chola lay in the Kaveri River Valley, a fertile region whose complex hydraulic system built over the centuries provided two rice harvests each year. In the core area, relatively strong state control lay in the people,

PARALLELS AND DIVERGENCES

Economic and Political Uses of Temples

Asian temples and monasteries served economic and political functions, as well as religious ones. They provided ways to focus economic activities of people near where they resided. Some regional temples and monasteries acquired sufficient influence to play significant political roles.

Indian temples often became economic centers. In southern India, for example, temple complexes employed large numbers of artisans to craft and repair sculptures, bronze works, and murals. Hewn blocks of granite formed the temple base and superstructure. Peasants also worked the agricultural lands owned by the temples, and some temples used the services of temple prostitutes, who plied their trade for the complex's economic well-being, as well as for religious rites like symbolizing nature's fertility. Many religious centers amassed great sums of money and lent some out to devotees.

Chinese Buddhist monasteries also benefited from the largess of faithful followers. Some monasteries developed pawn shops, banks, and credit unions, and many Buddhist temples also became large landowners. Chinese governments tended to look less favorably upon successful monasteries and sometimes forced them to return their lands to tax rolls. Peasants who worked these estates were also forced back into taxpaying. Indian monarchs tended to see monasteries as opportunities for economic and political support, paying close attention to establishing influence over them.

Southern Indian and Javanese temples also served direct political and religious purposes. The massive temple complex at Tanjore, the Chola capital, was completed early in the tenth century, impressing visitors and subjects with the ruler's political might. Similarly, Borobudur (a symbolic replica of India's holy Mount Meru) in central Java encompasses nine terraced tiers in a vast area. The artistry suggests Javanese mastery of Indian sculptural techniques but may also indicate the presence and active employment of Indian artisans. Whatever the origins, the immediate effect upon an observer is one of awesome majesty.

Japanese monarchs well understood the political influence of Buddhist monasteries. One emperor in the eighth century remarked that he could not control the throw of the dice, a local river that regularly flooded, and the warrior monks of nearby temples. He later moved the capital from Nara to Heian to get away from politically powerful monasteries. Civil and military leaders later appreciated the political influence of large temple complexes and helped persecute religious leaders who threatened the positions of the established sects.

---

but, in regions more distant, the pattern seen in Harsha's realm appeared. Local autonomy was permitted in exchange for loyalty and regular revenues flowing to the capital.

Within the south, patterns of regionalism and localism emerged similar to those of Europe and Asia. Overall unity was never achieved in the south, because one state ruled in competition with other governments. As in Europe, Zhou China, or Japan, there existed a feudal-like practice wherein a subordinate person pledged support to a dominant person in exchange for land. Revenues from trade, especially maritime commerce, gave monarchs sufficient funds to induce local rulers to remain loyal. When monies from these sources dried up, central control usually broke down completely. Thus, Indian regionalism resembled its European and East Asian counterparts.

REGIONALISM IN SOUTHEAST ASIA, AROUND 600–AROUND 1450

Some peoples of Southeast Asian states, including Funanese and Vietnamese, have been considered in Chapter 10. Our focus here will be on the Malays, Burmese, and Thais, all of whom were strongly influenced by Indian culture.

Island and Peninsular Southeast Asia

From the sixth to the fifteenth centuries, except for the time when the Chola state controlled trade in the eastern Indian Ocean, Malays generally dominated the maritime trade that ran from India to

China. Their ships and crews handled the bulk of goods that came through the sea lanes between southern and eastern Asia. At the same time, rulers of Malay states developed complex ruling systems that united and integrated river-valley and plains economic systems. As with the Indians, central to the successful policies of the Malay monarchs was the use of revenues from maritime trade to strengthen their control over different economic regions and skillful adoption of ideas and terminology from Indian religions. The Indian word *maharaja* ("great ruler") carried political and religious significance for Malays. Buddhist priests and Hindu *brahmans* traveled the Southeast Asian sea lanes and spread their religions throughout southeastern and eastern Asia. Muslim merchants and

missionaries followed the same routes and converted Malays in later centuries. Malay peoples inhabited the coastal areas of the Malay Peninsula, as well as the islands of Indonesia. The mainland Malays did not develop independent states, but the islands of Sumatra and Java became the centers of two contrasting governmental systems. The former supported maritime-based governments, and in the latter many agriculture-based polities developed.

Much of Southeast Asia's early trade with India was handled by the Funanese people of mainland Southeast Asia. In the fifth century, members of the elite in southern China responded to the loss of access to the silk-road trade by sending trading missions to Southeast Asia. Malays jumped at the

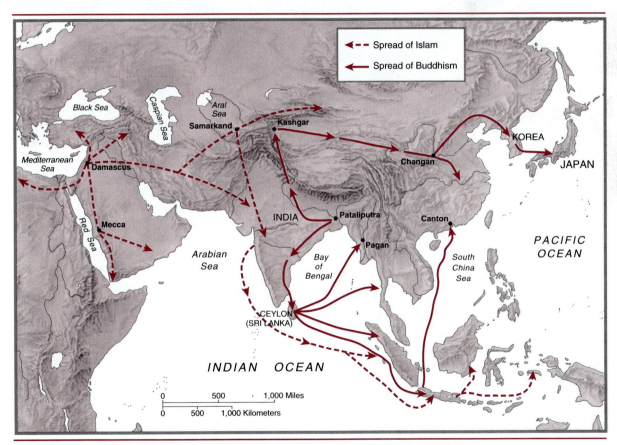

M A P 1 4 . 2 *The Spread of Islam and Buddhism, 200 B.C.–A.D. 1450.* *Islam and Buddhism followed similar land and maritime routes when they spread through Asia. Although conquest was important in the early spread of Islam, later conversions came largely through missionary activities, especially in Southeast Asia. Trade routes were crucial avenues for the transmission of both Islam and Buddhism. East Asia remained largely Buddhist, while other parts of Asia often became increasingly Islamic.*

FIGURE 14.3 **_Temple Complex at Borobudur._** *The architectural design of this immense Buddhist temple at Borobudur in Java reflects the steps on the path to nirvana. On the lower levels, relief and sculpture show the earthly life of desires, while the middle terraces portray the life and spiritual education of the Buddha. At the summit is an unfinished sculpture of Buddha, demonstrating the formless world of spiritual enlightenment. Thus, the temple symbolizes the Buddhist vision of the world, leading to knowledge beyond desire and form.*
Georg Gerster/Comstock.

opportunity, ignoring Funan as a way station to China and gradually dominating maritime trade with China.

In the seventh century, Srivijaya,[2] a state on the island of Sumatra, formed an empire with a strong commercial basis. A key element in Srivijaya's expansionist drive was the development of a port city and its use as a base for maritime trade. Upland products like timber were brought downriver and were sold or shipped overseas. Soon, Srivijaya extended its sway over peoples of other river valleys, first on the Sumatra coast and then on the Malay Peninsula.

Srivijaya monarchs borrowed from Indian culture, using Buddhism and Hinduism to legitimize their rule in Sumatra. For example, Srivijaya leaders adopted the title of *maharaja* and built temple complexes throughout their realms. In addition, both Buddhism and Hinduism were tolerant of indigenous religious cults and permitted the absorption of local deities into their pantheons.

Monarchs from Srivijaya also used maritime revenues to consolidate their rule over Malays on Sumatra and the Malay Peninsula. They lavishly endowed religious centers to gain and maintain support of the local people. Tax revenues, especially from maritime sources, were returned to the local temples in the form of annual religious dona-

[2]**Srivijaya:** shree vah JY yah

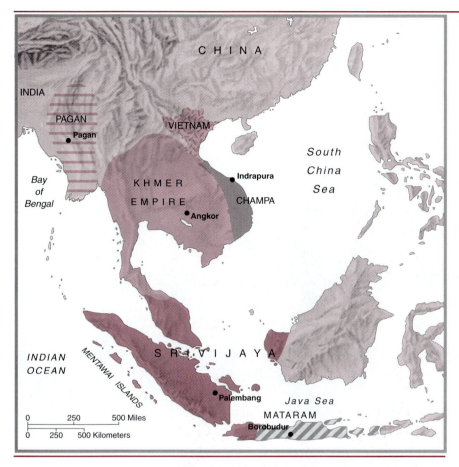

MAP 14.3 *Southeast Asian States around 1200.* *Many states flourished in twelfth- and thirteenth-century Southeast Asia, some prospering along the major trade routes between China and India. No one state or ruling group was able to unite either mainland or archipelago Southeast Asia. Buddhism was the dominant religion in this region until 1200, but thereafter gave way to the advance of Islam (spread by missionary and commercial efforts), especially on the islands.*

tions. The Srivijaya rulers also demanded that subordinates swear allegiance in exchange for continued rule of their domains, and failure to remain loyal brought military action and curses on the heads of recalcitrant leaders. A combination of fear and Srivijaya largess generally kept political harmony and stability.

Central Javanese kingdoms vied for influence and control of the agricultural lands. During the eighth century, the Sailendra[3] dynasty established itself in central Java and grew strong enough to build a massive temple complex at Borobudur, completed early in the ninth century. Borobudur displayed Buddhist artistic motifs, reflecting the power of Sailendra monarchs who admired Indian culture. About the same time as the completion of Borobudur, Sailendra monarchs negotiated a political alliance with the Srivijayans that linked the river valley and plains economies. The combined resources helped both semiautonomous

states and enhanced their maritime trade with China and India, which endured until the eleventh century, when the Cholas devastated the Srivijaya port cities and precipitated a two-century decline.

East Javanese kingdoms that rose and fell from the eighth to the fourteenth centuries formed and adopted Hindu- and Buddhist-inspired elite culture. By the fourteenth century, Muslims appeared in the waters of Indonesia and made inroads among the merchants, the courtiers, and the commoners. Islam had a growing impact on the Malays and spread through the Indonesian archipelago and into the southern Philippine Islands.

Other Southeast Asian States

A basic tension existed between peoples who lived in the hills and those who inhabited the river valley lowlands in many states of Southeast Asia. Lowlanders often came into a river valley and forced existing settlers out. Many refugees settled in the hills and mountains, where they eked out

[3] **Sailendra:** sy LEHN drah

FIGURE **14.4** *Ananda Temple at Pagan, Burma.* *Pagan became an important political and religious center in Burmese history. This temple, constructed in the eleventh century, captures the ornate splendor of Burmese Buddhism; it is still in use today.* Archaeological Survey of India.

livings by hunting and gathering. The Miao, Yao, Karens, Shan, and other hill peoples were thought of as savages by the sedentary lowlanders, who used force and discriminatory policies to maintain political dominance over them.

The Irrawaddy and Chao Praya river valleys supported agriculture-based local governments during the first millennium A.D. Historical records say little about these peoples, but it is known that they actively traded with Indian merchants and adopted Indian institutions.

Beginning in the ninth century, the Burmese peoples began moving from southern China into the Irrawaddy River Valley. Pagan,[4] a city in the middle of the Irrawaddy River Valley, became the capital, lending its name to a powerful Burmese state that unified most of the basin. The rulers of Pagan built thousands of Buddhist temples, many

of which still enchant visitors today. Some temple complexes became politically influential and successfully lobbied for favorable treatment from authorities.

In the tenth century, the Burmese rulers of Pagan began to develop an interest in maritime commerce because of the massive trade in the Bay of Bengal region and because the land route into China had been closed to them. A port city on the Irrawaddy River welcomed Indian, Malay, and a few Chinese ships and merchants beginning in the eleventh century. By the twelfth century, a major maritime trade center emerged and played a significant role in trade between Southeast Asians and Indians. After the collapse of the Pagan state in the thirteenth century, chaos reigned as other peoples moved south from China in the wake of the Mongol disruptions. Only in the sixteenth century did a new Burmese government control much of the former Pagan realm. One result of expansion

[4]**Pagan:** pah GAHN

of the new states from the sixteenth century was conflict with the Thais.

Like the Burmese, the Thai[5] people began moving south from China and took a different route that eventually left them in the lower reaches of the Chao Praya River. This migration, which began in the twelfth century, accelerated in the aftermath of the Mongol conquest of China's southwest. Soon, the Thais became the dominant group in the central lower river valley and established a capital at Ayuthia.[6] Eventually, many Thais converted to Theravada Buddhism. As the Ayuthia government grew powerful, it expanded Thai influence to the south and east. In the north and west, the Thais had to fend off attacks by the Burmese. Although the Burmese never established permanent control, they hastened the decline and collapse of the Ayuthia government.

Thai artists achieved great success in creating Buddhist statues, and the architecture of the Thai temples combined graceful sloping roofs with ornate temple decorations. These sculptures frequently had full-fleshed arms and legs that revealed curves of a sensual nature. A famous reclining Buddha at Ayuthia has long attracted both faithful Buddhist pilgrims and admiring travelers.

CHINESE REGIONALISM, 220–589

This section will focus on Chinese regionalism in a time of general political division, economic turmoil, and social conflict. Despite these unsettling conditions, writers and artists produced literature, literary criticism, calligraphy, and philosophy. Perhaps the political fragmentation and social upheaval allowed for a loosening of obligations imposed on individuals by governments, families, and clans.

Political Developments after the Third Century

When the Han Empire fell in 220, it was succeeded by three regional kingdoms, each of which was based in a self-contained economic area. The northern state, Wei,[7] united the Yellow River Valley and controlled a large sedentary population. The southeastern state, Wu, occupied much of the Lower Yangzi Valley, especially the agriculturally productive Yangzi Delta area. The southwestern kingdom, Shu, ruled the Upper Yangzi Valley. Although Wei managed to conquer and temporarily rule all three regions, it soon collapsed, and not until the late sixth century did a government reunite China.

The conquest and rule of northern China by non-Chinese peoples in the fourth century shocked many elite Chinese. How could the nomadic "barbarians" have wrested away the Yellow River Valley and the North China Plain? Some elite families remained in the north and accommodated themselves to the alien rulers, while others fled south of the Yangzi River.

The Huns, a branch of the Xiongnu[8] nomads, first overran Yellow River cities in the early fourth century. Non-Chinese peoples had often been encouraged to settle in the border areas, as long as they agreed to pay taxes, nominally follow Chinese practices, and help defend the frontier areas against nomadic raiders. Some Chinese abused their non-Chinese subjects and caused an uprising that weakened China's defenses and permitted the Huns to wrest control of the north from Chinese hands.

Various governments ruled north and south of the Yangzi River. In the north, for example, one Hun tribe conquered, ruled for one or two generations, and was then tossed out by another tribe. The loss of life in the often brutal campaigns was enormous. Economic activity was frequently disrupted as rulers either drove away the Chinese peasants or enslaved them. The Yangzi River Valley was colonized by refugees from the north. Local non-Chinese were chased away, absorbed, or exterminated by these peasant farmers, and agriculture, villages, towns, and temples were established. Soon a governmental administrative apparatus, including tax collectors, followed. The land was fertile, and the milder climate provided for a wider variety of crops and larger yields. Eventually, maritime trade between Chinese and Southeast Asians developed.

---

[5]**Thai:** ty
[6]**Ayuthia:** ay YOO thee yah

[7]**Wei:** way
[8]**Xiongnu:** sheeyahng nuh

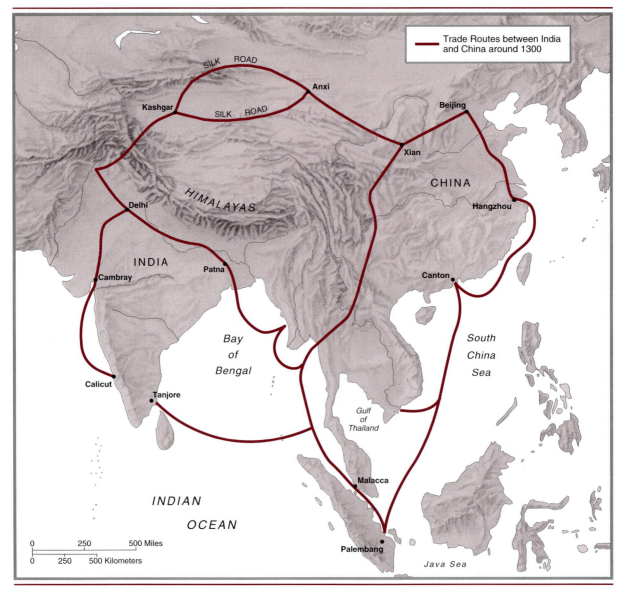

MAP 14.4 *Trade Routes between India and China around 1300.* *Following the Mongol conquest of much of East and Central Asia, support of commercial activity and the favoring of merchants by Mongol rulers stimulated trade across Eurasia. Bustling with trade venturers, both land and maritime routes were increasingly traveled during the period of regionalism, becoming even more crowded by 1300.*

Confucianism in the Regional Era

Confucianism, a system of ideas and practices that stressed family values, became more appreciated during the time of regionalism because it helped promote social stability. In northern China, after the conquests of the nomads, many extended families survived the vicissitudes of political turmoil because of their substantial social and economic resources. One key for social stability, as these families soon learned, was to inculcate Confucian values that stressed a tightly knit family structure. Social cohesion meant an increased chance of surviving alien governments that sometimes persecuted ethnic Chinese.

Confucian ideas benefited not only elite families but also certain regional rulers, who appreciated the sociopolitical aspects of Confucianism when carefully guided by the state. Time-tested Confucian values like filial piety, harmony, loyalty, and sincerity could be reinvigorated by a united local polity. Social stability could be strengthened because cohesive families tended to stay united no matter what political or economic pressures they faced. Regional monarchs appreciated a Confucian ideology that inspired attitudes of obedience in subjects and officials. Stable social conditions and loyal officials were results that appealed to all rulers.

Buddhism's Adaptation to Chinese Conditions

Buddhism arrived in China by land routes from Central Asia and by water routes from Southeast Asia from the first through the seventh centuries. It did not become popular, however, until the fall of the Han Dynasty in the third century. Buddhism gained influence through missionary activity and an accommodation effort by priests who wished to make it more appealing to the Chinese. For example, to overcome Chinese discomfort with Siddhartha Gautama (the Buddha), who abandoned his family to seek the meaning of life and suffering, new Buddhist scriptures emphasized that one could be a good Buddhist as well as a devoted husband, father, and son. These efforts were successful, and, by the early sixth century, it is estimated that China had about 30,000 temples and nearly 2 million monks and nuns. Buddhism was the religion of perhaps 90 percent of the northern Chinese. Many Chinese in the south also embraced Buddhism.

Some Buddhist monasteries possessed large land tracts and laborers to work them. These tax-free estates represented a liability to governments, which occasionally confiscated lands and forced religious people back onto the tax rolls. Of course, the interrelationship between religious activity and economic development was not peculiar to China. It may be seen also in Europe, India, and Southeast Asia.

Arts and Philosophy

The period of Chinese regionalism saw the continued development of the arts and philosophy. Chinese poetry became increasingly influenced by Buddhism, and poets often extolled the beauty of the natural landscape. Literary criticism first appeared, and long-lasting categories of literature were firmly established. The success of Buddhism provoked Daoists to imitate successful ways of the foreign religion.

FIGURE 14.5 *Education of Noblewomen.* *Attributed to Gu Kaizhi, a famous artist who lived in the fourth century, this painting is from a silk handscroll depicting the practice of teaching noblewomen proper etiquette. Additionally, many elite women were taught to read and write. The seal marks on the painting indicate its changing ownership over the centuries.* Courtesy of the Trustees of the British Museum.

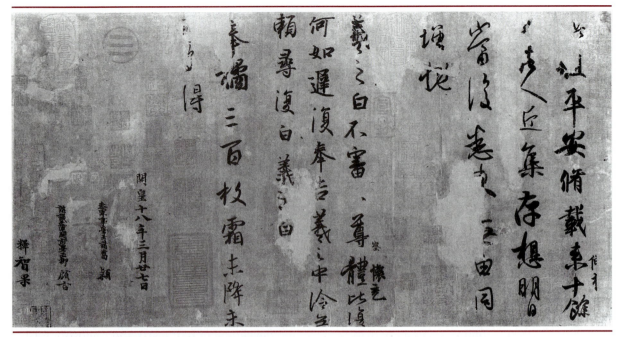

FIGURE 14.6   *Calligraphy of Wang Xizhi.* *Generally regarded as China's greatest callig-rapher, Wang Xizhi created this example of decorative writing sixteen centuries ago. Calligraphy, which Chinese scholars practiced as a mental and artistic exercise, was a means by which character could be judged.*   National Palace Museum, Taipei, Taiwan, Republic of China.

Literature is often regarded by Chinese schol-ars as the most important Chinese artistic form, and poetry is the most influential literary genre. The period under consideration is filled with important literary works, and one of the finest poets was Cao Zhi[9] (192–232), son of the founder of the Wei state. Cao Zhi was not in line to succeed to the throne, so he spent his days composing beau-tiful verse. Two significant poets, Tao Yuanming (365–427) and Xie Lingyun[10] (385–433), lived about midway through the era. Tao Yuanming was an official who became disgusted with bureaucratic life and returned home to live out his days as a gentleman farmer. Many of his poems celebrate the simple pleasures of rural life:

> I planted beans at the foot of the southern
>   mountain.
> Weeds flourished, but my bean shoots were few.
> I get up at dawn, work to clear away the tangle;
> Wrapped in moonlight, I shoulder my hoe
>   and come home.

> The path is narrow, grass and trees tall:
> The evening dew wets my clothes.
> Wet clothes—they're not worth the worry
> Just so my hopes aren't disappointed!

The line about shouldering his hoe and heading home is one of the most famous in Chinese litera-ture. Xie Lingyun's poems espoused Buddhist ideas and extolled the beauties of nature.

Literary criticism became well established with the appearance of the first treatise on the sub-ject, written by Liu Xie[11] (around 465–around 532). This work set forth categories and standards by which to judge literary pieces, and it examined the history and development of Chinese literature. Liu Xie's work is still regarded as a major reference of literary analysis.

Calligraphy received a powerful boost from Wang Xizhi[12] (321–379), who was considered China's greatest calligraphic master. Calligraphy meant various things to scholar-artists. Writing Chinese characters from memory helped focus the

[9] **Cao Zhi:** sow jur
[10] **Xie Lingyun:** sheeyeh lihng yoon

[11] **Liu Xie:** leeyoo sheeyeh
[12] **Wang Xizhi:** wahng shee jur

mind, and artists appreciated the close linkage between the sweep of one's cursive script and the lines of paintings. The Chinese also believed that one's handwriting revealed one's inner mind and character. Wang Xizhi's writing style became so highly prized that some of it was carved into stone.

Daoism's unfettered social philosophy attracted some adherents in the third and fourth centuries. These eccentrics protested the rigid forms of correct social behavior demanded by the Confucians, yet they also were escaping the dangerous times in which they survived by seeming to be foolish. One interesting group of third-century Daoist eccentrics was known as "The Seven Sages of the Bamboo Grove," a group of drinkers who enjoyed one another's company. One sage delighted in startling his houseguests by appearing in the nude. Another would roll his eyeballs until only the white parts showed, a favorite way to interrupt a boring conversation. Many of the "Sages" were competent poets and musicians who attracted attention for their entertaining verse.

Daoists competed with Buddhists, who successfully spread Buddhism in China. Daoist monasteries built in the era of regionalism were established to counter the influence of Buddhist monasteries. Daoist monks studied Daoist alchemy and philosophy. They also used their medical knowledge to cure people, at the same time proselytizing to their patients. Leaders of the two religions commenced a bitter rivalry that endured for centuries. In the sixth and seventh centuries, one attempt to bridge the chasm between Buddhism and Daoism resulted in the development of Zen Buddhism, a sect that combined Daoist and Buddhist elements.

JAPANESE REGIONALISM, AROUND 250–1333

Japanese leaders sought to create a powerful state, but they had to overcome strong economic and social factors that supported regionalism. Military conquest and the borrowing of Chinese political institutions helped create centralized rule. But court power struggles brought new families into the political arena, and the creation of private estates provided the economic basis for regionalism and feudalism.

Economic and Religious Factors

Although rudimentary agriculture had developed in the first millennium B.C., intensive agriculture came to Japan from mainland East Asia in the third century B.C. Paddy-field rice growing a few centuries later significantly increased grain yields. A village became the economic center for local peasants who lived there and farmed the surrounding paddy fields. Villages had walls to protect their inhabitants and to emphasize their separateness from other communities. Supporting this identity was the collective worship of a local deity, a ***kami***,[13] usually connected to fertility. Sometimes villages united into village networks for mutual protection. Over time, powerful clans gained control of village clusters and increased their influence. One such clan-village cluster and its *kami* were appropriated by the Yamato clan.

Before the sixth century, Shinto, Japan's indigenous religion, never developed an organized priesthood or a complex theology. Instead, it retained strong animistic elements, believing that natural objects were alive and worthy of veneration. Rocks as well as trees were thought to have life and should be appreciated. Shinto also possessed strong shamanistic traits because shamans—intermediaries who communicated with the spirit world—became essential to interpreting the will of the *kami*. In that sense, the head of the Yamato clan was also the head priest of Shinto.

The Yamato clan identified itself with the sun goddess, a potent deity among the Japanese people. The sun has figured prominently in the name "Japan" (place where the sun rises) and on many flags. Eventually, the myth developed that the Yamato emperor was a descendant of the sun goddess herself.

After the imperial system became relatively centralized in the seventh century, agricultural lands were taken over by the state. This public-land program began to be undermined in the succeeding century when private estates, ***shoen***,[14] were recognized by the central government. Over the course of time, more and more *shoen* were granted to individuals or to religious temples. By

[13] ***kami:*** kah mee
[14] ***shoen:*** shoh ehn

the twelfth century, *shoen* provided the economic support for several court factions. Military leaders, relying on the *shoen* system, declared independence from the imperial system and created a parallel political structure based on private estates.

The Imperial Age, around 250–858

We have already seen the early formation of the Japanese state by the Yamato family. Here our attention will center on the adoption of Chinese institutions to gain control of the rural population.

Although various Japanese monarchs conducted diplomatic relations with China in the early centuries of Yamato rule, the intensive period of borrowing from China came after 587, when Soga no Umako, head of the Soga clan, became the only court leader by ousting rival clans. Rather than assume power as the founder of a new dynasty, Umako manipulated the existing structure by placing pliant rulers on the throne. He also followed a common practice of marrying women of one's own clan to Yamato men in the hope that a male offspring of such a union would later ascend to the throne. This pattern was repeated many times in Japanese history.

IN THEIR OWN WORDS

Famine in the Japanese Feudal Age

Daily life in twelfth-century Japan was vividly portrayed by Kamo no Chomei in his work *An Account of My Hermitage*. Written in 1212, it presents the author's views and descriptions of everyday affairs in the imperial capital of Kyoto. The breakdown of imperial rule brought regionalism and severe economic problems. Long-distance trade collapsed during the fighting and resulting social chaos. This particular passage describes a famine of 1181 and 1182 and reflects Kamo's ardent Buddhist beliefs.

. . . there was a dreadful drought and famine that lasted for two years. Spring and summer brought drought, autumn was marked by typhoons and floods, one misfortune followed another so that none of the various types of grain ripened properly. . . . As a result, the people in the different provinces either abandoned their lands and migrated to other regions or left their homes and went to live in the mountains. . . .

It was customary for the capital to depend on the countryside for all its needs, and once supplies of provisions ceased to come in, the inhabitants found it impossible to live in their usual style. In desperation they brought out one after another of their various treasures, asking so little for them that they were all but throwing them away, but even then they could find no buyers. On the rare occasions when a transaction was arranged, gold counted for little, while grain was the prized item. Beggars lined the roadside, the sound of their pitiful cries dinning in one's ears.

So the first year came to an end, and it was expected that the new year would bring a return to normalcy. But instead epidemics broke out, adding to the suffering, and relief seemed nowhere in sight. People were now dying of hunger, and each day their plight worsened; they were like fish trapped in shallow water. . . . Beside the walls of the buildings and along the roads, the bodies of those who had starved to death were beyond count. Since nothing had been done to remove them, the stench soon filled the city, and the sight of them as they decayed was often too ghastly to look at. . . .

The woodcutters and other poor people by this time no longer had the strength to deliver firewood to the city, so persons with no other means of support broke up their own houses and peddled the wood in the markets. But as much wood as a man could carry did not bring enough to sustain life for a single day. Strangely enough, among the wood I saw bits of metal foil attached. When I investigated, I found that some people, lacking any other resort, were going to the old temples, stealing Buddhist images, ripping out the furnishings in the sacred halls, and breaking them up for firewood. Truly I was born into an age of defilement and evil to be witness to such heartless acts!

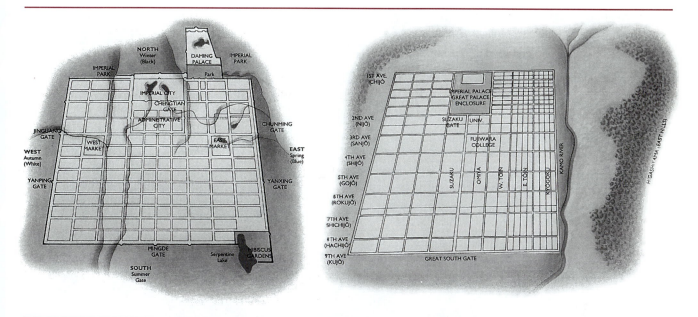

FIGURE 14.7 *The Japanese Capital at Kyoto.* *Like its predecessors, Kyoto, or Heian kyo (right), was built on the model of the Chinese capital, Changan (left). The imperial palace is located in the north-central part of the city, as the North Star is placed in the night sky. Streets are laid out on a grid pattern and run north-south and east-west.* From *Cradles of Civilization: China* (Norman: University of Oklahoma Press). Reproduced with permission.

Soga no Umako, Empress Suiko [15] (reign dates 593–627), and Prince Shotoku formed a ruling team that promoted borrowing institutions and ideas from the Chinese. One major development was the adoption of Buddhism as the religion not only of the Soga clan but also of the court. In the sixth century, Buddhism was introduced to the Japanese by a Korean monarch who desired a diplomatic and military alliance with the Japanese. By the eighth century, Buddhism became the state religion, and Buddhist temples were built in regional centers.

Although the Soga clan was ousted from power in 645, the borrowing from China continued. Many Japanese went to China on diplomatic and educational missions, and several students who stayed in China later became major reform leaders. The high point of Japanese borrowing came in the eighth century. During that time, the Japanese implemented a Chinese-style law code and established a bureaucracy. A replica of the Chinese imperial capital was built at Nara and another at Heian, [16] but the city was laid out on a smaller scale. The Japanese also wrote Chinese-style poetry and used Chinese characters to write their own language. Two histories of Japan, the *Kojiki* (*Record of Ancient Matters*) and *Nihon Shoki* (*History of Japan*), followed Chinese historiographical models.

Modification of Chinese institutions and practices also occurred. The Japanese, for example, added a religious bureau to the state because the monarchs were regarded as *kami* descended from the sun goddess. Japanese-style poetry was collected in an anthology, the *Collection of Myriad Poems*. It featured poems with Japanese themes by poets like Kakinomoto Hitomaro, one of Japan's great poets. An interesting feature of the *Collection of Myriad Poems* was the inclusion of anonymous poems, including many attributed to commoners. Because these people could not write, poets likely wrote down the oral compositions.

[15] **Suiko:** sooee koh

[16] **Heian:** hay yahn

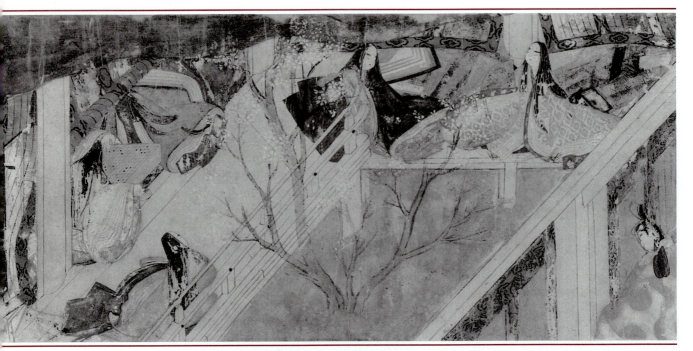

FIGURE 14.8   *Scene from* The Tale of Genji.   *The oldest complete novel written any-where in the world,* The Tale of Genji, *by the Japanese Lady Murasaki, is also considered to be one of the finest. Illustrations of the events of this famous book appeared soon after it was written in the first quarter of the eleventh century. This scene shows women playing* go, *a game of strategy based on an older Chinese game. Despite their cloistering by Japanese society, many aristocratic women acquired both cultural skills and education.*
The Tokugawa Art Museum, Nagoya.

The Aristocratic Age, 858–1160

The Fujiwara clan played a vital role in the development of the Japanese central government. After the mid–ninth century, members of that family garnered a succession of titles and power that created a family dictatorship. Marriage politics in the pattern of the Soga clan also played a crucial role in the ascendancy of the Fujiwara because certain of its female members married the Yamato emperors and princes. When the marriage system broke down, the Fujiwara could fall back on its domination of two regency posts. Along with a handful of other prominent aristocratic families, the Fujiwara dominated the imperial court.

At the same time that this sociopolitical process unfolded, an economic trend undermined the imperial system. The Fujiwara gained control of many *shoen* estates and isolated them from the imperial land-tax system. This process encouraged other families to create their own economic bases, especially in frontier areas.

Apart from the important aristocratic families that lived in the imperial capital, members of the social elite away from the capital dominated their respective areas. Like the gulf that separated the courtier aristocrats from the regional nobility, the provincial nobility lived far above the social level of the common folk. Noblewomen usually were much freer to own property. They were treated with respect because they might marry into a higher social level and thereby elevate a family's status.

In all cases, land served as the economic base undergirding social prominence. Estates provided revenues to the imperial government, to the local religious temple, and to the local socially elite families. Commonly, services were exchanged for access to revenues from land parcels.

Buddhism took new forms in the aristocratic era. The essential tendency was the spread of Buddhism to the common folk. Prior to the tenth century, Buddhism's complex message remained difficult to comprehend and generally inaccessible to ordinary Japanese, so a few priests began to emphasize faith rather than an esoteric knowledge of scriptures. Soon, Buddhist priests actively sought conversions in rural towns and villages, and singing and dancing often accompanied the proselytizing efforts of the more charismatic priests. At the same time, efforts were made to accommodate Shinto. *Kami* guarded Buddhist temples, and many Buddhas were interpreted as Shinto gods.

An indigenous Japanese literature matured in the Aristocratic Age. Writing Chinese-style poetry gradually declined, and native Japanese genres assumed more importance. Perhaps the most striking development was the Japanese novel, which reached a high degree of sophistication in the hands of Murasaki Shikibu (around 978–around 1015), an aristocratic woman who came from a minor branch of the Fujiwara family. Lady Murasaki wrote *The Tale of Genji*, a work that many scholars believe is Japan's greatest novel.

The Tale of Genji concerns the life and loves of a fictional imperial prince, Genji. At another level, it is the account of the imperial court: its values, its social life, and its varied activities. It reflects court patronage of the arts. The novel also contains hundreds of poems and quotations from Chinese and Japanese history; many additional poems are original. All of this suggests the vast learning and creative power of Lady Murasaki, who was a member of the court and the daughter of a midlevel Japanese official.

Architecture also reached a high level of development. One wooden structure, the Byodo-in (Phoenix Hall), still stands as a testament to the impressive building expertise of its architects. Built in the tenth century, the Byodo-in, which housed a sculpture of the Buddha, was constructed in graceful lines and accompanied by a reflecting pond.

The Development of Feudalism, 1160–1333

The breakdown of the central government accelerated with the rise and dominance of the military families. Indeed, the appearance of a new system of local power based on mutual and reciprocal allegiances led to the establishment of Japanese feudalism. The prevailing governmental structure was the **shogunate**, a military overlordship

headed by a *shogun*; it ruled in tandem with the Japanese monarchy, in an uneasy relationship.

The second half of the twelfth century in Japan was dominated by the power struggle between two military families, the Minamoto and the Taira.[17] Both had been established in provinces far away from the imperial capital, and court factions used the two families to provide military muscle. By the mid–twelfth century, however, power had shifted from the aristocratic families to the military houses. Between 1156 and 1185, the Taira and Minamoto vied for political supremacy, and the Taira initially prevailed. Each warrior house not only relied on branch houses whose members were blood kin, but they also used coalitions of other warrior families to increase their own strength. The warrior, a professional fighter, lived and died by the sword. A more familiar name for the warrior was **samurai**, meaning "the one who serves."

The Taira family preferred to work within the imperial system and, like the Soga and Fujiwara, married its women to the Yamato men. Taira revenues centered on *shoen* estates and maritime trade. By 1180, a Taira infant was placed on the throne, even though he was clearly a figurehead ruler. A disaffected imperial prince called on Minamoto warriors to fight the Taira, and the five-year Gempei War (1180–1185) commenced. By the end of the conflict, the Taira family had been destroyed, and Minamoto Yoritomo (1147–1199), head of the Minamoto family, had established a separate governmental system that became known as the Kamakura Shogunate.

Minamoto Yoritomo was one of Japan's most significant political figures because he did not choose to work within the imperial structure but opted to establish a separate government that handled the affairs of the military class. Because Yoritomo lacked the experienced personnel to govern all of Japan, he agreed to maintain the imperial system. To the warriors who offered him allegiance, Yoritomo gave land taken from the Taira and their allies. The land-based manor system underlay the interlocking web of personal relationships of warrior chiefs and their vassals. Unlike in the European and Chinese feudal systems, but similar to southern Indian feudalism, Japanese peasants were not tied to the land in serfdom.

[17] **Taira:** ty rah

Figure 14.9 *Minamoto Yoritomo.* *The founder of Japan's first shogunate, Minamoto Yoritomo is shown wearing formal court robes and not his military attire. Rather than directly involving himself in the affairs of the imperial court, Yoritomo created a separate administrative structure to handle warrior affairs, a policy that helped usher in the feudal age of Japanese history.* Tokyo National Museum.

Once established, the shogunal government weathered a series of crises, including the deaths of Yoritomo and his sons. Power passed to the Hojo family, a house of loyal retainers tied by marriage to the Minamoto. By early in the thirteenth century, Hojo regents ruled the shogunate in place of the Minamoto family. Perhaps the most able Hojo regent was Hojo Yasutoki (reign dates 1224–1242). Yasutoki brought a vigorous personal style to the post, and he forged an alliance with able subordinates to provide an effective administrative team. Consensus politics became a major part of Japan's political culture in the Hojo regency and remains important even today. Among Yasutoki's accomplishments was the supervision of the publication in 1232 of the *Joei*[18] *Law Code*, a set of guidelines and precedents for handling legal disputes. This document became the handbook for generations of judiciary members who staffed one of the most sophisticated trial systems in the world. The *Joei Law Code* was used in Japan as late as the nineteenth century.

Hojo regents provided effective government and justice for the Japanese people. In times of famine, for example, government rice stores were made available to the suffering people, and taxes were reduced or canceled for the most severely effected areas. One regent ardently followed Zen Buddhism.

Two Mongol invasion attempts helped undermine Hojo rule. As a result of two typhoons and fierce local resistance, both campaigns failed, and Japan was spared the onus of Mongol rule. Yet the *samurai* demanded rewards in land and money that the Hojo leaders could not deliver. Afterward, the government declined, falling in a time of social chaos in the fourteenth century.

Two major Buddhist sects, Zen and Nichiren,[19] became influential in the first phase of shogunal rule. Zen stresses strict discipline in the training of its adherents, and it places great emphasis on meditation. Nichiren Buddhism was named for its founder, Nichiren (1222–1282), who believed that Japan would become the center of "true" Bud-

[18] *Joei:* joh ay

[19] **Nichiren:** nee chee rehn

dhism, namely his own sect. Both Zen and Nichiren Buddhism appealed to some *samurai*, and each has remained important in Japanese life.

Zen had developed in China and had appeared in Japan prior to the twelfth century but had failed to take hold. In the 1100s, Japanese priests went to China and brought back their own interpretations of the Zen message. In the thirteenth century, some Hojo regents sponsored the building of a Zen center in Kamakura, the shogunal capital. With this patronage, Zen spread among the warriors, who valued its emphasis on discipline in a natural environment. Zen offered a way of coping with the horrors of battle and death, which were common occurrences in a *samurai*'s daily life. Along with Zen teachings and practices from China came tea, to which the Japanese became devoted.

Nichiren Buddhism argued that Buddhism had reached its highest form in Japan and asserted that the *Lotus Sutra*, a major Buddhist work, was its true text. Sincerely reciting the name of the *Lotus Sutra*, in fact, was said to grant the reciter a chance at salvation. Nichiren quarreled with other religious leaders and certain officials, resulting in his suffering persecution that helped increase his following. The Nichiren sect cultivated the warriors, many of whom liked its message.

Literature flourished in the early feudal age. Prose essays developed under the discipline of stylistic masters like Kamo no Chomei, who in 1212 wrote the much-admired *An Account of My Hermitage*. Women like Lady Nijo wrote memoirs, a major genre of the Warrior Age. She was a member of the aristocracy and was the concubine of a reigning monarch. Her *Confessions of Lady Nijo* was prized as an important social document.

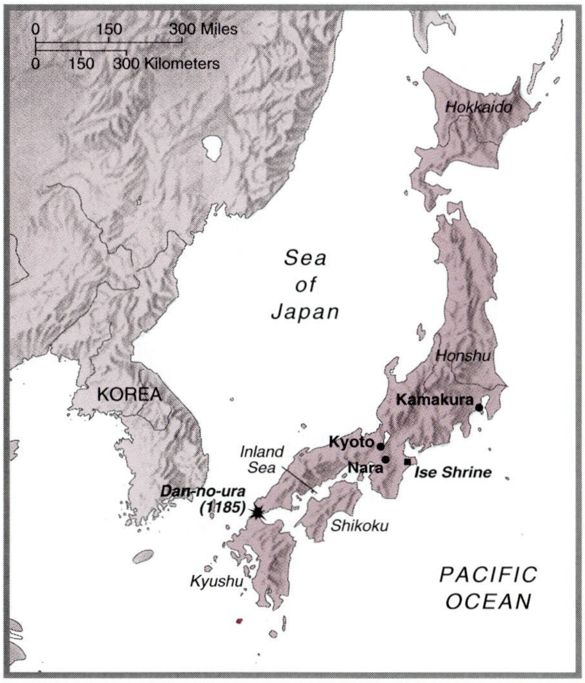

MAP 14.5 *Japan around 1200.* *The island of Honshu was where most significant political activity took place in the historical era. Nara was the capital for much of the eighth century; Kyoto was the capital until the late twelfth century. The Ise Shrine, dedicated to the sun goddess Amaterasu, is situated fifty miles east of Nara. After 1180, Kamakura became the capital of the warrior government set up by Minamoto Yoritomo. The Minamotos' political dominance was ensured by 1185.*

FIGURE 14.10 *Japanese Teapot.* *During the feudal age, the Japanese developed the tea ceremony, a formal ritual activity. It usually involved very simple but precise action, suggesting harmony and serenity in a time of political uncertainty. When* samurai *entered a tea house, they were obliged to leave their swords outside. The implements of the tea ceremony often were modest, but this seventeenth-century teapot is made of gold.* The Tokugawa Art Museum, Nagoya.

ENCOUNTERS
The Tea Ceremony

Tea is one of the most widely consumed beverages in the world, having been adopted by most societies around the globe. No one knows exactly where or when the tea plant was domesticated, although it clearly was somewhere in the area near the Southwest Chinese border. The first written record of tea comes from about A.D. 350, and it became a major tribute item four centuries later in the Chinese Empire. Tea came to Japan in 729 as a gift to Emperor Shomu, probably from the Chinese court. It spread to Southwest Asia through the Mongols, who had in turn adopted its use from the Chinese. The British became aware of tea through their contacts in China, and the drinking of tea in England and Europe began in the seventeenth century. Indeed, early English colonists in Massachusetts emigrated from England before tea drinking had become common there, and, when tea was introduced to Massachusetts, some were unfamiliar with how to prepare it and tried eating the leaves on bread. Tea was introduced to India by the English in the eighteenth century.

At various times, tea has been prepared in myriad ways. In addition to simply boiling or steeping the leaves, it has been flavored with substances like sugar, milk, salt, ginger, flowers, citrus peel, flour, butter, and fruit juices. The most common way of preparing tea in China and Japan, the areas with the longest tradition of tea drinking, however, is simply to brew it with hot water.

The first tea tax in China was imposed by the ruler in 780, but tea had not yet attained its eventual status of cultural symbol. To help elevate it, tea merchants later hired a poet, Lu Yu (1125–1210), to write a book popularizing it. His *Classic of Tea* made a point appreciated by Buddhist, Daoist, and Confucian alike: The simplicity and beauty of a well-ordered tea ceremony reflected the harmony and flow that ideally ordered the universe. Lu Yu's work presented essays on the pleasures and benefits of tea drinking, the proper method of preparation, the twenty-four utensils whose use he advocated, and practices for the formal presentation of tea.

From that time, the spread of tea has been accompanied by some version of the tea ceremony. The Mongols adopted elements of the ceremony and passed them to the Arabs and others to the west; the English adapted their version from that of China. Almost everywhere that tea is drunk, rules of etiquette order its consumption.

But nowhere else has such a formalized tea ceremony developed as in Japan. The tea practices that arose in the thirteenth century later grew into a showy and elaborate ceremony. The rise of Zen Buddhism and its philosophy of simplicity, however, made these ostentatious practices less appealing, and a major revision of the tea ceremony took place in 1588. Sen no Rikyu, an expert on the tea ceremony, reduced the ceremonial clutter to seven rules. He redesigned the physical setting of tea drinking, advocating a small tearoom and use of the simplest—but most elegant—of implements. The tenor of the tea ceremony was to be one of contrived tranquility. The modern Japanese tea ceremony continues this tradition.

The versions of tea drinking in China, Japan, and elsewhere, however, were adopted only by the elite or by those who aspired to that status. Less well-to-do folk typically consumed their tea with little or no ceremony, and much tea was drunk in commercial teahouses that were gathering places particularly for men. There they ate light foods, drank tea, relaxed, and chatted; the teahouses served much the same social function as the British pub or the American bar. Women were more likely to congregate at home, eating snacks, drinking tea, relaxing, and talking. In these informal, nonelite settings, the philosophical symbolism of the tea ceremony was largely absent, and the rules of etiquette—so much as they were known—were relaxed or ignored to maximize the pleasure of the event.

Japan experienced long eras of political division, not a few of which also saw chaos erupting from battles and campaigns of great ferocity. Yet these times of weak rule also witnessed the continuance of cultural forms produced by elite persons.

Women played even more active roles in the production of literature from these ages. A variety of Buddhist sects also appeared, and some appealed directly to the common folk. Buddhism's popular appeal helped keep it vibrant.

INDIA	SOUTHEAST ASIA	JAPAN	CHINA		
Indian regionalism, c. 180 B.C.– c. A.D. 320				200 B.C.	Fall of Maurya Empire, c. 180 B.C.
				A.D. 1	Buddhism in China, A.D. 57
			Chinese regionalism, 220–589	200	
					Chandra Gupta founds Gupta Empire, 320
		Imperial Age, c. 450– c. 850		400	
					Buddhism in Japan, c. 550
Harsha's rule, 606–647	Srivijaya-Sailendra Era, c. 650– c. 1100			600	Harsha begins conquest of North India, c. 606
	Burmese settle in Irrawaddy River Valley (Pagan Era), c. 800– c. 1350	Aristocratic Age, c. 850– c. 1160		800	Building of Borobudur temple in Java, ninth century
					Rajaraja I ascends to throne in Chola, 985
Chola state (south), c. 1000– c. 1300				1000	Indian fleet destroys Srivijayan navy, 1025
		Develop-ment of feudalism, after 1180		1200	Minamoto Yoritomo becomes *shogun*, 1192
					Nichiren founds new Buddhist sect, c. 1250
				1400	

SOME CAUSES AND CONSEQUENCES OF REGIONALISM

Regional tendencies frequently asserted themselves in Asia. Economic factors, like changes in trade and land management, played significant roles in the downfall of centralized polities. On occasion, feudalism resulted from the breakdown of political unity and the assertion of local interests. Despite the disappearance of centralized governments, most forms of art continued to flourish because of patronage from nonmonarchical elements, like merchants and temple priests. In addition, the weakening of the social fabric sometimes promoted social experimentation and an appreciation for ideologies that engendered social stability.

Economic developments strongly contributed to the collapse of imperial governments in Asia. Trade, especially long-distance trade, became inextricably linked to the fate of some states. The regime of Harsha aspired to duplicate the grandeur of his Gupta predecessors, but unlike them Harsha never controlled the trade routes running through the Indus River Valley. Similarly, loss of the silk-road trade contributed to the decline of the Han Empire, helping to foster regionalism in China. Maritime trade revenues increased dramatically after the sixth century and provided southern Indian and Southeast Asian monarchs with monies to purchase local rulers'

loyalties. Conversely, when these funds dwindled, control outside the core areas weakened.

Land management assumed a large role during these times. The development of private estates became the first step toward regional rule, because landlords usually succeeded in reducing or eliminating tax liabilities associated with their lands. Harsha gave land to officials and to temples, thereby accelerating regionalism. Temples owned large tax-exempt estates throughout Asia and deprived the state of important tax revenues.

Feudalism appeared in Japan during the time of regionalism. Not only did feudalism result from the breakdown of central authority, but it also emerged from the development of private estates. The decline of a dynasty sometimes resulted in the weakening of central control. At the same time, local control of private-estate revenues enhanced regional power groups. Monarchs who aspired to retain some form of unity used money and loyalty oaths to win support from lower levels. Minamoto Yoritomo insisted that subordinates faithfully serve their military leaders. Again, fear of a strong ruler and interest in rewards facilitated these feudal relationships.

Social controls enforced by states, clans, and families may be undermined or broken during the social upheaval accompanying an empire's collapse. During these eras, social experimentation, like that of the Seven Sages, sometimes occurs. The absence of normal social controls may lead to the development of new forms of literature or to the embracing of foreign religions, like Buddhism or Hinduism.

SUMMARY

1. When the Maurya Empire of India fell around 180 B.C., local and regional rule began in India. In the northwest, many states were founded by invaders who promoted Buddhism. In the northeast, Harsha became a major ruler in the seventh century. He promulgated policies that weakened his government and encouraged regionalism.

2. Southern India saw the rise and fall of many states, some of which depended heavily on agriculture and some of which based themselves more on trade, especially maritime commerce. Monarchs and merchants supported artists who pro-

duced spectacular sculptures and massive temple complexes. Hinduism became progressively more common there in the eighth and ninth centuries.

3. The Malay people often controlled the ocean waterways of Southeast Asia. On Sumatra and Java, societies based largely on maritime trade, Buddhist motifs became popular and are seen in the massive temple complex of Borobudur.

4. On the Southeast Asian mainland, the Burmese and Thai peoples migrated along major river valleys and displaced earlier peoples, some of

whom were forced into the mountains. The Burmese, like the Thais, adopted Theravada Buddhism. Both the Burmese and the Thais built governments that promoted Buddhist ideas and warred against each other. Temple-building projects took place in both areas and saw the development of distinctive Burmese and Thai artistic styles.

5. Chinese calligraphy, literary criticism, and poetry continued to develop in the era of Chinese regionalism.

6. The uncertain Chinese political climate from the third through the sixth centuries highlighted the importance of family networks to stand against or bend with difficult governments. Confucian ideas that supported a strong family system continued to be favored among the Chinese social elite.

7. Japanese villages became key economic units with the development of paddy-field agriculture in the third century. Clan networks gained control of the villages and increased their political influence. In the seventh and eighth centuries, Yamato monarchs implemented a modified Chinese imperial system that turned private land holdings into imperial lands.

8. The Japanese aristocratic and feudal eras saw the appearance of private estates that supported hierarchical allegiances and responsibilities. Thus, Japanese feudalism's rise came from the collapse of imperial rule. Minamoto Yoritomo played a key role in building feudalism.

9. Buddhism became accessible to the Japanese commoners with a stress on faith in the Buddhist message. In the feudal age, Zen and Nichiren Buddhism reached out to the warriors.

SUGGESTED READINGS

Devahuti, D. *Harsha*. Oxford, Eng.: Clarendon Press, 1970. A classic biography of a major figure in Indian history.

Needham, Joseph. *Science and Civilization in China*. Vol. I. Cambridge, Eng.: Cambridge University Press, 1954–84. A multivolume history of Chinese science and elite culture.

Tarling, Nicholas, ed. *The Cambridge History of Southeast Asia*. Vol. I. Cambridge, Eng.: Cambridge University Press, 1993. A collection of essays about early Southeast Asia.

Thakur, V. K. *The Historiography of Indian Feudalism*. New Delhi: Commonwealth Press, 1989. An examination of prominent theories about the development of Indian feudalism.

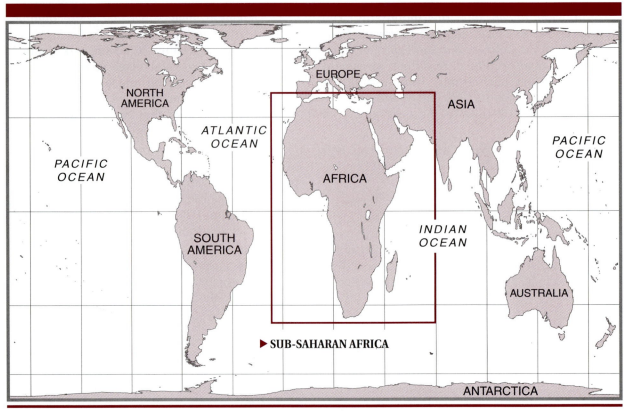

NORTH
AMERICA

EUROPE

ASIA

ATLANTIC
OCEAN

PACIFIC
OCEAN

PACIFIC
OCEAN

AFRICA

INDIAN
OCEAN

SOUTH
AMERICA

AUSTRALIA

▶ SUB-SAHARAN AFRICA

ANTARCTICA

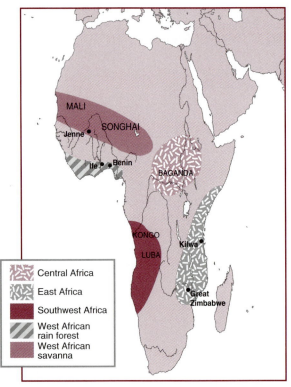

MALI

SONGHAI

Jenne

Ife   Benin

BAGANDA

KONGO

Kilwa

LUBA

Great
Zimbabwe

Central Africa

East Africa

Southwest Africa

West African
rain forest

West African
savanna

▶ SUB-SAHARAN AFRICA

CHAPTER **15**

Regional Kingdoms of Sub-Saharan Africa

around 200–around 1600

On his head he wears gold-embroidered caps covered with turbans of finest cotton. He gives audience to the people for the redressing of grievances in a hut, around which are placed ten horses bedecked with gold caparisons. Behind him stand ten slaves carrying shields and swords mounted with gold....

A Moorish scholar from Spain wrote these words to describe the majesty of the king of Ghana, a West African state, in 1067. Most of Africa south of the Sahara Desert was ruled by similar kings by this date.

One of Africa's historically most significant features is the Sahara, the largest desert in the world and one of the driest. Prior to 10,000 years ago, the Sahara was much wetter, and paintings on rock faces show that people, hippopotami, and other animals that need considerable amounts of water thrived there. Subsequently, however, the region has dried progressively, forcing out large-scale human habitation and forming a barrier that by 5000 B.C. stretched across the continent, separating North Africa and its Southwest Asian and European neighbors from the remainder of Africa.

The area south of the Sahara, known collectively as **sub-Saharan Africa**, had a wealth of indigenous states whose development often was stimulated by trade. These states varied greatly in size, with the smallest kingdoms having only a few thousand citizens and the largest having populations over one million. Regional states were the general rule, but a few empires developed and

371

were successful for a time. Largely cut off from the rest of the world, these states developed a distinctive African stamp.

Nestled among the sub-Saharan states, often in lands less suitable to successful agriculture, were a variety of band-, tribe-, and chiefdom-level societies. These societies typically interacted with the states, particularly through trade, but they were basically autonomous.

None of the sub-Saharan states or other societies developed writing, so documentary evidence is limited largely to their later history, particularly after the development of large-scale commerce with Arab and North African Muslims around 700. Archaeology can offer some assistance in reconstructing the earlier periods, but archaeological research in sub-Saharan Africa is made difficult by poor preservation of remains and too few archaeologists studying such a vast area. Thus, little is

known archaeologically about many regions, and no region is known so well as comparable areas of the other inhabited continents. This means that our knowledge of detailed events and processes in many areas is frustratingly incomplete.

SETTING THE STAGE FOR SUB-SAHARAN AFRICAN CIVILIZATION

Most of human evolution took place in Africa, as discussed in Chapter 2. By 30,000 B.C., Africans had spread to most of the corners of the continent. The reason for that spread lay largely in the success of their adaptation: Success led to larger populations, which in turn led to the search for new lands to support the overflow.

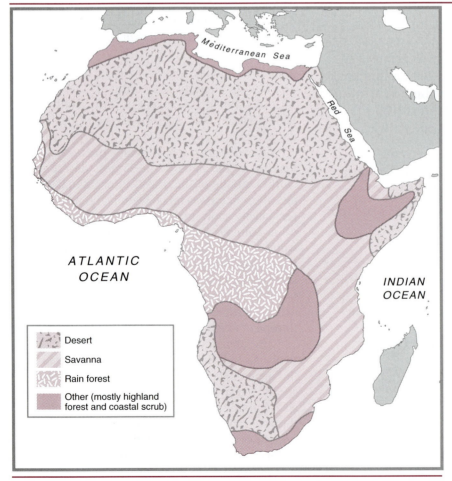

MAP 15.1 *Environmental Zones of Africa.* *Most of Africa is desert or savanna. Oases, coasts, and river valleys in the arid lands are moister than other areas. Trade between environmental zones was an important factor in African state formation.*

Legend:
- Desert
- Savanna
- Rain forest
- Other (mostly highland forest and coastal scrub)

Mediterranean Sea

Red Sea

ATLANTIC OCEAN

INDIAN OCEAN

UNDER THE LENS

The Banana Staple

Bananas were domesticated in India and came to Africa with the inventory of Asian crops that arrived around A.D. 200. Several types appear to have arrived at about the same time, including both sweet bananas and their starchier cousins, plantains. Most peoples that grow bananas use them sparingly in their diet, often as sweets. But several African societies have developed a special relationship with bananas, relying on them for a major portion of their nutrition.

Bananas present both advantages and challenges to those who rely heavily on them. On the one hand, they can be an incredibly productive crop, yielding more food per unit area planted than any other crop available in Africa until the 1500s; they also provide a good nutritional base with a moderate caloric content and a good range of vitamins and minerals. But there are three drawbacks. Bananas require a great deal of water, a resource scarce in much of East Africa, where bananas first were introduced; they are finicky about the climate they will grow in; and they deplete soil fertility. This means that they can be grown effectively only in areas with appropriate climate and by people ready to devote the labor required to irrigate them and use manure as fertilizer.

After becoming established in some of the coastal communities along East Africa, the banana was carried into the interior by agriculturalists who had managed to procure cuttings for their own horti-

cultural experiments. The earliest inland record of bananas is in Kenya about 250, around the Mount Kenya region. From there, they were carried eastward through some very inhospitable terrain until they arrived at the foot of Mount Kilimanjaro in present-day Tanzania, where they found a perfect setting.

There, the ancestors of the modern Chaga people applied traditional agricultural practices that included irrigation and manuring, and the result was phenomenal production. Eventually, they abandoned the yams that previously had been their mainstay to focus entirely on bananas. From there, the package of crop and cultivation practices spread to other places with appropriate climate throughout sub-Saharan Africa.

One of the places where bananas became a staple is in the Baganda kingdom of Uganda. The Baganda people prepared (and still do) a dish called *matoke*[a] that can be varied infinitely but has a consistent pattern. To make *matoke*, peel your bananas and wrap them in banana leaves, then steam or boil them. After they have been cooking about an hour and are very soft, mash them. To complete your *matoke*, mix the mashed bananas with cooked fish, or meat, or vegetables, or fruit, or seasonings. The more prosperous the diner, the more sumptuous the additions, but the banana remains the basis. For most Baganda, *matoke* is the main dish at every meal.

[a] *matoke:* mah TOH kee

In later periods, most Africans relied primarily on domesticated plants and animals for their food; this reliance permitted them to have greater control over their food supply and to increase the total amount of food. Local domestication of various plant foodstuffs began around 5000 B.C. or a bit earlier, a date comparable to that of domestication in Eurasia and the Americas. Black-eyed peas and cowpeas were local domesticates that provided protein. Sorghum (a grain), several types of millet (another grain), African rice, African yams, and *ackee* (a starchy fruit) were African staple crops that fueled the expansion of the sub-Saharan African population. Other local crops, such as

watermelon, coconut, many kinds of vegetable greens, and sesame, also were domesticated locally and filled out the culinary roster. Later, around A.D. 200, domesticated crops from India and Southeast Asia began appearing on the east coast of Africa and spread throughout sub-Saharan Africa. These included Asian yams, taro, and bananas, crops that could thrive in zones where African domesticates were less successful. Finally, various highly productive American crops, including peanuts, manioc, corn, and chilis, were introduced to sub-Saharan Africa by the Europeans in the sixteenth and following centuries. While plant foods always have provided the bulk of

African foods, meat also was available from early times in the form of domesticated cattle, goats, and guinea fowl. All of these crops and animals were integrated into a subsistence economy that was able to provide for large and expanding populations.

Iron was critical to the development of complex society in many parts of Africa. Tropical grasses that formed thick root mats essentially prevented cultivation with stone hoes, but iron implements could cut through the roots effectively, permitting the spread of large-scale agriculture to the vast African grasslands. The traditional viewpoint among archaeologists has been that the technology of working iron came to sub-Saharan Africa from outside, probably from Southwest Asia. In recent years, however, increasing information has muddied the picture. Clearly, West Africans were making and using iron by at least 500 B.C., a date previously thought a millennium too early. This technology may have been imported from outside or invented locally, but current evidence is inadequate to determine which.

By A.D. 200 or so, two processes appear to have coincided. First, iron making and using became popular in sub-Saharan Africa and spread over much of the continent. All of this technology followed similar patterns, and it is believed to be linked. Second, certain pottery styles began appearing in widely separated parts of the continent, and trade items became more common everywhere. Many scholars interpret this pair of phenomena as evidence of the **Bantu expansion**, the spread of Bantu-speaking peoples over most of sub-Saharan Africa, bringing their distinctive artifacts, iron technology, language, and culture with them. Some scholars, however, believe it more likely that this evidence signals the development of widespread trading links across Africa that were stimulated by the development of and commerce in iron. Regardless, this event is the final stone that paved the way for sub-Saharan African civilization.

As this chapter will show, civilizations developed in most parts of sub-Saharan Africa by the period between 200 and 1200, maybe earlier in some places. Certainly they all possessed the core elements of agricultural dependency, state government with its extended bureaucracy, urbanism, long-distance trade, class stratification, and occupational specialization. Many also possessed various of the secondary elements of civilization, including monumental architecture, a great art style, currency, and metallurgy. As noted earlier, no sub-Saharan African civilization developed writing, so we are dependent primarily on archaeology (and scanty oral tradition) for information on the period before 500, but there has been precious little archaeological research in that period. As a result, we are currently unable to determine how far back in time some of these civilizations reach.

WEST AND CENTRAL AFRICA

The environment of western and central Africa consists of three broad bands, extending from west to east. In the north is the Sahara Desert, with little rainfall or vegetation; **oases**, islands of lush vegetation usually fed by a spring, are the only places where human settlement has developed in the Sahara in the past several thousand years. Immediately to the south of the Sahara is the **savanna**, a semiarid grassland with occasional trees. Water is more abundant here, occurring in springs, seasonal and permanent rivers, and groundwater trapped in the soil; this zone also has abundant iron supplies, which were tapped by its occupants. Of all the zones, the savanna was the most densely populated. Finally, to the south of the savanna is the **tropical rain forest**, a dense tangle of trees and undergrowth with abundant—sometimes overabundant—water. The tropical rain forest poses three major challenges to human settlement: diseases that thrive in its saturated soils, transportation through tangled vegetation, and land clearance for agriculture. Despite these drawbacks, the tropical rain forest saw the development of several kingdoms.

The Rise of Civilization in West Africa: Jenne, around 200–around 700

At one time, historians saw the kingdoms of western and central Africa as direct outgrowths of contact with Arab traders around the year 700. This was understandable, because they could base their conclusions only on documents, and the documents were written by the Arabs after 700. The

FIGURE 15.1 *Jenne Warrior.* *This sculpture portrays a warrior or possibly a founding ancestor. The rich ornaments indicate that the individual is a member of the elite. The statue is about two feet tall and made of terra-cotta, lightly fired clay; its exact date is not known.*
Photo by Franco Khoury. National Museum of African Art,
Eliot Elifson Photographic Archives, Smithsonian Institution.

absence of earlier written evidence led scholars to believe that sub-Saharan civilization was inspired by, if not directly copied from, the Arabs who first recorded it. In recent years, however, a revolution has occurred in the interpretation of how these kingdoms developed, largely based on new archaeological finds. It now is clear that at least one region of West Africa had a functioning civilization by A.D. 200, centuries before the Arab trade commenced.

The story begins at the city of Jenne,[1] in the southern part of what is now the Mali Republic. The settlement of Jenne began around 300 B.C., but at this point it was merely one village among many in West Africa. By A.D. 200, however, the settlement had grown greatly, and, although precise estimates are not available, the population of Jenne probably was more than 10,000. Part of a settlement hierarchy, Jenne was urban.

Jenne's early urbanism is significant because there is no evidence of trade with areas north of the Sahara. There are abundant indications of trade within West Africa but no items traceable to Nubia, the Sudan, Egypt, or other parts of North Africa. This means that external stimulus cannot be invoked to explain the rise of Jenne.

Jenne's location at the southern edge of the savanna provides clues that may explain its development. This edge of the savanna has greater rainfall than areas farther north, providing more reliable agricultural yields to support a large population. Archaeological remains at Jenne show that the diet of its inhabitants was dominated by African rice, which grew well in the rich soils along the Niger River at Jenne. In addition, the inhabitants raised cattle and either sheep or goats and supplemented their diet of domesticated foods with wild plants and animals. This strong base permitted Jenne to invest in trading expeditions southward into the rain forest, probably initially trading surplus agricultural products for salt, a desperately needed necessity for agriculturalists with no access to the sea or its resources. Later, Jenne provided a broad range of products to the rain forest towns, including gold, iron, and ivory. In return, Jenne received salt, wood, dried fish, and perhaps slaves. Jenne's position at the southern periphery of the savanna, though poor for the

[1] **Jenne:** ZHEHN eh

trans-Sahara trade, was perfect for the savanna-forest trade.

While most of our knowledge of Jenne comes from later periods, archaeological evidence and oral tradition provide some peeks into life in early Jenne. Society was divided into tiers, with a small elite and a great mass of commoners; it is unknown whether slaves existed at this date. The elite were buried in tombs cut into bedrock, accompanied by platters of food, vessels of drink, and ornaments of various kinds. In later times, servants were sacrificed in the tombs, but there is no evidence of this in early Jenne. Markets apparently were held in the city on fixed days of the week, and farmers and others from areas around the city would bring their produce for sale or barter. In the early period at Jenne, there is no evidence of the use of currency.

Jenne is the only urban community of its sort known at this date in western or central Africa, but our present state of knowledge is admittedly poor. On the basis of available evidence, it seems to have possessed a state government, urbanism, and the other core criteria for civilization. Was it truly the isolated case that some scholars believe it to be, or is archaeological knowledge so incomplete that other contemporary civilizations remain unrecognized? There is no way at the moment to know, but there are intriguing hints that Jenne may have been the center of only one among several such early urban societies.

Later West and Central African Kingdoms: The Northern Stimulus, around 700–around 1600

Around 700, the first Muslim traders established commerce between the northern savanna regions of western and central Africa and their home bases north of the Sahara. This contact was permitted by two factors. The first was the camel, domesticated and used for several centuries in North Africa but not used south of the Sahara; the second was the gradually expanding fund of information on the Sahara, its routes, and its oases. By this date, the dangerous trial-and-error process of exploring the desert had revealed reliable knowledge that permitted caravans to advance from one oasis to the next all the way across the Sahara with limited danger of getting lost or running out of supplies.

By the 900s, trade between sub-Saharan Africa and the Muslim world was substantial and regular. Cloth, salt, steel swords, glass, and luxury goods flowed south, while gold, slaves, ostrich feathers, fine leathers, and fancy woods passed northward. The expansion of West and Central African commerce with the advent of the Dar al-Islam market fit nicely with the trade systems that had been set up earlier.

The **cola nut** held a special place in this trade. Indigenous only to sub-Saharan Africa, the cola nut was (and is) often chewed before a meal to stimulate appetite and digestion; sometimes it was powdered and used as a condiment during the meal. (This is the same cola nut that formerly flavored cola soft drinks.) It is a mild stimulant, and its significance lies in the fact that it is the only stimulant permitted strict Muslims. Consequently, when Arabs developed a taste for the cola nut, West Africa profited as its only source.

The trans-Sahara trade transformed western and central African kingdoms. Gold had been mined and worked in West Africa using indigenous technology since at least 800. With the coming of the Muslim trade, a new and profitable market opened, spurring increased production. Many other items that had some value locally were greatly desired in the north, and far higher prices could be charged the Arabs. This spurred the development of larger cities, a more powerful elite, greater class stratification, and stronger governments.

Another major change brought by the Arab and North African traders was Islam. Prior to this time, sub-Saharan Africans practiced religions based on polytheism and animism. After the coming of the Arabs, Islam spread widely in sub-Saharan Africa, especially in the savanna zone. While examples of forced conversion are known, they apparently were rare. This makes sense, because the Muslim intruders usually were a small, militarily negligible body, unable to force their hosts into anything. Far more common was voluntary conversion.

For certain groups, converting to Islam had important practical advantages, some of which have already been discussed in Chapter 12. Given a choice, Arab and North African merchants preferred to deal with other Muslims. Perhaps more important, Islam provided a code of ethics for traders of vastly different cultural backgrounds,

FIGURE 15.2 *Jingereber Mosque of Timbuktu.*
Timbuktu was a major trading center of West Africa.
Situated at the edge of the Sahara Desert, it provided
services to caravans and travelers who made the diffi-
cult crossing from the north, and served as a locus of
exchange for goods that originated farther south. With
the trade and travel across the Sahara came Islam. This
mosque, built as a house of Muslim worship around
1350, is one of the oldest still standing in West Africa.
Courtesy of Jean-Louis Bourgeois.

removed from the commoners. This distance was reflected both in social interactions and in habitations, as rulers and merchants came to live in a quarter of the city separated from the rest of the populace. The commoners themselves were the last to become Muslims, and their conversion sometimes was inspired by a charismatic Sufi preacher or the desire to avoid being captured and made a slave (because a Muslim could not be legally enslaved by another Muslim). In many cases the conversion of commoners was nominal only, and traditional religious practices continued little changed. Conversion of a people was not always complete, and sometimes a royal edict was required to convince the commoners of the good judgment of converting to Islam.

Later West and Central African Government and Civilization, around 700–around 1600

Throughout most of West and Central Africa after 700, government was similar. The so-called **Sudanic-type state** was ruled by a divine king, usually mythically descended from the creator god. This king had absolute authority over his subjects, and he was attributed divine characteristics. Particularly, he was believed to have no need to eat, and the smuggling of food into the palace, its preparation, and his consumption of it were guarded with secrecy. The king's status meant that he had contact with commoners rarely and only under ritually regulated circumstances. As a divine being, the king could not die a natural death, so he was ceremonially strangled or poisoned when near death. A king's successor was determined partly by descent and partly by the will of the titled officials who had attended the previous king.

The Sudanic-type state was highly bureaucratic. The king appointed a wide variety of officials, the most important of whom almost always were the Queen Mother, the Queen Sister, two or three Great Wives, and four Advisors (usually male). The Queen Mother, of course, was an office filled by the accident of being the mother of the king; there usually was room for choice of the Queen Sister, because any king might have several sisters; the Great Wives and Advisors were selected primarily for their wisdom and judgment. This system is distinctive in that it reserved many pivotal

enabling them to interact with trust and shared expectations and providing explicit ritual sanctions if ethical rules were broken. Islam assisted African and Arab merchants in dealing with one another, facilitating interregional trade.

Islam spread through most West and Central African kingdoms in a predictable manner. First to convert were the merchants, because they had the greatest incentive as well as the greatest contact with Muslim outsiders. Next to convert were the rulers, whose conversions usually were state events, with carefully planned ceremonies and speeches. As merchants gained greater wealth, they and the rulers came to share power to a greater extent, forming an elite that was further

Kanka Musa, whose name was prefaced by the respectful term, "Mansa," was the emperor of Mali in the early fourteenth century, near the end of the empire's height. He became famous for the opulent *hajj* that took him, an enormous entourage, and magnificent and precious art to Mecca for a pilgrimage. Ibn Fadl Allah al Omari,[a] a contemporary Egyptian scholar, collected information on Musa from a friend in Mali and published the following account of the splendor of the imperial court at Niani. Note the combination of African and Muslim symbols and elements.

> The sultan [ruler] of this kingdom presides in his palace in a great balcony called *bembe* where he has a great seat of ebony that is like a throne fit for a large and tall person; on either side it is flanked by elephant tusks turned towards each other. His

[a] **Ibn Fadl Allah al Omari:** IB uhn FAH duhl AHL uh ahl oh MAHR ee

weapons stand near him, being all of gold—saber, lance, quiver, bow, and arrows. He wears wide trousers made of about twenty pieces of material which he alone may wear. Behind him there stand about a score of Turkish or other pages that are bought for him in Cairo [in Egypt]; one of them, at his left, holds a silk umbrella surmounted by a dome and a bird of gold; the bird has the figure of a falcon. His officers are seated in a circle about him, in two rows, one to the right and one to the left; beyond them sit the chief commanders of his cavalry. In front of him there is a person who never leaves him and who is his executioner; also another who serves as a spokesman between the sovereign and his subjects, and who is named the herald. In front of them again, there are drummers. Others dance before their sovereign, who enjoys this, and make him laugh. Two banners are spread behind him. Before him they keep two saddled and bridled horses in case he should wish to ride.

advisory positions for women, something rare in state-level governments. Both men and women, chosen primarily for their abilities, composed this inner circle of advisors. This approach to government differs markedly from a strictly hereditary system of the sort found in many states elsewhere.

The government also supported a hierarchy of local officials, including provincial and district chiefs and other local administrators. Their primary duties were:

— raising tribute to support the opulent lifestyle of the king and his court;

— gathering commodities for long-distance trade, some of which was carried on under royal auspices; and

— seeing that royal edicts and wishes were carried out throughout the realm.

Kings gathered artisans to create works in the great art style that developed. Bronze castings of the West African kingdoms are particularly well known, probably because they survived the centuries well and became favorites of early-twentieth-century art collectors in Europe and North America. Other media were important, however, and

art included carved wooden sculptures, ivory carvings, cast gold, featherwork, and painted leather.

West and Central African kings directed great public works projects; few are still archaeologically visible, because they were made with unfired mud that served well in its time but has disintegrated over the centuries. Some known monumental works include royal tombs cut into bedrock, groups of large standing stones serving to mark elite burials, walled palaces, mosques, and great walls surrounding cities. Royal patronage also supported irrigation and drainage projects that permitted the growing of substantial surpluses of foodstuffs.

Political History in West and Central Africa

Little can be said about the political history of this area before documents. After the coming of the Arabs, it becomes much better known, and the picture becomes even clearer following the coming of the Portuguese and other Europeans after 1440.

Our first evidence, around 800, indicates that there were a great number of independent polities throughout the savannas of West and Central Africa. Most of these were small kingdoms with a central city or town and outlying towns and villages, usually with populations running in the tens of thousands. These kingdoms could be considered city-states comparable to those in Europe, Asia, and Central America.

An exception to this pattern was Ghana, an inland empire centered on the western portion of present-day Mali. Oral tradition states that Ghana had twenty kings before the time of Muhammad (around 600), and it is unclear how early the kingdom and empire may have begun or what was its process of formation. The Ghana state was destroyed by the Almoravids, a Berber group from North Africa bent on converting the Ghanaians to Islam and controlling the trans-Saharan trade. In 1054, the Almoravids captured critical trading centers in the north of Ghana, weakening that state enough so that it toppled by 1077. Almoravids held some kind of control over Ghana for a brief time, but by 1100 they had lost it. Ghana, however, had disintegrated and could not reunite itself, and for the next century the area was composed of many small states.

Around 1200, another empire developed, larger and richer than Ghana. The Mali Empire was centered on the city of Niani[2] in the old Ghana Empire and incorporated all that Ghana previously had controlled. Mali extended its empire beyond the borders of the old Ghana state in all directions, including westward to the Atlantic Ocean. Much of this extension was through military conquest, and therein lay the seeds of Mali's destruction. Mali's military was overextended, and it was tolerated by subject states only so long as it provided protection under which trade could proceed. When it failed in this purpose, however, these conquered states felt no ties of loyalty and seceded or joined rival empires. As more states defected from the empire, Mali was weakened and less able to fulfill its duties as protector. The empire began eroding by 1320.

The chief state to benefit from Mali's weakening was Songhai,[3] situated to the east of Mali. Once part of the Mali Empire, Songhai was an early defector that began building its own empire by around 1350. Most of the defector states from Mali became part of the Songhai Empire, either immediately or after a period of independence. Songhai relied on diplomacy as much as military action to build its empire, and this resulted in greater loyalty among its subjects. At its height in 1515, Songhai was the largest sub-Saharan African empire, with a population numbering well over one million. Songhai's rich province of Hausaland was lost after its local ethnic group staged a successful revolt there; subsequent internal dissension further weakened the Songhai Empire. In 1590, following civil strife over imperial succession, Moroccan forces conquered and occupied Songhai.

All of the states and empires discussed so far are from the savanna zone, but states also developed in the tropical rain forest zone. Here, Islam and its literary tradition took little hold, so most of our early information comes from archaeology.

FIGURE 15.3 *Queen Mother of Benin and Attendants.* *This cast bronze sculpture from the eighteenth century focuses on the Queen Mother with her large headgear and rich ornaments. She is surrounded by women servants, who themselves were probably nobles. In many sub-Saharan societies, the Queen Mother was one of several powerful female advisors to a king. This sculpture comes from Benin, in the coastal rain forest of West Africa.* Metropolitan Museum of Art, Gift of Mr. and Mrs. Klaus G. Perls, 1991.

[2] **Niani:** nee AHN ee
[3] **Songhai:** SOHNG HY

FIGURE 15.4 *Procession at the Court of Benin.* *Benin became rich through participation in the slave trade with Europeans. This seventeenth-century Dutch engraving shows the king of Benin on horseback, surrounded by musicians, attendants, and tame leopards; soldiers and nobles, also on horses, follow. Pictured leaving the palace, whose turrets are surmounted by brass ornaments in the form of birds, the procession is probably headed to a shrine where a ritual will be performed.* From Olfert Dapper, *Beschreibung von Afrika,* first published in Amsterdam in 1670.

Current information suggests that settlements in the forest zone were modest villages prior to around 600. By around 850, a handful of archaeological sites, such as Igbo Ukwu, show evidence of larger size, greater wealth, and the presence of an elite. Such sites contain some traded items from the Arabs, although their numbers are few, and most archaeologists believe they came there through trade links with the savanna kingdoms. Little is known about the government or economics of these early communities, although some scholars believe they were chiefdoms.

One point is clear: The development of large and complex polities came later to the forest than to the savanna. In fact, the rise of complexity par-

allels quite closely the rise of the large-scale trade networks of the savanna kingdoms to the north. It may very well be that the interregional trade carried on by Ghana and other states in the savanna led them to seek commodities from the forest communities; this, in turn, may have stimulated the development of a wealthy class that gained power and came to lead the forest communities.

Good evidence for kingdoms begins to appear by 1200, with the development of the Ife[4] state; shortly thereafter, Benin,[5] the other major state in the forest zone, also originated. Both Ife and Benin

[4] **Ife:** EE fay

[5] **Benin:** beh NEEN

had sophisticated royal courts and an extravagant cast-bronze sculptural tradition. The wealth of these states resulted directly from their control of trade between the coast and the savanna.

In 1440, the Portuguese began trading for slaves with the forest kingdoms of West Africa. Under this stimulus, these kingdoms expanded in size and power as they accumulated wealth from the European slave trade over the next centuries. While slavery had existed in West Africa centuries before and had expanded under Islam, its intensity increased and its nature changed markedly when the Europeans became involved. This event marked a turning point in the history of West and Central Africa.

EAST AFRICA

East Africa from present-day Somalia to Mozambique can be viewed as two great zones: the coast and the interior. From around 700 to 1600, coastal East Africans lived radically different lives from those of their interior cousins, yet the two were intimately linked by the ties of economy.

Coastal East Africa and the Indian Ocean Trade, around 700–around 1600

The coastal zone of East Africa is a narrow strip, scarcely five miles wide and more than a thousand miles long. The zone is generally favorable for human occupation, presenting a variety of food and other resources. But the most desirable point about the coast, at least from the 700s onward, was its accessibility to ships plying the trade routes of the Indian Ocean.

The east coast of Africa is only about 1,600 sea miles from India and closer still to Arabia. (In contrast, the west coast of Africa is about 3,000 sea miles from the nearest part of Europe.) Further, winds and currents between Africa and Asia are seasonal and they reverse direction every six months, making travel easy and relatively safe. (In contrast, the west coast was made inaccessible by contrary winds and currents that could not easily be overcome with maritime technology available before the fifteenth century.) Given this geography, it is little wonder that coastal East Africa had extensive contacts with Asia far earlier than coastal

West Africa had contact with Europe. Some of those early contacts on the eastern coast were discussed previously in terms of imported crops around 200, but even more pervasive contacts developed by 700.

The Axumites and contemporary southern Arabs had established some trade contacts with the coastal peoples of East Africa by around 300, but these were sporadic and limited. Around 700, the volume of trade between Asia and coastal East Africa increased considerably. Arabs, Persians, Indians, and Malays are documented as visiting the coast for trade, and Chinese may have done so as well. Ivory, tortoise shell, incense, spices, gold, iron, amber, slaves, ambergris (a fragrant secretion from whales, used in perfume making), and other perfume oils were major exports from East Africa; in return, Asia sent ceramics, soapstone pots, cloth, beads, and glass. Anxious to take advantage of this commerce, Africans developed cities and towns along the coast specifically as ports of trade. Many of these ports were preexisting villages, but some were new and located in areas that had excellent harbors but insufficient resources to provide food for a community.

As a result of this trade, the elite of these coastal communities became wealthy. They expended some of their wealth on fancy tombs and houses made of stone, and some of their houses even had indoor toilets. Meanwhile, other inhabitants, principally dock workers, fishermen, laborers, and servants, remained poor and continued living in the mud-and-thatch huts that had previously been the universal type of housing. Some of these settlements took on Arab or Persian names, and the local language—Swahili—adopted many Arabic words. Islam became the dominant religion, at least among the elite, and mosques were built. A recent archaeological survey has located 173 coastal settlements with stone structures for the elite.

It perhaps is not surprising that at one time scholars believed these to be Arab colonies, outposts set up in a foreign land to facilitate trading. Certainly the number of Arab characteristics is great, but the documents, oral history, and archaeological evidence all agree that these coastal settlements were local African developments, encouraged by trade.

Kilwa was one of the two or three largest of the coastal settlements. Gaspar Correa, a member of Vasco da Gama's Portuguese crew, wrote an account of his visit to Kilwa in 1514, in which he describes that place:

> The city is large and is of good buildings of stone and mortar with terraces, and the houses have much wood works. The city comes down to the shore, and is entirely surrounded by a wall and towers, within which there may be 12,000 inhabitants. The country all round is very luxuriant with many trees and gardens of all sorts of vegetables. . . . The streets of the city are very narrow, as the houses are very high, of three and four stories, and one can run along the tops of them upon the terraces, as the houses are very close together; and in the port there are many ships.

Correa focused his description on the elite portions of town, and Kilwa is noted for having a larger elite section than other port communities. We can be sure, however, that there was another side to Kilwa, where common people and slaves lived simpler lives in houses made of thatch and mud.

The form of government along the East African coast varied from place to place. In some cities and towns, authority was vested in a council of lineage heads; in others, local rulers were elected, and some of these were able to convert their positions into hereditary ones, leading to de facto kingship. In at least some cases, an Arab or Persian accepted a position as ruler, presumably a

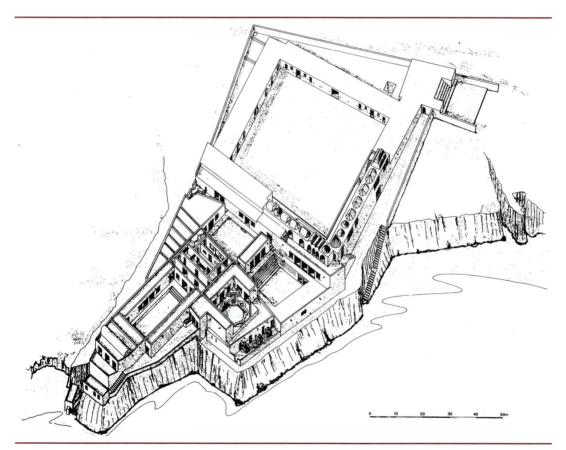

FIGURE 15.5 *The Palace of Husuni Kubwa.* *This reconstruction, drawn by an archaeologist who excavated there, shows the magnificent palace of Husuni Kubwa, constructed by the Mahdalis, a dynasty of rulers of Kilwa on the eastern coast of Africa. Trade with Arabs, among others, enriched this community and especially its rulers, who in the fourteenth century converted some of their wealth into this cliff-top palace overlooking the northern coast of Kilwa Island. The octagonal structure in the center foreground is a swimming pool, and the square depression to its right is a reception court with hundreds of niches for oil lamps. The largest structure, at the top of this drawing, was a warehouse for precious Mahdali goods waiting to be traded.* From *A Thousand Years of East Africa*, The British Institute in Eastern Africa. Reproduced with permission of the Institute.

compromise candidate when local factions could not agree. Rulers typically continued to live in their own houses, making them a bit more fancy by adding sculpture or other ornamentation. Each of these governmental systems was extended only to a single community, and there is no evidence of any attempt to incorporate several communities into a single polity. Not until the conclusion of the Portuguese conquest of the East African coast around 1640 would the region be united under a single government.

The Interior of East Africa, around 1150–around 1600

The settlements along the East African coast traded over great distances, and some of their inhabitants reaped the rewards in the form of wealth, but their economic success would have been impossible without the interior. Most of the people of this zone lived a more modest life than those we have discussed previously in this chapter, living in small villages with limited class stratification. One of their contributions to the coast was in providing food and other necessities not always available in the quantities required to support the coastal cities and towns. Some of these small-scale societies specialized in animal herding, others focused on agriculture, and still others practiced both. A second contribution of these peoples to the coastal lifestyle was in supplying many of the materials the coastal people traded with foreigners, particularly ivory and slaves. In return, they received salt, shell and glass beads, cotton cloth produced in the coastal towns, and perhaps some of the fancy cloth imported from Asia.

One exception to this characterization stands out starkly: Zimbabwe.[6] The ancient Zimbabwe state (around 1150–around 1600) in the highlands of present-day Zimbabwe (formerly Rhodesia) was centered on a major city, usually termed "Great Zimbabwe." This city consisted of several massive circular buildings of stone, as well as areas of thatched huts. The stone buildings have attracted a great deal of attention because of their size. The largest had an exterior wall of stone nearly 800 feet long, more than 15 feet thick, and about 31 feet high; this amounts to about 50,000 cubic feet of masonry. Put into perspective, this is enough masonry to face an Egyptian pyramid measuring

more than 200 feet at the base of each side. Further, the stone blocks are very finely cut and set together closely with mortar, reflecting high building standards.

Great Zimbabwe is the largest of the settlements of the historic Zimbabwe state, with an estimated population of 10,000 to 12,000 persons within its walls, but there also are nearly 200 other sites known that have similar stone structures. These cities and towns are generally believed to be regional centers under the capital at Great Zimbabwe. In addition, there are many village sites with no stone architecture of the sort that surrounds the larger settlements, representing the smallest unit in the settlement hierarchy. This clearly is an urban system.

The Zimbabwe state probably developed shortly before 1150, perhaps with an original capital at Mapungubwe,[7] shifting to Great Zimbabwe around 1250. While there are no documents to guide interpretation, oral history and archaeology suggest that the ancestors of the modern Shona people built and lived in Great Zimbabwe.

The great wealth of Zimbabwe is reflected both in its architecture and in some of the artifacts that have been found there. Persian bowls, Chinese ceramics, Southwest Asian glass, shell and glass beads, and a coin minted in Kilwa, all found at Great Zimbabwe, indicate wealth. They also point to the apparent source of that wealth: extensive trade with the coastal settlements.

Zimbabwe controlled areas rich in gold, and gold was perhaps the most sought-after commodity the coastal towns had to offer Asian traders. Evidence of Zimbabwean gold mines and processing areas have been found, and some historians believe that a fifteenth-century Portuguese account referring to gold mines in the kingdom of Butua may refer to Zimbabwe.

Little is known regarding the government of Zimbabwe. The assumption usually is that it was a state with a king and lesser district chiefs. Many scholars believe that trade was a royal monopoly, and some believe that the king was a hereditary ruler identified as the descendant of a god. These conclusions are supported by oral traditions, but there are no documents to corroborate them.

In the seventeenth century, Portuguese control of the East African coast became greater, and it began to extend inland. At the same time that its

[6] **Zimbabwe:** zihm BAHB way

[7] **Mapungubwe:** mah puhn GUHB way

FIGURE 15.6 *Great Enclosure at Great Zimbabwe.* *This aerial photograph shows the central portion of the archaeological site of Great Zimbabwe in the interior of eastern Africa. The Great Enclosure encircles an area of about 100 acres, believed to have been used largely for religious rituals and elite housing. Archaeologists estimate that 18,000 persons might have lived at this site, and nearly 200 similar though smaller sites are known. Great Zimbabwe was at its height in the first half of the second millennium.* Courtesy of the Department of Information, Rhodesia.

coastal partners were in the process of being conquered by a foreign power, for reasons presently unknown, Zimbabwe collapsed. First the gold trade languished, then the urban system broke down, and shortly thereafter elite culture at Zimbabwe disintegrated.

SOUTHWEST AFRICA

The southwestern portion of Africa, largely comprised of what is today Angola, has undergone tremendous environmental change in the past few centuries, largely as a result of human activity. Consequently, the present environments are not representative of those that would have been exploited by southwestern Africans at the time when states were first developing. Along the coast was a narrow, relatively moist strip; in the northern and southern parts of the interior was savanna; and between the savanna zones, in the central interior, was a zone of dense tropical rain forest. In the far south, the savanna graded into the inhospitable Kalahari Desert.

Agriculture became prominent in Southwest Africa sometime after A.D. 500, probably around 800. By 1000, it was practiced in all zones except the driest and those that were the most densely forested. Important crops were mostly derived from parts of Africa farther north and included sorghum, millet, yams, bananas, peanuts, and sugarcane. Fish were widely used in areas along the coast and fertile rivers, and land animals provided protein elsewhere.

Southwest Africa diverges from most of the rest of Africa in its degree of internal diversity. In most parts of Africa, the various peoples followed more or less similar lifestyles, changing in parallel over time as conditions in the region changed. In Southwest Africa, however, some peoples became intensive agriculturalists and developed states; others adopted agriculture but retained egalitarian political systems; still others retained hunting and gathering as the primary components of their subsistence. Some of these choices may be explained as reflecting the limitations or possibilities of the environment, but others seem to relate to other, as yet unrecognized, factors.

The Development of Early Southwest African Kingdoms, around 1000–around 1600

Those peoples who developed kingdoms in Southwest Africa followed more or less the same pattern of political development. In most parts of Southwest Africa, men heading lineages were also recognized to have a special relationship with the land. These individuals, known as **lords of the land**, simultaneously were leaders of their kinship groups and priests who dealt with spirits that inhabited various spots in their lineage territories. As some lineages prospered and their populations grew, lords of the land began to augment their kinship-religious duties with expanded political and economic powers. Prosperous lineages meant increased revenues for the lords of the land, who administered lineage finances; lords of the land became increasingly liberated from ordinary duties, and their image as special individuals grew. Eventually, they were wealthy and powerful and were revered as leaders in politics, as well as in religion and kinship. At this stage, some would declare themselves leaders of related lineages, deposing other lords of the land by political maneuvering or by force of arms. As this occurred, several villages would be united under a single coercive leader, who began acquiring an entourage of counselors, judges, ambassadors, and courtiers.

Probably the earliest of the Southwest African kingdoms was Luba in the interior southern savannas. According to oral tradition, the kingdom of Luba was founded by Kongolo, a lord of the land who subsumed several lineages into his own, appointing their former leaders as subordinates who, with his consent, could rule their lineages in

FIGURE 15.7 *Elite Grave from Luba.* *The Luba kingdom of southwestern Africa was characterized by the same sort of class stratification known throughout sub-Saharan Africa. This grave from the Lake Kisale region provides evidence of the wealth and high status of its occupant. The elaborate ceramic bowls were produced only for use in burials and probably contained food; the various iron weapons befit the warrior status of the elite male; finally, the ivory and iron jewelry indicate that this is the grave of a member of the elite. Graves such as this date from the eighth and ninth centuries.* Pierre de Maret, Africa Museum, Tervuren, Belgium.

his absence. Kongolo and his subordinate leaders were permitted to own slaves, although apparently no one else was permitted to do so. The system has been considered feudal by some scholars, because each level of the hierarchy delegated authority to the level below it, unless a crisis necessitated cooperative behavior to support the king. The Luba kingdom probably was formed between 1000 and 1100.

On the southern coast of Southwest Africa, another kingdom formed around 1200. This was the famous Kongo kingdom. Although not the largest or most powerful of the states in this region, it is the best known because of abundant oral tradition and sixteenth-century Portuguese accounts describing it. According to oral tradition, the Kongo state developed slowly, perhaps over a century or more beginning around 1200, as various lords of the land amalgamated their power to form a single king. Because Kongo is so well documented, we shall describe it as an example of kingdoms in Southwest Africa.

The Kingdom of Kongo, around 1200–around 1600

The king of Kongo usually inherited his position, probably from his father, although royal inheritance sometimes passed through female lines, in which case a king would inherit by virtue of being the son of the king's sister. There was no rule that the eldest son should be named king, and a group of nine to twelve electors had to select which son would become the new king. Rarely, they would be forced to go outside the royal family to select a king, if they judged all hereditary candidates to be incompetent.

The king had considerable, though not absolute, power. He was able to declare war, open or close trade routes, appoint governors and other officials, and collect taxes, but in all these tasks he was overseen by a council. The king and council maintained a delicate balance of power. On the one hand, the council could countermand a royal decree; on the other hand, the king appointed the council and could disband it or remove specific members. The system encouraged cooperation, because either of these actions would destabilize the country, laying it open to outside invasion from its neighbors, a constant threat.

The king ruled over a series of provinces, but each of these had its own governor who carried out everyday administration. Governors came into power by various mechanisms, most apparently inherited from when they were independent lineage territories. These included election by the people with the king's confirmation, inheritance from one's father, and royal appointment. Governors received salaries from the king, who was the only authority able to collect taxes. Beneath the governors were hereditary village chiefs, who also probably received stipends.

Banza was the capital city of Kongo, and it reportedly housed many thousands of people within its encircling stone walls. It served as a fortress to protect the king in times of trouble, as the control center for the trade between the coast and interior, and as a religious center (because the king was considered divine and retained important ceremonial obligations).

At Banza, the king held court. Seated on a ceremonial stool, wearing a headdress and bracelet of copper or ivory, and holding a tax purse, the king was surrounded by symbols of his various religious and secular roles. We know little about court life, only that several officials remained with the king at most times to serve his needs as soon as he voiced them.

The lifeways of the common people of Kongo are poorly known. Clearly, most people were farmers living in small villages spread throughout the kingdom. Along the Atlantic Ocean and some stretches of rivers, small villages were dominated by fishing, although it is unknown whether men, women, or both sexes worked in this occupation. It is known, however, that those who fished also produced pottery for trade. In addition, there were miners, metal workers, makers of **raffia** (a fabric made of palm fiber), salt manufacturers, and merchants. Each of the occupations probably had a traditional status associated with it.

It appears that much, perhaps all, trade was controlled by the king. *Nzimbu*[8] (a type of cowrie shell) were the official currency of Kongo; currency from neighboring states, including cross-shaped copper ingots and squares of raffia, probably also was accepted. Major articles traded included salt, iron, copper, woven goods, and pottery. It is clear, however, that this trade linked the coastal and interior sections of Southwest Africa but did not extend significantly beyond the region. While only limited archaeological study has been devoted to

[8] *Nzimbu:* NZIHM boo

FIGURE 15.8 ***Dutch Delegation at the Court of Kongo.*** *This Dutch engraving from 1642 depicts Dutch traders kneeling before the king of Kongo, a major kingdom of southwestern Africa. Courtiers in elite dress stand beside the seated king. There are several European items in this engraving: the chandelier hanging above the king, the king's leather boots, and a miniature cross dangling from the king's left elbow. These items probably were special gifts bestowed on the king by European traders, but it is possible that they were added by the engraver as artistic flourishes. The Latin inscription above the king's throne, which reads "Sir Alvare, King of Kongo," was almost certainly invented by the artist.* From Olfert Dapper, *Beschreibung von Africa*, Amsterdam, 1670.

this region, virtually none of the exotic products of long-distance trade have been found in Southwest Africa.

The family in the Kongo kingdom was largely oriented around the mother's line. It is probable that the basic family unit was the extended family, with sisters, their husbands, and children living together in a single house. Among the aristocracy, marriages were important political devices, because a series of good marriages could ally a man with several powerful lineages and propel him into a favorable position for a royal appointment.

Religion in Kongo, as throughout Southwest Africa, was local polytheism. Islam penetrated to this area only in the fifteenth century, and then not

as a serious competitor to local faiths. There were no commercial incentives to convert to Islam in Southwest Africa, because there was no major or direct trade with Dar al-Islam. In addition, the divine nature of the king might have been undermined by the introduction of a new religion, so it is unlikely that rulers—the typical leaders in national conversion—would have been inclined to support this new religion.

Trade, Civilization, and Southwest Africa

Southwest Africa stands apart in one respect from the other regions of Africa that have been discussed in this chapter: Its development received

The Recognition of Segmentary Opposition

Prior to the 1930s, British colonial administrators frequently complained that Africans were "capricious" or "unpredictable" in their political alliances. On one occasion, a village might carry on a violent feud with a neighboring village, but a few days later, the two might fight side by side against a coalition of more distant villages; the following month, all of these combatants might unite to fight the British. What the colonial administrators failed to realize was that these shifting coalitions were reflections of a widespread African approach to political organization.

In the early 1930s, E. E. Evans-Pritchard, a British anthropologist, was asked by the British colonial administrators of the Anglo-Egyptian Sudan to investigate this phenomenon and try to explain it. Evans-Pritchard spent two years with the Nuer tribe of the Sudan, and its members explained to him the workings of **segmentary opposition**.

The principle underlying segmentary opposition is simple. Each person is a member of a series of hierarchic groups, mostly based on kinship and village residence. The simplest element is a family within a village; next is the village itself; then comes a series of progressively larger groups consisting of ever-larger coalitions of villages; finally comes the entire Nuer tribe. In any conflict—violent, judicial, or otherwise—a person's loyalty rightfully is owed to the largest group that can array itself against the antagonist. In an argument over my neighbor's dog, the conflict involves my family against my neighbor's family; if someone from a neighboring village steals something from me, the conflict is seen as my village against the neighboring village. If my antagonist comes from a village that is involved in a high-level coalition opposing a similar coalition that includes my village, these coalitions would be the stage for the conflict. Finally, outsiders could find the entire Nuer tribe marshaled against themselves in a conflict. A person's political loyalties in a segmentary system were not simply to the state; rather, they were owed to a series of nested entities culminating in the chiefdom or state.

When Evans-Pritchard published his findings on segmentary opposition, colonial administrators began to understand previously baffling events. The Nuer, for example, were perennial enemies with the neighboring Dinka, constantly conducting feuds and raiding against each other; this enmity was underscored by mythological tales explaining their differences. Consequently, the British in the late nineteenth century believed they could count on Dinka aid to conquer the Nuer but were astonished when the Nuer and Dinka united unsuccessfully to resist British incursions. In reality, the Nuer and Dinka saw themselves as enemies when in mutual conflict and as allies when in conflict against a common enemy.

Scholars since the 1930s have realized that many states in sub-Saharan Africa were organized around the principle of segmentary opposition, permitting them the flexibility to quarrel yet effectively unite, depending on the circumstances. As so often is the case, behavior that seemed irrational was merely based on unfamiliar principles.

---

no significant stimulus from trade with distant places. While West Africa began its development of complexity with Jenne and before the advent of significant outside trade, the rise of trade with Dar al-Islam spurred growth in the savanna; at the same time, savanna-forest trade (and the later European slave trade) stimulated growth in the forests. Similarly, the Indian Ocean trade was crucial to the rise of complexity in East Africa. In Southwest Africa, however, there was no ready access to trade routes with foreign traders from distant lands, and trade within this area was sufficient to promote the development of civilization.

Trade is a potent force in stimulating complexity, and it matters little whether the trade is with far-away lands or with nearby ones.

SIMILARITY AMID DIVERSITY IN SUB-SAHARAN AFRICA

This chapter has focused on only a few of the many civilizations that flourished throughout sub-Saharan Africa. We have not touched on the Mongo, the Loango, the Mande, the Bachwezi, the

WEST AND CENTRAL AFRICA	EAST AFRICA	SOUTHWEST AFRICA		
Jenne, 200–700			**200**	Asian crops arrive in East Africa, spread of iron metallurgy, and Bantu expansion begins, c. 200
			–	
			–	Arab and Axumite trade with East Africa, c. 300
			–	
			400	
			–	
			–	
			–	
			600	
			–	
			–	Inception of Arab trade in West Africa, c. 700
			–	
			800	Agriculture becomes important in South-west Africa, c. 800
			–	
			–	Arab trade becomes common, c. 900
			–	
			1000	
		Luba Kingdom, 1000–1600	–	Conquest of Ghana, 1077
			–	
			–	
	Great Zimbabwe, 1150–1600		–	
			1200	
Mali, 1200–1400	Ife and Benin, 1200–1600	Kongo Kingdom, 1200–1600	–	
			–	
			–	
			1400	Portuguese open slave trade in West Africa, 1440
			–	
			–	American crops arrive in West Africa, c. 1500
			–	
			1600	

Mossi, and many others with long and important histories. The sampling of societies discussed in this chapter, however, shows two major patterns in sub-Saharan African civilizations.

On the one hand, there is great diversity from place to place. Certainly the stone cities and towns of the East African coast would not be confused with the wood-mud-grass houses of villages in Southwest Africa. The details of culture, mythology, and language differed from place to place, and these differences formed the basis by which individuals identified with their societies.

On the other hand, probably more than on any other continent after the development of civilization, there is an essential similarity, largely political, among sub-Saharan African civilizations. Characteristics of government typically shared by these civilizations are:

— a state whose ruler has strong but rarely absolute power;

— an institutionalized system of confirming royal succession, so that an inept or undesirable heir in line to the throne by virtue of heredity can be excluded from leadership;

— a broad and institutionalized system of advisors; and

— an unusually high degree of formal political participation on the part of women.

All of these characteristics tend to have made these governments more responsive to a broad range of opinion within the realm, presumably better serving the people. None of these governments had full consent of the governed, but all had a greater element of responsiveness to public interests than many of their counterparts elsewhere.

These political similarities may be rooted in the Bantu expansion, the result of a single political form spreading out from a center of dispersal and then changing only gradually and slightly over the centuries, resulting in parallel structures. Alternatively, they may be the result of convergence, as different societies found the same solutions to the common problems of survival in the generally semiarid lands south of the Sahara. The answer must await more and better archaeological study of the period before A.D. 200.

SUMMARY

1. There were many regional states and a few empires in precolonial sub-Saharan Africa. Many of these were urban civilizations.

2. African civilization was based on agriculture using both locally domesticated and imported crops. Trade was an important spur to the development of civilization in many places.

3. Iron technology allowed the expansion of agriculture into African lands previously unavailable for farming. The Bantu expansion may have carried iron technology with it.

4. In West and Central Africa, early states such as Jenne developed largely through trade within sub-Saharan Africa.

5. Following the inception of trans-Saharan trade with the Arabs and Muslims, West and Central African states developed stronger governments, more pronounced class stratification, and larger urban systems. Also, many adopted Islam, largely because of the economic advantages.

6. The Ghana, Mali, and Songhai empires were civilizations of the savanna zone of West Africa. Forest states in West Africa, such as Ife and Benin, developed into civilizations somewhat later than the savanna states.

7. In coastal East Africa, settlements took advantage of trade with Asia and other lands along the rim of the Indian Ocean to develop a local elite and considerable wealth. While they sometimes took on the trappings of Arabia, they were indigenous African developments.

8. In interior East Africa, most peoples were at the tribe or chiefdom level. Zimbabwe, however, was an urban state that traded gold with the coastal settlements in order to support a powerful elite.

9. In Southwest Africa, kingdoms such as Luba and Kongo developed out of lineages. They were stimulated by the growth of trade within the region but—unlike other parts of Africa—not by interregional trade.

SUGGESTED READINGS

Connah, Graham. *African Civilizations*. Cambridge, Eng.: Cambridge University Press, 1987. A good treatment of the archaeological evidence regarding sub-Saharan states.

Fage, J. D., and Roland Oliver, gen. eds. *The Cambridge History of Africa*. Eight vols., each with a volume ed. Cambridge, Eng.: Cambridge University Press, 1975–85. A basic source.

Sherratt, Andrew, ed. *The Cambridge Encyclopedia of Archaeology*. New York/Cambridge, Eng.: Crown Publishers/Cambridge University Press, 1980. An excellent overview of the civilizations discussed in this chapter, focusing on the archaeological evidence.

Summers, Roger. *Zimbabwe: A Rhodesian Mystery*. Johannesburg, South Africa: Thomas Nelson and Sons, 1965. A popular treatment of Zimbabwe by a competent professional archaeologist; most useful for details on the discovery and early (mis)interpretation of the site.

UNESCO. *General History of Africa*. Eight vols., each with a volume ed. Paris: UNESCO, 1981–88. (Also reprinted by various publishers.) A very detailed treatment, especially focusing on the role of Islam in Africa; volumes III and IV are especially useful.

Shogun's *Vassal*. In this detail from a thirteenth-century scroll, a Japanese vassal (center) reads aloud the document that describes his rights and privileges over a territory granted to him by the shogun. The household reacts with pleasure and anticipation at the wealth and social status that this land will bring them. If this territory were large enough, the vassal could divide it into smaller estates and grant it to subordinates, who would then become his *vassals*.   From the Eshi no Soshi (scroll), painting on silk, 13th century. Sakamoto Photo Research Laboratory, Tokyo.

Feudalism

I, John of Toul, affirm that I am the vassal of the Lady Beatrice, countess of Troyes, and of her son Theobald, count of Champagne, against every creature living or dead, excepting my allegiance to Lord Enjourand of Coucy, Lord John of Arcis, and the count of Grandpré. If it should happen that the count of Grandpré should be at war with the countess and count of Champagne . . . I will aid the count of Grandpré [myself] and will aid the count and countess of Champagne by sending them . . . knights. . . .

—JOHN OF TOUL

This excerpt comes from a document in which one medieval knight tried to work out the potentially conflicting obligations of serving more than one lord at a time. Many medieval knights had multiple obligations of service in feudal France, which was one of the most complex feudal structures in the world.

In Issue 2, we saw how models can be used to help us make comparisons and contrasts on a global level, and in this issue we will present a model of feudalism in order to compare several examples of empires or kingdoms that transformed to regional control. As with any model, generalizations sometimes camouflage the experiences of specific societies, but there is an advantage to these generalizations because they can help us see patterns and trends that are similar around the world. In feudalism's case, we can see how some overextended polities tried to maintain control over their territories.

THE FEUDAL MODEL

Feudalism is a decentralized sociopolitical structure in which a weak monarchy attempts to control the lands of the realm through reciprocal agreements with regional leaders. Some scholars do not like the term "feudalism" because it has been traditionally used to compare the history of medieval feudal France with the histories of other regions of the world, using Europe as the model, which limits the kind of comparisons one can make. If the term's definition takes on a more generic meaning, then European feudalism no longer acts as the paradigm by which other feudal systems are judged but becomes one among many feudal structures to study. In this issue we will use feudalism to examine several societies that experienced similar political episodes of regionalism in their histories.

The characteristics of a feudal society are:

— a decentralized administration indicative of weakened monarchical control (including an ineffective or nonexistent bureaucracy);

— regional leaders (members of an aristocratic warrior-elite) who receive land for use (economic exploitation, such as the collection of taxes, and jurisdictional authority, such as law courts, over large territories); and

— the receipt of these lands in exchange for loyalty oaths and military support of the monarch.

Feudalism usually emerges when a monarchy does not maintain central control over the realm. An example might be when empires expand to include vast territories that a monarch cannot easily control, resulting in the empire's breaking into regions with regional governance under a weak monarch. The breakup of an empire does not always end in feudalism but sometimes leads to a complete political collapse and the growth of new polities out of the remnants of the old. Feudalism, however, exists only in the presence of a nominal central ruler with limited power. If a monarch attempts centralization, regional leaders usually resist the efforts at encroachment onto their spheres of influence, sometimes resulting in hostilities that lead to a usurpation of the throne by a regional leader.

Feudal states include a system of land management wherein a monarch awards land use to a subordinate regional leader in return for a pledge of loyalty and military support. Additionally, the regional leader acts as a local governor, collecting taxes and tributes, maintaining judicial authority, and organizing local military units. The lands received are populated by peasants or commoners whose production financially supports the regional leader. In some cases, regional leaders reapportion lands to their own loyal followers, who become leaders of smaller areas; this process is called **subinfeudation**. In times of war, the monarch calls on the feudally obligated regional leaders (the aristocratic warrior-elite) to assemble with their vassals and fulfill their obligations of military aid. Regional leaders frequently take advantage of destabilization, occasionally engaging in rivalries or in challenges that end in outright rebellion. If the regional leader does not remain loyal to the monarch, theoretically the lands might be forfeited and granted to another, but only if the ruler is powerful enough to command his other regional leaders to fight on behalf of the monarchy.

FEUDAL SYSTEMS

Chinese, European, and Japanese societies all produced periods of feudalism. The feudal era in China dates from around 900 to around 400 B.C., in Europe from around A.D. 900 to around 1100, and in Japan from around A.D. 1200 to around 1600. Of course, because feudalism influences social structures and customs, many feudal elements continued to exist in these societies well after these dates. In each area, feudal relationships ebbed and flowed with the political tides of centralization and decentralization. A general review of Chinese, European, and Japanese histories reveals that their feudal structures were essentially the same and that a basic pattern of land use in exchange for military service is certainly present within the three societies.

China

The Late Zhou era (900–400 B.C.) was a period of decentralization in Chinese history. Our knowledge of these times is fragmentary, so we cannot precisely say how reciprocal relationships evolved and whether they extended much below the highest aristocratic level. Zhou rulers controlled their

FIGURE I.3.1 *Rebellious Vassals.* *Warfare in the Han Dynasty had changed little since China's feudal era. Occasionally, vassals seeking greater territories or privileges rose up against monarchs and their loyal vassals, as seen in this woodcut based on a second century A.D. carving. When ruling forces were defeated, dynasties changed or independent polities emerged. When loyal troops were victorious, rebel vassals lost both their lands and their lives, leaving their families dispossessed and orphaned.*

Stone Rubbing
from the Wu family shrine, Chia-hsiang, Shantung. From *Chin-shih-so.* Photo by Eileen Tweedy.

territories through their regional leaders, consisting of old allies and kinsmen. Similar to the earlier Shang Period, kinship was sometimes fictive or arranged through marital ties. A ceremony existed that included the presentation of handfuls of dirt, representing the lands awarded, for oaths of loyalty and promises of support. The exchange of land for loyalty fits the feudal model.

In periods of strong rulers, those whose allegiance was suspect were forced to migrate to areas of dependable loyalty. When Zhou rulers remained relatively strong, they had control of their landed aristocrats, but when the monarchy became weak, they lost revenues, resulting in less tribute to the Zhou treasury. In addition, the landed aristocrats became increasingly hostile toward the ruler and one another.

In the Early Zhou Period, an embryonic bureaucratic system had been created. Administrators served as clerks and overseers, keeping records and performing as advisors or department heads for regional leaders, as well as for the monarch. A skilled professional bureaucracy was developing and becoming an important aspect in Chinese government. Yet, after a few generations, and certainly by the ninth century B.C., central power dissipated, and the local lords wielded considerable independence of the monarchy. The loss of central authority by the Zhou monarchy and the loss of bureaucratic control fit the pattern of the feudal model.

Allied regional leaders defeated the Zhou ruler, and, although the Zhou dynasty continued under weaker successors, warring persisted as regional leaders fought among themselves. Central power all but evaporated; similarly to the French royal lands in the European feudal period, the lands directly under the control of the Zhou ruler shrank to include only the capital and its supporting rural lands. China then entered the prolonged Warring States Period (403–221 B.C.), when regional leaders engaged in deadly rivalries, vying for power and influence. Eventually the regional leaders abandoned the imperial structure, leading China out of feudalism. Private ownership of land replaced the feudal practice of awarding land for military support, and regional leaders developed state bureaucracies to govern their territories.

Europe

Aspects of Roman and Germanic practices and customs from roughly A.D. 500 contributed to European feudalism, but the feudal structure emerged after the invasions of the ninth and tenth centuries spurred decentralization and regionalism, particularly in France. Feudalism in Europe, therefore, was part of an evolving process and was

FIGURE I.3.2 *Land Grants.* *This castle in Yorkshire, in northern England, was a manor granted to a loyal vassal. The castle is located in the center of the estate, the village spreads out along the road, and the fields surround the castle and the village. This organization reflects their interrelationship between the lord and the peasants: In feudal society peasants worked the land and produced the wealth that sustained the lifestyle of the vassals.* Aerofilms, Ltd.

closely associated with the Germanic custom of the king as gift giver.

In general, European feudalism consisted of the awarding of lands, called **fiefs**, to regional leaders by the king, who received oaths of loyalty and military support in return. The one who granted land was a lord, and the one who received land was a vassal. A fief could include large agricultural lands (and the peasants and serfs who worked them), towns, villages, or even church properties. The vassal was expected to support the lord's interests on and off the battlefield. In return, the lord represented the vassal before the law or in social matters, such as arranging marriages. Vassals usually fell under the legal jurisdiction of their lords. European feudalism was a complicated system of rights and privileges, as well as of land use.

The reapportionment of granted lands by the regional lords became very complex over time. Lords sometimes acquired additional lands and wealth by making themselves vassals of other lords. The feudal network, therefore, was not only a vertical hierarchy but also a horizontal entanglement of relationships (as is evidenced in the example of John of Toul at the opening of this issue). Any lord could be the lord of many vassals and simultaneously be a vassal of many lords. The idea of **liege lord**, one who had a greater feudal claim,

gave vassals a means to choose which lord to serve if competing demands were claimed. Although European feudalism became increasingly complex, it conforms to the basic feudal structure.

The granting of fiefs was carefully orchestrated with family and kin groups. Many regional vassals kept tight control of lands by giving fiefs only to family members or to the church, whose bishops, abbots, or other ecclesiastical officials could not leave church lands to heirs. A formal ceremony, similar to that in China, was performed that signified the process of becoming a vassal. This ceremony involved the action of paying homage to the lord, signifying the lord's authority over the vassal. If the fief had been held by one family for several generations, the tendency was to view the fief as a hereditary right.

Although feudal customs continued to dominate much of medieval European history, monarchs pressed for centralization in the eleventh century and supported growing bureaucracies that regained control of revenues and governance.

Japan

In Japan there was a long-lived practice of the warrior-elite class giving out lands in exchange for gathering a group of retainers who owed loyalty

FIGURE 1.3.3 *Investiture Ceremony. This thirteenth-century work depicts the ninth-century emperor Charlemagne in the traditional posture of granting privileges to a vassal. The vassal kneels before the king; his weaponless hands, positioned in prayer, are a sign of submission. Traditionally, a clod of dirt or a banner was presented to symbolize the territories awarded to the vassal. A sword, representing the vassal's military obligation to his monarch, might also be given.* Bibliothèque nationale, Paris.

and service to their lord, an arrangement that directly compares to the feudal model. Early Japanese aristocratic society was organized around a clan structure with subordinate social and economic groups bound to the clans through fictive kinship ties. From the seventh to the twelfth centuries, Japanese monarchs and aristocrats borrowed the Chinese political system and imposed it on their subjects, but this system eventually disintegrated.

By the twelfth century, a warrior-elite supplanted aristocrats on some lands and created its own governmental structure. Aristocrats had taken advantage of a decentralized landholding system by appointing their own agents as overseers of land parcels. These agents collected rent monies from peasants who tilled the plots. In exchange, the aristocrats gave power to these subordinates to collect the rents and fees from the tillers. This system was essentially a bureaucracy. The warrior-elite, however, ended this bureaucracy and gained economic and jurisdictional control of their own regions. They then founded the shogunates, three successive regional leaders' families that controlled Japan through ineffective emperors from the twelfth through the nineteenth centuries.

During that time, a whole series of reciprocal relationships involving loyalty oaths and obligations evolved that follow the pattern of the feudal model. *Daimyo*, retainers of the *shogun*, further subdivided lands among their own retainers, the *samurai*. This pattern of subinfeudation was very

similar to Europe's, but *samurai* usually served only one *daimyo*.

Central control by the warrior groups was strong in the thirteenth century, but the Mongol invasions of the 1270s and 1280s severely weakened this feudal system because the retainers who responded to the *shogun*'s call to defeat the invading Mongols were not given lands in reward for their successful efforts. Because Mongol lands were distant from Japan and the operation was defensive, there was no conquered territory to award to feudal retainers. This lack of reward weakened the *shogun-daimyo* relationship. The first shogunate fell some decades later, in 1333. The next shogunate was impotent in terms of control, and this impotence led to the regional wars of 1467 to 1568. During the third shogunate in the seventeenth century, more and more *samurai* moved off their lands and lost economic control of their territories. This process of relocation essentially ended feudalism in Japan as centralization reemerged.

FEUDAL-LIKE SOCIETIES

There are many examples of societies that manifested one or more of the characteristics of feudalism, particularly weak monarchical control or a type of strong regionalism. A society cannot be feudal, however, without tension between royal privilege and local autonomy. The Early Shang

FIGURE I.3.4 Samurai.
This daimyo *(center top) has assembled the vassals of his territories—the* samurai. *Many* samurai *were actually clansmen of the* daimyo, *who was in turn the vassal of the* shogun. *In many feudal societies, vassalage followed family lineage, which helped to keep land grants intact and provided a base of support when challenging lords or monarchs.*
Stephen Turnbull/Japan Archive.

Period and the Early Zhou Empire in China, the Harsha Empire in India, the Byzantine Empire in southeastern Europe, and the Carolingian Empire in western Europe had relationships of vassalage and land management, but the rulers retained central bureaucratic administrations that impeded regional leaders' power in local areas.

Feudalism does not include those areas where no central authority exists and lands and power are vested solely in regional aristocrats, even if one regional leader dominates an alliance of several regional leaders. After the breakup of the Mongol Empire, the monarchy toppled and independent allied states appeared. Some societies had strong regional alliances dominated by one regional leader but never developed a monarchy or central authority. Scholars identify the states that demonstrate some of the characteristics of feudalism but not all as being feudal-like.

FEUDAL CODES

Examining the codes of behavior from feudal China, Europe, and Japan helps us to see how feudal relationships and responsibilities work. In part, these codes were products of the particular social customs and warrior mentality. All warriors are bound in some way to their superiors by oaths of loyalty. The Chinese warriors were bound by a code of honorable or righteous behavior, **li**, which under Confucian influences evolved into the virtues of the Chinese "gentleman." European knights were bound by a code of suitable behavior, **chivalry**, that encouraged the ideals of honesty, courtesy, and defense of the defenseless. The Japanese *samurai* were bound by a code of self-denial, indifference to adversity, and generosity to the less fortunate; in later centuries this code would be formalized as the **bushido** code. In each case, local customs and the lord's expectations influenced the codes.

Loyalty to one's superior was central to feudal structures in all three areas. The Chinese warrior was expected to travel many miles to attend the investiture ceremony, where allegiance and loyalty were pledged. Religious overtones helped to solidify the monarch's authority in the minds of the participants. It was not until later in the Warring States Period that regional leaders refused to go to the capital and participate in the ceremony. In Europe, as in China, a ceremony of investiture humbled the vassal in the presence of the lord. Kings expected their vassals to kiss their feet as an act of submission. In Japan, *samurai* were pledged to the service of their lord with extraordinary devotion.

They were never to question the instructions of their lord and were expected to shield him on the battlefield. The Japanese lord could even order the death of a *samurai* by ritual suicide.

In each feudal structure there was a variety of attention paid to the prescribed practices. But codes of behavior were not enough to control heavily armed warriors from taking advantage of the very people they were pledged to defend. Knights errant frequently broke the peace of Europe, for example, and their constant rivalries, in part, prompted religious leaders to initiate the First Crusade in order to establish peace. Like the legendary Robin Hood of England, Chinese knights errant championed the downtrodden and frequently challenged bureaucratic authority. Their exploits were popular in Chinese literature. Masterless *samurai* frequently bullied the local peasant populations and sometimes quarreled among themselves until violence settled the dispute. Loyalty to one's lord was usually observed when lords were able to dominate their retainers, but, when relationships changed, lords were increasingly unable to demand obedience. Often the oath taken was only as solid as the armor of the lord who demanded it.

COMPARING FEUDAL STRUCTURES

By comparing the feudal structures of China, Europe, and Japan, scholars can gain insight into how states have coped with decentralization and regionalism. General patterns can be used to create a model, which can then be used to study other societies facing similar challenges.

By definition, the basic characteristics of the model have to be found in all examples. In each of these cases, weak monarchies led to regionalism, and land was exchanged for the military support and loyalty of regional leaders to stop disintegration into smaller independent polities. Why would regional leaders retain a weak monarch? Comparison of the examples suggests one answer might be in the key characteristic of loyalty. Regional leaders often recognized the legitimacy of keeping weak monarchs through religious tenets of divine right of rule. In China the monarch ruled through the Mandate of Heaven, in Europe Christian monarchs ruled by the grace of God, and in Japan the *shogun* received legitimacy from the god-emperor.

In applying any model to a set of specific circumstances, however, instances of dissimilarity will be observed; the states studied here developed feudal practices that were not exactly alike. In European and Japanese feudalism, complex subinfeudation helped to organize and maintain several levels of the warrior-elite. In contrast, China probably did not develop an elaborate practice of subinfeudation; the feudal relationship remained at the highest aristocratic level. Unlike Chinese and Japanese feudal disputes, which led to periods of warring regions, European feudal disputes retreated from the battlefield into the emerging court system as monarchs regained central administration.

SUGGESTED READINGS

Bloch, Mark. *Feudal Society*. Two vols. Trans. by L. A. Manyon. Chicago: University of Chicago Press, 1961. This seminal work, first published in 1940, is still a standard on medieval feudalism.

Duus, Peter. *Japanese Feudalism*. Third edition. New York: Knopf/Random House, 1993. A standard work on Japanese feudalism.

Gernet, Jacques. *A History of Chinese Civilization*. Trans. by J. R. Foster. Cambridge, Eng.: Cambridge University Press, 1985. A general history of China.

Herlihy, David. *The History of Feudalism*. New York: Harper and Row, 1970; reprinted, London: Humanities Press, 1992. This primary sourcebook's selections clearly show elements of the European feudal structure.

Varley, H. Paul, Ivan Morris, and Nobuko Morris. *Samurai*. New York: Delacorte, 1970. A review of the Japanese *samurai* structure.

PART THREE EXAMINED REGIONALISM IN MANY parts of the world. Part Four will explore the resumption of empire building after times of regionalism in the Americas, Europe, and Asia. Political ambitions and desire for wealth propelled rulers to extend their domains far beyond their homelands. In fact, the new empires controlled larger areas than those discussed in Part Two. Control and expansion of trade routes brought commercial growth and economic prosperity on an unprecedented scale. Much of Eurasia and Africa was linked by a vibrant and thriving trade network that exchanged goods, technologies, ideas, and diseases at levels greater than ever.

Chapter 16 presents the empires of the Aztecs and Incas, governments that ruled vast areas. The Aztecs and Incas effectively integrated their subjects politically and economically into their empires. Europeans conquered these territories in the early sixteenth century. Chapter 17 examines the Byzantine Empire and assesses some of the reasons for its unusual longevity. The empire's domination of trade routes coming from Eurasia and Africa helped provide the economic foundation

	AMERICAS	EURASIA-AFRICA
400		
500		Byzantine Empire
600		
700		
800		
900		
1000		
1100		
1200		
1300		
1400	Aztec Empire	
1500	Inca Empire	
1600		

for the political longevity of the Byzantine state. Chapter 18 studies the reestablishment of imperial rule in East Asia. It also examines the unprecedented economic growth in China and the social changes generated by increasing economic opportunities. Chapter 19 analyzes the contradictory nature of the Mongol Empire, a state that was founded with great violence but one whose rulers encouraged commercial activity. The Mongols helped promote a trade network with sea and land routes linking Europe, Asia, and Africa. Economic prosperity affected many in these lands until a catastrophic epidemic effectively dampened transregional trade, causing political decay and economic bankruptcy.

PART FOUR

THE REEMERGENCE OF EXPANSIVE SOCIETIES

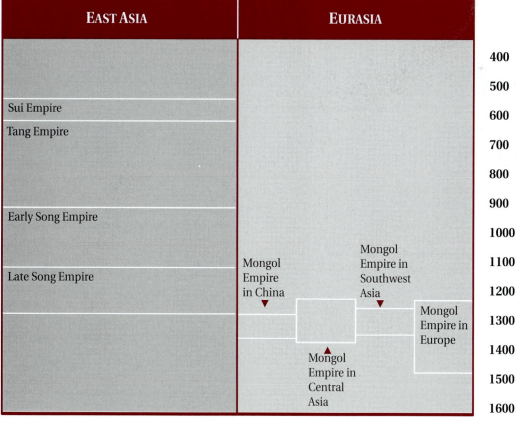

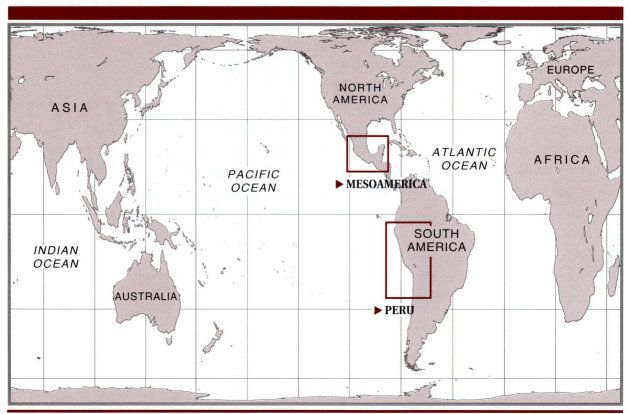

ASIA

EUROPE

NORTH
AMERICA

AFRICA

PACIFIC
OCEAN

ATLANTIC
OCEAN

▶ MESOAMERICA

INDIAN
OCEAN

SOUTH
AMERICA

AUSTRALIA

▶ PERU

AZTLÁN

Gulf of
Mexico

Culhuacán
Tenochtitlán
Tlaxcala

Usumacinta R.

PACIFIC
OCEAN

▶ MESOAMERICA

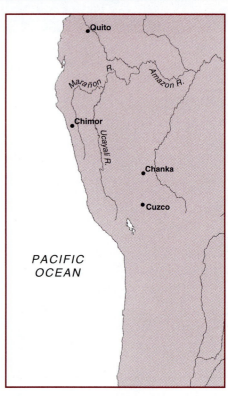

Quito

Marañon R.

Amazon R.

Chimor

Ucayali R.

Chanka

Cuzco

PACIFIC
OCEAN

▶ PERU

The Americas on the Eve of European Contact

around 1300–1532

Under the rising full moon and clear skies of October 11, 1492, Guacanagarí, the chief of the Caribbean island of Guanahani, gazed out over the ocean surrounding his realm. Unbeknownst to him, Christopher Columbus and a boatload of sailors were anchored beyond his vision. The next morning, they would come ashore and greet the local Indians, changing forever the course of history. What were the Americas like on that sultry night as Guacanagarí peered into the twilight?

This chapter focuses on the latest societies of the Americas before contact with Europeans, ones that arose isolated from the rest of the world and were functioning entities at the time of European contact. It relates an essentially American story, and Europeans enter into it only as the agents truncating the Native American tradition.

The Nuclear American civilizations discussed here, those of the Aztecs and Incas, were among the most complex of pre-Columbian civilizations. They were surrounded by many other civilizations. Similarly, the North American societies treated here, the Iroquois, Hopi, and Navajo, are only a few of the many North American Indian groups extant in the sixteenth century.

THE AZTEC EMPIRE, 1325–1521

The Valley of Mexico, the site of present-day Mexico City, saw the rise and fall of Teotihuacán, the Toltecs, and many other peoples and states prior

Figure 16.1 *Tenochtitlán in 1519.* *At the eve of the Spanish conquest, the Aztec capital of Tenochtitlán was a bustling city built around a central religious precinct, shown in this reconstruction. The Great Temple in the center had two stairways, one dedicated to Huitzilopochtli (the war god) and the other to Tlaloc (the rain god); other gods had separate temples or shrines within temples.* David Hiser/Photographers Aspen.

to A.D. 1300. This rich environment encouraged the growth of population and accumulation of wealth, allowing states to develop and expand. The richest, most powerful, and most expansive of the pre-Columbian states of the Valley of Mexico was the last: the Aztec Empire.

From Aztlán to Tenochtitlán

The Aztecs did not originate in the Valley of Mexico. Rather, they began somewhere in the north, in a place they mythically designated Aztlán. While the location of Aztlán is not known exactly and has been claimed for such unlikely places as present-day northeastern New Mexico and southern Wisconsin, it almost certainly was somewhere in northwestern Mexico, probably around Durango. The people of Aztlán were not yet known as Aztecs and went by a number of names, including "Mexica,"[1] which they called themselves. They were part of a larger category of northern peoples collectively known as Chichimecs.

The Chichimecs were mobile tribes that lived by hunting, gathering, farming, and raiding. While some scholars claim them to have been at the tribe

level, most believe that the Mexica were a chiefdom at this point. The Chichimecs had been in contact with the Valley of Mexico since the time of Teotihuacán, whose northern colonies and mining communities were raided almost constantly by the warlike Chichimecs.

The Mexica migration was demanded by Huitzilopochtli, a god who spoke through his priests. Oral histories, written down in the fifteenth or sixteenth century, place the departure from Aztlán in 1111 and the arrival in the Valley of Mexico in 1325. The long trek was marked by incessant privations and hostilities with the peoples through whose land they passed. Wherever the Mexica stopped temporarily, they built a temple dedicated to Huitzilopochtli, suggesting that their travel was perhaps more in the nature of conquest.

Legend states that Huitzilopochtli told the Mexica priests that they would recognize the proper place to settle by an eagle perched on a prickly pear cactus, a sight they finally saw in the Valley in Mexico. They settled there and founded their capital, Tenochtitlán,[2] meaning "place of the fruit of the prickly pear cactus." This mythic found-

---

[1] **Mexica:** meh SHEE kuh

[2] **Tenochtitlán:** teh nohch tee TLAHN

ing is pictured on the Mexican flag. Archaeology tells us that the Mexica founded short-lived settlements in the northern parts of the Valley of Mexico in their early years there and that Tenochtitlán was founded around the date indicated in the mythic history.

The Valley of Mexico was far from empty of people when the Mexica arrived. Immigrant Chichimecs of other tribes had swollen the already large population of the region, and the Mexica were not welcomed by the inhabitants. The Mexica were seen as competitors demanding land, and their military prowess was not lost on the local rulers. Further, the Mexica had customs that alienated their neighbors. One notable example occurred in 1325, when the daughter of Coxcox,[3] king of the neighboring state of Culhuacán,[4] was to wed a Mexica noble. The woman arrived at the Mexica city, and, under command from Huitzilopochtli, priests sacrificed her and removed her skin to be worn by a priest. Many Mesoamerican peoples sacrificed people, but even the Mexica rarely sacrificed a royal bride, and, when her father arrived the next day, he was understandably shocked. In his anger, Coxcox led his warriors against the Mexica, who were forced to move on.

By 1345, the Mexica had refined their diplomatic skills. They realized that they were feared by their neighbors, and they used their reputation to their own advantage. Through a skillful combination of treaties and warfare, the Mexica carved out their place in the Valley of Mexico, developed their capital city, and established their political control of the area. With this process they came to be known as the "Aztecs," and upon this basis they built the Aztec Empire.

Aztec Society

The Aztecs had only a short history of intensive agriculture. In their Chichimec past, they had practiced agriculture as an adjunct to hunting and gathering, but their new life in the Valley of Mexico demanded a greater food supply than the old ways could provide, so they developed new means of producing food. Mostly they adopted agricultural crops and techniques already in use in the Valley of Mexico. Of paramount importance were *chinampas*, fields formed by dredging nutrient-rich mud

from lake bottoms and forming fertile artificial islands by piling it in shallow water. *Chinampas* were very important to the Aztecs, who had been forced into areas with large numbers of lakes. The labor investment for *chinampas* was great, but so was the return: Aztec *chinampas* provided as much food per unit area as any agricultural technique known today. And in addition, *chinampas* were a self-sustaining system that required no fertilizing, irrigation, or flushing to remove salts deposited by irrigation. Largely forced into this labor-intensive strategy by the shortage of arable land, the Aztecs developed one of the most efficient forms of agriculture known anywhere in the world.

Religion permeated every aspect of Aztec life, especially for the elite. The Aztecs had many gods, chief of whom was Huitzilopochtli. Other important gods included Quetzalcóatl and Tlaloc (the rain god), both inherited from Teotihuacán and the Toltecs. These and other gods competed with one another for human attention, and all demanded sacrifices. Many of these sacrifices consisted of destroying inanimate objects, killing animals, or simply letting the blood of priests, but some of them required killing human beings. While human sacrifice was practiced by most Mesoamerican civilizations, the Aztecs conducted their sacrifices at a scale previously unknown, sometimes sacrificing thousands of people in a multiday ritual.

The reason underlying human sacrifice was simple: The gods were thought to demand sacrifices in return for continued well-being. The sun required blood to continue its transit; the seasons required blood to return on schedule; less important needs could be satisfied by a sacrifice of flowers or inanimate objects. But most important, the universe itself was renewed every fifty-two years, at the end of each calendric cycle, and failure to provide the proper sacrifices at this dangerous period could result in total destruction of the sort that had occurred several times before, according to Aztec mythology. Because of this context, sacrifice was considered an honor. Some people volunteered, others were selected on the basis of their merit, and warriors captured in battle—particularly valiant or noble ones—often were sacrificed. In fact, this need for captives probably was one incentive for the near-constant warfare that characterized Aztec history.

[3] **Coxcox:** KOSH kosh
[4] **Culhuacán:** kool hwah KAHN

Figure 16.2 *Modern* **Chinampa.** *In order to support their vast capital, the Aztecs needed to increase the agricultural productivity of the surrounding area. To do so, they developed* chinampas, *gardens made by piling mud into the shallow waters of Lake Texcoco, on which the island city of Tenochtitlán was built. Still in use, these* chinampas *increased the amount of land available for cultivation and created some of the most fertile farmland anywhere. Though sometimes called "floating gardens," they were firmly anchored to the lake bottom.* David Hiser/Photographers Aspen.

As well as sacrifices, the gods needed imposing places dedicated to their worship, and the temple-pyramids served this purpose. Clearly descendent from earlier Teotihuacano temple-pyramids, these huge stone edifices had temples on their tops, and this is where sacrifice and other devotions took place, including divination and the reading of omens. The scale and majesty of these pyramids awed the Spanish *conquistadores* who beheld them.

The gods also legitimized the hierarchy that permeated Aztec society. At the top were the nobles, viewed as descendants of Quetzalcóatl and sharing in his divine nature, and rulers could come only from this class. At the top of the noble class were the **tlatoani**,[5] the monarchs ruling cities and surrounding regions, and the Aztec emperor. Upon the death of a *tlatoani*, candidates would be named from the eligible family, and then the candidate deemed most capable would be elected by male nobles. This combination of hereditary kingship and election was established by Acamapichtli,[6] the first Aztec monarch.

The primary roles of noblewomen seem to have been as wives and mothers. The ideal noble-

[5] **tlatoani:** tlah toh AH nee
[6] **Acamapichtli:** ah kah mah PEECH tlee

woman was said to be respectful of her husband and unintrusive into his affairs. She was supposed to be quiet and decorous, and she was supposed to be a skilled weaver who practiced her art as a symbol of her domestic role. A woman in childbirth was thought of as a warrior of sorts and, if she died during the birth, was eligible for the heaven otherwise reserved for warriors who died in battle.

Beneath the *tlatoani* and other nobles were various categories of commoners, also in a hierarchy. Near the top were merchants and artisans, and below them were agriculturalists, laborers, and slaves. Slave status usually was acquired by selling oneself into slavery and was open to both men and women.

While slavery status was permanent, it was not passed on to one's children, and it was not particularly onerous. People selling themselves into slavery would be paid a certain amount one year before the slavery commenced; after that year, they became slaves, and their labor was controlled by their owners, who had certain obligations to them in terms of support. Slaves could own property (including other slaves), marry, and retain most of their legal rights. Most individuals selling themselves into slavery were impoverished, often from gambling, and used their payment to settle debts.

The Aztecs used art as one means of differentiating the different classes. **Sumptuary laws**, regulations stating what clothing and ornaments could be worn legally only by members of a certain class, provided a means by which a person's class immediately could be identified. Feather headdresses, for example, were reserved for the *tlatoani*. These magnificent constructions, often five or more feet high, were built on wooden frames and might contain 20,000 brightly colored feathers from tropical birds; some were so ornate and large that servants were needed to help support their massive weight.

One of the most highly valued arts was poetry. All elite men were expected to be skilled orators; in fact, *tlatoani* translates literally as "speaker." Nahuátl,[7] the language of the Aztecs, was much given to metaphor, and Aztec poetry pondered the meaning of life, the beauty of flowers, and the anguish of leaving one's home upon achieving

[7]**Nahuátl:** nah HWAHT

FIGURE 16.3 *Noble Aztec Headdress.* *The social position of an Aztec man was indicated by clothing and other symbols. The noble shown in this Aztec illustration wears a fancy but modest headdress in keeping with his station in life. The* tlatoani, *in contrast, wore a huge feather headdress mounted on a wooden frame, featuring rare feathers of the quetzal bird, attached with glue made from orchid roots and bound with hammered gold spacers and studs.* Bibliothèque nationale, Paris.

adulthood. Poetry and human sacrifice may seem incongruous to the modern reader, but they were perfectly harmonious to the Aztec elite.

Writing was a skill shared by most nobles and by those commoners whose profession demanded it. The written Nahuátl language was glyphic, so it looked like a series of pictures, each of which referred to a particular concept. The Aztecs, however, had no fixed rules regarding glyph order, and a certain amount of experience and creativity was necessary to read a passage. The Aztecs wrote books on society, morality, accounting, administration, poetry, science, and many other subjects, but most were destroyed by the Spanish during the conquest. Fortunately, a few have survived, as have some copies of earlier books with notes by Spanish priests that explain how these texts should be read.

The lifeways of commoners were less varied than those of the elite. Most commoner men were farmers or laborers; most commoner women ran a household and might also be weavers or physicians. For most of these commoners, the *calpulli*,[8] or residential unit, was the major orienting point. The *calpulli* was a district of a community, where land was held at least partly in common. *Calpulli* provided certain institutional services, including schools (for boys only) and temples. In addition, *calpulli* elected local officials and conducted taxing, censuses, and public works. For commoners, the *calpulli* was the most accessible level of government.

Politics and the Aztec Empire

The Aztecs passed gradually from a local state to an empire. The founding of the Aztec royal house was in 1372, when Acamapichtli ascended to the throne, justifying his legitimacy through the lineage of his mother, a princess of Culhuacán. Because *tlatoani* were elected, the Aztec rulership could and often did pass from brother to brother; women were excluded from rulership. As the Aztecs came to dominate the Valley of Mexico and beyond, the *tlatoani* of Tenochtitlán gradually became the Aztec emperors.

At its height just before 1520, the Aztec Empire extended from the Atlantic to the Pacific, from northern parts of present-day Guatemala to the northern edge of the central highlands of Mexico.

[8] *calpulli:* kahl POO lee

Although a few pockets of resistance successfully held out against the Aztecs, most notably the Tarascans on the west coast, most peoples within this area clearly were under Aztec domination.

The Aztecs integrated peoples who had been brought into the empire by military or diplomatic means. Conquered peoples were permitted to retain their own religion and government, but they took on obligations to the Aztecs. First, they had to provide tribute to the emperor. This tribute was explicitly specified in documents originating in Tenochtitlán and might consist of a mixture of everyday items (corn, cotton cloth, and animal hides) and luxury items (tropical feathers, cacao, and turquoise). Second, conquered peoples were expected to serve as allies in future wars. Third, they were expected to worship the central gods of the Aztecs, in addition to their own traditional gods. Finally, they were expected to contribute individuals for the human sacrifices required by Mesoamerican religions.

For many conquerors, establishing a stable empire is the primary goal, permitting the conqueror to reap the material benefits of conquest. While the demand for tribute shows that material benefit was important to the Aztecs, they had another need to fill: captives for sacrifice. Consequently, the Aztecs did not wish to consolidate their conquests to the point that further warfare would be unnecessary. Indeed, Tenochtitlán and Tlaxcala, a neighboring state, conducted ritualized warfare regularly for the express reasons of training troops and mutually obtaining captives for sacrifice.

The Aztec military was equipped with spears, arrows, swords with obsidian blades and tips, slings, and clubs, and was finely trained in their use. They wore cotton armor, which was very effective against most of these weapons. They were organized into military companies, some of which were based on *calpulli* and some of which were elite forces. Although books on tactics have not survived, warfare of the Aztecs clearly demonstrates that they had well-developed tactical theories.

In addition to their military strength, the Aztecs used *pochteca*, merchants who also served as diplomats and spies. The *pochteca* traveled widely outside the empire, because foreign trade was their specialty. While conducting their trade, they gathered information of potential military

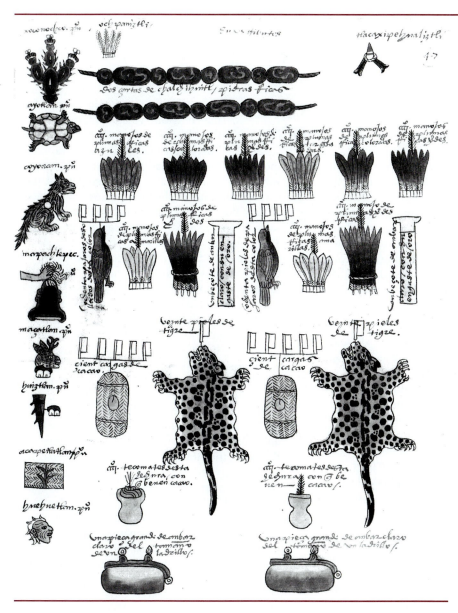

FIGURE 16.4 *Aztec Tribute List.* *The central imperial government of the Aztecs kept track of the tribute obligations of dependent allies through written documents. This copy of a tribute list was made just a few years after the Spanish conquest and shows some of the items rendered as payment, including jade beads, bundles of exotic feathers, cacao beans, and jaguar skins. The small feathers and flags projecting upward from the objects are Aztec glyphs indicating numbers; the images in the vertical row on the left are the names of tributary states; the Spanish writing is a sixteenth-century translation.* The Bodleian Library, University of Oxford.

value and sometimes negotiated with foreign powers. Once an area was conquered, their job was done; what had formerly come to Tenochtitlán as trade would then come as tribute. While the ideal *pochteca* was decorous and self-effacing, front teeth filed to points must have presented a fearsome appearance to potential trading and diplomatic partners, enhancing the *pochteca*'s reputation for being dangerous.

Montezuma II was elected to the posts of *tlatoani* of Tenochtitlán and Aztec emperor in 1502. By all accounts he was a generally able ruler,

extending the boundaries of the empire and maintaining the operation of the state. In 1519, a force of Spanish soldiers commanded by Hernando Cortés landed in eastern Mexico, bent on the conquest of Mexico. The Aztecs, of course, had no idea that the Spanish existed, and the sudden appearance of strange people in their territory was unsettling; this was especially true because rumors were circulating that the Spanish were gods, perhaps the Quetzalcóatl and his divine retinue, who myths said would return from the east someday. The Spanish advanced, collecting disaffected peoples

A few of the Aztec books, called **codices** (singular, **codex**), have survived intact, and one of these is the *Florentine Codex*. Named for the city where it was preserved after the conquest, the *Florentine Codex* discusses many aspects of Aztec life, including proper behavior, religious rituals, and professions. It was dictated to Spanish scribes in the Aztec language and written in Roman letters; a Spanish translation, marginal notes, and illustrations (some with Aztec writing included) were then added. The translated excerpts that follow describe a few of the sacrifices and divining practices that preceded the departure of a major trading expedition. They provide an insight into how thoroughly religion and trade were interwoven in the Aztec mind.

And when they [the merchants] were about to set out, then they sought a good day sign—One Serpent . . . One Crocodile, or One Monkey, or Seven Serpent.[a] The vanguard merchants who had read the day signs knew on which one they would set out. And when it was the day before they would set out on a good day sign, thereupon they once and for all washed their heads with soap and cut their hair here in Mexico. And all the time that they went traveling in Anauac, nevermore did they wash their hair with soap [or] cut their hair.[b] They only bathed up to their necks, not submerging in water; all the time they traveled abstaining. And when night had fallen, when the time of blowing shell trumpets[c] arrived, thereupon they began cutting lengths of paper. . . . Then they painted it with liquid rubber. They impaled the [lump of] rubber on a spit; thereupon they set it on fire. As it continued to burn, so they painted. And thus did they paint the paper: they gave it lips, nose, eyes. It resembled a man. Thus did they make a representation of the fire

[god]. [After cutting other paper representations of gods] all their offerings were arranged together in the middle of the courtyard, whereupon they entered their home [and] stood before the fire. There they beheaded a quail [to honor the fire]. When they had beheaded it, thereupon, with pointed obsidian blades, they pierced their ears, or they pierced their tongues. When the blood already flowed, they took it with their hands [and] said, "*Teonappa*,"[d] when they cast it into the fire. Thereupon they spattered the papers with it. . . . Thereupon he [the merchant] offered the paper to the fire. As he offered it, then he took white copal [incense] . . . then he inserted it among the papers so that it would blaze up well. And he stood watching it closely as it burned, taking good care of it. If the paper only smoked, when it did not burn well, he was much frightened. There he saw that perhaps a sickness would somewhere go to seize him. But if it burned quickly, so that it crackled [and] popped a great deal, he was greatly pleased thereby. He said within himself, "He hath been good to me, the master, our lord.[e] I shall indeed reach the place where I am to go." And when they had assembled indeed all the loads, they thereupon arranged them on carrying frames; they set one each on the hired burden-carriers to carry on their backs: Not very heavy, they put on only a limited amount. . . . Then they went forth [and] proceeded straightaway to the boats. None entered the women's quarters, neither did they turn back [or] look to one side. If perchance he had gone forgetting something, he might no more come to take it, nor might they still go to offer it to him. No longer could he do it. Neither did even one of all the old merchants [and] merchant women go following them. When one turned back they thought it an omen of evil—sinful; they regarded it as dangerous. In this manner did the vanguard merchants depart.

[a] These dates in the Aztec calendar were considered particularly auspicious for travel.
[b] This was a departure from normal behavior, because the Aztecs viewed personal hygiene and cleanliness as very important.
[c] Shell trumpets were sounded in Aztec cities at dusk.
[d] This word, although not fully translatable, begins with a root meaning "god."
[e] Referring to a patron god.

of the Aztec Empire with them as allies, and marched on Tenochtitlán. After initial setbacks, the Spanish captured Montezuma; his apparent capitulation alienated his subjects, and he died under mysterious circumstances—perhaps murdered by the Spanish, perhaps killed by his own people. (This mystery is examined in the "In Their Own Words" box in Chapter 1.)

By this time, the Aztecs had elected Cuitlahuac[9] as the new *tlatoani*, and he was able to rally his forces to drive the Spanish from the city. The success was only short lived, however, because Cuitlahuac and many other Aztecs had been infected with smallpox and died within a few months. The Spanish laid siege to Tenochtitlán and captured it in 1521, sacking it and massacring huge numbers of its inhabitants. This effectively crushed the Aztec Empire.

How could a force of only a few hundred Spanish conquer a major empire? Certainly Montezuma's initial vacillation was a factor. Spanish military technology also was superior to that of the Aztecs, and the horse gave the Spanish an advantage, but the most important factors probably were goals and disease. The Spanish were fighting a war of killing and conquest; the Aztecs were trying to take captives. Each was practicing war as experience dictated, and the ensuing interaction favored the Spanish. And perhaps most important, the Spanish brought smallpox and other germs with them, inadvertently but effectively destroying huge numbers of the Aztecs and mortally disrupting their society. Pockets of resistance held out for almost seventy years, but effective native rule of Mexico ended in 1521.

THE INCA EMPIRE, 1438–1532

At about the same time that the Aztecs were coming to dominate Mesoamerica, the Incas were rising in Peru. After the collapse of the Tiahuanaco Empire about A.D. 1100, Cuzco was one of the many regional kingdoms of Peru that took its place. In the four centuries that followed, Cuzco expanded to control the largest empire in the pre-Columbian Americas. From its position high in the Andes, Cuzco governed the Empire of Tawantinsuyu[10]—"Land of the Four Quarters"—commonly called the Inca Empire. ("**Inca**" accurately refers to the ruler of the empire, not the empire itself or its people, but we will follow the common practice of using "Inca" to describe the empire and people; the leader will be called the "the Inca emperor.") Because the Incas had no writing, events before the coming of the Spanish are based on legendary history and archaeology.

The Cuzco State Becomes the Inca Empire

Protected by mountains, Cuzco was a small and undistinguished state in southern Peru following the breakup of the Tiahuanaco Empire. Around 1438, Cuzco was ruled by a monarch named Viracocha.[11] Chanka, a neighboring state, was emboldened by Viracocha's weak response to their challenges and attacked Cuzco. Most of Cuzco's allies waited to see the outcome before committing themselves, and Viracocha and his heir abandoned the city to seek refuge in the mountains. Another of Viracocha's sons rallied the soldiers of Cuzco, who repulsed the Chanka, chased them to their homeland, and conquered them. The son was proclaimed the new ruler and assumed the name Pachacuti.[12] Pachacuti was a relentless conqueror, and within a few decades he and his heirs led military expeditions that extended the realm of Cuzco from Ecuador to northern Chile.

Of course, diplomacy went hand in glove with warfare. The Inca emperor had a standard course of action when he wished to bring a new state into the empire, as exemplified by the conquest of the Masqo.[13] The ruler first sent spies to ascertain the condition of the Masqo state, especially its military strength and alliances. Then he sent emissaries to the ruler of Masqo, offering gifts and privileges if Masqo voluntarily would become part of the empire. When the Masqo ruler refused, the Incas tried to woo away his allies, isolating Masqo. Only if a state still refused to join the empire would military action be taken against it.

---

[9]**Cuitlahuac:** kweht lah HOO ahk

[10]**Tawantinsuyu:** tah wahn tihn SOO yoo
[11]**Viracocha:** veer ah KOHCH uh
[12]**Pachacuti:** pah chah KOO tee
[13]**Masqo:** MAH skoh

The military forces of the Inca Empire were equipped and organized similarly to those of their enemies. Important weapons were clubs, slings, bows and arrows, and spears; leather armor and helmets were used by at least some soldiers. As the Incas absorbed conquered peoples, the ranks of the Inca armies swelled, so that they usually outnumbered their enemies in later years of the empire.

The Incas used both humane and brutal measures as alternatives in dealing with conquered peoples. They generally had a reputation for fair treatment of prisoners and conquered peoples. Typically, at the conquest of a state, prisoners were set free and leaders were given gifts, reducing any incentive to fight on indefinitely. Further, the local government usually was incorporated into the imperial government, and leaders often retained their positions under the changed circumstances. Such humane practices reportedly encouraged states and individuals to surrender to the Incas. These humane actions were more a matter of practicality than morality. In this way, an initially small state was able to extend dominion over a huge area, sometimes conquering states far stronger than it and generally avoiding exhausting its resources in protracted military actions.

But the Inca Empire was capable of drastic and brutal expedients: When regions persisted in rebelling, their populations could be relocated, often hundreds of miles away in a radically different environment. The challenges of survival became so great that political unrest was quelled. Sometimes this system of population relocations was applied immediately to a conquered province if it was felt that uprisings might be forthcoming; sometimes groups from established parts of the empire were relocated to newly conquered regions to serve as model citizens.

The Inca approach to empire building was very different from that of the Tiahuanaco Empire, which preceded it. While Tiahuanaco imposed its stamp heavily on conquered states, the Incas left them as intact as possible, using existing governmental organizations. Rather than recast a region, the Incas simply added it to the ever-growing imperial organization. The only requirements for a new province were four: It had to incorporate Inti[14] (the Incas' sun god) into its pantheon, it had to

FIGURE 16.5 *Inti, the Inca Sun God. Inti, depicted here in a woven tapestry from around 1450, was the supreme god of the Incas. His role in the maintenance of the universe was considered paramount, his worship was mandatory for any peoples entering Inca territory, and his likeness appeared throughout the Inca Empire.* British Museum/Photo by Derek Witty.

submit to the rule of the Inca emperor, it had to render tribute to Cuzco, and it had to participate in the economic exchange system controlled by the imperial government at Cuzco. In return, Cuzco extended imperial military protection, provided preferential trading agreements, and incorporated gods of conquered peoples into its ever-expanding pantheon.

Such a massive empire, especially in such rugged territory, required an efficient transporta-

[14]**Inti:** EEN tee

tion and communication system. The Inca roads and *chaski* (runners), discussed briefly in Chapter 3, provided this. The empire built thousands of miles of paved roads, hundreds of suspension bridges spanning dizzying chasms, and hundreds of staircases cut into the steep sides of mountains. *Chaski* were state employees who carried messages or small packages rapidly, each runner traveling only a couple of miles to the next. Slower transportation of bulkier items was over the same routes, using llamas or people as carriers. As elsewhere in the Americas, no wheeled vehicles were used; indeed, the steep slopes and stairs of many Inca roads would have prevented their safe or efficient use.

The Inca Empire was extremely successful, but it had a serious weakness: succession of the emperor. Rulers and their families were viewed as direct descendants of Inti, and only they were eligible for consideration as emperor. (To ensure divine blood, members of the ruler's family were permitted to marry only their siblings.) From within the royal family, however, any male could serve as the Inca emperor. In early times, the emperor designated his own successor, and that candidate was confirmed by the **ayllu**,[15] a kind of cabinet of nobles appointed by the ruler to advise him. As time went on, however, this system became unwieldy. Rulers tended to take more of the authority of appointing a successor, yet several emperors died unexpectedly in their youth and had designated no successor. These instances led to factionalism and civil war, factors that facilitated the Spanish conquest of Peru in the sixteenth century.

Inca Society

Inca society was based on the same food crops as its predecessors: potatoes, quinoa, corn, beans, and chilis. What changed under the Incas was the way these crops were distributed throughout the empire. In earlier periods, people ate foods that were available locally. If possible, a community farmed at different elevations to take advantage of the different climates and range of crops that could be grown; this agricultural strategy is called **verticality**. The Incas carried verticality one step farther, moving crops considerable distances over

[15] **ayllu:** EYE yoo

FIGURE 16.6 *Inca Bridge over the Apurímac River.*
The Andes are dissected by thousands of deep gorges between mountains, and the Inca road system had to provide ways to cross these efficiently. A common solution was to build bridges like the one shown here, a suspension bridge made of rope spun locally from grass fiber. This Inca bridge, and dozens of others like it, has been maintained for the last five centuries by local villagers. Loren McIntyre.

the excellent roads and allowing people in the coastal deserts of the north to eat highland foods.

This was not the only economic difference between the Inca Empire and its predecessors, nor even the most important. The Incas practiced public ownership and administration of land, and all production was viewed as the property of the state. Consequently, that production was gathered together, then redistributed by the state according to what it saw as need. On the one hand, this was a benign system, because it meant that a regional crop failure would have little effect on that region's inhabitants; surpluses from elsewhere could take up the slack. On the other hand, it was a powerful agent of control by the Inca government, which could withhold food from an area in order to force compliance with its policies.

The Inca Empire controlled the labor of its citizens. Most of the time, people were expected to go about their regular tasks, but for about one month out of a year, healthy men were obliged to contribute their time for the good of the state; this is known as *corvée* **labor.** *Corvée* labor was used primarily for military service and the construction of public works, such as roads. Sometimes *chaski* served under *corvée* labor.

Coca, the plant from which cocaine is extracted, grows abundantly in the Andes, and its production was controlled by the state. Men were allocated a modest amount of coca leaves for personal use, and most men seem to have been moderate in their use of it, though art occasionally depicts a glassy-eyed man with a wad of leaves in his mouth, apparently an abuser. Larger allocations were distributed to workers in particular industries, especially mining, to help them endure pain and increase their output.

As could be expected, given the nature of Inca conquest, religion varied tremendously from place to place. There were, however, a few commonalities. First, Inti was worshiped everywhere; this was necessary if the divine nature of the Inca emperor was to be acknowledged. Second, in most areas, there was a cult of the dead. Ancestors were revered, burial places were accorded special importance, and many corpses were wrapped and placed in such a manner that they became mummified. Third, human sacrifice took place, although on a small scale, particularly the sacrifice of children, whose youth was thought to ensure that they were uncorrupted by the vices of maturity.

An excellent example of the diversity of society and religion within the Inca Empire is the acceptance of homosexuality. In the deserts of the northern coastal part of the empire, the Chimú[16] people were a late addition to the Inca Empire, conquered only in the late fourteenth century. The Chimú not only tolerated homosexual behavior but required it in certain priestly rituals. Their mythology

FIGURE 16.7 *Inca Coca Users.* *The coca bush, from whose leaves cocaine is refined, is native to the Andes. The Incas and their predecessors used coca leaves as a drug. The leaves were chewed with lime, which was kept in a small dipping bottle dangling from the larger container for leaves, shown in this sixteenth-century drawing. The Inca government used coca as a tool of control, fostering addiction among miners and other state laborers engaged in particularly grueling work. The drug made the workers less susceptible to pain and incapable of serious uprisings.* Institut d'Ethnologie, Musée de l'Homme.

---

[16] **Chimú:** chee MOO

The Spaniards who chronicled their entry into the Americas were shocked by the human sacrifice they encountered, especially in Mexico and parts of the Caribbean and South America. They considered such practices to be proof of the natives' debased nature and evidence that they worshiped the devil. What they didn't realize was that human sacrifice at one time or another has been prominent in a wide range of societies on every inhabited continent, including the Spaniards' own Europe. Historically speaking, human sacrifice should be seen as a relatively common practice, not something restricted to a few aberrant societies.

As usually defined, human sacrifice is the killing of a person as part of a religious ritual. Peoples practicing human sacrifice usually have considered the victim an offering to a deity. Accordingly, the person offered must be a desirable, perhaps noble, person, certainly not a despised individual. Contrary to the popular impression, sacrificed individuals rarely were killed against their will; rather, as with the Christian martyrs under Roman persecution, dying in this prescribed manner was often seen as an honor that ensured one a place in heaven or its equivalent. Among the Aztecs, even captives taken in battle probably were honored by their sacrifice, because they worshiped the same gods and subscribed to the same general beliefs as the Aztecs.

The roster of societies that have practiced some form of human sacrifice is impressively long. The Sumerians sacrificed servants and others at the death of a king, and the sacrifices were buried with the king. The ancient Hebrews and their Phoenician neighbors sacrificed human beings in beseeching gods for favors or in atonement for great sins. People of the Roman Empire, especially under the influence of mystery cults, sacrificed people, as did those of ancient Egypt, Hindu India, first-millennium Japan, Zhou China, the Benin and Dahomey kingdoms of Africa, Polynesian kingdoms in Hawaii and New Zealand, Cahokia of pre-Columbian North America, native Australia, and Borneo. Europeans practiced human sacrifice as late as the medieval era, and the bog bodies discussed in Chapter 1 are an example of human sacrifices. The roster of societies practicing human sacrifice is so great that it cannot be viewed merely as an aberration.

Why has human sacrifice been so common? Probably the answer lies in the relationship that most societies have with their deities, who can be compelled—or at least encouraged—to provide something if the people who worship them perform the correct activity with the proper attitude. If a community is willing to give up one of its best to sacrifice, how can a god or goddess refuse them a favor? Sacrificing one person is thought to produce a divine obligation to stop the plague, to bring rain, or to send away the invaders. Sometimes the victim has been seen as a scapegoat, absorbing the wrongdoing of the entire community and cleansing it, but the essential petition to the deity remains the same.

included many examples of homosexual, transvestite, or androgynous deities, and their art commemorated these myths and rituals, often in graphic detail. In contrast, along the southern coast of the empire, homosexuality was generally frowned upon, certainly was not integrated into religious activities, and appears to have been relatively uncommon.

Through most of the Inca Empire, ceremonial centers with little or no permanent population served as centers for worship. In the highlands these featured temples made of huge, irregularly cut stones fit together very precisely; in the lowlands, temples were made of mudbrick. Many of the ceremonies were for the elite only, but commoners also made pilgrimages to these shrines.

The Inca approach to empire building did not encourage the development of a great art style. Indeed, provinces were encouraged to continue their traditional art styles, and representations of Inti around the empire took many forms.

Inca social structure was based on a hierarchy that placed the emperor and his family at the top, other nobles immediately below, and commoners

FIGURE 16.8 *Inca Architecture from Machu Picchu.* *Inca architecture throughout the highlands shares several distinctive characteristics. The wall at the left shows large blocks, carefully shaped so that they fit together with essentially no crevices between them; sometimes the blocks are six or more feet across. The peaked roof in the background is that of a brewing house where* chicha, *a corn beer, was made and sold. Machu Picchu is located on the eastern, rainy side of the Andes, and the peaked roofs help to keep the town dry during the rainy season.* Mireille Vautier/Woodfin Camp & Associates.

far below them. Beneath the commoners were **yanakuna**,[17] a status usually translated as "slaves," though little is known about them. The scant information we have on women suggests that they had very little political or economic power and were expected to find their primary roles as wives and mothers.

An Experiment in Private Ownership

While land in general was owned by the empire, the Incas did experiment with the private ownership of property. Beginning around 1480, members

of the nobility who had rendered special service to the empire were granted tracts of land in part of the Urubamba[18] Valley, near Cuzco. This healthful and pleasant area became a playground for the elite.

There is considerable disagreement about how to interpret this phenomenon. Some scholars believe that the land awarded the nobles was theirs to use but not to own. Others believe it was given to them outright, an outgrowth of the practice of royal gift giving, originally restricted to llamas, clothing, and other valuable items. Wives also were distributed according to this system.

[17] **yanakuna:** yah nah KOO nah

[18] **Urubamba:** oo roo BAHM bah

This experiment in private ownership may be significant, because it may mean that the Incas were moving toward a new economic system. But the Spanish conquest cut short whatever course they would have followed, and we will never know what the outcome would have been.

The Spanish Conquest

In 1527, the Inca emperor died, leaving two sons to compete for his position: Waskar in Cuzco and Atahualpa[19] in the northern city of Quito. The ensuing civil war ended in 1532, when Atahualpa's forces succeeded in killing Waskar in battle. By this time, Spanish forces under the command of Francisco Pizarro had landed on the coast of Peru. Within the year, the Inca Empire fell.

The excellent Inca communication system alerted Atahualpa to the presence of the Spanish before they even landed, and Atahualpa called to military service all able-bodied men near the Spanish landing site. This was partly to expand his own army, and partly to prevent disaffected regions from allying with the Spanish. Probably because their numbers were small—around 200 horsemen—the Spanish were permitted to penetrate the easily defensible passes surrounding Cuzco, and they entered the Inca capital.

At a confrontation, Atahualpa demanded that the Spanish return everything they had plundered on the trip to Cuzco. The Spanish refused and the next day lured Atahualpa and 2,000 of his top officials into an ambush, where Atahualpa was captured and the officials were, in the words of a *conquistador*, "killed like ants." Cuzco, while the nerve center of the empire, had a total population of only around 10,000 people, and there were no senior officials left to take command. Atahualpa was executed, and a puppet ruler was installed by the Spanish. In the course of a few hours, the back of the Inca Empire was broken, a consequence of its highly centralized imperial power structure.

As in Mesoamerica, the last empire of Peru was founded only shortly before the Spanish conquest. Far from entrenched in its ways, it was actively experimenting with new systems of economic organization and was grappling with the difficulties of royal succession. This empire, which so impressed the Spanish, was but in its infancy when it was strangled.

[19]**Atahualpa:** ah tah HWAHL pah

NATIVE AMERICAN SOCIETIES IN NORTH AMERICA

In the year 1500, there were more than 800 languages spoken in North America and about 1,000 different peoples. This level of cultural diversity was at least comparable to that in Eurasia at the same period and may have been greater, so it is impossible to select a few examples that do justice to that diversity. Nonetheless, the following treatment discusses four societies from three major culture areas of North America. There were no North American societies in this period that were urban states, so there were no civilizations. The three societies presented here exemplify the levels of complexity in this period.

The Eastern Woodlands: The Iroquois

The vast area to the east of the Mississippi River and along its western banks was characterized by dense forests and is known as the Eastern Woodlands. Except in the far north, where the growing season is too short, all societies here based their existence on maize-squash-beans agriculture, and all were at the tribe or chiefdom level. An example is the Iroquois.

The Iroquois are a group of closely related peoples living in and around New York State and the Canadian province of Ontario. The Iroquois way of life developed around 1050, spurred largely by the advent of a new form of corn that matured faster than its predecessors, allowing greater and more reliable yields and agricultural dependence. Settlement shifted to the fertile flood plains along rivers, and warfare increased as competition for these limited lands developed. Fortified towns developed as a response to increased hostilities.

Also as a result of this, five of the Iroquois tribes formed around 1300 a confederacy under Hiawatha. (Hiawatha probably was a real person who was instrumental in the formation of the confederacy, but later elaborations have transformed him into an almost superhuman hero.) This confederacy bound the tribes together in peaceful alliances and ensured their cooperation against outsiders. Later, in 1722, a refugee tribe from North Carolina was added to the confederacy, reforming it into the Six Nations of the present day. The Iroquois confederacy oversaw a highly efficient military organization, lauded by one English colonial

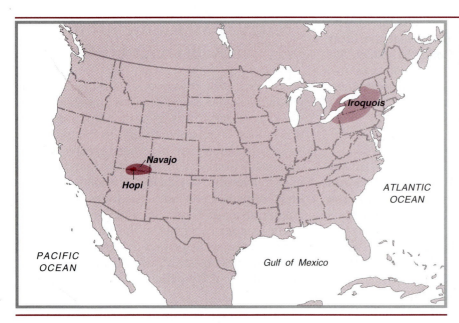

MAP 16.1 *Locations of Iroquois, Hopi, and Navajo.* *These tribes are only three of the nearly one thousand tribes that inhabited North America just before the arrival of Europeans.*

governor as the most powerful military force in North America in the 1750s.

But the Iroquois confederacy was more than a military machine. It also was a political system that provided for diplomat-ambassadors, elected chiefs, and a council whose members were elected by their tribe and made decisions for the confederacy as a whole. The confederacy had a body of rules and laws that organized its political functioning and guaranteed various rights to its citizenry.

While the Iroquois had no writing, they produced pictorial belts made of **wampum**, shell beads of different colors that were strung together in such a way that they formed pictures. The pictures served as memory aids, commemorating historic events and recording treaties. The exchanging of these belts at the time of a treaty or other agreement with a foreign power sealed the transaction, much in the same way that signing a written treaty or shaking hands might in other cultural contexts.

The Iroquois vested considerable power in women, who were the primary owners of land and were the focus of kinship organizations that were central to everyday life. They had the right to express views in the council; they also had the right to vote for office holders, though they were not normally permitted to hold elected office.

Iroquois religion was largely in the hands of kinship groups and voluntary societies that held ceremonies at fixed calendric dates. Six thanksgiving festivals, for example, were held at regular times of the year. The Planting Festival, held around May, was to bless the seeds of corn, squash, beans, and sunflowers that were being planted; the Strawberry Festival thanked nature for providing these first fruits of the warm months; the Harvest Festival in autumn welcomed the harvesting of the corn and its storage for the year. These and other ceremonies were organized and conducted by individuals as members of voluntary societies; there were no priests or similar full-time religious practitioners. Male and female healers, using both spiritual and herbal remedies, conducted healing rituals as needed.

As a major military power, the Iroquois were successful at resisting European domination for some time, though their ranks were decimated by European diseases. Their alliance with the English and their defeat in the American Revolution led to the downfall of the Iroquois in the United States, where they were reduced by harsh treaty settlements and vigilante attack.

The Southwest: The Hopi and the Navajo

The Southwest is characterized by arid and semiarid lands, particularly in the states of Arizona, New Mexico, Colorado, and Utah. This area was populated both by band-level hunter-gatherers and by tribe-level agriculturalists in this period.

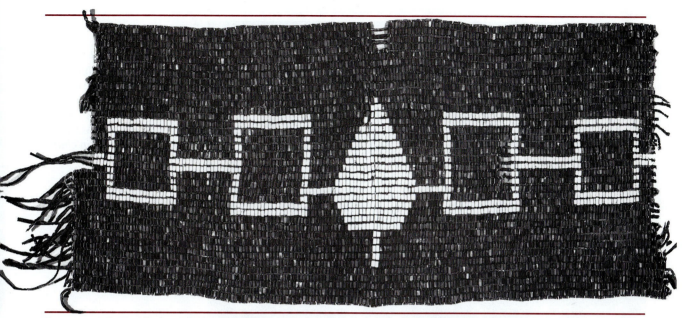

FIGURE 16.9 *Iroquois Wampum Belt.* *The Iroquois used beaded belts to commemorate and seal agreements. This belt, known as the Hiawatha Belt, records the original founding of the League of the Iroquois, the banding together of five tribes into a confederacy for mutual cooperation. Made of shell beads, it may date from as early as 1300. The squares represent four of the five tribes of the Iroquois, and the central figure represents the Onondaga tribe, whose territory is geographically central. The Onondaga symbol is interpreted both as a tree (representing the peace shared by the League members) and a heart (representing the central position of the Onondaga).* New York State Museum. Acquired May 24, 1927, by bequest of Emma Treadwell Thacher of Albany, N.Y. Courtesy of Chief Irving Powless Jr., Onondaga Nation.

The Hopi[20] are an example of tribe-level agriculturalists. Farming on the dry mesas where the Hopi lived was a laborious and precarious practice. A bad year could spell disaster, and bad years could be expected every seven to ten years.

To even the odds a bit, the Hopi took several precautions. First, they hand-watered their crops, because no streams large enough to support irrigation existed in their lands; this practice ensured that crops would receive sufficient water in all but the worst of times. Second, they established reciprocal relationships among villages, so that a village with a poor agricultural return one year could receive aid from a neighbor with better luck; another year, when fortunes were reversed, the aid would be returned. Third, the Hopi continued to hunt and gather foods as adjuncts to their diet. In bad years, these foraged foods would form a greater part of the diet. Finally, the Hopi had an agreement with the spirit world to ensure rain in response to ritual devotion. If rain did not materialize, clearly, as the Hopi saw it, the ritual had been performed poorly.

This agreement was based on the belief that there were mutual obligations between the Hopi and the spirits. If the Hopi performed rituals properly, the spirits were obligated to bring rain; this rain, in turn, obligated the Hopi to perform the rituals, completing the cycle. The rituals were not prayers requesting that the spirits provide rain; nor were they magic forcing them. Rather, the spirits were seen as equals with the Hopi in the sense that they, too, had social obligations that bound their actions. Men conducted (and still do conduct) the ceremonies privately in underground rooms called ***kivas***.[21]

Hopi population levels remained moderately low, never high enough to outstrip the available

[20] **Hopi:** HOH pee

[21] ***kivas:*** KEE vuhz

FIGURE 16.10 *Great Kiva at Aztec Ruins.*
The Hopi consider their kivas sacred places that may not be photographed; however, this reconstruction of a prehistoric non-Hopi kiva from northern New Mexico embodies all the main characteristics of a Hopi kiva. The round, sunken room had a bench along its periphery where participants could sit facing the sipapu, *a symbolic connection to the spirit world.*
George H. Huey

agricultural land; and the Hopi rarely engaged in warfare. Their multiroomed masonry houses (**pueblos**), sometimes reaching two or three stories high, look as if they might have been designed as defensive structures, but more likely they were designed for protection from the harsh seasonal temperatures of the region.

Living around the *pueblos* of the Hopi and other tribes were the Dene.[22] These relatively recent immigrants to the Southwest arrived from the north sometime after 1000 and led a nomadic way of life at the band level. They hunted and gathered their food without recourse to agriculture and lived in insubstantial houses designed to be used only for a night or two. Different groups of the Dene became the modern Apache and Navajo.[23]

The results of the European arrival in the Southwest were very dissimilar for the Navajo and *pueblo*-dwelling peoples (like the Hopi). Spanish missionaries focused their attentions on the *pueblo* dwellers, because they were sedentary and the establishment of a mission that exploited

Indian labor was practical. This meant that most *pueblo*-dwelling tribes had intensive missionary contact, resulting in rapid depopulation from disease, rapid modification of traditional religious and social systems, and, in some cases, virtual reduction to slave labor. The Hopi were one of the few *pueblo*-dwellers to escape most of these consequences, because their land was dry and at some distance from the rivers around which the Spanish concentrated their efforts. Of the twenty-three *pueblo*-dwelling tribes, only two were so lucky.

The Navajo fared very differently. As nomads, they avoided the most injurious Spanish attentions, adopting Spanish traits they found desirable and simply moving away if less desirable ones were being forced on them. Their most significant adoption from the Spanish was sheep raising. This pastoralism was based on domesticated sheep that had strayed from Spanish flocks or had been taken by Navajo raids. The sheep provided meat, an important adjunct to Navajo subsistence, and encouraged the Navajo to live in base camps, where limited farming was practical. The wool from the sheep formed the basis for weaving, an important occupation of Navajo women to this

[22] **Dene:** DEE neh
[23] **Navajo:** NAH vah hoh

NORTH AMERICA	MESOAMERICA		
		1000	Establishment of Iroquois lifestyle, c. 1000
		1100	Collapse of Tiahuanaco Empire, c. 1100
			Departure of Mexica from Aztlán, 1111
		1200	
Iroquois Confeder-acy, c. 1300–1600		**1300**	Founding of Iroquois confederacy, c. 1300
	Aztec Empire, c. 1325–1521		Mexica arrive in the Valley of Mexico, 1325
			Establishment of Aztec territory in the Valley of Mexico, 1345
			Founding of Aztec royal house, 1372
		1400	
	Inca Empire, c. 1438–1532		Viracocha conquers Chanka, 1438
			Urubamba privatization begins, 1480
		1500	Spanish conquest of Aztecs, 1519–1521
			Inca civil war, 1527–1532
			Spanish conquest of Inca, 1532
		1600	

UNDER THE LENS
The Hopi World Order

The Hopi view of the world and the place of the Hopi within it was founded in three basic principles: the bipartite universe, reciprocity with the spirits, and the system of correspondences. From these principles, the Hopi derived their basic moral, religious, and social order.

The Hopi recognized that there were two independent but similar worlds, one for the living Hopi and one for the spirits; this is the **bipartite universe**. The worlds were opposite to each other, so that summer in the spirit world was winter in the Hopi world, night in the Hopi world was day in the spirit world. In some manner, things in one world could transform into the other. The Hopi believed that after death, a person's spirit went to the spirit world to become a *kachina*[a] and that at birth, a baby was invested with a spirit that had been a *kachina*. Similarly and importantly, the *kachinas* had an essence (parallel to Hopi blood) called *navala*, which could migrate to the Hopi world and become rain, that much-needed commodity for desert farmers lacking rivers that could be harnessed for irrigation.

[a] *kachina:* kah CHEE nah

The spirit world and the Hopi world were related to each other by mutual obligations: **reciprocity with the spirits**. The Hopi were obligated to perform rituals for the *kachinas* (because the *kachinas* had provided *navala* in the form of rain), and the Hopis' rituals obligated the *kachinas* to continue providing *navala*. The cycle was neverending, as rain obligated the Hopi to perform the rituals, which in turn obligated the *kachinas* to provide the rain, and so forth. Without a full complement of properly performed rituals, the Hopi could expect only drought and death.

Finally, the **system of correspondences** was a complex symbol system that related cardinal directions, colors, types of clouds, ritual items, lightning, plants, animals, and many other things. The color for north, for example, was identified with forked lightning, yellow sweet corn, and butterflies, among others. The use or reference of any of these things during a ritual could stand for any of the others to which it corresponded. As a result, a collection of items on an altar could represent a complex series of relationships, prayers, and requests to the *kachinas*. This Hopi view of the world developed centuries ago and persists today among traditional Hopi.

day. Weaving also permitted many Navajo to enter the cash economy in the nineteenth century, when Euro-American markets developed after the coming of the railroad. Despite various episodes of clashes and mistreatment by European and American governments, these adaptations permitted the Navajo to thrive. In the past three centuries, they have transformed from a small group to the most populous Indian tribe in North America.

SUMMARY

1. The Aztecs descended from a seminomadic tribe that migrated to the Valley of Mexico around 1300.

2. Through a series of military and diplomatic maneuvers, the Aztecs established a large empire. Warfare maintained and expanded the empire, as well as providing captives for religiously mandated human sacrifice.

3. Aztec society was highly hierarchic, with nobles who were believed to be descended from gods. This hierarchic nature permeated Aztec life, affecting one's legal, economic, social, and political fortunes.

4. The Aztec Empire was conquered by the Spanish in 1521, largely as the result of the plummeting Aztec population owing to newly introduced diseases and the desertion of Aztec allies to the Spanish.

5. The kingdom of Cuzco in Peru expanded into the Inca Empire, also through warfare and

diplomacy. The Incas permitted newly conquered peoples to retain their ways of life and even their governmental hierarchies as they were incorporated into the Inca Empire, producing a heterogeneous empire.

6. The Incas generally rewarded rulers and states with gifts for surrendering to them. They also sometimes relocated large groups of people for imperial security.

7. The Inca Empire vested property ownership primarily in the government. *Corvée* labor, food redistribution, and population relocations were aspects of governmental control. The government also provided massive public works. A late experiment in private ownership was cut short by the Spanish conquest.

8. Leadership succession was a weakness of the Inca Empire, and the Spanish conquest was facilitated by a civil war over royal succession.

9. North America had a wide variety of societies at the time of European contact, including those of the Iroquois, Hopi, and Navajo. None of these had urban states.

SUGGESTED READINGS

Anderson, Arthur J., and Charles E. Dibble, ed. and trans. *Florentine Codex.* Monographs of the School of American Research, #14 (in 13 parts). Santa Fe, N.M.: The School of American Research and the University of Utah, 1951–81. An annotated translation of this important codex, written by Aztec scribes shortly after the Spanish conquest.

Baudin, Louis. *A Socialist Empire: The Incas of Peru.* New York: Van Nostrand, 1961. The classic Marxist interpretation of the Inca.

Berdan, Frances F. *The Aztecs of Central Mexico: An Imperial Society.* New York: Holt, Rinehart and Winston, 1982. A brief, readable, authoritative summary of Aztec society.

Brundage, Burr Cartwright. *Empire of the Inca.* Norman: University of Oklahoma Press, 1963. A general treatment of the Incas from the historical perspective.

Gillespie, Susan D. *Aztec Kings: The Construction of Rulership in Mexica History.* Tucson: University of Arizona Press, 1989. A feminist perspective on early Aztec history.

Kissam, Edward, and Michael Schmidt, trans. *Poems of the Aztec Peoples.* Ypsilanti, Mich.: Bilingual Press/Editorial Bilingüe, 1983. English translations of many Aztec poems.

Sturtevant, William C., ed. *Handbook of North American Indians.* Fifteen volumes. Washington, D.C.: Smithsonian Institution, 1978–present. The best single reference on North American Indians, containing authoritative articles with good bibliographies. To date, about two-thirds of the volumes have been published.

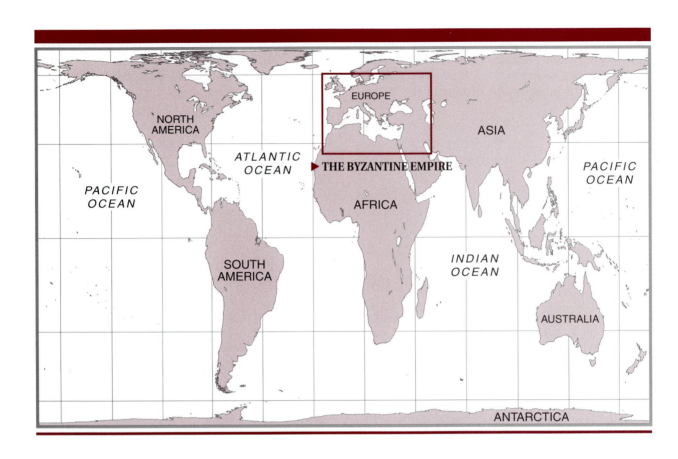

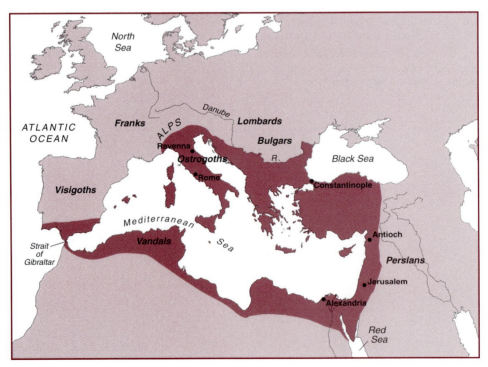

▶ **THE BYZANTINE EMPIRE**

The Byzantine Empire

around 450–1453

"The Golden Horn," observed a sixth-century writer, "is always calm." The bay of the ancient city of Byzantium acquired this name from the shape of its harbor and the commercial wealth that filled the purses of the city's citizens. In 330, Constantine renamed the city Constantinople (today called Istanbul) and established it as the new capital of the Roman Empire. Constantinople later became the seat of a new empire, which scholars have named the Byzantine Empire, after the original city of Byzantium.

The Byzantine Empire evolved over time, so a date of origin is difficult to identify. Some scholars date the empire as early as 330, when Constantine named Constantinople the new capital. Other scholars prefer the date of 395, which ended the last unification of the Roman Empire under Theodosius, or that of 476, when the last Western Roman Emperor was deposed by a German conqueror. Still other scholars prefer to see the origins of the Byzantine Empire from a nonpolitical perspective. Significant social, religious, and artistic differences between the western and eastern portions of the Roman Empire had existed long before the permanent political separation in the fifth century. It is perhaps best to recognize that the Byzantine Empire evolved from the previous Roman polity and accept a general date for its inception of around 450.

BYZANTINE SOCIETY

The Byzantine Empire is the longest-lasting empire in history, surviving well over 1,000 years. The various territories of the empire had long, illustrious histories before the fourth century. Many of the societies that you read about in Chapters 4, 7, and 8 occupied the same geographical areas.

Geography and Demography

The Byzantine Empire covered a vast territory. At the height of its power in the sixth century, the empire encompassed Greece, the Balkans south of the Danube River, Anatolia, Palestine, parts of North Africa, and the islands of the eastern Mediterranean and the Aegean seas. In addition, large portions of the earlier Western Roman Empire were reconquered by the Byzantine Emperor Justinian (reign dates 527–565), including much of Italy and southern Spain. Between the years 450 and 1453, the Byzantine Empire won and lost large portions of these areas.

Over the centuries, the Byzantine Empire was home to millions of ethnically diverse people. A conservative estimate places more than 30 million persons in the empire in the sixth century. The distribution approximated 8 million in Egypt, 9 million in the easternmost territories (Syria, Palestine, and parts of Mesopotamia), 10 million in the area of modern Turkey, and 3 to 4 million in the Balkans. Demographic shifts due to border hostilities from about the mid–seventh century to about the mid–ninth century caused some de-

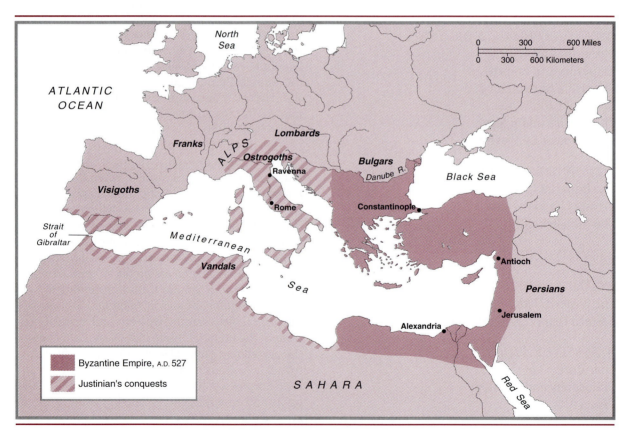

MAP 17.1 *The Byzantine Empire at Its Height.* *Under Justinian, the empire reached its greatest expanse by 565 A.D. A major campaign to reconquer western European territories was undertaken, achieving temporary results in some areas. By the end of the seventh century, eastern and southern Byzantine territories began to fall to Muslim invasions.*

urbanization. Many cities in Thrace, Greece, and the area of modern Turkey ceased to exist or survived only as small towns. Some urban centers relocated to safer sites.

Life in the Empire

The ideological link that provided unity for the empire was a religious one. Missionary activity had spread Christianity throughout the Roman Empire in the second century. When Emperor Theodosius declared Christianity the empire's only legal religion at the end of the fourth century, its influence as a unifying instrument became central to succeeding rulers. One monk, upon arriving in Thrace from an eastern territory in the ninth century, was challenged to prove he was a friend and not an enemy. His reply cited not his citizenship but rather that he, like his parents, followed the Christian faith. At the same time, belief in many different religions continued in private life. The practices of Judaism, Islam, Zoroastrianism, and local religious customs could be observed in any major urban center. Although animosity and persecution sometimes occurred against minority Christian sects that had been declared heretical, such as the Monophysites, the sects were tolerated when tolerance was politically expedient.

Generally, the lives of local people throughout the empire continued in much the same way as they always had in the centuries prior to the Byzantine Empire. Farmers plowed and harvested their fields, artisans made and sold their wares, the elite controlled wealth and wielded political influence, and imperial officers collected taxes and tried to keep the peace. Urban and rural living ebbed and flowed according to the economic and political factors of each generation.

Peasant life remained basically stable in the Byzantine Empire. In the fourth century, many farmers did not have free status, and others retained various levels of freedom. Sources show that there existed a variety of peasant statuses between the tenth and twelfth centuries. By the thirteenth to the fifteenth centuries, this pattern had not changed very much. There were certainly periods when peasants became serfs of great aristocrats or specific places where they were subjected to aristocratic control, but these patterns were not universal. The village community, made up of free landholding peasants, continued throughout Byzantine history. Usually these communities had relative independence from aristocratic control and governed themselves.

The merchants were the economic backbone of trade around the empire. Merchants bought and sold goods, sometimes as agents of the state and sometimes as independent traders. Some merchants became very wealthy, but merchants generally remained low on the social scale and were not allowed to hold important political offices. Seventh- and eighth-century deurbanization significantly reduced the number of merchants. By the eleventh century, however, urban renewal again stimulated merchant activities throughout the empire. Many merchants of Constantinople gained in wealth and social prestige, becoming a powerful political group within the city. Political power, however, was never sustained by merchants in most Byzantine areas. Many women in the thirteenth to the fifteenth centuries were merchants, retailing in cloth, beauty aids, and some foods. One Muslim source noted that the majority of artisans and sellers in the city of Constantinople were women.

BYZANTINE POLITICAL HISTORY

The Byzantine Empire inherited a system of law and an imperial structure from its Roman predecessor. Expansion concentrated on recapturing the Western Roman Empire's territories, and much of Justinian's efforts and the empire's resources were spent in Italy. During most of Byzantine history, emperors and armies fought to defend the far-flung borders of the empire, sometimes losing significant amounts of territory. Changes in administrative policies, however, prolonged the Byzantine Empire until 1453.

Byzantine Law

The early legal structure of the Byzantine Empire was inherited from Greek and Roman antecedents. Laws, however, were not systematically organized, and judges had no consistency in interpreting the law; many times inconsistencies surfaced, much to the frustration of those trying to adjudicate disputes. Several attempts at reconciling diverse

IN THEIR OWN WORDS

A Twelfth-Century Byzantine Market

Great markets constituted the heart of the trade centers in the Byzantine Empire. When the market commenced, great excitement ran through attenders of all ages. New clothes, jewelry, prepared foods, and fresh produce awaited the willing purchase of the marketgoers. The following excerpt is from an anonymous writer of the twelfth century. Although the work is fictional, this description of a market in Thessalonike in the territory of Macedonia reveals how these markets must have looked.

It is the most considerable . . . [market] among the inhabitants of Macedonia. Not only would the local population assemble there, but people from everywhere and of every sort would arrive. Greeks come from every place, as well as the neighboring tribes of . . . [Bulgars] who live as far as the Danube and the land of the Scythians, and the inhabitants of Campania, Italians, Spaniards and Portuguese, and Celts from beyond the Alps. . . . I for one . . . had until now no personal experience of the event and knew about it only from hearsay. So I desired to be a spectator of this sight and see everything without exception. With this purpose I climbed a hill located nearby and, sitting there, could observe the . . . [market] with ease. It looked like this: Tents of merchants were pitched in two lines facing one another. The lines ran a long distance, leaving between them a broad lane that allowed for the rush of the crowd. . . . Other tents were set up off this lane. They also formed lines, but not very long ones, as if they were the short legs of a crouching reptile. . . .

Looking down from my hill I saw all kinds of fabric and thread . . . of men's and women's garb produced both in Boeotia [Greece] and in the Peloponnese and carried on commercial ships from Italy to Greece. Also Phoenicia [Lebanon] sent many an object; Egypt and Spain . . . produced the best implements. Merchants brought all these things directly from their countries to old Macedonia and [Thessalonike]. But the Black Sea sent its produce first to . . . Byzantium and therefrom it was brought here and adorned the [market]. Numbers of horses and mules carried their load from there.

interpretations and pulling the myriad legal pronouncements together into collections had failed. Emperor Justinian, however, appointed a commission to create a new, authoritative law code, the *Codex Justinianus.* Shortly afterward, he commissioned a work to codify the works of Roman jurists. These and other legal reviews became known as the *Corpus Juris Civilis* (528–535), which was the foundation of law codes in most of Europe after the eleventh century.

Increasingly, Christianity influenced Byzantine law, as the church grew in size, wealth, and influence. The patriarch of Constantinople wielded great authority over legal practice. As Christian morality became the accepted pattern of behavior for the empire, Christian influence upon legislation increased, and civil law and canon law began to converge; this was similar to the influence of Islamic law in Muslim areas. Church courts remained independent of imperial courts, and the patriarch's court reserved the right of appeal of civil court decisions.

Emperors and Empresses

During Byzantine history, both the emperors and the empresses engaged in pomp and pageantry at court to demonstrate their elevated status and to display the emperor's religious authority. The foundation of imperial authority lay with past Roman emperors, but much of the Byzantine imperial persona came from Hellenistic and Christian influences that gave emperors even greater spiritual authority than their predecessors.

Solemn ceremonies and impressive pageantry created an ambience of otherworldliness and conferred power on the person of the emperor. The royal apparel for official occasions consisted of a long white tunic of silk with a purple cape, decorated on both sides with embroidered gold cloth. The imperial crown held precious jewels, such as pearls and rubies. One envoy to the court of a tenth-century Byzantine emperor observed the imperial grandeur. If his account is to be believed, he entered the great hall escorted by eunuchs and approached the emperor, who was seated on a magnificent throne. Mechanical birds sang and lions roared as the diplomat approached. After he prostrated himself three times before the emperor (a mandatory ritual), he looked up and saw that the throne and the emperor had ascended to the ceiling. He was forced to finish his interview peering heavenward. Other accounts by visiting Muslims describe beautiful Persian carpets, golden candelabra hung from silvered copper chains, and floors covered with ivy, rosemary, and roses. As one crossed the floor, perfume from crushed leaves and petals filled the room. Such theatrics dramatically conveyed magnificence and might.

Since the time of Constantine, Byzantine rulers viewed themselves as representatives of Christ, given divine authority to govern the Christian empire. Because of the political theory of divine selection, dynastic succession was not guaranteed to an emperor's heir. Selection was made by the army, the Senate of Constantinople, or the citizenry of Constantinople, each operating as a divine agent. In the later centuries of the empire, however, family succession became more common.

Imperial legitimacy came from the basic understanding that the emperor was chosen by the Christian God. Divine will, however, could turn against an emperor as surely as it favored his ascension to the throne (which was made painfully clear when usurpations were successful). Palace intrigues, plots, and assassinations fill the pages of Byzantine history during times of political crisis. Nearly one-half of Byzantine emperors died violently or fled to safety in monasteries. Most of those killed were poisoned, stabbed, or decapitated by rivals to the throne. One poor victim's head was publicly displayed on a pike. Another suffered multiple attacks to his person: He was chained and beaten, his teeth were knocked out with a hammer, one of his hands was cut off, he was paraded through Constantinople on a sick camel (symbolizing weakness, poverty, and humil-

FIGURE 17.1 *Emperor Justinian.* *This mosaic portrait of Justinian and his civil and ecclesiastical officials is found in the sixth-century Church of San Vitale in the city of Ravenna in northern Italy. Its place of prominence near the altar reminded worshipers of the emperor's exalted status in Christian society and of Justinian's claim of political authority over the city. Ravenna was one of the cities captured by the Byzantines in their reconquest of western territories during Justinian's reign. Eastern emperors after Justinian continued to claim the city as part of their empire until the conquests of Charlemagne in the eighth century.* Scala/Art Resource, N.Y.

iation), he had boiling water thrown in his face and one of his eyes plucked out, and he was finally hung up in the Hippodrome (a large arena used for sports) for even more torture. After pleading for relief, he was mercifully run through with a sword.

Emperors controlled many lands, incomes, and other material resources of the Christian

FIGURE 17.2 *Emperor John Cantacuzene.*
This portrayal of Emperor John Cantacuzene demonstrates his religious authority during a 1351 council of Eastern Orthodox bishops and monks. Although their religious power was often challenged by patriarchs, many emperors convened and directed council meetings, thereby influencing the development of church doctrine. Bibliothèque nationale, Paris.

church. They often determined ecclesiastical staffs or appointed bishops, including the patriarch of Constantinople. Emperors also called for or presided over church councils, at which they tried to impose their theological views. Emperors could not determine Christian doctrine by themselves; that could be accomplished only by bishops meeting in specially called church councils.

Empresses also played significant roles in the administration of the empire, albeit in more subtle ways, such as through regencies. Most empresses minted their own coins and controlled their own attendants, and they maintained parallel courts composed of elite women. Not every imperial wife gained the title of empress in the fourth and fifth centuries, however. Sometimes the title was given to an emperor's mother or sister instead of his wife.

Emperors' brides often came from distant lands as diplomatic ties wedded the interests of states together. By the twelfth century, wives gained the title of empress more consistently as dynastic succession regularly passed from father to son. Because of this, regencies became more common as young emperors waited to take the reins of power.

Although power usually resided in the emperor, or in the empress as regent, there were occasions when empresses ruled in their own names or influenced laws. Three examples are Irene (reign dates 797–802), Zoë (co-empress, 1042), and Theodora (co-empress, 1042; reign dates 1055–1056), all of whom ruled for brief periods. Irene began her rule as regent of her young son, between 780 and 797, but at his maturity she took the throne after blinding and deposing him. During the co-reign of the sisters Zoë and Theodora, the sale of offices was abolished and many people were elevated into the Senate. Decrees of the empresses demonstrate their influence in the running of the Byzantine state.

Empress Theodora (497–548), not to be confused with the co-empress Theodora, is perhaps the most famous empress in Byzantine history. A former actress, she married Emperor Justinian in 527. She endowed many churches, monasteries, orphanages, and hospitals. Her influence on Justinian's rule is hard to evaluate, but her participation in stemming the Nika Rebellion (see p. 439) suggests a relationship with significant influence. In addition, artifact inscriptions suggest equal reverence for both Justinian and Theodora. She received many letters from kings, one of whom she had instructed to write directly to her for matters to be placed before the emperor.

Byzantine Bureaucracy

A vast, effective bureaucracy aided the monarch in administration of the empire. Although its size fluctuated according to political necessity, the bureaucracy lasted throughout Byzantine history. Similarly to Muslim cities, most early Byzantine cities had governing councils that worked with imperial officials. In contrast to the Muslim councils, the councils of Byzantine cities were populated by wealthy local landowners instead of merchants.

Bishops also participated in the regulation of cities, because the local churches over which they

FIGURE 17.3 *Empress Theodora.* *Empress Theodora is depicted in similar fashion to her husband, the Emperor Justinian. Located on the wall opposite Justinian's portrait (Figure 17.1) in the Church of San Vitale, this mosaic demonstrates the imperial authority of the empress. Theodora is posed with her attendants in a mirror image of Justinian and his officials. Some scholars interpret the role of Theodora's court staff as a mirror bureaucracy that aided Justinian in governing the empire.* Bildarchiv Foto Marburg/Art Resource, N.Y.

presided usually possessed large amounts of land. As lack of participation in city councils plagued the late-sixth-century cities (because council members became personally responsible for tax payments to the state), bishops gradually filled the political gap, dispensing justice and raising taxes, sometimes functioning as governors.

Imperial Expansion

Justinian's armies had recaptured portions of what had been the Western Empire in the early sixth century. Belisarius, Justinian's able general, had put down a rebellion in North Africa in 534 and in the next year conquered Sicily and Dalmatia. Between 535 and 540, Belisarius wrestled Italy from the Germans, and Byzantine forces retook parts of Spain by 550. Continued fighting over Italy lasted until the capitulation of the Germans in Italy

in 555. It looked as if the Roman Empire would be resurrected.

By the end of the sixth century, however, most of Italy had fallen under the control of the Germanic Lombards. Byzantine emperors continued to claim authority over the western territories, and a Byzantine official residing in the northern Italian city of Ravenna claimed to govern the west in the name of the emperor. Most Italian cities were islands of independence fighting against Lombard encroachment. Because of border threats elsewhere in the Byzantine Empire, little aid was forthcoming.

The Empire under Siege

Throughout Byzantine history, raids and conquests threatened or redrew the empire's borders. Numerous invasions by different tribal groups from areas in Europe and Asia disrupted trade. In some cases, diplomacy brought peaceful resolution, but usually hostilities resulted in more bloodshed and territorial loss. Significant regional losses ensued under the conquests of the Arab Muslims and the Crusaders, but Byzantine resiliency maintained a smaller, yet still vital, Byzantine state. The final onslaught came from the conquering Ottoman Turks, but Byzantine influence continued to live in the cultures of the conquerors.

Although Justinian's period was one of expansion, he also dealt with raids on the northern and eastern borders of the empire. Raiders across the lines of defense along the Danube penetrated as far south as the Peloponnesus in Greece. The Persian Sassanians clashed with eastern imperial forces and gained control of Egypt, Palestine, and Syria for a brief time. Justinian responded to the multiple onslaught by reorganizing the administrative structure of the empire into provinces in order to give greater control to the central government. In the provinces, he secured the frontier areas with large fortified encampments from which the army could defend the borders. The reorganization saved the empire from conquest.

In the seventh and eighth centuries, continuing hostilities saw the loss of territory and another reorganization. The Byzantine Empire could not hold on to its farther eastern and southern provinces and, finally, lost them permanently to the Arab Muslims. Another reorganization of the empire's administration replaced the provinces and focused on smaller areas called *themes*,[1] old areas of land organization. The *themes* were now administered by generals exercising both military and civil power under the direct control of the emperor. The *theme* system allowed for greater military response to attacks on the borders. As time went on, the number of *themes* increased; by the mid–ninth century, there were more than twenty *themes* in existence, and, by the eleventh century, great landowners controlled some of them.

Arab Muslim conquest of some coastal areas broke the naval dominance of the eastern Mediterranean by the Byzantines, but trade continued to flow between Byzantine and Muslim areas. Constantinople itself was besieged twice by Arab Muslims in the seventh and eighth centuries but did not fall. In addition to Arab Muslim conflicts, Pepin the Short conquered most of the areas in Italy that had been captured by the Lombards or by Justinian. Pepin established the Papal States and set up an alliance with the pope. This loss of Italian territory essentially ended Byzantine imperial claims over the papacy; the pope increasingly turned to the Franks rather than to the Byzantines for military help.

During this same period, Bulgar forces (people from the territory along the northern border) repeatedly crossed the Danube and continued their raids into the next two centuries. The highly successful Byzantine dynasty of Macedonian emperors (857–1056) dealt with the brunt of these invasions. Basil II, the Bulgar-slayer (reign dates 976–1025), eventually stopped the Bulgar invasions; in 1014, he crushed the enemy's army and took between 14,000 and 15,000 prisoners. He blinded ninety-nine in every hundred, leaving one to guide his fellows back to their home territory. Basil then annexed Bulgaria, placing the entire Balkan population under imperial control. Basil had also achieved an alliance with the Russians, who had been threatening the empire in the tenth century. In 988, Russia's Prince Vladimir sealed a treaty by being baptized and marrying a Byzantine princess.

Various border skirmishes continued to stress the empire, as hostile peoples crossed the borders in the eleventh to the thirteenth centuries. In 1095, western Christians were called upon to aid in retaking Christian holy lands from the Arab Muslims at the request of the patriarch of Constantinople. The lands were retaken but not given back to Byzantine leaders; instead, Crusader States were established. In the late twelfth century, wayward European Crusaders under the influence of Pope Innocent III and Venetian economic interests set out for the holy lands on the Fourth Crusade. They soon became embroiled in Byzantine politics and ended up conquering Constantinople in 1204. Roman Catholics sat on the thrones of the Byzantine emperor and the patriarch. Only three areas of the empire retained independence from the crusaders: Nicea (on the west coast of Turkey), Epirus (on the west coast of Greece), and Trebizond (on the northeast coast of Turkey).

Crusaders held Constantinople for almost six decades. Niceans and Bulgars joined forces against their common western enemies and continually

---

[1] *themes:* THEHM ehs *or* THEEMZ

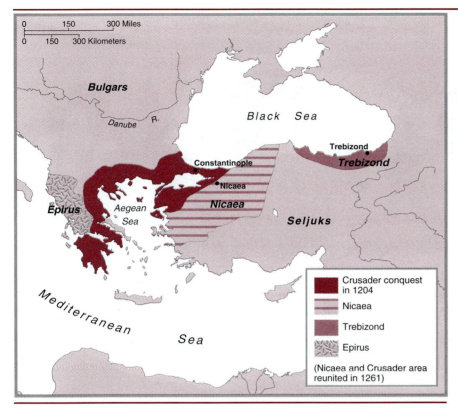

MAP 17.2 *Byzantine States around 1215.* *Medieval European crusaders' invasions and Muslims' conquests broke the Byzantine Empire into regional states by 1215. In the mid–thirteenth century, the areas that had fallen to the European crusaders were reunited with the Nicaean state under one polity.*

harassed them. Within a little more than fifty years, the coalition finally expelled the westerners from the sacred city. In 1261, Michael VIII established a new dynasty in Constantinople and reunited parts of the Byzantine Empire.

The expulsion of the crusaders, however, did not restore the Byzantine Empire to its former glory. Much of Constantinople lay in ruins, not only from the sacking and looting of 1204 but also from lack of maintenance. By the thirteenth century, the Italian commercial centers of Venice and Genoa held important economic routes, and Constantinople could not regain its economic footing. Michael VIII continually had to defend his diminished Byzantine Empire against western retaliation by the crusaders and the encroachment of the Serbs.

In the fourteenth and fifteenth centuries, the Byzantine Empire continued to be plagued by border skirmishes and a dire threat to its territories in Anatolia. The vigorous new state of the Ottomans was on the rise in the east, and Ottoman soldiers had captured most of the territory of Anatolia from the Byzantines by 1340. In another fifteen years,

the Ottoman Turks had gained a toehold in Europe. Parts of Thrace fell to them in the 1360s and most of Greece soon afterward.

The final assault occurred in 1453, when the Ottoman sultan, Mehmed[2] II (reign dates 1451–1481), laid siege to Constantinople with more than 80,000 troops. Emperor Constantine XI defended the city with 7,000 soldiers and twenty-six warships. The physical defenses of the city were formidable, but Mehmed had plans. He also had 120 ships with which to patrol the coastal waters. To circumvent the defensive chain stretched across the entrance to the Golden Horn, Mehmed had seventy of his vessels moved overland on rollers and then launched into the harbor to attack the north end of the city. Several of his forward observers spied out the wall defenses, and, with this information, Mehmed directed engineers to lay mines at strategic places and aim cannonballs to knock down the remaining walls. Gunpowder technology was the undoing of Constantinople's legendary walled defenses. The Byzantine Empire

[2] **Mehmed:** MEH mehd

FIGURE 17.4 *Muslim Defeat of Byzantine Army.* *In this scene, Muslim Turks defeat a retreating Byzantine force. The Muslim cavalry was superior to that of most Byzantine horsemen, who often lost territory to Muslim cavalry advances. The Byzantine Empire controlled many trade routes, and competitive states (especially Muslim) tried to capture Byzantine territories to extend their trade networks. When Dar al-Islam expanded into Anatolia, it competed with Byzantine religion and economics. By 1215, parts of the empire had fallen to invaders or were split into regional kingdoms.* Biblioteca Nacional, Madrid.

finally breathed its last as the emperor died with his troops in the final defense of the city; it had taken seven weeks for Constantinople to fall.

The Empire's Longevity

From the sixth to the fifteenth centuries, the Byzantine political structure experienced several organizational and administrative changes and aspects of governance underwent significant realignments as the empire adjusted to changing political conditions. The ability of Byzantine emperors and officials to remain flexible in their administration of the empire contributed significantly to its survival in the face of large territorial losses.

Emperors also changed socioreligious policies in attempts to defend the empire. For example, Monophysites (who had been deemed heretics by a church council in 451) were tolerated during periods of Persian and Arab invasions so as to keep them loyal to the empire and allow them to be conscripted into the army. Many Monophysites in Egypt and Syria, however, welcomed the Muslim conquerors as liberators from Byzantine policies.

CONSTANTINOPLE, THE SEAT OF EMPIRE

Constantine chose the site of the old city of Byzantium for his new capital for several reasons. It already functioned as a major commercial center, it sat strategically at the mouth of the Bosporus Strait, and it lay bordered on three sides by water, offering almost impenetrable protection when fortified. The city lasted as the Byzantine capital for almost the entire history of the Byzantine Empire, and, in many ways, the imperial city is a microcosm of Byzantine society.

The Imperial City

Because Constantinople lay at the crossroads of major overland trade routes, the city itself was a hub of activity. Although the official language of the city was Greek, as many as seventy-two languages could be heard as travelers wove their way through the throngs of people, carts, and animals along the twelve-foot-wide, two-mile-long main street of the teeming city. Constantinople resembled many major trade centers; the streets were crowded with shops and open-air bazaars, whose vendors barked out their bargains to passersby. Moneychangers guarded tables full of bags of foreign and local coins to exchange. Street entertainers added to the noise and confusion of the streets, where pickpockets and petty thieves probed at loose purses.

An incredible range of commodities could be found in the city. By the time of Justinian, silk was being produced by local silkworms, descendants of the first worms smuggled into Constantinople as eggs from China. Beautifully brocaded silk garments caught the eyes of many people, but few could afford them. Gold and silver ornaments, religious statues, and other trinkets tempted the traveler to part with some hard-earned money. Food stalls abounded, filled with exotic smells and delicacies from the various homelands of the colorful faces in the crowd. More traders and merchants entered every hour through the Great Golden Gate at the west end of the city; here merchants from the Adriatic coast and northern Greece arrived with their treasures.

The public works of Justinian were probably the most ambitious in the city's history. Projects during the early Roman Empire had included the erection of aqueducts to ensure an adequate water supply for the city, Roman baths to accommodate the citizens' desire for relaxation and entertainment, and the Hippodrome to stage public spectacles similar to those in the Colosseum or Circus Maximus of Rome. Constantine's construction projects had included many church buildings and a forum. Justinian's projects rebuilt sections of the city that had been destroyed in a fire and further fortified the city against enemy attack. Triple walls, 13 miles in circumference, protected the city; in some places these walls measured 25 feet in width. Multiple watchtowers held soldiers who scrutinized the approach of caravans and ships and observed travelers approaching the fifty gates of the city. A moat protected the only side of the city that was accessible by land, and a great

FIGURE 17.5 *Chariot on Silk. This seventh-century silk textile depicts a charioteer driving his horses in a race, perhaps in the Hippodrome in Constantinople. Elaborately designed textiles such as this found their way along the numerous trade routes far beyond Constantinople. The introduction of silkworm eggs from China into Constantinople allowed for local production that drove the price of silk merchandise down, making it more affordable to Europeans.* Musée du Moyen Age (Cluny), Paris, France. Giraudon/Art Resource, N.Y.

chain impeded unwanted ships in the Golden Horn.

Justinian's most celebrated building project, however, was the rebuilding of Hagia Sophia ("Holy Wisdom"), a church nearly destroyed by a fire in 532. The new edifice soared 180 feet, overshadowing the other churches of the city, and spread more than 100 feet across. It was the largest domed building in the world at that time. Ten thousand workers toiled six years to complete the project, and the result was magnificent. The rather bulky exterior belies the beauty of an interior flooded with light. Forty windows at the base of the dome allowed the sun's rays into the building from any angle, and the effect made it seem as if the dome floated in the air, as if a gift from heaven. Rose-colored dawns cast an ethereal light throughout, and a huge silk hanging depicting Christ

between the saints Peter and Paul shimmered in the light. The interior of the building was decorated with more than twenty tons of silver, the dome was covered in gold, and mosaics depicting various saints and religious figures adorned the massive walls and ceilings, complementing the marble surfaces. Tradition says that upon entering the church for the first time, Justinian exclaimed, "I have surpassed you, Solomon!" (alluding to Solomon's construction of the great temple of Jerusalem). After serving several centuries as a mosque, today Hagia Sophia is a museum.

Hagia Sophia held thousands of worshiping citizens and pilgrims. On Easter Sundays, the emperor himself participated in an impressive procession through the streets to the church, preceded by attendants dressed as the twelve apostles. The emperor wore a white robe, and, as he came into view, the population prostrated themselves in reverence to him. Here was Christ's representative on earth and the successor to Constantine, who had called himself the thirteenth apostle.

Imperial laws and restrictions governed trade in the city. Magistrates enforced strict import and export regulations on all raw materials and finished products. Some foreign merchants were limited to a certain number of days in the city, to help protect local merchants and control the markets. Certain dyes, especially royal purple, were restricted for use by only the imperial household. Restrictions applied to many professions as well. For example, butchers could not go outside the city to buy their goats, sheep, or pigs directly from herdsmen; they were forced to purchase them from a designated seller inside the city. They then butchered and sold what they had purchased for the day. Punishments for infractions of the restrictions on trade included expulsion from one's guild, flogging, or banishment.

Twenty-two guilds organized and controlled the workers of the city. In contrast to the independent guilds of Europe, Byzantine guilds came under the direct authority of the city's prefect (an imperially appointed official), who acted as chief justice, chief of police, and chief trade regulator. Each guild then supervised its own members, setting wages and work hours. This helped maintain strict price and supply controls. As with European guilds, each specialty was restricted to a particular area or block in the city. Grocers and others who sold perishable goods remained the only exception; they were allowed to set up business in various neighborhoods.

Because the city was a major trade center, myriad professions existed to employ the working population. The many artisan professions included metalworkers, shipbuilders, candlemakers, bakers, potters, and perfumers. Merchants sold the completed goods in the city's shops or exported them to faraway places. Most workers were men, but many women worked in the imperial silk factory and other textile-producing workshops. Fishing, working the docks, and providing menial labor filled the time of those on the lower end of the social scale. Slaves were imported from central and northern Europe and from Africa to be domestic servants, land workers, and workshop laborers.

Private Life in the City

The city of Constantinople enjoyed times of population growth and endured periods of plague in its lengthy history. From the sixth to the thirteenth centuries, the city's population numbered about one million people. Of these, some were the fortunate wealthy, who lived in relative comfort. Constantinople had no space for expansion, so excess population migrated to suburban areas that developed near the city, such as the northern shore of the Golden Horn. Most of the citizens lived in neighborhoods that were cramped and unsanitary. Alleys and narrow streets functioned as waste-disposal areas that often bred disease, which occasionally developed into epidemics that killed thousands.

The poor depended on the gifts of pilgrims and priests, and the homeless often found shelter in public spaces. Frequently those who had died during the night had to be removed before business could commence the next day. Following in Greek and Roman traditions of public charity, Justinian tried to remedy the predicament with a decree that distributed as many as 80,000 loaves of bread to the hungry every day. His public works projects, in part, were initiated to put the unemployed back to work.

Recreation could be found in various places around the city. The public baths afforded a place for rest and relaxation for all classes. As in Rome, people gathered there to exchange gossip, informally establish business ties, and meet new friends. The heat of the summer months often drove citizens to the baths more than once a day. The Hippodrome, by far, was the most popular place for entertainment, and everyone was admitted free of charge. The emperor and his subjects shouted encouragement to their champions in the competitions held there. In the early Byzantine Empire, chariot races offered the most popular sport. Animal fights and lighter entertainments by clowns, jugglers, and dancers also delighted the crowd between major events. Torture and executions of capital offenders also occasionally drew the curious to the Hippodrome, as did the emperor's speeches and heated political debates. By the early thirteenth century, crusaders from Europe amused the citizens with jousts between mounted knights. If the citizens wearied of the city noise and the roars of the Hippodrome crowd, they could walk the spacious parks and gardens found throughout the city.

Clothing indicated a person's social status, as in many places of the world. Within the city, various sects and professions wore distinctive clothing or colors. Two rival factions in the city wore characteristic bits of cloth on their shoulders to identify them as Green Party or Blue Party members, not unlike the gangs of Han Empire China and modern North America. The factions began as clubs associated with the Hippodrome, where they led the cheering fans of the green and blue teams. Members of these groups also acted as bodyguards to the emperor, for which they wore distinctive Hun-style clothing: cloaks and shoes, large-sleeved tunics gathered at the wrist, and a particular hairstyle, cropped in the front and long and flowing in the back. Rich merchants and citizens could afford the new styles, especially the silk clothing, so popular in Constantinople; their horses even sported embroidered saddlecloth. Long, elaborately decorated coats replaced Roman togas among the elite by the sixth century. Silver and gold threads woven into brocaded fabrics adorned the bodies of the wealthy, while ornate jewelry of silver and gold, mounted with precious gems, decorated their necks, arms, and hands. In contrast to the elite with their high fashions, commoners and slaves continued to wear knee-length tunics cinched at the waist.

Life in the city encompassed a broad spectrum of lifestyles. Some ethnic groups or religious sects lived in segregated neighborhoods; Jews were not allowed to live within the city walls but found shelter in the suburb north of the city. Most elite and merchant house construction centered on a courtyard, with windowless walls facing the street. Poorer houses consisted of multiple-story apartment buildings (sometimes nine stories high) that offered cramped quarters for multiple-family living. Food variety in families' diets was determined by wealth. Dried, cured, or fresh meats could be purchased, but few poor families could afford much meat. Fruits, such as apples, pears, grapes, figs, and melons, could be purchased from the markets in the city. Shoppers also found vegetables, such as cabbage, leeks, cucumbers, onions, and carrots. Elite dishes were flavored with honey, pepper, and cinnamon. Every household, large or small, helped consume the tons of fish from the bulging nets of fishing ships each day. Pastoralists supplied the milk products used in many households. A common dish for both rich and poor families consisted of a mixture of fish, cheese, and vegetables cooked in a casserole.

Most women in Constantinople experienced less freedom than men. Except for the empress, they could not attend the exciting sports events at the Hippodrome. Women could not participate in processions or parades or engage in the many public political debates and protests. All women, including the empress, were required to cover their heads and faces in public, in similar fashion to women in Muslim society. Women did control the households, however; whether the household was large or small, all domestic arrangements came under the authority of the wife and mother. Wealthier women employed servants or owned slaves to assist them in keeping the home comfortable. In poorer homes, younger girls learned domestic chores by working alongside their mothers.

Women were mentioned frequently in Byzantine law, and, during Justinian's reign, several changes in Byzantine law affected women. Wives could own property of equal value to their dowries, which, in some cases, was a considerable amount. In addition, widows retained the right to be guardians of their children, thus, in certain circumstances, controlling vast amounts of family wealth. Justinian complained that Constantinople housed too many brothels, staffed by young girls and innocent women enticed from rural areas, and he outlawed all houses of prostitution in the city. His edicts may have slowed prostitution but did not eliminate its practice. Divorce could be filed by a woman if her husband did not consummate the marriage within two years, made false claims of adultery against her, held her captive, or was unfaithful to her. A wife could not obtain a divorce for any other reason. Justinian did not accept mutual consent as grounds for divorce. These divorce laws, however, were repealed by Justinian's successor, who recognized them to be unpopular.

Children belonged to both fathers and mothers, particularly after Justinian issued his law code. Although the law limited the ages for marriage to fourteen years for boys and twelve years for girls, many families arranged marriages by the time the children were four or five years old. Sons of artisans were expected to follow in the same professions as their fathers. Children of concubines, as in Muslim society, received legal status and limited rights of inheritance.

FIGURE 17.7 *Danielis, a Wealthy Byzantine Woman.* *Danielis was a very wealthy Byzantine widow who lived in the ninth century. Her control of her own wealth demonstrates the financial freedom women enjoyed under Byzantine law. She was a sponsor and supporter of a young politician named Basil, who in* A.D. *867 became Emperor Basil I, founder of a new dynasty. Her close association with the emperor gave her influence in Byzantine society. Basil made her son, John, an official in his bureaucracy. When John died, Danielis left most of her great wealth to Leo VI, Basil's son and successor. In this drawing, Danielis visits Basil and presents him with gifts.* Biblioteca Nacional, Madrid.

The Nika Rebellion

Social unrest often exploded into riot and revolt in the city during periods of heavy taxation and economic distress. Tax payments took the form of gold from city dwellers and produce from rural-area dwellers. During Justinian's war with the Persians, taxes were increased to pay for the expenses of combat and interruption of trade. In January 532, rioting broke out at the instigation of the Greens and the Blues, who had gained some popular political influence. The disturbance began in the Hippodrome and spread to the streets and throughout the city. Shouts of "Nika!"[3] ("Victory!") filled the afternoon air as the proponents organized into a mob ready to fight for tax relief.

The Nika Rebellion incited full-scale looting that destroyed many businesses and ignited widespread fires that damaged many buildings, including the imperial palace. Soon the rebels were calling for a new imperial election, and the situation became desperate as the nephew of a previous emperor was elected by the crowd. Justinian wavered, considering whether to flee the city. It may have been Empress Theodora's persuasion that convinced him to stay, and he finally mobilized his army to his defense. Under Justinian's direction, the army wrested the city from the rebels and attacked and massacred nearly 30,000 of them in the Hippodrome. Justinian rebuilt the city after the Nika Rebellion; the construction projects put many unemployed people to work and helped calm political tensions.

BYZANTINE ECONOMY

The Byzantine economy centered on agriculture and trade. Agriculture was the mainstay of revenues for the government and supplied local people with the basic commodities for survival.

[3] **Nika:** NY kah

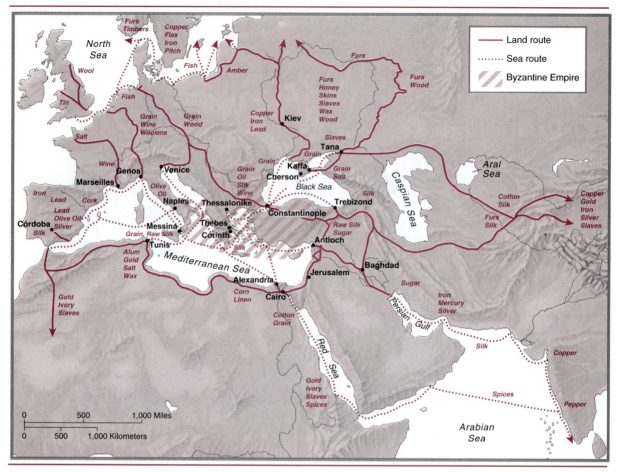

MAP 17.3 *Byzantine Trade.* *Byzantine trade served as a link between the European trade network and East Asian and Indian trade networks, with Constantinople as its hub. Silks, jewels, precious metals, sugar, and spices from eastern areas were brought along the silk road and spice routes to exchange for slaves, wood, honey, woolens, and grain from European areas.*

Trade took many merchants across the empire on their way to domestic markets in ships and along caravan routes. Few foreign trading expeditions were sent by the Byzantines, whose almost ideal placement at the crossroads of Eurasia and Africa afforded them a wealth of trade goods.

Landholders consisted of the state, the Christian Church, and individuals. Some landholders held large estates that rivaled the aristocratic villas of the Western Roman Empire or the manors of medieval Europe; poor farmers had small landholdings and could barely eke out a living. Some of these impoverished farmers became tenants of wealthier landowners. They were similar to the serfs of medieval Europe: They remained tied to the land that they worked and fell under the legal jurisdiction of the landowner. One-third of tenant harvests went to pay imperial taxes, leaving only two-thirds to pay rent to landlords and to meet all other expenses. Heavy taxation prompted many tenant farmers to abandon their allegiance to the Byzantine Empire when enemy soldiers invaded their territories. From the seventh to ninth centuries, border hostilities caused the breakup of large landholdings. By the tenth century, most farming was done by free farmers with small landholdings.

Most domestic trade was conducted in the major market cities of the empire, Constantinople, Thessalonike,[4] and Trebizond, where goods from various places were brought for sale. Generally, domestic trade was significant. Wine, oil, wool,

[4]**Thessalonike:** THEHS uh LOHN eh kah

metals, marble, timber, and finished products, such as cloth and leather goods, were exchanged at the major market cities. Local networks of trade between the empire's urban centers and rural areas supplied the subjects with various staples. The volume of trade between urban centers was greater in the eastern territories than it was in western areas, which tended to be more self-sufficient.

Long-distance trade was a central component of the Byzantine economy, and the location of major trade cities made the empire a natural center for the passage of goods moving between Europe and Asia. Long-distance trade brought spices, jewelry, and other products from China, Persia, and India as well as aromatics from Axum and rhinoceros-horn medicine from sub-Saharan Africa. Other items, such as grain, wine, honey, wax, furs, skins, gold, iron, ivory, and slaves, came from Europe and Africa. In addition, many raw materials came into the empire that then were transformed into finished products and later exported. Byzantine glassware, for example, was highly prized; emperors often sent pieces as gifts to foreign rulers. Goods moved overland from their places of origin into the empire through trade stations in Persia or north of the Caspian Sea into the Black Sea area. Water routes from Southeast Asia transported goods across the Bay of Bengal, the Arabian Sea, and either the Persian Gulf or the Red Sea into ports in Southwest Asia.

Byzantine trade fluctuated, depending upon the political circumstances and general economic conditions. The collapse of Axum in 650 cut off one area of trade from the Byzantines. The political and military reverses of the mid–seventh to mid–ninth centuries, which caused deurbanization in the empire, helped create a decline in the volume of trade. By the tenth century, lessened hostilities led to a revival of urbanism and trade after nearly three centuries of decline. Significant commerce between Dar al-Islam and the Byzantine Empire increased the number of available goods, slaves, and revenues. The eleventh and twelfth centuries experienced significant growth as urban centers sprawled and Italian markets flourished. Egyptian sources show that Byzantine products, such as brocades and finished furniture, became increasingly popular in Egypt.

In the thirteenth century, the Byzantine trade network experienced serious decline because of the competition of Italian trade networks, which controlled exclusive access to the markets of central and western Europe. The Italians regulated Byzantine exports of food and raw materials to the west and the imports of finished products of Italian and French cloth. By the fourteenth century, Byzantine trade, although still extensive, remained subsidiary to the growing Italian network. The fourteenth-century conquests of Byzantine lands by Ottoman Turks further challenged Byzantine trade. As with other empires we have reviewed, decline in trade and political disintegration often coincided.

Interregional trade treaties helped regulate the flow of goods around the empire, and some peace treaties had clauses attached to them that determined trade relations with neighboring polities. These documents established agreements on trade sites, terms of exchange, and certain privileges for merchants (like duty exemptions). A clause in the peace treaty of 562 with Persia, for example, specified that all trade be done at specific stations. Sometimes clauses designated where and for how long foreign merchants could reside in the cities. In 907, a treaty with the Russians specified that their merchants in Constantinople be housed at St. Mamas, a monastery in the southwestern section of the city, be permitted to receive supplies for six months, and be exempt from duties. The treaties with Italian cities were primarily commercial. The first was with Venice in 992, followed by treaties with most of the other Italian maritime centers.

FIGURE 17.8 *Byzantine Currency. The Nomisma coin of the Byzantine Empire was so stable that it became the currency of choice of most merchants in the Mediterranean Sea trade from around the tenth to the thirteenth centuries. Europeans used the coin, calling it a bezant. Devaluation of coins was often a major factor in the interruption of trade networks, and merchants preferred to be paid with currency they could trust.* British Museum/Photo by Derek Bayes.

Italian merchants enjoyed many privileges that others did not, including free access to many markets.

One major component of Byzantine trade was the stability of its coinage. The *Nomisma*, a Byzantine coin, became the preferred medium of exchange from Central Asia to western Europe. While its gold content fluctuated somewhat over the centuries, the coin remained a standard on which users could confidently rely. The eighth-century English historian Bede, wanting to demonstrate the purity of a local princess, described her as "pure as a bezant."

BYZANTINE CHRISTIANITY

Between the fourth and the seventh centuries, Christianity became entrenched as the major religion of the Byzantine Empire. Patriarchs (bishops) of Jerusalem, Antioch, Alexandria, Rome, and Constantinople emerged as leaders of the church. When Arab Muslim conquests of Byzantine territories came to include the cities of Jerusalem, Antioch, and Alexandria, the remaining patriarchs of Constantinople and Rome became the two most prominent Christian leaders. The patriarch of Rome (the pope) became the head of the western Christian church, and the patriarch of Constantinople became the leader of eastern Christians. The presence of powerful Christian emperors who also claimed spiritual authority, however, created a competition for control over the eastern church. The relationships between the patriarchs of Constantinople and the emperors were a mixture of mutual support and rivalry. The emperor often convened councils and intervened in spiritual matters, while the patriarch frequently intruded in imperial affairs and plotted with officials against the monarch. At most times, however, both worked for the mutual benefit of the Christian religion.

The Eastern Orthodox Church

Christians in the Eastern Roman Empire developed some theological perspectives and liturgical practices that differed profoundly from those of the Western Roman Empire. Religion is, above all, a cultural expression, and as the two halves of the empire diverged culturally down different paths, so did the Christian faith develop disparate practices in the two areas. A few examples of the variation in practices will help to explain the 1054 **schism**, a religious split caused by irreconcilable differences of opinion. The consequence of the schism was the formation of two major branches of Christianity: the Roman Catholic and the Eastern Orthodox.

Some examples of the practices that separated Christians are found in social attitudes, rituals, and theological opinions. For example, Byzantine men began abstaining from shaving in the seventh century, as beards became popular throughout the society. Beards were associated with manliness; emperors from the fourth century on increasingly wore beards, and beards at court distinguished powerful officials from court eunuchs. Byzantine monks always wore beards after biblical and monastic tradition. The shaving off of a beard came to be a severe punishment for any Byzantine man. By the eleventh century, the beardless Europeans were thought to be effeminate; clearly, beards translated into a matter of pride for Byzantine men. Some bearded Byzantine priests even refused to offer the bread and wine of the sacred meal to shaven (that is, western) communicants.

Another distinction between eastern and western Christianity was that of language. The traditional language of theology had been Greek. During the Roman Empire, the official language had become Latin, but many theologians continued to write in Greek. As time passed and the breakup of the Roman Empire commenced, western theologians came to accept Latin as their theological language. Byzantine theologians came to regard Latin treatises as unworthy of serious consideration because of translation difficulties in expressing the nuances of theology. Many of the theological arguments that led to the 1054 schism occurred as a result of misunderstandings because of language difficulties.

Many liturgical rituals differed between the two areas and clashes occurred over territorial control. One difference in ritual was the calculation of the celebration of Easter. The Council of Nicaea in 325 named the date for Easter as the first Sunday after the first full moon after the spring equinox (which tied it to the traditional celebration of the Jewish Passover feast). Differences between the dating of Easter, which falls sometime between March 21 and April 25, developed because Byzantines used different computations of astronomical tables. For example, Easter might be celebrated in Italy on April 18 and in Constantinople on April 25. (A discrepancy between the days of celebration still exists today.)

A major clash concerning territorial control erupted in the ninth century, challenging the traditional Byzantine view of the equality of patriarchs. The patriarch of Constantinople had been deposed by the Byzantine emperor, who placed Photius (his secretary) on the patriarchal throne. The pope objected and claimed the right to depose Photius and any priests who had supported him. This assertion of papal supremacy over the patriarch deeply offended many easterners and had a profound effect on strained relations between eastern and Roman Christians.

The most serious of the differences, however, were theological. The best example is the addition of the clause "and the Son" to the Nicene Creed (a statement of faith adopted from the First Council of Nicaea in 325), which was repeated by Christians at most worship services. The western church had added the clause to help explain the meaning of the Trinity. The Byzantine Christians agreed with the theology of the clause but objected on the grounds that language could be neither added to nor subtracted from the creed. The clause caused a conflict that reverberated throughout Christendom. Even the Byzantine emperor joined the fracas and had the original creed carved on silver tablets. The "and the Son" clause played a significant role in the theological arguments that led to the formal schism in 1054. Today, the clause remains a major stumbling block to Christian reunification.

The schism between eastern and western Christianity created the Roman Catholic Church in medieval Europe and the Eastern Orthodox Church in the Byzantine Empire. Each side claimed that it held the correct interpretation of scripture and was heir to Christian tradition. The very titles suggest this: The word "catholic" means universal and the word "orthodox" means correct belief. By the time the European crusaders entered Byzantine territories in the late eleventh century, great animosity already existed. The conquest of Constantinople by crusaders for a short time in the thirteenth century exacerbated the enmity of each side for the other.

Eastern Orthodox Monasticism

Christian monasticism began in the Eastern Roman Empire and continued to be a significant element of Byzantine Christianity. Although monasticism had originated with hermit monks in the eastern deserts, it soon became an urban phenomenon; one-third of the approximately 1,000 monasteries and nunneries were located within

FIGURE 17.9 *Greek Island Monastery.* *This is the Simonopetra Monastery on Mount Athos, an island off the Greek coast. There are many monasteries on the island, placed there because of its remoteness. The monasteries were built into steep cliffs that impeded access in order to preserve the seclusion of the monks living there. In the eleventh century, all women (and female animals) were banned from the island to keep the monks from being distracted by thoughts about sex and to preserve their spiritual focus. The ban remains in effect today.* Otis Imboden/ NGS Image Collection.

Constantinople. The population of these monasteries ranged from as few as three monks to as many as several hundred. The hermit attitude of renunciation of the world, however, continued in remote monasteries, such as those on Mount Athos. The ethnic diversity of the empire led to distinctive ethnic monasteries.

As with the monasteries of Roman Catholic Europe, Eastern Orthodox monasteries often owned extensive properties and contributed to the intricate trade system and economy of the empire. Some monasteries received special economic privileges from the state. They could inherit properties from private citizens, they remained protected against confiscation by covetous neighbors, and they could rent out their lands to farmers without paying new taxes. Monastery properties grew substantially in the tenth century. Some monks tried to curb the growth, fearing that the resulting wealth would tempt the monks from their spiritual duties. One emperor tried to restrict the purchase of new lands in 964, but monasteries continued to expand. In an attempt to redistribute monastic wealth and increase state revenues, emperors in the fourteenth century granted some monastic lands to soldiers as payment for their services.

Unlike their Roman Catholic counterparts, Eastern Orthodox monasteries did not establish particular orders, such as Benedictines or Cistercians. Each monastery remained under its own rule (which was patterned on generally accepted practices), and individuals exercised a level of autonomy. In contrast to the western model of monks' vowing obedience to their abbots, eastern monks frequently moved from monastery to monastery or out into hermitage, away from the community. Also in contrast to European monasteries, Byzantine monasteries did not develop a special focus on becoming educators, although intellectual pursuits did appeal to many monks. Much of the literature of the early Byzantine Empire, such as accounts of the lives of the saints and wise sayings of the desert hermits, came from the monasteries. Monks and nuns formed the majority of the educated in the ninth century. Scholars have estimated that 50 percent of Byzantine scribes in the tenth and eleventh centuries were monks. Literacy, of course, facilitated the reading of prayers and scriptures.

Eastern Orthodox monasteries, like their Roman Catholic counterparts, ran hospitals and orphanages in addition to performing various charitable services. Refugees found safe haven within their walls during times of political upheaval, and beggars and the dispossessed received food and clothing. Many monasteries also offered housing to pilgrims on the way to holy sites and housed prisoners living out sentences of banishment for their crimes.

Byzantine monasteries became great patrons of the arts, although monks usually did not produce visual art themselves. Manuscript illumination did not become a monastic occupation, as it had in western Christianity. Some of the best examples of Byzantine silver and gold vessels, visual art, and textiles were produced by artisans for monasteries. Architects and artists were usually imported to build and decorate the churches and residence halls.

Monasteries remained the primary residence for those seeking a spiritual life of prayer and devotion to God. Many Christian mystics experienced their spiritual encounters with the divine in monasteries, and many of their writings contributed to the development of Eastern Orthodox tradition.

BYZANTINE ELITE ARTS

Patronage of the arts in Byzantine society came primarily from the state and the Eastern Orthodox Church; significant patronage by individuals did not come until about the fifteenth century. The unique Byzantine style was influenced by Classical Greek, Roman, and Hellenistic literature, philosophy, and visual art. By the sixth century, Christian motifs and genres dominated the art of the empire.

Literature

Byzantine literature inherited styles from previous generations. With the advent of Christianity, some dramatic forms were abandoned because of their topics, which were perceived as immoral (such as the poetry of Sappho from ancient Greece). Poetry, as well, became attached to ritual in the form of hymns. The writing of sermons and wise sayings of holy individuals offered the reader a selection of devotional materials. Histories of various military and religious events became popular. Between about the mid–seventh century and the beginning of the ninth century, very little literature was produced beyond theological treatises.

Literature adopted an encyclopedic focus in the mid–ninth century, when compilations became popular. Many technical works dealt with the administration of the empire, such as military textbooks, treatises on taxation, documents on the imperial system, and law textbooks. Religious works continued to be produced, especially idealized biographies of saints' lives, **hagiographies**.[5] Other works included collections of Classical Greek and Roman literature.

A famous twelfth-century historian named Anna Komnene[6] (1083–1153) was the eldest daughter of an emperor. She wrote a history of her father's reign that scholars have found most helpful in analyzing the twelfth-century empire. During this same period, a new genre developed in literature that discussed the dual nature of good and evil in every individual; many characters showed attributes of both heroes and villains. Stories and poems about sex, chastity, and romance written by professional novelists and poets rather than government officials or monks entertained the literate of the empire. Hagiographies went out of style in this new literary climate.

From the thirteenth to the mid–fourteenth century, Byzantine literature experienced a revival of hagiography and a new pessimism in the representation of history—no great surprise since the empire was under much political and economic stress. Western literary styles had been imported into the area through the Crusader States in the twelfth and thirteenth centuries, and their influence appears in thirteenth-century Byzantine works. During this period, several intellectuals began translating Latin texts into Greek. Some traveled to Italy, where they translated into Latin Greek texts, especially philosophical works, that they had brought with them. Many of these intellectuals tried to preserve the ancient Classical Greek and Roman styles, a practice that may have helped to stimulate the Italian Renaissance.

Philosophy and Theology

Byzantine philosophy was closely associated with Christian topics. The philosopher and the monk had a lot in common; they both loved wisdom and both disciplined themselves to live a moral life. As with all Byzantine intellectual traditions, philoso-phy inherited and adopted Greco-Roman and Hellenistic traditions. In addition, philosophical speculation benefited from the Byzantine exchange, particularly that of Islamic philosophy. Christian theologians of the first four centuries A.D. gave Byzantine philosophers paradigms for what they saw as the "true" philosophical life: martyrdom and monasticism.

The prominent Byzantine philosopher John of Damascus (675–749) divided philosophy into two main branches: theoretical and practical. Theoretical philosophy consisted of physics, mathematics, and theology, and practical philosophy included ethics, economics, and politics. His division served as the basis for the study of philosophy in the Byzantine Empire. A Neoplatonic revival heavily influenced Byzantine philosophy, particularly through the works of John of Damascus. John is a good example of a Byzantine Christian philosopher; he wrote many polemical works, including some against Islam and heresies, as well as sermons, hymns, moral tracts, hagiographies, and biblical commentaries.

Eleventh-century philosophy benefited from a focus on education. For example, at the University of Constantinople (begun around the mid–eleventh century), the school of philosophy was headed by an influential teacher, Michael Psellos (1018–1081?). Psellos drew on a diverse offering of sources in his classes on philosophy, and he assembled topics from them in a short encyclopedia. Some of Psellos's works, as well as those of many of his successors, analyzed Aristotle's ethics, physics, and logic. In his classes, Psellos stressed physics, which he taught was created by God but functions according to the laws of nature. This conception left little room for miracles.

The eleventh to the mid–thirteenth centuries witnessed renewed interest in the philosophical works of Plato and the Neoplatonists, especially within Christian intellectual circles. Earlier mystical writings, such as those of the sixth-century mystic Pseudo Dionysius[7] the Areopagite, also became popular again. His works on mysticism were the most influential Christian writings on Neoplatonic ideas.

After the fall of Constantinople to crusaders in 1204, the focus of Byzantine philosophical activity shifted to Nicaea. A group of philosophers gathered there; their polemics covered all the subjects

---

[5] **hagiography:** HAW jee AHG ruh fee *or* HAY gee AHG ruh fee
[6] **Komnene:** kohm NEHN ay

[7] **Dionysius:** DY oh NIHS ee uhs

UNDER THE LENS

The Iconoclastic Controversy

Byzantine Christians venerated **icons** because they were the images of holy people, even Christ himself. One would not throw away or deface an icon, for example, because it represents the subject of its art. Like the stories of the saints in the hagiographies, the images inspire virtue; some described them as "silent writing," and in this sense, their destruction would be like ripping up a Bible or defacing the Qur'an. Icons are still produced today in Eastern Orthodoxy, and the attitude toward them is still one of respect.

In the eighth century, a controversy arose over the practice of venerating icons in the Byzantine Empire. Many individuals thought that people were worshiping the icons instead of giving them special respect; these objections were based upon older traditions of not making or worshiping false idols. The issue fixed particularly on making images of Christ and then spread to other images; some denounced the practice and asserted that it should be stopped. Several bishops condemned icons in the early eighth century, and their views fueled a formidable movement.

Emperor Leo III (reign dates 717–741) supported the movement and issued in 726 an edict demanding the destruction of a famous icon of Christ on a gate in Constantinople. The citizens rioted. Nevertheless, the **iconoclasts**, icon destroyers, gained momentum. By 730, Leo III deposed the dissenting patriarch of Constantinople and issued a decree demanding the destruction of all icons. In the ensuing years, hundreds of thousands of icons were destroyed. This destruction significantly defaced holy places because icons covered the walls, screens, and altars of every Eastern Orthodox Church and monastery. Almost every household also had icons used for daily devotionals, and placards with icon images were often carried in processions and parades. Many Monophysites applauded the emperor's decree, believing that Christ did not have a human body, and therefore no image of him could be made. Many monks, the most ardent defenders of icons, were forced to whitewash the images in their churches and monasteries; those who refused to do so were prosecuted.

In the following decades, other emperors continued iconoclastic policies. One emperor called a local council to condemn icon veneration as satanic. The issue extended beyond painted images and challenged the perception of the saints. Veneration of saints' relics was questioned as inappropriate, but this issue did not result in relic destruction. Many **iconophiles**, venerators of icons, who lived in isolated areas continued their practices; the farther away from the capital one lived, the less one observed the decree.

The iconoclastic controversy contributed to the hostilities between eastern and western Christendom that ended in the schism of 1054. A decree prohibiting religious images also was sent to the pope. Because there was a different artistic tradition in western Christianity that did not include veneration of icons, western Christians failed to understand the objection to simple representations of Christ and the saints. Heated debates between popes and Byzantine patriarchs and emperors commenced. The papacy was threatened if it did not comply, which helped to convince the pope at that time that the Franks were better allies than Byzantine emperors.

Although theological issues were at the heart of the controversy, scholars argue that economic and political motivations also spurred Leo III to act. Leo and succeeding emperors used the excuse of iconoclasm to confiscate monastic properties of those monasteries whose monks refused to comply with the decree; these monasteries continued to function under state control. Some scholars argue that the emperor needed to reassert his authority over the church, which might be accomplished by deposing the patriarch and forcing compliance with the decree. The iconoclastic controversy lost momentum in the ninth century as some emperors gave sympathetic support to iconophiles and finally ended with a formal compromise that icons were constructive representations of holy individuals. Icons are still a significant part of Eastern Orthodoxy today.

of philosophy. They particularly argued over the virtues and vices of Aristotle's ideas versus those of the Neoplatonists. Toward the end of the Byzantine Empire, the debate of first-century Christians about the relationship of Greek philosophy to Christianity rose again. The debate raged on, and the discipline of philosophy became suspect to many Byzantine intellectuals who came to believe there should be a separation between the disciplines of Greek philosophy and theology.

Visual Arts

The visual arts of the Byzantine Empire were rendered in such media as textiles, manuscript illustration, metalwork, painting, and mosaics. Many earlier styles and subjects influenced Byzantine arts, as did the exchange of styles with conquerors and peoples on the borders. A unique element of Byzantine religious art was the expected attitude of the viewer to the object; the artist was secondary to the religious person depicted. In addition, artistic style tended to remain consistent, and model books and artisan tradition served to keep the styles uniform.

Some changes did occur stylistically in Byzantine art, especially in painting during the eleventh to the fifteenth centuries. Scenes of everyday life appear in the eleventh century, augmenting the dominant religious themes and imperial portraits of preceding centuries. By the eleventh and twelfth centuries an attempt to display more emotion can be observed in paintings. New ideas influencing artists in the thirteenth century significantly altered the previous 150 years of Byzantine art, in part because of patronage by local officials. Uniformity of the previous centuries gave way to new expressions as the empire came to an end.

FIGURE 17.10 *Virgin of Vladimir. Icons decorated Byzantine churches and monasteries and were venerated during liturgical services. The Russian city of Kiev adopted Eastern Orthodoxy, which embraced iconographic art. This twelfth-century icon of the Virgin Mary and baby Jesus is from Constantinople. It was eventually taken to Russia, where it became one of the most famous icons of Russian Orthodoxy, known as the Virgin of Vladimir.* Sovfoto.

SUMMARY

1. The Byzantine Empire evolved out of the Eastern Roman Empire and soon developed a uniquely Byzantine culture. The empire at its height encompassed Greece, the Balkans up to the Danube River, the Turkish Peninsula, Palestine, parts of North Africa, and the islands of the eastern Mediterranean and the Aegean seas. The population of the empire in the sixth century has been estimated at more than 30 million people.

2. Christianity became the ideological link that united the Byzantine Empire. Everyday life in the empire remained largely unchanged as farmers, artisans, merchants, and others continued to live in much the same ways as those of previous generations.

3. Byzantine law was codified during Justinian's reign in the *Corpus Juris Civilis*, which became influential beyond the borders of the

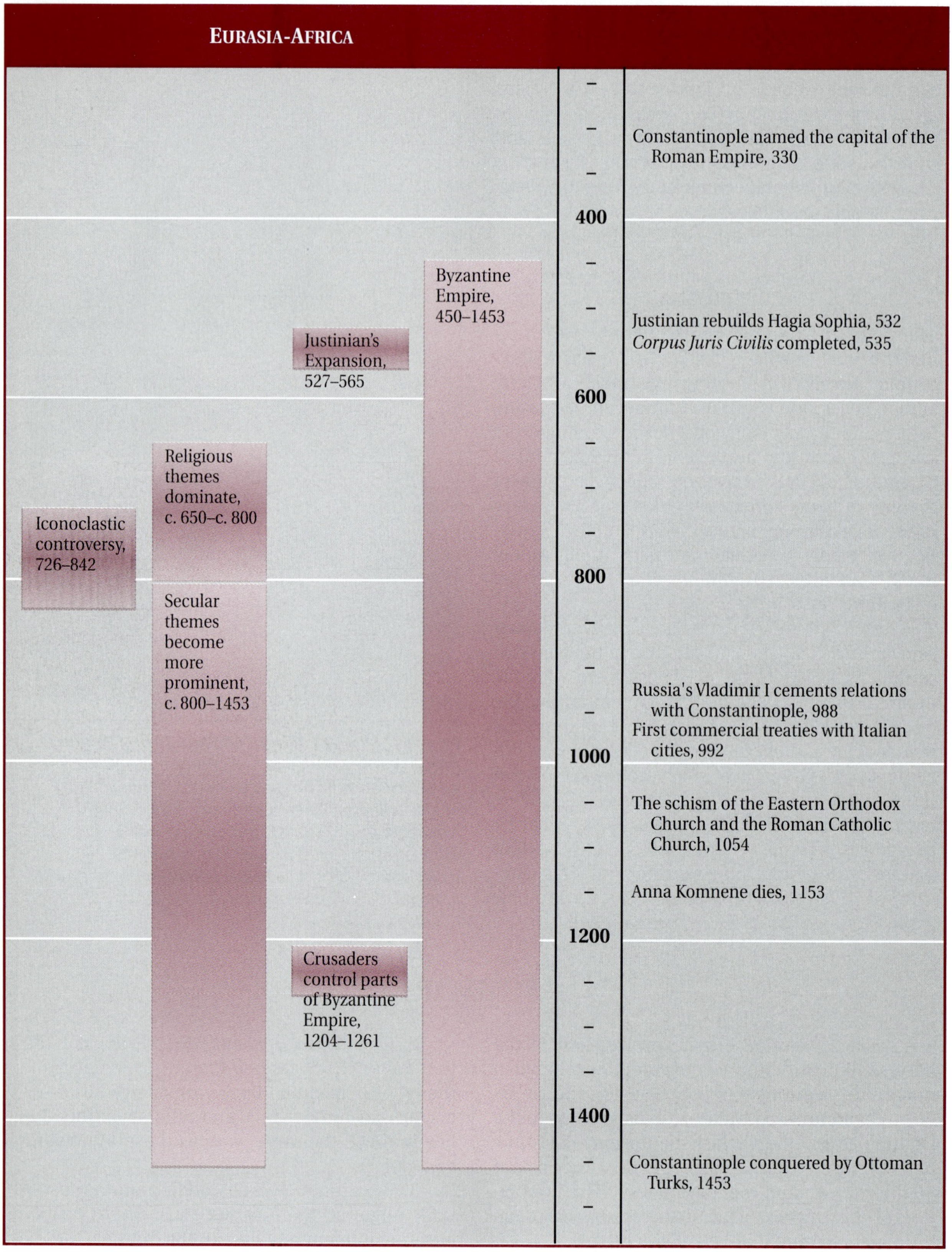

EURASIA-AFRICA

Constantinople named the capital of the Roman Empire, 330

400

Byzantine Empire, 450–1453

Justinian rebuilds Hagia Sophia, 532
Corpus Juris Civilis completed, 535

Justinian's Expansion, 527–565

600

Religious themes dominate, c. 650–c. 800

Iconoclastic controversy, 726–842

800

Secular themes become more prominent, c. 800–1453

Russia's Vladimir I cements relations with Constantinople, 988
First commercial treaties with Italian cities, 992

1000

The schism of the Eastern Orthodox Church and the Roman Catholic Church, 1054

Anna Komnene dies, 1153

1200

Crusaders control parts of Byzantine Empire, 1204–1261

1400

Constantinople conquered by Ottoman Turks, 1453

empire. The Christian Church influenced Byzantine law, and the patriarch's court functioned as the court of appeals.

4. Emperors and empresses played significant roles in the empire. Although emperors were thought to have been chosen by divine will, they were actually selected by the army, the Senate, or the citizens of Constantinople. Most empresses maintained parallel courts with elite women and influenced the policies of the emperors. Some empresses ruled for brief periods.

5. Many border raids disturbed the peace of the empire between 450 and 1453. Muslims conquered the eastern and southern portions of the Byzantine Empire, and crusaders conquered Constantinople in 1204. The Ottoman Turks conquered Constantinople in 1453, ending the Byzantine Empire.

6. Reorganization of the imperial administration into provinces occurred under Justinian. This system was replaced with the *theme* organization, which enabled better defense of the empire.

7. In 330, the city of Byzantium was chosen as the capital and renamed Constantinople by Constantine. Many ethnic groups populated the city, which was the hub of an extensive trade network. Many public works were erected by Justinian, including Hagia Sophia, the impressive church. Constantinople had formidable defenses: a three-wall system, water on three sides, and a moat that impeded the only land access.

8. Citizens numbered about one million in the city of Constantinople. All citizens could attend public recreation areas, such as the baths and gardens. Some women held control over vast fortunes and, if widowed, over their children. Social unrest broke out as the Nika Rebellion in 532, when the citizens of Constantinople looted and burned the city, after which Justinian ordered 30,000 rioters to be massacred in the Hippodrome.

9. The economic foundation of the Byzantine Empire was agriculture and trade. Both domestic trade and long-distance trade moved raw materials and finished products throughout the empire and beyond. Muslim and Italian competition inhibited Byzantine trade, and, after the thirteenth century, the empire never regained its extensive trade network.

10. Christianity remained the religion of the empire, and heresies were sometimes tolerated for political reasons. The Byzantine Empire's Christians developed different practices, rituals, and theologies that eventually brought them into conflict with western Christians. The pope and patriarch excommunicated each other in 1054, creating the Eastern Orthodox Church and the Roman Catholic Church. Monasticism was an important element of Eastern Orthodoxy. Most monasteries were patrons of the arts; monks usually hired artisans to build and decorate their churches and monasteries.

11. Patronage of the state and the church increased the production of Byzantine art. Literature, philosophy, and visual arts inherited Classical Greek, Roman, and Hellenistic antecedents, yet a distinctive Byzantine style developed. Christianity had great influence on the arts, supplying religious themes for expression.

SUGGESTED READINGS

Browning, Robert. *Justinian and Theodora*. New York: Thames and Hudson, 1987. An examination of the reign of Justinian and the influence of Theodora.

Haussig, H. W. *A History of Byzantine Civilization*. Trans. by J. M. Hussey. New York: Praeger Publishers, 1971. A thorough coverage of the Byzantine Empire.

Mango, Cyril. *Byzantium: The Empire of New Rome*. New York: Charles Scribner's Sons, 1980. A standard review of Byzantine history.

Meyendorff, John. *Byzantine Theology*. Second edition. New York: Fordham University Press, 1979. A standard work on Eastern Orthodoxy.

Rice, Tamara Talbot. *Everyday Life in Byzantium*. New York: Barnes and Noble, 1994. An informative review of life in the Byzantine Empire, especially in the early centuries.

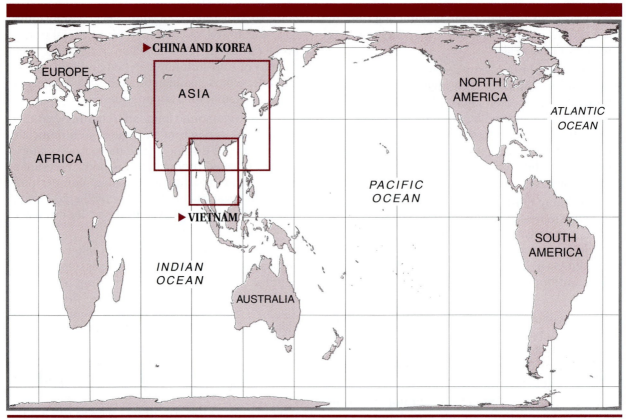

EUROPE

ASIA

► CHINA AND KOREA

AFRICA

► VIETNAM

NORTH
AMERICA

ATLANTIC
OCEAN

PACIFIC
OCEAN

INDIAN
OCEAN

SOUTH
AMERICA

AUSTRALIA

Talas

TIAN SHAN MTS.

*Nomadic Turkic
Peoples*

PAMIR MTS.

SILK ROAD

KUNLUN MTS.

Yellow R.

KOREA
(Silla
Dynasty)

JAPAN

TIBET

Yangzi R.

Changan

Hangzhou

CHINA
(Tang Empire)

*South
China
Sea*

NAN-CHAO

► **CHINA AND KOREA**

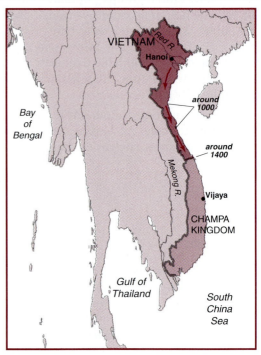

VIETNAM

Red R.

Hanoi

*around
1000*

*Bay
of
Bengal*

Mekong R.

*around
1400*

Vijaya

CHAMPA
KINGDOM

*Gulf
of
Thailand*

*South
China
Sea*

► **VIETNAM**

Empires and Other States in East Asia

589–1279

The Song Chinese naval commander confidently surveyed the enemy's fleet. Although outnumbered in ships and sailors, he had two secret weapons. One was a small number of paddle-wheel ships that could travel rapidly, terrifying people who could not discern the cause of the propulsion. The Chinese admiral also had tested gunpowder weapons of great destructive power. Both weapons would help him defeat this rival navy.

This account recalls a naval battle wherein Chinese ships smashed an invading force in 1161. It also suggests the success the Chinese had in adapting technological discoveries to military affairs, helping to fuel empire building.

In this chapter, we will see how the Sui dynastic house reunited China. Reestablishment of a centralized, bureaucratic state gave the political strength to conduct an expansionist foreign policy, including an attempted reassertion of Chinese domination over the Korean Peninsula and Central Asian trade routes. Later, several elements of China's domestic market flourished, and its maritime commerce, especially with Southeast Asia and South Asia, improved. While the Koreans and the Vietnamese ultimately became independent, they used their own versions of Chinese political and cultural forms to establish strong and stable polities.

CHINA REUNIFIED: THE SUI AND TANG EMPIRES, 589–907

Sui[1] and Tang[2] power dominated East Asia for nearly two centuries, before decline and internal crisis forced a redirection of imperial energies to internal matters. These two regimes harnessed their subjects by creating a stable government staffed with individuals chosen by a civil service examination system.

The Sui Empire, 589–618

The Sui Empire lasted only three decades but had significant achievements. It reunited China permanently, inaugurated an effective political recruitment system, strengthened central control over regional and local officials, reestablished strong frontier boundaries, and created a solid economic base.

The long national division began to come to an end in the 580s, when General Yang Jian[3] (reign dates 581–604) usurped power in one of the northern Chinese states. He slowly consolidated his position and expanded his conquest of North China. In 589, after a long period of planning, the conquest of South China began. Sui partisans made and distributed tens of thousands of leaflets denouncing the southern monarch. A combined land and river attack began in Central China, passed through the Yangzi River gorges, and continued to the river's mouth. The Sui fleet numbered in the thousands, including large ramming ships. Once the waterborne effort was victorious, the land defenses crumbled, and the captured southern monarch was sent north to the Sui capital, where he peacefully lived out his life in exile.

Most of Yang Jian's activities were devoted to building a powerful government and consolidating unified rule over the north and the south. He was a skilled judge of talented people and an empire builder, but he was given to fits of temper (he once beat a man to death with a horse whip). Because he came to power by a palace coup, Yang Jian grew suspicious of everyone, including his sons. Yet for

[1] **Sui:** SWAY
[2] **Tang:** TAHNG
[3] **Yang Jian:** YAHNG JEE yahn

FIGURE 18.1 *Shrine to the Amida Buddha.* *Cast in 593, this bronze Amida Buddha illuminates the importance of Buddhism for the Sui Empire. Aiding those who called on him for help, protected by guardian deities, and surrounded by adoring animals, the Amida Buddha gained a widespread following in China, especially among the poor. Over the next century and a half, Buddhism became the dominant religion of China, uniting northerners and southerners as well as upper and lower classes.* Gift of Mrs. W. Scott Fitz. Courtesy of the Museum of Fine Arts, Boston.

all his faults, Yang Jian was a strong and successful monarch who monitored his officials by requiring them to write regular reports about their actions. He knew that only through the reestablishment of a centralized, bureaucratic administration would the unity last, but he paid a stiff price in personally having to read mountains of reports.

One of Yang Jian's most reliable and astute advisors was his wife, the Sui empress Dugu Jielo, who shared her husband's political vision, his tough-minded governing style, and his thrifty ways. She insisted on his not having other wives and was a sole partner in marriage as well as a chief advisor in politics. One of her major political acts was to persuade her husband to name her second (and favorite) son, Yang Guang (reign dates 604–618), as heir apparent.

Yang Jian established uniform practices for government and society. Weights and measures were standardized once again, and laws were codified. Standardized written tests were given to prospective office holders in order to find the most capable people. Begun in 589, this practice commenced the establishment of a civil service examination system. Administrative offices were thus staffed by capable individuals who owed their positions and loyalty to the monarch. To prevent regional and local officials from building local power bases, Yang Jian refused them permission to serve in the areas of their birth. To ensure that officials were honest and efficient, inspectors were regularly dispatched to distant places. These "eyes and ears of the ruler" became an indispensable administrative tool.

Buddhism, the personal belief system of Yang Jian, was used by the Sui leaders as a unifying force because it was established pervasively in both North and South China. Imperial support of monks and temples throughout the empire brought a measure of assurance to people in South China. Yang Jian also supported Confucianism because it stressed loyalty, honesty, and hard work by Confucian-trained officials. Because Confucianism stressed family unity, it helped foster social stability.

Building projects consumed much Sui attention and resources and contributed to the long-term economic well-being of the Chinese people. Roads connecting distant parts of the empire were built or resurfaced. The capital, Changan, was con-structed near the site of the previous imperial capital and was laid out on a north-south grid, measuring about six miles east to west and more than five miles north to south. Rebuilding of the Great Wall began in the north.

Yang Jian spent his last years without the empress, who died of natural causes. When the ruler became ill in 604, Yang Guang, the heir apparent, may have killed his father in order to facilitate the transition. Yang Guang's early years saw a continuation of his father's policies: Civil service examinations were held, building projects continued, and able government followed. One project was the construction of the Grand Canal, a waterway system connecting the Yangzi and Yellow river systems and, more important, two vital

FIGURE 18.2 *Emperor Yang Guang on the Grand Canal. Dragon boats plied the Grand Canal in the Sui era, carrying Emperor Yang Guang and his courtiers. These multideck ships relied on sails or human labor to move. This eighteenth-century painting captures the lively activity on the major north-south waterway linking key economic areas. Although the labor and material resources of the empire were heavily taxed to produce the canal, the long-range vision of Sui monarchs provided some of the means to keep the empire united.* Bibliothèque nationale, Paris/ET Archive.

economic centers. Thus, economic unity underlay political unity, and water transport flourished in a network of canals and natural waterways.

Yang Guang continued an expansive foreign policy against Eastern Turks and Koreans, but, although he was successful against the former, he failed miserably against the latter. Campaigns against the Koreans were mounted in 612, 613, and 614. Each was a military disaster stemming from strong Korean resistance, unfavorable weather conditions, and formidable logistical problems. The heavy taxes to supply these campaigns brought the Chinese people to starvation levels and prompted revolts that spread over much of North China. The massive building projects and cruel treatment of laborers caused widespread hatred of the state. Defeat also depressed the monarch, who submerged his sorrows in sensual pleasures. By 618, large parts of the empire were under rebel control, and the Sui Empire passed from the scene. Its legacy of unity was passed to its successor state, the Tang Empire.

The Early Tang Empire, 618–762

The Chinese people have a saying, "Qin–Han, Sui–Tang." It means that the short-lived Qin state (221–207 B.C.) accomplished much that was inherited by its successor state, the Han Empire, just as the short-lived Sui Empire left a significant heritage to the Tang state. The Tang Empire is important in another way: Its great power and prestige in East Asia caused its political system and cultural patterns to become models—followed with modifications—for the Koreans, Japanese, and Vietnamese.

The Tang Empire was founded by an aristocrat, Li Yuan (reign dates 618–627), who took command of a rebel force to maintain some influence for his family and for a major section of the Sui political elite. Within a year, Li Yuan's forces, some of which were led by his sons, defeated the major rebel contenders. The Tang Empire was proclaimed, and the founder inherited and modified the Sui institutions.

FIGURE 18.3 *Tang Era Woman Riding.* *Tang artisans were famed for their colorful ceramic ware. This piece depicts a woman riding the solidly built horse typically represented in the fine arts of the seventh and eighth centuries. Especially in the early decades of the empire, elite women often rode on horseback. A few, such as Empress Wu, also wielded considerable power in the imperial administration.* Laurie Platt Winfrey, Inc.

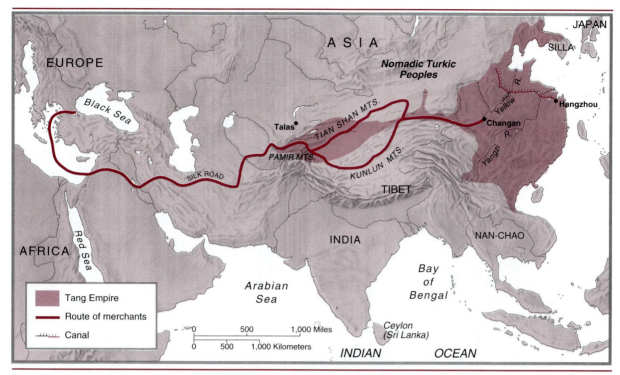

MAP 18.1 *China around 750.* *The Tang Empire occupied the largest amount of territory under Chinese rule in East and Central Asia until the eighteenth century. At its greatest extent in 750, the Tang Empire controlled the famed silk roads and permitted Chinese merchants to trade directly throughout Central Asia. Control of these roads was lost soon after the Talas River Battle in 751, significantly reducing income for the Tang court.*

Li Shimin,[4] the second son of the emperor, became increasingly hostile to his brother, the heir apparent. Li Shimin, a brilliant commander, formed a group of skilled advisors. In 627, the hostility between the two brothers led to bloodshed, when Li Shimin's allies plotted an ambush of the heir apparent within the palace walls. Li Shimin soon dethroned his father and became the second Tang emperor (reign dates 627–649).

Li Shimin pacified the frontiers, revised the law codes, consulted widely among his officials, and presided over an efficient administration. Like the Sui founder, Li Shimin controlled his officials by meticulously reviewing their mandated reports. Top officials were commanded to sleep in their offices in shifts so that the monarch might consult them when necessary. By the end of his reign the nation was peaceful and prosperous.

[4]**Li Shimin:** LEE SHER mihn

Only three women in Chinese history exercised direct political power, and one was Empress Wu (627–705). Wu began her court life as a minor concubine in Li Shimin's inner palace. When he died, she—along with other childless court women—was sent to a nunnery, and on one occasion the new emperor visited that holy place and became infatuated with his father's concubine. Wu was brought to the palace and eventually displaced the reigning empress. As imperial consort, Empress Wu not only provided male heirs, but she also aided her husband in ruling when he suffered from declining eyesight. Over time, she became the de facto ruler and purged her political rivals. At the time of the emperor's death, her son succeeded to the throne, and Wu ruled as a regent for her sons until she usurped power for herself.

In 690, Empress Wu proclaimed herself emperor (a title reserved for men), and to ensure her succession she had long prepared popular

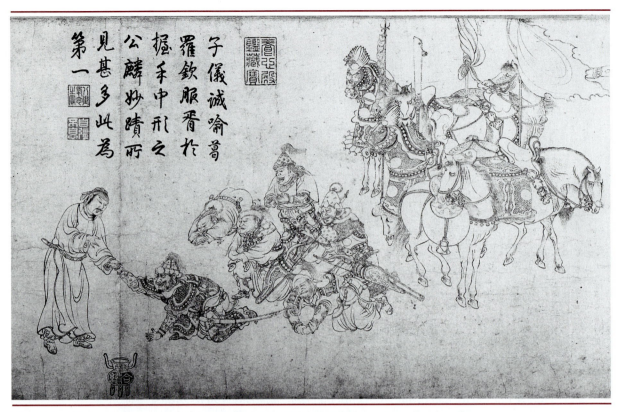

第一見甚多此為公麟妙睹而掘手中形之羅欽服膺於子儀誠喻曾

FIGURE 18.4 *Relations between Chinese and Central Asians.* *China developed a series of complex relations with the states and peoples of Central Asia. This line drawing of the Song era depicts the Tang general Guo Ziyi receiving the homage of Uighur Turks. General Guo had served with these soldiers in Central Asia, and later, when Uighur armies threatened China, the general went unarmed into the enemy camp. Guo's former allies paid homage to him and later supported the Tang monarchy in its bid to regain power. The drawing also illustrates the Chinese ideal of foreign powers submitting to a culture that leads by moral force rather than by force of arms.* National Palace Museum, Taiwan, Republic of China.

opinion by granting amnesties and tax relief to various groups. She used the examination system to select a new generation of officials who were capable as well as personally loyal to her. At the same time, the aristocrats' strong grip on power was undermined. Despite the fact that purges were undertaken to cow or eliminate opponents, China was generally tranquil. After Wu had been in power for several years, old age and senility led to her forced retirement.

Xuanzong[5] (reign dates 712–756), the next major ruler, was an able monarch, and during the first three decades of his rule, he presided over a vigorous administration staffed with effective officials. Thousands of musicians, artists, and poets performed their tasks at the emperor's command. It was a prosperous time, during which Chinese armies roamed as far west as Central Asia beyond the famed silk roads.

Scholars have noted that the highlight of this age was reflected in poetry, because three of China's greatest poets wrote during this time. For centuries, poetry had remained the most prestigious of the literary genres, and scholars who circulated in the capital used their poems to introduce themselves to potential patrons. Wang Wei, a nature poet, also became a painter who founded a school of painting. Li Bo cultivated an eccentric persona, one linked with drinking and carousing. Du Fu often wrote lyrics of biting social commentary that partly reflected his own impoverished circumstances.

[5]**Xuanzong:** SHOO wahn zoong

Dynastic crisis owing to multiple causes nearly toppled the empire in the 750s. Declining revenues, a result of tax evasion, had grown to significant proportions, and the existing funds no longer supported the emperor's court. Central to this fiasco was the breakdown of the land-tenure system that had been in effect since Sui times. People were ignoring imperial laws and avoiding taxes by bribing officials. Another element in the fiscal crisis was an imperial ego that demanded more and more expensive entertainments and luxurious living at a time of reduced tax receipts.

IN THEIR OWN WORDS

Poetry of China's Three Masters

Tang Xuanzong's era produced significant poets, including Wang Wei, Li Bo, and Du Fu. Wang Wei (699–759) has been revered for his poems of natural settings, especially mountains:

Bamboo Lodge

I sit alone in the dark bamboo grove,
Playing the zither and whistling long.
In this deep wood no one would know—
Only the bright moon comes to shine.

My Retreat at Mount Zhungnan

In my mid-age I loved greatly the Path,
In late years I made my home by the Southern Hill.
When the spirit moves, I often wander alone
Among lovely scenes known only to myself.
I ramble where the stream ends,
Then sit and watch the clouds rise.
Occasionally I meet an old man in the woods,
So we talk and laugh without thinking of going home.

Li Bo (701–762) came from Southwest China and became adept in the martial arts. Li Bo loved to drink, and a story (probably untrue) has a drunken Li Bo adrift in a river leaning out of his watercraft to embrace the moon's reflection in the water. The boat capsized and the poet drowned. Li Bo often followed a Daoist path, and, like Wang Wei, he loved mountains:

Summer Day in the Mountains

Lazily I wave a white feather fan,
And lie naked in the green forest;
I hang my cap on a crag,
My bare head sprinkled by the pine wind.

Du Fu (710–770) tried for much of his adult life to get an official position. His ambitions played a tragic role in Du Fu's family life as reflected in his lines:

My old wife stays in a strange land,
Our ten mouths separated by wind and snow.
Who would have left them long uncared for?
So I went home to share their hunger and thirst.
Entering the door, I heard a loud wail;
Our youngest boy had died of starvation.
. . . .
Ashamed I am to be a father
That the lack of food should have caused his death.

Perhaps because of his own suffering, Du Fu's poems expressed great concern with the suffering of the common people and a strong Confucian anger about their troubles:

The silk that was bestowed at the vermilion court
Came originally from some poor shivering women;
. . . .
Inside the vermilion gate wine and meat are stinking;
On the roadside lie the bones of people frozen to death.

The vermilion gate and court meant the imperial palace. And the rotting wine and meat show the luxurious palace in the time of Emperor Xuanzong, when tens of thousands lived in the imperial palace complex of the forbidden city.

The contrasting scenes of poor people and sumptuous court life show Du Fu to be a moralist critic of his government at a time of failing imperial power. The poor, however, suffered both in prosperous and in impoverished times. The poetic tone shifted from a love of the natural environment for its particular beauty to a stark portrayal of a government feeding on its people.

The frontiers had also become increasingly unstable, and this instability undermined the state's aura of invincibility. In 751, a Muslim army defeated the Chinese at the Talas River in Central Asia. Coupled with this reversal was the northward expansion of the Tibetans, who cut off China's access to the silk roads and deprived the government of the lucrative revenues from western trade. In the southwestern part of the empire, a Thai army inflicted a serious defeat in 754 on the Tang frontier forces. General An Lushan, who commanded a significant frontier army in the northeast and could count on the support of other northern frontier commanders, also rebelled. By themselves, any one of these uprisings or defeats would not have been decisive, but over a five-year period, the cumulative effect shook the Tang state to its foundations.

The An Lushan Uprising (755–763) nearly toppled the Tang Dynasty. Rebel forces marched rapidly toward the capital but were stopped by the defenders at the major eastern pass leading into the metropolitan region. One chief official, in what must have been one of history's great blunders, ordered the defenders to attack the stymied rebels. The engagement led to a total defeat for the imperial forces and opened the capital to the rebels. The emperor, his favorite concubine, her cousin, and a few courtiers fled to the south. The palace guard blamed the mistress and her cousin for the debacle and threatened to mutiny unless they were killed, and the emperor reluctantly complied with his guards' demand.

After many difficult years, the rebels were defeated and the ruling house was restored, yet circumstances after the restoration were quite different from those of earlier times. For example, the tax base had shrunk dramatically, and many areas of the empire had passed out of the central government's control. Before 755, Chinese rulers were more confident and expansive; now they became more wary and introspective. The aristocracy played a smaller role in politics. The scholar-official who earned a position in the government by passing a series of civil service examinations became a major political, cultural, and social player. Buddhism was weakened after a series of purges, and Confucianism emerged as the dominant ideology for both the state and the scholar-official.

The Late Tang Empire, 763–907

Beginning in 780 and lasting for about four decades, a series of effective Tang monarchs recaptured some of the lost court power and influence. They quelled new rebellions and reclaimed some measure of imperial authority over distant provinces, and the dynasty seemed to rebound. During that time some major historical works appeared, and the beginning of a reinterpretation of Confucianism surfaced. Significant writers included Han Yu (768–824), who developed a form of prose called the **Ancient Style**, which demanded that essays be clear, lucid, and simple in contrast to the more florid style of the writers of his day. The Ancient Style soon became the prevalent writing method.

By the early ninth century, several factors combined to weaken imperial influence. The later monarchs failed to lead effectively and found themselves the pawns of court factions. Another factor in the decline of the court was the growing power and eventual dominance of the eunuchs. One emperor tried to rally soldiers to slay the eunuch leaders, but the plot was discovered and crushed. With the decline of imperial rule came the dominance of local military leaders, who became semi-independent warlords and fought with one another for dominance.

In the mid–ninth century, Buddhism was dealt a serious blow. The reigning monarch believed that the monasteries were too large and, because they were tax exempt, that large amounts of potential tax receipts were unavailable to the state. In addition, tens of thousands of potential taxpayers were working for the monasteries. From 841 to 846, a series of court decrees closed hundreds of monasteries, led to the confiscation of their properties, and returned their monks and nuns to the tax rolls. In addition, thousands of gold, silver, and other metal statues were melted down. These actions severely weakened the economic foundation of Buddhist influence.

Late in the century, a major uprising left the Tang state reeling. During the ten years of fighting, nearly all of the remaining imperial forces evolved into warlord units similar to the armies at the end of the Han era. By 907, the last Tang leader was ousted, and a brief period of division and turmoil gripped China.

The period of division between the Tang and Song[6] dynasties (907–960) was a time when non-Chinese peoples ruled parts of North China and artistic development flourished. During this relatively brief time of political fragmentation, intense political rivalries developed.

THE SONG EMPIRE, 960–1279

Scholars have been fascinated by the contradictions of the Song period. Some have argued that the Song Empire's military weakness permitted the north and eventually all of China to be conquered and ruled by non-Chinese. Yet others have asserted that the Song Empire also established a powerful economic base that maintained independence and kept non-Chinese groups like the Mongols at bay for decades. The government, staffed by civil service appointees, ran smoothly and oversaw a long era of political stability.

Early Political Stability, 960–1127

Most of the early Song monarchs were effective rulers, and they presided over a centralized, unified bureaucratic state. Key to government stability was a group of officials who attained their positions by passing a series of rigorous examinations. Numbering in the thousands, officials who passed these tests were the majority of bureaucrats, providing a loyal, hardworking, talented workforce that was united in Confucian outlook. Despite several efforts at reform and growing political factionalism, the general tenor of rule was stable and efficient.

In 960, General Zhao Guangyin[7] (reign dates 960–978) overthrew his ruler, and for the next two decades he and his successor brother established the Song Empire (960–1279). Determined to avoid challenges from his own top officers, Emperor Zhao invited them to a banquet, thanking them but remarking that he felt uneasy on the throne. Emperor Zhao added that he feared being toppled by one of those in attendance, and when the drunken officers professed their loyalties, the emperor proposed that they all retire the next day.

Yet in safeguarding the throne, the army lost most of its experienced commanders. The transfer of the best units from the frontiers to the capital also forestalled challenges from ambitious generals, but the lack of stable northern borders plagued the founder's successors.

Many top Song officials were outstanding writers. Underlying elite cultural development was the growing use of printing, first by government, then by private interests. **Block printing**, the carving and inking of text on a wooden surface to reproduce many copies, was perfected during the Song era. Tang artisans had first used block printing for Buddhist scriptures. In the Song era, editions of the classical Confucian texts, the standard histories, and new works of literature were printed. Inexpensive books became generally available, sparking great interest in scholarly endeavors.

Su Shi[8] (1036–1101), who came from an illustrious family—his father and brother were talented prose and poetry stylists—has usually been regarded as the outstanding Song poet. Much in the manner of Li Bo of the previous dynasty, Su's poems often had a carefree air:

> Spring night—one hour worth a thousand gold coins;
> clear scent of flowers, shadowy moon.
> Songs and flutes upstairs—threads of sound;
> in the garden, a swing, where night is deep and still.

Political tragedy overtook Su Shi because of his opposition to court policies. He was exiled to Hainan Island in the distant south, and, although a tropical paradise not unlike the Hawaiian Islands, Hainan was far from Chinese civilization. Exile there was a cultural if not physical death sentence.

The poet Ouyang Xiu[9] (1007–1072) wrote in the eleventh century. Not only were his poems widely praised, but Ouyang's prose was admired even more because he further perfected the Ancient Style begun in the Tang era. Beyond poetry and prose, Ouyang devoted considerable attention to philosophy and the writing of histories, one of which was the *New Tang History*.

The greatest historian of the Song era was Sima Guang[10] (1019–1086). By his time, most of the

---

[6] **Song:** SOHNG
[7] **Zhao Guangyin:** JOW GWAHNG yihn

[8] **Su Shi:** SOO sher
[9] **Ouyang Xiu:** OH yahng SEE yuh
[10] **Sima Guang:** SEE mah GWAHNG

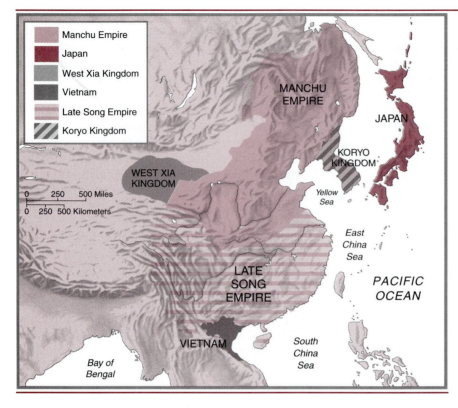

Manchu Empire
Japan
West Xia Kingdom
Vietnam
Late Song Empire
Koryo Kingdom

MANCHU EMPIRE

JAPAN

KORYO KINGDOM

WEST XIA KINGDOM

Yellow Sea

East China Sea

LATE SONG EMPIRE

PACIFIC OCEAN

VIETNAM

South China Sea

Bay of Bengal

MAP 18.2 *East Asia around 1200.* *The territory under Chinese control was significantly reduced after the invasion of the Manchus in 1127. Vietnam had become an independent state in the tenth century, and Korea was ruled by the Koryo dynasty. The West Xia Kingdom had been established by Tibetans in the tenth century, ruling much of Northwest China. All of these states existed in an uneasy balance of power until the Mongol invasions of the thirteenth century.*

official histories were dynasty-centered, and although such divisions of time are natural in one political perspective, they are limited in the broader chronological sweep. Sima Guang undertook a monumental effort, the writing of a chronological history from 403 B.C. to A.D. 959. It was titled *Comprehensive Mirror for Aid in Government* and was admired not only for its factual accuracy but also for its balanced, objective assessments.

Confucianism received much attention and energy from Song scholars. Not only did Ouyang Xiu reinvigorate Confucius's ideas, but also major Confucian thinkers interacted to lay the groundwork for the grand reinterpretation of Confucian philosophy in the next century. A key influence for this development was Buddhism, which offered a metaphysical interpretation largely foreign to Confucian thought.

The Late Song Era, 1127–1279

Conquest and rule of North China by invaders forced the Song state to move south. Although it controlled much less territory than its predecessor state, the Late Song government established a stable political order and a rather prosperous economy before succumbing to the Mongols in 1279. The military capabilities of the new government have been derided by some scholars, yet the Late Song government resisted the Mongols for four decades.

The government revived the use of paper money and the payment of taxes in currency. Officials also encouraged the development of local and regional trade. Some manufacturing took place in cottage industries rather than in large-scale manufacturing centers, but other industries were state-run, including the salt and porcelain industries.

In philosophy, new interpretations of Confucian ideas were synthesized into a system called Neo-Confucianism. The scholar Zhu Xi[11] (1130–1200) integrated the strands developed by earlier thinkers into one coherent system. Zhu Xi also interpreted the basic works of Confucius and his successors, and he wrote many historical commentaries. Although Zhu Xi was a political opponent of the government during his own time, his

[11] **Zhu Xi:** JOO shee

ideas and interpretations became the official view by the fourteenth century. In order to pass the imperial examinations between 1313 and 1905, scholars had to use Zhu Xi's ideas.

Landscape painting remained fascinating for many Chinese artists in Late Song times. Both professional and scholarly painters followed their Early Song predecessors in concentrating on the landscape style, which had developed earlier. Natural settings have captivated Chinese; Wang Wei of the Tang created many admired landscapes. Ma Yuan (who flourished in the thirteenth century) mastered the landscape form in which human beings are tiny within the great expanse of mountains and lakes. Ma Yuan followed the tradition of presenting nature and people in a harmonious relationship. This kind of painting continued into Mongol times and beyond. Chinese also continued painting still lifes, portraits, and cityscapes.

After long battles with the Mongols, who persistently tried to conquer the south, the Song government succumbed in 1279. Fierce resistance brought the Mongols' vengeance against southern cities and discrimination toward southern scholars who sought positions in the Mongol government. The extensive land holdings of the Chinese empires of Sui and Tang had been lost, and all lands north and south of the Yangzi River fell to the Mongols, with the result that no territory remained under Chinese control in the last two decades of the thirteenth century. Instead, the non-Chinese Mongols ruled an empire that spanned from eastern Europe to Korea; that development is examined in Chapter 19.

Scientific and Technological Developments

A cluster of discoveries and applications came in the Song era, many of which were publicized in print. Some discoveries came because of government interest and support, while others developed from private inspiration.

The measurement of time was vital to the Chinese emperor and his bureaucrats. For example, the monarch insisted that all peoples who sought diplomatic relations adhere to the Chinese calendar (and, presumably, China's view of the world). Highly reliable star charts were produced in the Song era, and one astronomer invented a mechanical clockwork. It was in the form of a water-driven

FIGURE 18.5 *Chinese Medicine. Traveling doctors treated rural patients during the Song era. Although the introduction of exams and licensing of practitioners brought sophistication to Chinese medicine during this time, much medicine was practiced by doctors who went from village to village. This scene depicts a peasant needing to be held down while he receives treatment. A physician's assistant looks on, awaiting instructions.* National Palace Museum, Taiwan, Republic of China.

clock tower that rotated a wheel linked by gears to a celestial globe that mapped the sky. The whole apparatus moved at precise, regulated intervals.

Chinese astronomers knew of the regular periods of Halley's comet and described sunspots long before anyone else did. In 1054, the Chinese recorded the great nova explosion in the Crab Nebula. They noted the appearance of the gold-colored "guest star" and observed it through the twenty-seven days of its visibility. By that time, their accurate calculations measured the solar year at 365.2445 days, which is only four minutes off modern measurements.

Medical knowledge was also greatly advanced in the Song period. Chinese physicians carefully studied the patterns of epidemics and persuaded politicians to promote good hygienic practices.

Pharmacology benefited from the widespread use of drugs, and physicians systematically collected the results of their treatment of diseases. Numerous illnesses were described and catalogued with the recommended treatments, and this information was published by block-printing methods for distribution to government medical offices. Although the first recorded dissection of a human cadaver occurred in China during the first century A.D., the systematic study of human anatomy occurred during the Song era. The book *Diagrams of Internal Organs and Blood Vessels* was compiled and printed early in the twelfth century. Eventually it became available to Rashid al-Din, a Persian physician and historian who was serving in China and carried the work home, whence it passed to Europe.

CHINA'S ECONOMIC DEVELOPMENT, 589–1279

From the sixth to the twelfth centuries, China's economy changed dramatically, reaching a level of development similar to that of Europe in the eighteenth century. Not only did agricultural production expand, but crop specialization and trade intensified as well. Commerce generally blossomed both domestically and regionally; an East Asian and Southeast Asian network of expanded commercial relationships developed by the late thirteenth century. At the same time, mass manufacturing produced enormous quantities of products for the state and for trade. China seemed poised on the edge of what modern economists refer to as self-sustaining economic growth.

Chinese Agriculture

The Sui and Tang monarchs sought to maintain control of the peasants and landlords through a policy forbidding private landownership. Rights to the land were granted to subjects by the state in fixed allotments. Regular censuses were taken, and the lands were redistributed based on demographic changes. Taxes and service obligations (labor and military) were also determined according to land allotments and census findings. The system worked, from the state's perspective, until the mid–eighth century, when it collapsed during

the An Lushan Uprising. From that point, private landowning became the dominant agricultural pattern, and a landlord class gradually emerged by the Song era.

Private markets contributed to the commercialization of agriculture. After the mid–eighth century, a weakened Tang state lost control of markets, and private markets began to appear. Gradually, through improved distribution systems and wider circulation of coinage, the commercialization of agriculture grew. By Song times, some local districts turned to crop or product specialization. In the southeast, for example, farmers produced only fruits like oranges or lychees for export and had to trade these products for rice and other staples. Others grew timber for commercial markets.

By the Song era, the Chinese had mastered the **paddy-field method** of growing rice—wet-field rice cultivation by the use of dams, irrigation ditches, sluice-gates, and the treadle water pump. Enormous amounts of labor and financial resources were used to prepare the paddy fields. Rice was a staple in Central and South China, and the paddy-field method allowed for yields that were three times greater than those obtained by conventional methods. In addition, Chinese farmers experimented with growing different varieties and strains of rice to develop more productive and disease-resistant yields.

Agriculture's development had a significant impact on other economic and social sectors. The familiar pattern of a dozen or so agricultural villages served by a market town began in Tang times, expanded in the Song era, and continued into the twentieth century. In addition, growing agricultural prosperity and productive capacity permitted Chinese cities to enlarge to one million or more persons, largely through the spread of suburbs outside city walls.

Commercial Expansion

The Tang imperial system of state-controlled trade through the establishment of governmental markets ultimately gave way to a mixed system of state-run and private markets. Early in Sui and Tang times, Chinese monarchs attempted to dominate the exchange of goods to limit the numbers of wealthy merchants, to forestall hoarding, and to control prices. This system remained in place until the mid–Tang era, when the An Lushan Uprising

FIGURE 18.6   *Rice Paddy Farming.* *Large rice yields prompted farmers to pursue the paddy-field method, which depended on water-control techniques, especially pumping. This painting shows human and animal power being used to transfer water between fields.* © Wan-go Weng.

greatly weakened the imperial court. Private markets grew up and slipped out of government control, although officials still licensed trade officials and worked with merchant and artisan guilds and associations to ensure regularity and fairness of market sales.

Sui and Tang emperors also attempted to open and maintain the land trade routes between China and Central Asia. The second Sui monarch, Yang Guang, spent a vast amount of money to secure the allegiance or acquiescence of western tribes that controlled the silk roads, achieving limited success by his diplomatic effort. The second Tang emperor, Li Shimin, directed the westward expansion of Chinese military forces that brought the silk roads under direct control, as they remained until the defeat of the Chinese army at the Talas River Battle in 751. The loss of trade routes after that date reduced Tang government revenues, leading to declining state control over commerce.

Another element in commercial growth was the improvement in transportation. Here again, the state played an essential role in the upkeep of roads and bridges, although privately built roads also came into existence. One area of development was the public building of canals and related transportation waterways. Water transport was a cheap and efficient way to convey goods. At least 40,000 vessels of various sizes plied the Grand Canal, and, by Song times, more than 30,000 miles of connected inland waterways interlaced heavily populated sections of Central China. Boat-building techniques improved, and Chinese craft effectively sailed on inland and maritime waters. Chinese ships used iron nails, waterproofing, buoyancy chambers, nautical compasses, and a variety of technical design elements in their construction and operation by the twelfth century. In fact, travelers in East, Southeast, and South Asian waters usually preferred to take Chinese vessels because of their technological superiority.

Fiscal measures gradually developed to keep pace with the burgeoning commercial growth, especially after the fall of Tang. Tang officials could not make enough coins to keep in circulation, but the Song government oversaw improved mining operations and ore extraction for silver and copper to produce sufficient coinage for the economy. Song copper coins were regularly used in Korea, Japan, and Vietnam by the twelfth century. In addition, the Song government expanded the printing of paper money backed by government reserves. Bills of transfer and exchange also were used, and deposit shops issued checks for people who placed bullion in their establishments. Monetary devices were as important to commerce as blood is to the body.

The Development of Manufacturing

The Chinese increased their emphasis on manufacturing to produce large quantities of iron and steel. By the onset of the eleventh century, 100,000 to 150,000 tons of those materials were produced annually, and most were used in making weapons and armor for the armed forces. Mining of other metals, like copper, also increased dramatically in the Song era. Production of porcelain ("china") also grew extensively in the Song period.

The state ran many manufacturing centers, partly because of the enormous funds and sup-

plies needed. Deforestation in much of northern China forced the Chinese to use coal and coke to fuel blast furnaces. The water transport system that linked major economic regions to the capital also provided for a relatively inexpensive means to carry finished products.

The textile industry, largely privately run, benefited from technological developments to improve production. By the eleventh century, water-powered machines spun hemp thread. In addition, a spinning wheel with multiple spindles and driven by a foot treadle spun cotton thread. A cotton gin was developed to facilitate the separation of cotton seeds from cotton fibers. And by the twelfth century, a silk-reeling machine had been perfected and placed in production. It saved labor costs and replaced many women workers.

Despite the development of an impressive economic base that annually produced more than 100,000 tons of iron and steel, North China was overrun by Manchus (called Ruzhen) early in the twelfth century. The Manchus initially had little use for such industrial operations and permitted them to rust away.

ENCOUNTERS
The Talas River Battle of 751

In the mid–eighth century, two expanding peoples, the Arabs and the Chinese, met and fought in Central Asia. The Arabs came from Southwest Asia and confidently expected to defeat all challengers. The Chinese were retracing the steps of earlier Chinese expeditionary forces into Central Asia and expected to be triumphant, like their predecessors of eight centuries earlier. The Arabs won, and many far-reaching trends were started by this watershed event.

The Chinese force dispatched by Tang Xuanzong had conquered the famed silk roads and pushed beyond the formidable Central Asian mountain ranges to the Talas River. In 751, the Chinese army, led by a Korean, Gao Xianzhi, met a grievous defeat and suffered the loss of most of its forces. The Talas River defeat forced Chinese forces to regroup hundreds of miles to the east. Yet Tibetan forces closed off China's corridor route to the silk roads and other western points. China's attention drew ever more

toward domestic matters and toward the South China Sea. For more than a millennium no army dispatched by a government of China reclaimed the silk roads.

China's defeat sparked many developments in Eurasia. Many Chinese were captured by the Arab-led force, and one scholar noted that through these prisoners of war, China's expertise in the manufacture of paper passed throughout Eurasia, being spread by Muslims. The Central Asians and Arabs benefited from these technologies, which later passed along to the Indians, Africans, and Europeans. Presumably these developments facilitated the spread of knowledge and the growth of the intellectual elite.

Islam had been expanding rapidly in many directions during the previous century, and the Arab-led force had been dispatched by the Umayyad caliph in Damascus. Although the Arabs did not capitalize on their victory by settling in Central Asia, Islam became deeply rooted there several centuries later.

FIGURE 18.7 *Song Naval Warfare.* *The rear section of this boat is for steering and propulsion; the front, stacked with gunpowder-filled weapons, could be detached and set adrift toward enemy vessels, to explode with devastating effect. Gunpowder, invented in the tenth century, was seldom used in warfare until the twelfth century. Firearms and cannons were not developed until the next century.* From the *Wu bei zhi* (Records of military preparations), 1621.

ELEMENTS OF CHINESE SOCIETY

In this period, significant social changes occurred in China. Political control and social influence slipped from the aristocrats to the landlords, while the peasants retained their position of second on the social scale. Artisans and merchants were commoners. By the twelfth century, some landlords were becoming merchants and manufacturers in order to earn money and to support their families. Neo-Confucianism was hostile to independent women and enforced the belief that all women should be under some form of male control. When Neo-Confucianism spread to Japan and Vietnam, for example, the position of Japanese and Vietnamese women worsened. Ethnic minorities also suffered from discrimination by the Chinese people.

China's Social Classes

China developed an ideology of a four-class social system by the second century B.C. The four (scholars, peasants, artisans, and merchants) were positioned in hierarchical order with the scholars at the top and the merchants at the bottom. By the Song era, this social classification remained, but the components of the scholar elite had changed.

Both the Sui and Tang empires were dominated by scholars who came from the aristocracy. Great aristocratic clans from Northwest China had provided the leadership for the rise to power of both the Sui and Tang dynasties. As a reward for their support and continued allegiance, the rulers maintained official lists and rankings of the elite families and clans. In addition, government officials frequently came from these families, who educated their sons to follow the Confucian code. Although the examination system began earlier, the *yin* **privilege**, the exemption of high officials' sons from the civil service examinations, maintained an aristocratic character in officialdom.

Several factors, however, worked against permanent aristocratic social and political dominance. Empress Wu, for example, reduced the influence of the northwestern clans by favoring candidates from Northeast China. In addition, Chinese law fostered an equal division of property among male heirs. This worked against the long-term stability of great clans, because of the splitting of land over several generations. Many great clans also disappeared in the wars of the eighth, ninth, and tenth centuries.

The growth of the examination system as a major recruitment instrument by the state, especially in the Song era, also had important social consequences. For nearly a century, many Song officials were scholars who used the *yin* privilege to maintain their families' political and social predominance. Most lived in the capital and served as a social and political elite there. By the mid–eleventh century, however, restriction of the *yin* privilege, success of southerners in the examination system, and political purges destroyed most of the families' and clans' political and social influence.

By the twelfth century, many scholarly families firmly established themselves in their local areas. In doing so, they responded to the reduction in the number of scholars being taken into the government. Some became landlords, teachers, market superintendents, or merchants. Many scholarly merchants took advantage of their writing and mathematical skills to benefit from the burgeoning economy. Eventually, scholars became an unofficial governing class beneath the lowest level of normal bureaucratic activity.

Peasants were socially high but economically low. Peasants remained second on the social scale, a position that meant little to their daily lives. Although enterprising peasants might escape the daily struggles for survival, the vast mass of peasants toiled in the same conditions as their ancestors.

Artisans and merchants were excluded from the examination system until the Late Song period. Artisans, although often highly skilled, were usually illiterate and did not take the exams. Their technical knowledge might be passed on to sons or apprentices, but they did not build large family or clan networks. They received a certain amount of social largess from their guilds, which were often organized along kinship lines. Merchants also formed guilds and trade networks, sometimes accumulating fortunes but having little social standing or political power.

Gender Issues

Men dominated all aspects of public life in China; they became officials, produced most artistic works, performed most economic tasks outside the home, and presided over social institutions, including the family. Their social position was recognized by law; it was relatively easy for a man to divorce a woman and extremely difficult for a woman to divorce a man.

Exceptional women certainly attained limited recognition in histories and other works. The first empress of the Sui era and Empress Wu of the Tang period played key political roles. Lady Yang effectively acted the part of Emperor Xuanzong's favorite concubine in the mid–eighth century, but she has been remembered as causing the emperor's downfall. Li Qingchao[12] wrote beautiful poetry in the Song period.

[12] **Li Qingchao:** LEE CHEENG chee yow

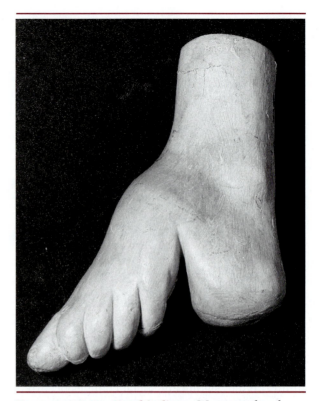

FIGURE 18.8 *Footbinding. Women endured footbinding to satisfy men's desire that they possess unnaturally small "lotus" feet. This cast conveys the ideal foot, doubled on itself into the tiniest size possible. This practice spread throughout all classes and involved a years-long process that caused excruciating pain. A woman's suitability as a marriage partner was jeopardized if she did not conform to this standard. In China's male-dominated society, where women had few options besides marriage, the ideal of the bound foot lasted for a thousand years.* Wellcome Institute Library, London.

Commoner women often lived under control of men throughout their lives. Perhaps the most infamous practice was footbinding, the prevention of the natural growth of women's feet through tight binding. Men thought the tiny feet to be erotic, helping to create a centuries-long fashion. Elite women initially and, eventually, women of the lower classes suffered permanent crippling. Over time perhaps one billion women suffered from this custom. Widows increasingly were expected not to remarry, and they either lived with their in-laws or returned home without prospect of marriage. Women wove at home and handled a variety of domestic chores, like the pickling of foods for preservation. They also toiled in a variety of occupations, especially those associated with the silk industry. But they lost jobs to machines that could do the work of many and at cheaper cost. Women not only were bound by foot wrappings; their lack of education and inferior status bound them to men.

Ethnic Minorities in China

China has had a long and significant experience with ethnic minorities. In times of prosperity and strong government, foreign merchants and other aliens received good treatment from the Chinese. They often resided in foreign enclaves of major cities, including the capital, and even established temples where they worshiped their deities. From the sixth to the thirteenth centuries, however, the Chinese expanded from north to south and treated non-Chinese with assimilation, encapsulation, or expulsion measures.

Because of their larger numbers the Chinese believed that they could intermarry with and absorb ethnic minorities. Large numbers of Manchu people, for example, were ultimately assimilated by the Chinese people. When conquering a new region, the Chinese sent in colonists, many of whom married the non-Chinese. At the

PARALLELS AND DIVERGENCES

The "Other" before 1600

Most societies have designated one or more social groups as deserving of contempt and discrimination. Often racial, ethnic, or caste groups, these unfortunates were seen as the antithesis of the rest of the societies in which they resided. In recognition of this, modern social theorists have come to call such groups "the other."

Chinese and Mesoamericans, for example, used the term "dog" to symbolize contempt for another group. Chinese characters employed to write the names of non-Chinese people sometimes contain a component that means dog. Because the dog was a beast and had negative connotations to the Chinese, their use of its name indicated their utter contempt for the non-Chinese peoples. Similarly, when the Aztecs first moved into the Valley of Mexico, indigenous peoples sometimes referred to them as *chichimecs* or "sons of dogs." This pejorative usage, however, took on a more favorable tone when the Aztecs became powerful.

The Japanese also had at least two kinds of "others." One was the Ainu[a] people, a North Asian people. For centuries, the Japanese fought the Ainu and pushed them out of Honshu. Many Ainu died in these campaigns, and those who escaped to the northern island of Hokkaido eventually were forced to live away from the Japanese. In the sixteenth century, however, the local Japanese warlord who had jurisdiction over the Ainu developed a policy of tolerance that lasted for three hundred years. Rather than subjugate and annihilate the Ainu chiefdoms, the feudal lord took a peaceful approach to relations, emphasizing conciliation and noninterference in Ainu life. By the nineteenth century, the Japanese government continued the previous policy, treating the Ainu as a principal asset to the northern island. Throughout, the Ainu were regarded with sympathy and humanity.

The *eta*,[b] members of a Japanese caste group, were forced to live in ghettoes attached to towns or cities. The *eta* performed socially useful but degrading occupations, like butchering, leather working, burying human bodies, and waste removal. Because Shinto beliefs excoriated "polluting" activities, like waste removal, people who performed these tasks suffered religious condemnation. Only in the nineteenth century were the *eta* granted legal equality. The Koreans had their own outcast group whose members performed similar useful societal functions.

Low caste members in India and Jews in Europe also suffered discrimination despite the fact that they performed necessary social or economic jobs. Members of India's low castes frequently handled "polluting" tasks such as removing dead bodies. Jews provided financing opportunities to Christian merchants, officials, and monarchs because Christians were forbidden by their religion to participate in usury. Both groups suffered religious discrimination, including being forced to live in ghettoes.

[a]**Ainu:** EYE noo

[b]***eta:*** EH tah

same time, the Chinese established Confucian schools and encouraged members of indigenous elites to study there. The Koreans and Vietnamese resisted assimilation, despite their borrowing of Chinese culture and institutions.

Encapsulation occurred when ethnic groups were driven into the hills and then were surrounded or encapsulated by the Chinese, who took over the nearby lowlands that were more suitable for agriculture. The Miao and Yao peoples of South China suffered encapsulation, a fate they and other ethnic minorities faced in parts of Southeast Asia, too.

In Southwest China, expulsion was often a familiar pattern for dealing with ethnic groups. Both the Burmese and Thai peoples, for example, had polities along the Chinese frontier and on occasion raided or destroyed Chinese settlements. In the Song era, when the Chinese moved farther south, the Burmese and Thais were forced out of their homelands and migrated to Southeast Asia.

KOREA CREATES AN INDEPENDENT STATE

Geographical elements have played a key role in the history of Korea. Near both China and Japan, Korea has long suffered from the expansionist tendencies of both countries. One effective long-term Korean strategy was to ally with the Chinese and adopt some Chinese state institutions to govern themselves.

China has influenced Korea for more than two millennia. During the Warring States Period (403–221 B.C.), for example, Chinese refugees from the unification wars fled to territory where Koreans lived. In the late second century B.C., Chinese armies conquered and ruled parts of Korea for four centuries. Three Chinese districts in Korea later succumbed to Korean forces, but the fourth, Lolang, remained in Chinese hands until A.D. 313. After the Koreans regained control of their peninsula, three kingdoms emerged, and they contended with one another for domination of the peninsula.

Japan also fought with the Koreans because of competing trade and diplomatic interests. Some historians have asserted that the Japanese long held a toehold colony, Mimana or Kaya, on the peninsula. According to ancient Japanese chroni-

FIGURE 18.9 *Korean Crown.* *Korean artisans produced dazzling pieces, including this seventh-century crown recovered from a Silla tomb in southeastern Korea. Made of cut sheet gold and jade pieces, the highly stylized elements of its design seem to represent trees and antler shapes that were especially striking when illuminated. Silla monarchs united the peninsula and ruled for centuries.* National Museum of Korea, Seoul.

cles, several semihistorical figures, including the legendary Japanese Empress Sujun, invaded or conquered parts of Korea. Whatever the facts, there has been a long and often contentious relationship between the Koreans and Japanese.

In the sixth and seventh centuries, the Chinese, Koreans, and Japanese began to interact in many ways. In the sixth century, Koreans and Japanese crossed the strait between them, bearing gifts and information, and much of Japan's early knowledge of China came from Korea. Buddhism came from China via Korean monarchs, who tried to impress the Japanese in the hope of forging an alliance against the other kingdoms.

In the seventh century, growing Chinese military power threatened Korea, when the second Sui emperor unsuccessfully tried to conquer it. The second Tang emperor also failed to impose Chinese rule on the peninsula. The third Tang emperor and Empress Wu attempted several campaigns in Korea. In 661, Chinese and Japanese naval forces fought a battle near the Kumgum

River because both sides wanted to dominate the peninsula. The Japanese suffered a major defeat and retreated to their islands.

China seemed victorious and prepared to take Korea, yet the Korean king rallied his people against Chinese rule, and by 668, the beleaguered Chinese forces were forced to abandon their conquests. The Korean monarch proclaimed his rule over Korea and adopted some Chinese political and cultural forms that had proved effective in ruling large populations. The dominance of the Korean aristocracy, however, meant that many Chinese institutions, like the examination system, were ignored or significantly modified. The new Silla[13] Dynasty lasted until 918, when it was replaced by the Koryo Dynasty. The Koryo monarchs ruled with a modified Chinese system with many indigenous practices. The dynasty briefly resisted the Mongols but finally capitulated, surviving until 1388.

VIETNAM CREATES AN IMPERIAL AND EXPANSIONIST STATE

Like the Koreans, the Vietnamese people endured Chinese rule and often rebelled against their overlords. In the tenth century, under the leadership of patriots, the Vietnamese threw off the Chinese yoke and established a powerful polity.

Successive Vietnamese governments, like those in Korea and Japan, freely borrowed from the Chinese and modified various practices to suit themselves. Centralized rule wielded by scholar-officials, who had to pass a series of civil service examinations, became the norm. These political and social elite members, like their Chinese counterparts, wrote Chinese-style poems in the Chinese language. In addition, like Chinese Confucians, Vietnamese scholars promoted values of filial piety, loyalty, and humane behavior. They occupied the top rung of the Chinese-style social scale and praised the Vietnamese peasants, who occupied the second rung. Vietnamese merchants, like their Chinese counterparts, suffered the scorn of scholars and officials.

The Vietnamese government embarked on a long-range expansion southward. The Vietnamese conquered various states along the southern borders and annexed them. From the tenth to the thirteenth centuries, the Vietnamese fashioned an empire stretching hundreds of miles beside the South China Sea. A key part of this expansion was the resettlement of Vietnamese peasant villages long distances from their original homes in the north. The strong village cohesiveness and peasant militancy in defense of their new lands facilitated this process. As the distances between the Vietnamese capital and the southern frontiers lengthened, a desire for local autonomy was enhanced. Under weak monarchs, this regionalism led to the weakening of the Vietnamese Empire.

Both the Chinese and Mongols attempted to conquer Vietnam in later times but failed. The Mongols launched three unsuccessful invasions of Vietnam; each withered before tropical diseases

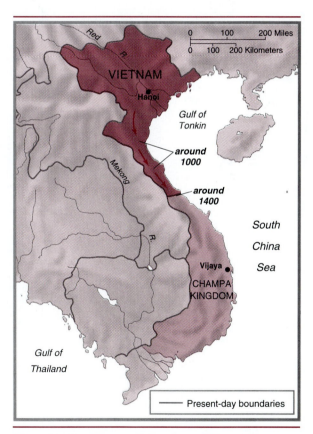

M A P 1 8 . 3 *Vietnam's Southward Expansion, to 1400. Vietnamese monarchs and peoples expanded southward steadily between the tenth and thirteenth centuries. Mountains to the west confined the migration to the coast and river plains. The Vietnamese assimilated many other cultures in their march south.*

[13] **Silla:** SHEE yihl ah

CHINA	KOREA	VIETNAM		
			–	
			–	
			–	
Sui Empire, 589–618			600	Yang Jian unites China, 589
Tang Empire, 618–907	Silla Dynasty, 668–918		–	Yang Guang's last Korean campaign fails, 616
				Korea is united, 668
			–	
			–	An Lushan Uprising begins, 755
			800	
			–	
	Koryo Dynasty, 918–1388		–	Gunpowder invented in China, c. 900
Early Song Empire, 960–1127		Ly Empire, 969–1408	–	Vietnam gains independence, 969
			1000	Ouyang Xiu born, 1007
			–	
			–	Manchus overrun northern China, 1127
Late Song Empire, 1127–1279			–	
			1200	Zhu Xi dies, 1200
			–	
			–	Vietnamese defeat Mongols, 1287
			–	
			1400	
		Le Empire, 1428–1802	–	
			–	
			–	

and guerrilla resistance by the Vietnamese. In the 1280s, Tran Hung Dao, a hero to later generations of Vietnamese patriots, commanded the successful resistance to the Mongols.

The Chinese failed to impose permanent control, while the peoples south of Vietnam could not resist the steady encroachment of Vietnamese influence. Vietnam has sometimes been called by scholars the "Lesser Dragon," meaning that it is a smaller version of China. Certainly, in its Chinese-style institutions and expansive foreign policy, that designation is apt.

SUMMARY

1. After a lengthy period of division, Yang Jian, a general in a northern Chinese kingdom, usurped the throne, pacified the north, and soon conquered South China. The Sui Empire lasted for nearly three decades and established the basis for a unified Chinese state. Among the unifying elements were the Grand Canal, an examination system, and the promotion of Buddhism.

2. The Sui Empire fell after failing to conquer Korea, and the Tang Empire succeeded to power. The Tang emperors expanded their control of Central Asia and conquered many tribes. The Tang Empire also saw the rise of an exceptionally talented trio of poets, Wang Wei, Li Bo, and Du Fu, who left an enduring poetic legacy. During the second half of the Tang era, regional warlords wrested control from the central government.

3. Following a brief time of disunity, a northern general, Zhao Guangyin, usurped power, pacified the north, then conquered the south. The Song Empire never aspired to the imperial legacy of the Han, Sui, and Tang empires, but it effectively ruled the central area of the Yellow and Yangzi river valleys. Key to the strength of the Song Empire's success was a polity resting firmly on an imperial examination system that selected talented scholars who mastered the ideas of Confucianism.

4. The Song era also saw the appearance of a sophisticated economic system of large-scale industrial manufacturing, high levels of agricultural productivity, and significant levels of commercial activity. The considerable technological advances of the eleventh century were aided by the use of printing to spread knowledge. The conquest of the north by non-Chinese aborted this development.

5. Although the four-class system (scholars, peasants, artisans, and merchants) remained in effect, the scholar class changed in social content. Aristocrats were eventually replaced by local landlord scholars. China's ethnic minorities endured a variety of discriminatory policies, including assimilation, encapsulation, and expulsion.

6. Since around 100 B.C., Korea had been influenced by China, experiencing four centuries of direct Chinese rule. After ousting the Chinese, the Koreans formed three regional governments that were united through conquest in the seventh century. Both the Chinese and Japanese had attempted to control parts of Korea but failed. Korean independence meant some use of political institutions and ideas borrowed from China.

7. The Vietnamese threw off a millennium of Chinese control in the tenth century and followed some Chinese practices. The Vietnamese commenced a long era of southward imperial expansion.

SUGGESTED READINGS

Ebrey, Patricia. *The Inner Quarters*. Berkeley: University of California Press, 1993. An interpretation of women's roles in the Song imperial period.

Hall, John, ed. *Japan before Tokugawa*. Princeton, N.J.: Princeton University Press, 1986. Essays about feudal Japanese society and its economic foundation.

Lee, K. B. *A New History of Korea*. Trans. by E. Wagner. Cambridge, Mass.: Harvard University Press, 1985. An important interpretative history of Korea.

Lo, W. W. *An Introduction to the Civil Service of Sung China*. Honolulu: University of Hawaii Press, 1987. A look at the examination system and its impact on China's social system.

Woodside, A. B. *Vietnam and the Chinese Model*. Cambridge, Mass.: Harvard University Press, 1968. A classic study of Vietnam's cultural relations with China.

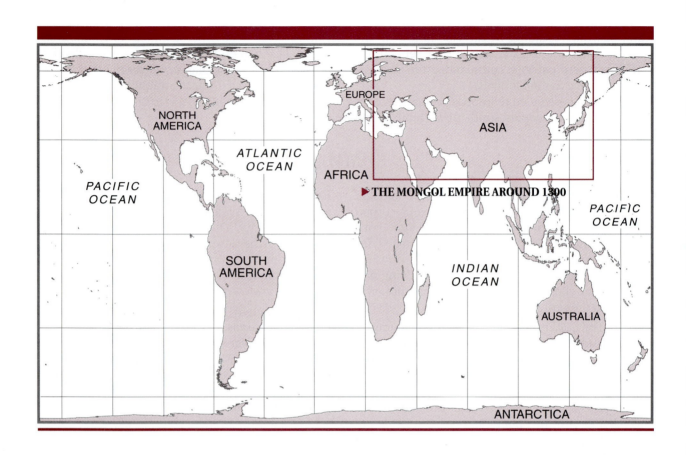

▶ THE MONGOL EMPIRE AROUND 1300

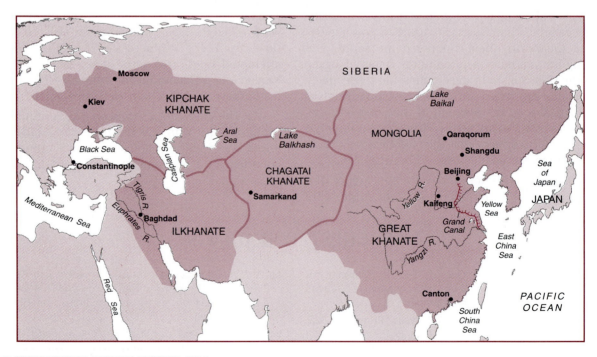

▶ THE MONGOL EMPIRE AROUND 1300

The Mongol Empire: Ascendancy, Domination, and Decline in Eurasia

1206–1480

The Korean navigator trembled before the Mongol general. A great storm was coming, and it would threaten the invasion fleet. Thousands of Mongols were beginning to push off the beachhead and threaten a full-scale rout of the Japanese defenders. The Mongol commander scowled and ordered the fleet to stay anchored another day.

This scene in 1274 recounts the beginnings of the great disaster that thwarted one thrust of Mongol imperial expansion. A typhoon struck the Mongol ships and killed tens of thousands, saving Japan from Mongol rule. Although failing to conquer Japan, the Mongols won and ruled an empire stretching across much of central Eurasia.

Civilizations have traditionally been based in cities. Some Mongol leaders, however, retained a nomadic lifestyle even as other Mongols built an empire. They originated in the Asian **steppe**, the grasslands of Inner Asia (Manchuria, Mongolia, and eastern Turkestan). Although Mongol nomads usually distrusted settled peoples, they traded with agricultural peoples who lived generally south of Mongolia. In the thirteenth century, under the leadership of a great warrior, Chinggis[1] Khan (sometimes spelled Genghis Khan), the Mongols swept south, east, and west to conquer much of Asia and part of Europe. In the process they fashioned one of the largest empires in history. At the same time, because the Mongols united much of

[1] **Chinggis:** JIHNG guhs

473

East, Central, and Southwest Asia and because they favored merchants, land-based commerce flourished as never before. The reuniting of China also revived a vast maritime trade stretching from the South China Sea to the Indian Ocean and the Red Sea.

In this chapter, we will examine the rise of the Mongols and survey their rapid defeat of numerous states in Asia and Europe. In Eurasia, only the Indian subcontinent, the area of Europe west of the Danube River, and Siberia escaped the great Mongol army. We will look at the Mongol leadership, the war machine, and the administrative system that permitted the Mongols to control a vast domain. Then we will survey the polities and societies of the four regions they ruled: East Asia (China, Mongolia, and Korea), Central Asia, the Kipchak Khanate (Russia and the adjacent eastern steppelands), and Southwest Asia (Persia). The Mongols destroyed a Central Asian civilization in their rise to imperial rule, yet they effectively preserved long-established civilizations in East and Southwest Asia.

CHINGGIS KHAN AND THE RISE OF THE MONGOLS

Temujin[2] (around 1162–1227), who is better known by his title Chinggis Khan ("Illustrious Leader of the Mongols"), united the various clans and tribes that dwelled in the area known today as Mongolia. For the purpose of simplicity, we will refer to this man as Chinggis Khan throughout this chapter, even though the title was not claimed until 1206. Chinggis Khan came from a noble tribal family, and the unification effort occupied much of his adult life. Despite many setbacks, Chinggis Khan gathered a group of talented followers and united his tribe. Warring followed, but the military skills of Chinggis Khan helped unite the peoples of Mongolia.

Before examining the great conference of leaders that assembled in 1206 to recognize Temujin as Chinggis Khan, we should survey the peoples he subdued early. The great majority herded sheep, cattle, camels, yaks (shaggy-haired oxen), and horses. Their diet featured beef, mutton, and milk.

[2]**Temujin:** teh MUH jeen

One favored drink was fermented mare's milk. Because the Mongolian nomads tended herds, they had to move from pasture to pasture in a regular fashion in order to prevent overgrazing. In addition, they feared the vagaries of weather that might bring drought and an end to the herds' food supplies or animal diseases that might swiftly destroy a herd. The mobile life prevented storage of quantities of goods that could ease the ravages of the elements.

Hunting supplied food to supplement the daily diet. The hunt was conducted like a military operation, as various units of a tribe surrounded a

FIGURE 19.1 *Mongol and Horse. The cavalry was a key element of the Mongols' success. A close relationship to horses was cultivated from childhood, and strict attention was paid to their proper use and well-being. The combination of well-trained riders and dependable horses gave the Mongol forces superior speed and maneuverability over most of the armies they encountered. This Chinese painting captures the relation of rider and horse as an archer stops to retrieve the animal he has brought down. Mongol archers were skilled at firing long distances and from the saddle.* Louvre © R. M. N.

game-filled area where disciplined maneuvering herded the creatures into a killing zone. Chinggis Khan used these activities as war games and severely punished leaders who failed to play their assigned parts.

The horse was significant in the Mongol conquest, and the Mongol cavalry represented two millennia of improvement in the use of the horse in warfare. Mongols learned to ride horses at a young age, and they quickly became expert riders. They earned the reputation of enduring great privation during a campaign and were said to be able to ride for ten consecutive days, eating while in the saddle. In one campaign in eastern Europe, Mongols rode about fifty miles per day.

The constant warfare between tribes before 1206 often became fierce. In the manner of his predecessors, Chinggis Khan might kill all of the adult males from a defeated tribe in order to forestall a possible retributive strike at a later time. If allowed to live, warriors from tribes were often conscripted and interspersed among the main military units. Women, especially attractive ones, could expect to be taken as wives by victorious men; even married women who might be pregnant could be subject to this practice. Sons born soon after coming into a new father's tent generally experienced the same treatment accorded his biological children.

Women of the Mongol upper class sometimes asserted themselves politically. Chabi,[3] the main wife of Khubilai[4] Khan, became a major advisor to her husband. The second wife of one khan played a masterful political role in a succession dispute and served as regent for her son. Other aristocratic Mongol women effectively administered vast personal domains. And a few women fought alongside men in battle.

Although the overwhelming number of people united by 1206 spoke Mongol, some traced their ancestry to other ethnic groups, like the Turks. When Chinggis Khan met with the dignitaries of the Mongols in 1206, he decreed that the spoken Mongol language (previously unwritten) be written down in a Turkic script, a practice that is still followed.

In 1206, a great gathering of the tribal leaders and members of the political elite proclaimed Chinggis Khan to be the preeminent Mongol ruler

[3] **Chabi:** CHAH bee
[4] **Khubilai:** KOO bihl ayh

FIGURE 19.2 Mongol Battle Scene. *This Persian miniature depicts a young Chinggis Khan riding into battle accompanied by his mother (in white). Mongol elite women sometimes played active political roles and fought alongside their sons, fathers, or husbands. Chinggis's father, a chieftain, was killed when the future khan was still a boy, and another family seized tribal leadership. Widow and children existed for the next few years on the fringes of society, until Chinggis began his rise to power.* © United Nations Educational, Scientific and Cultural Organization (UNESCO), Paris.

and then pledged to follow him with absolute obedience. To solidify his position, which was based on a succession of military and political victories, Chinggis Khan promoted the religious interpretation that he was the choice of Tengri, the Mongol deity; he was said to have granted Chinggis Khan the power to conquer the world. To give a more permanent base for Mongol unity, Chinggis Khan

FIGURE 19.3   *Relics of Chinggis Khan.*   *The nomadic Mongol peoples of Central Asia
kept their property ready for frequent moves. Their dwellings, called* yurts, *were comprised of
a portable, cylindrical framework made of willow that supported a felt or skin covering. This
1930s photo taken in Inner Mongolia shows the* yurt *that holds the relics of the Great Khan,
revered by Mongols for centuries.*   Peabody Museum, Harvard University. Photo by Owen Lattimore.

also compiled and proclaimed the ***Yasa***,[5] a binding
legal code taken from Mongol customs, ancestral
traditions, and additional decrees promulgated by
the new monarch. For example, the annual hunt
was strictly regulated by the *Yasa.* Another major
innovation commencing in 1206 was the establishment of a relay postal or message system, like the
American Pony Express. This communication network carried important messages rapidly from one
part of the realm to another and became renowned
across Asia.

Certainly an element of good fortune accompanied Chinggis Khan's successes. Many of the
enemy states he conquered had ineffective rulers
or had been weakened by internal problems. Yet,
fortune aside, Chinggis Khan became a skilled military commander, and he possessed the great talent of identifying outstanding individuals and

placing them where their assets benefited him
most. Finally, as the events of 1206 indicate, Chinggis Khan possessed effective organizational abilities. The Mongol government and its army would
conquer and hold sway through much of Asia for
generations.

THE CONQUEST AND RULE OF CHINA AND KOREA

Chinggis Khan began a major invasion of Chinese
territory in 1211, and the collapse of the last Chinese resistance took place in 1279. During the
interim, although Mongol attention was often
diverted elsewhere, the Mongols periodically
returned to renew their military campaign. One
Mongol ploy was an appeal for the Jidan people to
revolt against the Manchus, who had conquered

[5] ***Yasa:*** YAH sah

and ruled the Jidan. The Jidan, a group ethnically kindred to the Mongols, responded favorably to the Mongol call in that part of China. As seen in Chapter 18, parts of North China had long been under foreign domination, and in that sense the Mongols were another group seeking to control China.

The Conquest of North China

By 1215, the Mongols had advanced across North China to the city that eventually became known as Beijing. Beijing, like most large cities, was walled, and siege warfare was needed to capture the city.

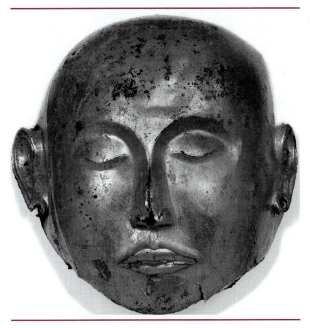

FIGURE 19.4 *Jidan Funerary Mask.* *The Jidan people came from Northeast Asia and ruled Northeast China for almost two centuries. This death mask of bronze and gold shows an artistic style more North Asian than Chinese, the result of a conscious effort of the Jidan to retain their ethnic identity against Chinese influences. While in possession of Northeast China, rather than use the Chinese language, they created a new writing system to record their own language. The Jidan were ethnically related to the Mongols and some Jidan later served Chinggis Khan and his successors in ruling China and other states.* From *Empires Beyond the Great Wall: The Heritage of Genghis Khan* (Natural History Museum of Los Angeles County, 1994). Courtesy of the Zhelimu League Museum, Inner Mongolia Autonomous Region, People's Republic of China. Photo by Marc Carter.

The Beijing siege endured for months and infuriated the impatient Mongols, who, in more than thirty days of pillage and looting, killed large numbers of Chinese and Manchus after the city fell to them. This massacre also may have shown the Mongol fear of a possible counterattack from the large numbers of people who dwelled in cities. Later, when a small Mongol force returned to their steppe pasture to the north, they slaughtered their captive Chinese prisoners. Some have argued that the Mongols did not wish to be slowed by the horseless Chinese, while others noted that the Mongol escorting party might have feared an uprising by the large number of captives. Later, the Mongols used terror in the form of wholesale massacres to awe their enemies, and several cities surrendered to the approaching Mongols rather than face widespread killing. The campaigns in North China continued with little pause until the Manchus were defeated in 1234.

The Campaigns of Khubilai Khan

It took another forty-five years before South China fell to the Mongols in 1279, leading to the Mongol Empire (1279–1368), because the Late Song Empire put up a strong resistance to the nomads. Khubilai Khan (1215–1294), a grandson of Chinggis Khan, presided over the conquest and ruled over most of East Asia until his death in 1294. He was a remarkable ruler of China because he attempted to straddle both the Mongol and Chinese elements in his armies and government. Khubilai Khan understood that while China might be conquered on horseback, it had to be ruled in the traditional manner of bureaucratic control developed during the previous few centuries. Consequently, Khubilai Khan invited Chinese scholars and officials into his administration, but because he did not wish to rely solely on the Chinese, he also invited people like Marco Polo, the European adventurer, to serve in his government. The non-Chinese were given the designation of "Colored-Eye People," presumably because the irises of their eyes bore colors other than the dark brown common to the Mongols.

Khubilai Khan also attempted to further expand through conquest the boundaries of his domain. In that way, he faithfully adhered to his grandfather's admonition to conquer the known

UNDER THE LENS

Yehluchucai: A Jidan Advisor to Chinggis Khan

The Mongols' nomadic origins made them suspicious of urban centers and agrarian societies. Chinggis Khan developed a strict code of laws to guide and bind the Mongols, but he and his successors needed to rely on others for advice and techniques for ruling large agrarian states.

Yehluchucai[a] came from a noble Jidan family whose men long had served the Manchus ruling North China. Yehluchucai's father reached the top level of the government, and his son could have relied on the *yin* privilege to avoid taking the imperial exams. Being a proud man, Yehluchucai decided to forgo the *yin* privilege and prepared for the exams. The year he took them, Yehluchucai ranked number one in the empire and thereby merited a choice government position, in which he served for a few years. Then the Mongols attacked the city in which the young Jidan lived. The carnage of the siege and the subsequent Mongol slaughter of many residents compelled Yehluchucai to seek refuge in a Buddhist monastery. Within three years, he attained spiritual enlightenment, and because of his Jidan heritage (tribal kinship to the Mongols), Chinggis Khan summoned him.

In the initial meeting, the Jidan's frank manner and impressive figure caused Chinggis Khan to seek his counsel. Over the years, Yehluchucai often interceded on behalf of conquered peoples by asking that they not be killed. Many survived because of Yehluchucai's skillful pleas, and perhaps his greatest success came in the 1230s.

As more of northern China came under Mongol control, the Mongol leaders debated about what to do with the vast lands under their possession. One faction argued for turning the territory into a pastureland, which would have necessitated slaughtering millions of Chinese. Yehluchucai and others argued that by taxing the people instead of killing them, the Mongols could gain all of the riches that they desired. Yehluchucai also reckoned an amount that could be garnered by levying a tax. Ögödei permitted Yehluchucai to implement the proposal, and the tallies squared with the estimates. Millions of lives were spared by Yehluchucai's clever arguments. Shortly thereafter, he became a major advisor to the monarch. Over time, Yehluchucai brought in many Chinese officials and organized a Chinese-style administration that became a basis for the Chinese system finally implemented under Khubilai Khan after 1260.

[a] **Yehluchucai:** YEH loo CHOO sy

---

world. In addition, the continued campaigning provided the ever-restless Mongol warriors outlets for their energies; better to have them focused outward, Khubilai Khan's thinking went, than plotting some kind of internal uprising. Besides, new conquests meant new chances for glory and booty from the defeated peoples.

Khubilai Khan twice attempted to conquer Japan. In 1274, more than 30,000 warriors and support personnel sailed from Korea to Japan. After the Mongol landing on the southern island of Kyushu, fierce resistance by Japanese *samurai* slowed the invaders. A typhoon smashed the hapless fleet and wrecked the Mongols' hope for a victory. A combined Mongol and Chinese fleet with around 150,000 people launched a second inva-

sion in 1281 and was ravaged by another typhoon. Khubilai Khan called off a third effort in the mid-1280s.

Further campaigns were launched against Southeast Asian states by Khubilai Khan. In the 1280s, two major invasions attempted to annex Vietnam, but resistance by the Vietnamese was too strong. (An earlier Mongol invasion of Vietnam had been thwarted by heat, insects, and tropical diseases.) A Mongol armada sailed to the islands of the Southeast Asian coast, including Java, but this campaign also failed to take its military objectives.

Despite the string of defeats along the periphery of the Asian mainland, Khubilai Khan remained in firm control of China. There he laid the foundation for a rule lasting nearly one century. One major legacy was the rebuilding of the Grand Canal, which permitted Khubilai Khan and others to ship grain from the prosperous south.

China under Khubilai Khan's Successors

While violent court intrigues occupied the Mongols, the local Chinese populace experienced moderate rule. In fact, much power passed into the hands of educated Chinese landowners who acted as unpaid officials, often keeping order and mediating in clan or family disputes. This quasi-administrative system characterized Chinese society until early in the twentieth century and enabled governments to rule tens of millions of people with a mere 20,000 officials.

The Mongols appreciated the artisan and merchant classes, two groups that in theory languished at the bottom of the Chinese social scale. Artisans were organized and protected by the state, and they were exempted from certain taxes. In addition, the state allocated them rations of food, clothing, and salt. Physicians, too, were seen as artisans and favorably treated. They worked in imperial hospitals and practiced Islamic as well as

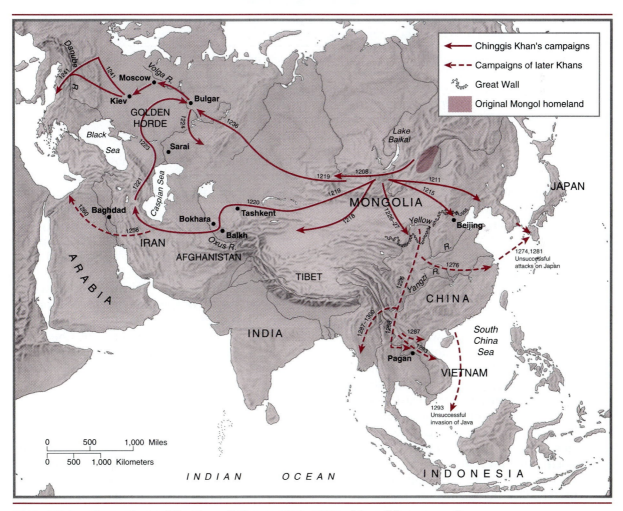

M A P 19.1   *Campaigns of the Mongol Khans, 1206–1300.* *Mongol forces ranged across much of Asia and parts of Europe. Naval expeditions did not achieve the success of the land campaigns, which—with the exception of those waged against the Mamluks and Vietnamese—were usually victorious.*

FIGURE 19.5 *Mongol Naval Battle Scene.* *While attempting two unsuccessful invasions of Japan, the Mongols fought several naval engagements. This Japanese painting shows a Mongol vessel being boarded by samurai, *bearing swords and wearing layered armor. Japanese* samurai *tended to prefer individual combat, while the Mongols usually fought in group formations.* Imperial Household Collection, Kyoto/Laurie Platt Winfrey, Inc.

traditional Chinese medicine. Merchants were accorded high status all over the Mongol realm and were eligible for state loans at the low annual interest of 10 percent. For this reason and others, domestic and international commerce mushroomed.

Artistic forms flourished during Mongol rule. A new poetic form that was closely tied to folksongs dominated versification during the Mongol era. Storytelling became a popular art form in the Chinese cities as professionals plied their narrative trades, sometimes for days or weeks in one neighborhood. The books used by the storytellers occasionally became the foundation for the emergence of Chinese novels. Opera developed, and more than 150 play manuscripts still exist. They were written in colloquial Chinese, reflecting close ties to the common people. Painting, especially in the landscape genre, closely followed the tradition established in the previous Song era and reached new levels of expression in the hands of a few Chinese masters, like Zhao Mengfu,[6] whose canvases inspired generations of artists in China, Korea, and Japan.

[6]**Zhao Mengfu:** JOW MEHNG foo

Khubilai's successors did not always share his preference for ruling from the cities, and some of them reverted to the traditional Mongol nomadic life. During the first half of the fourteenth century, Mongol factions representing the sedentary and nomadic lifestyles contended at the imperial court, and some rulers were assassinated after only a few months in power.

In 1368, the Mongol government fell to a Chinese rebellion led by a commoner. Those Mongols who survived the terrible battles of the 1360s returned to the steppelands north of China and contented themselves with periodic sorties into the agrarian domain they once ruled. Never again did the Mongols conquer China.

The Conquest of Korea

Korea, like China, fell to the Mongols in the thirteenth century. Although the initial invasion began in 1218, it took the Mongols until the late 1250s to subdue the tenacious Korean people completely. The Koryo Dynasty (935–1392) had long ruled Korea and was in a weakened state when the Mongols swept into the peninsula. The Mongols could lay waste to the cities, but they could not persuade the Korean monarch to surrender. Indeed, the royal family fled to an island off the coast and stayed there for many years despite numerous Mongol efforts to entice them to return. As long as there was a focus of Korean resistance, guerrilla fighters harassed the nomads.

In 1259, the last opposition to the Mongols disappeared and an accommodation was negotiated with the Korean court. In exchange for tribute items, like clothing, horses, and animal skins, the Koreans were permitted much local autonomy. On occasion, the Mongols demanded and received Korean soldiers to fight in their wars, especially during the failed invasions of Japan, and, in the large military campaigns, units from parts of Eurasia fought alongside Mongol soldiers.

Korea also became a base from which the invasions of Japan were launched. Each invasion severely drained the resources available in Korea and led to great suffering. Pleas from the Korean monarch persuaded Khubilai Khan to cancel plans for a third invasion. From that time until the mid–fourteenth century, when Mongol rule collapsed in much of East Asia, the Koreans were treated mildly by their nomadic overlords.

DEVASTATION AND RULE IN CENTRAL ASIA, 1219–1370

In 1219, much of Central Asia was ruled by a polity headed by Ala al-Din Muhammad, a Muslim ruler (shah), who had once planned to conquer China. After seeing that the Mongols had begun their invasion of North China, the shah sent observers

FIGURE 19.6 *"Autumn Colors on the Zhiao and Hua Mountains." Zhao Mengfu (1254–1322) excelled at painting landscapes, such as this scene of a marshy plain of willows, boats, and scattered houses, backed by hills covered in fall color, dated 1295. Zhao was related to the ruling family of the Song Empire and briefly retired when the Mongols took over. Responding to an appeal from Kubilai Khan, he returned to court life. Zhao was criticized by fellow Chinese as a collaborator, but this did not deter him from lending his considerable prestige to the group of artists serving the Mongols.* National Palace Museum, Taiwan, Republic of China.

PARALLELS AND DIVERGENCES
The Reliance of Pastoralists on Settled Peoples

Nineteenth-century anthropologists argued that pastoralism was a less complex way of life than agriculture and that pastoralists developed at an earlier date in human prehistory. Modern archaeology, however, has shown that pastoralism is the most recent form of subsistence to evolve, appearing only after agriculture has become well established in a region. Studies of historic and modern pastoralists indicate that herding simply cannot produce the quantity and especially the diversity of products needed to ensure survival; pastoralists always rely heavily on farmers.

Herders produce mostly meat, milk and milk products, and fiber from their animals' coats. They may supplement their herding with the hunting of wild animals and the gathering of wild plants, but their primary emphasis must be on their herd animals. A major problem, of course, is that they must limit the number of animals slaughtered to ensure that their herds remain large, so a meat surplus is rare; in fact, most pastoralists do not produce enough meat to keep themselves alive, if that were the only food they relied on. The demands of their animals force them to move regularly for fresh pasturage, so pastoralists have little opportunity to grow crops to supplement their food supply.

Instead, pastoralists typically obtain major portions of their food and other goods from nearby agriculturalists. Much of this is obtained by trade, because farmers usually relish the meat and cheese supplied by the pastoralists and will trade quantities of their agricultural produce for these products. In addition, wool and other pastoralist products can be traded to the sedentary farmers and urbanites for goods otherwise unavailable to the herders.

In some periods, pastoralists also have used their mobility and endurance to superior military advantage, seizing desired goods by raiding. As a result of trading and raiding, some pastoralists became quite wealthy, and some settled down in older age, opting for the less strenuous life of the city. This reliance on settled peoples has led one anthropologist to refer to pastoralists as "part-societies," recognizing that they could not persist without their sedentary economic partners.

The Mongols viewed empires with suspicion because they were convinced that the Chinese and others cheated them. Mongols hated the tolls and fees at their borders and bristled at the violations of Mongol-Chinese agreements. City folk were not to be trusted and perhaps were to be eradicated. Had the Mongol attempts been more concerted and successful, the Mongols would have found their own way of life threatened. Pastoralists soon realized that raiding could be conducted only in a limited manner, being sure to skim only some wealth from settled peoples; if weakened too much, agriculturalists could not have supported the pastoralists. In short, successful pastoralists have contented themselves with being traders and limited predators.

---

to ascertain the power of this new military group. Chinggis Khan also learned of his formidable neighbor and wanted to establish friendly relations with the shah. With that in mind, the Mongol leader dispatched diplomats to offer a friendly alliance between the ruler of the west and the ruler of the east. Soon thereafter, a wealth-laden caravan under Mongol protection arrived in one of the eastern cities of the shah's realm. A subordinate of the shah killed a Mongol envoy and confiscated the convoy's goods, and the shah did not repudiate the action of his official. Chinggis Khan and his successors regarded this action as a personal affront and swore vengeance against the offending state and its ruler. In 1219, Chinggis Khan headed a large invasion force that probably numbered over 100,000 soldiers. Over the next two years, the Mongols systematically destroyed Ala al-Din Muhammad's Central Asian empire and hounded him all across his lands. Although they failed to capture him, they did make his life thoroughly miserable.

The campaign had all of the elements of most Mongol invasions except that the destructiveness seemed to go beyond the usual limits of Mongol warring. To derive the maximum effectiveness of

FIGURE 19.7 *Ruins of the Citadel of Herat. During their conquest of Central Asia, the Mongols destroyed many cities and settlements. To avoid army casualties, Mongol forces usually spared cities that surrendered without resistance, while the inhabitants of those that resisted were massacred as a warning to others. Reports claim that only twenty-five people survived the attack on the citadel of Herat in Afghanistan, built on the site of a fort raised by Alexander the Great.* © 1992 John Adderley.

the arrayed armies, the Mongols relied on strict discipline to maneuver so that all units converged on a designated place at a given time. When the Mongols lost an important leader or a prince to an enemy, they warred without mercy. One city in the southern part of the shah's empire managed to kill one of Chinggis's grandsons. The town was taken, the inhabitants were slaughtered, the buildings were burned, and the surviving urban structures were pulled down. Resistance to the Mongols continued. When another city fell after a long siege, all of its men, women, and children were beheaded and each group's severed heads were formed into a separate pyramid. On at least three occasions, after the Mongol forces withdrew, a trailing Mongol force suddenly returned and killed all those who had returned or left their hiding places. It became a common practice of Mongol warfare for soldiers to single out artisans in a town, spare them from death, and march them off to service, usually in the Mongol homeland. When Samarkand fell in 1220, around 30,000 artisans and engineers were spared. By the end of this campaign little remained of the vibrant civilization there.

Rule over the Central Asian lands passed to the eldest son of Chinggis Khan. Prosperity slowly returned to towns and cities because many vital trade routes passed through them. A key stretch of the Mongol post road also went through Central Asia, and many travelers and couriers visited scenic or otherwise famous sites.

THE KIPCHAK KHANATE AND THE DOMINATION OF RUSSIA, 1221–1480

Russia had no major leader when the Mongols arrived in the 1220s. The government of Kiev (around 900–1240) had long since passed its prime and disintegrated into warring princely factions. Some Kievan princes went north and northeast to settle the vast forest areas there. Indeed, the wooden houses and buildings in many northeast towns and villages resembled the log dwellings across the North American frontier of the eighteenth and early nineteenth centuries. Russia, in fact, in the early decades of the thirteenth century, was a patchwork of independent principalities and city-states that stretched west to east from the Baltic Sea to the Ural Mountains and north to south from the White Sea to the Black Sea.

The initial Mongol thrust in 1221 was more of a scouting expedition by two of Chinggis Khan's able commanders. They had trailed Ala al-Din Muhammad, the fugitive Central Asian sultan, to the Caspian Sea area, and, after assuring themselves that he had perished, they decided to cross the Caucasus Mountains and explore the northern reaches of the steppe. News of their plundering in the kingdom of Georgia and elsewhere gave Russian princes time to mobilize a large army to meet them. Outnumbered, the Mongols used a ploy that had often worked in the past. They charged the Russian positions and then broke off the attack to take flight. Like many other Mongol opponents, the Russians could not resist chasing the fleeing cavalry. After an extended ride, the Mongol forces swung around and were joined by hidden forces that entrapped the pursuers. The enemy was annihilated, and the Mongols returned to finish off the remaining forces. Fortunately for the Mongols, the rivalries among the surviving Russian princes brought counterattacks in a piecemeal fashion. Soon the Russians were severely defeated, and the Mongol army heeded the command of Chinggis Khan to return to Central Asia.

The Conquest of the Bulgars, Kipchaks, and Russians

The second main incursion into Russia came around fifteen years later when a large Mongol army, numbering perhaps 120,000 soldiers, attacked. Batu,[7] another grandson of Chinggis, headed this expedition accompanied by many key Mongol leaders and princes, including representatives of the lines of Chinggis Khan's four sons. It was a carefully planned major thrust into Europe and relied heavily on intelligence gathered by merchant-spies.

The first attack came against Bulgars, who lived along the Volga River and who had served as a buffer between the Russians and the steppe peoples. By autumn 1236, the Mongols destroyed the Bulgars and rebuilt their capital. Some Bulgars fled to Russia, where they were granted asylum.

A second expedition along the Volga targeted the Kipchak people, who were a loose confederation of Turkish tribes. After a brief, hard-hitting attack, the Kipchaks were defeated, and many joined with the Mongols in their attacks against the Russians. When the Mongol leader, Batu, established his domain, the Kipchak component of his subjects inspired the name Kipchak Khanate for this section of the Mongol Empire.

With most of the Volga River Valley secured, the Mongols turned to the Russians. Once again, because of internal rivalries, Russian leaders failed to lay coordinated defensive plans. The initial operation went through the winter of 1237 and 1238 and brought the towns and cities of the northeast under Mongol domination. The usual thorough destruction was conducted throughout the area, and only the city-state of Novgorod in the northwest was spared because a spring thaw undermined cavalry operations. Batu then spent the next year and a half resupplying men and materials as well as defeating remnant opposition forces in the south.

By 1240, the Mongols resumed their march toward Kiev and then into eastern Europe. One Mongol commander wished to spare Kiev from utter destruction and offered peace terms. The defenders replied by executing the Mongol envoys. This infuriated the Mongols, who gathered their entire attacking force before the city. The fight was ferocious and ended in Mongol victory. As might

[7]**Batu:** BAH too

FIGURE 19.8 *King Bela of Hungary Facing the Mongols.* *On April 10, 1241, a Hungarian force led by King Bela was defeated by the Mongols, under Batu Khan. In this European-painted scene, Batu, grandson of Chinggis Khan, faces the Hungarians at the bridge over the Sajo River, captured with the aid of artillery barrages. The Mongol forces conquered most of eastern Europe (southern Poland to the Adriatic, at Bosnia) and were on the brink of invading the west when the death of the Great Khan in December 1241 sent Batu back east to help select a successor.* Osterreichische Nationalbibliothek.

be expected, the city suffered great destruction, including the ravaging of tombs of Russian saints and dignitaries, whose bones were exhumed and scattered on the streets. The Mongols then rode toward the heart of Europe.

The Attack on the Hungarians

Hungary, the main target in Europe, was ruled by an otherwise capable monarch who was so unwise as to execute some Mongol envoys. That action, as well as the king's refusal to surrender the Kipchaks who had fled from the Mongols, assured the Mongol invasion of his land. At the same time, to protect their northern flank, the Mongols launched a strike by a force of about 30,000 men into Poland and Bohemia. That expedition saw fierce fighting, including one savage encounter during which the

Mongols severed the ears of their slain enemies. Nine bags of ears were collected as war trophies. Several other Mongol units advanced through the Carpathian Mountains into Hungary in a coordinated effort. The decisive battle, in April 1241, brought utter defeat for the Hungarian monarch, who fled to the Adriatic Sea. He was pursued by a detachment of Mongols who arrived at the Mediterranean seacoast but could not follow the monarch to his island retreat. Some months later in Mongolia, the death of the Great Khan (head of the Mongols) Ögödei[8] (1229–1241) forced a withdrawal of the Mongol armies from Europe. They never returned to the western campaign. Instead they withdrew to the Volga steppe region, where Batu established his headquarters. From there, he

[8] **Ögödei:** OOH geh day

IN THEIR OWN WORDS
Humanitarian Elements of Mongol Rule

People may think of Mongols as barbaric, but they also had humanitarian traits. Warfare, of course, has caused great suffering throughout history, but the Mongol rulers seemed unusually destructive of life and property. Our view of the Mongols comes from others because the Mongols never wrote about themselves.

One perspective is provided by the historian Ala-ad-Din Ata-Malik Juvaini (1226–1283), who records some humanitarian acts of Mongol rulers, especially Ögödei Khan. Juvaini actually held mixed views about the Mongols, who destroyed much of his beloved Persian culture. In his *History of the World-Conqueror*, he discusses Mongol atrocities and mentions their humanitarian deeds. In the following selections, we can see how Ögödei treated commoners.

A poor man, who was unable to earn a living and had learned no trade, sharpened pieces of iron into the shape of awls and mounted them on pieces of wood. He then sat down where the retinue of the Khan would pass and waited. The Khan caught sight of him from afar and sent one of his attendants to him. The poor man told him of the weakness of his condition, the smallness of his property, and the largeness of his family and gave him the awls. But when the messenger saw his clumsy awls, . . . hardly . . . worth a barleycorn, he thought them unworthy of being presented to the Khan and so left them . . . and [returning] told what he had seen. The Khan ordered him [to go back and] bring all the awls that the man had with him. . . . taking them in his hand he said: "Even this kind will serve for herdmen to mend . . . seams . . . with." And for each awl he gave the man an [ingot of gold or silver].

A poor man came to his court with ten thongs tied to a stick. He opened his mouth in prayer [for the Khan] and stood at a distance. The royal glance fell upon him and when the officers inquired about his business, he said, "I had a kid [goat] in my household. I made its flesh the sustenance of my family, and out of its hide I fashioned thongs for the men-at-arms, which I have brought with me." The Khan took the thongs and said: "This poor fellow has brought us what is better than goats." And he ordered him to be given a hundred ingots and a thousand head of sheep. And he added that when this was consumed, [the man] should come again, and he would give him more.

An Indian woman with two children on her back was passing by a gate. The Khan, who had just returned from the country, caught sight of her and ordered the treasurer to give her five ingots. He took them to her at once, but put one in his pocket and gave her only four. The woman noticed that one was missing and pleaded with him to give it to her. The Khan asked him what the woman had been saying. He replied that she was a woman with a family and was uttering a prayer. The Khan then asked, "What family has she?" "Two small orphans," replied the treasurer. The Khan went to the treasury and ordered the woman to be summoned. Then he commanded her to take every kind of clothing that pleased her fancy, as many embroidered garments as a rich and wealthy man would wear.

---

and his successors demanded that the Russians render various services common to subject peoples elsewhere in the expanding empire.

Mongol Administration of Russia

The Great Khan Möngke[9] (reign dates 1251–1259) ordered a census of the Russian population in the 1250s for tax and service purposes. This was part of a general effort by Möngke to maximize the employment of the empire's human and material resources. The initial population count commenced in 1257 and expanded to all areas by 1260. Some evidence suggests that the Mongols imposed agricultural and commercial taxes on the Russians, although it is unclear what rates were demanded. In addition, the Mongols divided the population into administrative units for conscription purposes, with each unit responsible for supplying a certain number of soldiers when called upon.

When ruling Russia, Mongol leaders like Batu relied heavily on local Russian princes who col-

[9]**Möngke:** MEHNG keh

lected taxes and then remitted them to the capital, Sarai. Initially, the khans demanded that princes appear at regular intervals so that they might renew their pledges of allegiance to the khan, and sometimes the Russians accompanied the tax revenues. The Mongols permitted much self-government. Indeed, one reason for the rise to power of the Moscow princes in the fourteenth century was their use of excess funds collected for the Mongols to finance local building and other projects. Moscow sovereigns continued to curry favor with their Mongol overlords, so that they might benefit from being the khan's officials.

In the late fourteenth century, one Moscow prince, Dmitri, briefly challenged Mongol domination by refusing to acknowledge Mongol overlordship. In addition, an army of a Central Asian leader who claimed descent from Chinggis Khan attacked the Kipchak Khanate and inflicted serious damage upon it. Several tribal confederations broke off to form the Kazan Khanate, the Siberian Khanate, and the Crimean Khanate. By 1480, the Kipchak Khanate's weakened condition enabled the Moscow prince Ivan III to renounce Mongol overlordship and resist the efforts of a Mongol army to punish him. In that campaign, the Crimean Mongols aligned with Ivan III.

Mongol rule in Russia brought many political changes to the Russian people. Initially, great destruction devastated the land and its peoples. One chronicle of the time said that after the Mongols passed through, no one was left to mourn the fallen. Yet their relatively lax ruling policies permitted the growth of local administration and the consolidation of power by the Moscow princes. The extended era of peace permitted a rebound and some material prosperity among the nobility and the merchants. Mongol rulers often preferred hunting to ruling; their soldiers were splendid warriors but ineffective administrators.

THE MONGOLS IN SOUTHWEST ASIA, 1258–AROUND 1350

Southwest Asia was composed of a multitude of polities at the time of the Mongol invasion and conquest in the 1250s. The Abbasid Caliphate, which had loosely ruled over the Islamic world for

centuries, and the Saljuq[10] Turks, who had long dominated the Persian lands, were in a weakened state when the Mongols arrived. In fact, much of the area was in the hands of petty rulers who fought one another and vied for control of larger domains.

In the mid-1250s, the Mongol leadership decided to subjugate Southwest Asia, which had experienced haphazard Mongol rule, much in the manner of the great campaign of the 1230s and 1240s in Russia and eastern Europe. Command of the operation was given to Hülegü,[11] one of the Great Khan's younger brothers. In addition, all Mongol and allied sovereigns were expected to supply specified numbers of men or supplies. Failure to respond signaled disloyalty and invited swift retaliation by the Mongols.

Hülegü took a long time in arriving in Persia, the first focus of his conquest, because his large force of more than 100,000 needed time to cross rivers and traverse difficult mountain ranges and other natural obstacles. Hülegü's army also traveled with large siege machines that could not be quickly or easily transported.

Once in Persia, the commander began probing the formidable mountain fortifications of the Ismaili sect (popularly known as the Assassins). This group had long been identified as a major obstacle to unification of the region, and, over the succeeding months, castles and other forts of the Ismailis were systematically destroyed. Other Mongol forces began conquering parts of Persia to the south.

After subduing the Ismaili sect, Hülegü conquered the Abbasid Caliphate. In the normal pattern of the Mongols, smaller towns around the great capital, Baghdad, were first taken and plundered, and then came the assault on the capital itself. As they had done on many previous occasions, the Mongols built a wooden palisade surrounding the capital to keep the townspeople from escaping. In addition, Hülegü drove many captives ahead of the attacking forces to break the will of the besieged as well as to minimize the attackers' losses. Once the city fell in early 1258, the slaughter began, and some sources note that part of the savage killing came from Georgian units of the Caucasus Mountains region that fought alongside the Mongols. These Georgian soldiers avenged

---

[10] **Saljuq:** sehl JUHK
[11] **Hülegü:** HOO leh guh

FIGURE 19.9 *Mongol Siege of Baghdad.* *Baghdad fell to Mongol forces under Hülegü in 1258, ending the Abbasid Caliphate. The Mongols built a wall around the city to prevent escape during the siege, in which the caliph and over 500,000 inhabitants were killed. The conquerors later made pyramids of the heads of slain inhabitants to deter further resistance to their rule.* Bibliothèque nationale, Paris.

themselves on their former Muslim overlords. As in previous conquests, artisans were spared; most of them were rounded up for the long trek to the Mongol capital, Qaraqorum.[12]

Mongol forces ranged over most of Southwest Asia and even managed to take Damascus for a brief time. Their ability to maintain a lasting presence along the eastern Mediterranean coast was continually frustrated by the rulers of Egypt. In the seesaw fighting for the extreme western part of Southwest Asia, the European monarchs and the European crusaders, who controlled some cities and areas, refused to cooperate with the Mongols against their common Muslim enemy.

[12] **Qaraqorum:** kah rah KOHR uhm

Hülegü and his successors ruled Persia, Mesopotamia, and parts of the Caucasus region for nearly a century. The economy of Persia and the surrounding territories was devastated in the thirteenth century by the Mongol conquest and the Mongols' harsh taxation policies. Warfare, famine, and disease sharply reduced the population, which slowly recovered to pre-Mongol levels in the last decade of the thirteenth century. There was some influx of Turkish and Mongol settlers, but they lived in nomadic communities and had little effect on either agriculture or urban life.

From the 1290s to the mid-1330s, there was a spurt of economic growth, especially in agriculture and trade. Owing to the adoption of lighter taxes, small-scale peasant landholding increased and helped to promote agricultural prosperity. Cities gradually became active economic centers, though nothing in commerce or agriculture reached the levels of pre-Mongol times. Trade routes running through much of Asia lay in the control of the Mongols, and the increased commercial volume also improved the fortunes of artisans and merchants in Persian cities. Chinese products once again reached Persia, and Persian traders and advisors often traveled to China.

The arts experienced some interruption with the destruction of the great cities of Southwest Asia. Poetry, which had long flourished under previous governments, went into decline after the Mongols arrived. This was largely linked to the poets' loss of elite patronage, as well as to the urban devastation. Nevertheless, certain forms that included mystical poetry continued under the Mongols.

The Mongols supported the writing of historical works in an attempt to immortalize themselves. Certain Persian Muslim historians are key sources for our knowledge of the Mongol era; Juvaini and Rashid al-Din (1247–1318) deserve special mention. Both men served in Mongol administrations; Juvaini came from a long line of top government officials in Central Asia, while Rashid al-Din was a physician. Juvaini's history contained highly polished prose and poetry. Written in pieces over the span of a decade, this history has been an invaluable source of information about the Mongols because of the variety of people Juvaini knew. Rashid al-Din wrote long after the Mongol conquest, and his style lacks the flair of Juvaini's. Rashid al-Din's major historical work, however, developed from a wide range of sources. He assembled a resource team of two Chinese scholars, a Buddhist monk from South Asia, a spe-

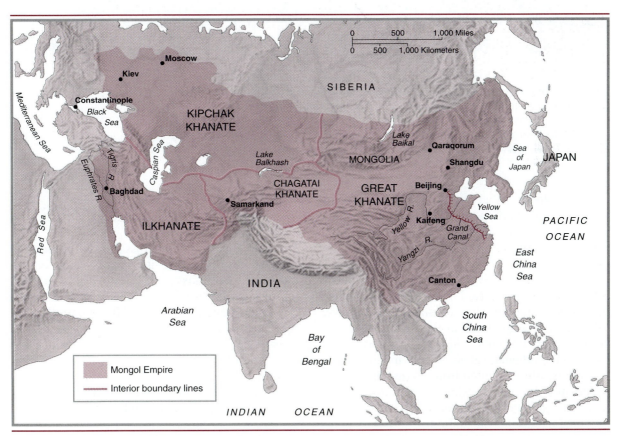

MAP 19.2 *The Mongol Empire around 1300.* *The empire became so large that it broke into four khanates centered in Persia, Russia, Central Asia, and East Asia. Despite this division, trade continued to flow smoothly across Eurasia.*

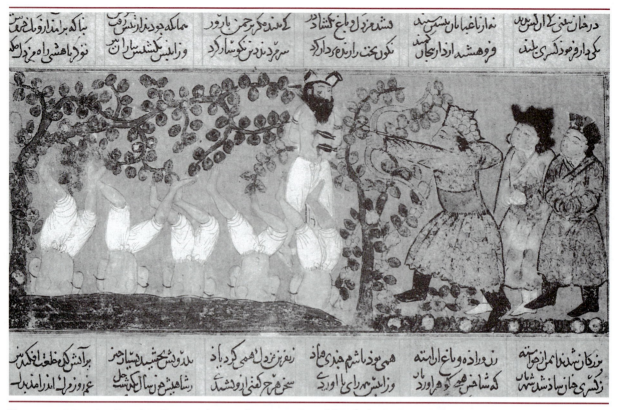

FIGURE 19.10   *Persian Perspective on the Mongols.   After their state was overrun by the Mongols, some Persians wrote or painted what they saw or heard of the atrocities committed by the conquerors. This manuscript illustrates one prisoner being executed with arrows, while others are buried alive, head down. While many kinds of brutality were inflicted by the Mongols, fear, rumor, and imagination may have played a role in creating this scene, and others.*   Chester Beatty Library and Gallery of Oriental Art, Dublin.

cialist on Mongol tribal traditions, and a European traveler. Thus, perhaps more than any previous scholar, Rashid al-Din conveyed a Eurasian perspective, ranging far beyond the geographic limits of Islam.

Mathematics and science continued to flourish in the Mongol period. A few Persian mathematicians explored algebra and trigonometry, following in the footsteps of their Muslim predecessors. The Persians laid the foundation for important mathematical discoveries in later times. Astronomy also benefited from the erection of an observatory by Hülegü, who was interested more in astrology than in astronomy. The observatory provided a place for the gathering of astronomers and facilitated their continued scholarly research, which reached new heights.

THE MONGOL EXCHANGE

The Mongols exploded across Eurasia in the thirteenth century and united a vast area of the Eurasian landmass while providing nearly unprecedented security for merchants and travelers. At the same time, Mongol fleets patrolled the sea lanes of the East China Sea and the South China Sea, thereby facilitating maritime trade between India and China. The growth of the China market added a vital piece to the puzzle of Eurasian trade. South China's trade, both internally and externally, flourished prior to the Mongol conquest. The Southern Song government, for example, opened nine Chinese port cities to maritime trade. Thereafter, once the cities recovered

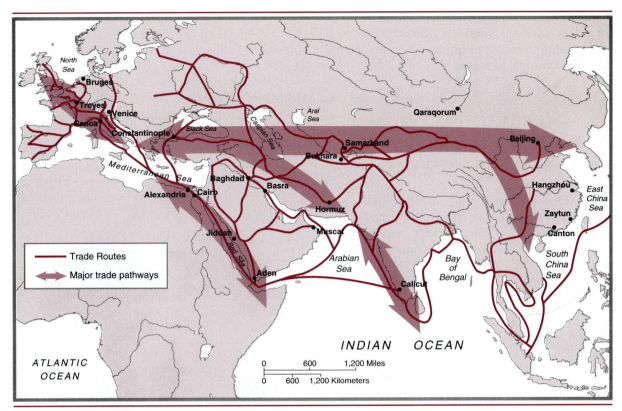

MAP 19.3 *The Mongol Empire and Trade around 1340.* *The Mongol exchange
benefited from the growth of land and maritime trade across Eurasia and parts of Africa.
Mongol leaders favored merchants and actively promoted commerce. As a result, caravans
traversed the silk roads and convoys of merchant ships plied the seas and oceans off Asia
and Africa. The volume of trade was unparalleled until the seventeenth century.*

from the destruction of warfare, the increase of
commerce accelerated. It was aided by the Mongol
appreciation for trade and merchants. A reunited
China became a major exporter and importer, thus
becoming a significant impetus to a burgeoning
trade that brought hemispheric prosperity until
the mid–fourteenth century. Europeans sent furs,
grain, and merchants eastward. Indeed, the inter-
mixing of people, goods, ideas, and diseases created the basis for what may be called the Mongol
exchange.

One great benefit of the Mongol unity was the
increased trade between regions of Eurasia. Like
most nomadic groups that needed to exchange
goods in order to survive, the Mongols promoted
trade and supported merchants who traveled from
place to place in search of profitable exchanges.
European merchants, like Marco Polo and his

uncles, as well as Muslim merchants traveled to
China in pursuit of business profits and adventure.

Traders, soldiers, and officials served in distant parts of the Mongol Empire. Russians fought
in China, while Chinese, Turks, and Persians
worked in places like Mongolia, China, and Russia.
Some of these subjects returned home with new
ideas and ways of doing things. Marco Polo governed an area of southern China and returned to
Venice with tales of coal being used as a fuel and
paper currency being employed as a major
exchange medium.

Knowledge of the compass and of gunpowder
technology, along with many other technological
wonders, moved from east to west, with the compass arriving in the 1200s and gunpowder reaching
Europe in the 1300s. Some in the Islamic world
gained access to the compass and gunpowder, but

it was the Europeans who employed the compass to aid in their explorations overseas and who employed gunpowder technology to enhance the power of state governments.

SOME COMPARISONS BETWEEN THE MONGOLS AND THE MUSLIMS

Both Mongols (1200s) and Muslims (600s and 700s) rapidly conquered vast areas of the eastern hemisphere in their early decades of power, and there are some fruitful comparisons to be made

about their rule and legacies. After a century or more of rule in their domains, the Mongols settled in, while the Muslims continued to expand, generally by peaceful means.

Despite the devastation brought about by their conquests, both the Mongols and Muslims adopted many political institutions of their newly conquered subjects. Certainly, the Mongols used terror as a means to cow their enemies, and cities

FIGURE 19.11 *Astronomical Chart of the Mongol Era.* *Mongol leaders in Southwest Asia employed many scholars from among conquered peoples, drawing on the rich resources of the Muslim scientific tradition. This constellation chart comes from a Persian manuscript written by Nasr al-Din Tusi, a famous astronomer and mathematician. Tusi not only survived the invasion of his homeland but went on to achieve high office, build an observatory, and write many important works in his various fields of expertise. Although Mongol leaders were more interested in astrology than astronomy, both continued to flourish under foreign rule.* Reproduced by permission of the Harvard-Yenching Institute.

FIGURE 19.12 *Yuan Dynasty Vase.* *This vase was created around 1350 by Chinese artisans working under Mongol rule. During this time, potters were encouraged to increase production of their wares, resulting in new techniques, new levels of sophistication, and new markets. White pottery, which was the most popular, included vases, dishes, and figurines that could be painted and glazed or incised with decorative patterns. Widespread distribution of this work was facilitated by the stimulation of trade during the era of the Mongol exchange.* Victoria and Albert Museum.

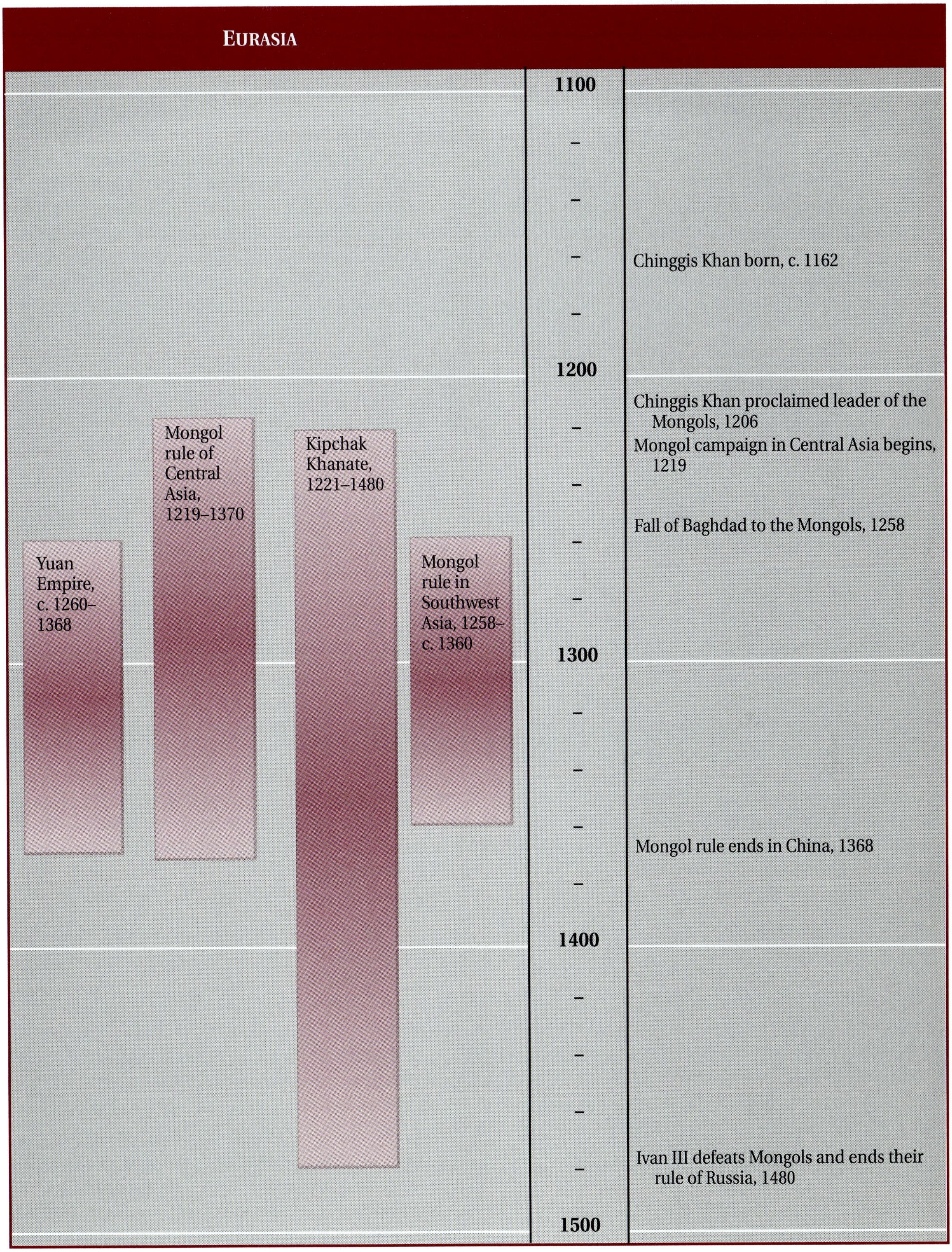

EURASIA

1100

Chinggis Khan born, c. 1162

1200

Chinggis Khan proclaimed leader of the Mongols, 1206

Mongol campaign in Central Asia begins, 1219

Fall of Baghdad to the Mongols, 1258

Yuan Empire, c. 1260–1368

Mongol rule of Central Asia, 1219–1370

Kipchak Khanate, 1221–1480

Mongol rule in Southwest Asia, 1258–c. 1360

1300

Mongol rule ends in China, 1368

1400

Ivan III defeats Mongols and ends their rule of Russia, 1480

1500

that resisted Mongol demands suffered grave population losses. Although losses did accompany the Muslim conquests, terror was more sporadic. Muslims generally left irrigation systems alone, while the Mongols destroyed them in parts of Central Asia. Once in power, both groups tolerated local religions, although Muslim rulers imposed special taxes on nonbelievers. The Mongols realized that winning the local religious leaders' support through tax exemptions and other means facilitated rule over the common people.

Muslims continued to spread their religion long after their initial conquests, unlike the Mongols. In that sense, the peaceful expansion of the religion of Islam continued over the centuries and the miles of land and sea. Judges, merchants, and Sufis roamed over continents and found converts from the western Pacific to the eastern Atlantic basins. Dar al-Islam was a realm of sociocultural unity that the Mongol domain never achieved. Indeed, Mongols in Southwest and Central Asia often adopted Islam, Christianity, and Buddhism as their own religions.

Both Mongols and Muslims appreciated trade and presided over eras of significant commercial growth. Chinggis Khan usually favored merchants and artisans because he understood the benefits of business ventures. Muhammad and many members of the Muslim ruling class were themselves merchants and pushed Islamic expansion along long-distance trade routes. Muslim merchants were often favored by Islamic governments spurring trade and encouraging non-Muslim business people to convert. Unity in the Mongol and Muslim empires also created the stability and peace necessary for successful commercial ventures.

The Mongol and Islamic exchanges brought many ideas, foodstuffs, and textiles to diverse parts of the hemisphere. Muslim astronomers served Chinese, Indian, and Arab monarchs. Chinese paper makers found a home in Baghdad, and from there paper making and its use spread across Dar al-Islam. Gunpowder was taken by the Mongols into Southwest Asia and from there passed to Europe. All regions eventually were transformed by this technology.

Perhaps the greatest difference and permanent legacy related to religion. The Mongols were tolerant of the religions of others. The Muslims ardently practiced their faith and carried it everywhere they went. Today, hundreds of millions of Muslims reside in Eurasia and are a living testimony to the enduring legacy of Islam. Mongols either assimilated into the societies that they ruled or returned to Mongolia, where their descendants still reside.

SUMMARY

1. Mongol unity came in 1206, when Chinggis Khan was proclaimed the leader of the Mongols. At that time, he also gave the Mongols a law code and began working on a courier system to transmit messages rapidly throughout his empire.

2. China was a major target of Chinggis Khan, whose campaign against it began in 1211. The conquest of North China concluded in 1234, and all of China fell into Mongol hands by 1279. With the example of Khubilai Khan, the Mongols came to rule China like traditional monarchs, although one faction preferred to maintain a nomadic identity.

3. Mongol factional strife in China led to a weak government, and revolts in the mid–fourteenth century finally toppled the Mongols there.

4. Central Asia fell to the Mongols in 1221 after a bitter struggle that shattered the urban civilization there. The Mongols often deliberately employed terror as a weapon to facilitate their conquests in Central Asia and elsewhere. Rule over Central Asia passed to one line of Chinggis's sons and lasted for over a century.

5. Russia fell to the Mongols during a three-year campaign marked by frightful massacres. Control passed to Batu, the leader of the expedition, and the Mongol rule lasted for more than two centuries.

6. Local rule was encouraged by the Mongols and permitted the growth of influence by the Chinese gentry landlords and the Moscow princes.

7. Persia and the rest of Southwest Asia endured successive invasions by the Mongols from the 1220s through the 1250s. Although Mongol conquest and rule initially devastated the region's people and economy, some return to pre-Mongol

prosperity occurred from the 1290s to the 1330s. History writing expanded owing to Mongol patronage, and some forms of poetry flourished.

8. Despite the destruction caused by many Mongol invasions, the rule brought peaceful conditions and the growth of trade. A Mongol exchange between Asia and Europe occurred, and goods, technologies, and foodstuffs spread across that vast domain.

9. The Mongols came from the steppelands of Asia and followed a nomadic lifestyle, spurring the development of civilization in much of Eurasia.

SUGGESTED READINGS

Boyle, John. *The Mongol World Empire, 1206–1370*. London: Variorum Reprints, 1977. A classic examination of the Mongol realm in light of Eurasian politics and society.

Cleaves, Francis, trans. *The Secret History of the Mongols*. Cambridge, Mass.: Harvard University Press, 1982. An accurate translation of and insightful commentary on a major source of Mongol history.

Dardess, John. *Conquerors and Confucians*. New York: Columbia University Press, 1973. A classic interpretation of the Mongol rule of China.

Luc, Kwanten. *Imperial Nomads: A History of Central Asia, 500–1500*. Philadelphia: University of Pennsylvania Press, 1979. A standard look at the geopolitical context of Central Asia and the Mongol role within it.

Rossabi, Morris. *Khubilai Khan*. Berkeley: University of California Press, 1988. An examination of later Mongol rule in East Asia.

Buddha.   This cave-temple carving of the Buddha is nearly forty-five feet tall and was commissioned by the Wei emperors, who ruled China from the fourth to the sixth century. The artistic style shows the Buddha with Asian features, demonstrating the acculturation of Buddhism in China. The earliest known Buddhist community in China dates from around A.D. 65; scholars believe Buddhism followed the silk road and the southern sea routes to Asian territories.   George Holton/Photo Researchers, Inc.

World Religions and Their Spread

At the end of the tenth century, Vladimire I of Russia faced a religious quandary. People in his realm practiced myriad polytheistic customs that helped to impede cultural uniformity and remained in stark contrast to the cohesiveness of the neighboring monotheistic states. Vladimire chose eastern Christianity over Judaism, Islam, or western Christianity primarily because of the close commercial ties his realm enjoyed with the Byzantine Empire and the diplomatic advantages the conversion would bring to his court. Vladimire was baptized, married the Byzantine emperor's sister, and commenced the conversion of his subjects to eastern Christianity in 988. This conversion of Russia is one example of how world religions spread.

A religion becomes a **world religion** when it gains significant numbers of adherents across broad geographical expanses. The world religions of Judaism, Hinduism, Buddhism, Christianity, and Islam all moved across continents and into new cultural areas, where they were adopted and adapted by new peoples.

The effects of the dissemination of world religions are numerous. As a religion spread beyond its point of origin, its structure, theology, and practice often changed as believers integrated it into their own cultural perspectives. In addition, the religion affected the society to which it came, sometimes changing or altogether eliminating local practices. In this chapter we will examine the ways in which world religions spread and discuss some of the consequential effects of their spread.

THE WAYS IN WHICH RELIGIONS SPREAD

Religions spread as a result of conquests and coercion, missionary activities, migrations, and trade and cultural interactions. Expansion of a religion as a result of conquest may coerce or encourage a subject population to accept a new religion or entice the conquerors to adopt a new religion. Dissemination through missionary activity entails a concentrated effort to persuade indigenous people to convert. Transporting a religion through migration brings it to new areas, as individuals carry their religion with them when they move. Finally, the spread of religion through trade and cultural interaction occurs whenever people of different cultures meet and exchange ideas and customs. Some combination of these four factors was almost always present in the spread of the world religions under examination here.

Conquest and Coercion

Because many peoples consider their belief system superior to those of others, conquerors sometimes desired to spread their religion to those they conquered. In addition, forced conversions helped the new regime to organize and control the subdued population through ideology. A unified belief system was more efficient for maintaining control and legitimizing rule. Uniform belief helped to ensure an obedient population, and kings and emperors often claimed to rule through divine mandate.

Examples of the spread of religion through violence or coercion are relatively rare, but cases can be identified. During the seventh-century Muslim expansion, there were incidents of forced conversion as the Arabs swept through Southwest Asia. In addition, Spanish *conquistadores* compelled many indigenous people in Mexico to convert to Christianity, and Portuguese colonists in

FIGURE I.4.1 *Conversion.* *Conversion was often a matter of political or social circumstances rather than a result of personal choice. In this scene from medieval Europe, King Clovis is baptized by a Christian missionary. Soon after Clovis's conversion and baptism, hundreds of his subjects were also baptized. As the Franks conquered new territories in Europe, they demanded that local populations convert to Christianity. This gave Frankish kings, like Charlemagne, a religious ideology to unite the realm and the religious sanction to rule by the grace of God.* Musée Condée, Chantilly/Laurie Platt Winfrey, Inc.

Asia forced Hindus to convert to Christianity. Monarchs often used coercion to convert their populations in order to unify them. When the Sui monarch reunited China through conquest in the late sixth century, he championed Buddhism as a way to link the peoples of the north and south together with one ideology. Germanic kings, like Clovis and Charlemagne, forced their tribes to convert to Christianity because it gave them divine right of rule and helped establish hereditary succession.

Conquerors were also converted when they came in contact with the cultures of their subjects. If the indigenous religion unified the polity and aided in governance, monarchs benefited by converting. By the eleventh century, Turks had conquered the Arabian territories of Syria and Palestine, as well as a large portion of Persia. Islam, already entrenched in these areas, spread to the conquerors, and the Turks became Muslims. Hun conquerors of northern China converted to Buddhism through their use of Buddhists in the government, and Mongol conquerors of Southeast Asia soon adopted Islam through contact with the Muslim population there. The adoption of Islam aided in Mongol rule.

Missionary Activity

In addition to conquests, missionary activity has contributed significantly to the spread of world religions. A **missionary** is a person who purposely sets out to preach, teach, and persuade individuals or groups to consciously accept the belief system or theology of the religion. This kind of activity is called **proselytizing**. Most world religions have included some element of proselytizing.

Although Buddhism is found throughout the world today, its main geographical focus has been in Central, East, South, and Southeast Asia, and it owes its spread largely to missionaries. This development began during the time of Ashoka, who commanded Buddhist priests to carry the message of the Buddha to distant lands in the third century B.C. Buddhism then spread to the rest of India, to Central Asia, to China, and to Southeast Asia. Missionaries used a variety of techniques, including illusion, singing, and dancing, to convey the potency of their message.

Missionaries, mostly monks, took Christian belief beyond the geographical area of ancient Palestine, spreading Christianity among Greeks, Romans, and other peoples of the Mediterranean region in the first to the fourth centuries A.D. Various missionary activities continued to expand Christianity to medieval Europe in the fifth and sixth centuries and beyond. Missionary activities later extended to Arabia, India, China, and the Americas. When some Europeans arrived in China on trading expeditions, they met Asian Christians whose ancestors had been converted by early missionaries.

Islamic missionary activity followed the roads of conquest and trade. Most proselytizing centered on the cities, and missionary activity in the countryside occurred at a slower pace. Wandering Sufi mystics spread Islam throughout Africa, Europe, and Asia, sometimes moving into unconquered territories by themselves. These itinerant missionaries expanded Islam far beyond the borders of Muslim states. Most conversions to Islam were the result of missionary activities.

Not every world religion has a tradition of proselytizing. Judaism traditionally did not support missionary activity, although some people did convert to Judaism in different periods and in different places when they came in contact with Jews. Some Roman intellectuals became Jews while living in Palestine during the Roman Empire. Most conversions to Judaism arose from marriage.

Migration

Significant numbers of peoples throughout the centuries migrated into new areas, resulting in the spread of religious practices to the newly adopted homeland. Immigrants often settled in neighborhoods where they felt more comfortable among those who shared their cultural heritage. As they interacted with the indigenous population, ideas and customs dispersed. Descendants sometimes moved away from ethnic neighborhoods into the surrounding population, spreading their religious heritage through social contact and marriage.

Migration was closely linked with cultural interaction because it offered two opportunities for exchange: It exposed both the indigenous and the migrating populations to each others' religious practices. One example of this is the Jewish **diaspora**, the forced migration of a people. Thousands of Jews were forced to relocate from Palestine to the city of Babylon in the sixth century B.C., where

Figure I.4.2 *Joden Savannah.* *Jews relocated to many areas of the globe during periods of persecution and expulsion. In northern South America, near the banks of the Surinam River, a state called Joden Savannah (the Jewish Savannah) was carved out of the forest by emigrating Jews. The central community was named Jerusalem-on-the-River, in memory of the ancient Jewish homeland. As depicted in this nineteenth-century drawing of a storefront, the Jewish community traded with indigenous peoples. The Jews also established farms that produced sugar, coffee, and cotton.* Beth Hatefutsoth, The Nahum Goldmann Museum of the Jewish Diaspora, Tel-Aviv.

they intermarried with local people. Jewish theology was influenced by local cosmology, and, when Jews migrated back to their homeland in Palestine, they brought some Babylonian ideas with them. Another diaspora occurred in A.D. 70, when the Romans broke up a rebellion in Palestine; some migrated westward to Europe and others eastward to territories of Southwest Asia or southward to parts of Africa. Some moved to Ethiopia, where indigenous people converted to Judaism, producing a large Jewish population there, the Felasha. In the following centuries, Jews migrated into the Turkish Peninsula, an area where various peoples from Central Asia came in contact with them. In India, the cities of Calcutta and Bombay also had

numerous Jews, who were mostly immigrants from Baghdad. The Jewish populations are largest in Europe, and some scholars argue that most European Jews are descendants of Khazar emigrants to eastern Europe.

In addition, other world religions spread into new areas through migration. Hindus migrated to Southeast Asia, sometimes moving their entire families when they found employment as advisors to the Khmers of Southeast Asia. Christian migration occurred in significant numbers during and after the centuries of European colonization. Many Muslim scholars, teachers, administrators, and judges followed Sufi missionaries and traders into Africa. An example of this is the settlement of

Timbuktu, on the bend of the Niger River in West Africa, which originated around 1100 as a commercial center but by 1400 had become an important Muslim intellectual center.

Trade and Cultural Interaction

The spread of religion through trade and cultural interaction is the most complex of the four factors in the spread of world religions. Although it was closely linked with conquest, missionary activity, and migration, occasionally cultural interaction alone brought conversion. Cultural interaction occurs when travelers, such as merchants or immigrants, bring their religious practices with them into an area. One very important factor in the decision to convert is the perception of the status of the persons in the religion. The politically powerful and the wealthy, such as traders and rulers, were the most likely to serve as models.

Perhaps the most significant catalyst in the spread of world religions was that of trade. Merchants facilitated the spread of religion as they followed the trade routes throughout the globe. Trade, coupled with migration, spread Judaism to China, where a group of Jews resided in the capital city of Song China after receiving permission from the emperor to build a synagogue there. Buddhist merchants from India actively traded in the cities of Southeast Asia and carried their religious practices with them, converting many people. In Dar al-Islam, non-Muslim merchants often converted because an injunction in the Qur'an regarding moral behavior and social interaction made commercial contacts easier and more lucrative for Muslims. In other states, many peoples came into contact with Islam as Muslim traders and merchants traversed the trade routes. Conversions to Islam in Southeast Asia and in sub-Saharan Africa, for example, were primarily the result of the growth of trade. From the eighth century on, Islam spread rapidly along the various trade networks of the fourteenth and fifteenth centuries.

Conversion to a new religion was often a practical economic or political decision. Some Jews in Europe converted to Christianity so that they could protect their property from anti-Jewish mobs or own land. Muslim law forbade the ownership of Muslims as slaves, and conversions in West Africa became common as indigenous people tried to avoid being sold as slaves to Muslim traders. Many people in the Roman Empire converted to Christianity, especially in the first five centuries A.D., because of the unrestricted charitable services offered by Christians to the poor. After the conversion of Constantine in the fourth century, Christians were awarded tax exemptions, and priests were even given monetary grants. People also converted to Islam to avoid the sometimes oppressive taxes on nonbelievers. An intriguing example of mass conversion comes from the eighth century. The king of Khazar (located roughly between the Caucasus mountains and the Volga River) adopted Judaism as the state religion in 740. Many scholars have speculated that this conversion was prompted for political ends. The

FIGURE I.4.3 *Pagoda Mosque.* *Islam traveled with Muslim traders into many areas of the world. In China, Muslims took control of major western trade routes during the eighth century. Converts to Islam employed the local architecture when constructing their mosques. Many pagoda mosques can be found today in northwestern China.* China Features, Beijing.

Khazar state was situated in a strategic military and commercial position, and Byzantine and Muslim interests threatened Khazar independence; one Khazar princess had married a Byzantine emperor to help cement political relations. Khazars may have converted to Judaism to unify the state with a single ideology that was distinct from that of its closest neighbors, making it more difficult to assimilate the Khazar population.

Many people have converted to a new religion for cultural reasons, sometimes because they admire those who practice the religion. Koreans and Japanese in the fourth and sixth centuries, for example, converted to Buddhism because they believed it came from China, and they highly respected Chinese ways. When the Emperor Constantine converted to Christianity, many members of the Roman elite converted in order to gain political advancement. In the Americas, some indigenous peoples living close to European settlements gave up their traditional lifeways and became Christians when they accepted European cultural practices and technology. Some Romans converted to Judaism because they believed monotheism to be more logical than polytheism.

WHEN RELIGIONS AND SOCIETIES MEET

The effects of new religious ideas entering a society often involved changes both in the society and in the practice of the religion. Local customs were blended into religious practice, and social behaviors frequently changed to accommodate the new religious sensibilities. Certain kinds of rituals and attitudes affected lifestyle changes. Particular kinds of clothing were adopted, new foods or the abstinence from foods was introduced, and the prohibition of alcohol or the ritualistic consumption of alcohol was initiated.

Adopting and Adapting New Religions

The adoption of a new religion sometimes met with resistance, affecting how it was integrated with local custom. Buddhism had a difficult time being accepted by the Chinese because of translation problems and social differences. Because Siddhartha Gautama had left his family in order to

seek the meaning of existence, Chinese who believed in loyalty to one's family deplored his actions. Also, in China pork is a favorite food, and many Chinese dishes use it as an ingredient. Muslims, however, are forbidden to eat pork. This cultural barrier caused a serious conflict with Chinese acceptance of Islam. As a consequence, there are few Muslims living in the traditional pork-raising areas of southern China but many more Muslims who populate the traditional sheep-raising western areas. Buddhism sometimes encountered cultural resistance to its promotion of vegetarianism because the consumption of meat was associated with high status and affluence in China, Korea, and Japan.

Often, the culture changed the religion. The prominence of militancy in Japan changed Buddhism, which had initially stressed nonviolence. The warrior-monk became a familiar figure in Japanese politics by the eighth century and caused much bloodshed until the sixteenth century, when the militant sects were destroyed. Zen Buddhism appealed to *samurai* warriors, and Zen priests developed the Japanese martial arts of *karate* and *judo*.

In most cases of the spread of world religions there has been at least some level of adoption or adaptation of ideas and practices. This blending has created new customs and rituals. Some Japanese practiced Buddhism and Shintoism at the same time, mingling elements of both into their daily practices. Originally, December 25 was celebrated by peoples in the Roman Empire as the winter solstice, and, in the fourth century, Christians adopted the date to celebrate Jesus' birth. The adoption of the non-Christian festival date allowed the observance to continue among a population reluctant to abandon a popular festival and transformed this local custom into one of the most celebrated of Christian holy days. The Chinese were influenced by Buddhist ideas, such as the notion of reincarnation. In eastern Mexico, native populations incorporated their own religious beliefs into Christianity, and many native religious elements continue in the practice of Christianity there today.

Syncretic Religions

In some instances a new religion will form, using elements of both the earlier, traditional religion and the newly introduced religion. Such a religion

FIGURE 1.4.4 *The Last Supper.* *Many religions were influenced by the new cultures with which they came in contact. This scene, portraying the passover meal just prior to Jesus' crucifixion, is a common theme in Christian art. The disciples are gathered around the table in traditional poses, but the food is more appropriate to South American palates than to Jewish diets of the first century A.D. or to European Christians. The platter holds a guinea pig, a delicacy to Andean Indians.* South American Pictures.

is called **syncretic**, and an excellent example comes from the Iroquois of the Great Lakes region of Canada and the United States. This example will be given fuller review in order to demonstrate the process of forming a syncretic religion.

Prior to the American Revolution, the six tribes of the Iroquois confederacy thrived. But the Iroquois had allied with the British in the American Revolution, and they received the harshest treatment of all loyalists after the British defeat. Their lands were reduced, orchards were chopped down in retribution, and their livelihood was generally restricted. These disasters led to a tailspin of despair, alcoholism, and general breakdown of the

traditional moral order. By the end of the eighteenth century, the Iroquois were a pale reflection of their former selves, living their lives in what one scholar has termed "slums in the wilderness."

Then, in 1799, an Iroquois named Handsome Lake had the first of several religious visions. In narrating the first vision, Handsome Lake described angels in the form of Iroquois men in ceremonial dress who came to him and instructed him as to the role he was destined to play in the rebirth of the Iroquois people. He was to be a prophet, to instruct the people in morals, and to lead them back to a path of righteousness and prosperity. Those who rejected his message would be relegated to a smoky, hot damnation. Later visions provided more detail about how the Iroquois should reform themselves, what rituals were most important, and what spirits would assist the Iroquois in their victory over circumstances.

Handsome Lake became a well-known prophet of and preacher to the Iroquois. His fame as a preacher became so great that Iroquois traveled far by foot to hear him speak, and his charisma attracted thousands of adherents. He had four main visions before his death in 1815, and from these visions he developed a new religion that drew its inspiration jointly from traditional Iroquois religion and from Christianity.

In general, Handsome Lake advocated the return to practices based on traditional Iroquois values, particularly advocating that Iroquois abstain from alcohol, witchcraft, birth control, gossiping, and domestic violence, all of which had been on the rise in the dark years following the end of the American Revolution. In addition, Iroquois were encouraged to be industrious in seeking work to support their families and in maintaining tribal lands to form a haven against European culture. Handsome Lake advocated adopting a few European ways, mostly regarding education and agricultural technology, but he strongly rejected commercialism and profit, private ownership, and gambling.

In some cases, Handsome Lake's views were adopted so fully that the tribal government enforced his moral code. The primary sanctions against violating this morality, however, came from Christianity. Jesus was one of the spirits that appeared to Handsome Lake, and he and other spirits described a hereafter that had a lovely, restful glade for good Iroquois and a smoky, fiery pit for the bad—clearly the visions of heaven and hell in contemporary Christianity. Sinners, if they repented and wanted to avoid the scorching eternity of hell, could be forgiven after public confession. Confession, heaven, hell, Jesus, and angels all were Christian elements that had no equivalent in earlier Iroquois religion.

Handsome Lake had several disciples, and they preached his teachings after his death. For some years, the religion he preached was practiced by many Iroquois as simply a revised version of their traditional faith, but, around 1840, it was formalized into the modern church called "Longhouse Religion." The name comes from the ceremonial building where many services are held, and the cross that appears inside it speaks eloquently to the merger of the Iroquois cross formed by the junction of the sacred four directions and the Christian cross on which Jesus was crucified. Longhouse Religion is practiced today by perhaps a quarter of the Iroquois.

TOLERANCE AND INTOLERANCE IN WORLD RELIGIONS

Many theological, economic, and political factors affect whether a society will exercise intolerance or encourage tolerance of other religions. In some instances intolerance was the result of monotheism or the idea of holy war. In other instances it was a result of cultural bias. Religious tolerance fostered peace within an empire that included people of diverse religious practices. Tolerance also enabled trade to flow without interruption.

Some theological intolerance stemmed from monotheistic religions' exclusivity. Polytheistic religions, such as Hinduism and Buddhism, typically have no theology that impedes the acceptance of other religious practices, so adherents had no compunction about being intolerant or forcing conversions. According to ancient Jewish tradition, Jews were forbidden to intermarry with non-Jews and often discriminated against those who did. In medieval Europe, Jews were frequently subjected to violence, in which their businesses, their homes, and their lives were destroyed. Jews in many European cities were also forced to live in **ghettoes** (an Italian word that means the Jewish section of a city).

Intolerance was sometimes a consequence of wars of conquest by conquerors who believed in the superiority of their religion and believed that they were fighting a holy war. When ancient Jews conquered the area of Canaan in ancient Palestine, they believed that it was necessary to eliminate non-Jews in order to keep their religion pure from what they saw as contamination through cultural interaction. When Muslims expanded into India during *jihad* (Muslim holy war), they destroyed or defaced many Buddhist and Hindu temples and statues. One raiding party destroyed the university at Nalanda in 1193. Christian crusaders from medieval Europe conquered the Palestine area in a holy war to extract ancient Christian sites from Arab Muslim control. In all these examples, holy war was the extreme expression of intolerance.

In many areas, however, tolerance of a variety of religious practices prevailed. Muslims tolerated both Jews and Christians as "people of protection" or "people of the book," referring to the scriptures shared by the three monotheistic traditions. Jews and Christians were tolerated but not given equal status in Muslim countries. In contrast to other areas in Europe, the Muslim city of Toledo, Spain, in the tenth century tolerated Judaism and had more than 10,000 Jewish citizens. Many non-Muslims found living under Islamic law tolerable but converted anyway for financial or social advantages. In the twelfth century, toleration of Jews and Muslims was a policy of the Norman kings of Sicily, in part because of trade connections. Also, several Christian missionary societies worked against the political and social exploitation of the European colonizers in the seventeenth and eighteenth centuries because they believed the practices violated Christian principles.

SUGGESTED READINGS

Chadwick, Henry, and G. R. Evans, eds. *Atlas of the Christian Church.* Oxford, Eng.: Equinox, 1987. A well-illustrated history of the development and spread of Christianity.

Faruqi, Isma'il Ragial, and David Sopher, eds. *Historical Atlas of the Religions of the World.* New York: Macmillan, 1974. A good review of world religions, with excellent maps.

Fisher, Sydney, and William Ochsenwald, eds. *The Middle East: A History.* Fourth edition. New York: McGraw-Hill, 1990. A history of the spread of Islam within the broader context of Dar al-Islam expansion.

McManners, John. *The Oxford Illustrated History of Christianity.* New York: Oxford University Press, 1990. A general history of Christianity in all parts of the world through the twentieth century.

Monroe, Charles R. *World Religions.* Amherst, N.Y.: Prometheus Books, 1995. A good general survey of major religions and philosophies.

THE PRECEDING PAGES HAVE TRACED THE HUMAN STORY from some millions of years ago to around A.D.1500. They have scrutinized some periods and peoples, and they have examined others more lightly. Even this vastly simplified version of the past is very complicated, and it is easy to get mired in the details, losing sight of the main currents of development. Part Five tries to place this vast period in perspective, searching out patterns and trends over time. It draws attention to events that are the last gasps of a changing order and other events that foreshadow the modern era to come.

Chapter 20 looks at this period from the focused perspective of science and technology. How well were the processes of the natural world understood? How skilled were people at harnessing the natural world to control them? How much did science and technology influence each other?

PART FIVE

PERSPECTIVES

Chapter 21 examines the broad sweep of human existence, focusing on issues that have had profound effects in shaping the world. Oriented around the growth of population as a long-term and consistent trend, this chapter links many developments to their demographic basis. How has the inexorable growth of human population affected history? How have people met their obligations to increasingly demanding governments? What role has trade played in the unfolding of human history? How have people's self-conceptions and allegiances changed in response to a more complicated world? And, finally, how much environmental degradation have human beings wreaked on their planet?

Medieval European Farming. *Around the world, technology has transformed everyday life. This fourteenth-century illustration shows a medieval European farmer using a horse-drawn harrow to till a field. The domestication of animals and the use of iron tools (the blades of the plows and harrows used to turn the soil and the blades of the scythes used to harvest grain) increased productivity. In the background, a scarecrow dressed as an archer guards a planted field.*
Giraudon/Art Resource, N.Y.

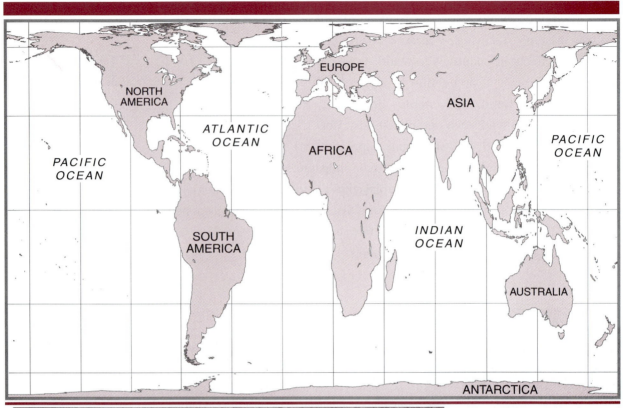

A Traditional Blacksmith from Ghana. *Using a bellows to raise the heat of his fire, a blacksmith shapes iron in a manner that can be traced back many centuries.* Larry Burrrows, *Life* Magazine, ©Time Inc.

Technology and Science

Before 1500

A sweaty blacksmith, skin caked with soot, heats his iron to a dull red. He murmurs a prayer, then slides a willow sapling among the coals and tosses on a small cup of bull urine. He nestles the iron into its fiery bed, confident that it will be strong.

For centuries, practical technologists such as this blacksmith followed arcane procedures to control the fashioning of products. Occasionally, accident or ingenuity sparked a new discovery, with widespread impact.

Historians often focus on political, military, and economic events. The expansion of a state into an empire, the conquest of neighboring lands, the creation of a middle class—developments like these sometimes dominate history texts, but it is important to remember that many of these changes were made possible by new technology. Some of these critical technological developments have been discussed in the previous chapters, including irrigation, iron, paper, and gunpowder. This chapter will investigate some of these and other technological feats further and will consider the relationship between technology and science in the period before 1500.

THE RELATIONSHIP BETWEEN TECHNOLOGY AND SCIENCE

Technology and science seem so enmeshed today that many people think of the two as an inseparable pair, but a major distinction can be drawn between them. As used in this chapter, **technology** is the study of making devices that serve a purpose; **science**, on the other hand, is the quest to understand phenomena, to learn how things work and the reasons behind their operation. Technology is interested only in making something that serves a purpose, regardless of whether the principles behind the device are understood; science is concerned with knowledge, both general principles and specific facts. Technology is interested only in *whether* a device operates; science is interested in *how* and *why* things operate. Technology is applied; science is theoretical.

This distinction, of course, has not always been made by historic societies. Medieval Europe, for example, made less of a distinction between science and technology, considering both to be aspects of natural philosophy; Islamic science in this period fused science, technology, and religion together into a single category of knowledge; and other societies have had their own unique ways of conceiving of the relationship between applied and theoretical activities.

Historians of science, too, differ in how they conceive of science and technology. Some distinguish between science and technology on the basis of goals, as we do here; others distinguish on the basis of methodology; still others focus on whether practitioners reached conclusions similar to those reached by modern science. One school of thinking suggests that any distinction made between science and technology is misleading, because the overlaps are so great. All of these viewpoints lead to valuable insights, but we believe that seeing science and technology as distinguished by their goals will help point out a broad pattern in this period.

The magnetic compass provides an example of the dichotomy between science and technology. It was well known by the twelfth century in China and most of Eurasia that a piece of magnetite ("lodestone") would always point southward if suspended by a string or floated on a tiny raft in a bowl of water. How to make and use the compass—the domain of technology—was firmly established. For about a century, however, why the compass worked—the domain of science—was considered mysterious. In the thirteenth century, scholars in Europe and China seized upon the scientific issue and attempted to explain magnetism. Although these thirteenth-century attempts invoked different principles from those involved in the modern explanation established by physics in the nineteenth century, they still are scientific, because they tried to explain systematically why the magnetic compass operated.

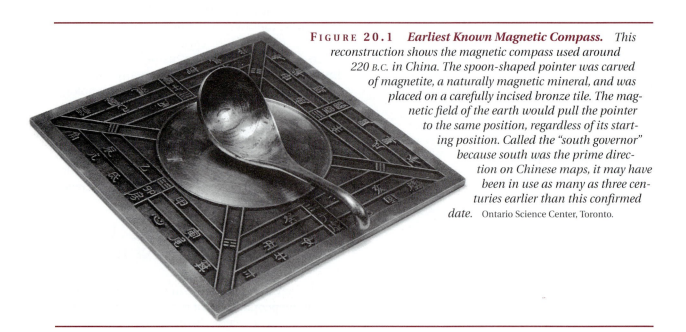

FIGURE 20.1 *Earliest Known Magnetic Compass.* *This reconstruction shows the magnetic compass used around 220 B.C. in China. The spoon-shaped pointer was carved of magnetite, a naturally magnetic mineral, and was placed on a carefully incised bronze tile. The magnetic field of the earth would pull the pointer to the same position, regardless of its starting position. Called the "south governor" because south was the prime direction on Chinese maps, it may have been in use as many as three centuries earlier than this confirmed date.* Ontario Science Center, Toronto.

EXAMPLES OF TECHNOLOGICAL INNOVATION

From the thousands of examples of technological discoveries before 1500, a few cases illustrate some of the common threads that run through them and the diversity that separates them.

Domesticated Plants and Animals

We do not normally think of agriculture and pastoralism as technological achievements, probably because we usually focus on the great changes in human behavior that came about with these modes of subsistence. Nonetheless, new and improved devices were involved: the crops and livestock themselves. We have discussed agriculture at some length in Chapter 3, and here we focus only on aspects relating directly to science and technology.

Recall that "domestication" refers to the act of genetically modifying a plant or animal from its wild ancestor so that it will be more useful to human beings. The first corn plants had only a few tiny seeds and required a long growing season; they were modified for greater production and more rapid maturation. The first wheat plants had seeds with brittle connections to their stalks, meaning that much grain was lost in harvesting because it fell to the ground at the slightest movement of the plant; they were modified to produce a tough connection that would withstand the rigors of harvesting. Hundreds of other crops have been transformed to increase their production, improve their quality, or modify their growing requirements so that they can be grown in a wider range of environments.

Even more critical were the modifications that had to be made in domesticating animals. While a corn plant with only a few kernels might have been a nuisance, it was not dangerous. Cattle or swine with the aggressive temperament and nasty disposition of their wild ancestors, however, were quite another matter. Most of the animals that have been domesticated for human use were quite savage in the wild, and it would have been critical to tame them before they could become a major part of human economies. Taming individual animals would have been time consuming and only imperfectly effective, because the aggressive behavioral traits were instinctual.

How did early domesticators go about modifying their crops and livestock? Because all early

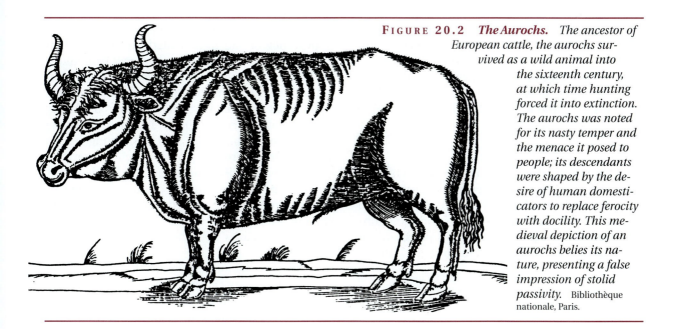

FIGURE 20.2 *The Aurochs.* *The ancestor of European cattle, the aurochs survived as a wild animal into the sixteenth century, at which time hunting forced it into extinction. The aurochs was noted for its nasty temper and the menace it posed to people; its descendants were shaped by the desire of human domesticators to replace ferocity with docility. This medieval depiction of an aurochs belies its nature, presenting a false impression of stolid passivity.* Bibliothèque nationale, Paris.

domestication took place long before writing, we must rely upon indirect evidence. It may be reasonable to assume that modern hunters and gatherers might have a similar knowledge of plant and animal breeding to that of the earliest domesticators. The twentieth-century !Kung[1] of Southwest Africa eat *magongo*[2] nuts, the fruit of a wild tree, but they normally consume only the smaller nuts. The larger nuts are thrown into ravines, where the greater moisture encourages their germination. As the !Kung say, the bigger nuts are likely to produce trees that produce bigger nuts. Similarly, various hunters might have tried to kill the most aggressive of wild animals, arguing that removal of such animals from a population would make animals in future generations less hostile and easier to hunt.

All hunters and gatherers have recognized that offspring will resemble their parents, among plants and animals, as well as people. This is an example of scientific recognition, because it invokes a general principle to explain why something happens. Presumably, early domesticators used scientific recognition to see that the plants and animals with the most desired traits were bred for the next generation, while those with unwanted characteristics were killed before they could reproduce.

Probably the practical knowledge of inherited traits was discovered as it related to people, then extended to animals, then to plants. Alternatively, it may have been discovered as people observed the results of their propagation of plants or animals. Either way, it was a scientific recognition important for domestication, despite the fact that these early domesticators had no knowledge of genes, chromosomes, heredity, or other modern concepts of reproductive biology.

Iron and Steel

Iron has many advantages over other metals for the making of tools. If treated properly, iron can be very hard and durable, and it can be sharpened to a keen edge. In addition, iron is a common substance and can be produced in most places. But it also has some significant technological draw-

[1]**!Kung:** KUNG, preceded by a click produced by sucking air out from under the sides of the tongue; many Westerners pronounce the word without the click.
[2]*magongo:* mah GOHNG goh

backs: It requires a more sophisticated process for refining than do the other metals that were commonly used for tools in antiquity (copper, tin, zinc, lead, silver, and gold), and it will be soft, malleable, or brittle if not treated properly. Before going into the historical aspects of iron making, we shall review the technological factors that are involved in its manufacture.

Iron on our planet occurs almost exclusively as **ore**, compounds in which the metal is chemically bonded to other elements. (The exceptions are mostly meteorites that have struck earth while passing through space, and they were used to make ornaments before iron was used for tools.) Before the iron from ore can be used, the other elements must be removed by smelting. Copper or lead ores can be smelted at low temperatures, of the sort obtained in a hot campfire, but iron ores require a much higher temperature. To obtain this temperature, air must be pumped onto the fire through bellows or some other mechanism, increasing the oxygen concentration and the heat of combustion. In addition, only certain fuels will attain the necessary temperature, notably hardwood charcoal.

Once the iron ore has been smelted, the impure iron is allowed to run out of the smelter, forming a rocky mass called the **bloom**. This bloom can be refined further simply by hammering it when hot, mechanically forcing the glassy impurities from it. When enough impurities have been removed so that the iron attains a metallic appearance, it can be reheated and poured into molds. This form of iron is called **cast iron** and is useful for some purposes, such as cauldrons, but it is brittle and soft, making it of little use for most tools. Cast iron can be made more useful by reheating it and continuing to hammer it, driving out still more impurities and converting it into **wrought iron**. Wrought iron is much harder than cast iron, but it still has a tendency to brittleness or malleability. If the worker pounds the heated wrought iron into the desired shape and plunges it, still hot, into water to cool it rapidly, the resulting iron will be harder still; this process is known as **annealing**.

One more factor determines the quality of the iron produced: its carbide content. Pure iron, no matter how it is treated, is not a terribly hard metal. But small amounts of iron carbide, formed by the chemical bonding of iron and carbon, produce **steel**, a much harder and more useful substance. Hence, to produce harder iron—steel—the smelter must introduce free carbon into the iron while it is molten or at least heated to a high temperature.

This is an impressive suite of techniques that must be controlled to produce high-quality iron tools. High-temperature fires are needed in the smelting; free carbon must be introduced into the molten iron; the iron must be cast, then wrought; and finally it must be annealed. To make matters worse, few of these techniques could be borrowed from earlier metallurgical practice because metals used earlier had different characteristics and required different treatment. Quenching hot copper or bronze rapidly in water, for example, actually makes it softer and less useful.

The earliest smelting of iron appears to have taken place in Anatolia, around 2000 B.C., about the time of the Hittite rise to power there. From this start, iron smelting spread around the eastern Mediterranean—to India, to Europe, and eventually to the Americas after Columbus. The Chinese began making iron around the seventh century B.C.; theirs was probably an independent invention of iron-making technology. African iron making may have been either invented independently or carried from India by traders.

Our best documentary information on early iron making comes from Southwest Asia and, later, Europe. There, literature tells us that swords often received names and were thought of as having individual characteristics, almost like personalities. Literature from *The Odyssey* onward describes the particular attributes of specific swords, and one of the more fabled swords, the Excalibur of Britain's King Arthur, was described as "a most excellent sword." These descriptions were not just literary contrivances of the authors or delusions of the warriors. Indeed, different weapons varied greatly in their qualities, largely related to the quality of the metal from which they were made. For iron swords, the critical variables usually were the amount of iron carbide in them and the techniques employed by their makers.

Contemporary accounts of early iron making are understandably rare, because the iron makers wished to retain their trade secrets. We do know, however, that there were many procedures in-

FIGURE 20.3 *Forging a* **Samurai** *Sword.* *The early forging of edged weapons of iron was attended in most places by complicated rituals that lay somewhere between magic and science, and Japan was no exception. This painting from the sixteenth century shows several Japanese swordmakers performing the range of operations necessary—including prayer—to produce a good* samurai *sword. While the men make swords, a woman makes tea.* Werner Forman/Art Resource, N.Y.

volved that to the modern mind seem unrelated to the manufacture of iron. Hittite blacksmiths, for example, were required to abstain from sexual activity with women before making a sword. Their contemporaries in Mesopotamia had incantations that had to be recited during the making of the sword, as did thirteenth-century Japanese smiths. And almost everywhere there were seemingly useless additions to the smelting vessel or the bed of coals where the iron was heated for hammering. The recitation of an incantation might serve the practical purpose of ensuring that a process lasts a certain amount of time, but most of these actions seem better explained as attempts to infuse the

UNDER THE LENS
Recipes for Fine Iron

Detailed accounts of iron working in premedieval times are rare. Most iron workers were illiterate, and their work was judged degrading and was unlikely to catch the attention of the literate elite. Further, there was little incentive to write down detailed accounts, because many of the practices were trade secrets, jealously guarded rather than indiscriminately advertised.

From later periods, however, after time had erased much of the secrecy associated with iron working, there are many accounts of how to produce the best iron. Most of these are excellent examples of how physics and metaphysics blended in early science.

An example comes from medieval Poland. A remarkable ninety-two-page poem extolling iron and its makers was published around 1598 by Walenty Roździeński,[a] a Polish smith. This work, the *Officina Ferraria*, includes explanations for the mechanisms by which the quality of the iron can be controlled. A few quotations illustrate that physical and magical mechanisms were considered to control the process.

> Certain tests, they say, show that the iron of no other country [than Spain] is sharper. It is obviously the water in which the smiths quench the iron that brings this about. . . . The iron here has an especial substance, but the water is stronger than iron itself; quenching in it increases the sharpness of the iron.

Modern physics tells us that the strength of iron is related to how quickly it is annealed ("quenched"), not some special property of the water in which it is quenched.

> In Styria also they dig ore with the property of yielding both steel and plain iron; but steel has to be smelted twice, while iron is smelted only once.

The carbide content—the discriminating feature between iron and steel—resides not in the ore but in the carbon introduced, in this case, during the second smelting. And in discussing the Polish ore from Nikwa, Roździeński notes that steel can be made from it, but only if the smith uses "charcoal from young pine trees, since charcoal from other kinds of wood won't do." The young pines, with their greater sap content, presumably burned slowly enough to liberate free carbon that could incorporate with the iron to produce steel.

> In olden times some elves . . . used to haunt forges. . . . Those forgemasters whose forges they haunted had great luck, everything went well for them, almost according to what they had in mind, both in the craft of ironwork and in everything else.

[a]**Walenty Roździeński:** vah LEHN tee ROHZH dzee EHN skee

---

iron with the perceived characteristics of a particular material.

An example of these actions is the so-called **green withy**[3] **smelting** of pre-Roman Britain. In this process, fresh twigs of willow and similar plants ("withies") were added to the molten iron shortly before it was poured out. In this manner, the withies would burn just sufficiently to yield free carbon that converted the iron to steel. From the point of view of the iron makers, however, the withies were important for their mystical properties, giving the resulting iron flexibility, like the willow from which the withies came. This connection, of course, makes no sense in terms of modern scientific conceptions, but it clearly is a scientific explanation. It seeks a general principle that explains *why* a procedure works.

Shortly after Southwest Asia was developing iron technology, so was China. There, wrought iron was being produced by the seventh century B.C., cast-iron tools by the sixth century B.C., and steel by the second century B.C. Unlike in Southwest Asia, Europe, or Africa, iron working in China very rapidly attained mass production, largely because the required technological elements already existed and needed only to be brought together. Efficient furnaces that could be used for iron smelting had been developed for the manufacture of fine pottery, bellows had been used in bronze casting, and fluxes (agents to reduce the melting temperature of something) were known from ceramic manufacture.

[3]**withy:** WIHTH ee

Chinese iron making also followed scientific principles, although those principles again were different from modern ones. For example, swords were classed according to the number of "refinings," that is, how many times their iron had been folded and hammered together when heated. Texts inform us that contemporary Chinese believed that swords with greater numbers of refinings were stronger, yet the physical principle underlying their strength related to their carbide content, which is essentially unrelated to the number of refinings.

Wherever iron was made, its quality improved over time. In any area, the earliest iron was the most variable, including pieces that were scarcely usable. With time, however, the softest and most brittle pieces became less common, and the finest iron was superior to that of a generation before. This pattern is evidence that the iron makers were attentive to the results of their procedures, adjusting their techniques when they saw improvement. At the same time, however, there is little evidence that theoretical, scientific understanding of iron metallurgy kept pace.

Although iron in most areas became an incredibly important material shortly after the onset of its use, especially for military purposes, there is no evidence that scholars took much interest in it during this period. This may relate to the traditional status of blacksmiths from India through Southwest Asia, the Mediterranean, and Europe. While recognized as critical to society, blacksmiths were viewed as degraded as a result of their profession. In India, ironworkers formed one of the lowest castes, and less rigid social systems elsewhere relegated them to similar lowly positions. Perhaps scholars were reluctant to show interest in such an undervalued subject.

Ships and Shipbuilding

The oldest known archaeological remains of a boat come from northern Europe about 12,000 years ago. However, water transportation is known to be much older. The peopling of Australia 50,000 or more years ago must have been accomplished by boats of some sort, because there never was a land bridge connecting Australia to Asia. These early boats, however, presumably were small and simple, probably rafts or dugout canoes. Such simple conveyances would have been suggested the first time someone saw a log or a mat of vegetation floating down a river, and they would have required little genius or special skill to develop.

Later vessels, however, became larger, particularly as long-distance trade burgeoned and these ships became the vehicles for much of that trade. All of the ancient civilizations with access to waterways achieved a certain level of shipbuilding skill, but the Greeks stand out as particularly capable. Given the geography of Greece, with its long and convoluted coastline and almost all of its ancient population along the sea, it is not surprising that ancient Greeks relied heavily on maritime transportation. In addition, their large population and limited agricultural base forced them to trade with the outside world for food.

Ships of the Greek Classical period were of two types, named for their shapes: long ships and round ships. **Long ships** were long and narrow, with a typical length-to-width ratio of 10:1. Such ships were fast, yet they had great difficulties weathering storms and had limited space on board. (The space was so limited that there were neither stores nor galley, so the ship had to send its crew ashore twice daily to forage for meals.) Used almost exclusively for military purposes by governments or pirates, these warships were equipped with a bronze ram at the prow and were propelled by one or more banks of rowers. The most effective of these long ships, the **trireme**,[4] had three banks of rowers and could attain speeds of approximately 8 to 10 miles per hour for prolonged periods and spurts up to nearly 15 miles per hour. Triremes typically were about 120 feet long and carried a crew of around 170 rowers and 30 officers and marines.

The other principal type of ancient Greek ship was the **round ship**, which was much broader, usually with a length-to-width ratio around 4:1. This made it less sleek than its long ship cousin, and it was much slower. On the other hand, it had much more space on board, so it was used primarily as a trading vessel. An added virtue of its squat shape was its ability to survive stormy weather, especially if it was fully burdened and rode low in the water. Round ships usually were considerably larger than long ships, often running 150 to 200 feet in length. Powered by sails exclusively, round ships averaged about 4 miles per hour.

[4]**trireme:** TRY reem

FIGURE 20.4 *Greek Trireme.* *This full-scale replica of a Greek trireme was produced as part of an experiment to assess the difficulties of making and using such a long ship. A full complement of rowers propelled this vessel in the Mediterranean Sea. The experiment showed that the trireme was less seaworthy and more fragile than documentary records had suggested.* Trireme Trust, Courtesy of John Coates.

The Greeks experimented widely with ship design. One experimental vessel built in the third century B.C. was reported to have been more than 400 feet long and to have carried more than 4,000 rowers. This mammoth vessel survived its initial tests, but it was so difficult either to power or maneuver that it was kept permanently in port as a monument to Ptolemy IV, the Greek ruler of Egypt who had commissioned its construction. Other experiments, less ambitious but more practical, produced innovative arrangements to increase the number of rowers, improved steering systems, and assembled masts and sails in ways that permitted sailing farther away from the direction of the wind. Some of these were successful and were incorporated into future designs, while others were mercifully forgotten.

At the same time that shipbuilders were developing the Greek fleets, scholars were exploring the physics of water pressure and buoyancy. The most noteworthy and influential of these was Archimedes[5] (287–212 B.C.), whose interest in the subject is traced in a story recounted by his contemporaries. Archimedes was entering his bath in a public bathing house and sloshed water out of the tub. Suddenly recognizing that the amount of water displaced was equal to the volume of his body, he rushed home to work on his idea, shouting "*Eureka!*" ("I have found it!"). Unfortunately, he neglected to clothe himself and was remembered ever after for his famous nude dash through Syracuse.

Archimedes studied how water was displaced by solids immersed in it, how density affected whether a solid would float or sink, and how the shape of the lower portion of a floating solid

[5]**Archimedes:** ahr kih MEE deez

affected its stability. Another of his studies examined the relationship between the length of a lever and its efficiency. All of these areas of study could have been directly applicable to shipbuilding, and Archimedes even used examples of oars and masts to discuss his principles of leverage. Nonetheless, these scholarly findings were never translated into improved vessels. Archimedes' discoveries were the closest ancient Greeks came to bridging the gap between scholarly science and applied technology, yet even he didn't use these principles to improve Greek shipbuilding.

Why were these revolutionary and potentially valuable insights not applied to the practical world of shipbuilding? The answers lie partly in the division of labor, partly in economics, and partly in the philosophy of ancient Greece. First, the shipbuilders were of a vastly different class from Archimedes, and probably few or none ever read scholarly discussions of science or took part in discussions of it. They most likely were unaware that Archimedes' principles even existed.

Second, some of the improvements that Archimedes' findings might have prompted were of little benefit to the Greek economic system. Improving the efficiency of delivering power from rower to oar to vessel was not a major concern, because labor was abundant and cheap. Slave economies are not always attuned to labor-saving devices or machines that use power more efficiently. In fact, such devices sometimes have been considered dangerous, because they threaten to idle huge numbers of slaves, giving them time to contemplate rebellion.

Third, ancient Greek philosophers made a major distinction between material things and essential things. Codified by Plato but really existing before him, this distinction held that you could hold a real rock (a material thing), but that the essence of "rockness" was a concept that could be treated only in thought. Plato's famous analogy was that we see only the shadows thrown onto the wall of the cave by something passing between a fire and the wall. The shadow is the material thing; the unseen body that casts the shadow is the essential thing.

By definition and inclination, Greek scholars dealt with essential things. Their discussions, therefore, were on a logical plane, dealing with general principles, and there was a general disdain for application of those principles to everyday things, even for most empirical testing. Their preferred mode of operation was to ponder a problem, come up with a logical explanation, and then move on to another problem. Hero, probably a contemporary of Archimedes, actually conducted a few experiments in the physics of water pressure, but he was a rare exception, and his conclusions had no more effect on shipbuilding than those of his colleagues.

Gunpowder

The first explosive to be successfully produced and used, gunpowder is simply a finely ground mixture of three common substances: charcoal, sulphur, and saltpeter. Charcoal can be produced anywhere there is wood; sulphur can be mined from most volcanic deposits; and saltpeter can be either mined or scraped from the bottom of dung heaps or from old mortar, where it forms naturally. Chemically speaking, the sulphur serves to instigate a reaction, because its flash point is low and it can be set off by a low-temperature flame. The heat released from the burning sulphur then forces the saltpeter to liberate oxygen, which supports the ignition of the charcoal to a high temperature. These joint reactions occur very rapidly and release large volumes of gases, creating the rapid expansion that we call an explosion. In an open area, ignited gunpowder burns with a great hissing, but, if enclosed, the gases expand outward, rupturing their container. If a single outlet is provided, most of the force of the expansion will funnel through that outlet, carrying a cannonball or other missile with it.

Gunpowder was invented in China, probably around the ninth century, and appears first in a Daoist text warning others to avoid the author's accidental destruction of his house by mixing together three seemingly innocent substances. By 950 it was being used for **flare weapons**, tubes that projected the fiery flash of a gunpowder explosion toward an enemy; a century later, it was used also for bombs, rockets, and land mines; by 1270, Mongols were using Chinese cannons to propel projectiles at enemies.

Although the use of gunpowder weapons in China was widespread in the centuries following their invention, their impact on Chinese society was surprisingly minor. The Chinese political and economic systems persisted with little disruption, and gunpowder weapons became simply some of the many devices available for use in war. In fact,

FIGURE 20.5 *Early Chinese Incendiary Device.* *This sixteenth-century drawing shows "the enemy-of-ten-thousand-men," a gunpowder device for the defense of fortified cities. A contemporary document states that it should be used "to defend remotely located small cities, in which the cannons are either weak in firing power or too heavy and clumsy to be effective weapons." This device was said to kill with its flame and poisonous smoke. Gunpowder weapons appeared first in China, but later became more important tools of war in Europe.* R. B. Fleming.

gunpowder weaponry waned in importance in China, with the result that seventeenth-century Jesuits from Europe were employed by the Chinese government to instruct in casting cannons, a skill apparently lost in the four centuries since the invention of cannons in China.

Unlike in China, the military use of gunpowder in Europe had far-reaching effects. Gunpowder came to the Arab world and to Europe by the thirteenth century. In Europe, its use quickly stimulated the construction of firearms, although it is unclear whether these were independently invented or copied from Chinese models. By 1326, guns were mentioned in an Italian manuscript, and a gun was illustrated in an English document the following year.

Clockmakers were the first European gun and cannon makers, and they transferred many of their precise technological skills directly to the making of various sorts of firearms. **Bombs,** fully enclosed vessels filled with gunpowder and ignited with a slow fuse, could be surreptitiously placed against a fortification or could be delivered from the air by a kite with a long string release. **Firepots** were pot-like vessels with modest amounts of gunpowder and fist-sized stones or metal darts that could be directed toward a light fortification or a mass of soldiers. Firepots were made larger and larger, until recognizable cannons were in use by 1346. Another modification of these firepots that appeared in Belgium by 1337 was a massing of up to 144 narrow firepots, projecting missiles the size of an egg or smaller. Mounted together on a frame, they were a potent killing system that could be fired quite rapidly. By 1374 the English had dismantled this weapon, mounted its barrels on sep-

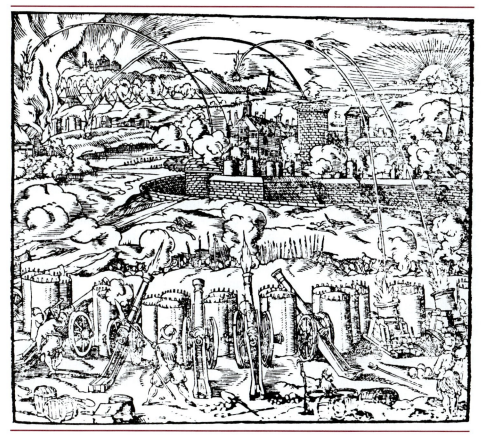

FIGURE 20.6   *A European Siege.*   *In this sixteenth-century engraving, cannons and mortars besiege a walled city. The arcs of flight of the projectiles are reminders of the importance of ballistics, a branch of applied mathematics being developed at that time.*
Courtesy of Ian Hogg.

arate wooden stocks, and distributed them to foot soldiers; these were the ancestors of the modern rifle. All these weapons were unwieldy and inaccurate, but they (and their improved successors) revolutionized warfare.

The European understanding of the chemistry of gunpowder was framed by the scientific understanding of the day. Matter was seen as composed of four essential elements, and the explosive nature of gunpowder was associated with hot and dry elements. The association of sulphur with hell and volcanoes was not lost on Europeans, nor was the great heat with which charcoal burned. The role of saltpeter, a white powder that tastes salty and has no obvious connection to explosives, was less well understood. As a result, European gunpowder makers maximized the content of sulphur, actually using almost twice the optimal percentage. Saltpeter, in contrast, was minimized. These decisions were based on current understanding of

science, but their practical effect was that the explosive was about 15 percent less powerful than the optimal mixture. Only in 1790, when scholars produced a greatly different conception of the chemical reactions taking place, did Europeans adjust the formula for gunpowder to achieve maximum effect. (Chinese gunpowder makers, too, underestimated the role of saltpeter, using insufficient amounts until around 1300.)

Gunpowder had different effects on the development of various branches of European scholarship. While the science of chemistry received little impetus from gunpowder technology, the branch of mathematics and physics that dealt with cannonball propulsion was greatly stimulated. This study, **ballistics**, had begun with the catapults and other war engines of earlier periods, but their inherent inaccuracy made intensive ballistic study irrelevant. Cannons, however, could be aimed more accurately, and elevating the shot appropriately

FIGURE 20.7 *German Saltpeter Factory. Saltpeter was a critical component of gunpowder, but it was the one most difficult for medieval Europeans to acquire in quantity. Vast mineral deposits of saltpeter in South America were unavailable to them, and saltpeter in Europe had to be laboriously collected from beneath dung piles, from excrescences on mortared walls, or from low-quality mineral deposits mixed with earth. This sixteenth-century engraving shows the German process for refining mineral deposits, based on leaching out saltpeter with water that was later evaporated.* Image Select, London.

became a major challenge. Elaborate tables and graphs of proper elevations for given charges and ball weights were compiled. These ballistic tables included the results of both trial and error and the utilization of mathematical principles.

EXAMPLES OF SCHOLARLY SCIENCE

Not every society has had scholars. There were, however, several well-established scholarly traditions in the world prior to 1500, and this section presents examples of their scholarship.

Chinese Astronomy

From the Han Dynasty onward, Chinese rulers maintained programs of astronomical research that employed dozens, sometimes hundreds, of astronomers. Two incentives generated this intense interest.

First, one means of legitimizing a royal house was through the establishment and maintenance of the calendar. The solar year consists of slightly more than 365 days, 365.2422 days to be more exact, and this means that any calendar will naturally get out of step with the stars over time. To avoid this, days were added periodically, and properly doing so was seen as a measure of the legitimacy of rule.

Second, celestial bodies were seen in a direct and unchanging relationship to the earthly and human world. Different constellations, for example, were seen as associated with different Chinese provinces, and different portions of the sky were thought to be connected to different feudal states or dynasties. Positions of stars and planets were seen as favoring or disfavoring particular kinds of activities. They were seen as the Mandate of Heaven (the deity) in physical manifestation, transmitted on to people through the stars. As stated in the *I Ching*,[6] a Chinese treatise written in the eleventh century B.C., "the heavens manifest good and evil signs through the celestial phenomena." In short, the Chinese study of celestial bodies was seen as necessary for astrology, the predicting the course of the future and the determination of divine will through the examination of celestial movements.

Given these incentives, Chinese scholars understandably were highly concerned with the prediction of astronomical events. They divided such events into one class that was inherently predictable (such as the rising of Venus) and one class that was difficult or impossible to predict (such as eclipses and supernovas). Prediction was based on the recognition of number series and their reduction to algebraic formulas. This procedure bore no implications in terms of actual positions or movements of the celestial bodies involved, and there was no official theory of movements of stars and planets. Scholars debated possibilities, but the governmental bureaucracy remained silent on the issue.

[6]*I Ching:* EE CHIHNG

S ima Qian, a Chinese scholar of the first century B.C., specialized in both astronomy and history. He summarized his view of the relationship between humanity and the heavens in the following excerpt, which sheds light on the ancient Chinese association between earthly and celestial events.

IN THEIR OWN WORDS
The Chinese Heavens

> Since the beginning, when humankind came into being, rulers in successive eras have observed the motions of the sun, moon, and stars. Through the reigns of the Five Emperors and Three Kings [i.e., throughout antiquity], as the effort was continued their knowledge became clearer. [China, the land of] the ceremonial cap and belt, was considered "inside," and [the lands of] the other peoples considered "outside." The Middle Lands were divided into twelve provinces. Looking up, they contemplated the signs in the sky. Looking downward, they found analogues to these on the earth. In the sky there were the sun and moon; on earth, *yin* and *yang*. In the sky there were the Five Planets; on earth, the Five Elements. In the sky there were the lunar mansions [i.e., constellations]; on earth, the territorial divisions. The Three Luminaries [i.e., the sun, moon, and planets] are the seminal *qi*[a] of *yin* and *yang*. The *qi* [i.e., material essence] originally resides on earth, and the Sages unify and organize it. Since the time of Kings Yu and Li of the Zhou era, the ruling house of each state used different means of divination to find a way to conform to the exigencies of the time as manifested in celestial omens. From their documents and books no rules whatever for portents can be extracted. Therefore when Confucius laid out the Six Classics, he merely recorded abnormal phenomena and did not write down interpretations.

[a]*qi:* CHEE

While their techniques were largely descriptive rather than explanatory, Chinese scholars were quite successful in their predictions. By around 100 B.C., Chinese astronomers were able to predict accurately the period of Halley's comet and the occurrence of lunar eclipses. Around A.D. 400, Chinese astronomers developed a mechanical device to represent the stars in their positions in the sky, and by 1088 they had developed a water-driven clock tower to show the stars' movements. As celestial movements became more predictable, their value in astrology became lessened.

Using our distinction of technology and science, ancient Chinese astronomy was a mixture of the two. On the one hand, it sought out and described regularities in natural phenomena, making it science. On the other hand, it incorporated little interest in explaining the phenomena, instead focusing more on the practical implications for calendrics and astrology, and in that sense it was technology.

Indian Dietetics

Charaka is the traditional author of a scholarly treatise that appeared in India around 50 B.C. Charaka may have been a single individual or a

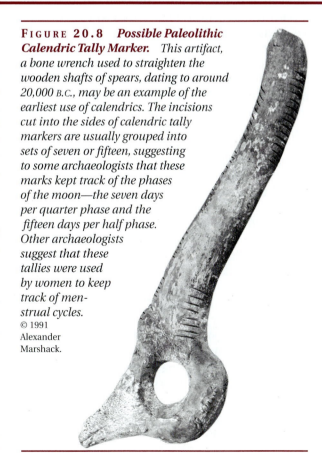

FIGURE 20.8 *Possible Paleolithic Calendric Tally Marker. This artifact, a bone wrench used to straighten the wooden shafts of spears, dating to around 20,000 B.C., may be an example of the earliest use of calendrics. The incisions cut into the sides of calendric tally markers are usually grouped into sets of seven or fifteen, suggesting to some archaeologists that these marks kept track of the phases of the moon—the seven days per quarter phase and the fifteen days per half phase. Other archaeologists suggest that these tallies were used by women to keep track of menstrual cycles.*
© 1991 Alexander Marshack.

composite of several, but his *Samhita*[7] formed the basis for Indian medicine in the period before 1500. Much of what Charaka codified probably had been derived earlier.

At the base of Charaka's system was a classification of five states of matter, the different combinations of which could produce various characteristics. A person's food was composed of a mixture of those five states, and one's diet affected one's person. Proper eating, therefore, was the route to proper health.

Proper eating, however, was not simple. The goal was to achieve a balance of the states of matter, but many factors affected that balance. Each person, for example, had a different constitution that was dominated by one of several states. A rajasic[8] person, for example, was dominated by a hot nature, expressed in enthusiasm, energy, impulsiveness, and greed. That person naturally should avoid foods with predominantly hot natures. On the other hand, another person's constitution might be deficient in rajasic elements and demand hot foods to achieve balance. A person suffering from chills might require additional hot foods, but a person with a fever might need to avoid them. The season, physical environment, and other factors also went into this complex mix.

How could one determine what states of matter dominated a food? The answer lay in the taste of the food, but there were no simple rules. A hot food, for example, could possess that quality by virtue of several characteristics, including irritating spiciness, acidity, or oiliness. Further, the habitat of the plant or animal that produced the food could have an effect, as with waterfowl, which are thought to be less hot than terrestrial birds. Needless to say, any food had the potential to be interpreted differently by different dieticians, and this was exactly what happened. The two millennia since the writing of the *Samhita* have seen continual debate, revision, and criticism of food classifications.

Imbalances in states of matter were considered the primary cause of disease, whether major and debilitating or minor and transitory. The chief role of physicians, therefore, was to diagnose what imbalance was causing a problem and prescribe appropriate changes. This system led to the merging of the concepts of food and medicine, and improvement could be effected either by changing the diet or by giving the patient powerful doses of substances that were not normally eaten but contained large amounts of the necessary attribute. In another society, these would have been called medicine.

This dietetic system was scientific in its explanatory nature, but it also was technological, because it had a practical goal and its efficacy was assessed on the basis of empirical results. Finally, it became part of folk culture, passing from scholars to the lay public through religious teachers.

Muslim Optical Physics

Ancient Greek scholars like Aristotle and Euclid had developed a notion that vision came about because a person's eye emitted some form of ray that shot outward and intercepted objects. When this ray encountered something, some sort of signal was sent back to the eye, where vision occurred. According to this idea, light as such did not exist in nature; it was created by the eye. This explanation held sway in European and Southwest Asian scholarship until the research of Abu Ali Hassan ibn al-Haytham[9] (965?–1039).

Ibn al-Haytham originated an alternative explanation that admitted to the existence of light independent of the eye. In his theory, any object that can be seen sends light out, either by producing it or by reflecting it. This light then travels to the eye, where it is perceived. He suggested that the mechanism of perception encompassed the eye, optic nerve, and front part of the brain. The light passed through the cornea of the eye, which focused it; it somehow was transmitted along the optic nerve; and finally it was perceived in the brain. Ibn al-Haytham's ideas are similar enough to our modern conception of vision that their monumental significance may not be easily grasped. In essence, he divorced optics from the human condition, conceiving of light as a phenomenon that exists independently of human intervention.

Ibn al-Haytham also created an innovative methodology. Rather than merely present the logic of his conception, as most of his predecessors did,

---

[7]***Samhita:*** sahm HEE tah
[8]**rajasic:** rah JAH sihk

[9]**Abu Ali Hassan ibn al-Haytham:** AH boo AH lee hah SAHN IHB uhn ahl HY tohm

he set up elaborate experiments to test his ideas. In all essentials, this was hypothesis testing of the modern sort. Ibn al-Haytham's experiments were carefully thought out, and great care was put into their implementation and the recording of their results.

Ibn al-Haytham's scholarship was scientific by virtually any standard. Certainly it sought systematic explanations, and it anticipated many methods of later science. So far as we know, however, it had no connection with any technological application.

European Alchemy

Alchemy, the field of endeavor dedicated to transmuting baser metals into gold, probably developed in Hellenistic Egypt and was passed on to Dar al-Islam and finally Europe. The reasoning behind alchemy was simple enough: Nature shows abundant examples of one thing changing into another, so it should be possible to control the process. In a frequently cited example, a lamb can transform water and grass into wool and meat. Similarly, it was thought, it should be possible to turn lead into gold.

Central to alchemy was the conception of all matter being essentially the same, differing only in details. Alchemists usually worked within the framework of Aristotle's four elemental qualities—hot, cold, wet, and dry—which were believed to make up all matter. Alchemists reasoned that lead and gold shared many characteristics and had to be similar in qualities. If they could manipulate the qualities just a little, they thought, it should be possible to turn a lowly valued metal into gold, the epitome of value and purity in medieval philosophy.

In practical terms, alchemists operated by trying to reduce base metals to their simplest forms, then reconstituting them as gold. This was begun through the "stripping off" of everything except the essence of the metal, usually through some process involving heat or distillation. Then, substances were added in an attempt to add the Aristotelian qualities thought necessary to produce gold. While alchemists never achieved their goals, they developed and refined many chemical processes, including fermentation, distillation, and dissolution. The equipment they invented became useful for many later chemical and other operations.

In terms of modern scientific understanding, the goal of alchemy was unattainable. Nonetheless, it was a wedding of practical processes (technology) and theories to explain the results (science). In late medieval times, alchemy became more mystical, devoting more of its efforts to finding the elixir of life, an agent that purportedly would bring immortality. Although there had been critics of the enterprise of alchemy since the tenth century, late medieval alchemy fell from general scholarly acceptance because of its increasing mysticism.

SCIENCE AND TECHNOLOGY BEFORE 1500

The examples in this chapter illustrate some of the major relationships between science and technology in the period before 1500. Their specific details have a certain value, but more important are the patterns they reveal.

First, science and technology were not seen as wedded in the sense that they are today. Some craftspeople, such as Greek shipbuilders, worked exclusively in technology and neither contributed to nor drew upon the existing fund of scientific knowledge. Other craftspeople derived scientific principles that directed their actions, as when Saxon smiths added green withies to a forge's fire. Similarly, scholars had varying involvement with science and technology. At one extreme, Chinese astronomers directed most of their attentions to the technological implications of their work; at the other extreme, Ibn al-Haytham's optical findings apparently had no impact on technology. While alchemists' scientific theories had little impact on technology, their practical inventions supported the development of various technologies, including the manufacture of brandy and the production of certain types of perfume.

Second, in the period before 1500, there typically was a strong division of labor between scholars and craftspeople. Scholars and craftspeople had little contact in this period. Often working under royal or other patronage, scholars were members of an intellectual (and often socioeconomic) elite; craftspeople typically had less formal education, less wealth, and less prestige. Scholars communicated with one another through the writ-

FIGURE 20.9 *Roger Bacon. Bacon was a thirteenth-century English monk known best for championing the experimental method of science. He was one of the most successful scholars to find practical uses for academic ideas. Here he performs an incendiary experiment.* Science Museum, London.

ten word, but craftspeople rarely had access to these writings; the widespread illiteracy of craftspeople usually would have made access a moot point. It is difficult to envision many occasions when the two could have exchanged ideas on common problems.

The incentives motivating scholars and craftspeople were largely different, too. Scholars could enhance their personal reputations by an interesting idea or way of explaining something. Their patrons would appreciate such fame, because it reflected favorably upon them. Thus, scholars of this era most favored grand interpretations, explanations that were at a high level of abstraction and

might have no practical use. Ibn al-Haytham's remarkable theory of vision and light was an example: It illuminated scholarship, but it led to no improved technology. Craftspeople, on the other hand, were grounded in practical interests that could be translated into improved products or production methods.

Third, science in this period was very different from the science of today, and explanations in science and technology often included factors that today would be considered magical. **Magic** refers to the manipulation of the physical world through practices that have a spiritual or mystical connection, rather than a physical one. That a Hittite blacksmith should avoid sexual contact with a woman before forging an iron sword is such a magical factor, related to the efficacy of the forging only through a complex reasoning based on the sword being a masculine symbol. The sword was used by men for violent activity, and it was used for thrusting, thus relating to the male genitalia; such a potent male object could be polluted, the thinking went, if its creator were to have sexual relations with a woman and transmit her femininity. Such factors would not even be considered as part of the modern scientific explanation of how steel becomes hardened, but they were regularly invoked as explanatory factors in science and technology in this period.

This leads to a philosophical issue: Just because early science used factors that modern science considers irrelevant, does that make it nonscientific? The most important issue in science as defined in this chapter is the search for an explanation that covers a series of similar cases. Sexual contamination, as envisioned by the Hittites, would occur every time the appropriate conditions existed and, therefore, is scientific, even though it includes factors that modern scientists would consider ludicrous.

Fourth, science and technology before 1500 contained the seeds that would lead to modern science in the following centuries. The experimental method pioneered by Ibn al-Haytham attempted to codify procedures to make it unlikely that false explanations would be accepted, through accident, self-delusion, or purposeful deceit. The experimental method was laid out in Europe by Roger Bacon (1214?–1294?) and some of his contemporaries, and it increasingly became a hallmark of the modern scientific method.

SUMMARY

1. Science is the theoretical study of why and how phenomena operate, and technology is the practical design of devices.

2. The domestication of plants and animals was permitted by a rudimentary scientific knowledge of the rules of biological inheritance underlying it.

3. Iron and steel production was complex and usually included various ritual and magical practices. Scientific principles underlay these and other practices, though they were quite different from those recognized in modern times.

4. Both shipbuilding technology and the scientific study of buoyancy were quite sophisticated in Classical Greece, but there was little linkage between the two.

5. Gunpowder was developed in China and was used for weapons there; it then passed to Dar al-Islam and Europe. Scientific principles underlay the formulation of gunpowder, but they were quite unlike those recognized today and resulted in a less efficient explosive. The needs of artillery led to the science of ballistics, as accurate aiming of cannons became important.

6. Chinese astronomy was oriented mostly toward prediction of events for astrological and calendric purposes, not toward their explanation. In that sense, it was more technological than scientific.

7. Indian dietetics, based on conceptions of states of matter and their balance in the body, was scientific in theory and technological in practice.

8. Ibn al-Haytham developed a light-oriented theory of vision. This scientific breakthrough had no apparent impact on technology.

9. European alchemy tried to transmute base metals into gold. While it failed, it was a mixture of science and technology that developed processes and equipment that facilitated later endeavors.

10. Before 1500, science and technology occurred in various mixes in both scholarly and practical research.

11. The worlds of scholars and craftspeople were separate in this period, and the work of one group rarely influenced the other. Practitioners of both occupations used scientific explanations.

12. Magic was important in both technology and science in this period.

13. Science and technology in this period contained the seeds of experimentation and other elements that would come together in the modern version of the scientific method.

SUGGESTED READINGS

Cippola, Carlo M., and Derek Birdsall. *The Technology of Man: A Visual History.* New York: Holt, Rinehart and Winston, 1979. A highly readable and well-illustrated discussion of technology, particularly before 1600.

Hill, Donald R. *Islamic Science and Engineering.* Edinburgh: Edinburgh University Press, 1993. A basic survey of Islamic science and technology.

Landels, J. G. *Engineering in the Ancient World.* Berkeley: University of California Press, 1978. Really treating only Classical Greece and Rome, this small volume has an excellent section on ships and shipbuilding as well as good treatments of power sources, engineering machines, and theoretical knowledge.

Lindberg, David C. *The Beginnings of Western Science.* Chicago: University of Chicago Press, 1992. An influential synthesis that urges that premodern science not be judged by modern criteria.

Needham, Joseph. *Science in Traditional China: A Comparative Perspective.* Cambridge, Mass./Hong Kong: Harvard University Press/The Chinese University Press, 1981. A well-illustrated series of essays discussing Chinese scientific and technological accomplishments prior to 1600.

Singer, Charles, E. J. Holmyard, A. R. Hall, and Trevor I. Williams, eds. *History of Technology.* Five vols. Oxford, Eng.: Oxford University Press, 1954–58. This imposing multivolume treatment of world technology provides information and references on most topics of interest. Very authoritative and technical.

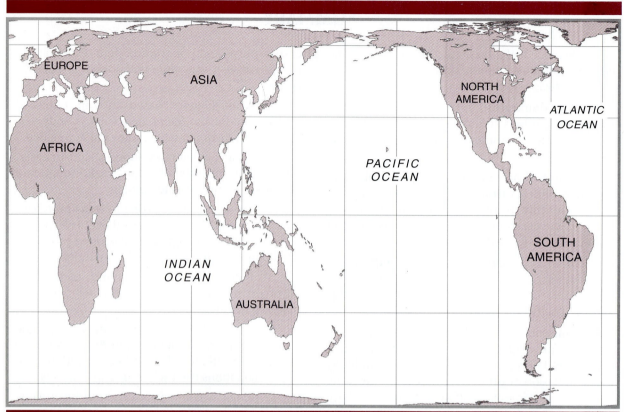

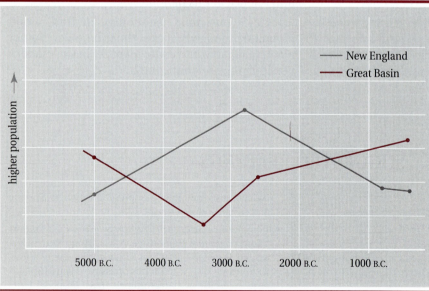

higher population →

5000 B.C.   4000 B.C.   3000 B.C.   2000 B.C.   1000 B.C.

New England
Great Basin

Population Change during a Dry, Warm Climatic Period.
New England and its moist forests profited as the warmth increased and extended the growing season, allowing the production of more food. The Great Basin and its desert, on the other hand, became even drier than before, limiting food and forcing depopulation. Note that the peak in New England population in this period occurred within a short time after the lowest dip in the Great Basin population.

Population Sparks Human Change

History is often seen as the tricks that the dead have played on the living, but we may also see it as the tricks which the living play on the dead.

Although these sentiments are not attributed to one person, they have often been used by historians to tease students into thinking about the problems of historical interpretation. In this chapter, we will develop a few perspectives on the period before 1500.

DEMOGRAPHIC PERSPECTIVES

Human population growth and its resulting pressures often sparked the development of agriculture, urbanization, and significant environmental degradation. Modern human beings with brain capacities equivalent to those of people today evolved around 100,000 B.C. and began to populate the earth. Indeed, these ancestors of ours were as intelligent as anyone found today in Boston, Calcutta, or Cairo. From 100,000 B.C. onward, most of the seminal human changes arose ultimately from growing densities of people as well as from climatic and geographical factors. The increasing complexity of human relationships often sparked key developments.

Population Growth

Over thousands and thousands of years, human population growth has continued despite numerous periods of climatic change. Changing temperatures benefited or hindered humans depending on local conditions. In North America, the northeastern New England region saw significant population growth during a time of rising temperatures and little rainfall, but in the west, the Great Basin suffered a population decline as the desert became drier and hotter. (See the graph on p. 526.)

Looking at Figure 21.1, one sees that between 70,000 and 10,000 B.C. the global population size grew very slowly. Glaciation and warming alternated through that period until the past 12,000 years, when a milder climatic pattern reigned. In the earlier time, the population ranged between 500,000 and a few million people, but the often unfavorable climate kept population growth slow.

After 10,000 B.C., the milder climate and concentration of human populations forced people to alter significantly their economic patterns. Traditional ways of hunting and gathering no longer sufficed to feed the larger numbers. In places with suitable growing conditions and sizeable populations, agriculture appeared. People began to produce more food, and they even experimented with sowing and harvesting plants that provided storable foodstuffs. In the Americas, Africa, and Eurasia, for example, people settled in fixed locations and grew dependent on grains and vegetables like maize, sorghum, wheat, and rice.

As people in more areas began to devote more attention and energies to agriculture, the populations grew more rapidly. Figure 21.2 shows the dramatic population swell between 8000 B.C. and 4000 B.C. Total global population estimates represented by these figures range from around 5 million people to well over 86 million people in that 4,000-year span. By 4000 B.C., farming villages dotted landscapes and agricultural surpluses supported the rise of modest-sized urban centers. In Southwest Asia, Egypt, India, Mexico, and China, humans invented pottery, metallurgy, numerical systems, and written languages in response to the challenges of urban living. Pottery opened up the range of food products that could be stored and cooked. Metallurgy offered farmers better agricultural implements to increase the sizes of their harvests, soldiers better weapons with which to defend the towns, and household managers improved vessels in which to cook and store foodstuffs. Numerical and written systems afforded rulers ways with which to control their subject populations and merchants the means to keep track of their goods.

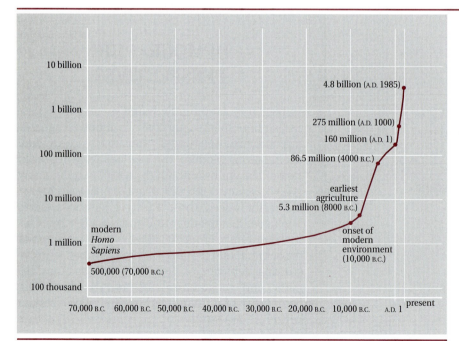

FIGURE 21.1 *World Population, 70,000 B.C. to the Present.* *The rate of population increase was modest throughout most of the existence of modern* Homo sapiens, *but improved environmental conditions and the development of agriculture between 10,000 and 8000 B.C. spurred rapid, exponential growth. Despite wars, plagues, and other local demographic disasters, population has continued to grow at an ever-increasing rate since that time.*

Checks on Population Growth

As people moved into cities, they also became more vulnerable to the vicissitudes of war, famine, and disease. Cities tended to attract enemy armies that desired the wealth and supplies lying within city walls. Indeed, the walls themselves are testimony to attempts by military forces to conquer cities. At the same time, living in close proximity allowed the increased spread of germs and disease. Furthermore, poor waste disposal created unsanitary conditions.

Large-scale warfare occasionally devastated cities and their surrounding regions, especially when commanders conducted sustained campaigns. The Mongol forces fought on and off in China for nearly six decades; their efforts significantly weakened farming populations and caused widespread loss of life. One scholar noted that the population of China was well above 100 million before Mongol rule and around half that about a generation after the Mongols were expelled from China. (Some of the population decrease resulted from a series of famines and epidemics not related to the warfare.) Although the total number of deaths was significantly lower, the population decrease caused by the Inca conquest of the Chanka people was a proportionally comparable to

that in China. This level of death through warfare, of course, occurred in many parts of the world.

Famine sometimes stalked city and countryside in the period before 1500. All cities were heavily dependent on agricultural products, and a drop in farming production severely threatened the well-being of urban dwellers. Floods and droughts regularly reduced harvests and led to malnutrition or famine in countryside and city alike. Warfare, especially siege warfare, also significantly reduced or severed urban access to outside foodstuffs. Even if people survived famine, they occasionally fell to diseases they contracted because of their weakened physical constitutions. Decomposing corpses and disruption of urban sanitation systems aggravated health problems.

Disease often became an efficient killer and population check. The close concentrations of people in armies seemed especially conducive to the transmission of communicable diseases. For example, two extended epidemics, from A.D. 165 to 180 and from 251 to 266, rocked the Roman Empire and demoralized the Roman leaders and commoners; the latter was known as the "crisis of the third century." The first epidemic came with returning soldiers who had fought in the eastern provinces. Not only did continual outbreaks of disease in the cities over both periods keep

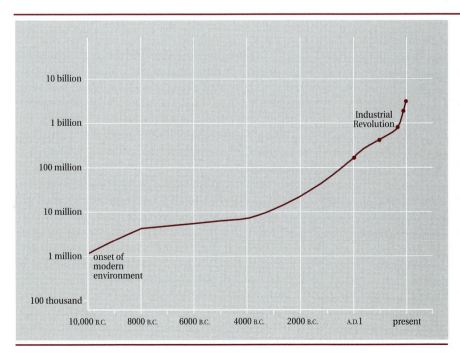

FIGURE 21.2 *World Population, 10,000 B.C. to Present.* *This graph is an enlargement of the latest portion of Figure 21.1. This more detailed version shows more changes in the rate of population growth, occasioned by various events and processes. The rapid population increase between 4000 B.C. and A.D. 1, for example, resulted largely from improved and expanded agriculture; the slower rate of increase between A.D. 1 and 1700 resulted largely from massive epidemics that characterized that period.*

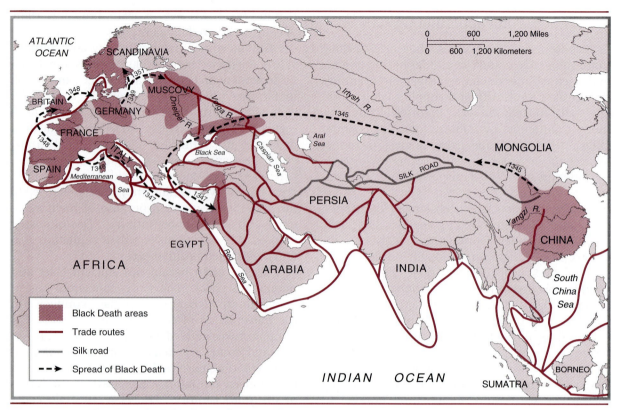

M A P 2 1 . 1　*The Spread of Black Death, around 1350.*　*The occurrence of the plague and its spread from town to town along the trade routes of Asia, Africa, and Europe alerted scholars to the connection between trade and the spread of disease. Disease-carrying hosts traveled the great intercontinental roads, infecting other people as they passed from China through Central Asia and on to Europe and Africa.*

population levels lower, but the seemingly random nature of the deaths also undermined public morale. Wartime refugees also became vulnerable to malnutrition, disease, and death.

A massive epidemic, the Black Death of the fourteenth century, brought loss of life in the tens of millions of people and catastrophic debilitation to commerce and agriculture across Eurasia and North Africa. The bubonic plague seems to have initially irrupted into Chinese populations beginning in the 1320s. It spread in many parts of China until the 1350s with great loss of life. At the same time, it seems to have been carried into Mongolia and across the steppes into the Crimea. Two Central Asian areas, one inhabited by the Nestorian Christians and the other by the Uzbek Muslims, were devastated by the plague before it struck in Europe, Southwest Asia, and Northwest Africa. Travel along Chinese and Central Asian trade routes facilitated the spread of this deadly disease.

The Mongols played a key role in the spread of the plague to Europe and elsewhere. In fact, they launched one of the earliest biological warfare operations in history. The tactic came at the Mongol siege of the Genoan port of Caffra on the Crimean Peninsula in 1246. During the campaign, bubonic plague struck the Mongol forces, and before lifting the attack the commanding Mongol prince ordered that diseased corpses be launched by catapult into the city. Although many survived the siege, Caffra citizens soon contracted the plague. Thereafter, the epidemic spread by maritime trade routes through the Mediterranean and then by land and sea northward. Its southward march was effectively halted by the Sahara Desert because of the absence of people.

Alexandria, the major Egyptian port, was the next target of the plague, which soon spread along the Nile River as well as along the southern and eastern coasts of the Mediterranean Sea. The

FIGURE 21.3 *Plague in Europe.* *The Black Death ravaged Europe in the mid-fourteenth century. This painting shows a scene in Florence, Italy, where a group composed mostly of women mourns the dead; others bury shrouded bodies while priests preside over the interment. Later, the death rates from the plague grew so high in some places that these activities ceased or took on a haphazard quality.* Bibliothèque nationale/Explorer, Paris.

effects proved catastrophic for both cities and rural areas, which were left with insufficient numbers of people to support critical operations. In fact, Egyptian agriculture took ten generations to recover fully from the depredations of the epidemic.

The transmission across Europe came by a variety of trade routes, reaching the British Isles and Scandinavia and sparing parts of eastern Europe and Russia. The plague's severity varied from place to place; in England, for example, it took a century for the population to recover to pre-plague levels. Both cities and countrysides might be hard hit. Although estimates of the population loss have varied, this widespread epidemic cost more than 20 million lives by most reliable accounts. Thus, the population of many areas was severely reduced for generations by this disease. The massive death toll created labor shortages and increased wages for artisans and farmers.

Population Restructuring

Population growth affected the structure of human populations themselves. Some of this restructuring related to changes in life expectancy patterns for all groups. Other kinds of changes can be classified according to people's age or gender.

From around 100,000 to around 10,000 B.C., the structure of hunter-gatherer societies changed little. People living in groups could be expected to live into their thirties, with women enduring until their early thirties and men generally surviving until their late thirties. The large number of women dying in childbirth accounted for much of this difference.

The development of agriculture brought people into villages and effected certain structural changes. Life expectancy rates increased by about five years because of overall better nutrition and health. Gender differences still remained, owing to the continuance of deaths in childbirth for women. A related consequence was that more older people, especially older men, inhabited villages.

Once cities began to appear, between 4000 B.C. and A.D. 300, population structure changed further. General life expectancy rates remained about the same initially, gradually increasing over time. The major change came with the appearance of differentiated social groups. A gap developed and grew, for example, between the wealthy and the poor. Women from wealthy families began living longer because they received better health care, had fewer children, and did not work. Over time, the population of older people grew, especially in wealthy households. Charity expanded beyond family concerns and gradually became a focus of city governments.

Despite some urban problems, cities remained sites of opportunity for enterprising people. Not only did cities increase in size, but also they tended to exhibit remarkable resiliency in weathering the disastrous effects of warfare and disease. A chief cause of this urban ability to bounce back demographically was the swelling or restoring of a population by migration from the countryside into the city.

URBAN TRANSFORMATIONS

Urban populations dominated political and economic life over four millennia, even though the population of nearly all states was mostly rural. Rural people sometimes played significant political and social roles, but the urban elite tended to dominate decision making in most kingdoms and empires. Merchants thrived in cities and often wielded political influence commensurate with their financial strength. In Mesoamerica, for example, merchants played key roles in political and social life.

City-states

Cities became the political center of most polities. In city-states, the city was perceived as the heart and soul of the broader polity. Over time, governments grew more professional in their staffing,

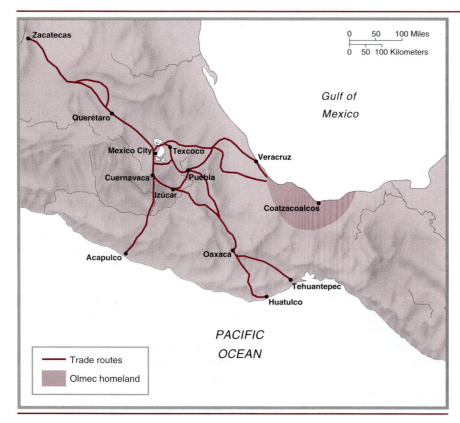

MAP 21.2 *Trade Routes in Mesoamerica around 1500.* *Trade routes of the Aztec Empire crisscrossed Mesoamerica, especially present-day Mexico. The routes connected port cities along the Gulf of Mexico with ports along the Pacific Ocean, as well as the northern parts of Mexico with Central America. Some of the routes followed trails of earlier centuries, including those of the Olmecs from the first millennium B.C.*

evaluation procedures, and ruling techniques. Officials, whatever their social or local origins, usually received an education in urban schools and closely identified with the capital's sociocultural environment.

The most common type of city-state was the pristine city-state. The Greek *polis*, for example, remained dominant for centuries in the first millennium B.C. In addition, city-states became a common pattern in the Mayan civilization of Mesoamerica during the first millennium A.D. as well as in other places and times. Although the Greeks and Mayans each had common cultural patterns and traditions, they had no lasting, overarching political structure. Each city-state retained its own identity.

Another form of city-state, the derived city-state, emerged from the breakdown of an empire. These city-states had existed in South India, for example, after the fall of the Pallava or Chola empires. When the imperial government collapsed, the capital city managed to retain control of its surrounding countryside.

Early city-states generally resembled those that survived the fall of empires. Populations of both identified primarily with their urban centers, and urban life retained its features of social stratification and economic specialization. A significant difference was that the derived city-state enjoyed the benefits of the preceding imperial infrastructure, especially a superior transportation system.

Trade and Empire

Cities tended to dominate trade relations within and between polities. They were the starting and ending points of exchanges of goods, because the significant funds necessary for long-distance trade could usually be found there. Furthermore, the large urban populations provided lucrative markets for merchants' goods, and each city established and regulated market centers. Sometimes states directly sponsored commercial activity, but, more often, they permitted organizations of merchants to finance large-scale trading ventures.

Long-distance trade in Mesoamerica began quite early. The Olmec trade, for example, ranged from the Gulf of Mexico to the Pacific coast by the first millennium B.C. The Teotihuacanos relied on obsidian as a major trade good to help build their trading network in the next millennium. The Aztecs later used roads and routes developed by their predecessors to great effect.

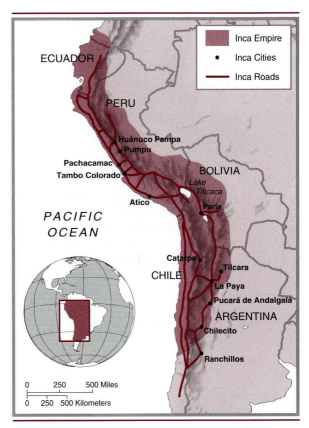

MAP 21.3 *Trade Routes in South America around 1500.* *The Incas built an extensive road system that ran along the Pacific coast and wove through the Andes. Information and goods moved along the remarkable road network to all parts of western South America. Major roads passed through Cuzco, the Inca capital, located at the midpoint of the north-south highway.*

In many other world areas, there has been a close relationship between trade and empire. In India, for example, Mauryas, Guptas, and Cholas all sought control of major trade routes in their rise to power. Ashoka's bloody Kalinga War in the mid–third century B.C. began over his intention of dominating land and maritime trade routes running through Kalinga, a coastal state. The Gupta conquest of the Indus Valley opened key trade routes to imperial control, as did the Chola campaigns along the southwestern coast of India. Trade revenues then played a vital role in funding lavish court styles and in financing large bureaucracies or payoffs to important local leaders. Conversely, when these revenues declined or evaporated, imperial statecraft was undermined, and, a few decades later, the empires collapsed. Similar patterns may be discerned for the Axum and Srivijaya empires in Africa and Southeast Asia.

Artisan and Merchant Guilds

Artisans tended to band together in guilds for security and lobbied officials for beneficial treatment of guild members in long-range trading ventures or in establishing market dominance. These craft organizations helped their members find employment and maintained some kind of standards for finished products, because quality goods sold better both domestically and regionally. Sometimes guilds provided limited social welfare benefits in hard times; they might help a member in times of sickness or survivors in times of a member's death. Artisan guilds also became centers for Sufi missionaries in Dar al-Islam; these mystics used the guilds as bases for their religious brotherhoods, where they found social comfort and spiritual support.

Merchants frequently organized themselves into guilds as well. They used their societies to raise money for a variety of commercial ventures.

In addition, merchant guilds lobbied for laws favorable to themselves or against exorbitant taxes. In the Byzantine Empire, for example, merchants successfully won special trading privileges, some of which were negotiated in treaties with other states. Artisans and merchants, especially those from foreign lands, frequently lived in special sections of cities and even adopted corporate governance in regulating their lives.

Some cities did not have guilds. Minoan merchants and artisans did not feel the need to organize themselves into mutual-support networks because the state provided for their needs. In addition, Aztec artisans and merchants felt no need for occupational guilds because the imperial state and kinship organizations took care of their needs, including those related to social welfare. After 1200, Southwest African kingdoms had no guilds because occupational specialists were organized along kin lines and looked after their relatives.

Urban Elites and Attitudes about Cities

Cities created large elite groups. People were needed to run state and urban governments, priests were needed to run various religious centers, and architects and artists helped design and decorate state buildings and monuments. Periclean Athens, Ptolemaic Alexandria, Ashokan Pataliputra, and Fujiwaran Kyoto were dynamic centers of elite culture and general prosperity. Seen from these lofty perspectives, life in the rural areas, especially in villages, seemed nasty, brutish, and short. Villages, of course, seldom possessed elite groups of the variety, complexity, or formal education of those found at the capitals. Exile of members of the urban elite from their cities was often regarded as a horrible punishment.

A variety of attitudes developed about cities and their inhabitants. Peasants often saw cities as centers of predatory officials or swindling merchants, and they frequently avoided travel to the cities except when compelled by economic motives. Most rural folk avoided taking complaints to the towns or cities because justice favored city folk. Pastoralists frequently viewed cities and city folk with distrust, frequently believing that cheating on commercial agreements was an urban trait. In addition, farmers rarely left their home areas; at most they might venture into regional market

FIGURE 21.4 *Aztec Artisan at Work.* *This codex illustration shows an artisan in Mesoamerica working with feathers, an important commodity for a people that highly valued feathered costumes. Because the state looked after the needs of its artisans, guild networks were not established during the Aztec imperial era.* Biblioteca Medicea Laurenziana.

FIGURE 21.5 *Peasants at Market.* *Rural folk had an ambivalent attitude toward crowded, bustling cities: The places where they were compelled to sell their produce or handicrafts were also places where they might be robbed or swindled. Pictured here are sixteenth-century peasants selling their wares in a city market.* Alinari/Art Resource, N.Y.

towns for business or the purchase of supplies. And yet, cities remained places of opportunity and fortune for people willing to take risks. Thus, a steady stream of immigrants came into the cities, especially larger political and economic centers.

ROLES AND RELATIONSHIPS

A **role** is an affiliation and a set of rights and obligations that someone assumes, and the examination of roles is a way of exploring the numerous obligations that people had in their lifetimes, especially as populations grew. All people fill multiple roles; some are of primary importance, others lesser. During one's life, roles change in number and significance; and in complex organizations related to civilizations, people have often acquired a large variety of roles.

Family Roles

Kinship involves a complexity of roles for an individual. The family is perhaps the most important social institution in history, and all people have been identified by the familial roles they have played. In fact, families had members who played multiple roles. A person might be a daughter and a mother as well as a sister or aunt, all at the same time. Through most of history, kinship has provided people with clearly defined roles and with different power associated with them. Individuals have specific identities and social places; they know who they are and often derive some form of security from that knowledge. The family or clan to which one belonged might have closely regulated one's life, yet it also might have provided some form of security against a state that demanded much from an individual. In hard times, a family or clan might also provide a kind of safety net of charity or other assistance.

Gender Roles

Within the family and the larger social environment, one's gender roles determined how a person might be treated and regarded. Tribe-level societies that practiced intensive agriculture tended to be relatively egalitarian in the distribution of political influence, social position, and economic wealth. Tribal men and women benefited more or less equally in these matters. Civilizations, on the other hand, were usually male-dominated, with females relegated to lower-status roles. Mothers were subordinated to fathers, wives to husbands, and sisters to brothers. Mother-in-law and daughter-in-law conflicts were a common pattern in families, with much friction reported as women competed for the attention of their men. During times when poor people faced economic ruin, female infanticide was often practiced. Girls were also sold into prostitution or slavery in times of hardship or to earn money.

In political realms, exceptional women might gain an opportunity to wield political power, but their position usually rested on their acceptance by males who defined the political roles. Successful women politicians might be biologically female, but they ruled like men; they were politically male. Monarchs, like Queen Hatshepsut of Egypt, even resorted to wearing false beards in order to play the male-defined role in a more realistic manner.

Women might play economic roles, but they also acted within carefully circumscribed limits. In some cases, wives became business managers, but only when their husbands died. During the Qin Empire, for example, Widow Jing became a prominent mining industrialist after her husband died. Single women seldom were permitted to start their own businesses.

Certain occupations and trades became and remained largely the preserve of women. In Greece of the Classical era, prostitution houses were run by women, and in Mesopotamia women dominated some trades, such as brewing beer. Weaving and certain forms of textile production remained in the hands of women. From China to India to Mesoamerica, women wove at home and worked in cottage industries that made cloth. Chinese empresses symbolically wove a piece of material, as did Aztec empresses. Both Chinese and Byzan-

FIGURE 21.6 *Incan Weaver. This Incan woman weaves cloth on a belt loom. Usually fastened to a tree, the loom was used to produce woven goods demanded by the state as annual tribute. Each family had to produce a required amount, a form of taxation. In many societies women did the great majority of this work.* Musée de l'Homme, Institut d'Ethnologie.

tine textile manufacturers employed large numbers of women. These jobs were usually extensions of traditional sex roles.

Patron-Client Relationships

The patron-client relationship was found in most societies. Rich and powerful patrons often assembled groups of supporters who were tied to them socially, politically, and economically. In exchange for loyal support on a variety of issues, the clients received financial assistance, job-seeking support, legal protection, or employment security. Frequently, these relationships centered on a specific patron, but in more complex social or political situations, a hierarchy of patrons might be established. Feudal Europe and Japan, for example, saw alliances bind clients (warriors) to lords who were themselves clients of large territorial magnates.

One type of patron-client connection involved eunuchs and flourished primarily in Eurasia. Castrated males served in the women's quarters of a

FIGURE 21.7 *Eunuchs Serving the State. Many imperial courts required the assistance of eunuchs. In this scene a key official, the chief black eunuch (lower left), escorts a prince to the place where he is to be circumcised. During the Ottoman Empire, black eunuchs became powerful because of their access to the princes and emperors whom they had befriended.* Topkapi Saray Museum.

palace and were chosen for that role because they could not impregnate the emperor's women. Sovereigns commonly employed eunuch clients as a corps of advisors in personal bureaucracies in order to circumvent regular government agencies that might resist or thwart royal initiatives. Monarchs used eunuchs as a means to control others because the eunuchs were generally loyal and easy to control. Eunuchs could not found a dynasty.

Religious Roles

When a foreign religion came to a new area (as when Buddhism came to Japan), there were two common approaches to it. The religion had either to accommodate the local beliefs or to outlaw them. Sometimes, however, missionaries converted a prominent political or social elite member to encourage their clients or subjects to accept the new religion. When Muslims came to West Africa in the ninth century, for example, they deliberately converted a few rulers and watched many in the ruler's domain convert as well.

Clergy members often assumed secular roles when tending to the needs of their congregations. Byzantine bishops, for example, handled a variety of duties for the emperor. They helped administer the laws, collect taxes, and maintain law and order in their jurisdictions. They also participated in charitable activities to help their members. In Mesoamerica, priests of the Aztec religion handled some tribute records and transactions because they could read, write, and calculate. Because many civilizations had this type of arrangement, there was no separation of church and state. Indeed, secular and religious activities often formed a seamless web.

Ethnic Identities

An additional role concerns one's ethnic identity. Many peoples saw themselves as culturally superior to peoples who did not adopt their languages and social practices. They believed these peoples to be barbarians without culture and inferior to themselves. The Ptolemaic Greek rulers of Egypt, for example, refused to intermarry with Egyptians and maintained a closely knit ruling elite.

Another feature of civilizations involved the shifting roles brought by local rule, regional rule, or imperial rule. In times of political change, a local town might find itself under a prince who then might be defeated and have his territory incorporated into a regional kingdom. Within a lifespan, that larger entity might succumb to a successful emperor who built a transregional realm. Similarly, the decline of an empire might mean a rapid return to some form of regional or local control.

ENVIRONMENTAL DEGRADATION

One of the consequences of demographic complexity found in densely populated cities was the degradation of the urban and surrounding environments. Human-waste removal presented difficult problems to city officials, and by-products of metallurgical production fouled land storage sites and nearby waterways. Deforestation, often resulting from the clearing of land for agriculture, sometimes led to erosion.

Pollution and the Environment

Tens of thousands or more of closely packed people created nightmares of human-waste disposal. Most often sewage removal or treatment was haphazard; disease flourished in towns and cities where sewage and drinking-water sources intermingled. City planners and politicians in the period before 1500 were ignorant of the causes of disease. In some Persian cities, for example, local farmers regularly gathered untreated human-waste products for use as fertilizers for their farmlands, unaware of the risks of transmitting disease.

Cities also had problems with the disposal of dead bodies, which were sources of disease. In many places, especially in Asia, people who handled the corpses and carted them to burial sites or to crematoriums suffered discrimination. Outcast groups performing these necessary societal functions could be found in Japan, Korea, and India.

Metallurgy, a major feature of civilizations, resulted in a variety of hazardous wastes. Disposal of waste by-products troubled some city managers, but most ignored the growing refuse sites or moved the factories to other places. Iron slag heaps, for example, marred the local landscape of

FIGURE 21.8 *Crowded City Life. One of the nightmares of urban crowding was the disposal of human waste. This fifteenth-century French miniature shows a man using a makeshift toilet between two houses. Above him is a second-story latrine with a hole in its floor, through which human waste dropped. This lack of sanitation caused great personal discomfort and created ideal conditions for the breeding of disease.* Bibliothèque de l'Arsenal.

FIGURE 21.9 *Deforestation in China.* *This woodcut depicts Chinese logging efforts during the Ming Empire (1368–1644). Two groups of loggers chop at standing trees, while another group trims the trunk of a fallen tree. At the lower left, a supervisor addresses a group of kneeling workers. Deforestation denuded many parts of China, although at times the Chinese replanted and harvested trees as they did grains.* From *Chung-kwo pan-hua-hsuan.* Photo by Eileen Tweedy.

Nubia. Furthermore, **leaching**, the movement of chemicals as water runs off topsoil, rapidly contaminated subterranean water supplies because slag heaps typically contained extremely toxic concentrations of arsenic, antimony, lead, and radium. Ironically, waste-disposal centers have provided archaeologists with fertile grounds for amassing artifacts to understand and interpret civilizations.

Irrigation systems were developed to increase agricultural production, but they caused their own problem. Over time, salt in irrigation waters settled on farmlands, rendering them inhospitable to growing plants. One reason for the decline of the Indus River Valley civilization was overuse of irrigation, leading to a salting of the land.

Deforestation

People in this period relied heavily on wood for fuels and building materials, so densely populated places frequently denuded forest lands. China suffered the rapid loss of trees as people claimed the trees for their energy and building needs. A few ancient Chinese texts lamented the environmental destruction and the termination of a mythical era of harmonious interaction among humans, other animals, and the environment. One scholar noted that in the early Middle Ages, European cities seemed like islands in a sea of forests, but at the end of the late Middle Ages, forests appeared to be islands in a sea of towns, cities, and fields. Slash-and-burn agriculture also reduced forests and trees in many parts of the world. In addition, water runoff in deforested areas caused erosion and the silting of rivers. These effects hampered agriculture and river transport.

Agriculture Transforms Landscapes

Agricultural techniques became more complex and began to alter local environments significantly. Apart from forests falling to farmers' axes, deep-plowing techniques sometimes resulted in massive erosion. Exploitation of the Ethiopian highlands ecosystem of East Africa by the Axumite civilization brought dire consequences. Axumites harvested trees and severely reduced the forests of the highlands. The ecosystem changed dramatically over several centuries, and, when rainfall cycles became less predictable and produced more torrential deluges, mud slides carried off villages and buried parts of the capital. Key export items were also lost as forest animals retreated or disappeared. The combined losses accelerated the decline of the Axum Empire, and the region has still not fully recovered from the environmental degradation. Although this was a unique case, similar destruction by agriculture occurred all over the world.

Environmental degradation had affected numerous societies long before the Industrial Revolution of the eighteenth and nineteenth centuries. Many of the ecological problems faced in recent times have ancient historical roots.

SUMMARY

1. Modern human beings appeared about 100,000 years ago and gradually adapted culturally to their environments. Their numbers grew slowly until the development of agriculture, after which the pace accelerated rapidly.

2. Although warfare and disease reduced human populations, there was steady growth. Warfare killed great numbers of warriors and civilians. Disease proved to be an even more lethal curb on human numbers. The Black Death was by far the worst demographic catastrophe prior to the sixteenth century and killed over 20 million people.

3. Cities became the centers of city-states, federations, kingdoms, and empires. Some political trends were toward centralization, while others were toward decentralization.

4. Cities also became hubs in the trade routes that evolved into continent-wide systems by the first millennium A.D. The Mayans and Aztecs used them in Mesoamerica, while Muslims plied the caravan routes across Asia and Africa.

5. Artisans and merchants organized guilds to support their own self-interests. These craft networks helped control the quality of manufactured goods. At the same time, they offered social benefits, especially to the less fortunate of their members in troubled times.

6. City folk had their own social hierarchies and usually despised rural folk. The latter sometimes returned the scorn and distrust of urban folk.

7. A variety of roles and relationships governed the individual in society. Most related to the family and one's gender, and others related to patron-client relations, religious obligations, or ethnic identity.

8. The natural environment was dramatically changed by humankind in premodern times. Cities produced huge amounts of waste. Agriculture reduced forests, and irrigation canals also brought significant environmental alterations.

SUGGESTED READINGS

Adas, Michael, ed. *Islamic and European Expansion.* Philadelphia: Temple University Press, 1993. A series of essays examining broad issues of Eurasian history.

Chaudhuri, K. N. *Trade and Civilization in the Indian Ocean.* Cambridge, Eng.: Cambridge University Press, 1985. A major survey and interpretation of trading patterns in the Indian Ocean.

McNeill, William. *Plagues and Peoples.* Garden City, N.Y.: Anchor Press, 1976. A classic treatment of the role of disease in history.

Tuchman, Barbara. *A Distant Mirror.* New York: Ballantine Books, 1978. A survey of European history, focusing on the Black Death and its consequences.

ACKNOWLEDGMENTS

Chapter 1

Excerpt from *His Five Letters of Relation to the Emperor Charles V* by Hernando Cortés, edited and translated by Francis Augustus (A. H. Clark, 1908).

Excerpt from *The War of Conquest, How It Was Waged Here in Mexico* by Bernardino de Sahagún, edited and translated by Arthur J. O. Anderson and Charles E. Dibble (Salt Lake City: University of Utah Press, 1978).

Excerpt from *The History of the New Indies and Spain* by Diego Durán (New York: Orion Press, 1964).

Chapter 2

Excerpt from the Iroquois creation myth, as told to Russell Barber.

Chapter 3

Excerpt from *The Florentine Codex, Book 9,* edited and translated by Arthur J. O. Anderson and Charles E. Dibble. (Santa Fe: School of American Research; Salt Lake City: University of Utah Press, 1978). Copyright © 1982 by the School of American Research. Reprinted by permission.

Chapter 4

Excerpt from *The Code of Hammurabi,* translated by Robert Harper (Chicago: University of Chicago Press, 1904).

Chapter 5

Excerpt from *Anthology of Chinese Literature,* edited by Cyril Birch. Copyright © 1965 by Grove Press. Used with the permission of Grove/Atlantic, Inc.

Chapter 6

Excerpt from *A Forest of Kings: The Untold Story of the Ancient Maya* by Linda Schele and David Freidel (New York: William Morrow and Company, 1990).

Chapter 7

Excerpt from *The Aeneid of Virgil,* translated by Allen Mandelbaum. Translation copyright © 1971 by Allen Mandelbaum. Used by permission of Bantam Books, a division of Bantam Doubleday Dell Publishing Group, Inc.

Excerpt from *The Odyssey of Homer,* translated by Richmond Lattimore. Copyright © 1965, 1967 by Richmond Lattimore. Copyright renewed. Reprinted by permission of HarperCollins Publishers, Inc.

Chapter 8

Excerpt from *The Letters of Pliny the Younger,* translated by B. Radier. Copyright © 1969 by B. Radier. Reprinted with the permission of Penguin Books, Ltd.

Chapter 9

Excerpt from *The African Past: Chronicles from Antiquity to Modern Times,* edited by Basil Davidson (Boston: Little, Brown and Company, 1964), pp. 55–56. Copyright © 1964 by Basil Davidson. Reprinted with the permission of Curtis Brown, Ltd.

Chapter 10

Excerpt from *Translation of the Edicts of Ashoka* by Romila Thapar. Copyright © by Romila Thapar. Used by permission of Oxford University Press, Inc.

Chapter 11

Excerpt from *Han Agriculture* by Hsu Cho-yun. Copyright © 1980 by University of Washington Press. Reprinted with permission from the publisher.

Chapter 12

Excerpt from *Say I Am You,* edited and translated by John Moyne and Coleman Barks (Athens, GA: Maypop Books, 1994), pp. 22–23. Copyright © 1994 by Coleman Barks. Reprinted with the permission of Coleman Barks.

Chapter 13

Excerpt from *Medieval Women Writers* by Katharina M. Wilson. Copyright © 1984 by University of Georgia Press, Athens. Reprinted with permission from the publisher.

Chapter 14

Excerpt from *Four Huts: Asian Writings on the Simple Life,* edited and translated by Burton Watson (Boston: Shambhala Publications, 1994), pp. 73–77. Copyright © 1994 by Burton Watson. Reprinted with the permission of Shambhala Publications, Inc., Horticultural Hall, 300 Massachusetts Avenue, Boston, MA 02115.

Chapter 15

Excerpt from *The African Past: Chronicles from Antiquity to Modern Times,* edited by Basil Davidson (Boston: Little, Brown and Company, 1964), p. 78. Copyright © 1964 by Basil Davidson. Reprinted with the permission of Curtis Brown, Ltd.

Chapter 16

Excerpt from *The Florentine Codex, Book 9, Chapter 3,* edited and translated by Arthur J. O. Anderson and Charles E. Dibble (Santa Fe: School of American Research; Salt Lake City: University of Utah Press, 1978). Copyright 1982 by the School of American Research. Reprinted by permission.

Chapter 17

Excerpt from *Change in Byzantine Culture in the Eleventh and Twelfth Centuries* by A. P. Kazhadan and Ann Wharton Epstein, University of California Press, Berkeley.

Chapter 18

Excerpt from *An Introduction to Chinese Literature* by W. C. Liu. Copyright © 1966 by Indiana University Press. Reprinted with the permission of Indiana University Press.

Chapter 19

Excerpt from *The History of the World Conquerer* by Allah-ad-din Atha-Malil Juvaini, translated by John Andrew Boyle. Copyright © 1958 by the President and Fellows of Harvard College. Reprinted with the permission of Harvard University Press.

Chapter 20

Excerpt from "The Chinese Concept of Nature" by Mitsukuni Yoshida in *Chinese Science: Explorations of an Ancient Tradition,* edited by Shigeru Nakayama and Nathan Sivin. Copyright © 1971 by the Massachusetts Institute of Technology Press. Reprinted with permission of the Massachusetts Institute of Technology Press.

Global Change from Prehistory to the 1500s

Full-Color Maps

These color maps are here for your reference. We hope you will have reason to consult them over the course of your study of world history. You might use them to remind yourself of dates and locations in which certain civilizations thrived. They might cause you to notice which cultures flourished simultaneously and which bordered one another. At times, you might find yourself comparing these maps to the map of the world today and thinking about the historical influences on the world we now live in. We also hope you turn to this appendix whenever you need to find a good map quickly.

On each two-page spread you will find maps that illustrate the changes that came to one geographical area over the period of time covered in Chapters 1–21. These areas are Southwest Asia, India, East and Southeast Asia, the Americas, Europe, the Mediterranean, and Africa. The final map illustrates the spread of world religions from 450 to 1450.

Southwest Asia and the Mediterranean, around 2700 B.C.–331 B.C.

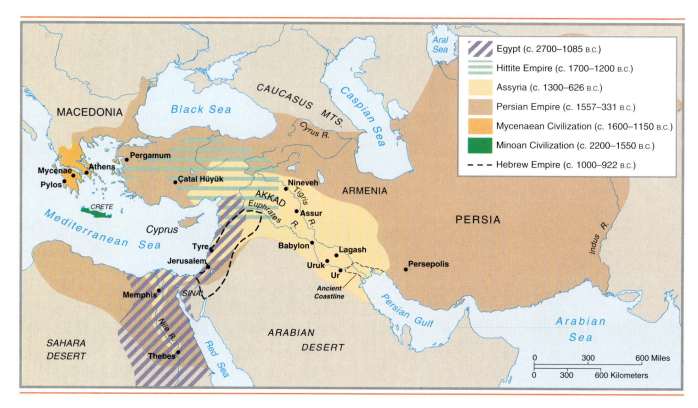

Legend:

- Egypt (c. 2700–1085 B.C.)
- Hittite Empire (c. 1700–1200 B.C.)
- Assyria (c. 1300–626 B.C.)
- Persian Empire (c. 1557–331 B.C.)
- Mycenaean Civilization (c. 1600–1150 B.C.)
- Minoan Civilization (c. 2200–1550 B.C.)
- Hebrew Empire (c. 1000–922 B.C.)

▶ **ANCIENT SOUTHWEST ASIA AND THE EASTERN MEDITERRANEAN, 2700–331 B.C.**

ANCIENT SOUTHWEST ASIA (CH. 4) SAW THE RISE OF numerous states, some of which developed into empires. In some cases these empires united several cultural groups and civilizations. The Persian Empire stretched from the Indus River Valley (Ch. 5) to Egypt, uniting various peoples under one polity and controlling major trade routes. Alexander, a Macedonian general, conquered the Persian Empire, creating an empire that was vast but short-lived (Ch. 8). Unity dissolved after Alexander's death, creating a patchwork of smaller polities. These areas would never again be united under a single state.

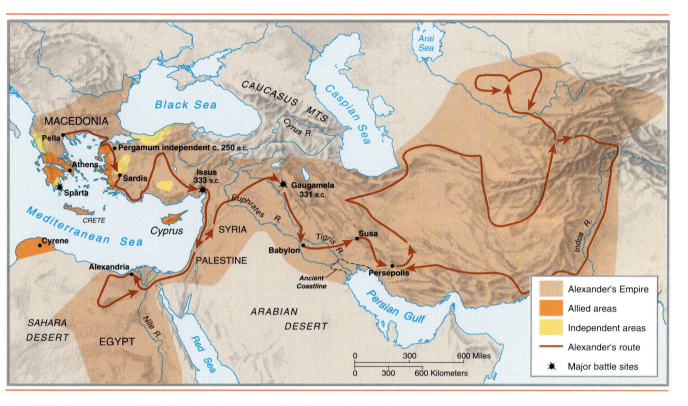

Black Sea

CAUCASUS MTS.

Aral Sea

Caspian Sea

MACEDONIA

Pella

Pergamum independent c. 250 B.C.

Cyrus R.

Athens

Sardis

Issus 333 B.C.

Gaugamela 331 B.C.

Sparta

Mediterranean Sea

CRETE

Cyprus

SYRIA

Euphrates R.

Tigris R.

Susa

Babylon

Indus R.

Cyrene

PALESTINE

Persepolis

Alexandria

Ancient Coastline

Persian Gulf

SAHARA DESERT

ARABIAN DESERT

EGYPT

Nile R.

Red Sea

Alexander's Empire

Allied areas

Independent areas

Alexander's route

Major battle sites

0   300   600 Miles

0   300   600 Kilometers

▶ **ALEXANDER'S EMPIRE AND THE SUCCESSOR STATES, 334–331 B.C.**

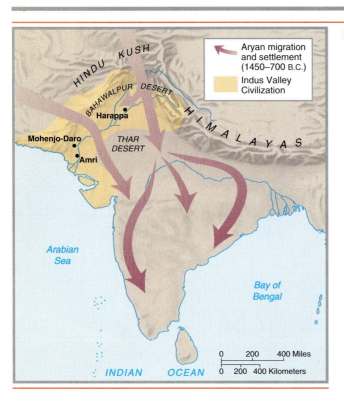

Aryan migration and settlement (1450–700 B.C.)

Indus Valley Civilization

HINDU KUSH

BAHAWALPUR DESERT

Harappa

HIMALAYAS

Mohenjo-Daro

THAR DESERT

Amri

Arabian Sea

Bay of Bengal

0   200   400 Miles
0 200 400 Kilometers

INDIAN   OCEAN

▶ **INDIA, 320 B.C.–A.D. 550**

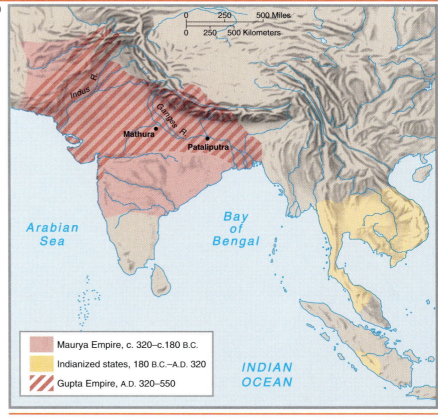

0   250   500 Miles
0   250   500 Kilometers

Indus R.

Ganges R.

Mathura

Pataliputra

Arabian Sea

Bay of Bengal

Maurya Empire, c. 320–c.180 B.C.

Indianized states, 180 B.C.–A.D. 320

Gupta Empire, A.D. 320–550

INDIAN OCEAN

South and Southeast Asia, around 2500 B.C.–A.D. 1350

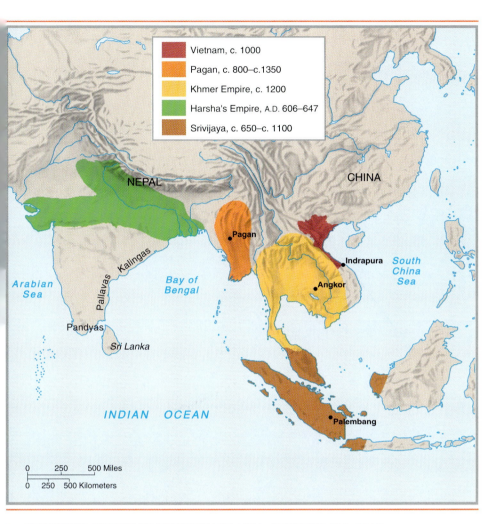

Legend
Vietnam, c. 1000
Pagan, c. 800–c. 1350
Khmer Empire, c. 1200
Harsha's Empire, A.D. 606–647
Srivijaya, c. 650–c. 1100

NEPAL

CHINA

Pagan

Indrapura

South China Sea

Angkor

Arabian Sea

Kalingas

Pallavas

Bay of Bengal

Pandyas

Sri Lanka

INDIAN OCEAN

Palembang

0   250   500 Miles
0   250   500 Kilometers

▶ **REGIONAL STATES IN SOUTHEAST ASIA, AROUND 606–1350**

INDIA SAW THE EARLIEST STATE FORMATION IN South and Southeast Asia (Ch. 14). The Indus Valley civilization flourished for centuries, then collapsed. Only after the Aryan migrations from Southwest and Central Asia did Indian states form, especially in the Ganges Valley. The Maurya, classical-age Gupta, and Harsha empires ruled over large sections of India (Ch. 10). After the seventh century, regionalism became the dominant trend. State building also began in the early centuries A.D. in Southeast Asia. By 1200, major states had appeared on mainland and inland Southeast Asia (Ch. 14). The Burmese, Khmer, Vietnamese, and Malays had established viable polities.

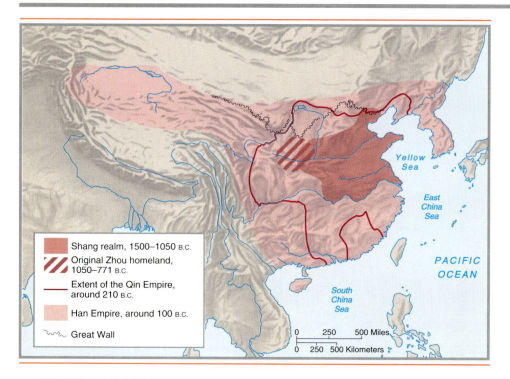

▶ ANCIENT AND EARLY IMPERIAL CHINA, 1500–AROUND 100 B.C.

Shang realm, 1500–1050 B.C.
Original Zhou homeland, 1050–771 B.C.
Extent of the Qin Empire, around 210 B.C.
Han Empire, around 100 B.C.
Great Wall

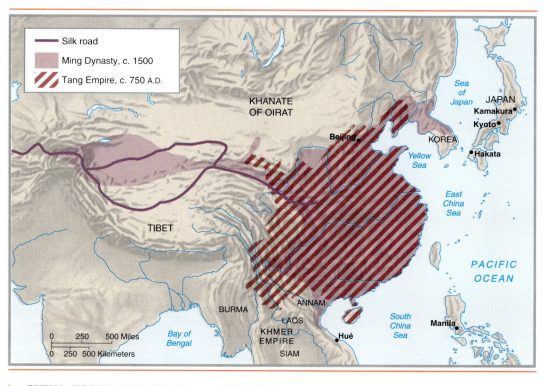

▶ CHINA, KOREA, AND JAPAN, A.D. 750–1500

Silk road
Ming Dynasty, c. 1500
Tang Empire, c. 750 A.D.

East and Central Asia, around 1500 B.C.–A.D. 1340

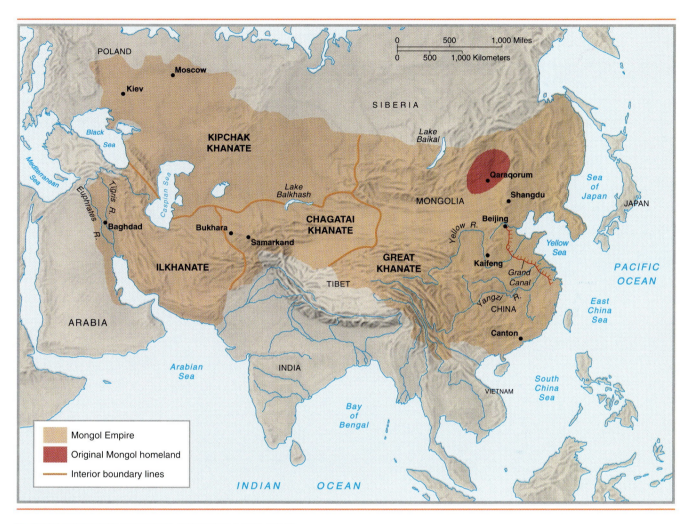

▶ **THE MONGOL EMPIRE AROUND 1206–1340**

S UCCESSIVE DYNASTIES EXPANDED CONTROL of areas making up part of modern China (Ch. 5). The Shang realm included much of the Yellow River Valley and the North China Plain. The Zhou territory included lands once controlled by Shang and expanded southward to the Yangzi River. Qin emperors added new domains, especially to the south, while the Han Empire controlled part of Korea, Southwest China, and areas to the west. By 762, Chinese control over the western region had been lost, regained, and lost again. By 1500, nonwestern lands ruled by Tang emperors (Ch. 18) were retained by their Ming counterparts (Ch. 28). The Mongols (Ch. 19) conquered and ruled a vast domain, covering most of Asia and a small part of Europe. This was one of the few times general unity was achieved in Asia.

The Americas, around 4000 B.C.–A.D. 1532

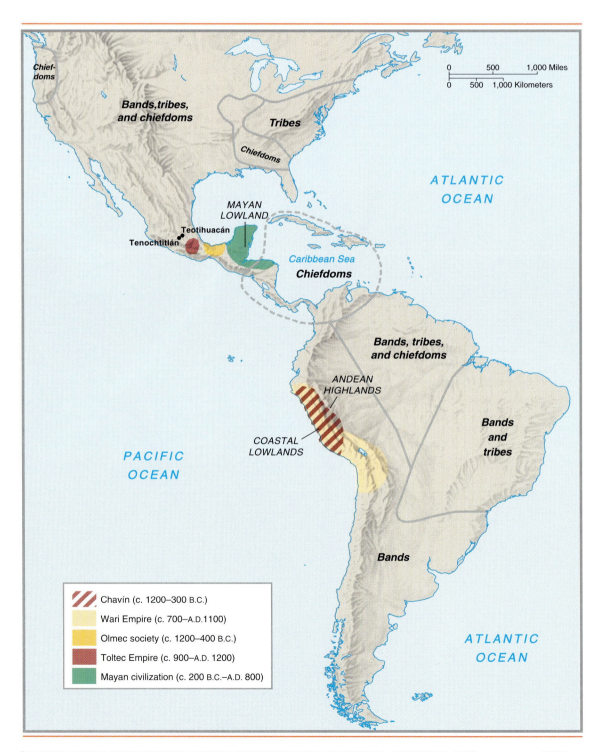

Chief-doms

Bands, tribes, and chiefdoms

Tribes

Chiefdoms

ATLANTIC OCEAN

MAYAN LOWLAND

Teotihuacán

Tenochtitlán

Caribbean Sea

Chiefdoms

Bands, tribes, and chiefdoms

ANDEAN HIGHLANDS

COASTAL LOWLANDS

PACIFIC OCEAN

Bands and tribes

Bands

ATLANTIC OCEAN

0   500   1,000 Miles
0   500   1,000 Kilometers

Chavín (c. 1200–300 B.C.)

Wari Empire (c. 700–A.D.1100)

Olmec society (c. 1200–400 B.C.)

Toltec Empire (c. 900–A.D. 1200)

Mayan civilization (c. 200 B.C.–A.D. 800)

▶ THE DEVELOPMENT OF CIVILIZATION IN THE AMERICAS, AROUND 4000 B.C.–A.D. 1200

_DURING MOST OF THE PERIOD WHEN THE **Americas** were isolated from the rest of the world, they were organized into regional and local political units. There were periods, however, when interregional empires developed. The largest empires, those of the Aztecs and Incas (Ch. 16), were in the latest period. Other peoples, like the Maya (Ch. 6), were unified by similar culture but were divided into many antagonistic states.

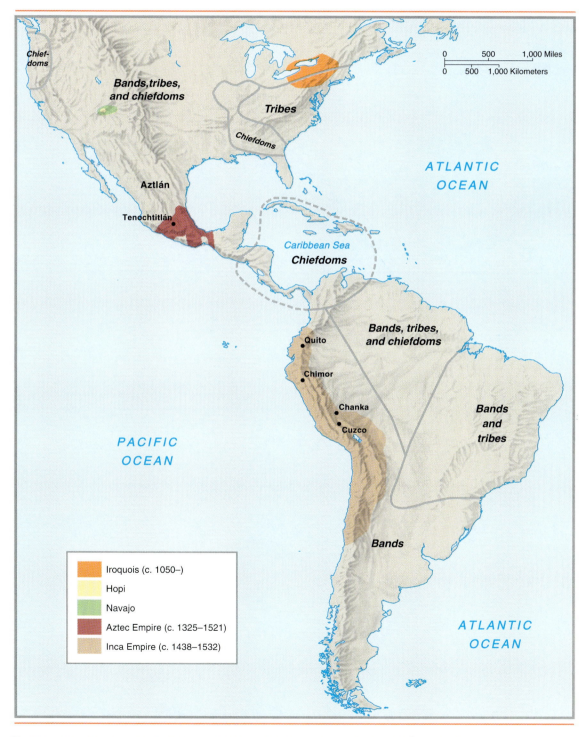

Chief-doms

Bands, tribes, and chiefdoms

Tribes

Chiefdoms

ATLANTIC OCEAN

Aztlán

Tenochtitlán

Caribbean Sea
Chiefdoms

Bands, tribes, and chiefdoms

Quito

Chimor

Chanka

Cuzco

Bands and tribes

PACIFIC OCEAN

Bands

ATLANTIC OCEAN

▮	Iroquois (c. 1050–)
▮	Hopi
▮	Navajo
▮	Aztec Empire (c. 1325–1521)
▮	Inca Empire (c. 1438–1532)

0   500   1,000 Miles
0   500   1,000 Kilometers

▶ **THE AMERICAS ON THE EVE OF EUROPEAN CONTACT, AROUND 1300–1532**

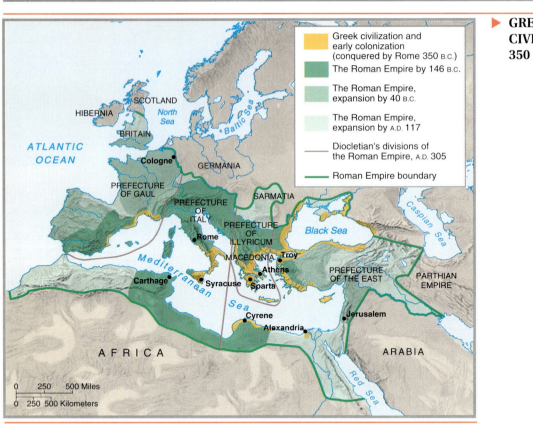

GREEK AND ROMAN CIVILIZATIONS, 350 B.C.–A.D. 305

Greek civilization and early colonization (conquered by Rome 350 B.C.)

The Roman Empire by 146 B.C.

The Roman Empire, expansion by 40 B.C.

The Roman Empire, expansion by A.D. 117

Diocletian's divisions of the Roman Empire, A.D. 305

Roman Empire boundary

ATLANTIC OCEAN

SCOTLAND
HIBERNIA
BRITAIN
North Sea
Baltic Sea

Cologne
GERMANIA
PREFECTURE OF GAUL
SARMATIA
PREFECTURE OF ITALY
Rome
PREFECTURE OF ILLYRICUM
Black Sea
Caspian Sea
MACEDONIA
Troy
Athens
PREFECTURE OF THE EAST
PARTHIAN EMPIRE
Carthage
Mediterranean Sea
Syracuse
Sparta
Cyrene
Jerusalem
Alexandria
AFRICA
ARABIA
Red Sea

0   250   500 Miles
0   250   500 Kilometers

EUROPE, SOUTHWEST ASIA, AND NORTH AFRICA, 500–843

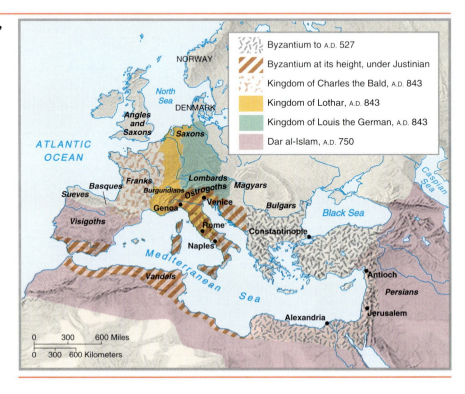

Byzantium to A.D. 527

Byzantium at its height, under Justinian

Kingdom of Charles the Bald, A.D. 843

Kingdom of Lothar, A.D. 843

Kingdom of Louis the German, A.D. 843

Dar al-Islam, A.D. 750

NORWAY
DENMARK
North Sea
Angles and Saxons
Saxons
ATLANTIC OCEAN
Basques
Sueves
Franks
Burgundians
Lombards
Ostrogoths
Magyars
Genoa
Venice
Bulgars
Black Sea
Caspian Sea
Visigoths
Rome
Naples
Constantinople
Mediterranean Sea
Vandals
Antioch
Persians
Alexandria
Jerusalem

0   300   600 Miles
0   300   600 Kilometers

Europe, Southwest Asia, and North Africa, around 350 B.C.–A.D. 1200

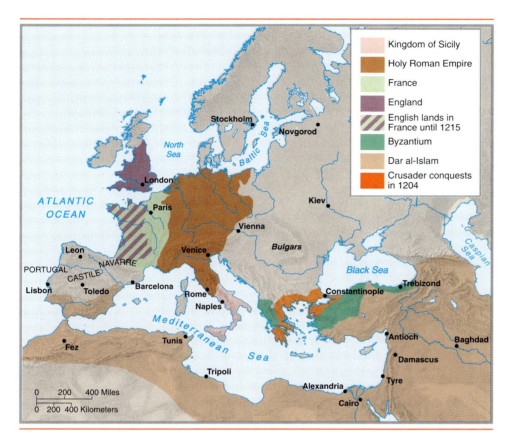

Legend:
- Kingdom of Sicily
- Holy Roman Empire
- France
- England
- English lands in France until 1215
- Byzantium
- Dar al-Islam
- Crusader conquests in 1204

▶ **MEDIEVAL EUROPE, BYZANTIUM, AND MUSLIM STATES, AROUND 1200**

THE HISTORIES OF EUROPE, SOUTHWEST ASIA, and North Africa were united for a significant period during the Roman and Byzantine empires (Ch. 17). Trade flourished in the homogeneous political zones during peacetime, and goods and ideas flowed freely among cultures. Regional polities emerged as migrating peoples challenged political unity. After a period of transition between the fourth and fifth centuries (Ch. 13), the Roman Empire (Chs. 7 and 8) broke into a patchwork of Germanic states in the west and the new state of Byzantium in the east. After the rise of Islam in the seventh century (Ch. 12), North Africa and most of Southwest Asia remained united under Dar al-Islam but divided into regional polities.

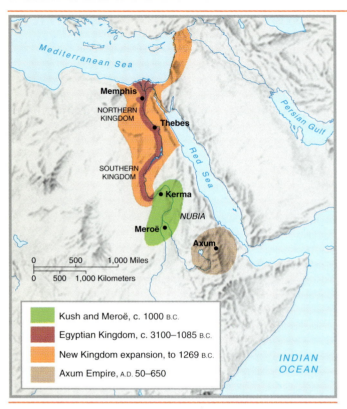

ANCIENT AFRICAN CIVILIZATIONS, 3100 B.C.–A.D. 650

Kush and Meroë, c. 1000 B.C.

Egyptian Kingdom, c. 3100–1085 B.C.

New Kingdom expansion, to 1269 B.C.

Axum Empire, A.D. 50–650

AFRICA AND DAR AL-ISLAM, AROUND 50–1200

Axum, A.D. 50–650

Ghana, A.D. 300–1200

Dar al-Islam, A.D. 750

Islamic expansion

Africa and Dar al-Islam, around 3100 B.C.–A.D. 1550

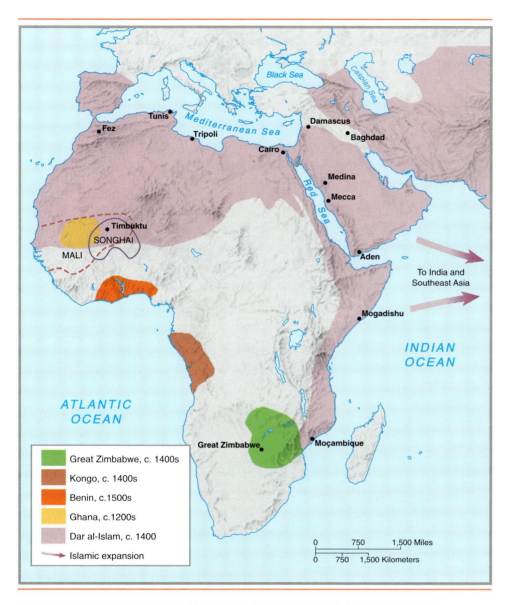

Great Zimbabwe, c. 1400s
Kongo, c. 1400s
Benin, c.1500s
Ghana, c.1200s
Dar al-Islam, c. 1400
Islamic expansion

▶ **LATER AFRICA AND DAR AL-ISLAM, AROUND 1100–AROUND 1550**

THE EARLIEST CIVILIZATIONS IN AFRICA DEVELOPED in the northeastern part of the continent (Ch. 9). Later, internal developments and the influence of Islam stimulated the origin of many civilizations south of the Sahara Desert (Chs. 12 and 15). The spread of Islam led to the development of Dar al-Islam (Ch. 12), those lands that shared Islamic culture.

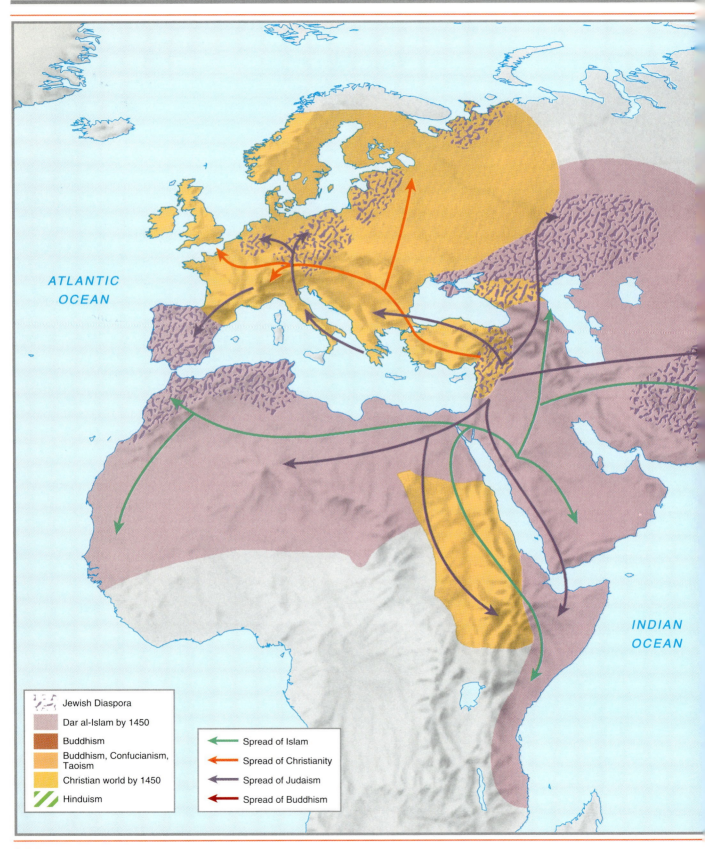

ATLANTIC
OCEAN

INDIAN
OCEAN

Jewish Diaspora

Dar al-Islam by 1450

Buddhism

Buddhism, Confucianism,
Taoism

Christian world by 1450

Hinduism

Spread of Islam

Spread of Christianity

Spread of Judaism

Spread of Buddhism

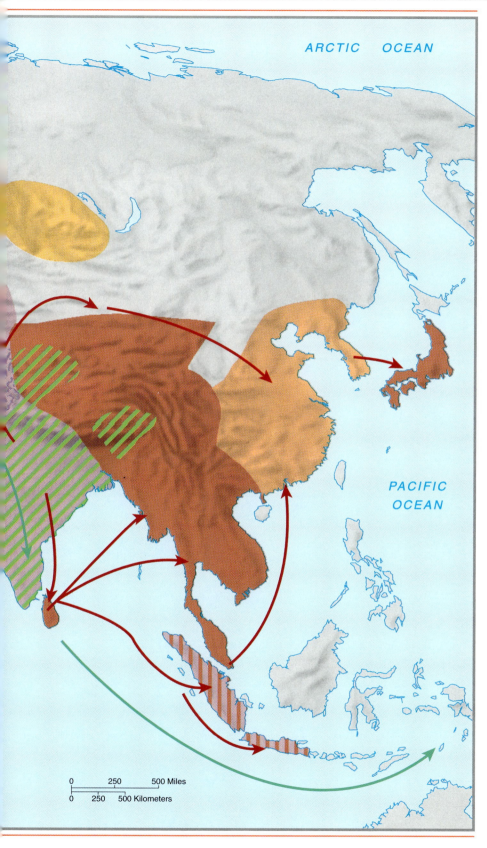

The Spread of Religions in Eurasia and Africa, around A.D. 450–1450

THIS MAP SHOWS the major avenues of world religions' spread from their points of origin into new areas (Issue 4). Religions expanded through conquest, missionary activity, and exchange of ideas. In many cases, more than one religion spread into a geographical area. For example, both Buddhism and Islam were introduced, at different times, into Southeast Asia. The map shows the predominant religions in each area by about 1450; for example, both India and China had Christian populations, but their numbers remained small.

ARCTIC OCEAN

PACIFIC OCEAN

0   250   500 Miles

0   250   500 Kilometers

Glossary of Terms

A

acropolis   a high area in early Greek cities that served as a gathering place for safety against raids

Afrocentrism   the view that Africa is the primary location of important cultural innovations that subsequently spread into Western civilization and were adopted around the world

agora   a central market area in early Greek cities

ahimsa   the Jain doctrine of causing no harm to any living soul

alchemy   the field of endeavor dedicated to transmuting baser metals into gold

Allah   the Islamic deity

alloying   the mixing of metals to produce a metal with characteristics different from those of any of its components

alphabetic writing   writing that uses a limited number of symbols to represent the component sounds of a language

Ancient Style   a form of prose that developed during the later Tang Empire of China (763–907) that required essays to be clear and simple

animism   the worship of deities thought to reside in natural forces and objects such as rivers, trees, and mountains

annealing   heating and gradually cooling a metal to reduce internal stresses and make it harder and more durable

anthropomorphism   the practice of attributing human characteristics, such as physique or temperament, to deities or other nonhuman entities

Apedemak (ah PEH deh mak)   the local Nubian lion god

applied mathematics   the mathematical study of measurement and prediction, used to solve real-world problems

aqueduct   an artificial channel that carries drinking water

archaeology   the study of the human past, primarily through material remains

archons (AWR kahnz)   officials who ran the day-to-day government in early Athens

Areopagite Council (air ee OH pah gyt)   a group of aristocrats who governed ancient Athens

astrology   the prediction of the future on the basis of the alignments of stars and planets

avatar   an incarnation of a Hindu god

ayllu (EYE yoo)   a cabinet of advisors appointed by the ruler of the Inca Empire

B

ballistics   the branch of mathematics and physics that deals with the propulsion of projectiles

band   a group of around 30 to 200 people living together with little or no formal government; a band derives food from hunting, fishing, and the gathering of plant foods

Bantu expansion   the spread of Bantu speakers, with their distinctive artifacts, iron technology, language, and culture, throughout most of sub-Saharan Africa

barter   the trading of one item for another

Bering Land Bridge   a stretch of dry land that once connected North America and Asia, allowing people to migrate by foot to the Americas

bias   factors that affect one's ability to observe and understand

biological evolution   the concept, advocated by Charles Darwin in *On the Origin of Species*, that one species of plant or animal can (and did) change into another over long periods of time

bipartite universe   the universe of the Hopis, who believe in two independent, similar worlds—one for the living Hopi and one for the spirits

block printing   the carving and inking of a page of text onto a wooden surface in order to reproduce many copies

bloom   a rocky mass of impure iron formed by smelting iron ore

Bo   a vassal group in Zhou China that ruled small territories

bomb   a fully enclosed vessel filled with gunpowder and ignited with a slow fuse

brahmans   the caste of Aryan priests in ancient India

Buddha   Prince Siddhartha Gautama, who lived in imperial India from around 563 to 480 B.C. and who is believed by Buddhists to be "the enlightened one"

bureaucracy a hierarchy in which officials represent the state and its ruler in many interactions

bushido a code of behavior for Japanese *samurai* that required self-denial, indifference to adversity, and generosity to the less fortunate

C

calendar system a system of dates and years that is based on astronomy

caliph an Islamic political and religious leader

calpulli (kahl POO lee) the residential district of Aztec commoners, in which land was held at least partly in common; also the people who live in such a district

canon law church laws regulated by church officials in Christianity

cast iron molded and somewhat refined iron that remains brittle and soft

caste a hierarchical system of social categories in India that determines one's status, occupation, rights, and duties

casting producing shaped objects by melting metal and pouring it into a mold, where it hardens

central places places where people from surrounding communities go to procure goods and services unavailable in smaller settlements

century an ancient Etruscan and Roman military organization, consisting of 100 soldiers

ceremonial center a place with little or no permanent population that is reserved for religious activities

chiefdom a group of around 1,000 to 10,000 people organized under a leader with true coercive power and having several layers of wealth, authority, and prestige, often with named classes and many different occupations

chinampas Aztec fields, formed by dredging nutrient-rich mud from lake bottoms and piling it in shallow water

chivalry a code of behavior for European feudal knights that encouraged honesty, courtesy, and the defense of the defenseless

circuses large arenas for races and major sporting events in the Roman Empire

city-state an urban system, including a city and its surrounding supportive villages and farms, that is united under a single government

civet a musky substance, derived from the civet cat and used in perfumes

civilization the final stage of cultural evolution, characterized by dependence upon agriculture, long-distance trade, state government, occupational specialization, urbanism, and class stratification

class a segment of society with a distinctive level of wealth, prestige, and power

class stratification the condition under which members of a society have differential access to resources and power

coca the plant from which cocaine is extracted; it grows abundantly in the Andes

codex (plural: **codices**) a handwritten book; the term is usually reserved for Mesoamerican, Islamic, and European examples

cola nut a nut, indigenous to sub-Saharan Africa, that can be chewed before a meal to stimulate appetite and digestion, or ground into a powder and used as a condiment

colossal heads large Olmec sculptures probably representing rulers

comitatus (koh mee TAH toos) a Germanic friendship structure that compelled kings to rule in consultation with their warriors; warriors owed advice, political support, and military allegiance to their kings

commandery a large administrative district of the Qin Empire

Confucianism the most significant philosophy in Chinese history; founded by Confucius (551–479 B.C.), it stressed a human-centered, moral-based life

consul a military leader in ancient Rome who held the power to command the troops and to execute the law

Contemplative Daoism the most mystical and anarchistic philosophy of China's Classical Age, asserting that the best government is no government and the best social conventions are no social conventions

corvée labor the practice of requiring healthy men to contribute their labor for about one month out of every year for the good of the state

covenant a contractual agreement between a people and their deity whereby the deity agrees to bless and protect the people in return for worship and devotion

cultural evolution the idea that there is a general tendency over time for cultures to become more complex

cultural relativism a concept developed by Franz Boas that all cultures should be viewed as equal in sophistication and value

culture the learned behavior and values that characterize each human group

cuneiform (koo NAY ih form) an ideographic system of writing with some alphabetic (or syllabic) elements that developed in Sumeria around 4500 B.C.

cyclical time a conception of time in which a sequence of stages is seen as repeating forever

Cynicism a philosophy, popular in ancient Greece, that called for a return to the simple life of the early Greek city-state; its followers idealized the life of poverty, wearing rags and eating only what was given to them

D

daimyo (DY mee yoh) a Japanese territorial lord who was a retainer of a *shogun* in feudal Japan

Dao (DOW)   in Daoist philosophy, the path or the way; metaphorically, the origin of all things

Dar al-Islam   the Islamic territory during the height of Islamic expansion, culturally connecting Asia, Africa, and Europe

deffufa (duh FOO fuh)   a massive mudbrick tower near the city of Kerma in central Nubia that was used for storing goods

Delian League   a coalition formed in Greece following the Persian Wars in order to provide for the common defense and the liberation of any Greeks who remained under Persian control

democracy   a political system that places government in the hands of all its citizens or their elected representatives

descriptive model   a model that focuses on how a process operates

dharma (DAHR mah)   the Buddhist concept of cosmic law, truth, and proper living through ethical conduct and social responsibility

diaspora (dy AS poh ruh)   the forced migration and dispersion of a people

dynastic succession   a succession of rulers from the same family

E

economic trade   trade conducted in order to obtain an otherwise unavailable item

Eightfold Path   the Buddhist concept for the correct path that one must follow in order to eliminate desire and suffering; it includes correct views, aspirations, speech, conduct, livelihood, effort, mindfulness, and meditation

elite culture   the cultural elements distinctive to the upper classes

empire   a state that controls a large area that encompasses societies culturally different from itself; also, a group of states or territories that is ruled by a single power

encephalization index   a measure of the average brain size for a species, adjusted for its body size

enclave   a distinct area of a city in which a segregated population group lives

Epicureanism   a Greek philosophy of the fourth century B.C. that was based on the belief that the senses are the foundation for all knowledge

ethnocentrism   the belief that one's own ideas, values, culture, and cherished behavior patterns are socially, morally, or religiously correct and superior to others

eunuch   a castrated human male

Eve hypothesis   the theory that all human beings evolved from a single female ancestor in the last 100,000 years

ever-normal granary system   a system of the Qin-Han Empire of China whereby the government collected grain from various regions of the empire into warehouses and redistributed it to the people as required

exchange   any process by which goods flow between people; also a period of transmission of ideas, species, and technology

explanatory model   a model that focuses on the motivations or underlying causes of a process

F

fact   a description of an event or action that is generally agreed to be true on the basis of present evidence

faunal succession   a method for dating a deposit by dating the fossil within it

feudalism   a decentralized sociopolitical structure in which a weak monarchy attempts to control the lands of the realm through reciprocal agreements with regional leaders

feudalization of the church   the process, in medieval Europe, through which church lands fell into the hands of kings and great lords, who then made vassals of bishops and granted properties to the church

fief   a gift of land awarded to a regional leader by the king, who in return received an oath of loyalty and military support

filial piety   honor to one's parents; a vital part of Confucius's teachings

filioque clause   a particular clause ("and the Son") in the Christian Nicean Creed that contributed to serious disagreement between the Roman Catholic Church and the Eastern Orthodox Church

firepot   a potlike weapon filled with gunpowder, stones, and darts, which was used in fourteenth-century Europe

flare weapon   a tube that projected a flash of gunpowder and was first used in China in the tenth century

folk culture   the cultural elements embraced by the lower classes

Four Noble Truths   the basis of Buddhism, stating that (1) life is suffering; (2) suffering has a cause; (3) the cause is desire; (4) desire and suffering may be eliminated by following the correct path

G

Ge'ez (GHEE ehz)   the script used to write the language of Axum

gentleman   the ideal Confucian type; a person of noble character who treats others humanely, helps the weak and the poor, reviews and criticizes his own actions daily, and radiates moral force

genus   a taxonomical category of moderately to closely related species

geography   the study of the ways in which people have used the planet's land and resources

ghetto originally, the Jewish section of an Italian city; any segregated enclave in cities around the world

great art style an art style that occurs over a broad geographic area and is the dominant and often the only style within a culture, other than family-based folk art

green withy smelting the process employed in pre-Roman Britain of making steel by adding fresh twigs to molten iron shortly before pouring it out

guild system a hierarchical organization of merchants and artisans that regulated production of goods and worked for the common political, economic, and social interests of its members

Gung blood relatives of the ruling house in Zhou China

H

hagiography (HAW jee AHG ruh fee, *or* HAY gee AHG ruh fee) in Christianity, the laudatory biography of a saint

hajj the pilgrimage made by Muslims to Mecca

Hellenes the Greek name for the Greeks, from about the seventh century B.C.

Hellenization the spread of Greek culture

helots war prisoners of ancient Sparta who were farmers, were restricted in their rights, and were constantly guarded by Spartan soldiers

hijra (HEEJ rah) the migration of Muhammad and his followers from Mecca to Medina in 622

history the study of the human past, primarily through the interpretation of documents

hominid any member of the family of animals that includes human beings

hoplite a citizen-soldier in ancient Greece

humoral medicine the philosophy that bodily substances have inherent qualities that must be balanced in order to maintain health

I

icon a representation of a holy person

iconoclast one who destroys holy images

iconophile one who venerates holy images

Ideals Plato's changeless, eternal, and nonmaterial forms in the mind of the Platonic god

ideograph a hieroglyph representing an entire word or complex idea

ideographic writing a form of writing in which each symbol represents an idea, irrespective of the pronunciation of the spoken word

ideology the complex of ideas and philosophy that directs one's goals, expectations, and actions

immortal the ideal type in Contemplative Daoism; an entity that lives in the mountains, possesses magical attributes, subsists on simple foods, drinks dew from plants, is able to fly, and cannot be destroyed

imperial referring to an empire

imperialism the process of forming, extending, or maintaining an empire; an economic and political colonial system of an industrial country needing raw materials and markets

Inca the ruler of the Empire of Tawantinsuyu; also commonly used to describe the empire itself or its people

inquisition originally, an inquiry into what was being taught or preached by lay preachers in medieval Christianity; later, the inquiry by a designated church official into whether anyone held "correct" beliefs

intelligence the ability to learn, reason, and create; one of the characteristics of human beings

interpretation an inference that is consistent with the facts and extends knowledge beyond them by the use of logic, analogy, or some other method of reasoning

intrinsic growth the increase in population as a result of families' having more than two children who survive to adulthood and become parents

investiture the medieval European procedure whereby lords awarded land grants and symbols of secular and holy office

irrigation the practice of bringing water to agricultural fields through canals or similar devices

J

jati a social classification system of India's imperial age, in which an individual's social status was defined by birth and ritual position, which included one's job

jihad (jee HAHD) an Islamic holy war; a holy struggle by the Islamic Ottoman Turks against their Christian or Muslim enemies

K

k-selection the reproductive pattern practiced by animals that have few young and invest a great deal of care in each one

kachinas inhabitants of the Hopi spirit world

kami (kah mee) an early Japanese local deity, usually associated with fertility

karma the Buddhist belief that the residue of a person's actions attaches to the person's soul

kivas (KEE vuhz) underground rooms where Hopi men conduct private ceremonies of ritual devotion to the spirits in order to ensure rainfall

kraal a government capital in southern and southwestern Africa

kshatriyas (KSHAH tree ahs) the caste of warriors in ancient India

L

lactose intolerance   the genetic inability to digest the sugar (lactose) in milk

leaching   the movement of chemicals through soils, caused by water runoffs

Legalists   philosophers and bureaucrats in Warring States China who believed that government must be powerful both militarily and economically

li   a code of honorable or righteous behavior for Chinese feudal warriors

liege   the lord, usually the king, with the greatest feudal claim on a vassal in the European feudal system, which allowed a vassal to serve many lords

lifeways   typical behaviors for a society

linear time   a conception of time in which time passes inexorably forward with no repetition of cycles

logic   the methodology of using systematic reasoning to discover truth

long ship   a long, narrow ship of the Classical Greek period; such ships were fast but unstable

lords of the land   Southwest African men who simultaneously were leaders of their kinship groups and priests who dealt with spirits that inhabited various spots in their lineage territories

lugal   a war leader elected during periods of emergency in ancient Sumeria

M

magic   the supposed manipulation of the physical world through practices that have a spiritual or mystical connection, rather than a physical one

Magna Carta   a charter signed by King John of England in 1215 that reiterated traditional English aristocratic rights, one being to participate in the rule of England

Mahabharata (mah hah BAH rah tah)   the world's longest poem and one of the epic works of Indian civilization

maharaja   a great ruler in India

Mandate of Heaven   an idea begun in ancient China by Zhou rulers, who argued that the former Shang rulers had lost their legitimacy and that the time for a new regime had come; later it became synonymous with popular support

manioc   a starchy, calorie-rich root crop that is widely grown in Mesoamerica; it is also known by its Spanish name, *yuca*

manorialism   a self-sufficient economic system based on a lord's feudal manor with agricultural workers who are often bound to the land

manumission   the freeing of a slave

Mesoamerica   an area in pre-Columbian Mexico and Central America where certain distinctive cultural traits were present: corn-squash-beans agriculture, pyramids as bases for temples, a hieroglyphic writing system, a common calendar, a distinctive ball game, and human sacrifice

metallurgy   the set of skills, practices, and knowledge that relate to the working of metals

military model of government   a centralized political system with a chain of command, emphasizing strict obedience

"missing link"   a hypothetical human-ape that could bridge the evolutionary gap between modern human beings and our proposed apelike ancestors

missionary   a person who purposely sets out to preach, teach, and persuade individuals or groups consciously to accept the belief system or theology of the missionary's religion

model   a picture of how or why a general process works

Monophysite   a form of Christianity whose adherents believe that Jesus has a single, unitary nature, not the dual natures of man and God that mainstream Christianity claims

monotheism   the belief that only one god exists

monumental architecture   large and impressive buildings and similar structures erected at public expense

Moors   North Africans of mixed Berber and Arab parentage

mosque   a Muslim place of worship

N

nagashi   an individual who led several clans during the rise of the Axum kingdom in Ethiopia

navala   the essence of the Hopi spirit world, which could migrate to the Hopi world in the form of rain

nirvana   for Buddhists, the state at which existence ceases and the soul no longer needs to be reborn

nomarch   the governor of a provincial area in ancient Egypt

nome   a provincial area in ancient Egypt

noneconomic trade   trade conducted to cement friendships and other ties

Nuclear America   the area in the Americas, composed of Mesoamerica and Peru, that first developed complex societies

nzimbu (NZIHM boo)   a type of shell that was the official currency of the kingdom of Kongo

O

oasis   an island of lush vegetation in a desert, usually fed by a spring

obsidian   the delicate volcanic glass required in making the fancy and sharp Mayan tools

occupational specialization   the division of labor into specific jobs

oikos (OY kohs)   the ancient Greek household unit, which consisted of the family, land, slaves or tenants, buildings, and livestock of a single farmer

Oldowan tools   tools comprised of a piece of stone with one to five flakes removed to form a sharp edge; these crude and early tools, fashioned by *Homo habilis*, were unearthed in the Olduvai Gorge in Tanzania

oligarchy   rule by a few influential members of the elite

Optimate Party (AHP tih mayt)   the ancient Roman traditionalists who supported aristocratic control through old family alliances and senatorial contacts

oracle bones   bones used in ancient China to predict the future; the earliest evidence of Chinese writing remains on these bones

oral accounts   stories and descriptions of the past preserved by word of mouth

ore   compounds in which a metal is chemically bonded to other elements

"out-of-Africa" theory   the argument that the evolution to modern *Homo sapiens* took place only once and in Africa; from there, according to this view, modern people spread to the rest of the world, outcompeting earlier local hominids, who became extinct

outcaste   the lowest hereditary social group in India, which performed polluting tasks, such as waste removal

P

paddy-field method   a very productive method for growing rice that was perfected in the Chinese Song era; wet-field rice was cultivated through the use of dams, irrigation ditches, sluice-gates, and the treadle water-pump

Paleo-Indians   the earliest native Americans

paleomagnetic dating   a method for dating fossils by reading their preserved magnetic fields and comparing them with known magnetic fields at different dates

papal monarchy   the central administrative bureaucracy of the Roman Catholic Church that rivaled those of European kings in the period from roughly the end of the eleventh to the end of the thirteenth century

Parthenon   the temple of Athena in ancient Athens

pastoralism   the herding of domesticated animals

patriarch   a bishop of one of five particularly important Christian cities (Jerusalem, Antioch, Alexandria, Rome, and Constantinople)

patricians   the wealthy class in early Rome

patron deity   a particular god or goddess believed to protect a city and to be superior to all other deities

pax Romana   the long period of peace during Augustus's reign from 31 B.C. to A.D. 14

peasant   a farmer who works lands owned by the family or a landlord

period   a span of time, defined by scholars for convenience, during which conditions, events, and lifeways remained more or less similar and were distinctive from those of preceding and succeeding periods

Peru   a cultural area in pre-Columbian South America consisting of the highland and coastal portions of modern Peru, as well as the adjacent highland and coastal areas of Ecuador, Bolivia, and Chile

phalanx (FAY langks)   a block of infantry soldiers in ancient Greece consisting of as many as 100 men lined up in rows as many as eight deep

pharoah (FAIR oh)   an ancient Egyptian king who embodied all authority and was believed to be god incarnate

philosophy   the pursuit of wisdom or knowledge

physical remains   material items that are left behind by past peoples and preserved

plating   the production of a thin layer of one metal on another; usually a less valuable metal is plated with a precious one

plaza   a flat open area between buildings

plebeians   the commoner class in early Rome

pochteca (pohch TEH kuh)   Aztec merchants who also served as diplomats and spies

pogrom   an official riot in which bureaucrats led and incited mobs to persecute Jews in Europe

polis (plural: **poleis**, POH lee ihs)   an early Greek city-state

polity   a state government

polytheism   the worship of many gods

pontifex maximus   the chief priest in the ancient Roman government

Populares Party (pahp yoo LAHR ehs)   a political party in ancient Rome that manipulated the citizens' votes in exchange for reforms and handouts

potassium-argon dating   a method for dating a rock by measuring the amount of argon in it

primary source   a document that was written by a participant in or an eyewitness to the event, activity, or process being described or analyzed

primates   the order of animals that includes human beings, apes (such as gorillas, chimpanzees, and orangutans), and monkeys

principate system   an imperial monarchy in Rome that was established by Caesar Augustus and was based on traditional titles and offices

projection   a systematic mathematical transformation that provides rules for drawing a two-dimensional map from three-dimensional data

prophet a person believed to have been called by a deity to act as its representative

proselytizing the activity of preaching to, teaching, and persuading individuals or groups to accept a particular belief system or theology

pueblo a multiroomed masonry house in Hopi culture that sometimes reaches two or three stories high

purchase trade that uses currency

pure mathematics the abstract study of numbers, logic, and spatial forms

Purposive Daoism a philosophy of China's Classical Age, favoring minimal social regulation, limited government, and patience in personal relationships

Q

quinoa (KEE nwuh) a grain from the amaranth plant that was an important part of the ancient Peruvian diet

Qur'an (KOOR ahn) the holy book of Islam

R

radiocarbon dating a method for dating materials that were once alive by measuring the amount of radioactive carbon within them

raffia a fabric made of palm fiber that was manufactured in the kingdom of Kongo and elsewhere

raja a common term for the monarch in Indian history

Ramayana (RAH mah yah nah) an epic poem from ancient Indian civilization

reciprocity with the spirits mutual obligation between the human Hopi world and the spirit world

reincarnation the belief that people have past and future lives

Renaissance an era of artistic, sociopolitical, and economic change that occurred in Europe from around 1350 to around 1600; it was characterized by an interest in Classical Greco-Roman forms

rhetoric the art of argument

role an affiliation and a set of rights and obligations assumed by a person in a particular social context

Roman exchange traditional commercial products, previously unavailable commodities, styles, and ideas that coursed through the Roman Empire and its trading partners in great volumes

Romanization the emulation of Roman ways

round ship a slow, sturdy, spacious ship of the Greek Classical period

S

sacbes (SAWK bayz) earthen roads raised above the surface of the jungle floor in Mayan civilization

samanta **system** a system in seventh-century India that granted semiautonomous rule to recently conquered territories and their rulers

samurai a professional warrior in feudal Japan; literally, "one who serves"

Sanhedrin (san HE drihn) the religious council and highest seat of Jewish justice in Jerusalem until A.D. 90

saqia (SAH kee uh) an ox-powered waterwheel used to lift water from the Nile to agricultural fields in the Nubian kingdom of Meröe

satrap (SAY trap) a governor of an ancient Persian province

satrapy a province in ancient Persia

savanna a semiarid grassland with occasional trees

schism a split; often used to refer specifically to a religious split caused by differences of opinion

scholasticism a medieval philosophy involving the use of reason to develop faith and understanding of the created universe

science the quest to understand natural phenomena and to learn how and why things work as they do

secondary source a document in which information that has been gathered from primary sources is analyzed and digested, providing an interpretation of the event or process

sedentary a term that describes people who live in a single, permanent settlement

segmentary opposition a widespread African approach to political organization in which each individual, as a member of a series of hierarchic groups based on kinship and village residence, is politically loyal to the largest hierarchic group that can array itself against the antagonist in a conflict

Senate a council of ancient Rome that advised the government leaders, over whom it exerted considerable influence

serf a worker whose labor is owed to someone else, usually a feudal lord, and whose status is inherited by children, but who also retains certain personal rights and is not conceived of as "owned"

shadouf (shah DOOF) a technology devised in ancient Egypt, consisting of an upright support with a swinging lever that was used to lift buckets of water from irrigation canals

shah a ruler of Muslim Persia; the leader of the Persian Empire

Shi'a (SHEE ah) a prominent Islamic sect

Shih a vassal group in Zhou China that often fought for the higher lords or served as officials

shoen (shoh ehn) private estates in eighth-century Japan and after

shogunate a military overlordship and the dominant governmental structure in feudal Japan

shovel-shaped incisors   front teeth with side edges that curl slightly backward, a genetic trait distinctive to East Asians and American Indians

shudras (SHOO druhs)   the class of menial workers and indigenous peoples in ancient India

sign   a marker that indicates meaning but is not arbitrary

Sikhism (SEEK ihz um)   a monotheistic religion founded in sixteenth-century northern India; it began as an attempt to bridge the religious differences between Islam and Hinduism and was transformed into a religion of resistance to Mughal oppression

Skepticism   a philosophy popular in ancient Greece that was based on the belief that there is no ultimate pattern by which to order one's life

smelting   the rendering of ores to derive pure metals from compounds

social history   the study of everyday life in the past

social sciences   the disciplines that study human culture and behavior

sophists   itinerant paid instructors in ancient Greece whose teaching emphasized advancement in the professions of politics, law, teaching, and playwriting

source analysis   a set of procedures developed by historians to determine whether a particular document is legitimate and accurate

stages   patterns of cultural characteristics that are common to societies of a similar level of complexity

state government   a government with strong leadership, a supporting bureaucracy, and a supportive ideology

steel   a hard and useful metal formed by the chemical bonding of iron and carbon

stela parks   elite Axumite cemeteries with tall stones as markers

stelae (singular: **stela**)   large stones with low-relief carvings on their flat surfaces

steppe   grasslands, particularly in Inner Asia

Stoicism   a Greco-Roman philosophy beginning in the fourth century B.C. that was based on the belief that human happiness grows out of self-control and the performance of duty, rather than from the mere pursuit of pleasure

subinfeudation   the practice of reapportioning regional lands to leaders of smaller areas in a feudal system

sub-Saharan Africa   the area south of the Sahara Desert

Sudanic-type state   a form of government in West and Central Africa after 700 in which the state was ruled by a divine king who was believed to be descended from the creator god

sultan   an Islamic ruler, outside of Persia; the leader of the Ottoman Empire

sumptuary laws   regulations stating what clothing and ornaments may be worn by members of each social class

survival of the fittest   the concept that individuals with traits that aid in their survival will live long enough to pass those traits on to their offspring, and individuals with undesirable traits will be weeded out because those traits will lead to their deaths before they have the opportunity to pass the traits on to offspring

sutra   a treatise, in poetry or prose, on some issue in Buddhism

suttee (SUH tee)   the Hindu practice of burning widows on the funeral pyres of their husbands

symbol   in linguistics, an arbitrary marker that stands for something else

syncretic   a descriptor applied to a newly formed religion that uses elements of both an earlier, traditional religion and a newly introduced religion

system of correspondences   a complex Hopi system of symbols that relates cardinal directions, colors, types of clouds, ritual items, lightning, plants, animals, and many other things to each other

T

tax farming   the selling of tax-collecting authority by the state

technology   the production of material items; the study of making devices that serve a purpose

tef   a milletlike grain that was domesticated by Ethiopians

theme (THEHM eh *or* THEEM)   in the Byzantine Empire, an area administered by generals exercising both military and civil power

theocracy   a form of government that recognizes a deity as the head of the government and a high religious official as the interpreter of that deity's will

tlatoani (tlah toh AH nee)   the Aztec emperor

trellis theory   the argument that modern *Homo sapiens* evolved locally from preexisting *Homo erectus* populations

tribe   a community with leadership by example, usually consisting of 100 to 2,000 people who have settled in a single, permanent village and get most of their food through the growing of crops

tribunes   the representatives of the plebeians, elected after the plebeian boycott in ancient Rome

tribute   the rendering of goods to a powerful individual or state by a subordinate

trireme (TRY reem)   a long ship of the Greek Classical period with three banks of rowers that could travel fast and steadily

tropical rain forest   a dense tangle of low-latitude trees and undergrowth with abundant water

tyranny   originally, the usurpation of rule by an individual who has widespread support and is brought into power by citizens in opposition to oppressive oligarchical control in ancient Greece

U

Upanishads   ancient Sanskrit discourses that speculate about the nature of reality

upright bipedalism   the ability to walk on two legs, characteristic of the earliest known hominids and possibly developed in response to the need to carry infants away from danger

urbanism   the condition in which the settlement system in a region consists of some relatively large settlements that are internally diverse and that serve as central places

urbanization   the development of cities

usury   loaning funds out at a particularly high interest rate

V

vaishyas (VAY shee ahs)   the caste of commoners in ancient India

varna   an Aryan social classification system of India's imperial age

vassal   a military retainer of the king in a feudal system; vassals usually took an oath of loyalty to the king in return for control of lands given to them by the king

Vedas (VAY duhs)   a series of religious and historical works transmitted orally by the Aryans until they were transcribed around 500 B.C.

verticality   the strategy of farming at different elevations in order to grow a variety of crops that thrive in different climates

W

wampum   shell beads of different colors that the Iroquois strung together to form pictorial belts

well-field system   the manorial system in Zhou China, in which the plots were laid out like a tic-tac-toe schematic (#), resembling the Chinese character for "well"

were-babies   a common motif in Olmec art consisting of human babies with fangs and jaguar paws

world religion   a religion that has gained significant numbers of adherents across broad geographical expanses; world religions include Judaism, Hinduism, Buddhism, Christianity, and Islam

wrought iron   a form of refined iron that is harder and less brittle than cast iron but remains somewhat malleable

Y

yanakuna (yah nah KOO nah)   in the Inca Empire, a class of people who were lower than commoners; usually translated as "slaves"

Yasa (YAH sah)   a binding legal code promulgated by the Mongol leader Chinggis Khan and derived from Mongol customs, ancestral traditions, and additional decrees

yin **privilege**   the exemption of high officials' sons from civil service examinations during the Chinese Sui and Tang eras

Z

ziggurat   a tiered temple near the center of a Mesopotamian city

Index

A note about the index:

Pages containing main coverage or description of a topic or person are set in bold-face for easy reference. Entries include dates for important events and major figures as well as brief identifications, alternate names, and pronunciation guides when appropriate.

Parenthetical notations following pages refer to:
- (illus.)   for illustrations and graphs
- (map)   for maps
- (table)   for tables